AF605934

GALEAZZO CIANO

Galeazzo Ciano

The Fascist Pretender

TOBIAS HOF

UNIVERSITY OF TORONTO PRESS
Toronto Buffalo London

Toronto Buffalo London
utorontopress.com
Printed in the U.S.A.

ISBN 978-1-4875-0798-5 (cloth)
ISBN 978-1-4875-3731-9 (EPUB)
ISBN 978-1-4875-3730-2 (PDF)

Toronto Italian Studies

Library and Archives Canada Cataloguing in Publication

Title: Galeazzo Ciano : the fascist pretender / Tobias Hof.
Names: Hof, Tobias, author.
Series: Toronto Italian studies.
Description: Series statement: Toronto Italian studies | Includes bibliographical references and index.
Identifiers: Canadiana (print) 20210112719 | Canadiana (ebook) 20210112824 | ISBN 9781487507985 (cloth) | ISBN 9781487537319 (EPUB) | ISBN 9781487537302 (PDF)
Subjects: LCSH: Ciano, Galeazzo, conte, 1903–1944. | LCSH: Diplomats – Italy – Biography. | LCSH: Foreign ministers – Italy – Biography. | LCSH: Fascists – Italy – Biography. | LCSH: Fascism – Italy – History – 20th century. | LCSH: Italy – History – 1922–1945. | LCGFT: Biographies.
Classification: LCC DG575.C52 H64 2021 | DDC 945.091092 – dc23

Printed with the support of the Gerda Henkel Foundation, Düsseldorf.

University of Toronto Press acknowledges the financial assistance to its publishing program of the Canada Council for the Arts and the Ontario Arts Council, an agency of the Government of Ontario.

Canada Council for the Arts
Conseil des Arts du Canada

Funded by the Government of Canada
Financé par le gouvernement du Canada

Contents

Illustrations

Acknowledgments

I was extremely fortunate to receive the support of so many people and institutions during the prolonged period of research and writing of this book, a period that retrospectively feels longer than the lifespan of its protagonist Galeazzo Ciano. Without their help this book would not have been possible, and therefore I owe them a great deal of thanks.

First and foremost, I would like to thank my mentors at the Ludwig-Maximilians-Universität in Munich, Xosé Manoel Núñez Seixas, Margit Szöllösi-Janze, Martin Baumeister, and Christiane Lemke. Their excellent advice and constant support were indispensable for the success of the work. Without their assistance and suggestions as well as their willingness to discuss the status of my manuscript at any time, I would not have been able to successfully finish the arduous task of writing a habilitation thesis.

During my research I had the pleasure of working at several outstanding research institutions and universities in Germany and the United States of America. I am indebted to my friends and colleagues at the Institute for Contemporary History in Munich, Washington University in St. Louis, and the University of North Carolina (UNC) at Chapel Hill. They all listened to me discuss my research in exhausting detail and provided the rich intellectual environment and supportive atmosphere that made this book possible. In particular, I am sincerely thankful to Karen Auerbach, Melissa Bullard, Susanne Cowan, Karen Hagemann, Konrad Jarausch, Lauren Jarvis, Ryan Jones, Susan Pennybacker, Sonja Schilcher, Thomas Schlemmer, and Hans Woller. Johannes Hürter deserves special mention for his excellent guidance during all these years and his calm advice when dealing with the challenges of academia. My deepest gratitude to the directors of the institute and the department chairs who made it possible for me to enjoy this excellent atmosphere, namely Jean Allman, Fitz Brundage, Lisa Lindsay, Horst Möller, and Andreas Wirsching.

Questions of content have been discussed at conferences, lectures, workshops, and during numerous coffee breaks with many scholars who have been immensely helpful in clarifying my ideas and pointing me in the right direction. In particular, I would like to thank Shelley Baranowski, Arnd Bauerkämper, Mathias Beer, Sandra Berger, Dirk Bonker, Benjamin Claude Brower, H. James Burgwyn, Marcus Gräser, Sebastian Jobs, Hillel Kieval, MacGregor Knox, Paul Michael Lützeler, Ronald Suny, and Anika Walke.

Particular thanks need to be extended to the Gerda Henkel Foundation. Without the foundation's generous fellowship, I would never have been able to embark on my journey to decipher Galeazzo Ciano's life. Their prompt and straightforward handling of any issue that arose during my research and their support for the publication of this book were truly outstanding and deserve special mention. In addition, I am very grateful for the grant I received from the German Historical Institute in Washington, DC, which allowed me to conduct my research in the United States. And finally, the support of the Volkswagen Foundation and the visiting professorship program of the German Academic Exchange Service allowed me to work at Washington University and at UNC Chapel Hill, where I found the time and necessary support to finish my book.

The nature of this book necessitated an archival scavenger hunt in several countries. Thus, special thanks are due to the staffs of the many archives and libraries that I visited during my research, including the Archivio Centrale dello Stato and the Archivio Storico Ministero Affari Esteri in Rome, the Bundesarchiv Berlin-Lichterfelde, the Franklin D. Roosevelt Library and Archive, the Institute for Contemporary History in Munich, the Library of Congress in Washington, DC, the UK National Archives in Kew, the US National Archives and Record Administration at College Park, the Politisches Archiv des Auswärtigen Amts, and the US Holocaust Memorial Museum in Washington, DC. Without their experienced and encouraging staff and their friendly professionalism this book would never have been completed.

Particularly, I would like to extend special thanks to Derek Holmgren who took upon himself the ungrateful task of copy-editing the first versions of the manuscript. His attention to detail, his numerous helpful comments on both style and substance, and his abhorrence of redundancies taught many a lesson in copy-editing and good English. To him goes my unending gratitude and to me the blame for any remaining flaws. Many other watchful eyes have looked over the manuscript and cleared up the chaos in the notes, and I am very grateful for their excellent support, in particular the support of Genevieve Cecil, Konrad Frenzl, and Max Metz. Nor could I have asked for better care and guidance from my editor at the University of Toronto Press (UTP), Stephen Shapiro, and my copy-editor, Carolyn Zapf. Together they all have done superb work transforming my manuscript into this beautifully produced book. Additional thanks to the anonymous reviewers who took the time to read and engage with my work.

Finally, I would like to thank all my friends at home and abroad who have always been there for me and have given me the moral support necessary to master the day-to-day trials and tribulations of writing a book. They have contributed more to the successful completion of this book than they might be aware of. Words utterly fail to express my gratitude to my parents and my brother, who always believed in me, put up with my moods, and gave me all the support I needed. Without them this book would never have been written. The book is dedicated to them.

GALEAZZO CIANO

Introduction

He never considered himself to be very political, much less rebellious.[1] As a worker at the *Fabbrica Italiana Automobili Torino* (FIAT) factory, he never joined the trade unions or the socialists. It was only in 1921 that he decided to support the new fascist movement. He was scolded by his co-workers, friends left him, and many others accused him of betraying the future and solidarity of the workers. But he did not care. He was hooked by the fascists' promises to fight corruption, to end patronage and nepotism, and to lead Italy into a brighter future. In those days, he never understood why people opposed them. Should not everyone be happy that somebody was finally brave enough to stand up to the corrupt establishment? It was only years later that he came to the painful realization that promises and pledges are great to listen to, but political decisions should not be based solely on pleasant feelings. It was late on a chilly evening in October 1936 when he decided he had to act. He sat down at his desk and started to write a short note, trying to conceal his own handwriting by scribbling almost-illegible letters. He put it in an envelope, sealed it, and put his jacket on. Under cover of darkness, he left his apartment and took several detours to his destination: the post office at the Turin main station. On his way back, he made sure that he was not being followed, haunted by the thought of how Benito Mussolini would react when he read the sentences anonymously sent to him:

> Excellency, I remind you that the scandalous propaganda in favour of your son-in-law, this idiot, is making the whole nation vomit ... The days of nepotism in Italy are over, and the nation's patience is limited. You and He must be careful of making false moves. Especially He![2]

A quick change of scene whisks us to Oberallmannshausen, southern Germany, in the summer of 1943. Hanns Johst, author and president of the *Reichsschrifttumskammer* (Reich Literature Chamber), was enjoying the day in his garden – or trying to. He had intended to escape the hectic heat of Munich, the "City of the Movement," but the family who had recently taken over the villa formerly occupied by the noble and peaceable Sayn-Wittgenstein put an end to any thoughts of peace and literary productivity. Day after day Johst was forced to endure the shouting, complaining, crying, and all the other nonsense. But the redoubtable Reichsführer-SS Heinrich Himmler had asked him to keep an eye on the family. Rather than starting a new poem, Johst instead wrote Himmler a litany of complaints regarding his new neighbours:

> He gestured to me for an hour, telling me three times ... that as a new neighbour and a Christian heart I have a damnable duty to tell the Führer and you his wish to be received. Apparently, he dared to write memoirs that interest the whole world ... Even the backdrops of vanity bend for so much shoddiness. I flipped through the world literature and found no allegory for this kind of cheapest indignity.[3]

Almost seven years and 700 kilometres separate these two letters, and yet they both discuss the same person: Galeazzo Ciano, Count of Cortellazzo and Buccari, son-in-law of Benito Mussolini. He rose to the height of power for a decade before his execution in 1944 and was one of the most dazzling and controversial figures of Italian fascism.[4] Only a handful of twentieth-century Italian politicians continuously held important positions in government for almost ten years and adorned the front pages of newspapers and magazines. This spectacular life story is not, however, the only reason why writing a biography about him presents tremendous challenges. Ciano was more than the sum of his experiences. His positions and presence during this critical moment in history are key to understanding the rise and fall of fascism in Italy and the nature of fascist regimes more generally. Through the prism of Ciano's life – both professional and private – we can examine in depth the establishment and constant renegotiation of internal and external power relations in Italian fascism, the limits of the "totalitarian experiment" (Emilio Gentile), and Italy's position in relation to the other regimes and fascist movements of twentieth-century Europe.

Galeazzo Ciano was born in Livorno to Admiral and future fascist minister Costanzo Ciano and Carolina Pini on 18 March 1903.[5] During the First World War, he attended the Foscari Gymnasium in the city of Venice. Before the end of the war, he moved with his mother and his younger sister Maria to Genoa, where he received a classical secondary school education and graduated as the second best of his year in all of Italy. Scholarship in hand, he enrolled at the prestigious Sapienza University of Rome in 1921 to study law. In addition to his law studies, which he completed at the end of 1924, Ciano wrote as a literary and theatre critic for the newspapers *Il Paese*, *La Tribuna*, *Il Nuovo Paese*, and *L'Impero*.[6]

In 1925 Ciano joined the diplomatic service. After basic training he worked in the Foreign Ministry's Cipher Department before he was appointed vice consul in Rio de Janeiro under Ambassador Giulio Cesare Montagna. In the summer of the following year, he became second embassy secretary at the Italian embassy in Buenos Aires, serving Ambassador Alberto Martin Franklin. In May 1927 Ciano moved to Beijing, where he became embassy secretary under Ambassador Daniele Varè. Three years later he was posted to the newly established embassy in the Vatican under the direction of Ambassador Cesare Maria De Vecchi. In March 1930 he married Edda Mussolini, Benito Mussolini's eldest daughter, in Rome, and after a honeymoon on Capri, the young couple moved to Shanghai in September, where Ciano worked at the Italian diplomatic mission for the next three years. In Shanghai he became the head of a local League of Nations' commission to investigate and report on the attack of Japanese forces on the city in early 1932.[7]

On 1 August 1933 Mussolini made Ciano his personal press chief. The appointment was an open invitation for the ambitious Ciano to enter the inner circle of fascist power. On 25 June 1935 he climbed yet another step up the career ladder: at his insistence, the State Secretariat for Press and Propaganda, which had been created in 1934, was transformed into a ministry, and he was raised to the rank of minister. Thus, after just nine months working for the regime in Rome, Ciano became its youngest minister.[8] After his promotion, he participated as a bomber squadron commander in the Ethiopian War, which lasted from October 1935 to May 1936.

On 11 June 1936 the *Duce* named his thirty-three-year-old son-in-law foreign minister – the youngest foreign minister Europe had ever seen. After his appointment, an alleged policy of moderate revisionism was replaced by a more aggressive foreign policy. Under Ciano's leadership, this change took place at a rapid, seemingly irreversible pace and led to the German-Italian alliance, the so-called Pact of Steel, in May 1939, and Italy's entry into the Second World War on 10 June 1940.[9]

Thanks to the offices he held and his relationship with Mussolini, many contemporary observers at home and abroad saw Ciano as the *Duce*'s designated heir. For them, his ultimate fate was as surprising as his rapid rise. In the spring of 1943 Ciano was dismissed as foreign minister and transferred to the post of ambassador at the Holy See.

After the *Gran Consiglio del Fascismo* (Fascist Grand Council) revoked the *Duce*'s military supreme command on 25 July 1943, Ciano and his family tried to flee abroad. However, the Germans handed him over to Mussolini, who had established the *Repubblica Sociale Italiana* (RSI; Italian Social Republic) and kept fascism alive in northern and central Italy. On 19 October 1943 Ciano was arrested in Verona and imprisoned. He was found guilty of high treason and executed on 11 January 1944 at the age of forty.

From his appointment as press secretary until his execution, Ciano was one of the most prominent figures in the fascist regime. His belief in dynamic progress, in youth as a historical force, and in the *Duce*'s charisma shaped Italy's domestic and foreign policy for years. A biographical study of him provides new insights into the attempted fascistization of society and politics, the persistence of traditional structures and ideas under fascism, the inner mechanisms and machinations of fascist rule, performative diplomacy in peace and wartime, and fascism's succession problem. But how to write a biography of Ciano?

Writing the Biography of a Fascist Hierarch

For decades political biographies, especially those about powerful (white) men, suffered from a poor reputation among historians. Social historians in particular argued that biographies are traditionally conservative, unreflective, and poor in theory.[10] Although opinions on how to write a biography vary widely, the many outstanding biographies that have been written in the last few decades have convinced most scholars of the genre's potential when it comes to understanding not only the lives of individuals, but also the times in which they lived and how they are remembered. Moreover, historians such as Lucy Riall and Margit Szöllösi-Janze have also refined our methodological toolbox when it comes to engaging with an individual's life.[11]

The few existing biographies on Galeazzo Ciano, however, have largely ignored the paradigmatic shifts within historiography. They adhere to a traditional, chronological structure that provides the readers with many details and anecdotes about Ciano's life.[12] Even more recent studies have failed to relate his life to the latest research on Italian and European fascism and its insights into various key areas, including occupation and racial policy, youth education, transnational networks, and performative (foreign) policy.[13] Unfortunately, the biographies of Ciano are not the exception. We still have almost no thoroughly researched academic studies of any of the leading figures of the Italian fascist regime besides Mussolini.[14]

The failure to carefully engage with Ciano and other members of the inner circle has far-reaching consequences for our understanding of Italian fascism. It propagates the narrative of Mussolini as the almighty dictator, a narrative that consistently dominates the historiography on Italian fascism.[15] By analysing other members of the fascist elite, including Ciano, we are better able to understand the contradictions and complexity of fascist domestic and foreign policy – rather than dismissing them as the result of Mussolini's machinations or some stereotypical Italian mentality. The importance of source-based and analytical studies on the key figures of a fascist system is exemplified by the historiography of Nazi Germany. Works on the "second guard" of the Third Reich have massively enriched and revolutionized our understanding of National Socialism.[16]

Following these examples, my biography on Galeazzo Ciano is intended to provide a new perspective on one of the major figures of Italian fascism and to debunk some of the "urban legends" that concern him and his family. The book will help us better understand the dynamics of the fascist dictatorship on a personal, social, international, and cultural level. Doing so offers a fresh perspective on key issues that I hope will encourage readers to rethink Italian and European fascism.

I decided a thematic approach best suited this biography, which is intended to provide a more nuanced understanding of Ciano's character and work rather than an exhaustive but superficial overview of his life. To help accustom the reader to this approach, I selected four topics that form the cornerstones of Ciano's life. These topics, outlined in more detail further on, are Ciano's family and friends; Ciano as a member of the political elite; Ciano as a diplomat; and Ciano as the presumed heir. Using this thematic structure has several advantages.

First, it reduces the risk of portraying and analysing the subject's life along a deterministic line from his childhood to his execution in 1944. Ciano, like most of us, did not lead a linear life but, rather, one that was connected to, influenced by, and responsive to the individuals and circumstances he encountered. A chronological structure, however, could lead to what Pierre Bourdieu calls the "biographical illusion" of a coherent life.[17] Focusing on specific elements of his life, however, shows us "the existence of 'multiple selves' in any individual life that can be altered to suit the times, the setting and/or the demands of a particular audience."[18]

Second, such an approach saves us from the false assumption that we are actually capable of capturing someone's entire life between the covers of a book. Such a book would either prove unreadable in its minutiae or, as many extant biographies demonstrate, lead the author to reiterate a number of well-known facts in order to shape a more coherent narrative. While there is nothing inherently wrong with the latter approach, it does tend to obscure nuances that could open new lines of enquiry. The available Ciano biographies often stray from their subject by offering extensive descriptions of Italian foreign and/or domestic policy, subordinating Ciano to the events in which he was involved. A thematic approach allows us to balance an analysis of the subject with the broader historical context, which French historian Jacques LeGoff insists is one of the crucial tasks of any biographer.[19]

And third, in addition to being the cornerstones of Ciano's life, these themes help us to examine the "cracks in the totalitarian facade" (Alexander De Grand) of the Italian fascist regime more thoroughly than if they were buried in a chronological retelling of Ciano's life. By revealing the limitations of the "totalitarian experiment" through these lenses, we can better understand the functioning of the regime, its demise, and, especially in comparison with Nazi Germany, how Italy might have been less radical than its German counterpart even though its rhetoric was sometimes more bombastic and inhumane.

In order to illustrate, analyse, and understand the limits of the "totalitarian experiment," we must delve into the issue of internal and external power relations, which touch on the functionality of the Italian fascist regime as a whole. In Italian fascism, power was neither totally centred in Mussolini nor uniformly dispersed but was instead concentrated in various centres such as organizations (for example, the fascist party; ministries) and individuals (like Ciano). This idea of power as distributed across various centres, which in turn may form alliances and become embedded in hierarchies that wax and wane with time, pushes us to examine Ciano's methods for accumulating and concentrating power.[20] The aforementioned four themes I have selected as the cornerstones of Ciano's life enable a meticulous and detailed analysis of his rise and fall within the contemporaneous historical context.

Better than any other academic genre, the biography allows us to combine various methodologies in order to thoroughly analyse the study's subject from manifold angles.[21] Given the nature of Ciano's life and activities, I use approaches from political, diplomatic, and social history to examine his institutional networks, the importance of his family, his friends and clientele networks, as well as the significance of wealth and ideology. In addition, I examine Ciano's charismatic aura by applying Max Weber's concepts of authority and use ideas taken from performance theories. Since both these approaches will feature predominantly in my study and are closely intertwined, I will explain them in more detail here.

Since Weber developed his concept of a charismatic authority, which describes the emergence of an extraordinary leader during a crisis, it has been consistently modified and refined to address criticism of his original concept.[22] The existence of a charismatic leader – and Mussolini is often regarded as the archetype – rests on "the nature of the charismatic personality" and "factors which have allegedly helped to create and sustain the charismatic bond."[23] Thus, a charismatic leader had to follow a mission that would guide his actions. Moreover, he must be able to project a natural, positive aura and appear as an energetic and dynamic personality capable of leading the nation out of its perceived crisis. The achievement of this mission would bring about the rebirth of a great and powerful nation, and thus in Italy would compensate for the weak national self-confidence that had haunted the Italians since unification in the nineteenth century.

Yet, such a cult of personality could only function as a tool of leadership when the charisma was granted to the leader by the people and the party. It was therefore essential for a charismatic leader to be a "man of the people" and to embrace the necessary symbiotic relationship.[24] Charismatic personalities can only rise in certain sociopolitical, cultural, and historical situations. Of particular importance is a communal sense of crisis at a given moment. Even though there must be an underlying reality to such a crisis, it can be either moderated or aggravated by skilful propaganda. In such instances, people would demand a strong leader whose rise would be facilitated by authoritarianism already embedded in the political culture or the collective national memory.[25]

Properly understanding Fascist Italy through the lens of Weber's concept requires three correctives. First, many studies based on Weber's ideas focus on the dominant fascist leaders and thus cement a hierarchical understanding of the fascist system.[26] Richard Griffin and others, however, have pointed out that, after the First World War, "new types" of politicians emerged, coming from such diverse backgrounds as the military and the arts and sciences. Thanks to their energetic personalities and actions, these individuals convinced a broad constituency that they were capable of leading the community out of the crisis du jour. They constructed an aura of legitimacy based on personal charisma rather than political experience that entitled them to lead. In Italy the warrior-poet and nationalist Gabriele D'Annunzio or fascist *ras* (local leaders) such as Dino Grandi in Bologna and Italo Balbo in Ferrara are excellent examples of this phenomenon.[27]

Second, Griffin's micro-level approach allows us to better explain the rapid rise and influence of diverse protagonists of the fascist elite in addition to Mussolini. In the constant struggle for power, charisma constituted one resource among many; others included what Weber labelled traditional or legal authority along with wealth, knowledge, institutional background, and personal networks. Thus, although the actual leader possessed charismatic authority, he could be challenged by other individuals and thus needed to constantly defend and renegotiate his appeal. Mussolini's charismatic authority was indeed challenged by subordinates, whose national and international prestige constituted a major threat to the *Duce*'s reputation. Figures like Italo Balbo and Galeazzo Ciano spent considerable time and energy trying to manufacture their own version of a charismatic authority, hoping to increase their own influence.

Finally, as historians Christopher Duggan and Paul Corner have shown, fascism in Italy was based on a mix of coercion and consensus, and not only on violence and suppression. They have demonstrated that, whereas the *Partito Nazionale Fascista* (PNF; National Fascist Party) was unable to generate a lasting bond between the party and the people, Mussolini as the charismatic leader functioned for a long time as the most crucial bridge between the people and the regime. Thus a loss of charisma would undermine the legitimacy not only of the leader but also that of the entire regime.[28]

My use of performance theory reflects the fact that under fascism performative politics successively replaced referential, programmatic politics.[29] Cultural historians in particular have described in detail the various ceremonies and events during the fascist regime.[30] Thus it is no surprise that performance also played a key role in Galeazzo Ciano's life and work, including his control of the state's propaganda apparatus, his conduct of foreign policy, and his attempts to construct his own self-image.

According to performance theory, acts can create meaning, order, and stability. They are conditioned by symbols and concepts such as nationality and gender, and must be consistently repeated in order to confirm, refresh, and even modify existing rules. As they can influence and potentially change the current order and shape a "new" reality, performative acts are not just mirroring the existing social and political structure. Rather they can, for example, include certain groups and exclude others; they can imply an inward sense of belonging and give an outward suggestion of strength; they can be used to construct and demonstrate the power of a state or an individual; and they can also create solidarity in places where there is no consensus.[31] But why and how are they able to do this?

Performative acts can appear in many different forms ranging from dress codes to official state propaganda. Particularly important as a form of symbolic communication to control and dominate societies are so-called political rituals, including mass demonstrations and state receptions. Performative acts consolidate different, sometimes complicated and even contradictory, meanings into an easily understandable one. Their vagueness allows various groups to interpret them differently. Thus they are multifocal in that they always remain ambivalent and allow the audience to project their preferred interpretation.[32]

To measure whether Ciano was able to use performative acts as a power resource, we must closely examine if he achieved the intended effect – if he, in other words, was able to construct a "new" reality. Since the ambivalent nature of such acts makes it difficult to use objective criteria to measure possible success, the intentions of everyone involved – the actors who directly participated in the performance, the persons responsible for the staging, and the intended audience – must all be considered. Only by examining all three of these levels can we gain a better understanding of whether Ciano benefitted from performative acts or not.

Structure and Sources

The book is divided into four chapters, each dealing with a certain fragment of Galeazzo Ciano's life that helps to illustrate the limits of the "totalitarian experiment" in divergent areas of public and private life and also highlights the existence of Ciano's multiple selves. The first chapter, "The Family," focuses on Ciano's intimate relationships, including his relatives and close circle of friends. What role did his father, Costanzo Ciano, a celebrated hero of the First World War and prominent figure of the fascist regime, play in his son's life and career? How important was Costanzo's charismatic authority and the patron-client network he created in his hometown? Did Ciano also attempt to build a patronage network of friends, relatives, and clients in an effort to acquire, maintain, and expand his power? What were the consequences of his marriage to Edda Mussolini? What does it reveal about public and private life in a fascist dictatorship, and how did it affect Ciano's position within the regime and Italian society? This chapter provides the first-ever critical portrait of the rise of the Ciano family beginning in the late nineteenth century and an analysis of the role of family in Galeazzo Ciano's social and political standing.

In the second chapter, "The Politician," I examine Ciano's role within the fascist movement and regime to gain insights into the mechanism of the fascist system. Central aspects of this chapter are his career and leadership as a minister, his ambivalent and often-tense relations with the fascist movement and the PNF, his alliances and networks involving Mussolini and other members of the fascist elite, and his dealings with the Catholic Church and the royal family. To better understand Ciano's position within the inner circle, it is essential to thoroughly analyse his personal relationship with the fascist movement from his teens and how his work as a minister influenced his reputation among the fascist elite and the Italian people.

After analysing Ciano's domestic political activities, the third chapter, "The Diplomat," focuses on his foreign policy. By examining his diplomatic training, his first diplomatic missions in Latin America and China, his parallel diplomacy as minister of propaganda, and his tenure as foreign minister, this chapter addresses the question of how Ciano defined and situated Italy's role in the world. In contrast to the many studies on Italian foreign policy that often chronologically recount diplomatic meetings and focus on Mussolini as its chief architect, I examine Ciano's diplomacy through three lenses: first, his worldview and strategy; second, his preference for performative diplomacy; and third, his use of both parallel and secret diplomacy.

In the fourth chapter, "The Successor," I analyse whether and, if so, how Ciano was perceived as a potential successor to the *Duce* by examining what kind of self-image he or others promoted and invented in public, how it changed over time, and how society viewed him. By looking at a selection of his public self-images, ranging from the "deputy *Duce*" to the athlete, soldier, and victim, I unmask the ways in which he attempted to create these specific images and whether these constructed images were persuasive in public. Thereby, Ciano's diary is an especially important source, not only for its record of his thoughts but more for how he used it as a way of "deliberate self-fashioning" in order to "preserve and control his place in popular memory."[33] Using Ciano as a case study, this chapter touches on the crucial issue of succession in Fascist Italy, because it reveals an inconsistency at the core of fascism: What does a fascist transfer of power actually look like? After all, should someone not seize power through struggle, rather than having it bequeathed to them by the *Duce* through a hereditary line or a last will?

The epilogue, "A Man of His Time," not only summarizes the main findings of this book and highlights how Ciano's life exposes the limits of the "totalitarian experiment" in Italy, but also addresses the question of whether labels such as "fascist" or "conservative" are sufficient to characterize Ciano. By examining various cornerstones of Ciano's life and analysing what his actions, reactions, and relicts tell us about the time and place in which he lived, I argue that it is more fruitful to interpret and frame Ciano's life – and with him Italian fascism – through a generational lens.

When it comes to primary sources for this project, I of course relied on Ciano's personal diaries (1937–43), published in various editions and languages since 1946. But in addition to the diaries, I also turned to archival records from eight different countries and the relevant published editions of the Foreign Ministry records for Belgium, France, Germany, Great Britain, Italy, Switzerland, and the United States. These sources were immensely helpful in contextualizing the contents of Ciano's diaries, as Italian memoirs, diaries, and autobiographies are often so fragmented and problematic that one might be inclined to disregard them out of hand.[34] Many historians do have such reservations about personal memoirs and diaries, yet all the current biographies of Ciano are based on an uncritical and sometimes careless use of several of the poorly published versions of the diary.[35] Given the nature of this study and my awareness of these inferior published editions, I decided to focus on the original photographs of the diary from the years 1939–43, which were taken by the American Office of Strategic Services at the end of the Second World War and kept in several public archives.[36]

Unfortunately, these photographs entail manifold gaps and erasures that hint at potentially deliberate alteration of the text by Ciano and/or his wife. Though the authenticity of the diary is not in question, the many unresolved issues with the original photographs should caution those historians who rely solely on the published versions for their research. There is no doubt that Ciano's diary is a treasure trove for catchy quotes, and thus it would be tempting to quote from it at length. However, given the diary's problematic nature, one should be careful not to overemphasize Ciano's voice. This problem is another reason why I chose to augment and contextualize the diary photographs with archival and Foreign Ministry documents as well as a wide selection of published and unpublished documents and primary sources. Such an approach allows for a far more critical examination of Ciano's complex and contradictory personality while minimizing the pitfalls of translation errors and deliberate misdirection.[37]

In addition to the just-mentioned sources, I examined many Italian and foreign daily and weekly newspapers, photographs, and film materials to build a better picture of the propaganda and the performative dimension of Ciano's domestic and foreign politics and their impact. In this area too, this study breaks new ground, given that visual sources have not yet been included in biographies of Italian fascist personalities. A study on Ciano in particular offers the opportunity – and I would argue even demands – the use of images and film materials as more than a means of illustration. These items help to contextualize and sometimes visualize written documents; and more often than not, they also point to additional aspects that are lost or omitted from written records, including the "performativity of social actions and behaviour."[38]

This material provides a broad and more-than-sufficient source base for a thorough analysis of Ciano's personality, character, and politics, despite the many problems and questions that still surround Ciano's diary and the absence of personal papers from the Ciano family. One note of caution, however: because Ciano's personal notes primarily cover the period from the summer of 1937 to February 1943, we still have to deal with an imbalance in the available source material. As a result, outside this time period this study relies predominantly on statements given by third parties when assessing Ciano's personality, which always carry a hint of pure speculation and bias.[39]

British historian and Mussolini biographer Denis Mack Smith once wrote that the *Duce*'s entourage was "less than competent" and is therefore not worth studying.[40] Galeazzo Ciano's life and career, however, illustrates that it is time to move past such derision. The thematic analysis of Ciano, who was caught up between the high expectations of his peer group and his subsequent desire to maintain the status quo, reveals a multifaceted character who invented various self-images for specific circumstances that transcended apodictic categories like "fascist" and "conservative." The study of Ciano's life, career, and beliefs also reveals the heterogeneity of the fascist elite. Ciano's biography lifts the curtain of the almighty Mussolini and in doing so offers a better understanding of the inner functioning of fascist rule, the machinations within the upper echelon of power, the fascistization of Italian society, and the foreign policy of the fascist era, thus highlighting the limits of the totalitarian experiment.

1
The Family

The Son of a Hero

In the early summer of 1939, Europe was on the brink of war. After Germany had occupied Prague in March and Italy had invaded Albania in April, relations between Great Britain and France, on the one hand, and the Axis powers, on the other, reached a low point. A few statesmen and diplomats still desperately tried their best to prevent the outbreak of an armed conflict in Europe. For Galeazzo Ciano, however, the fear of an impending war played only a minor role; instead, he was paralyzed by his personal grief over the death of his father, Costanzo Ciano, on 26 June 1939. He "felt something was torn away from ... [his] physical being," and he only now realized how "real and deep and indestructible ... ties of blood" were. "You, Father," he wrote in his diary, "you have known me from my infancy, my admiring love for you, you alone can thoroughly understand my sorrow. You are with me in my spirit, inseparable forever."[1]

These sentences illustrate Galeazzo Ciano's close attachment to and admiration for his father. They gain further significance considering that Ciano usually described and commented on political events in his diary; to mourn his father, however, he often made exceptions.[2] Thus, in order to understand Galeazzo's life and persona, it is necessary to first examine the life and work of his father. Who was Costanzo Ciano, whose son showed him so much respect and affection, and who called him the "glory of imperial Italy?"[3]

The date and place of birth of a person and thus the sociopolitical and cultural environment are essential for understanding someone's life.[4] This point is especially true for Italy. Politicians and intellectuals of the *Risorgimento* failed to overcome regional linguistic, cultural, social, and economic differences and to replace local identities with a national one.[5] Even at the beginning of the twentieth century the famous dictum, "We have made Italy. Now we must make the Italians!"[6] which was attributed to Massimo d'Azeglio, had not been realized. Italians often felt a greater loyalty and commitment to their own hometown than to the abstract idea of an Italian nation-state. Recognizing Italy's regional differences and mentalities is therefore the first step in understanding the life and people in Italy.[7] In the case of the Ciano family, it leads us to Tuscany, more precisely to Livorno, the birthplace of Costanzo and Galeazzo Ciano.

During the seventeenth and eighteenth century, tax privileges enabled Livorno to become a cosmopolitan seaport. The city attracted merchants from all over Europe, creating a multicultural mix of Italians, British, French, Greeks, and Spaniards. Due to the inhabitants' well-known liberal attitude, the city also accommodated one of the largest Jewish communities in Italy.[8] For the French philologist Charles de Brosses, all this diversity contributed to the special charm of the city. He enthused that one can find all peoples of Europe and Asia in the city and hear the languages of the "Tower of Babel" on the streets and squares.[9] His compatriot, the philosopher Charles Montesquieu, admired the "beautiful city" and praised "the Grand Dukes, who have done such a great and good job here, creating a thriving city and advantageous port."[10]

After Italian unification, however, the city lost all fiscal privileges, ultimately leading to its economic decline. In the newly created kingdom, Livorno, the former pride of the west coast, unsuccessfully competed with Rome, the new capital; with Florence, the city of arts and culture; with Milan, the heart of the Italian economy and the press, and seat of the national stock exchange; and with Turin, the city of the Royal House of Savoy and the centre of heavy industry.[11] The American writer Henry James, otherwise known for his love of Italy, wrote that Livorno "may claim the distinction, unique in Italy, of being the city of no pictures."[12]

Instead of sights, the city was characterized by economic recession, high unemployment, and increasing emigration. Yet, Livorno was not the only city struggling with these challenges.[13] Throughout Italy, the adventurous times of the Italian national movement had been replaced "by the sober prose of a daily routine and unsuccessful nationhood."[14] The governments in Rome had failed to pacify the country's tense social and political situation and to control the increasing irredentist demands. Since the 1880s several politicians had promoted the colonization of Somalia and Eritrea to distract from these domestic problems. This expansionist policy led to the enlargement of the army and navy, and to a state subsidy for heavy industry.[15]

Eventually, one of the beneficiaries of this new policy was Livorno. State support and the resources on the island of Elba helped to establish a prosperous shipbuilding and steel industry. By the turn of the century, the city had largely overcome its decline and successfully transformed from a commercial into an industrial city. In 1866 Luigi Orlando, a native of Palermo, founded the *Navali Orlando* shipyard in Livorno together with his brothers. Thanks to the aggressive imperialist policy under Prime Minister Francesco Crispi, who came into office in 1887, the shipyard won numerous contracts.[16] In the following years, the Orlando family took over the entire shipbuilding business and metal industry in the city. Their economic success eventually led to more political influence at the local and national level. In 1914 Rosolino Orlando was elected mayor of Livorno, and already in 1904, Salvatore Orlando had won a seat in the Chamber of Deputies in Rome. In 1918 the latter was appointed secretary of state in the Ministry of Maritime and Railroad Transport, and two years later he became a member of the Senate. Their support of the governments in Rome earned the Orlandos political and economic favours from several ministers. This patronage, in turn, enabled them to increase their wealth and expand their position in Livorno. For the time being, the family became the patron of the city.[17] After the First World War, the fate of the Orlandos would be closely linked to the rise of another son of the city: Costanzo Ciano.

Even today we possess only limited information about Costanzo Ciano's adolescence, his education, and his early military and political career. In 1932 he turned down an offer by the publisher Arnaldo Mondadori to write his memoir.[18] The little we do know is often distorted by glorification and thus of dubious historical validity, allowing many myths about his life to live on as no scholar really seems to challenge them. Since the 1920s more than twenty-five hagiographic monographs about Costanzo Ciano have been published: he became the subject of an official cult, enshrined in a fifteen-minute-long documentary by the state-run *L'Unione Cinematografica Educativa* (LUCE) about his life, which was released after his death.[19] But why did leading fascists like Roberto Farinacci posthumously glorify him so enthusiastically? A glance at Ciano's life and career until the "March on Rome" in 1922 and at the role his public image and charisma played in his rise will provide answers to this question.

Costanzo Ciano was born on 30 August 1876 to Raimondo and Argia Ciano. His father, a simple sailor for the Coast Guard, had to support a family of fifteen. The extended family lived in a small house in the impoverished Borgo dei Cappuccini district, reflecting the precarious socioeconomic conditions in Livorno at the time. While modernization and industrialization gave rise to nuclear families in some parts of Italy, in structurally weak regions, such as Livorno, children of extended families still had to make a significant contribution to the family income.[20] In November 1891 Costanzo Ciano joined the Naval Academy in Livorno.[21] At that time the academy was open to applicants of all social classes, and fathers from socially disadvantaged backgrounds, such as Raimondo Ciano, hoped that military training would provide a better future for their sons.[22]

During his training Costanzo Ciano was taught traditional values such as discipline, willpower, and monarchical-hierarchical thinking.[23] On 16 July 1896 he graduated from the academy as a naval cadet. In 1901 he was promoted to first lieutenant and married Carolina Pini, who belonged to one of Livorno's wealthy middle-class families. Ciano's social advancement was also reflected in the couple's family planning. Since children no longer seemed necessary to provide financial security, Carolina Ciano only gave birth to two children: Galeazzo (18 March 1903) and Maria (27 February 1913).[24] Within a generation, the Ciano family – like many other families in Italy's urban centres – had successfully transitioned from a poverty-stricken extended family to a bourgeois nuclear family.[25]

Costanzo Ciano's first job was at the Navy Signal and Radio Academy in Porto Venere, a small coastal village near La Spezia. During this time, he made friends who would play an important role in his later life, including Guglielmo Marconi, the Nobel Prize winner in physics in 1909, and Admiral Domenico Cavagnari. As an officer of the Royal Navy, Costanzo also participated in the Libyan War (1911–12). According to Farinacci, the invasion of Libya offered Ciano, who was driven by "painful patriotism," the opportunity to show the world Italy's glory and to fight against the country's decay.[26] Farinacci's comments illustrate Italian nationalists' longing to finally be recognized as a great power and thus give insight into a specific Italian national identity, a mix of a "feeling of superiority" and a "lack of self-confidence." Even though this feeling would later legitimize the palingenetic ultranationalism propagated by fascists, it was not exclusively fascist to begin with, but firmly rooted in Italy's collective memory.[27]

After Italy entered the First World War, Costanzo Ciano was sent to Venice.[28] Together with his family, he moved into an apartment in Piazza Santa Maria del Giglio. Poverty, disease, and Italy's highest suicide rate, on the one hand, and romanticism, tourism, culture, and intellectuals like Gabriele D'Annunzio, on the other, shaped the city's ambivalent image that Thomas Mann used for his book *Tod in Venedig* (*Death in Venice*).[29] In the first decade of the twentieth century, the city saw the rise of Giuseppe Volpi, a fervent interventionist and businessman with close ties to American industrialists and contacts with the local fascist group operating under Giovanni Giuriati. Like the Orlando family in Livorno, his economic position made him the city's patron, the last "Doge of Venice." Volpi, governor of Tripolitania from 1921 to 1925 and minister of finance from 1925 to 1928, would also play an important role in the lives of the Cianos.[30]

In Venice, Costanzo Ciano was primarily in charge of small torpedo boats, the *Motoscafo Armato Silurante* (MAS).[31] In November 1917 Ciano, commander of seven destroyers and three MAS, defeated an Austro-Hungarian unit near Cortellazzo that was superior in number and fighting strength. This victory helped to stabilize the front line after the Italian troops had suffered a devastating defeat at Caporetto on 24 October 1917.[32] "Never before," Farinacci extolled, "has one seen such a daring and glorious sea battle: in broad daylight an attack of two peanut-sized crafts against twelve ships, the smallest of which was so strong that it could have destroyed the attackers with a few targeted shots."[33]

In February 1918 Ciano secured another victory. With three MAS he launched several torpedoes against four steamers in the Bay of Buccari. Although no serious damage was done, the surprise attack was a moral victory for the Italian fleet and humiliated the Austro-Hungarians.[34] Thanks to D'Annunzio, who was present during the attack, the raid – known as the *beffa di Buccari* (mockery of Buccari) – became enshrined in Italy's collective memory as one of the boldest maritime operations during the war, and his commander, Costanzo Ciano, was thereafter remembered as a hero. D'Annunzio spontaneously redefined the acronym MAS into *Memento Audere Semper* ("Remember to be always brave") and declared it to be Ciano's official motto. In the following months he constantly praised his idol's daring deeds in newspapers, public speeches, and on the radio.[35] As early as 1921, fascist propaganda organs ran with these stories, in large part because D'Annunzio's description of Ciano matched those of the ideal fascist officer: always at the head of his unit; upright, calm, and determined; never shunning a confrontation and even disappointed when he was denied a fight. By doing so the fascist propaganda further popularized the myth surrounding Ciano.[36]

After the war, Costanzo Ciano – like many of his comrades – faced demobilization despite the numerous orders of merit he had received for his military actions.[37] When he was denied a promotion in February 1919, he was placed in the reserve at his own request. In May 1919 he accepted an offer from industrialist Giovanni Agnelli to manage the *Il Mare* company in Genoa. The new position promised job security and a much more lucrative income than that of a navy officer.[38]

Even though Ciano's military career ended in 1919, the myth surrounding him laid the foundation for his political career. In the general election of November 1919 he made his first, yet unsuccessful, attempt to enter politics, running for the conservative *Unione Democratico* (UD) in Livorno.[39] The present historiography offers a simple narrative for why he decided to enter politics in the first place: friends like D'Annunzio urged him to take up this "burden."[40] Yet, crediting Ciano's political commitment primarily to external pressure is hardly convincing. Three reasons present themselves to explain why he had lost confidence in the political elite and wanted to offer an alternative.

First, during the First World War, Venice suffered severely under aerial bombardments. As a result, citizens lived under the constant strain of death and violence. The local administration ordered a blackout of the city as well as the closure of public institutions. When, after the "Catastrophe of Caporetto," no precise information about the situation at the front reached the city, many inhabitants fled inland. Unable to provide reliable protection, even Ciano sent his family to Genoa. The remaining citizens, including Ciano himself, accused the government of abandoning Venice to its fate.[41]

Second, Ciano blamed the same politicians for not resolving acute crises, including the return of war veterans and the growing influence of the socialists.[42] He felt that it was now his duty as a war hero to overcome this dilettantism. He believed that his determination and success during the war were enough to legitimize his candidacy. Internalizing Carl von Clausewitz's dictum, Ciano regarded politics as nothing more than the continuation of war in times of peace.[43]

And third, Ciano accused the political elite of betraying Italy's victory during the Paris Peace Conference negotiations. He was not alone. Many nationalists suffered from what they considered Italy's *"vittoria mutilata"* ("mutilated victory"), the notion that after the war Italy had not received everything promised in the Treaty of London (1915). The term was allegedly coined by D'Annunzio, and its devastating impact can be compared to the "stab-in-the-back-myth" of the Weimar Republic.[44] D'Annunzio, however, did not only verbally attack the government in Rome: from 12 September 1919 to 29 December 1920, he occupied the city of Fiume, which – according to him – rightfully belonged to Italy.[45] Fiume and D'Annunzio became a powerful rallying point for attacks on the supposedly unjust peace treaties. Many nationalists openly showed their solidarity with the poet by visiting Fiume. Among them were Benito Mussolini, the futurist Filippo Tommaso Marinetti, and Guglielmo Marconi. In November 1920 the famous conductor Arturo Toscanini gave a concert in the city. By turning these visits into spectacular gatherings, D'Annunzio not only set new standards for public events but assured that his revisionist demands were heard around the world. As a leading representative of the avant-garde theatre, it is hardly surprising that he became a pioneer of the performative political style.[46]

Although Costanzo Ciano did not travel to Fiume, he showed his support for the occupiers and defended D'Annunzio's action in his political program, which resembled more a mishmash of demands than a cohesive agenda.[47] By addressing the occupation of Fiume he was working with a topic that emotionally touched the citizens in Livorno. The city had already experienced several violent clashes between its citizens and the French troops stationed in the city after the First World War. The government in Paris was not only seen as an obstacle to Italy's rightful territorial claims in the Adriatic because it advocated a free Fiume state and supported the new Yugoslavian state. Rather, the dispute over Fiume served as an outlet for a fanatical irredentism in Livorno, which was directed in particular against the French presence in Corsica.[48]

Despite his electoral defeat, Ciano remained convinced that "new times would require new people."[49] He was forced to acknowledge that he was not as popular in his hometown as he had believed. To be victorious in the next general election in May 1921, he had to increase his presence in and commitment to Livorno. Moreover, he realized that an inexperienced politician like himself had no chance in a party dominated by members of the traditional elite. To succeed, he had to join a new political force. At that time, several ultranationalist movements fascinated many people in Europe, who hoped that they would put an end to the perceived crisis of their nation. Their "pervasive, palingenetic, modernist ethos," according to Roger Griffin, "meant that many individuals ... were predisposed to 'jump ship' so as to be protagonists of what could easily be seen as a new rather than a dying world, and so be able to join in the making of history."[50] One of these groups was Benito Mussolini's fascists.

By 1919 about twenty *fasci di combattimento* had been founded in Italy by revolutionary socialists and syndicalists who left the *Partito Socialista Italiano* (PSI; Italian Socialist Party), demobilized soldiers and officers, members of the petit bourgeoisie, and students, journalists, and avant-garde artists.[51] On 23 March 1919 Mussolini summoned their representatives to Milan to unite them into a national political movement. His goal was ambitious, considering that the participants shared more a common, emotional mental attitude than a joint political platform or consistent ideology. This mindset was multifaceted. Fascism was a youth and renewal movement. It was supported by a younger generation who rejected an encrusted and inflexible political, economic, and social system. The middle class also saw fascism as a chance for social advancement and emancipation, hoping to expand its social and political influence at the expense of the traditional elites. And fascists believed in a crude form of vague ultranationalism. They wanted to fight back against what they perceived as a humiliation they had experienced after the war.[52] In addition, there were other characteristics, which varied from region to region, resulting in a great heterogeneity of the movement. In industrial cities such as Turin, fascism was primarily a counter-revolutionary phenomenon. There, industrial and traditional elites sought an alliance with the fascists to oppose the revolutionary forces of the Left. In border regions such as Venezia Giulia, racism played a more important role in gaining a large following. The fascists presented themselves as defenders of *italianità* and their combat troops (*squadristi* or Blackshirts) carried out brutal attacks against Slavs.[53]

The political scene in Livorno had been dominated for some time by conservative forces. However, in the regional elections of 7 November 1920 they suffered a bitter defeat. The socialist Uberto Mondolfi became the new mayor and replaced the local government under Rosolino Orlando (UD).[54] Ten days later the local *fascio di combattimento* was founded, consisting mainly of the lower middle-class, white-collar workers and officer cadets of the Naval Academy.[55] On 20 January 1921 the first issue of the local party newspaper *A NOI!* was published, in which editor-in-chief Paolo Pedani explained the political program. He explicitly distanced himself from traditional parties and called for the privatization of the economy, the abolition of the monarchy, the subordination of workers' interests to the common good, and the dissolution of autonomous trade unions. Pedani also called for a "peaceful" expansion into the eastern Adriatic – a demand that enjoyed wide support among irredentists.[56]

Considering the importance of *ras* (local charismatic leaders) like Roberto Farinacci in Cremona for the success of the fascist movements, the *fascio* in Livorno had one fundamental problem. While these *ras* were able to unite their heterogeneous following and turn their "provinces into true states within the state,"[57] the fascists in Livorno lacked such a dominant personality. While the *fascio* had been one of the strongest groups in Tuscany when it was founded, one year later it ranked last.[58] Even the violent attacks on offices and politicians of the PSI could not stop its demise. It was not for nothing that contemporaries considered Livorno as a PSI stronghold, calling it "little Russia."[59]

In the end, the Livorno *fascio* benefitted from two factors. First, the socialists were unable to overcome their internal strife. During the Second Congress of the PSI in Livorno, the left wing of the party split off and founded the *Partito Comunista Italiano* (Italian Communist Party) on 21 January 1921. Second, many industrialists and members of nationalist groups and the UD regarded the fascists as a potential tool for opposing the socialists and regaining power.[60] Terrified by the recurring strikes and with no help forthcoming from the government in Rome, many industrialists like Giuseppe Orlando were convinced that "they had to take their cause into their own hands."[61] By entering the *fascio*, the establishment sought to moderate the radical fascists and impose their political will upon the movement. One of them was Costanzo Ciano, who joined the party on 20 March 1921.[62]

Ciano's fame as a war hero and his allegiance to Livorno gave the *fascio* their long-desired personality. Thus far, historians have barely analysed his motives for joining the fascists due to the lack of personal documents and statements.[63] There is no doubt that Ciano must have been fascinated by the new political force, which he wanted to use for his own career.[64] But what about a personal ideological affinity for fascism? Ciano was a staunch monarchist, so Pedani's anti-royalist stance was hardly something with which he agreed. Other points of the party platform, however, were more appealing to him, including the privatization of the economy, the strengthening of employers, the nationalist tone, and the foreign policy objectives.[65] With the help of the fascists Ciano also hoped to secure and expand his social and financial position in Livorno, which he saw threatened by the Left. We should keep in mind that he was an upstart, eager to defend his new social status. The perceived threat to his own standing ultimately turned Ciano into a fierce anti-communist.[66]

In May 1921 the leadership of the UD and of the local *fascio* agreed to form an alliance, the *Blocco Nazionale*, for the upcoming election. However, only two people on the joint voter list were natives of Livorno: the industrialist Guido Donegani and Costanzo Ciano. The fascist and conservative press highly praised the latter's pure blood, his heroism and patriotism.[67] He especially enjoyed the backing of the Orlando family, the Livorno-born Senator Florestano De Larderel, and his old admirer, Gabriele D'Annunzio. Dino Perrone Compagni, the "grand duke" of the Tuscan fascists, supported him too. He hoped that a fascist takeover in Livorno would bring the shipbuilding industry under his control and thus destroy the last stronghold of the socialists. Ciano was integral to this plan thanks to his good relations with the Naval Academy and the industrial elite.[68] In the end, the *Blocco Nazionale* became the strongest political force in Livorno with 36.7 per cent of the votes; nationwide, the alliance gained 275 seats in the Chamber of Deputies in Rome – 35 of which went to the fascists, among them Costanzo Ciano.[69]

After the election nationwide riots erupted between fascists and leftists. In reaction to the violence, trade unions declared a general strike for the summer of 1922 with fatal consequences. The fear of a revolution drove the urban bourgeoisie and the conservative elite further into the arms of the fascists. Some *fasci* seized the opportunity, taking over cities like Ferrara and Cremona. In Livorno, too, the strike led to an even closer alliance between conservatives and fascists. Costanzo Ciano worked tirelessly in the background to make this cooperation possible. When the Republicans ended their collaboration with the Left, accusing them of a Sovietization of Italy, and joined the local *fascio*, the fascists in Livorno also dared a coup.[70]

Perrone Compagni began to assemble fascists from all over Tuscany in Livorno. Costanzo Ciano himself travelled from Rome to Livorno on 2 August 1922 in order to participate in the "seizure of power." He declared that it was the duty of every Italian to protect the homeland, freedom, and the family against the subversive elements in the country. He called on his fellow citizens to join the fascists to stop the "murder" of the *patria*.[71] These martial statements notwithstanding, Ciano still represented the moderate fascists who enjoyed the support of the city's economic and conservative elites. This allegiance was also evident in Ciano's public appearances. He was usually dressed in a bourgeois suit, even during the "conquest" of Livorno's city hall, and in the following years he was rarely seen wearing a fascist militia uniform.[72]

On 3 August 1922 the socialist mayor, Uberto Mondolfi, resigned from his post and handed the city to Costanzo Ciano and the fascists. He had bowed to the fascist demands after Perrone Compagni threatened to storm the city hall and hurt Mondolfi's family if he refused to resign.[73] In their own historiography, the fascists declared the year 1922 as the "Year of the Victim." Ignoring the internal rivalries, they exaggerated the threat posed by local "subversives." They claimed that anarchists had hunted down fascists in Livorno and that only the "blood of martyrs" had ensured the survival of the *fascio*.[74] By claiming to have been victims, they were able to portray their violence in purely defensive terms and, by doing so, legitimized it in the eyes of the conservative elites.

The reality was different: the fascists did not prevail because of "their own blood"; much more important for their ultimate victory was the tolerance and active support of the local security forces, the Naval Academy, and the conservative elites. The fascists in Livorno were primarily a counter-revolutionary force, which allowed them to convince the political and industrial establishment to join them in their struggle against a common enemy on the Left. Moreover, they successfully applied a dual strategy, which was also used by Mussolini: they resorted to revolutionary violence and publicly adopted a conciliatory position at the same time.[75]

After the turbulent days of August 1922, the fascists quickly restored public order in Livorno. Anxious to demonstrate that they were actually able to do so, they turned to the Orlando shipyard, the largest employer in the city. The Orlandos had decided to close their firm after the government failed to settle outstanding payments. Prefect Edoardo Verdinois suspected that they primarily wanted to put pressure on the government, because the closure of the shipyard would have pushed the city into further turmoil. The fascists were aware that the reopening and thus the continued employment of many workers not only would be met with broad approval by the population but would also be a harsh blow to the socialists. The importance they attached to this situation was evidenced by the calibre of individuals entrusted with handling the affair: Perrone Compagni, Costanzo Ciano, and the deputy secretary of the PNF, Giuseppe Bastianini.[76] Once again, the fascists adopted their double strategy. While Perrone Compagni threatened to use violence against the Orlandos, Ciano and Bastianini negotiated with them.[77]

On 12 October the owners of the shipyard agreed to resume operations and assured Ciano that only the fascist trade union would be allowed to represent their workers.[78] In return, the fascists promised to reimburse the Orlandos for all their payment claims. The fascist leaning newspaper *Gazzetta Livornese* lauded the solution and stated that all citizens were pleased that the decent and hard-working employees enjoyed – once again – peace and security.[79] The historian Frank Snowden rightly dismissed the seriousness of the threats against the shipyard, arguing that the personal ties between the fascists and the Orlando family were too close.[80] Rather, the threats allowed the Orlandos to justify their break with the traditional trade unions in the eyes of their workers and the people in Livorno. Overall, it was a huge success for the fascists in general, who were able to put an end to the socialist influence in Livorno's most important industry, and for Costanzo Ciano in particular, who was once again able to portray himself as the moderate element of the fascist movement.[81]

Costanzo Ciano's life, from the son of a simple sailor to a war hero to a fascist leader, was predestined for fascist propaganda. Farinacci wrote that Ciano had always worked with all his might and with dedication for the good of Italy; only interested in breaking Italy's "shackles," he had worked tirelessly to conquer an Italian *Mare Nostrum* in order to secure the survival of his homeland.[82] Distorting the causal links, the fascists used Ciano's life as a perfect example to show how a highly decorated naval officer and First World War hero was cast aside by the liberal government and then joined the fascists out of his "deep love" for the Italian nation.[83] According to numerous glorifying depictions, Costanzo Ciano's decision was hardly surprising. Farinacci even claimed that Ciano was a fascist before the first Italian *fascio* had been founded; he was one of the first, most resolute, and loyal fascists and made a name for himself as irrepressible, assertive, and proud. As a result, Ciano had left his "bourgeois life" behind him and become a "political hero" of Fascist Italy.[84] Thus, following Benito Mussolini's and Giovanni Gentile's credo that deeds are more important than words, Ciano's life offered all facets to present him as the role model for future generations.[85]

From the 1920s, the fascist propaganda exploited Costanzo Ciano's military and political career to emphasize the existence of a strong bond between the old, conservative elite and the new fascist movement. By portraying him as a First World War hero and as a hero of the fascist revolution – or, as Farinacci wrote, Costanzo Ciano represented "tradition" and "revolution" simultaneously – the propagandists tried to appeal to both groups.[86] While Ciano's success as a naval officer attracted monarchical, military, and conservative elites, his role during the fascist coup in Livorno earned him the respect of the fascists. Both narratives, which Ciano himself promoted during his lifetime, were also circulated after his death and especially during the Second World War. Despite renewed tensions between conservatives and fascists due to Rome's entry into the war, Costanzo Ciano was still held in high esteem by both groups. By using his career and his character, fascist propagandists wanted to call to mind the strong bond between conservatives and fascists that had once existed.[87]

It is unknown whether Galeazzo Ciano noticed the important role his father played for the fascist propaganda. However, his actions prove that he intended to maintain, defend, and – if possible – even further his father's reputation. After all, did not his father bring "honour to the party; a soldier, a fascist, a Christian?"[88] In particular, Galeazzo employed several strategies to preserve if not grow his father's legacy. As propaganda and foreign minister, he intervened in the ways his father was depicted. He censored every critical tone, publicly reprimanded critical authors, and threatened them with professional and personal consequences, thus demonstrating how important his father's prestige was to him. Even when he was under house arrest in the summer of 1943 and people began to publicly condemn his father's corruption, he defended his father's reputation.[89] Galeazzo also organized several festivities in Livorno to commemorate his father's heroic deeds, including ceremonies for the anniversary of the *beffa di Buccari* and his death.[90] And most importantly, he used buildings, monuments, public squares, and streets to remind the public of his father and further the cult surrounding him.

After Costanzo Ciano's death, his son planned to build a tomb that "will rise from the top of the hill. It will be a monument that will recall your war and your heroism. On top of it will be a beacon which will be lit every night so that we may all be reminded from a distance of your immortal spirit."[91] Although the mausoleum's construction was started immediately after Costanzo Ciano's burial in the summer of 1939, it was never completed. Today visitors can only see the pedestal, on which the marble statue of Costanzo Ciano should have been placed.[92] The monument's mock-up, however, demonstrates how the mausoleum and the statue were modelled after the image of the heroic admiral, as it was handed down to us by D'Annunzio: Costanzo Ciano stands high up on the ship's bow, defying all dangers and obstacles.[93]

Besides building a magnificent mausoleum Galeazzo Ciano also intended to renovate his father's "modest" birth house in Livorno and turn it into a "holy place."[94] Both buildings – birth house and tomb – were supposed to become pilgrimage sites for his father's admirers, contributing to the cult-like worship that developed after his death. Ciano's plans remind us of the important role religious symbolism played in the political strategy of Italian fascists, a fact that supports the conceptualization of fascism as a "political religion," as suggested by historians such as Emilio Gentile.[95]

Galeazzo Ciano also ensured that, even outside of Livorno, prestigious buildings, squares, and entire towns were named after his father, including a grammar school in Naples, the village of Ponte a Moriano, and a square in Tirana.[96] In addition, streets and squares surrounding the *Palazzo Montecitorio* in Rome, the seat of the Chamber of Fasci and Cooperations, were named after his father's greatest accomplishments.[97] Near Cortellazzo, the scene of Costanzo Ciano's first "heroic" deed, a new fishing village was built to commemorate his father's naval victory.[98] In La Spezia and Genoa tall statues of his father were erected during the Second World War, using a similar iconography that could already be seen with the plans for the mausoleum: Costanzo Ciano was depicted as the daring admiral, standing on a pedestal that resembled a ship's bow, looking fearlessly into the distance (figure 1).

Although Galeazzo Ciano was not particularly happy with the artistic design, both statues were created by well-known sculptors such as Francesco Messina.[99] LUCE recorded and broadcasted both inauguration ceremonies, which were attended by large crowds, Galeazzo Ciano, and other dignitaries of the regime. The coverage of the ceremonies alternated with scenes of torpedo boats – Costanzo Ciano's famous MAS – while the commentators reminded the viewers of Ciano's great victories in the First World War. Their intention, however, was not only to commemorate a hero of a past war; they also wanted to spread courage and confidence in a time of particular distress. Their message was easy to understand. Bravery, boldness, and refinement – and thus all characteristics that distinguished Costanzo Ciano in the First World War – would eventually bring victory in the Second World War. The newspaper *La Stampa* even wrote that Ciano had finally returned to help the nation in peril. Italy was indeed in desperate need of a war hero, and the regime enshrined Costanzo Ciano in that role.[100]

It is hardly surprising that Galeazzo Ciano had a personal interest in preserving and constantly protecting his father's reputation and honour. First, he was well aware of how important his father's charismatic authority was for his career. Second, he hoped that the eulogies about Costanzo Ciano would positively impact his own – or at least the family's – reputation. Indeed, in several newspaper reports he was always described as the hero's son.[101] He assumed that by defending his father's honour he would preserve one of the central pillars of his family's influence. In Italy's patriarchal society under fascism, the family's prestige was still closely connected with the reputation of the male head of the family. And third, the family – and thus the prestige and honour of all its members – had always played an outstanding role in Mediterranean societies. Protecting the family's honour was a nearly sacred duty for all its members since it was a key element for an effective patronage system, which ultimately determined the family's power. Failing to defend the family's honour could cause the family's downfall, a fact that still held true during the fascist period.[102]

However, the high esteem for Costanzo Ciano came at a price to his son because traits such as honour and prestige are bound to one specific person. Although it is understandable that Galeazzo Ciano tried everything to preserve and maintain his father's memory, he could

Figure 1. Statue of Costanzo Ciano in La Spezia, 1940. Ullstein Bild #01072609.

not just claim his father's reputation for himself – personal charisma, unlike office charisma, cannot be transferred.[103] In addition, he was continually compared to his father, a comparison he was never able to live up to, given the glorification Costanzo received. Galeazzo Ciano thus faced a huge dilemma, which he was unable to resolve. The more he praised his father's deeds in order to defend his reputation, the more he contributed to an impossibly idealized image of his father against which he paled in comparison. Thus, his father's charisma was not only a blessing for the family, but also a heavy burden for his son.[104]

The Ciano Family in Livorno

On 27 October 1922 Benito Mussolini openly attempted to seize power and mobilized the Blackshirts near Rome, while he himself stayed in Milan by the telephone. Prime Minister Luigi Facta and his cabinet were largely isolated. They resigned and hoped to defy fascism at the last minute by declaring a state of emergency. However, King Vittorio Emanuele III refused to declare a state of emergency. Nevertheless, he still tried to prevent a Mussolini government by entrusting Antonio Salandra with the formation of a new cabinet. Moderate fascists such as Costanzo Ciano and Cesare Maria De Vecchi began negotiations with Salandra and welcomed his proposal to offer Mussolini the post of minister of the interior. To their discontent Mussolini declined and demanded the position of prime minister.[105] After negotiations failed, the way was clear for Mussolini. Although the legendary "March on Rome" was never, as the fascists later claimed, a revolution that overthrew the constitutional order, the event nevertheless had far-reaching consequences for Italy and for the whole of Europe, as contemporaries like the German diplomat and writer Harry Graf Kessler realized.[106]

On 30 October 1922 Benito Mussolini presented his new government, which had three fascist ministers – Giovanni Giuriati (minister for the occupied territories), Alberto De' Stefani (minister of finance), and Aldo Oviglio (minister of justice). Mussolini himself assumed the post of prime minister, and he also headed the Ministry of Foreign Affairs and the Ministry of the Interior.[107] Nevertheless, the constitution did not grant him a special status among his cabinet colleagues. As prime minister it was his task to mediate between ministers and find a political consensus. That he ultimately prevailed as leader of the fascist movement and became the key figure for holding together the extremely heterogeneous movement was due to his political experience, his oratory skills, and his charismatic authority. None of his rivals, including Italo

Balbo, Roberto Farinacci, and Dino Grandi, were able to compete with him in these regards at that time on a national level.[108]

Despite his role during the fascist takeover in Livorno, Costanzo Ciano was only appointed as secretary of state for the merchant navy. Even though fascist historiography would posthumously exaggerate the importance of this office and depict Ciano as one of the main pillars of the new regime, it cannot be ignored that his position granted him little power to influence major political decisions.[109] Balbo and De Vecchi, as quadrumvirs, were responsible for the planning and execution of the "March on Rome" and were also original members of the Fascist Grand Council, founded in January 1923. Grandi, the leader of the *fascio* in Bologna, was appointed state secretary in the Ministry of the Interior in 1923 and served directly under Mussolini. And even Farinacci maintained his clout within the fascist party under Achille Starace. Unlike Costanzo Ciano, whose network and standing in Livorno was still in its infancy, the others had possessed undisputed power in their hometowns for some time, a fact Mussolini could not ignore. To avoid unrest on the periphery and to strengthen his regime's influence into the regions, he had to integrate these powerful *ras* into his regime. Towards Ciano, however, Mussolini did not need to show any consideration, especially since the man from Livorno had often voted against his proposals and clashed with radical fascists like Farinacci.[110]

In the following years, however, Costanzo Ciano's influence continued to grow. On 3 February 1924 Mussolini appointed him as the minister of post and telecommunications, and three months later Ciano took over the newly created Ministry of Communications, which he headed for almost ten years. On 24 September 1930 the *Duce* made him a permanent member of the Fascist Grand Council.[111] In April 1934 Ciano was nominated as the new president of the Chamber of Deputies, which was restructured into the Chamber of Fasci and Cooperations in 1939. Ciano's organizational skills, his commitment to the fascist regime, and his loyalty to the *Duce* were partly responsible for his career. Thereby, it was beneficial to him that he was in charge of the Italian railway system, as the new punctuality of Italian trains became – thanks to fascist propaganda – a symbol of the regime's effectiveness on a national and international level.[112] One key factor, however, that has so far received little scholarly attention, is Ciano's increasing standing in Livorno.[113]

Costanzo Ciano established a sophisticated patronage system in his hometown that helped to expand his own influence and limit the power of potential rivals. He increasingly intruded in political, economic, and social affairs, even though he resided far away in Rome. By doing so he slowly supplanted the Orlando family, which had controlled the city's destiny for years. Since the nineteenth century, patronage had been an integral part of the country's political culture and was widely used by ambitious families and individuals to acquire, maintain, and expand their influence. The lack of a collective national identity, a great mistrust towards the state institutions in Rome, and the inability of central governments to control the periphery had favoured this system. Local power became a valuable status symbol that increased one's influence on a national level and allowed one to oppose others and champion one's own interests in Rome.[114]

The patronage system was based on the exchange of goods between patron and client. The patron offered economic and political favours as well as protection; in return he secured the solidarity and loyalty of his client. This asymmetric game increased the influence and standing of all parties involved. A client was much more inclined to voluntarily enter into a dependency when the patron possessed a high prestige, as it guaranteed that the patron would most likely provide the promised protection and favours. Costanzo Ciano's exceptional reputation among conservatives and fascists alike made him an excellent target for any client. The system collapsed as soon as one side did not keep its part of the agreement and ended – for whatever reasons – the exchange of resources.[115]

After the First World War the fascists promised to abolish local power structures, to fight patronage, and to end corruption in the country. They cultivated an image as political outsiders in order to attack the establishment – a tactic that was and still is used by populist authoritarian movements.[116] A closer look, however, reveals that Costanzo Ciano represented exactly the person the fascists wanted to eliminate. As other studies have shown, he was no exception either. Several ministers, functionaries, and politicians of the fascist regime as well as party officials – from Grandi, to Farinacci, to Balbo – were anxious to defend their own patron-client networks. Such networks were the foundation of their influence and power, and losing them would have put their political survival in peril.[117]

But what did Costanzo Ciano actually do to build and maintain his own patron-client network in Livorno? First of all, he utilized his status within the local fascist party to distribute political favours and create dependencies. The vice secretary, Umberto Rodinis, for instance, owed his political career to Ciano's support and protection. In return, Rodinis informed him about internal affairs, potential rivals, and critics. Angelo Giuseppe Barbieri, Livorno's prefect from 1922 to 1925, was another of Ciano's protégés, who notified the *ras* about local politics and social affairs. Ciano's constant surveillance and control of local party and state institutions reduced their mutual rivalry in Livorno, which is typical of a polycratic system. And finally, it helped Ciano to expand and eventually preserve his powerful position in his hometown and to remain the only influential politician from Livorno on the national stage. No local politician, no matter how ambitious, was able to meddle in national affairs as long as Costanzo Ciano was alive.[118]

Family members played a particularly important role within Costanzo Ciano's patronage system. They helped to build and strengthen the ties between the Cianos and ordinary citizens as well as the local elites in Livorno.[119] So far, scholars have widely neglected the importance of family members and relatives when it comes to the functionality of patron-client networks during the fascist period, and have thus largely failed to offer a clear explanation of the local power dynamics.[120] Ciano's family extended into Livorno's cultural, social, and economic spheres. His mother Argia, his wife Carolina, his daughter Maria, and even the wife of his nephew Dino Grotta held honorary offices in charitable organizations, highlighting their attachment to Livorno. Costanzo Ciano often visited his hometown, accepted honorary memberships in various social, political, and cultural groups, and was sometimes the best man at local weddings to demonstrate his proximity to the people.[121] These examples illustrate the importance of non-material favours for a functioning patron-client network.[122]

Furthermore, Costanzo Ciano increased his and his family's fortunes and strengthened his personal contacts to Livorno's industry by becoming a member of various executive boards or by owning shares of local businesses. Yet, Ciano did not always interfere directly in the companies' affairs. Very often he acted through his brothers, Arturo and Alessandro, to rebut accusations of personal enrichment and corruption. The list of companies in which at least one of the Cianos was a member of the administrative body includes – among others – *Montecatini*, *Romana Elettricità*, and *Valdarno*.[123]

Even before the First World War it was common practice for wealthy individuals and a few corporations to be shareholders of several companies at the same time. As a consequence, the wealth and thus the economic power were restricted to a small group of influential individuals and companies.[124] The Ciano family serves as proof that this system continued to exist during the fascist era, despite the fascists' promise to fight corruption at all levels of government.

A particularly close relationship existed between the Ciano and the Orlando families, exemplifying the sophisticated entanglement between private relationships, industrial enrichment, and public offices. Giuseppe Orlando, owner of the Orlando shipyard, was able to acquire the Fiume company *Ganz & Danubius* with the help of the Cianos in 1920. Costanzo Ciano's close friendship with D'Annunzio, who occupied Fiume at the time, was key to making the deal. Alessandro Ciano, then head of the cabinet of the Ministry of the Navy, provided the necessary bureaucratic support. The newly acquired company was integrated into the *Società Esercizio Stabilimenti Whitehead* a few years later. Arturo and Alessandro Ciano, as well as members of the Orlando family, sat on its supervisory board. When in 1923 Costanzo Ciano decided to provide state subsidies for the shipping industry, he ensured that the Orlandos received a generous share.[125] Despite this special treatment, the Orlandos still fell into financial troubles. Thanks to Ciano's intervention, they were able to recoup their financial losses by investing in the growing radio and electrical businesses.[126]

In March 1934 Arturo Ciano used capital from the Whitehead Group to establish the *Società Anonima Motofides* in Livorno, which produced motorcycles and torpedoes. The largest private shareholders were once again the Ciano and Orlando families. The founding of *Motofides* was backed up by several laws introduced by Costanzo Ciano in Rome. These legislative measures guaranteed that enough funds were available to modernize the port and industrial quarter in Livorno, where the new company was built.[127] The plans to reconstruct the city's harbour were not new; but only when Ciano was a member of the government was he able to split the costs equally between Livorno and Rome.[128] The port's expansion was part of the city council's larger plans to convert Livorno into a prestigious metropolis in Tuscany. This project, however, was not only about glamorizing the city and boosting its economy; the intentions behind it were much more far-reaching. Settlement projects would allow for easier surveillance of and better control over the citizenry, especially the workforce. In 1927 the plans were finalized with Costanzo Ciano's blessing and implemented two years later.[129]

By personally sponsoring local industries and thus securing and creating jobs, Ciano hoped to gain the citizens' trust and sympathy. In doing so, he did not shy away from a confrontation with his former employer Agnelli. When Ciano learned that the American car company Ford wanted to build a new production facility in Livorno, promising hundreds of new jobs, he was thrilled. It would be a huge boost for the stagnating city's economy and, of course, for Ciano's reputation. Agnelli, however, feared negative consequences for FIAT and intervened with Mussolini. He appealed to national pride and argued that the Italian car industry must be protected from foreign competition. To Ciano's regret, the *Duce* sided with Agnelli and stopped the plans of the US car manufacturer.[130]

Costanzo Ciano's influence over his hometown and its citizens was almost encompassing. In 1923 Livorno's local government demanded the extension of its provincial borders at the expense of other regions. "Livorno," it stated in a letter to the government in Rome, "has become an important city with its industry, its new railway lines, its research facilities, its workers, and its economy. It can no longer be the smallest province of the kingdom."[131] Their request was granted, and Livorno acquired new areas from Pisa and Genoa. On 15 November 1925 the politicians in Livorno thanked Costanzo Ciano for his support, which was crucial for securing the regime's approval.[132]

As the city's patriarch Ciano was also involved in many other areas, including architecture, culture, and sport. He supported the Catholic convent in Livorno, and often supervised new constructions. According to fascist propaganda there was no new building he had not initiated.[133] Be that as it may, Ciano definitely knew about the propagandistic benefits architecture offered him. Refurbishments and the construction of the new *Palazzo del Governo* and the Telegraph Office earned him, once again, the sympathy of the citizens.[134] In the following years, Ciano continued lobbying in Rome to obtain the necessary support for the expensive modernization of Livorno. In numerous discussions he won over the ministers of finance and public buildings, and was able to engage renowned architects and urban planners such as Marcello Piacentini and Ghino Venturi. The latter undertook the construction of new residential homes in the city and built Italy's most modern hospital in Livorno, which was named after Costanzo Ciano.[135] In 1933 yet another prestige object of the family was completed, the sports stadium Edda Ciano Mussolini. Despite financial constraints and structural difficulties, there was never any doubt that it would be completed. A report about the stadium project stressed that Livorno required a sports facility that not only met the needs of the population but would also do justice to the prestige of the *ras* of Livorno.[136] The stadium became home to the *AS Livorno* soccer club, which experienced its most successful period in club history under the auspices of the Cianos.[137]

Costanzo Ciano also supported numerous other sporting events, well aware of their propagandistic significance. In 1927 he had taken over the patronage of the *Coppa Montenero* car race, which was renamed the *Coppa Ciano*. In several reports, news agencies praised him as the organizer of this event and published several images showing him mingling with the crowd and the race drivers, thus portraying him as a man of the people.[138] Moreover, car racing resembled a genuine fascist sport: it represented a combination of progress and modernity as well as athleticism, daring, and courage. Ciano also revived the *Palio Marinaro*, a boat race from the early seventeenth century, to remind residents of Renaissance-era glory; promoted the tourist industry in Livorno; and began to supervise the local hunting festival *Cacciatura* in 1937. And once again he used his ministerial office to Livorno's benefit: after he was appointed minister of communications in 1924, he lowered the price of train tickets in order to enable as many people as possible to participate in these local events.[139]

Costanzo Ciano, however, knew that he also needed the means to spread the image of a charitable, sports-loving, and patriotic family. Therefore, in 1925 he bought the newspaper *Il Telegrafo*.[140] On 1 June 1936 Giovanni Ansaldo became its editor-in-chief. As a journalist for the Turin-based newspaper *La Stampa* he had previously criticized the fascist regime. In 1926 Mussolini personally ordered his arrest in the course of an intensified campaign to suppress the freedom of the press. Ansaldo was sentenced to five years *confino* (exile).[141] However, after he voluntarily joined the PNF in 1935 it was possible for him to join the Ciano-owned paper *Il Telegrafo*. Within a few years he increased the circulation, hired renowned journalists, and led the newspaper to national and international prominence.[142] During his tenure he was well aware of how important the newspaper was for the prestige and therefore the influence of the Cianos. As the "unofficial" spokesman of the family, he maintained very good and close relations with Costanzo and later with Galeazzo Ciano.[143]

In life Costanzo Ciano controlled the fate of his hometown Livorno, imitating the traditional patronage system of nineteenth-century Italy. He successful defended his standing against local rivals and attempted – whenever the occasion would arise – to increase his regional influence. Ciano rewarded loyalty, provided protection, and presented himself as a charitable patron for all of the city's needs; disobedience and disloyal behaviour were rigorously sanctioned. Thanks to this "carrot and stick" tactic he became the patriarch of a "big family" for many of Livorno's citizens, his friends, and subordinates.[144] Moreover, he knew perfectly well that local and national power were closely interlinked. The more influence he possessed in Livorno, the more easily he could impose his interests at the national level. And whenever he used his position in Rome for his hometown's advantage, he would increase his backing in Livorno, which would in turn strengthen his national standing.

On 26 June 1939 Costanzo Ciano, the patriarch of Livorno, died suddenly at the age of sixty-two in the village of Ponte a Moriano. Shortly after his death was announced, King Vittorio Emanuele III, Mussolini, and Achille Starace arrived to pay their last respects.[145] Other prominent figures of the regime, including Italo Balbo, Giuseppe Bottai, and Cesare Maria De Vecchi, also attended "one of the most impressive funerals in Fascist history" at the Cathedral of Livorno.[146] Galeazzo Ciano was so moved by the condolences and sympathies that he compared the city to an "immense temple of sorrow."[147] Many citizens regarded Costanzo Ciano as a "real son" of the city, a true "Livornese," as he supposedly embodied local virtues and characteristics.[148]

As discussed earlier, a successful patron-client network relies on charisma, and thus on reputation and honour. We can therefore pose the questions: Did Costanzo Ciano's death and the subsequent absence of his charismatic authority affect his son's position in Livorno? Was the family network in Livorno strong enough to survive the sudden loss of Costanzo Ciano? Did Galeazzo Ciano continue to benefit from the family's patronage system, and did he recognize how important a stable local patron-client network was for his national power? One way to address these questions is to ask whether he used the same or similar tools that his father so successfully implemented over the years, and if so, what was the result.

In the 1930s Galeazzo Ciano only sporadically visited his hometown. These visits were short and usually took place during the summer months, a time when political and public life in Italy often ground to a halt. It is thus hardly surprising that we do not know of any major building projects in Livorno that are only associated with his name. Whereas his father used architecture to demonstrate the family's power and his personal benevolence, Galeazzo Ciano himself seemed not to care except when he sought to preserve his father's reputation. It should not be forgotten, of course, that Italy's entry into the Second World War made it considerably more difficult to carry out larger building projects, which might explain why Galeazzo Ciano's name was missing from the architectural records. Notably, however, his lack of interest in the affairs of his hometown can also be seen in other areas such as sports. He did not regularly attend local sporting events, including the *Coppa Ciano*. Instead of showing his support for local sports, culture, and traditions, highlighting his proximity to the citizens of Livorno, Galeazzo preferred the salons in the capital and the soccer matches of *Lazio Roma*.[149]

The different amounts of attention father and son paid to Livorno and its people had far-reaching consequences. While the citizens celebrated Costanzo Ciano as a hero, a true child of the city, they began to criticize his son early on. Such anonymous critics of the *ras*'s son risked severe punishment if they were discovered. Nevertheless, some citizens strongly disapproved of Galeazzo Ciano's foreign policy and were particularly appalled by his publicly indifferent behaviour during the German annexation of Austria in 1938. They even accused him, as one graffiti at the Edda Ciano Mussolini Stadium showed, of betraying his father's legacy and "heroic deed of Buccari."[150]

Galeazzo Ciano's relationship to his hometown seemed to change after Italy entered the Second World War. He began to visit Livorno more often, commented on the atmosphere in the city, and described compassionately the numerous problems the citizens faced, including food shortages and war-weariness.[151] Furthermore, he sometimes spent – as was the case in the summer of 1942 – several months in Livorno recovering from a supposed illness. However, he still did not tend his family networks and thus weakened the foundation of his family's influence. Instead, he went to Livorno to escape the chaos in Rome at a time when he had lost Mussolini's confidence and was more and more a target of criticism. Livorno became his self-chosen place of exile.[152]

Whereas Galeazzo Ciano neglected his relationship with the ordinary citizens in Livorno and was often conspicuous in his absence, he still tried to keep his contacts with local politicians and party officials. According to his diary, he was sporadically in touch with vice secretary Rodinis, who informed him about local affairs. But it seems that Rodinis's personal loyalty to Ciano's father was much stronger, given he was the latter's protégé.[153] The rise of the Livornese Umberto Ajello, who became *federale* of Livorno and would eventually join the RSI in 1943, illustrates further Galeazzo Ciano's loss of influence in his own city. In 1939 Ajello became *consigliere nazionale* of the Chamber of Fasci and Corporations in Rome and, as a result, achieved recognition beyond the regional confines of Livorno. Whereas Ciano's father always prevented Livornese from becoming active in national politics, Galeazzo Ciano was much less cautious. As a consequence, he lost the unique and important status of being the only nationally known figure from Livorno; this loss, in turn, challenged at least theoretically his standing as the *ras* of his hometown.[154]

But what about Galeazzo Ciano's contacts in local industry, given that the close relationship between the Cianos and the city's economy was crucial for the family's wealth and influence? In the 1930s Arturo and Alessandro Ciano still controlled the local industry, which especially benefitted from the regime's high demand for ships and torpedoes as a result of the Ethiopian War. In May 1936 the brothers were even able to take over the entire *Whitehead* company.[155] As a minister Galeazzo Ciano, like his father, might have influenced decisions in Rome in favour of Livornese companies and his family. Unfortunately, a lack of reputable sources makes ascertaining his precise role in awarding state contracts difficult. It seems more likely that he manipulated events from the sidelines in order to avoid accusations of nepotism and corruption. It was also convenient that Domenico Cavagnari, a close friend of the family, was navy chief of staff. That position gave him considerable influence over government contracts for shipyards and weapons manufactures.[156]

One can also speculate that Ciano maintained close links with the local industry through his uncles Arturo and Alessandro Ciano. However, a closer look at his relationship to his own family indicates otherwise. He only kept a distant connection with Gino Ciano – his father's youngest brother – and his mother Carolina Ciano, both of whom were involved in Livornese social associations.[157] According to a police report from 1941, Alessandro Ciano accused his nephew of ruining the family's name and, by doing so, jeopardizing the family patronage network.[158] Today we do not have any information that would refute these familial disagreements. As a matter of fact, Galeazzo Ciano did not mention Alessandro or Arturo Ciano in his diary at all.

Despite familial tensions, it became apparent at the end of the war that the fate of the family was still closely intertwined with Livorno's industry. Beginning in the summer of 1943, the Allies began to bombard the city's port and its industrial quarters, especially the Ciano-controlled *Motofides* factory. The destruction eliminated one of the most important sources of income for the Cianos and, as a consequence, endangered one of the pillars of the family's patronage network. Their inability to care for and protect the city led to the swift demise of one of Italy's wealthiest and most influential families.[159] Unable to cope with the situation and afraid of the corruption investigations by the Badoglio government, Arturo Ciano committed suicide in August 1943; two years later his brother Alessandro Ciano also died.[160]

These examples illustrate that, unlike his father, Galeazzo Ciano was never the undisputed head of the family. Even though he was the male heir, he never wielded his father's authority and did not therefore benefit from the family networks to the same degree. Even during fascism, familial structures and hierarchies remained fluid and had to be constantly renegotiated. It simply was not possible to inherit, part and parcel, one's predecessor's influence and reputation.[161]

Unable to exercise the same influence over his own family and the family's network, Galeazzo Ciano ultimately undermined his local power base. Other prominent figures of the regime – including Grandi, Farinacci, and Balbo – fiercely defended their power as a *ras* to the bitter end. Several reasons present themselves to explain why Ciano acted differently. The unexpected death of Costanzo Ciano left a void in the family hierarchy that he was unable to fill. It also shattered the patronage system to the core, based as it was for years on his father's personal charisma and the cult surrounding it. Galeazzo Ciano could not replace his father as the patron within the network as he was unable to don his father's mantel of charm and authority.

But he was also to blame. Unlike his father, he did not regularly provide material and idealistic favours for Livorno's citizens. Bearing in mind that a successful patron-client network is based on an exchange of resources, Galeazzo failed to deliver his side of the bargain. As a result, the people of Livorno felt no obligation to accept Galeazzo Ciano as the city patron who deserved their loyalty and unwavering support.

Another reason why Ciano neglected the local power base his family possessed in Livorno may be found in his own rapidly advancing career. His father and other high-ranking fascists only reached the upper echelon of the state apparatus after they had secured their power in the periphery. Thus, they had experienced first-hand the importance of the local power, an experience Galeazzo Ciano lacked. As Mussolini's press chief in 1933, he more or less began his political career in the centre of the regime. As a result, he failed to recognize how important regional power still was for political survival in Fascist Italy. Through a combination of self and circumstance, he was unable to follow his father's path, and Galeazzo – apparently unbothered by it – turned to two other strategies: He tried to establish his own national patron-client network that would go far beyond his family's local contacts. In addition, he attempted to trade on his close proximity and direct access to the Mussolini family after he married Edda Mussolini in 1930.

Ciano's Friends

Whereas Galeazzo Ciano was unaware of the importance of local power, he was very well aware of Costanzo Ciano's personal contacts and how important they were for the family and his father's career.[162] His father made friends with influential personalities in business, politics, and the military, who supported his career; in turn, he aided friends and relatives in obtaining jobs and money. This give-and-take formed the basis of a nationwide network that, together with his local patron-client network, strengthened his influence in Rome. Crucially, however, the national situation differed from conditions in Livorno, because the power asymmetry between the parties involved was much smaller, at times non-existent.

Furthermore, the power distribution was far more fluid, often exposed to external influences Costanzo Ciano himself could not control such as changing alliances and institutional connections. Thus, his relations on a national level more closely resembled a network with various centres than a distinct patron-client system. Costanzo Ciano's contacts and connections were known to Italians and foreigners alike. His opponents quickly accused him of being one of the most corrupt ministers of the fascist regime.[163] A British diplomat called the *Gruppo Ciano* a gang of thieves enriched thanks to the corrupt and greedy Ciano's insider information.[164] This group included fascist dignitaries such as De Vecchi and Leandro Arpinati; entrepreneurs like Agnelli, Volpi, and Marconi; military figures such as Cavagnari; and the poet D'Annunzio.[165]

The analysis of Costanzo Ciano's dealings with Guglielmo Marconi and Giovanni Agnelli offer excellent insight into how the *Gruppo Ciano* operated. As minister of communications Ciano showed great interest in the new medium of radio and promoted the distribution of radios in Italy.[166] In November 1924 the *Società Italiana Radio Audizioni Circolori* and Marconi's *Società Anonima Radiofono* were awarded the contract for radio broadcasts in Italy. Thanks to Ciano's mediation both companies had already merged to become the *Unione Radiofonica Italiana* (URI) in August, with Marconi's agency holding 85 per cent of the shares. Enrico Marchesi, who enjoyed Ciano's backing, became the president of the new company. Since Marchesi was a former official of the FIAT group, Ciano indirectly enabled his former employer Agnelli to become involved in the radio business too. As a result, URI became an industrial complex that was in charge of developing the Italian radio network and providing the necessary radios.[167] Due to the high demand – within two years about one million households in Italy were equipped with radios – URI was restructured and assumed the name *Ente Italiano per le Audizioni Radiofoniche* (EIAR) in 1927.[168]

When Galeazzo and Edda Ciano lived in Shanghai in the early 1930s, it was Marconi's opportunity to thank Costanzo Ciano for his support. He personally made sure that a radio connection between Italy and the Chinese city was built and upgraded.[169] Marconi's death in July 1937 did not end the interpersonal contract between the Ciano and Marconi families. When his daughter Degna Marconi was in financial distress, she turned to Galeazzo Ciano and asked him to help her and her brother. Even though we have no information about Ciano's reaction, after his appointment as foreign minister he – and not his father – was apparently the first member of the Ciano family such individuals would contact.[170]

Costanzo Ciano repeatedly used his contacts to benefit his son. This practice was particularly the case regarding Galeazzo Ciano's education and professional training. Since the late nineteenth century, fathers exerted major influence over their sons' careers, and Costanzo Ciano was no exception. Their intentions, however, were not solely altruistic; not only should their contacts assist their children with job placement, but the final position should also complement the existing family network. It was therefore preferable that the male child enter a prestigious profession such as navy or army officer, lawyer or diplomat.[171]

In 1921 Galeazzo Ciano began his law studies at the Sapienza University of Rome. He graduated in late 1924. During his time at the university he also worked as a literary and theatre critic for various Roman newspapers on a voluntary basis. It was his father who arranged these jobs for him.[172]

After graduation Costanzo intended to send his son to Livorno to become a lawyer. His local networks would have made it easy for Galeazzo to find clients and start a successful career. However, the latter was less than thrilled about the idea of working in the province. In the end it was agreed that Galeazzo would pursue a diplomatic career. His father only complied because he held the diplomatic career, its traditions, and loyalty to the royal family in high regard.[173]

Galeazzo Ciano was one of 600 candidates who applied for the 35 trainee positions at the Foreign Ministry in 1925.[174] Throughout Europe – and Italy was no exception – diplomats formed an elitist, self-contained group, which was dominated by the aristocracy even after the First World War.[175] Ciano, however, was a representative of the bourgeoisie, since his father was only knighted on 28 October 1928.[176] As a social outsider, eyed by the career diplomats with suspicion, he was in need of excellent recommendations when he applied. It was Giuseppe Bastianini who wrote a recommendation to support Galeazzo's admission as a favour to Costanzo, who was one of his close companions since the events in Livorno in 1922.[177] Due to Bastianini's position within the PNF his letter was extremely valuable. Thanks to such a strong advocate it was not necessary for Costanzo Ciano, then minister of communication, to pull more strings and intervene in the selection process of another ministry. Galeazzo was accepted and began his diplomatic training in the fall of 1925.[178]

Besides Bastianini, other friends of Costanzo Ciano, such as Domenico Cavagnari and Leandro Arpinati, played an important role in Galeazzo's career even after Costanzo's death. Cavagnari, who was born in 1876 in Genoa and owed his military career to Costanzo Ciano, was appointed chief of staff of the Italian navy in 1934.[179] During the *non belligeranza* (non-belligerence) period, Cavagnari was one of the most committed and loyal supporters of Galeazzo Ciano's non-interventionist policy.[180]

When Galeazzo Ciano's influence in Rome diminished, he desperately sought to contact other close confidants of his father, such as Arpinati. The former deputy general secretary of the fascist party and chairman of the *Comitato Olimpico Nazionale Italiano*, Arpinati had fallen from grace in 1930 and was exiled to Lipari.[181] Ciano, however, still saw in him a "man of honour" who had always enjoyed his father's respect.[182]

Galeazzo Ciano's relationships with Cavagnari and Arpinati illustrate that he maintained contact with some of his father's friends; however, he did not feel equally committed to all of Costanzo's friends. One example would be Cesare Maria De Vecchi, his superior at the Italian embassy in the Vatican in the early 1930s. In his memoirs, published in 1983, De Vecchi stated that "after a happy beginning, Ciano became again who he was, a gossip full of vanity and an uninhibited slacker."[183] Of course, we should treat this statement with caution. When De Vecchi wrote his memoirs, Ciano's diary – including the not very flattering comments about De Vecchi – had already been published.[184] Did De Vecchi use his memoirs to get back at Ciano, who was already dead?[185] To find an answer to this question we must consult the ambassador's own diary, which was partially published in 1998.

On 13 February 1930 De Vecchi wrote that Ciano was a "decent boy and an excellent official."[186] The ambassador became upset when he learned that Ciano had gone behind his back and informed the *Duce* about internal affairs at the Vatican. Ciano accepted the criticism and tried to flatter his superior by pointing out how deeply Mussolini relied on and valued De Vecchi's judgment.[187] Not surprisingly Ciano's strategy worked. For what greater praise could one receive than the *Duce*'s recognition? De Vecchi's diary entries illustrate that his memoirs should not only be read as a work of revenge. The relationship between Galeazzo Ciano and De Vecchi was indeed strained following their time together at the Vatican. Obviously, Ciano was willing to engage in nearly Machiavellian behaviour by abandoning friends of his father whenever he saw an opportunity to get closer to Mussolini. Compared to the *Duce*, De Vecchi and those like him could offer Ciano considerably less.

His father's conduct, however, was not the only instructive example of the importance of personal networks. At least as relevant was his experience as a diplomat in China during the late 1920s and early 1930s. There, he was able to observe first-hand the importance of two principles in particular, which centred on the individual person (*renzhi*) and interpersonal relationships (*guanxi*). Favours were used to build personal networks, which in turn helped ensure one's political survival. This practice led to a highly personalized political culture in China, dominated by emotional devotion and loyalty.[188] In his personal and professional interactions at home, Ciano began to adapt those rituals, which favoured more informal factors over legal norms and administrative structures. In the following years Ciano invested time and money to establish his own patronage networks, many of which included childhood friends, friends from university, and members of the Roman aristocracy.

In order to fully appreciate the diversity of these networks, it is first worth examining Ciano's relationships with Giorgio Amendola and Curzio Malaparte, before moving on to his contacts in the nobility. He met Amendola, the son of the liberal politician Giovanni Amendola murdered by fascists in 1926, in Rome in the early 1920s. Political differences were not a hindrance to Ciano in making friends – he also became friends with the Argentinean writer and bearer of the Lenin Peace Prize María Rosa Oliver and with the attaché at the Soviet embassy in Rome, Leon B. Helfand.[189] In his memoirs, published in 1976, Amendola stressed that he and Ciano often discussed politics, argued about issues, polemicized, but it never hurt their friendship, which only ended when he had to go into exile due to political persecution in Italy. He also described how Ciano protected him from a fascist mob after Anteo Zamboni's failed assassination attempt against Mussolini on 31 October 1926.[190] This anecdote served the purpose of strengthening Ciano's post-war image of the "good fascist" and confirming Ciano's commitment to his friends despite their sometimes widely different political views, though it is very likely that this episode never happened. When Zamboni's assassination attempt occurred, Ciano was working in South America.[191]

The author Curzio Malaparte joined the fascist party on 30 September 1922, shortly before the "March on Rome." He probably met Ciano in Rome around 1923, when both worked for the newspaper *L'Impero*. After repeatedly criticizing Benito Mussolini, the fascist party, and later especially Italo Balbo, Malaparte was exiled to Lipari for five years in 1933. He was released only one year into his sentence after Ciano personally intervened. He was placed under "special observation" in Ischia and later in Forte di Marmi.[192] In his semi-autobiographical work *Kaputt*, Malaparte wrote how Ciano defended him against everyone, and in a letter to former British Ambassador Sir Percy Loraine in 1947, he did not deny that he was a close friend of Ciano.[193] He emphasized, however, that he did not benefit in any way from the friendship and assured the ambassador that he had been a staunch anti-fascist since the 1930s. Malaparte not only hid his own involvement with the fascist movement but also thought it opportune after the Second World War to downplay his proximity to Ciano. Ciano's numerous interventions on behalf of Malaparte are yet another example of how Ciano used his political influence for the benefit and protection of his friends.[194]

Amendola and Malaparte are not isolated cases. Ciano had already begun to do favours for friends, colleagues, and acquaintances when he reviewed books and plays for the Roman press as a student. He positively reviewed works by his friend Orio Vergani and by Guelfo Civinini, a friend of his father.[195] After Ciano entered the inner circle of the regime in 1933, he, like his father, used his political power to help his friends even if it challenged fascist norms.[196] In February 1934, for example, he aided his friend Filippo Anfuso in securing a job at the Italian embassy in Athens, shortly after Anfuso had told him that he wanted to return to Europe from Asia.[197] In 1935 Ciano asked Renato Ricci, minister of education, about the school performance of the children of Celso Luciano, head of the *Segreteria Particolare* at Ciano's State Secretariat for Press and Propaganda. He expressed his wish that the "education" of Luciano's children would be "benevolently" promoted. Ricci assured him that everything had been taken care of.[198] In the same year Ciano assisted Oreste Bonomi, his employee at the Ministry of Propaganda, who wished to participate in the Ethiopian War.[199] In April 1938 he supported a former comrade from the Ethiopian War to find a job in the Italian railway.[200] And in 1939 he appointed his childhood friend Zenone Benini as state secretary for Albanian affairs in the Foreign Ministry.[201]

Galeazzo Ciano also had numerous contacts among the aristocracy. When he moved to Rome in 1921, old, established noble families such as the Colonnas, the Pamphiljs, and the Borghese still dominated the city's political and social life.[202] All governors of Rome between December 1926 and 1945 – with the exception of Giuseppe Bottai (1935–36) – were members of these families: Ludovico Spada Veralli Potenziani (1926–28), Francesco Boncompagni-Ludovisi (1928–35), Piero Colonna (1936–39), Gian Giacomo Borghese (1939–43), and Filippo Andrea VI Doria Pamphilj (1944–45).[203] The *Risorgimento* and the social turmoil during the First World War destroyed neither their political power nor their social capital. Whereas in other European cities a new, bourgeois public began to take over, the salons of the nobility remained the centre of social life in Rome.[204]

Aristocratic families like the Borghese and the Colonna were unwilling to admit an outsider into their milieu. Their social status threatened by up-and-coming industrialist and bourgeois families, by the Italian gentry, who were more than willing to marry into the wealthy upper-middle class, and by an increasing number of new nobles who were knighted after the First World War, they tried to preserve a "collective identity" distinct from the rest of society.[205] They strongly identified with their families and ancestors, and displayed an exaggerated self-esteem irrespective of actual wealth.[206] Although they successfully defended their status and influence in the city for the time being, the gentry, the upper-middle class, and the new nobles began to erode the once-strict social structures in Rome. Social advancement and social decline became much easier after the war, resulting in a much more diverse Roman establishment.

Galeazzo Ciano longed to be part of this establishment.[207] Being a member of the new nobility and a wealthy and influential politician, he viewed acceptance into the Roman aristocracy as a confirmation and a consolidation of his social status.[208] Thus, he tried various means of making contact with the old aristocratic families. The first opportunities occurred during his time at the Sapienza University. Legal studies enjoyed great popularity among many aristocrats, who viewed it as a way to access influential positions in politics after the bureaucratization and professionalization of the civil service and, by doing so, to display and keep their social status.[209] Moreover, Ciano's diplomatic training also offered him many chances to interact with the nobility. It was the diplomat Massimo Magistrati, born in 1899 and a member of an aristocratic family from Piedmont, who introduced Ciano to the salons of the Roman establishment. Magistrati had married Galeazzo's sister Maria on 5 November 1931.[210] Finally, Ciano was a huge admirer of golf and hunting, two leisure activities popular with the aristocracy. He regularly visited the Acquasanta Golf Club near Rome, which became one of the key watering holes of the Roman establishment.[211]

In the following years Galeazzo Ciano maintained good relationships with noble families such as the Balestra, the Borromeo d'Adda, the di Belmote, the di Bagno, and the Borghese.[212] But above all, Ciano frequented the salons of Isabelle Helena Colonna and Anna Laetitia Pecci-Blunt.[213] Isabelle Colonna originated from the Lebanese aristocratic family Sursock and in 1909 married Marcantonio Colonna, the head of the Colonna family. Malaparte wrote in his semi-autobiographical novel *Kaputt* that her table was adorned by the "smiling faces, rosy cheeks and strawberry lips of young women whom Isabelle offered as royal bounties to the insatiable vanity of Galeazzo."[214] According to Malaparte, Isabelle Colonna initially met the fascist regime with an "honest, smiling reserve" and showed "minute etiquette" and "strict protocol"[215] towards fascism. In the 1930s, however, she abandoned her restraint and began to establish closer contacts with members of the fascist leadership, including Balbo and Galeazzo Ciano. Her motives for this behavioural shift are unclear even today. She might have been looking for allies at a time when Mussolini intensified his verbal attacks against the aristocracy and the bourgeoisie.[216]

Due to her reputation, Isabelle Colonna was a perfect door-opener for the ambitious Ciano to become part of the social and political elite in the capital. Malaparte saw in her one of the most powerful personalities in Rome. "No one," he argued, "not even Mussolini, could have ruled in Rome against Isabelle. In the field of the conquest of power, Isabelle had nothing to learn from anyone: she had carried out her March on Rome from a much more distant base, almost twenty years earlier than Mussolini."[217] Ciano, too, was no match for the cunning Isabelle, who "reigned as queen without for a moment renouncing an ancient, amiable and mischievous predisposition for tyranny. Within that world Galeazzo appeared more as a tool of tyranny than a tyrant."[218]

Anna Laetitia Pecci-Blunt was married to Cecil Charles Blumenthal, a wealthy American Jew, and in the 1930s became one of the most influential art patrons in Rome. She held annual spring concerts with prominent figures like Igor Stravinsky and opened the *Galleria della Cometa* in April 1935, which showcased works by Giorgio de Chirico. When Mussolini started his radical reconstruction of Rome, she created an extensive collection of old city maps of Rome.[219] In the wake of the anti-Semitic laws of 1938, Mussolini forbade his son-in-law to attend the galas hosted by Pecci-Blunt, who had to close her gallery shortly thereafter and emigrated to New York.[220]

Galeazzo Ciano was not the only high-ranking fascist with personal contacts among Jews. Mussolini became particularly angry when he learned that Roberto Farinacci, "leader of the anti-Semitic movement … [had] a Jewish secretary ... This is the kind of thing," the *Duce* complained, "which foreigners see as proof of a lack of seriousness in many Italians."[221] Mussolini's anger did not prevent Ciano or other hierarchs from occasionally ignoring the race laws whenever people they knew were affected. In November 1938 Ciano intervened in favour of a Jew "who was at school with me … I phoned to Buffarini to call his attention to the case of the Jew with an Aryan wife. I think that this gesture of detachment from the Jewish nation and religion should be rewarded with special treatment. If the family's nucleus is to be protected," wrote Ciano, who believed in patriarchal family structures, "the father must not be placed in a position of inferiority in respect to his children."[222]

Galeazzo Ciano's contacts with the aristocracy resembled less of a patron-client network, as the power asymmetry between the parties involved was marginal or non-existent, and more a symbiotic alliance. Whereas the nobility hoped to halt further fascistization of society out of fear of losing their status, Ciano wanted to confirm his family's social advancement and protect his standing within the regime. Radical fascists harshly criticized Ciano's relationship with the Roman aristocracy, mostly because they regarded the nobility as a reactionary force that obstructed the establishment of a true fascist society. Mussolini repeatedly boasted about a "second revolution" to sweep away the aristocracy he despised. Everyone who did not belong to the class of workers and peasants – subsumed by the *Duce* in the category of the bourgeoisie – would have to yield to the fascist revolution.[223] In her autobiography, Rachele Mussolini criticized Ciano's obsession with the aristocracy and thus with the social milieu she hated. Even if personal envy might have clouded her judgment, there is no doubt that she – the daughter of a farmer – always held a grudge against the privileged social classes.[224] And even Berlin was concerned about Isabelle Colonna's activities and her proximity to Ciano. A report from January 1941, which can be found in the files of the German embassy in Rome, stated:

> Isabella [*sic*!] Colonna ... seeks to attract as many personalities from politics and the state as possible to her salon. She devotes her very special attention and extraordinary interest to some of them, including Ciano ... The responsible authority in the Ministry of the Interior fears ... that Isabella [*sic*!] Colonna is working for the English and is perhaps the most important spy of the English secret service in Italy, who is probably able to work through the American embassy. The Duce shall be informed of the matter.[225]

Although Ciano knew that radical fascists did not like his proximity to the aristocracy, he did not seem to mind.[226] He enjoyed being part of the establishment, a world that embraced prosperity, consumption, and leisure. Ciano explained to Bottai that "between the hegemony of the Germans or the English ... he preferred the latter; the hegemony of golf, whisky, comfort."[227]

One reason Galeazzo Ciano did not comprehend the severe rivalry between fascists and the Roman establishment may have stemmed from his understanding of the term "bourgeoisie." He preferred a "psychological definition" of the bourgeoisie in the spirit of French writer Gustave Flaubert: "Bourgeois," Ciano wrote in his diary, "is anything that is vulgar."[228] This very vague definition allowed him to fill the socially connoted idea of "bourgeoisie" with a positive meaning whenever he, his family, the upper-middle class, and the Roman aristocracy were concerned. When his sister died in October 1939, he proudly recalled the modest bourgeois life of an officer's family in Livorno.[229] In May 1942 he rhetorically asked whether it was really necessary to "strike at [the bourgeoisie] every day and harass it to the point of making it an implacable enemy of the regime."[230] He continued to claim that the bourgeoisie, the "backbone" of the nation, was enduring the greatest sacrifices in the war. While he once again failed to offer a precise definition of the term, he explicitly mentioned the bearers of the Supreme Order of the Most Holy Annunciation and the members of the Acquasanta Golf Club, who were subjected to the PNF's capriciousness and suppression like the attempt to close all golf courses. Thus, there is no doubt that he perceived himself to be a member of the bourgeoisie given that he belonged to both groups.[231]

As Ciano's political influence grew so did the number of his presumed friends, as it was no secret that he looked after them well. However, childhood friends like Susanna Agnelli noted bitterly that Ciano had no understanding of human nature. She complained that he felt honoured by these "flatterers" and failed to realize that they were using him to their own advantage.[232] Some contemporaries even spoke of a new disease that had broken out in Italy, the so-called *Cianismo*. Everyone tried to become Ciano's friend or claimed that he was related to them in order to gain more influence.[233] However, with Ciano's downfall in the summer of 1943 the entire structure of his personal network abruptly collapsed.

Only a few people remained loyal and tried to help him, including aristocrats such as Isabelle Colonna as well as long-standing friends such as Leonardo Vitetti and Susanna Agnelli.[234] Ciano's relationship with all of them was personal and far from the typical patron-client relationship. Ciano, however, lost more or less all of the contacts that comprised the bulk of his patron-client system. When his national influence diminished, he was no longer in a position to offer protection and favours in exchange for solidarity and loyalty. In an exclusively national patronage system – in contrast to his father's national and local system – the power asymmetry between everyone involved was significantly smaller. Thus, even minor fluctuations in Ciano's standing affected the delicate power balance between patron and client and could even turn it upside down. Several former friends and protégés like Filippo Anfuso emancipated themselves from him during the Second World War, and when Ciano lost his former clout, they turned completely against him in the summer of 1943. Ciano's personal vanity and his delight in pleasing others blinded him to this dilemma. In the end it was Galeazzo who gave, and his "friends" who took.

The Fascist Family

Dynasty and Nepotism

On 27 January 1930 a profound change took place in Galeazzo Ciano's life. The young diplomat had just returned to Italy and begun his service at the Italian embassy in the Vatican when he met then nineteen-year-old

Edda Mussolini at a party. Edda, born on 1 September 1910 in Forli, was the eldest child of Benito and Rachele Mussolini. There are several, sometimes contradictory, stories about how the marriage actually came to be. According to many studies, it was Mussolini himself who ordered Ciano's return from China, because he saw him as a possible husband for his daughter.[235] This interpretation is contradicted by the actual chronology. When Italian Ambassador Daniele Varè returned from the funeral of Sun Yat-Sen in Beijing on 6 June 1929, he found a telegram on his desk, which contained Ciano's recall.[236] At that time, there was no reason for the *Duce* to look for a suitable husband for his daughter. Edda Mussolini, with her parents' blessing, was in a relationship with Pier Francesco Orsi Mangelli, which only ended in January 1930.[237] We might come closer to the truth if we examine the temporal proximity between the recall notice and the establishment of the Italian embassy in the Vatican, the site of Ciano's new job. The embassy was opened in June 1929 and was headed by Costanzo Ciano's friend De Vecchi. As we know how his father helped Galeazzo with his education and career, it seems likely that Costanzo again used his influence to bring his son back to Rome when the opportunity presented itself.[238]

There are also manifold accounts of the first meeting between Edda Mussolini and Galeazzo Ciano. Benito Mussolini and his brother Arnaldo as well as Costanzo and Maria Ciano are mentioned as potential matchmakers.[239] All the various stories nonetheless share one thing: the belief that their first encounter was no coincidence. Edda wrote to a cousin that love had struck like lightning when she saw Galeazzo. When Ciano, eight years older than her, proposed to her two weeks later, she immediately told her apparently astonished but enthusiastic father.[240] Ciano was also ecstatic and could not wait to announce his engagement to his superior, Ambassador De Vecchi.[241] Without completely ignoring Edda and Galeazzo's feelings, the "love at first sight" story seems to paint the actual events in an overly romantic light. Mussolini most likely knew about his daughter's contact with Ciano. He monitored her moves through the Italian secret service *Organizzazione per la Vigilanza e la Repressione dell'Antifascismo* and kept a close eye on all letters she received.[242] When on 15 February Galeazzo Ciano officially asked for Edda's hand, Mussolini was certainly aware of the relationship and had already given his implicit blessing.[243]

Benito Mussolini and Costanzo Ciano's interference was not unusual. Even before the fascists came to power, parents usually had a say about whom their children wanted to marry. Moreover, the still valid Italian Civil Code of 1865 codified that sons under twenty-five years and daughters under twenty-one years could only marry with the consent of their parents. Although Galeazzo Ciano was twenty-six at the time, Edda was only nineteen and thus needed her parents' blessing. Compared to other couples of the era, both were relatively young when they got married. The average age of marriage in Italy during the liberal and fascist era was twenty-eight years for men and close to twenty-five years for women.[244]

The wedding took place on 24 April 1930 in the church of San Giuseppe. The best men were Dino Grandi and De Vecchi for Galeazzo Ciano and Arnaldo Mussolini and Don Giovanni Torlonia for Edda Mussolini. The former cardinal secretary Pietro Gasparri, who had signed the Lateran Treaty in 1929, officiated the wedding.[245] Following a Catholic tradition, the newly-weds visited St. Peter's Basilica after the ceremony.[246] Beforehand, the *Duce* had instructed the press to report about the wedding in moderation and to emphasize its private character. Obviously, he was very keen to present an image of a typical family wedding ceremony.[247] His instructions were ignored: over 4,000 spectators took part in the festivities. Numerous celebrities congratulated the couple, and the fascist press outdid itself with congratulations and praise. Several delegations of the fascist youth groups, the fascist militia, and the *Carabinieri* were also present.[248]

Despite Mussolini's publicly displayed modesty, he secretly enjoyed and welcomed the attention the wedding received. Two months before, Umberto of Savoy, the oldest son of King Vittorio Emanuele III and designated heir to the Italian throne, had married Princess Marie José of Belgium. Over 3,000 guests from the European aristocracy attended the opulent royal wedding, which lasted for a week and ended with extraordinary fireworks. Although more than 100,000 onlookers followed the ceremony, the organizers separated the nobles from the commoners.[249] By contrast, the fascist regime used Galeazzo and Edda Ciano's wedding to highlight family values and to express their affinity for the Italian people.

Even though the actual protocol adopted in each event differed, the motifs chosen were similar. The marriage between Prince Umberto and Princess Marie José – and thus the union between two European royal families – was supposed to secure and expand the rule of the House of Savoy. The marriage between Edda and Galeazzo was constructed as a fascist counterpart, symbolizing a popularly based fascist dynasty that paralleled the Savoy family.[250] The arranged marriage of descendants and the establishment of a dynastic succession – phenomena that gradually disappeared after the First World War – were obviously mechanisms used during fascism to preserve and expand the influence of a family.[251] Costanzo Ciano, the head of the Ciano family, hoped to strengthen the family's position within the regime by marrying his son to the *Duce*'s daughter. Mussolini, on the other hand, hoped to reinforce his ties to the moderate circles of the fascist hierarchy, of which Costanzo was a prominent member.[252]

Several contemporaries acknowledged the political side of the marriage. De Vecchi stated that "this wedding ... is very good: the son of a hero like Costanzo Ciano with the daughter of the Duce!"[253] He also supported the marriage for dynastic reasons and noted that even the usually critical public reacted positively.[254] The press in Livorno repeatedly emphasized the image of a fascist dynasty. The newspaper *Il Corriere di Tirreno* praised Edda Ciano's presence at the *Palio Marinario* in the summer of 1933 and pointed out the "devotion and love of the Livornese for their Minister and for Edda Ciano Mussolini."[255]

In the following years Galeazzo Ciano did not shy away from any expense and effort to promote the image of a wealthy and powerful dynasty. First, he attempted to affirm the dynastic claim by publishing pictures of his entire family in national and international newspapers, including photographs of his children:[256] Fabrizio Ciano, born on 1 October 1931 in Shanghai; Raimonda Ciano, born on 12 December 1933 in Rome; and Marzio Ciano, born on 18 December 1937 in Rome and nicknamed Mogli after the main character in Rudyard Kipling's *Jungle Book*.

Second, he hired world-renowned artists, such as the sculptor Francesco Messina and the painter Giorgio de Chirico, to produce busts or paint portraits of him and his wife (figure 2).[257] Whereas de Chirico painted Edda Ciano in a simple but elegant dress, he portrayed Galeazzo in the official uniform of the foreign minister. The abundant details in the paintings, among them the medals and badges, and the jewels around Edda Ciano's neck, were meant to highlight the status and wealth of the subjects. Antique busts and statues can be seen in the background in both paintings – elements that were particularly popular in baroque portraits. The reference to the baroque and classical eras was not coincidental. Images of rulers in general, and busts and portraits in particular, were used by the aristocracy, clergy, merchants, and other members of the *nouveau riche* to emphasize their social status.[258]

After his marriage to the *Duce*'s daughter, Ciano found himself thrust into the limelight of the national and international stage. Within a few years Ciano became Italy's most important politician behind Mussolini. His marriage gave Ciano access to the inner circle of the fascist hierarchy and, more importantly, to Mussolini himself – a significant career boost. When he was promoted to minister of press and propaganda at the age of thirty-two, the Italian press praised Ciano's organizational skills and his great merits for the fascist movement in order to give

Figure 2. Portraits of Edda Mussolini and Galeazzo Ciano by Giorgio de Chirico, 1942. Cristallini, "De Chirico's Disregarded E42 Invitation," 184. © VG Bild-Kunst, Bonn 2020.

the promotion a logical rational.[259] Some Italians, however, had already begun to question Ciano's rise. "The nation applauds," an anonymous critic wrote to the *Duce*, "the continuing scandals which the fascist regime inflicts on our beloved country by nominating Galeazzo Ciano to minister."[260] Accusations of nepotism slowly began to trickle into the public discourse and have since been inseparably linked to Ciano's career. Even when he was appointed foreign minister in June 1936, the emphatic national and international praise failed to silence the critics.[261]

Ciano's awards like the Supreme Order of the Most Holy Annunciation, which he received for the part he played in the occupation of Albania, were interpreted as clear signs of Italy's moral decay.[262] However, critics not only implied that Ciano received his ministerial posts because he was Mussolini's son-in-law; they also claimed that those family ties were the only reason he remained in said posts. This allegation was the only logical explanation for why Ciano was not removed from office even when he disagreed with the *Duce* and was accused of disastrous decisions such as the attack on Greece in autumn 1940.[263]

Like many Italian politicians before him, the *Duce* deliberately used family members to expand and maintain his authority. Ciano, as his son-in-law, was no exception. Mussolini also put other relatives in charge of key positions in the media in order to control the regime's propaganda apparatus. Arnaldo Mussolini was the editor-in-chief of the party newspaper *Il Popolo d'Italia* from 1922 until his death in 1931; Arnaldo's son, Vito Mussolini, succeeded him.[264] Foreign observers also noted Mussolini's inclination for integrating relatives into the government and stated that nepotism was one of his greatest weaknesses.[265]

Nevertheless, the accusations of nepotism illustrate that at least parts of the Italian population no longer accepted the traditional system of power acquisition. This criticism was all the more significant given that the fascists had promised to eradicate nepotism in Italy. The fact that they were unable – or unwilling – to fulfil their pledges damaged the reputations of numerous fascist hierarchs.[266] Such allegations also illustrate that the marriage between Galeazzo Ciano and Edda Mussolini should not only be analysed in light of power gains for those involved. The negative aspects can be illustrated in two other ways: first, in the claim to represent the "fascist model family"; and second, through the intrigues within the Mussolini family.

Fascist Family and Gender Roles

While nepotism was a widespread phenomenon during the liberal and the fascist eras, liberal governments had only tentatively tried to penetrate the privacy of the family. The Civil Code of 1865 defined the family as a hierarchical and patriarchal structure, but other legislative interventions were largely missing. Nevertheless, this family model prevailed and dominated Italian bourgeois society in the nineteenth and early twentieth century due to the moral clout of the Vatican. The Catholic Church strongly supported the state's family policy, thereby helping to shape a patriarchal society that embraced specific gender roles.[267] While the woman embodied passivity, emotionality, and motherliness, the man represented activity, rationality, and professional orientation.[268]

Beginning in the late 1920s Mussolini's regime embarked on an attempt to fascistize society and penetrate the private sphere of Italians. The family was supposed to become one with the state, a true reflection of the "dignity of the homeland."[269] The fascists' prime concern was to define gender roles, increase the birth rate in light of demographic stagnation, and propagate an ideal image of the fascist family as a counter-model to the bourgeois nuclear family, which they disparaged as individualistic, selfish, feminist, and pacifist.[270]

The fascists retained the patriarchal structure of the liberal era in its entirety and placed a strong emphasis on masculinity and the glorification of men as the "arms bearers" of the nation; women, on the other hand, were supposed to give the nation many children.[271] They also adopted the Catholic notion that giving birth to children was the most important part of a marriage. The regime went yet a significant step further. It enacted several laws that codified this idea and thus penetrated into the private lives of Italians. The government rewarded families with many children; punished childless, single Italians and homosexuals; encouraged early marriage; restricted opportunities for women to work outside their homes; and proclaimed 24 December as "Mother and Child Day." These legislative interventions transformed childbirth, once a private affair, into a public affair and, by doing so, indirectly raised the status of women as mothers of the nation.[272] Once again theory had little in common with reality. The regime failed to keep women out of the agricultural and industrial sectors, and many women assumed, often unofficially, roles in politics, though this practice contradicted the patriarchal self-image of many fascists.[273]

In their hatred of everything bourgeois, the fascists also attempted to break the personal emotional ties that had been a typical characteristic of the bourgeoisie since the late nineteenth century. They wanted to replace these bonds between parents and their children with shared feelings of community and comradeship. On 4 April 1926 they founded the youth organization *Opera Nazionale Balilla* to educate children between the ages of eight and eighteen, which expanded after 1934 to include children from six to eighteen. Three years later the youth organization was restructured under the new umbrella organization *Gioventù Italiana del Littorio*.[274] By separating children from their parents the fascists sought to destroy the bourgeois family, which they perceived as an obstacle to the establishment of a totalitarian state.[275]

To boost awareness and encourage compliance with these legislative measures, they were accompanied by a huge propaganda campaign to spread the fascist notion of familial roles. And what better way to do so than by showing off a model family, one well known to the general public? In Nazi Germany, Joseph Goebbels and his family filled this role;[276] in Italy, where better to look than to Edda and Galeazzo Ciano? But were the Cianos able to live up to expectations? To answer this question, I will examine aspects of their private life and public appearances: the affairs of both spouses; gender roles, especially with regard to Edda Ciano; and the upbringing of their children.

On 12 September 1930, Galeazzo and Edda Ciano set off for Shanghai.[277] With more than three million inhabitants and one of the densest settlements in the world, Shanghai was already a legend, the "bridgehead of the West" in China.[278] It attracted people from all social classes and countries, including refugees, adventurers, criminals, charlatans, and traders. The vibrant nightlife of Shanghai, the "whore of the Far East," was legendary: "In no city, West and East," British writer Aldous Huxley marvelled, "have I ever had such an impression of dense, rank, rich clotted life ... It is Life itself. Nothing more intensely living can be imagined."[279] After the Second Opium War (1856–60) the Imperial Chinese government had to grant foreigners legal and economic privileges, which enabled foreigners to strongly influence the city's social, economic, and political life, even though they only accounted for 3 per cent of the total population.[280] "In the pursuit of profit," Harriet Sergeant argues, the Western powers "made the most international metropolis the world had ever seen."[281] However, Western influence and the economic boom also had their dark side. The trade and consumption of opium became inseparable from the city's fortune.[282]

Edda and Galeazzo Ciano apparently enjoyed their time in Shanghai, which was more liberal and progressive than Italy. In Shanghai they lived in a magnificent villa, which quickly became a centre of the city's glamorous social life.[283] Far away from home, cracks soon appeared in their private life, and both began to go their own way. Rumours circulated about Galeazzo Ciano's affairs with other women.[284] After their return to Italy in 1933, the Cianos continued their open relationship. Although extramarital affairs were not unusual within the Roman establishment, they stood in opposition to the official fascist and Catholic family models.[285] Galeazzo and Edda Ciano quickly became the subject of Italian and foreign tabloids. The press speculated about his lovers, ranging from the wife of his co-worker Marcello Del Drago, to the actress Vivi Gioi, to the radio presenter Lisa Sergio.[286]

Thus, it seems hardly surprising that it was commonly believed the Cianos would separate. However, according to Edda Ciano, such a step was never seriously discussed.[287] This adherence to the status quo was most likely driven by a mix of personal, legal, and political factors. Neither the dogmas of the Catholic Church nor Roman law at that time allowed a divorce.[288] And while a separation might have led to Ciano's political and social demise, it can also be assumed that Benito Mussolini was opposed to such a step.[289] The *Duce* himself had several extramarital affairs, including with Margherita Sarfatti and Claretta Petacci; other fascist dignitaries such as Alessandro Pavolini and Roberto

Farinacci imitated their leader's example. All these affairs were hardly a secret but were a topic of public discourse.[290] A split between Edda and Galeazzo Ciano would have put the *Duce* and other prominent fascists in a tight spot and also discredited the publicly propagated family policy. Thus, it was in Mussolini's interest to keep up the appearance that his daughter led a perfect family life according to fascist dogmas.

Galeazzo Ciano's affairs even occupied foreign secret services and politicians. In 1944 the *Schutzstaffel* (SS) Special Representative for Italy, Eugen Dollmann, told the American art historian Bernard Berenson that the first time Ciano "dined as minister of foreign affairs at the German embassy, he started making love to the Ambassadress, Frau von Mackensen, in a way so disgusting that she loathed him ever after."[291] Most of Ciano's "adventures" began and took place at the Acquasanta Golf Club.[292] In his semi-autobiographical novel *Kaputt*, Curzio Malaparte described how the "young Roman women marched under the eyes of Galeazzo Ciano and his court."[293] During a lunch in honour of high-ranking diplomats, Ciano, according to American diplomat Jay Pierrepont Moffat, only had eyes and ears for the ladies.[294] The US ambassador in London, Joseph Kennedy, sardonically stated that he "came away with the belief that we would accomplish much more by sending a dozen beautiful chorus girls to Rome than a flock of diplomats and a fleet of airplanes."[295] Officials at the British Foreign Office were amused by Kennedy's assessment, but doubted his idea would actually pay off.[296]

Whereas the British and Americans only theoretically considered taking advantage of Ciano's weakness for attractive women, Germany may well have put this idea into practice. In Berlin, the SS owned the noble brothel Salon Kitty. The prostitutes were supposed to extract information from their clients, who often included diplomats as well as personalities from industry and politics, and pass it on to the secret service. Apparently, Ciano was a regular guest of this establishment whenever he visited the German capital. Due to a lack of concrete sources, it is more or less impossible to judge whether this strategy was successful and, if so, to what extent.[297] Nevertheless, US diplomats were convinced that the Germans used tactics in a similar vain to get valuable information out of Ciano. They possessed information that Ann-Mari Tengbom, wife of the German embassy secretary in Rome – Otto II von Bismarck – was deliberately sent to the Eternal City to exploit Ciano's weakness for women.[298]

While "every day there was a greater number of Galeazzo's widows, those simple-minded favourites who had fallen into disfavour with Count Ciano,"[299] Edda Ciano was also accused of having an affair with

Emilio Pucci. The then air force officer and later fashion tsar accompanied her when she spent the winter months in the posh ski resort of Cortina D'Ampezzo.[300] Unfortunately, there is no comprehensive study of her, so her relationship with Pucci and other alleged affairs cannot be verified.[301] Nevertheless, in her memoirs she complained that historians and journalists have treated her unfairly. "In a word," she wrote, "I was at one and the same time the Chinese Empress, Tz'u His, Catherine the Second from Russia, Catherine de Medici, Richelieu, Fouché, Queen Victoria, Mata Hari, et cetera."[302] She did not deny that she had a "strong will" and that she definitely was not a "submissive person." But she claimed that she had accepted and lived by the social constraints that shaped the life of every woman in Italy.[303]

Elisabetta Cerruti, wife of diplomat Vittorio Cerruti, disagreed: Edda's entire nature was "un-Italian," and she harmed the manners and morals of her fellow citizens. Countess Ciano, Cerruti claimed, hated the existing social order, had a bossy demeanour, and did not tolerate any contradiction.[304] Cerruti's characterization might have been clouded by her personal aversion to the *Duce*'s daughter. Yet, Romano Mussolini also stated that his sister did not adhere to social conventions. She wore tight swimsuits and expensive clothes, preferred French perfume, drove a car, and liked to party.[305] Edda Ciano indulged in the pleasures of poker, alcohol, and opium. Gambling became a true obsession, and she carried the resulting debts for years.[306] Although Ciano did not tolerate his wife's gambling addiction, he was unable to put an end to her habit. Once in a while he, Arnaldo Mussolini, or Osvaldo Sebastiani, the *Duce*'s private secretary, had to help Edda pay off her debts.[307] In 1936 Joseph Goebbels found that the daughter of the *Duce* was "terribly painted. Like almost all Italians. ... These are not women," he concluded, "who give the nation healthy children."[308] And finally, Ciano himself suggested that his wife did not strictly follow the fascists' gender conventions. He characterized her as an "excellent person" with "rare and great qualities," but she was apparently not popular among Italians because she was "too free and easy."[309] Above all, he might have been afraid that, given Italy's patriarchal society, rumours of her excessive sexual behaviour could damage his honour and prestige as her husband.[310]

All these statements suggest that Edda Ciano's own account should be treated with caution. Rather than embody the fascist social and gender norms, she appeared to rebel against them. Like many women of Italy's upper class, she was fascinated by the commercialization and glamour of Hollywood actresses, who were regarded as symbols of a modern life. She was exposed to these ideals during her time at the boarding school *Santissima Annunziata* in Florence, a private school mainly attended by children of British and American diplomats.[311] The glamorous social life in Shanghai further strengthened her non-conformist way of life. These Anglo-American values challenged and undermined fascist gender models as well as the traditional Catholic family model.[312] Fascist propagandists were well aware of this attraction. In 1933 they forbade the "publication of photographs or drawings of 'female figures who look artificially emaciated or masculinized and represent the type of sterile woman of decadent Western civilization.'"[313] The fact that it was Edda Ciano, the "first lady" of the regime, who emulated this image of a "decadent" Western woman might well have rendered these propaganda efforts futile anyway.[314]

Politics were another area in which Edda Ciano ignored fascist norms. With her father's blessing, she played an important role in the German-Italian relations, often unofficially sounding out Berlin's standing and potentially paving the way for official meetings.[315] One example is her visit to Germany in the summer of 1936. According to her memoirs, she wanted to see her relatives, Maria and Massimo Magistrati, and attend the preparations for the Olympic Games.[316] Given her meetings with leading National Socialists, including Hitler and Goebbels, contemporary observers were quick to dismiss the characterization of her visit as exclusively private.[317] London believed that, on behalf of her father, Edda proposed closer bilateral cooperation, discussed Austria's sovereignty with her hosts, and promised better treatment of the German-speaking population in South Tyrol.[318] Because we do not have any official transcripts of these conversations, we cannot verify these suspicions. Goebbels vaguely mentioned "interesting conversations" in his diary that also touched on the question of the German-Austrian relationship.[319] But Mussolini was evidently ready to turn words into deeds. While Edda stayed in Germany, he dismissed the state secretary in the Foreign Ministry, Fulvio Suvich, and appointed Galeazzo Ciano as the new foreign minister. After this change, high-ranking Germans like Goebbels lost their scepticism about Mussolini's intentions, for they suspected that Ciano wholeheartedly disliked Austria.[320]

The British ambassador in Berlin, Sir Eric Phipps, was amused to see Hitler, Goebbels, and other figures of the Nazi regime competing against each other to pay the greatest attention to the *Duce*'s daughter and wife of the new Italian foreign minister.[321] Phipps failed to realize that this personal homage, however exaggerated it may have been to the neutral observer, was the key to winning the Italians. It restored their self-esteem after decades of harbouring a feeling of inferiority towards the great European powers. Edda Ciano obviously enjoyed the courtesy and friendliness she received in Berlin:

> I was treated as the wife of the Italian Foreign Minister and given special consideration, similar to that reserved for us by protocol in my country, but with the addition of that solemnity and ponderous seriousness that is so much a part of German nature.[322]

When Edda Ciano visited Germany, alone or at her husband's side, she was greeted with great honours and fanfare. While her visits were initially welcomed, beginning in mid-1942 they turned into an embarrassment: she insisted on going to areas that were affected by the war; she intervened in favour of Italian foreign workers in Germany; and she was shocked when she saw the poverty of the German population while the elite was rolling in luxury.[323] Despite these negative experiences, she never lost her admiration for the leaders of Nazi Germany. In September 1943 she personally expressed her thanks to Heinrich Himmler for giving her an honorary SS membership. And even after the Second World War she made no secret of her admiration for Hitler.[324]

Galeazzo Ciano was not amused about his wife's political engagement. Although he welcomed Edda's company when he went abroad or hosted social events, he categorically opposed his wife's autonomous meddling in political affairs. He demanded that she stay out of politics and instead devote herself to the fine arts.[325] To understand his objections, we must consider two things. First, even though fascism in particular stressed the apolitical role of women in society, politics had always been the domain of men in Italy. Several entries in Ciano's diary reveal that he firmly believed in this patriarchal worldview.[326] Yet, it was not his attachment to traditional values alone that made Ciano weary of Edda's political machinations. The second, more serious concern for him was that she repeatedly criticized his policies and attitude as foreign minister. This position became particularly evident during the Second World War when she described the policy of *non belligeranza*, favoured and supported by her husband, as a disgrace for Italy.[327] And then there were other rumours that she was the true architect of Italian foreign policy and would wield significant power over Ciano's decisions.[328]

Despite her stubbornness and strong personality, Edda Ciano frequently participated in the regime's propaganda events such as the *Giornata della Fede* on 18 December 1935.[329] In light of the sanctions imposed by the League of Nations during the Ethiopian War, a large fundraising campaign took place all over Italy. During the ceremony Italians handed over their gold wedding rings to the regime. The fascists wanted to show the world that the entire population, without exception, spontaneously supported the government by making a symbolic financial contribution to the war. To thunderous applause Edda Ciano also donated her wedding ring on the *Piazza Venezia*. But it would be wrong to interpret her gesture as voluntary or exceptional. Rachele Mussolini and the Italian Queen Elena of Montenegro had already given their rings. The latter even opened the *Giornata della Fede* and, by doing so, put considerable pressure on Mussolini's wife and Edda Ciano. Edda had no real choice but to follow suit if she wanted to keep her reputation as the "first lady" of Fascist Italy.[330]

During the Second World War, Edda Ciano worked as a nurse for the Italian Red Cross and was stationed on various hospital ships.[331] According to the official fascist doctrine, the uniform of the Red Cross was the only one women were allowed to wear.[332] When her ship was attacked and sunk by British bombers in March 1941, fascist propaganda exploited the situation for political gains. It praised Edda's dedication to her homeland and – in the same breath – lauded Mussolini's commitment to the nation, which they suggested was so profound that he did not shy away from endangering his own daughter. Ciano, however, strongly disagreed with the *Duce*'s decision to risk the life of his own daughter and thus the mother of Ciano's children.[333]

Edda's decision to enlist as a nurse to help Italian soldiers should not be misunderstood as genuinely fascist. Gender studies have shown that in Western, non-communist societies, the nurse's uniform was the only way for women to participate in armed conflicts. Although their willingness to join the Red Cross was portrayed as an ideal embodiment of female self-sacrifice and selfless duty for the fatherland, it indirectly enshrined established gender roles in that the women still supported the fighting men.[334] In particular, members of the aristocracy had been involved in humanitarian organizations like the Red Cross for decades. Princess Marie José of Belgium, for example, worked as a nurse for the Italian Red Cross during the Ethiopian War and chaired the organization from 1936 to 1941. Once again, Edda had to follow suit if she wanted to convince the public of her dedication to Italy. Thus, instead of fulfilling exclusively fascist norms, she followed "traditional notions of female participation in the social system" and banked on political and social gains.[335]

The "new woman," and thus also Edda Ciano, had one primary task in fascist Italy: to give birth to multiple children in order to end Italy's demographic stagnation. The fascist pro-natalist policy was yet another area that fascist leaders massively propagated, but one to which, when it came to their own families, they did not follow. On average, the fascist elite had 1.9 children.[336] The Cianos may have exceeded average family size with their three children, but they were no match for the

Goebbels family in Germany and also fell short of propaganda expectations in Italy. And, once again, Edda Ciano seems to have deliberately defied the fascist norms. She stated in her memoirs that, after the birth of her first son, Fabrizio, she did not want to have any more children. Raimonda and Marzio Ciano were "accidents."[337]

Galeazzo Ciano did not shy away from exploiting his children for fascist propaganda – illustrated by their names and their membership in the fascist youth organizations. The youngest Ciano offspring, Marzio, was named after the ancient Roman god of war. The Italian public interpreted this gesture as a clear sign of support for the belligerent policy of the regime, and Ciano did not deny it. In addition, Mussolini was even enthusiastic about the name of Ciano's firstborn, Fabrizio.[338] He speculated that the name had its origin in the Italian word "*fabbro*" ("blacksmith").[339] Considering Mussolini's constant complaints that the Italian people had been "anvils" for too long, it is obvious that he saw a propagandistic potential in his grandson's name.[340]

When the new school year began in October 1938, Ciano was eager to show the public how important his children's membership in the fascist youth organization was to him. Photographs were published in the press and video footage produced that showed him and Fabrizio, who was wearing the *Balilla* uniform (figure 3). Ciano was portrayed as a responsible father who apparently entrusted fascist institutions with the education of his children. It is worth noting, however, that Ciano himself was the only person in the photograph wearing civilian dress. This contrast could be interpreted as a generational transfer from the "old" to the "new," where the future – personified by the children in their uniforms – was fascist. A diary entry by diplomat Luca Pietromarchi illustrates that the fascist education had at least some impact on Fabrizio. Pietromarchi described him as a "good boy with character" who had difficulties only when it came to shake hands, mostly because the fascist youth organizations only taught him the Roman salute.[341]

Was Galeazzo Ciano really following fascist education standards though? It was unanimously reported that he was an excellent father and idolized his children.[342] He preferred a strict upbringing, demanded discipline and decency, and paid attention to traditional values such as comradeship, obedience, and diligence. At the same time, he praised his children, demonstrated his confidence, and showed affection.[343] It seems that his educational methods closely resembled those of his own father, as Ciano described them in his diary.[344] Immediately after Costanzo Ciano's death, he looked back on his childhood days: "Do

Figure 3. Galeazzo and Fabrizio Ciano, October 1938. Ullstein Bild #01086820.

you recall," he asked his deceased father, "how I bade you goodbye every time you left … I was unable to speak and my eyes filled with tears; but I restrained myself as long as you were present, I did not want to show my weakness to a great soldier."[345] Ciano's words paint the picture of a strict upbringing in which emotions were regarded as a sign of weakness.

The few diary entries that deal with his own family illustrate Galeazzo Ciano's closeness and devotion to his children.[346] In November 1937 he happily stated that, for the first time, "the children ate at table with us. That very much gives one the feeling of family. For that reason, I like it."[347] Having dinner together as a family not only illustrated Ciano's affection for his children and showed him that he had succeeded as a father on his own father's terms, but also sitting at the same table and complying with certain rules during the evening meal was an important status symbol of middle-class nuclear families in the late nineteenth century.[348] In addition, Ciano hired a nanny for his children, again, a status symbol of the wealthy bourgeoisie. And last but not least, he made sure his children received a staunchly Catholic education. They were baptized and regularly attended mass, accompanied by Galeazzo and Edda Ciano. These examples show that Ciano's idea of education was heavily shaped by bourgeois traditions.[349]

Galeazzo Ciano did not hide his bourgeois educational methods from the public. Quite the contrary: the fascist media showed him as a caring father who paid considerable attention to bourgeois values. This negligence on the part of the propaganda apparatus suggests that the people responsible for curating Ciano's image were not aware of potential negative consequences for fascist family values. The photographs and video footage of Fabrizio Ciano's first day at school in 1937 are a perfect example. Comparing Fabrizio Ciano with Bruno Bottai, who was Giuseppe Bottai's son, reveals fundamental differences in their appearance (figure 4).[350] Whereas Fabrizio, who joined the fascist youth at the age of six, was dressed in a bourgeois suit, Bottai wore his *Balilla* uniform at school and during classes. These photographs and videos depict more than just the friendship between the sons of two key ministers of the regime; they also create the impression that Galeazzo Ciano did not wholeheartedly support a fascistization policy when it came to his own family – and he let the public know it by dressing his son in typical bourgeois clothing at a time when the anti-bourgeois campaign was in full swing.[351]

Galeazzo Ciano did not want to break the intergenerational emotional bond with his children as demanded by fascist doctrine. He sought and encouraged an inner devotion to his children and thus the exact affection between parents and their offspring that had developed in bourgeois families during the late nineteenth century. Numerous photographs show the entire Ciano family on vacation, at the beach, or in the garden of their holiday home. These pictures demonstrate the proximity between parents and children, an evident source of pride for Ciano (figure 5).[352]

Another excellent example of the Cianos' attachment to bourgeois tradition is a photograph taken by Ghitta Carrell.[353] It shows Edda Ciano with her three children; Edda, depicted as a caring mother who looks after her children, is dressed in white – the colour of purity. Marzio, the youngest child, sits on his mother's lap, the symbol of the family. Again, the posing in this photograph is not fascist in nature but rather follows conventions seen from the end of the nineteenth century onward. It illustrated the shift in family structures towards the bourgeois nuclear family. The children were shown as an integral part of the family, protected and cared for, who no longer had to make a living on their own.[354]

Figure 4. Bruno Bottai (left) and Fabrizio Ciano (right), October 1937.

Figure 5. Galeazzo Ciano with his family in Viareggio, 1938.
Ullstein Bild #00310851.

Intrigues and Corruption

Whether concerning wedding preparations or the education of his children, Galeazzo Ciano adopted several bourgeois traditions. In one aspect, however, he departed from traditional family norms: usually the wife would become part of her husband's family, which enjoyed a higher significance in Italy's patriarchal society.[355] In Ciano's case, however, the Mussolini family represented the much stronger centre of gravity, and from the beginning Galeazzo sought a close relationship with his father-in-law. Belonging to the Mussolini family was an important power source at the national level.

Ciano's diary gives us only a few insights into his private relationship with the *Duce*. After the death of his father and sister in 1939, we find some clues that suggest at least some short-lived kind of "father-son relationship" between Ciano and Mussolini.[356] The *Duce*'s earlier personal relationship with Ciano is even more difficult to measure. The telegrams Mussolini sent to Shanghai between 1930 and 1933 show a great devotion to his daughter but provide little useful information about his relationship to Ciano. An often-anxious *Duce* spoke about his own family life, wrote about his sons' travels, and reported on sporting events. Mussolini also asked about his daughter's well-being, sent warm greetings to "Galeazzo," and congratulated the couple on their wedding anniversary and on Fabrizio Ciano's birth. He also showed interest in the political events in China and Japan, and repeatedly urged his daughter to keep a diary, but to no avail.[357] The fact that he often addressed his son-in-law by his first name may be an indication of personal closeness or of reinforcing a certain hierarchy between Mussolini and Ciano; however, its importance should not be exaggerated as the fascist propaganda had tried for years to ban the more formal address "Lei" from Italian parlance.

Overall, we can summarize that Mussolini maintained a good but distant personal relationship to Galeazzo Ciano. Ciano was apparently not surprised, since it would have been not in Mussolini's "harsh character" to express affection.[358] Margherita Sarfatti claimed that the *Duce* was actually incapable of establishing an emotional bond with another person: "His family did bring him pride. He wanted them respected but only as a projection of his all-powerful ego."[359] Today, some scholars go even further and argue that, in contrast to the image spread by the fascist media, Mussolini was ashamed of his family, including Rachele and his sons. He only showed personal feelings towards his daughter Edda.[360]

In the spring of 1941 a shadow fell over the private relations between the Cianos and the Mussolinis when two groups increasingly tried to manipulate the *Duce*.[361] The first one, the "Clan of the Romagna," was led by Benito Mussolini's wife, Rachele, and the building contractor, Dario Pater;[362] the second one consisted of the family of Mussolini's lover, Claretta Petacci, who wanted to replace the members of the Ciano-Mussolini families.[363] Leading fascists, such as Giuseppe Bottai, Achille Starace, and Osvaldo Sebastiani, were deeply concerned about the power struggles within Mussolini's family and their effects on political affairs.[364] Galeazzo Ciano initially wanted "to keep out of this."[365] It was perhaps a noble but overall utopian wish. He did not realize that he was one of the main rivals for both groups in their attempts to win Mussolini's favour. It was an open secret that Rachele Mussolini had never liked Ciano, although she respected his father.[366] In the summer of 1941 Ciano, surprised by Rachele's constant verbal attacks, noted in his diary that she should stay out of politics.[367] However, he was still clueless about her true motives: she envied his proximity to Mussolini and thus the influence this *parvenu* held over the *Duce*.[368] Her hatred seemed to know no boundaries. Beginning in the summer of 1942 she regularly denounced Ciano to the Germans and warned them about his subversive and anti-German schemes.[369] In addition, the strained mother-daughter relationship between Rachele and Edda Mussolini did nothing to calm the situation, but might have even increased the tensions between Ciano and Rachele.[370]

Benito Mussolini met Claretta Petacci, the daughter of the papal personal physician, in 1932.[371] While his affair with Petacci may have violated the Catholic and the fascist understanding of marriage, it enabled the *Duce* to publicly show off his masculinity and sexual vigour.[372] This stance reveals the hypocrisy that can be found in the Italian society during fascism. Whereas ordinary Italians and even some fascist dignitaries had to comply with the fascist norms or face retribution, the *Duce*, the charismatic leader of the regime, was exempt. The control of public discourse through censorship and propaganda even enabled him to turn the obvious violation of norms into something positive. Petacci, on the other hand, used her intimacy with Mussolini to provide her family with lucrative jobs.[373] Little is known, however, about her initial relationship with Ciano. In her diary he plays little role, and one can read a certain reservation between the lines when he is mentioned.[374] In Ciano's own notes, Petacci appears for the first time in the spring of 1941, when Bottai told him about the intrigues between Rachele Mussolini and the Petaccis.[375] German journalist Fritz Heymann spoke of an antipathy between Galeazzo Ciano and the Petacci family, who continuously worked against Ciano and tried to turn Mussolini against his son-in-law.[376]

In April 1942 Mussolini's sister, Edvige Mussolini, approached Ciano and urged him to stop the Petacci family. She argued that their meddling was no longer a private problem, but that it had become a national issue. Ciano still insisted that he did not want to get involved. He stated that he could do nothing about it as long as the Petacci family was protected by Buffarini Guidi and Mussolini's new secretary, Nicola De Cesare.[377] However, slowly realizing that their machinations massively affected his own standing, he patiently waited for a good opportunity to strike at the Petacci family. Finally, in mid-June 1942 he thought his time had come. The minister of foreign trade, Raffaello Riccardi, provided him with information about imminent, illegal gold trafficking, which involved Buffarini Guidi and Claretta's brother, Marcello Petacci. Ciano informed Police Chief Carmine Senise and asked him to confiscate the gold. Although Buffarini Guidi and Petacci complained to the *Duce*, the gold was not returned to them.[378]

But it turned out to be only a pyrrhic victory for Ciano. His own friends, such as Leandro Arpinati, became the preferred targets of the Petacci family. Some of them, like Arturo Osio, director of *Banca Nazionale del Lavoro*, even lost their jobs.[379] Mussolini also made it clear in public that the Petacci family enjoyed his full support. Ciano was dumbfounded when the *Duce* showed more interest in Claretta Petacci's sister's wedding than in the marriage of his own children.[380] And even the joint efforts of high-ranking fascists and family members to restrict Claretta's access to Mussolini were only partially successful as the relationship between him and Claretta, who skilfully portrayed herself as a committed fascist and showered the *Duce*'s ego with praise, dragged on.[381]

In January 1943 Ciano was directly challenged by the Petacci family. He was asked – one could even say ordered – to appoint one of Petacci's trusted friends to the Italian legation in Spain. Ciano refused.[382] This episode may have led Edda Ciano to claim that the Petacci family was to blame for Ciano's ousting in February 1943. But we do not possess any records that would verify this allegation; it is just one example of the well-known personal rivalry between Edda and Claretta – a rivalry that was mirrored in their opposing public images. While Edda resembled the modern, neurotic woman, Claretta appeared as the fascist role model.[383]

Marcello and Claretta Petacci's financial dealings were no exceptions in fascist Italy, where corruption and bribery were part of the patronage system of the ruling class. As yet, however, their significance to the functioning of the fascist system has only recently attracted scholars. Richard Bosworth argued that the widespread acceptance and use of corruption undermined and damaged the totalitarian experiment in Fascist Italy.[384] When reading Bosworth's article, however, one finds the name of one family, whose wealth and luxury were a constant source of public gossip, is missing: the Cianos. Galeazzo Ciano made no secret that he had mastered the art of bribery, corruption, and tax evasion. The "personal benefits," he noted, "will frequently silence even the most noble feelings."[385]

It is difficult today to assess the exact wealth of the Cianos due to missing documents and contradictory information. According to several studies, they owned an apartment in the Parioli district, one of the most expensive in Rome; three other apartments in the capital; a villa in Capri; a country house near Ponte a Moriano; and a house near Livorno.[386] In the summer of 1943, Ciano handed over a list of his family's assets to the new government under Pietro Badoglio. The accuracy of this document, however, should be questioned. Ciano provided the information in order to refute allegations of corruption and illegal enrichment that he and his family faced.[387] The new regime of the RSI carried out an estimate of the value of Ciano's property in their area. This document provides at least one, albeit vague, idea about Ciano's wealth: He was a partner of the *Bombrini Parodi* company, and the value of the family's property in Ponte a Moriano amounted to two million lire. Moreover, his mother, Carolina, had bought another house in Saltocchio in 1941; the property was now valued at 300,000 lire.[388] After Ciano's execution, the authorities confiscated the family property in Livorno, but they made no estimate of its value.[389]

Three explanations present themselves for why there are only estimates of Ciano's wealth. First, goods and property were often not registered in Galeazzo's name but in the name of his mother or his sons.[390] Second, before the collapse of the regime Ciano tried to transfer much of his money abroad, especially to Switzerland. In this venture, Alberto D'Agostino, director general of the *Banca Nazionale del Lavoro*, played an important role. In the 1920s D'Agostino had invested in the *Whitehead* and *Motofides* companies and thus enjoyed a close partnership with the Cianos.[391] In the late summer of 1942 and with Ciano's blessing, he went to Switzerland in order to establish relations with the Swiss banks. A month later, Ciano had a meeting with the Swiss banker and diplomat Peter Vieli. Yet, while we have records of such encounters, we do not possess any documentation that would verify the transfer of Ciano's money to Switzerland.[392] Third, the more the Italian population suffered under the regime and the war, the more Ciano's critics exaggerated his wealth and luxury. Abstruse estimates circulated in public that put Ciano's wealth between 800 million and one trillion lire.[393] They told stories of how Galeazzo Ciano equipped his houses with marble floors, precious mosaics, and expensive furniture from China. Moreover, it was rumoured that the Cianos had owned railway lines, roads, and various newspapers, including the *Corriere della Sera* in Milan, which, however, was never in Ciano's possession.[394]

There were also rumours about Ciano's connection to the *Esposizione Universale di Roma* (EUR; World Exhibition Rome), which was supposed to take place in 1942. Critics claimed that the Cianos had bought the land of the EUR area for a very cheap price before its location was officially announced. Afterwards the value of the land skyrocketed, and the family sold their land at 100 times the original price.[395] According to information the British had, Ciano's land speculation was the only reason why he tried to keep Italy out of the Second World War. Italy's involvement in the war would have meant the end of the world exhibition and resulted in a huge financial loss for the family.[396] That speculation has two weaknesses: First, the regime officially began the construction of the EUR at the end of 1938. If Ciano wanted to make money from land speculation, he had to have sold his land by then. His *non belligeranza* policy, however, only began in August 1939. Second, despite all our knowledge of the Ciano family's widespread corruption and shady business deals, there is no evidence as of now to prove any land speculation in connection with the EUR. We do know, however, that Ciano intervened when the members of the preparatory committee for the EUR were chosen. This action, at least in theory, would have given him access to valuable insider information, including financial information.[397]

The Ciano family was the focus of attention in Italy. That was one of the reasons why the fascist propaganda machine used them as a role model in the attempt to spread fascist norms about family life and gender roles. This endeavour failed. The family was unable to fulfil these expectations in almost any area at almost any time. Instead, the couple led a modern, non-conformist life that became a topic of public debate and gossip. At first, the Cianos, the new fascist dynasty, might have eagerly welcomed their private life taking centre place in the limelight. Yet, the public's attention became an issue as soon as negative stories and scandalous details about their life, including rumours about love affairs, luxury, and corruption, began to dominate the public discourse.

It is difficult to determine the exact impact these rumours had on the success or failure of the fascistization of the Italian society. Elisabetta Cerruti claimed that the "boorish behaviour" of the Cianos was imitated by an entire generation, despite the efforts of the fascist propaganda.[398] However, the Cianos' lifestyle might have become a model for Italians precisely because it showed a familiar form of society, and the propaganda apparatus failed in effectively filtering what they presented to the public. In their obsession to report on the life and times of the Cianos, they seemed to have forgotten that the Cianos led lives that in fact contradicted fascist norms. Thus, the Cianos offered Italians a glimpse into a social life that was different from the society and family model preached by fascist purists – a social life, however, that, at least on the surface, was evocative of the Italian "white telephone" comedies, popular movies that often evolved around commercial culture and traditional, Catholic ideas, motifs, and ethos of paternalism, regionalism, and class privilege.[399] By doing so, whether consciously or not, the Cianos undermined attempts to establish a totalitarian regime in Italy, which wanted to penetrate private life by defining family and gender roles. As such, it was not important that many allegations against the Cianos were exaggerated or not true at all; what was more important was that these rumours circulated in the general public and that many Italians believed them.

These contradictions between the fascist ideal and salacious rumours harmed not only the totalitarian experiment but also Galeazzo Ciano himself. Between 1933 and 1936 he was responsible for the fascist propaganda apparatus. Under his guidance the propaganda issued numerous directives and instructions dealing with the ideal fascist family, the demographic campaign, and gender roles. The fact that he demanded Italians comply with these rules while he and his wife disregarded them led – in contrast to Mussolini, who was often regarded as standing above the ordinary political scramble – to an immense loss of credibility and respect among the Italian public.[400]

Shaping Italian Society

When Benito Mussolini was appointed prime minister of Italy in October 1922, he wanted nothing less than to revolutionize Italy's social and political structure. He was convinced that the traditional bourgeois society could not solve the serious grievances of the time and was therefore doomed. He promised to eliminate all the evils and vices that weakened the liberal society in Italy, including clientelism, corruption, nepotism, individualism, feminism, regionalism, and the class struggle. He also boasted that he would eradicate the social milieus that he blamed for the decline of his homeland: the bourgeoisie and the aristocracy. Mussolini aimed to overthrow the old system and replace it with a state-controlled society in which family and gender models were exclusively shaped by fascist ideas. "The fascist concept of a state," Benito Mussolini and Giovanni Gentile wrote in *La dottrina del fascismo* (1932), "is all-encompassing; no human or spiritual values can exist outside the state ... Fascism is totalitarian."[401]

Whether and, if so, how the fascist regime succeeded in replacing traditional structures with a totalitarian model of society is still debated among scholars. While Anglo-American historians like Christopher Duggan, Richard Bosworth, and Paul Corner look at the limits of this policy, Italian and German historians such as Emilio Gentile and Wolfgang Schieder highlight the efforts and successes of the totalitarian experiment.[402] How can we place the Ciano family, one of the most important and influential families of Fascist Italy, within this debate, and what can their story tell us about Italian society under fascism as a whole?

The rise of the Ciano family is closely linked to Costanzo Ciano. Thanks to his military career and his leading role during the fascist "seizure of power" in Livorno, he gradually established a charismatic authority among conservatives as well as fascists that enabled him to unify the heterogeneous fascist movement in Livorno. Costanzo Ciano belonged to a new class of politician who challenged the traditional establishment throughout Europe after the First World War. They were no longer part of the conservative and aristocratic milieu, but were often artists like D'Annunzio, journalists like Mussolini, or officers like Ferenc Szálasi in Hungary and Jure Francetić in Croatia. "These careers," according to Roger Griffin, "had ... fostered in them a sense of the decay of modern society and convinced them of the need for a radical transformation that would root out the decadent forces which conventional politicians seemed impotent to deal with."[403]

Costanzo Ciano expanded his power and that of his family by using traditional methods that had been an integral part of Italy's political culture since the nineteenth century, including the establishment of a local power base, nepotism, patronage, and corruption. His career illustrates that fascists, like many populist movements in the past and today, postulated a radical break with the past, but their leadership reinforced old grievances. Moreover, authoritarian systems limit the access to resources and thus strengthen an already existing patron-client network. As a result, power and wealth remained in the hands of the few families that possessed and controlled these resources. In turn, these families and the proximity to them would also become an important resource for the political struggle in Fascist Italy.[404]

Two other factors also contributed to the fact that clientelism and nepotism remained such powerful tools in Fascist Italy. First, new parties such as the fascists used patronage and corruption in order to broaden their base. Both the party program of the *fascio* in Livorno and the "Fascist Manifesto" (1919) were deliberately vague in order to appeal to many different groups.[405] This ambiguity enabled Costanzo Ciano and his son to select and adapt certain ideas, while totally ignoring others. Second, the fascist movement and the patronage system had an important similarity: both relied on a leader, a person who promised protection and a better future for his subordinates. Thus, instead of abolishing an already existing and efficient system, it was more convenient for the fascists to keep and exploit it for their own benefit.[406] In Livorno, Costanzo Ciano would eventually assume the roles of a traditional patron of his hometown and of a fascist *ras*.

Even during fascism, the power of a family was massively increased if its members were able to assume important positions within the military, economic, and political areas. Costanzo Ciano's family exemplifies this phenomenon. He strategically placed relatives to consolidate his own position in Livorno and to maintain close contacts with the local industry and the citizens. By doing so, his family enabled him to control the political and social affairs in his hometown while he was living in Rome. Using his strong local power base, Ciano eventually became more and more involved in national affairs. At the national level, he established contacts with other influential fascists and was able to defend his position thanks to alliances and mutual favours.

Costanzo Ciano's preference for nepotism, corruption, and patronage brought him into opposition with Augusto Turati, party secretary of the PNF between 1926 and 1930, who wanted to break the power of the *ras*. In his confrontation with the local fascist leaders, however, Turati finally lost and was dismissed in 1930. After Turati's ousting, rumours circulated in Italy that Ciano himself was responsible for his dismissal. Although there is no evidence of it, such suspicions testified to how much power was attributed to Ciano in 1930.[407] Thus, despite his more or less unimportant government posts, Costanzo Ciano – not least because of his long career – must be regarded as a significant personality of the fascist power apparatus in Italy.[408]

His son, Galeazzo Ciano, was well aware that the family's fortunes were based on his father's networks, reputation, and wealth. Consequently, he was very keen to preserve and defend his father's memory. And once again, we can observe how traditional and fascist structures overlap: in Mediterranean societies, honour and prestige had traditionally been important pillars of an efficient patron-client network. Nonetheless, Galeazzo Ciano failed to benefit from his father's reputation after Costanzo's death in the summer of 1939. He falsely assumed that his father's reputation could be transferred to him. In reality, his father's prestige instead became a burden. Not only was Galeazzo Ciano always compared to his father, but the myth was created that Costanzo Ciano – unlike his son – could have stopped Italy's entry into the Second World War and Italy's division in the summer of 1943.[409]

Galeazzo Ciano furthermore neglected his own family and the family's position in Livorno. As a result, he lost his local and family support, deprived himself of a possible safe haven, and was at the total mercy of the vicissitudes of national politics – an area that was much more difficult to control, simply because of the large number of different actors involved. Only when he realized his national isolation in the summer of 1941 would he try to reclaim a position of power in Livorno, the former stronghold of the Ciano family.

It is too simple to blame naivety or excessive self-confidence as the main reasons for Galeazzo Ciano's behaviour. Unlike his father, he never had to build a local power base from scratch and thus might have misjudged the importance of close ties to Livorno and his own family.

Compared to other members of the fascist elite, Ciano's failure to keep his local power base was unique. Yet, no other personality of the regime had to master the task of transferring local power from one generation to the next.

His marriage to Edda Mussolini catapulted Galeazzo Ciano onto the national stage within a few months. The Cianos' archenemy, Turati, is said to have exclaimed at the wedding: "Who will save us now from the Cianos' dynasty?"[410] Ciano's entry into the Mussolini family – and thus his direct access to one of the most important families in Italy at the time – was essential for his political career. Yet, less well known is that his becoming part of the Mussolini family also undermined many of his other resources, including the ties to his own family, which remained predominantly in Livorno. He realized only relatively late that Mussolini employed nepotism as a way to strengthen and ultimately defend his own power. The *Duce* did not feel obliged to Ciano because of some kind of personal attachment or sympathy, but rather valued his relationship to Ciano primarily based on cost-benefit considerations. Initially, Ciano had extraordinary standing as his daughter's husband for social and political reasons. The marriage not only provided the opportunity to begin a new fascist dynasty, but the young Ciano-Mussolini family could also be exploited as a model for the fascist family. When no progress was apparent in either area, Ciano began to realize that he was just one of many people vying for the *Duce*'s favour. In particular, groups around Rachele Mussolini and the Petacci family successfully intrigued against Ciano. If one had privileged access to Mussolini, one could influence his political decisions, and the son-in-law could not compete with the wife or the mistress. These struggles within the family were therefore never merely of a private nature, but directly affected political life in Italy. Thus, the Ciano-Mussolini familial relations illustrate the close entanglement between private affairs, public offices, and politics that existed during fascism.

Galeazzo Ciano also attempted to build close relationships with the Roman establishment and aristocracy in order to preserve and possibly expand his influence. However, Ciano faced a delicate dilemma described by Pierre Bourdieu: social newcomers, such as the Ciano family, who had belonged to the nobility only since 1928, were trapped in two worlds. Whereas they wanted to become part of the new social milieu to receive acknowledgment for their social advancement, the old aristocratic families, who distinguished themselves from the rest of society through a dynastic identity, were reserved and often hostile to the new nobility.[411] Ciano's entire life demonstrates that he was not able to solve this dilemma. While he distanced himself from his social origins, he was never fully accepted by the establishment. This failure partly explains why he never truly and permanently benefitted from his friendships with nobles, including Isabelle Colonna and Anna Laetitia Pecci-Blunt.

Nevertheless, Galeazzo Ciano's strong desire to become part of the establishment shows that, even during fascism, the attraction of the aristocratic milieu had not faded. Access to the establishment remained an important status symbol that conferred social and also political influence. Thus, it should not come as a surprise that many leaders and high-ranking officials of the regime sought a close relationship with the aristocratic milieu.[412] A stark contrast or divide between fascists and aristocrats, as demanded by radical fascist rhetoric and propagated after the Second World War by members of the nobility, never existed. Rather, a sophisticated network of personal and professional contacts prevailed that might have thwarted the totalitarian experiment but overall stabilized the political system.

The life of the Cianos took place in public in no small part because of their self-promotion of their own images. Their lavish lifestyle was an integral part of Roman gossip circles. It is less the truth of these insinuations that mattered, but how the rumours affected Galeazzo Ciano's reputation. His closeness to the Roman establishment drew criticism and anger from fascist purists. They saw in Ciano the decadent, individualistic bourgeois that fascism had set out to eliminate. His behaviour as a fascist minister and his coziness with the aristocracy were thus perceived as a betrayal of the original ideas of fascism. Moreover, his lifestyle violated not only fascist family and gender norms but also traditional Italian morality as propagated by the Catholic Church. Although a double standard regarding marriage and fidelity prevailed, especially among the Italian elite, the numerous rumours about Ciano's affairs and his alleged weakness towards his wife offered a welcome target for conservative critics. However, the Cianos' non-conformist lifestyle was in line with a trend that can be observed during fascism, particularly in the cities, where the younger generation lived and supported a diverse lifestyle.[413]

Galeazzo Ciano's rise and fall shows that Italian society under fascism was heavily influenced by traditional social models, which were mainly exemplified by the Catholic Church, the aristocracy, and the monarchy. Those traditional models and customs tended to overlap with fascist doctrine in many areas, making it difficult for fascism to sufficiently distinguish itself from them in order to justify a revolutionary push for the fascistization of society.[414] In addition, fascist doctrine could do little to counter modern Western family and social values, which had fascinated the Italian upper class since the 1920s. It is likely Mussolini realized that fascism's failure to offer new social models in key areas like gender roles and patriarchal society undermined his attempt to establish a totalitarian control over society, which is why he sought ways to eliminate the influence of the aristocracy and the Catholic Church.

The Cianos' behaviour also illustrates how leading fascists did not follow the dogmas propagated by party leadership, thus exposing the fascists' glaring double standards. Moreover, they never tried to hide their hypocrisy but instead publicized their lavish private life in order to remain in the limelight and conceivably increase their public appeal and reputation. This method revealed the "cracks in the facade," as De Grand put it, of the totalitarian experiment, and showed niches in which one could escape the fascist norms.[415] As a result, the foundations of the political culture and society of the liberal era endured. Fascism had promised to banish the power of the family, the patronage system, corruption, and nepotism from Italy and to revolutionize the traditional family image. After over twenty years of fascist rule, however, the old ways flourished more strongly than ever.[416]

Ciano's life illustrates that traditional social structures (for example, corruption, patronage networks, family, and gender roles) and models were not only fundamental to his rise to power but also functioned as a counter-narrative to the fascist propaganda machine, limiting its effectiveness. In turn, the continued existence of these structures enabled the key players of nineteenth-century Italy – especially the Catholic Church and the aristocracy – and their social models to survive and sometimes even thrive under fascism. Though radical fascists always boasted about eliminating stereotypical vices, and though party officials like Turati tried to break traditional habits of nepotism and clientelism, they ultimately failed.

This failure is a good indication of the sophisticated symbiotic relationship between the establishment and those fascist hierarchs who began to embrace the elitist way of life. It exposes how closely the conservative establishment, and above all the nobility, was connected to the fascist elite and how influential they were in shaping social norms. To fully grasp their potential influence and power during the fascist area, to understand their agency, and to deconstruct their own whitewashing after the Second World War, more studies on the role of the conservative elite during this time period are desperately needed.

The social entanglement between traditional and new models built the foundation for the political collaboration between the Catholic Church, the monarchy, and some fascists, which I examine in more detail in the following chapter of the book. Thus, a complete break with the traditional social structures would also have jeopardized this fragile alliance, which was essential for the survival of many high-ranking fascists and thus the system. Becoming an influential member of the fascist inner circle meant embracing traditional social norms, something Galeazzo Ciano realized when he described his father as a "soldier, a fascist, a Christian," and thus a person who was at home in all the major social circles. The continuing existence and influence of traditional models and structures suggest that fascism was never an anomaly in Italian history, as Benedetto Croce wrote in 1943.[417] Examining Ciano's life illustrates that fascism should instead be understood as a logical, albeit not irreversible, development of a hyper-masculine patriarchal society, which was perceived as threatened by the political Left after the First World War.

2
The Politician

The Minister

When Benito Mussolini was editor-in-chief of the Socialist Party's newspaper *Avanti!* his judgment of Italy's capital was not very flattering. He described Rome as a "parasitic city of cheap low-grade hotelkeepers, shoeshine boys, prostitutes, priests, and bureaucrats."[1] Although this harsh assessment was ideologically motivated and did not correspond to reality, Rome indeed had little glamour to offer when Galeazzo Ciano and his father moved to the capital in 1921. The age of rapid industrialization and modernized banking that has shaped so many urban centres since the late nineteenth century had no real impact on Rome. Bureaucracy, real estate speculation, and housing shortages dominated the city. It primarily benefitted from its former glory as the centre of the ancient Roman Empire and attracted curious tourists from all over the world.[2]

Yet, Rome was the capital and the political centre of Italy. The Chamber of Deputies, the Senate, and the seat of government were located there; in the mid-1920s, the PNF moved its headquarters from Milan to Rome. The city was also the seat of the Italian general staff and of King Vittorio Emanuele III, and some of Italy's most respected and influential aristocratic families lived there. Finally, Rome – or more precisely the Vatican – was the centre of Catholicism and the seat of the papacy. Thus, the city symbolized a microcosm of the political landscape during the fascist era. But how did Galeazzo Ciano interact with this environment?

On 1 August 1933 Ciano entered these inner circles of Rome's politics when he took over the *Ufficio Stampa del Capo del Governo* (USCG; Press Office) from Gaetano Polverelli. After only a few days in office, he asked his staff to prepare an internal memo concerning the creation of a new propaganda office. They concluded that efficient propaganda is possible only if all relevant institutions are united under the roof of the Press Office.[3] Ciano followed up with a detailed memorandum on the German Reich Ministry for Popular Enlightenment and Propaganda. The report focused on questions of budgeting and provided a list of other institutions that were responsible for propaganda activities in Germany. It emphasized structural rather than ideological aspects, thereby highlighting the authority and central position of Joseph Goebbels within the Nazi propaganda apparatus. The memorandum left little doubt as to Ciano's intentions: he wanted to lead a new, powerful, and financially independent organization with wide-ranging responsibilities.[4]

Ciano's first major test as the new head of the USCG came on 14 and 15 June 1934. Mussolini had invited Adolf Hitler to come to Venice after the German chancellor had pressed for a meeting with the *Duce*.[5] The visit, however, turned into an unpleasant affair from a propagandistic perspective; and together with the failed coup against Engelbert Dollfuß in Vienna in July 1934, during which Dollfuß was killed, it offered Ciano the perfect opportunity to bring the entire fascist propaganda under his control.[6] He intended to imitate the Nazi model in order to ultimately surpass Berlin, because for him Germany was both a role model and a rival.[7] Ciano's intentions became apparent in July 1934, when the Press Office moved into the prestigious *Palazzo Balestra* on Via Vittorio Veneto. Mussolini and several fascist notables attended the inauguration of the new headquarters, and Ciano, dressed in his fascist militia uniform, proudly presented every detail of the premises to them.[8]

On 10 September 1934 the USCG was upgraded to the State Secretary for Press and Propaganda with three directorates-general overseeing domestic press (*Direzione Generale per la Stampa Italiana*; DGSI), foreign press (*Direzione Generale per la Stampa Estera*; DGSE), and propaganda (*Direzione Generale per la Propaganda*; DGP). The name of the new agency indicates that Ciano still considered print media the main propaganda tool, despite widespread illiteracy in Italy. However, he also intended to use traditional forms of cultural education such as theatre, as well as new media such as film and radio.[9] He immediately began to interfere in the program of the radio station *Radio Bari*, using it to spread anti-British propaganda in the Arab world, although it was nominally under the control of the EIAR.[10] Ciano, however, was not bothered by such bureaucratic obstacles. Thanks to his father's personal contacts, such interference was relatively easy for him.[11] Wishing to operate at least semi-independently of his father's and father-in-law's networks in the future, Ciano obtained the necessary authorization on 15 September 1934 to enact decrees that would deal with propaganda in the broadest sense, as well as the right to attend meetings of the Council of Ministers as a secretary of state.[12]

The main tasks of the DGSI, the DGSE, and the DGP were to spread the "fascist truth" and inform the world about the "gigantic works of the regime."[13] In order to do so, the directorates-general reviewed and evaluated over 11,000 Italian news outlets, screened the foreign press, and provided over 135 foreign correspondents with information. To fulfil their ambitious and time-consuming work, they had large sums of money; press offices at the prefectures in Rome, Milan, Turin, Genoa, Bologna, Naples, and Palermo; their own press attachés at fourteen Italian embassies, all of which reported directly to Ciano; and they intensified cooperation with the Italian press agency *Agenzia Stefani*.[14] They also became increasingly involved in the professional affairs of journalists. At the end of his tenure as minister of propaganda, Ciano noted with satisfaction: "Journalism ... has ceased to be a private matter in order to become an instrument of civilization in the service of the Fatherland and a powerful educational tool."[15]

Because the directorates-general played a key role in disseminating fascist propaganda, Ciano made sure they were led by loyal confidants. The DGP was headed by Ottavio De Peppo, whom Ciano knew from their time together at the embassy in Rio de Janeiro, and he was assisted by Raffaele Casertano. Casertano, born in Naples in 1897, married aristocrat Maria Beatrice del Prete in 1934, with Ciano as his best man, and became one of Ciano's close collaborators.[16] Emanuele Grazzi was the head of the DGSE. Ciano was full of praise for Grazzi, noting that he was an expert on political issues, an excellent organizer, and respected by foreign diplomats.[17] The DGSI was under the leadership of Neos Dinale, followed by Francesco Felice in 1935 and Gherardo Casini in 1936, a trusted friend of Giuseppe Bottai and the Cianos.[18]

Ciano quickly began the *Gleichschaltung* (coordination) of the propaganda institutions.[19] In September 1934 he created the Directorate-General for Film and Film Censorship and appointed Luigi Freddi to administer it; previously the Ministry of Corporations and the Ministry of the Interior had been responsible for these areas.[20] Two months later, Ciano set up a fifth directorate-general under Oreste Bonomi to deal with all issues related to tourism, a task that was previously carried out by the *Commissariato per il Turismo*.[21] In 1935 he created the *Ispettorato per il Teatro*, which was responsible for music and theatre – areas that were previously in the hands of the Ministry of Corporations, the Ministry of National Education, and the Ministry of the Interior.[22]

The other ministries did not oppose Ciano's energetic pursuits – hardly surprising given that Mussolini himself led most of them. Only the *Ministero dell'Educazione Nazionale*, then headed by De Vecchi, remained independent, though its minister also expressed no objection to Ciano's plans. During these early stages, Ciano proved to be a determined organizer. He showed little consideration for the sensitivities of others while relying on the backing of his father and Mussolini. But it also became clear that he was neither creative nor innovative, as most of his ideas had been discussed earlier or were in use in Germany, France, the United States, and Great Britain.[23]

The *Sottosegretariato* under Galeazzo Ciano quickly grew in importance and size. The increased influence was reflected in the enormous expansion of responsibilities and the state's budget, which amounted to about 3 per cent of the fascist regime's total expenditure in 1934–35.[24] When Ciano moved to the Foreign Ministry in 1936, the Ministry of Press and Propaganda employed over 680 people; by contrast, his predecessor Gaetano Polverelli had been responsible for 35 people.[25] Bigger, however, does not mean better: a lack of consultation between the different directorates-general often prevented them from effective collaboration, as their areas of competence were not always clearly defined. Therefore, on 25 September 1934 Ciano created the *Segreteria Particolare* under Celso Luciano to better streamline the various offices' efforts.[26]

The heads of the directorates-general were mainly responsible for organizing their departments and had little decision-making power. They received instructions from Ciano via the *Segreteria Particolare*, which in turn consulted with the *Duce* on a daily basis. In rare cases, Mussolini directly contacted the directors-general. Mussolini usually talked to Ciano after he had met with officials from other departments and ministries, which laid the foundations for the propaganda measures later initiated by Ciano.[27]

Contemporary reports on Ciano's work and his relationship with his staff are rare. The head of the Directorate-General for Tourism, Oreste Bonomi, enthusiastically praised the social and professional skills of his superior, who, he felt, led the ministry with calm, vision, and kindness.[28] Such a glowing assessment must be treated with caution as it was part of a letter Bonomi wrote to Ciano himself. Still, other employees and numerous journalists were also impressed by the young minister's open and sometimes jovial disposition.[29] Especially in contrast to his predecessor, Ciano surprised many with his friendly treatment of subordinates and press representatives. Many of his so-called *veline* (circular letters) were formulated more like well-intentioned instructions than orders.[30] By doing so, he managed to create a positive image and earn a reputation as a supposedly non-partisan superior. Yet, his ministry was also fractured by envy and competition among the employees. Whether Ciano consciously promoted these rivalries is not known, but according to the principle *divide et impera*, he may well have taken advantage of such disputes that strengthened his own position as a potential mediator.[31]

Ciano was responsible for the propaganda apparatus, one of the most delicate and important areas of fascist politics, from 1933 to 1936. Scholars agree that this time period was crucial for the development of fascist culture and propaganda.[32] Instructions, prohibitions, surveillance, favours, and censorship were the means Ciano used to indoctrinate the Italian population and to portray Italy as a great power abroad. Many studies, especially written by cultural historians, have detailed the various means the fascist regime applied over time to achieve this goal, examining areas ranging from architecture, movies, literature, opera, and sports – topics I reference throughout this book whenever Ciano was directly involved.[33] However, the goal of this section is not to detail Ciano's areas of propagandistic expertise, but rather to show how he led other institutions down this road and was responsible for the centralization, monopolization, and enormous expansion of the propaganda apparatus, a topic that has so far not received the necessary attention. By doing so, Ciano gained valuable experience in the organization and management of a ministry as well as in daily dealings with other government organizations – skills that came in handy when he took over the *Palazzo Chigi* in June 1936.

As foreign minister Ciano immediately began to replace key personnel. Within just a few months, twenty-three positions were affected as Ciano tried to rejuvenate the Foreign Ministry and place loyal followers into important positions.[34] For example, his father's confidant, Giuseppe Bastianini, succeeded Fulvio Suvich as state secretary.[35] Bastianini, advocate of a "fascist international" and a fascist of the first generation, had been ambassador in Warsaw since 1932. He was considered the exact opposite of Ciano: serious, almost grim, calm, and reserved. Bastianini complained in his memoirs, published in 1959, that he had had little influence on foreign policy decisions. In an attempt to repair his reputation following the Second World War, he claimed that he was merely responsible for administrative matters.[36] In September 1939 Ciano sent him to London as an ambassador, and the post of state secretary remained vacant until Ciano's own dismissal in February 1943.[37]

Another significant change took place in the *Gabinetto*. Pompeo Aloisi, who had been head of this office since 1932, was replaced by Ciano's protégé Ottavio De Peppo.[38] Two years later, De Peppo was sent to the embassy in Ankara and replaced by Filippo Anfuso, whom Ciano had known since his training as a diplomatic officer. Anfuso was considered an intelligent and capable diplomat with a reputation for being a fervent fascist, cynic, and admirer of Mussolini.[39] He remained in this post until his transfer to Budapest in April 1942, when he was succeeded by Marquis Blasco Lanza D'Ajeta. D'Ajeta, born in Florence in 1907, joined the diplomatic service in 1932 and was initially a member of the Italian delegation to the League of Nations. When Ciano was sent to the embassy in the Vatican in February 1943, D'Ajeta followed him as embassy secretary.[40]

With the position of secretary of state vacant, the heads of the cabinet became the second most influential persons in the *Palazzo Chigi*, answerable only to the minister. They met with Ciano four times a day and presented him with reports of the diplomatic missions and the directorates-general. Ciano in turn decided which documents should be presented to the *Duce* and which should not. In this way, he exercised immense influence on Italian foreign policy – an influence that not only brought with it a great responsibility but also the theoretical possibility of manipulating the *Duce*.[41] Moreover, the heads of the *Gabinetto* always substituted for Ciano when the minister was absent from Rome, and he was considered by many contemporaries to represent the direction of the regime's foreign policy.[42] While some observers, for example, saw the appointment of D'Ajeta in 1942 as a positive new beginning for Italian foreign policy, in that Ciano had finally freed himself from the negative influence of Anfuso, Berlin was shocked.[43] While the Germans regarded Anfuso as a loyal supporter of the Axis, they were sceptical of D'Ajeta's commitment, as he was related to the US diplomat Sumner Welles and close to the Italian royal family.[44]

Within the *Gabinetto*, Ciano created the *Segreteria Particolare del Ministero*. Filippo Anfuso, who was replaced by Umberto Natali in 1938, was initially in charge. Natali held the post until February 1943, when he was sent to Lugano, Switzerland, as consul general. At that time, the American embassy in Bern classified him as a "100 per cent fascist."[45] The *Segreteria Particolare* facilitated Ciano's control over and coordination of the ever-growing *Gabinetto*, which in 1940 resembled a "ministry within the ministry."[46] The number of cabinet employees rose from eleven in 1939 to forty-two in 1942. Most of them were quite young, and formed a kind of elite of the diplomatic corps.[47]

Ciano repeatedly set up ad hoc subdivisions such as the *Ufficio Spagna* within the *Gabinetto*.[48] It was created on 8 December 1936 under the direction of Luca Pietromarchi and was responsible for coordinating the Italian intervention in the Spanish Civil War.[49] Pietromarchi, born in 1895 into an old aristocratic family, was considered a staunch Catholic, revisionist, and nationalist, but had little understanding of the Nazi ideology. His diplomatic experience, his conscientious methods, and his contacts within the Roman nobility made him one of Ciano's most important and trusted collaborators.[50]

Thus, it comes as no surprise that, when the *Ufficio Spagna* was dissolved on 1 January 1940, Pietromarchi remained in the *Gabinetto* and took over the *Ufficio Guerra Economica*, which existed until 10 June 1940 and dealt with the economic impact of the British trade blockade imposed on Italy.[51] After the French surrender, Ciano created the *Ufficio Armistizio e Pace* on 23 June 1940 to regulate the modalities of the ceasefire between Italy and France, and to take over the administration of the occupied territories. At the time, Ciano did not have any exact ideas of how this task was to be achieved; it was much more important to bring the administration of occupied areas under his control.[52] This office, also headed by Pietromarchi, was renamed *Ufficio Armistizio e Territori Occupati* in the summer of 1941 and became responsible for the occupied territories in Greece and the Balkans as well.[53] According to historian Davide Rodogno, this office oversaw the economic and political administration of occupied areas and gathered all the relevant information, thus becoming the centre of Italian occupation policy.[54]

On 1 August 1936 Ciano modified the structure of the directorates-general in the Foreign Ministry by the so-called *ordinamento Ciano*. By doing so, Ciano reinstated the structures that Carlo Sforza had introduced before the fascists took over. The *ordinamento* re-established six directorates-general, responsible either for geographical areas (*Direzione Generale degli Affari d'Europa e del Mediterraneo; Direzione Generale degli Affari Transoceanici*) or for administrative tasks (*Direzione Generale degli Affari Generali; Direzione Generale del Personale e dell'Amministrazione Interna; Direzione Generale degli Affari Commerciali; Direzione Generale degli Italiani all'Estero*).[55]

Former diplomats and scholars often argued that the directorates-general's influence within the *Palazzo Chigi* greatly diminished under Ciano. To prove their point, they referred to the *Direzione Generale degli Affari Transoceanici* (DGAT), which was headed by Luigi Cortese (1936), Emanuele Grazzi (1936–39), and Renato Prunas (1939–43).[56] They argued that the DGAT was not responsible for all the regions that were nominally part of its geographical mandate, such as Italian East Africa. Furthermore, they pointed out that the tenures of the individual department heads were often very short, thus weakening their authority.[57] However, historian Gianluca Borzoni showed the influence that Prunas – one of the most experienced diplomats under Ciano – was able to exert on foreign policy, given Ciano's great interest in South America and Asia. Ciano attached great importance to Argentina,

Brazil, Japan, and China, not only because of his personal ties to these countries but also because of their positions within his global foreign policy strategy.[58] Moreover, it should be remembered that Ciano created the position of the Directorate-General for Transoceanic Affairs; there had never been a comparable post before.[59] The case of the DGAT actually illustrates that the directorates-general preserved their importance and asserted their influence over Italian diplomacy.

In addition to these structural and personnel changes at the *Palazzo Chigi* in Rome, the personnel changes at Italy's major diplomatic missions abroad must be examined. The influence of ambassadors and consuls on foreign policy under Ciano is still debated. Former ambassadors repeatedly claimed that they were almost powerless and sent abroad without any specific instructions.[60] Other contemporaries such as Giorgio Nelson Page, however, argued that the ambassadors still fulfilled a delicate political function;[61] certainly, Dino Grandi seemed to be aware of the influence he, as an ambassador, possessed over the decisions in the *Palazzo Chigi*.[62] So what is the correct assessment?

It is instructive to first consider the issue from a purely administrative perspective. Ciano did not significantly change the number of diplomatic missions. When Italy entered the Second World War in June 1940, fifty-eight of the original sixty embassies that represented Italy's interests worldwide when Ciano took office still existed.[63] Of course, one cannot avoid the impression that Ciano removed inconvenient diplomats from the *Palazzo Chigi* by sending them to embassies on the periphery.[64] Raffaele Guariglia and Fulvio Suvich, who were sent to the embassies in Buenos Aires and Washington, DC, respectively, are typical examples. While it is certainly true that Ciano removed potential rivals from Rome, these embassy posts should not a priori be classified as insignificant. Argentina was home to the largest Italian diaspora in the world, and the country played a significant role, like the United States, in Ciano's foreign policy. Moreover, Suvich deliberately picked his new position, another sign that his relocation was not an "act of revenge."[65]

Ciano kept most Italian ambassadors at the major diplomatic missions in Europe, including Dino Grandi in London, Vittorio Cerruti in Paris, and Bernardo Attolico in Berlin.[66] Attolico, who was married to Eleonora Pietromarchi, advocated closer cooperation between Italy and the Third Reich. He was assisted by Ciano's brother-in-law, Massimo Magistrati, leading to speculation that Magistrati was keeping an eye on Attolico on Ciano's behalf.[67] However, there is no convincing proof that this was the case. After all, Magistrati had been in Berlin since 1933 and had already worked with Attolico at the embassy in Rio de Janeiro in the late 1920s.[68]

At the end of 1937, Ciano expressed satisfaction with his reassignments and restructuring measures. After fifteen years of work, he noted in his diary, the *Palazzo Chigi* has been finally "conquered." "And only I know," Ciano continued, "what a struggle I have had to make these goats keep step to the fascist march."[69] Even though Ciano had been minister for only one and a half years, Suvich noted that those whom Ciano promoted within the diplomatic service were predominantly party members. Suvich criticized this fascistization of the Foreign Ministry and added that, in his own defence, such a personnel policy had never existed during his tenure.[70] Yet, in light of Ciano's personnel and structural changes just reviewed, a more ambivalent picture emerges, which justifies neither Ciano's self-congratulations nor Suvich's criticism.

With the help of the structural measures Ciano intended to – as he did when he was minister for press and propaganda – control the entire decision-making process. He desired the sole authority to issue directives and make decisions within his ministry, thus imitating the power Mussolini attempted to exert over the Council of Ministers. In Ciano's eyes the officials in the *Palazzo Chigi* and the Italian envoys abroad should only play an advisory role; and many diplomats would later claim that Ciano robbed them even of that role. They used their memoirs as a means to deflect blame for an ultimately catastrophic foreign policy between 1936 and 1943 onto a single person: Galeazzo Ciano, the upstart and son-in-law of the *Duce*. Still today, their interpretation dominates the collective memory of the Italian Foreign Ministry from 1936 to 1943. Only recently have scholars cautioned against accepting these allegations and begun to take a more nuanced view of Ciano's politics.[71]

Ciano's personnel policy was not as one-sided as Suvich suggested. The attempts to fascistize the diplomatic corps began under Secretary of State Grandi, who integrated the foreign organization of the fascist party (*Ufficio Centrale per i Fasci all'Estero*, UCFE) into the ministry and reformed the admission procedure in 1927–28. He wanted to block alleged anti-fascists from entering the foreign service and instead fill the ranks of diplomats with staunch fascists, the *ventottisti*.[72] But even under Ciano, traditional career diplomats kept their special position within the Foreign Ministry. For Ciano, it was less an individual's fascist conviction that decided his diplomatic career and more that individual's loyalty, experience, networks, and reliability. Of course, Ciano's criteria were not innovative; they corresponded to traditional customs dating back to the times of Crispi.[73]

This reorganization ultimately meant that Ciano surrounded himself with a very heterogeneous group of people in terms of their ideological convictions, diplomatic experience, and family background. He promoted former friends and acquaintances from his youth and student days, such as Ottavio De Peppo and Filippo Anfuso.[74] Other employees, such as Blasco Lanza D'Ajeta, Marcello Del Drago, and Luigi Cortese, were close friends and therefore often accused of being promoted beyond their competence. However, they were all trained diplomats whose careers had already begun under Suvich. Only Ciano's childhood friend Zenone Benini held – as state secretary for Albanian affairs – an important position in the ministry without previous diplomatic training. Gino Buti, Luca Pietromarchi, Renato Prunas, and Leonardo Vitetti had also served in the diplomatic corps for an extended period. And even though Ciano personally did not like Prunas and Buti, he nevertheless respected their experience, took them on numerous trips abroad, and appointed them to important positions.[75] The appointments of D'Ajeta, Del Drago, and Pietromarchi demonstrate that Ciano also relied on the nobility, a traditional recruitment pool for diplomats. This practice offered him – as will be explained in detail later – the opportunity to use the networks of the European aristocracy to further his diplomacy.

As was the case at the German Foreign Office, career diplomats and party hardliners working for the *Palazzo Chigi* shared some interests. The similarities between the two groups were much greater than the differences when it came to such issues as the building of an empire in the Mediterranean and the revision of the Paris Peace Treaties. However, comparing the personnel in the Italian and German foreign ministries also reveals important differences. For instance, Ciano recruited his most trusted employees from a broader social base than did his counterparts in Berlin, where the thorough Nazification of the diplomatic corps began under Konstantin von Neurath and was enforced under Joachim von Ribbentrop.[76] Furthermore, only two influential Italian diplomats, Serafino Mazzolini and Filippo Anfuso, who owed their careers to Ciano, joined the RSI in autumn 1943; all other high-ranking diplomats remained loyal to the Italian king. Ciano's relationship with both individuals was already tense before the meeting of the Grand Council in July 1943, as evidenced by their lukewarm reactions to Ciano's dismissal as foreign minister.[77]

Ciano's self-congratulating delusion that he headed a fascist ministry in which a "fascist pace" prevailed must not be taken too credulously. The *Palazzo Chigi* was hardly an institution where radical fascists dominated the day-to-day activities; rather, Ciano intended to illustrate that the ministry was strictly hierarchically structured and would unconditionally execute the minister's orders – that is, his orders. Ciano's personnel policy and his restructuring measures were primarily driven by his hunger for recognition; they were only fascist in the sense that they centralized power and promoted an authoritarian style of leadership. It thus remains to be determined whether and to what extent Ciano's manner of diplomacy and foreign policy ideas were influenced by fascist ideology.[78]

The importance Ciano attached to a centralized ministry also becomes clear when we contextualize his remarks. At the same time as Ciano praised his own work, he complained that the foreign policy of the Third Reich was completely unpredictable because of the interference of numerous people and institutions.[79] Ciano wanted to avoid such a clash of competencies in what he considered to be his responsibility, and certainly did not let other ministers or the party intervene in his ministry. Judging by his actions in general and his personnel policy in particular, he succeeded partially in the years 1937 and 1938. His control over his ministry was a clear sign of his prominent position within the regime; if, upon reversion, someone tried or actually did meddle in his jurisdiction, it was a sign of Ciano's diminishing power.

The first test of Ciano's control arose when Jews were successively excluded from the Italian civil service. Besides the Ministry of the Interior under State Secretary Buffarini Guidi, it was above all the Ministry of Education under Giuseppe Bottai and the Ministry of Popular Culture under Dino Alfieri that radically implemented this policy.[80] In August 1938 the *Duce* also demanded that Ciano dismiss all Jews from the diplomatic service. According to Ciano's diary, he played for time and initially intended only to order the Jewish staff back to Rome.[81] In the same month, the head of the *Direzione Generale Demografia e Razza*, Antonio Le Pera, wrote to all the ministries enquiring about the measures taken against the Jewish staff.[82] Only a week later, in a personal letter to Buffarini Guidi, Ciano declared that he had reassigned all persons not belonging to the "Italian race." In this letter, however, he did not mention the word "Jew" once. However, he assured Buffarini Guidi that, after all measures had been implemented, the staff of his ministry would totally comply with the expectations of the Ministry of the Interior.[83] In the spring of 1939 it became apparent that Ciano's ministry did not proceed with the same vigour as other ministries, nor had he done what he had led Buffarini Guidi to believe. In reference to Le Pera's August letter, all ministries were again asked in March 1939 to report all measures taken against the Jews. Ciano's employee Luigi Vidau replied that Le Pera's circular had never reached the ministry.[84] Was it possible that Ciano had blocked the instructions in order to prevent anti-Jewish actions in his ministry? Considering Ciano's position within the regime at the time, we should assume that political considerations were more decisive than humanitarian motives. While he regularly intervened in the affairs of other ministries, he fended off any external interference in his ministry.

Nevertheless, the *Palazzo Chigi* had taken some measures against Jews. In December 1938 a circular was sent to all Italian legations asking the ambassadors and consuls to report all Jews in their service.[85] Little is known about the reaction of the heads of the diplomatic missions abroad, as the relevant documents are incomplete. Two examples show, however, that this instruction was not very well received, at least in the West. For example, the consul general in Liverpool vouched for the vice consul in Bradford, who was married to a Jew.[86] The Italian honorary consul in Belfast, Raymond Burke, was also acquitted of any suspicion of belonging to the Jewish "race."[87]

In Italy and in countries with authoritarian regimes, however, the *Palazzo Chigi* acted more resolutely. At the ministry's instigation the Jews were expelled from Italian companies in Budapest and from the International Institute for Agriculture in 1938.[88] The title of the holding in the archive of the Italian Foreign Ministry, *Dispensa del servizio di funzionari ebrei 1939*, suggests that Jews were or should at least be removed from the diplomatic service.[89] The different treatment of the Jewish employees in Italy and in Western countries shows that the *Palazzo Chigi* did not want to lose local expertise and cause even more criticism from the West.

Until the autumn of 1939, Ciano blocked any external interference into his ministry – at least there are no sources suggesting otherwise. This situation changed with Italy's decision to enter into the Second World War. The first and most prominent target was Italian Ambassador Attolico, who was transferred from Berlin to the Vatican on 27 April 1940 against Ciano's will. Hitler had demanded his dismissal from Mussolini and wanted either Roberto Farinacci or Dino Alfieri as his successor; the *Duce* eventually chose Alfieri.[90] In the summer of 1941, Ciano had to sack Zenone Benini and abolish the State Secretariat for Albania after Mussolini asked him to do so.

By personalizing and centring Italian foreign policy – and previously fascist propaganda – on himself, Ciano hoped to be perceived as the sole architect of a successful policy, even if he never secured that perception. A pompous appearance, careful staging, and a display of fascist zeal put Ciano in the public limelight,[91] but the fixation on his person alone posed certain dangers. It not only made people from all social classes envious, but it also put Ciano at risk of being held solely responsible for diplomatic failures. Moreover, US Ambassador William

Phillips reported that "Ciano kept everything in his own hands to such an extent that the works seem to have stopped in his absence."[92]

Such complaints highlight some of the negative consequences of Ciano's restructuring. Senior officials were only responsible for their specific portfolios. They did not have an overall view of Italian foreign policy, which made it difficult to constructively enact the policy. At the same time, however, Ciano's absence gave officials the opportunity to hide behind a lack of instructions and supposed ignorance. By pointing out that only Ciano knew the guidelines of foreign policy, his employees could evade political responsibility. Covered by the minister, they were free to act as they saw fit without fear of repercussions. A similar pattern also existed in other areas of the fascist government.[93]

The Fascist

In the early 1920s fascist student groups formed spontaneously at many Italian universities, and the first attempts were made to create a national fascist student association. The first larger groups emerged at the end of 1921 at the universities of Bologna, Florence, and Milan.[94] Several Italian universities, including the Sapienza University of Rome, saw violent clashes between fascist and anti-fascist students. It was in those days that Giuseppe Bottai, who had been introduced to a Roman *fascio* in 1919 by Filippo Tommaso Marinetti, and Galeazzo Ciano attended the Sapienza University.[95]

Little is known about Ciano's student years. Most of what we do know is based on the memoirs of old friends like Giorgio Amendola and Orio Vergani. Ciano biographers have uncritically recounted all their stories and anecdotes, subordinating them into a simple narrative: Ciano was neither interested in politics in general nor in fascism in particular; he was not a member of a *fascio*, and his membership card for the fascist group *La Disperata*, dated 1 May 1921, was forged ten years later in order to construct a fascist past for career reasons; and he did not participate in the "March on Rome."[96] According to that narrative, Ciano maintained close contacts with anti-fascists and devoted himself to the supposedly most apolitical of all occupations imaginable: the arts, theatre, and writing. The years 1921 to 1925 were, according to his biographer Giordano Bruno Guerri, "the literary period of Galeazzo Ciano."[97] Ciano is presented to us as an apolitical free spirit in order to draw a deterministic line from his youthful disinterest in fascism to his vote in the Grand Council in July 1943. Without fascist convictions and political instincts, Ciano was clearly not suited to manage and overcome all the later challenges in his life; his execution in 1944 seemed like the only logical outcome. But how much truth is there to these judgments?

The greatest obstacle for historians when dealing with Ciano's youth is the quality of the sources from the early period of the fascist movement. Either they are inaccurate, partly post-dated, or simply missing. Credible contemporary records about Ciano's early membership in a *fascio* are just as rare as materials concerning his participation in the "March on Rome." Another problem is that, although Livorno was the hometown of the Cianos, Galeazzo and his father spent the years of violent conflict in Genoa, and after his father's election success, both went to Rome. They visited Livorno only during the summer months, which may explain why neither his nor his father's name appears on a list published in 1923 recognizing all citizens of Livorno who participated in the "March on Rome." However, Ciano's childhood friend Zenone Benini is mentioned, making it likely that Ciano had early contact with the fascists.[98] After all, Galeazzo Ciano belonged to the war youth generation, which in the early days accounted for the second-largest group of members within the fascist movement.[99]

There are more indications that Ciano was indeed closer to the fascist movement than just his name being present on the controversial lists of members of the *fascio* in Livorno or Alessandro Pavolini's book, *Disperata*, published in 1937.[100] For example, it is unlikely that a young student like Ciano was not affected by the violent clashes at his university. Moreover, many contemporaries would later remember that as a student he was or at least could have been a supporter of fascism. The journalist Alfredo Signoretti did not regard the young Ciano as a "brilliant fascist zealot," but nevertheless saw him as a fascist who enjoyed being part of the young, intellectual fascist "rebels."[101] Even Vergani, who is often used as a witness to prove Ciano's apolitical attitude, did not categorically rule out the possibility that Ciano was a fascist of the "first hour."[102] But do we find additional evidence for Ciano's contacts with the fascist movement that go beyond these speculations and retrospective stories?

As a student Ciano worked for Carlo Bazzi's government-loyal newspaper *Il Nuovo Paese*, one of the leading presses calling for a "moral revolution" in Italy and, like Bottai, part of the revisionist faction of fascism.[103] After finishing his studies, Ciano worked for *L'Impero* under Mario Carlí and Emilio Settimelli until April 1925.[104] The assertion that he also wrote for Giovanni Amendola's *Il Mondo*, however, is one of the numerous attempts to construct the image of an anti-fascist Ciano. This often-quoted allegation refers to an anecdote that Giorgio Nelson Page retold in his autobiography. According to that story, the liberal politician Dino Philipson claimed that he saw Ciano in the editorial office of

Il Mondo. But even Nelson Page stated that Philipson's insinuation was a pure fantasy and likely meant as a provocation.[105]

For Ciano, the journalistic activity was not enough; it satisfied neither his ambitions nor his expectations. So he decided to write plays and fiction himself. He wrote a total of six stories, a comedy, and the drama *La felicità di Amleto*. The reviews for his plays were – apart from a benevolent comment in *Il Nuovo Paese*, for which he himself worked – not very flattering.[106] At the end of 1924, Ciano decided to give up writing.[107] Since his decision coincided with the end of his studies, it is obvious that Ciano considered writing primarily a leisure activity and did not see it as rebellion against his father. Nor should we argue that Ciano failed as a writer and that this failure had a lasting impact on his character, because it is abundantly clear that he never viewed writing as a suitable means of earning either money or fame.[108]

However, his writing was never an attempt to indulge in the life of a non-political, anti-fascist free spirit. The erroneousness of this view is apparent when we examine the people who were close to him in the years 1921 to 1925 and his own literary works. The centre of his social life was the *Café Aragno* in Via del Corso no. 180, a meeting place for young writers, intellectuals, and artists. Authors and journalists such as Emilio Cecchi, Guelfo Civinini, Curzio Malaparte, Mario Panunzio, and Orio Vergani; the editors of *L'Impero*, Carlí and Settimelli; and the renowned artists Giorgio de Chirico and Filippo Tommaso Marinetti frequented the place. In addition, Ciano was also in contact with people such as the head of the futurist avant-garde in Rome, Anton Giulio Bragaglia, and the fascist philosopher Julius Evola.[109]

Many of these intellectuals were close to Futurism or at least influenced by it in their work. Recurring leitmotifs of the futurists were themes of the "superhuman," "death," and "willingness to self-sacrifice" – topics that Ciano also used in his works.[110] For example, he had one of his fictional characters explain in a farewell letter that "there will be no doubt that he, who commits suicide, is better than all other people."[111] Only self-sacrifice, according to Ciano, elevates an individual to the level of a "better man," a "new man." To portray this outlook merely as the death wish of an otherwise cheerful young man or as a gloomy premonition of his early death misses the point.[112] The relationship between a willingness to make sacrifices and the "new man" was a recurring theme, not only in Expressionist dramas, such as Georg Kaiser's play *Die Bürger von Calais* (*The Burghers of Calais*), but also in Italian Futurism. Due to his poor literary œuvre, we should not include Ciano in the list of futurists, but he was nevertheless fascinated by the futuristic art movement.[113]

The artistic-aesthetic influence of the futurists is only one side of the coin; since Futurism has always been a political art movement, a political influence can also be assumed. In 1919 several futurists joined the first *fasci*. Futurism was to become the official fascist state art, and its theory of avant-garde theatre with its focus on performative actions heavily shaped the fascists' understanding of politics.[114] Although many futurists subsequently left the party because they were disappointed with the less revolutionary development of the PNF, Futurism endured as an artistic and political movement. This gravitation towards revolutionary fascism was particularly evident after the assassination of socialist opposition leader Giacomo Matteotti on 10 June 1924, which triggered a political radicalization among young intellectuals and numerous futurists who saw the killing of Matteotti as a welcome opportunity to initiate a second revolution and get rid of the church and monarchy once and for all. Even in the *Café Aragno* more and more guests publicly wore the fascist uniform.[115]

Leading futurists such as Carlí, Malaparte, and Settimelli voiced the strongest criticism of Mussolini.[116] Malaparte argued that the Matteotti crisis offered a unique opportunity to show the true revolutionary potential of the PNF.[117] He reminded Mussolini that he did not possess a royal mandate, but a "revolutionary" one from the "fascist provinces."[118] Settimelli and Carlí, in turn, used their newspaper *L'Impero* to demand the purging of the "bourgeois fascists" who had exchanged their army boots for comfortable slippers and stopped their fight against the conservative elites.[119] Although right-wing fascists such as Settimelli and Carlí and left-wing fascists such as Malaparte took opposing views, they joined forces to fight what they considered "bourgeois fascism" during the Matteotti crisis. They demanded that the *Duce* establish a totalitarian fascist regime and called on Mussolini to resign if he was unwilling to push the fascist revolution further.[120]

Galeazzo Ciano offers us a glimpse into his attitude towards the conflict in a letter he wrote to then-lover Mimy Aylmer at the end of June 1924:

> Finally, the horizon seems to clear up, and within us the fear is fading. This fear, spontaneously and justifiably, established itself in the spirit of every Italian who with a trembling heart did not so much care about the fate of a party or a government, but about the sublime and pure fate of his country. But now everything seems to have changed and everything seems to have gone well and I am extremely happy.[121]

However, it is not only the passage's brevity that makes it difficult to extract Ciano's political views. Typically, politics are not central components of love letters, especially when one's love is not reciprocated – but this was exactly such a letter. Nevertheless, two vague clues can be found. For one thing, Ciano showed national pride. He cared for the good of the Italian nation to the point that it was much more important to him than any government or party. Second, especially between June and August 1924, signs indicated that a "second wave" of the fascist revolution was imminent.[122] Did Ciano therefore support such a development by claiming that the "horizon seems to clear up" and "fear is fading"? Or was he only inadequately informed about the political events?

Looking at Ciano's relationship with his father at the time of the Matteotti crisis, it becomes clearer that he was sympathetic to the more radical fascists. While Costanzo Ciano remained loyal to the *Duce*, there were increasing rumours that his son had directly criticized Mussolini and that there had been numerous disputes between father and son.[123] These disagreements were not rooted in Ciano's obsession with writing – as has been claimed so far – but in different political convictions.[124] Consequently, Costanzo Ciano tried to prevent any political engagement on the part of his son as long as Galeazzo was close to the radical fascists. But Costanzo's objection was not fundamentally about whether Galeazzo could be politically active; that was fine, provided Galeazzo moderated his views.[125]

As late as November 1924 Galeazzo Ciano had contact with groups that voiced some of the harshest criticism against the *Duce*. To apodictically characterize his literary work as apolitical misunderstands the connection between culture and politics in the futuristic self-image. In particular, the editors of *L'Impero*, Carlí and Settimelli, fascinated Ciano and other members of the war youth generation with their unwavering idealism.[126] Although Ciano's exact relationship to fascism as a teen and a student can only be roughly reconstructed, the previous claim that he had no contact with fascism and rejected fascist slogans and promises at the time must be dismissed – which does not exclude, of course, that his fascist past was later exaggerated. On the contrary, his own literary work and his circle of friends indicate that he had contact with the fascist movement and was attracted by some of its ideas.

When Ciano undertook his first diplomatic missions abroad at the end of 1925, he only maintained loose contact with the fascist movement in Italy. For the next seven years, he was far from his home country and only rudimentarily informed about political developments in Italy. The few available telegrams he received related mostly to the personal experiences of his friends and family;[127] detailed information, however, about the systematic expansion of the fascist party and its sub-organizations under party secretaries Augusto Turati (1926–30), Giovanni Giuriati (1930–31), and Achille Starace (1931–39) was scarce thousands of miles away.[128]

Nevertheless, Ciano was not completely cut off from the fascist movement. Mussolini had done everything possible to help fascism achieve an international breakthrough, as he was convinced that fascism in its "idea, doctrine and implementation ... is universal."[129] He targeted the numerous Italian emigrants and in particular the *fasci all'estero* in the Italian exclaves in order to spread the idea of fascism, the "only powerful and genuine idea of the present century."[130] Such *fasci* were also active in Brazil, Argentina, and China, the countries in which Ciano gained his first experiences as a diplomat.[131] In Brazil, a relatively strong fascist movement had undertaken intensive cultural propaganda since 1923 in an effort to maintain links with its Italian homeland.[132] The *fascio* in Buenos Aires had been founded before the "March on Rome" and was one of the largest in South America.[133] In China, the Italian community was rather small – only 430 people. Nevertheless, the community comprised almost exclusively fascists: around 400 fascists were organized in the country's two *fasci all'estero*, both of which were founded in 1924.[134]

Details about Ciano's contacts with the local *fasci* in South America and China are rare.[135] It seems likely that he was neither very involved in the *fasci* nor participated in their foundation, due less to his lack of interest in fascism than to the tense relationship between the *fasci* and the diplomatic missions.[136] Diplomats perceived the missionary zeal of the fascists as a danger to bilateral relations, while the fascists accused the ambassadors and consuls of obstruction.[137] Regardless of the internal rivalry, Ciano was confronted with an increasing interest in fascism worldwide, both positive and negative. As a representative of Fascist Italy, he faced hostility from local anti-fascists and political exiles from Italy.[138] Since the 1920s, violent and sometimes fatal clashes between fascists and anti-fascists had been taking place in many major cities worldwide.[139]

Ciano was treated with respect when foreign politicians hoped to gain an advantage by forging a better relationship with Italy. The political leaders in China hoped to solicit Italian aid in order to break free from the influence of Japan and European powers such as France and Great Britain.[140] After Japan used the Mukden incident in September 1931 as an excuse to invade Manchuria, Chiang Kai-Shek approached the League of Nations and asked Ciano whether Mussolini could mediate in the conflict. The fact that he first contacted Ciano before he approached representatives from other powers proved Italy's increased influence and the *Duce*'s reputation in Chinese nationalist circles. Mussolini regarded the Chinese enquiry as a further confirmation of Italy's worldwide power and as a loss of prestige for the League of Nations. Although he refused Chiang Kai-Shek's request, he intended to use it propagandistically at a later date.[141]

After Ciano returned to Italy, he took over the USCG in the summer of 1933. His journalistic and diplomatic experience, openness to modern media, loyalty, and kinship all played a role in why Mussolini entrusted his son-in-law with this post.[142] Yet, one precondition seemed to be missing: a specifically fascist reputation. Ciano had neither held a leading position within the fascist movement nor had he come to the forefront as a fascist ideologue. Up to this point, he had never commented on the nature, characteristics, and goals of fascism. According to some contemporaries, this deficiency was no issue, as he was only expected to execute the *Duce*'s orders to the letter.[143] The hierarchy between Mussolini, the creative spirit, and Ciano, the worker, was captured in a photograph: Above Ciano, who sits at a desk and holds a pen in his hand as a sign of the executing henchman, is an oversized picture of Mussolini. The *Duce*, in turn, is depicted with a steel helmet – to underline his militant nature and determination – and looks into the distance towards the future of Italy, which was known only to him (figure 6).

Consideration of Ciano's work, however, reveals that he increasingly came up with his own ideas and heavily influenced the content and form of the propaganda.[144] He interfered in sports reporting as well as in reports on the demographic campaign;[145] he prescribed the language journalists should use by banning the use of foreign terms;[146] he banned reports about accidents from newspapers, forbade the use of the word "crisis," and gradually expanded the mechanisms of censorship;[147] he intervened in cultural programs, in the scientific community, and in the film industry.[148] The aim was to present a powerful and united Italy to national and international audiences and to indoctrinate Italian society with fascist ideals such as courage, will, and community. In this sense, as already mentioned, Ciano also instructed other institutions and was responsible for the centralization and enormous expansion of the propaganda apparatus. By doing so, however, he became a rival of the one institution that claimed to have the sole power to define genuine fascist values: the *Partito Nazionale Fascista*, then under Secretary Achille Starace. Conflicts between the two were therefore unavoidable.

That Ciano was critical of Starace and his activities became clear during the Ethiopian War. At the end of 1935 Ciano used the negative word

Figure 6. Galeazzo Ciano as the head of the Ufficio Stampa del Capo del Governo (USCG), 1934. Ullstein Bild #010822177.

"staracizzata" to describe what he considered to be the poor course of the war. Taking into account Starace's work as party secretary, this neologism was used to characterize a sometimes brutal, wasteful, unsubstantial, unsuccessful, and ultimately misguided policy.[149] Despite this obvious potential for conflict, Ciano rose in the hierarchy of the fascist militia. In May 1936 he was appointed consul of the fascist militia, and was promoted to general five months later.[150] The nearly simultaneous exaggeration of his fascist past, including him attending in the first row ceremonies in Florence to honour the *fascio Disperata*, further demonstrates that, immediately after the Ethiopian War, he sought to publicly display his closeness to the party for career reasons. This projected image even led to rumours that Mussolini would appoint Ciano as the next secretary of the PNF.[151] Still, in his diary – and thus after the summer 1937 – he did not mention any concrete activities in the party or the fascist militia, which reinforces the thesis that his party and militia memberships were more of a facade than an indication that he supported the party's policies under Starace. Nevertheless, he thought it was a prerequisite to be accepted by the other high-ranking fascists and to preserve his status within the ruling class.

After Ciano took over the *Palazzo Chigi* in June 1936, the relationship between him and Starace eased for a short time. There are two reasons for their evident rapprochement. First, they were no longer direct competitors when it came to the interpretation and dissemination of fascist values; and second, both supported improved relations with Berlin at that time.[152] This period of conciliation ended with the annexation of Austria in 1938, when Ciano's scepticism towards Berlin continuously increased.[153] At the end of 1938, Guido Buffarini Guidi approached Ciano and criticized Starace's attempts to meddle "in all areas of national life."[154] Ciano agreed and, in addition, rebuked Starace's anti-Catholic and anti-bourgeois policies, as well as the "atmosphere of persecution" that Starace had created. However, he refused to interfere directly in the dispute between the PNF and the Ministry of the Interior.[155] Considering Ciano's previous relationship with Starace, his criticism should not come as a surprise. While he continued to reject Starace's actions, he did not publicly side with the Ministry of the Interior; on the contrary, the rivalry between the PNF and the ministry was convenient for him. It weakened their influence and in turn strengthened his own standing.

It was only in the summer of 1939 that Ciano publicly stood against Starace and the party when he opposed a possible entry into the Second World War. While Ciano and Starace once again disagreed about the extent of the PNF's intervention in society, the Germanophile Starace now attacked Ciano's decision to stay out of the war.[156] Whereas Ciano and his allies told the *Duce* that the Italians were hostile to Germany and would welcome the *non belligeranza* policy, Starace claimed that the population could not wait to wage war.[157] Ciano knew that Mussolini would believe this talk much more than the warnings and sceptical impressions that Police Chief Arturo Bocchini gave the *Duce*.[158] He therefore pushed – ultimately successfully – for dismissing Starace, whose *squadrismo* he considered outdated and dangerous.[159] On 31 October Ciano's protégé, Ettore Muti, took over the position of party secretary. Muti was an opponent of the war and loyal follower who enjoyed popularity in Italy thanks to his actions during the Ethiopian War, the Spanish Civil War, and the occupation of Albania in April 1939.[160]

Having manoeuvred Starace out of office, Ciano was convinced that he could guide Muti to significantly influence the PNF's development. According to him, Muti was "still inexperienced in politics";[161] but Ciano was convinced that, since Muti was "naturally gifted and willing," he would follow him "like a child."[162] Raffaele Casertano, another of Ciano's close confidantes, was assigned to Muti as his private secretary.

He regularly informed Ciano about the party's internal affairs without telling his superior Muti.[163] Muti and Casertano's placement seemed to be a very clever move by Ciano. He was able to oust one key figure of the fascist regime, Starace, and indirectly control the PNF, his fiercest critic. After all, both Muti and Casertano owned him their careers, and in the spirit of the traditional patronage system, Ciano expected their loyalty in return. With the backing of Ciano, Muti immediately replaced numerous leaders of the local *fasci* with loyal followers, leading, according to German observers, to the party's decline.[164]

However, Ciano's success turned out to be a pyrrhic victory. He quickly lost control of Muti, who had gained power and influence as party secretary and was no longer dependent on Ciano;[165] and the policy of *non belligeranza* proved costly for Ciano. He had not succeeded in disposing of all the warmongers within the party, such as Roberto Farinacci, and by November 1939 Starace had returned as chief of staff of the fascist militia.[166] In January 1940 Muti sided with the interventionists, to Ciano's chagrined surprise.[167] As soon as Ciano realized that he had lost control of Muti, he unsuccessfully attempted to have him replaced.[168]

The disagreement between Ciano and Muti and the end of their friendship remained a topic of conversation on both the national and international level for months.[169] During the campaign in Greece, Ciano told the *Duce* that Italy would soon face difficult times and it would be necessary to replace Muti with a reliable party secretary – such as Giuseppe Bottai or Dino Grandi. Naturally, Ciano did not mention that Muti's fall would eliminate one of his main rivals. When Mussolini finally recalled Muti on 30 October 1940, he ignored Ciano's suggested replacements and appointed Adelchi Serena as the new head of the PNF.[170] The fact that the *Duce* took this step as late as October was yet another indication of Ciano's waning influence.

Although we possess little information about the relationship between the new party secretary Serena and Ciano, the strongest criticism against Ciano still came from the PNF and its sub-organizations.[171] Starace in particular discredited him in front of the Germans as an enemy of Berlin who only pretended to be friendly. There were even indications that the directorate of the fascist party had demanded Ciano's removal.[172] However, the German diplomats in Rome still considered Ciano powerful enough to resist these attacks.[173] Although they did not believe these accusations, they passed them on to Berlin, where they found in Joachim von Ribbentrop a sympathetic listener.[174]

On 26 December 1941 Mussolini appointed without any warning the twenty-six-year-old unknown Aldo Vidussoni as party secretary.[175]

Ciano could not explain Mussolini's actions, even if he initially had a positive impression of the new man. Given the tense domestic situation, however, Ciano doubted the choice to entrust such a delicate position to a young and inexperienced person, and he predicted that Vidussoni "will sweat blood in that environment of old whores which is the Fascist party."[176] However, after only a short time Ciano's verdict on the PNF in general and its new leader in particular deteriorated even further.[177] Vidussoni became a cipher for the strained relationship between Ciano and the PNF, as well as with the fascist hardliners. Conflicts arose over the generational question within the fascist regime and over the relationship between the state and the church, which is addressed in greater detail in the following sections.

Given his troubled relationship with the PNF and Vidussoni, Ciano was visibly irritated when he heard rumours that he was the real mastermind behind Vidussoni's appointment. "Let it be clear," he noted, "that he has come of Mussolini's mind as Minerva sprang from Jupiter's brow."[178] And indeed, there was and is no proof that Ciano was involved in Vidussoni's promotion. But once again Ciano was cast in the role of public scapegoat for Mussolini's decision.

Ill will between the party and Ciano was mutual. On 22 March 1942 an assassination attempt against him was uncovered, which allegedly was planned by students of the *Gruppi Universitari Fascisti* (GUF). While Ciano was convinced that the "hotheadedness of these young men will be cooled off" by exile or imprisonment, he had no explanation for this inner-party conspiracy. Were they anti-fascists hiding behind the party badge? Or was it perhaps a sign that the party no longer had its young members under control?[179] Ciano was convinced that the party had not taken enough care of the youth. For years, he argued, the party was only interested in pomp and circumstance. The distribution of uniforms, caps, and colourful handkerchiefs had, according to Ciano, replaced a more substantial policy.[180]

Ciano was not alone in offering a damning verdict on the fascist party. *Carabinieri* officers assured him that the PNF would no longer play a role in the lives of ordinary Italians, and fascists of the old guard also expressed concern and suggested a return to the "beginnings" of the movement.[181] Ciano agreed and considered anti-Bolshevism and a traditionalist worldview that respected family, property, and the church as the origins of fascism.[182] This remark is one of the few that illustrates Ciano's understanding of fascism, which was very similar to his father's view. A closer reading reveals, however, the incompatibility of Ciano's understanding with the notion of a totalitarian fascist state, which propagated both the penetration of privacy, the seizure of church property, and a constant revolution – in short, the fascistization of the entire Italian society.[183]

Ciano's total abandonment of the party and its leadership became obvious in the autumn of 1942. Severe food shortages, domestic turmoil, and bad news from the front devastated the public mood in Italy. High-ranking fascists, such as the leader of the fascist militia Enzo Emilio Galbiati, became aware of this explosive mix of problems, and in a conversation with Ciano, Galbiati assured him that he had already come up with plans to suppress potential unrest. Ciano seemed less than impressed and explicitly rejected the idea that the party and its militia should be used to maintain public order; instead he trusted the state police and the *Carabinieri*.[184] Nevertheless, the growing discontent among the Italian public forced the party to close ranks with Ciano and to find common ground with their long-time rival. When Mario Farnesi, the new vice secretary of the PNF, met with Ciano in November 1942, Ciano told him that he did not agree with the party in many respects, but he also did not want to "slam the door" and would remain open to further discussions. In contrast to his open posture towards the PNF, Ciano revealed his opposition in private, stating that he thought the party leadership "will be short-lived, and for my part I am not going to help them keep their jobs."[185]

The relationship between Ciano and the fascist party remained complex and subject to constant change until the end of Ciano's tenure as foreign minister. The rivalry, however, does not mean that Ciano categorically rejected fascist ideology. Anti-communism, the emphasis on youth as a historical force, and an exaggerated nationalism always held his interest. But once at the centre of power he had totally abandoned any revolutionary zeal he might have held as an admirer of Futurism, and he showed no missionary fervour to carry out a totalitarian project in Italy, as both would have threatened his position. Ciano's strained relationship with the PNF illustrates that, in what Robert Paxton identified as the "exercise of power" stage,[186] fascism had lost none of its heterogeneity, which had been part of the first *fascio di combattimento* in 1919 and still complicates a generally accepted definition of fascism today. This heterogeneity was also mirrored by the machinations within the upper echelons of the regime's officials, an issue I am going to address in the following section.

The Elite

Contemporaries associated Galeazzo Ciano with a heterogeneous, even chaotic, set of groups and networks during his political career. Sometimes he was a companion of moderate fascists, and sometimes he was their greatest opponent; sometimes he was part of groups dedicated to a "second revolution," and sometimes his name was on a list of fascist traditionalists; sometimes he was surrounded by fascists of the old guard, and sometimes he was admired by the young guard.[187] Such speculations illustrate the complex and constantly changing alliances among the fascist ruling class. Identifying and evaluating the individual factions proved immensely difficult even for contemporaries. The dynamism of shifting factions resulted from the constant and necessary cultivation of coalitions by those who belonged or who wanted to belong to the fascist leadership.[188]

In December 1925 Mussolini had achieved a dictatorial monopoly through his "Law on the Competencies and Prerogatives of the Head of Government." According to scholars, at that point (if not earlier) the goal of factional competition within the fascist elite was to gain the *Duce*'s favour and thus to rise in the regime. Davide Rodogno has coined the phrase "to work towards the *Duce*," following what Ian Kershaw identified as State Secretary Werner Willikens's maxim of "working in the Führer's spirit towards him."[189] The decree in 1925 undermined the rule of law and elevated the head of government above both parliament and cabinet. From that point on, the Council of Ministers was reduced to a committee of "technical advisors," and Mussolini was accountable only to the king. However, in the shadow of the *Duce*'s monopolization of state power, the opportunities for and power of the bureaucracy and the patrimonial rulers also increased. This situation led to a competition and a dynamic in everyday politics, enabling the civil servants, ministers, and state secretaries to work unchecked and unaccountable.[190] The following section considers Ciano's position in this power structure.

The Bearer of Hope

Upon his appointment as head of the USCG, Ciano became one of the most important persons within the regime thanks to his daily contact with the *Duce*. Their closeness was less due to his familial proximity and more to Ciano's actual function within the regime. By the end of the 1920s, Mussolini was increasingly reliant on propaganda given the looming danger of economic and social stagnation in Italy.[191] This state of affairs inevitably increased the importance of the head of the USCG, who gradually became one of the key figures in the consolidation of the regime.[192] When Ciano was appointed secretary of state for press and propaganda in 1934, he stepped out of the shadow of his father, who had just been dismissed as minister of communications and appointed president of the Chamber of Deputies – a prestigious, but politically less influential office. From Mussolini's perspective, the elder Ciano's demotion was necessary to prevent the accumulation of power in one family that might stir resistance in other parts of the fascist hierarchy and consequently endanger the *Duce*'s position.[193]

Now the most important member of his family, Galeazzo enjoyed a meteoric rise that gave him a great deal of autonomy, so that he saw his role "as dominant within the entire state, and he wanted to interfere in all government issues."[194] Through a network of press attachés and agents, he intervened in the work of the PNF and in foreign affairs. However, his ambitions were far from secret, given his reckless and unmindful behaviour. As early as January 1936, the German Ambassador Ulrich von Hassell was convinced that Ciano wanted to take over the post of then state secretary in the Foreign Ministry, Fulvio Suvich.[195] When Marcello Del Drago informed Ciano that he would be named the new minister of foreign affairs on 9 June 1936, Ciano told him: "Ah, I knew it, but I didn't know how and when."[196]

Ciano's successful work as minister of press and propaganda during the Ethiopian War, combined with the end of the League of Nations' sanctions and the recognition of the Italian Empire by numerous states shortly after he took over the *Palazzo Chigi*, earned him respect among high-ranking fascists. Encouragement from parliamentarians, members of the Grand Council, and the *Duce* indicated that Ciano had consolidated his position within the power apparatus, which he continuously used to interfere in areas beyond his jurisdiction.[197]

Ciano coordinated the Italian intervention in the Spanish Civil War and interfered in the Ministry of Press and Propaganda – which was renamed the Ministry of Popular Culture in May 1937 – during Dino Alfieri's and Alessandro Pavolini's tenure.[198] Ciano expected loyalty and support from his protégés and sought to establish a kind of patronage system at the ministerial level. Nevertheless, he failed to realize that people such as Alfieri and Pavolini had gained power through their promotion and that an asymmetric power gap, necessary for the existence of a patron-client network, thus no longer existed. Ciano's former protégés no longer required his protection, but instead could and did turn to other ministers or to the *Duce*. This relationship change did not stop Ciano from continuing to interfere in many different areas, making enemies among the fascists, the army, and the public.[199] As a result he had to tie his own position and his future even more closely to the *Duce*.

Despite his self-confidence, Ciano knew exactly who had enabled his precipitous career: his father and Mussolini. Friends and colleagues reported that Ciano behaved submissively in the presence of the *Duce* and idolized Mussolini, sometimes in ridiculous ways. During personal meetings and telephone conversations with the *Duce* he adopted a devoted and reverent attitude.[200] Although some stories may be exaggerated, they nevertheless describe Ciano's principal behaviour. Ciano's father taught him to display obedience to older family members and superiors; Mussolini was both father-in-law and the *Duce* of the regime. Moreover, Ciano had great confidence in Mussolini's abilities, and even saw the *Duce* as a tool of the divine providence.[201] Ciano's diary entries for the year 1937 and for much of 1938 speak volumes: Mussolini has "always been right," was "unshakable as a rock," and possessed an infallible instinct. When the *Duce* praised him, Ciano was so confused "that I can't even think." "Basically," he wrote, "one works only to satisfy him: If it works, this is the greatest reward." "When I heard his voice [on the radio]," Ciano confessed, "I started crying like a child."[202] A final highlight of Ciano's uncritical idolatry can be found during the Munich Conference in September 1938. The course of the conference significantly restored Ciano's belief in the *Duce*'s genius, given Mussolini's alleged determination and goal-orientated actions.[203]

What advantage did Mussolini hope to gain by promoting his son-in-law's career? Even though he privately stated that he appreciated Ciano's talent, three factors were more important to him.[204] First, he assumed that Ciano, especially after his brother Arnaldo Mussolini's surprising death in 1931, would be a loyal follower because of his kinship.[205] Second, when Ciano began as Mussolini's press chief he undoubtedly possessed some innate skills and qualities, but he lacked experience. For this reason, the first months of his ministerial career were a kind of apprenticeship during which Mussolini could instruct and shape Ciano according to his ideas.[206] Third, Mussolini brought Ciano into his cabinet when fascists of a younger generation began to criticize the government. They complained that the regime had reached an ideological dead end and had betrayed the "fascist revolution."[207] Indeed, while the fascists were successful in pushing some projects to fascistize the Italian society, numerous others initiatives had ground to a halt: the fascists were unable to end their alliances with the old elites, including industry, church, and monarchy; nor were they even close to creating the "new man" through the "fascist revolution."[208] The *Duce* was accused of turning his regime into an ordinary and thus corrupt, reprehensible dictatorship.[209]

Mussolini could not simply ignore this discontent, given that fascism, following futurist dogma, staged itself as a youth movement and an alternative to the old structures. Youth was more than just an abstract potential recruitment pool for future fascists. It was one of the central pillars on which the legitimacy of fascist ideology was based.[210] High-ranking fascists reacted to this criticism and supported the idea of a "second revolution" carried out by the youth. Giuseppe Bottai in particular insisted that the old guard needed to step down in favour of the younger generation. Only a "new elite" of young people could master the future task.[211] "The regime," Mussolini declared on 21 January 1930, "is and intends to remain a regime of youth."[212]

Ciano's appointment was enthusiastically welcomed by the younger generation. For journalist Asvero Gravelli, Ciano was the ideal person, since he belonged to the same generation and represented "the dynamic element of the European fascist action."[213] Ciano symbolized the young fascists on whose shoulders the renewal and future of fascism rested.[214] He was chosen, together with his peer group – the war youth – to take over the regime. Thus, Mussolini skilfully used Ciano to demonstrate his commitment to involving the younger generation in government and to put pressure on the older fascists and slowly disempower them.[215] For Ciano himself, the fascists' obsession with youth offered the chance to legitimize his rapid rise. He could use his age as a power resource and counter allegations that his inexperience meant he was not up to the task. The best way to illustrate the rivalry between Ciano and representatives of the old guard is by examining his relationship with his two biggest rivals of the 1930s: Italo Balbo and Dino Grandi.[216]

Although the mutual aversion between Ciano and Balbo originated in a dispute between Ciano's friend Curzio Malaparte and Balbo, it was Ciano's envy of Balbo that drove his enmity. Popular at home and abroad, Balbo had won the public's favour with his transatlantic flights in 1930 and 1933.[217] Although there is still little clarity as to Balbo's ambitions, his immense popularity posed a serious threat to Mussolini's charismatic rule. Worried by Balbo's success, the *Duce* sent him to Libya as governor in 1934.[218] It was not until the summer of 1937 that Balbo reappeared in Ciano's life as he tried to forge closer ties with the up-and-coming minister.[219] He obviously toyed with the idea of regaining influence in Rome with Ciano's assistance, after he was "exiled" to Libya.[220] He thought that Ciano's ambition would ultimately lead him to clash with the *Duce*, and the longer Balbo cultivated Ciano, the more the latter seemed to agree with his former opponent. Ciano felt flattered; he loved – as diplomat Roberto Ducci once wrote – to be liked.[221]

This mutual rapprochement was interrupted when Italy joined the Anti-Comintern Pact in November 1937; by doing so, Ciano secured a major diplomatic success. Afterwards Ciano was convinced that he could keep his position within the regime without Balbo's help.

In addition, Balbo criticized Rome's rapprochement with Germany. Ciano's about-face regarding Balbo is therefore hardly surprising. He now described Balbo as unreliable and embittered, an opponent of the Rome-Berlin Axis, and a man with a "miserable mind," whom he considered deeply inferior.[222] In addition, Ciano now reported Balbo's criticism to the *Duce* and was pleased that Mussolini reacted "very badly."[223] As Ciano strengthened his position within the regime and Balbo continued to fall out of favour, Ciano sought new allies – it was at this time that he briefly reconciled with Achille Starace, who was known for his Germanophile streak and his opposition to Balbo.[224]

Competition between Ciano and Balbo also played a role in Balbo's attempt to demand Italian citizenship for all Libyans in the autumn of 1938. Scholars often interpreted his request as a sign of his tolerance towards Africans and his opposition to the regime's new racial policy.[225] Balbo, however, primarily wanted to secure the support of the local population in North Africa in order to strengthen his position in the regime. It is therefore hardly surprising that, in addition to rejection by staunch racists such as Farinacci and Starace, the plan was also opposed by Galeazzo Ciano, who hitherto had not been considered a radical racist.[226]

Pinpointing the exact beginning of the relationship between Dino Grandi and Ciano is more difficult. Grandi, once Ciano's superior at the *Palazzo Chigi*, was demoted to ambassador in London in 1932, but the Italian public and many fascist leaders regarded him as far more competent than Ciano. Furthermore, as ambassador, Grandi gained the trust of the conservative establishment in Great Britain and presented himself as a protagonist of Italian-British rapprochement, thereby gaining recognition nationally and internationally.[227] Even after the Second World War he used every opportunity available to cultivate this image at the expense of Ciano.[228]

Ciano was suspicious and envious of Grandi, and began to complain about the autonomous actions of the man who was now his subordinate.[229] Yet, Ciano neither removed Grandi nor tried to undermine his efforts; rather, he attempted to present himself as the real architect of the Italian-British reconciliation.[230] Ciano knew that these talks with London were well received by the Italian public, and he felt threatened by Grandi's growing prestige and by reports that he should be replaced by the ambassador.[231]

Although the origins of these rumours remain unclear, Ciano's reaction indicates that they exacerbated the divide between him and Grandi, preventing a potential alliance between the two hierarchs whose political ideas were often closer than generally assumed. Their rivalry eased after Grandi was dismissed from his ambassadorship and appointed minister of justice in July and president of the *Camera dei fasci e delle corporazioni* in November 1939, where he succeeded Ciano's father. Grandi and Ciano's activity in different political fields, which overlapped only slightly and thus offered little potential for conflict, paved the way for a rapprochement between the two politicians.[232]

At the end of 1938, a shadow began to fall over the relationship between Ciano and Mussolini. It did not happen abruptly, but Ciano gradually alienated himself from the *Duce* when he began to realize that his political goals were not entirely congruent with Mussolini's plans. Until then, he had believed that he always acted with the full support and trust of Mussolini and had executed his plans to the letter; in short, he believed that he was an instrument of the *Duce*'s "fascist genius."[233] However, international events such as the annexation of Austria and the occupation of Prague, which Mussolini accepted or even endorsed indifferently in order to not jeopardize his friendship with Hitler, highlighted their growing differences.[234] In addition, Berlin's expansionist policies put Ciano under increasing pressure, as prominent fascists and the public blamed him and not the *Duce* for the alleged impotence of Italian foreign policy. His subsequent efforts to defend the Germans were less a declaration of loyalty to Berlin than an attempt to justify his policy in order to assert his position in Italy. However, his explanations were not very persuasive as he repeatedly contradicted himself.[235] Ciano also realized that his attachment to Mussolini did nothing to protect him from the resulting hostility. Even though the *Duce* did not blame Ciano personally, he did nothing to shield his son-in-law from the accusations.[236]

The growing opposition towards the regime's foreign policy gradually damaged Ciano's wunderkind aura. Hoping to disprove his critics, Ciano desperately sought a dramatic personal success to re-solidify his position.[237] He therefore pushed for the annexation of Albania in April 1939.[238] The move won Mussolini's praise, but the Italian public and many of his colleagues remained hostile to him. Many perceived the invasion of Albania as Ciano's personal crusade that would do nothing to benefit Italy. Moreover, parts of the fascist elite continued to criticize Ciano's autocratic behaviour, his continued adherence to the Axis, and his repeated interference in other ministries.[239]

In the summer of 1939, Ciano had to align himself even closer with the *Duce*, even though their political views were quickly diverging. Ciano's diminishing influence was reflected in widespread rumours of his dismissal and a possible army revolt against him.[240] In addition,

Costanzo Ciano's death took with it the support of the regime's moderates. That Ciano was nevertheless able to weather the storm was mainly due to international affairs. When Ciano finally realized in August 1939 that the Third Reich was unswervingly driving towards war, the fascist elite split into two camps.[241] One side, represented by Benito Mussolini, repeatedly emphasized Rome's loyalty to Berlin in order to counter accusations of another "1915," and argued that Italy could not avoid a European conflict.[242] The opposing side, represented by Ciano, who was wounded in his pride and vanity, outright rejected a war at Germany's side. Ciano noted in his diary that he was alone in his fight, but that did not change his attitude because he was convinced of his good cause.[243] Of course, this theatrical statement should be treated with caution. Neither Mussolini nor Ciano was the only representative of his respective side, nor was there a public confrontation between them, though Ciano claimed to have spoken with "brutal openness."[244] Nevertheless, Giovanni Ansaldo was surprised that Ciano now publicly pursued a policy different to the one Mussolini promoted.[245]

Ciano's policy of *non belligeranza* was initially supported by a heterogeneous coalition that included the king, the Catholic Church, industrial magnates such as Alberto Pirelli, officers around Pietro Badoglio and Giacomo Carboni, and numerous fascist ministers, including Giuseppe Bottai, Italo Balbo, Dino Grandi, and Luigi Federzoni.[246] A proud and relieved Ciano also noted in his diary that the Italian public was vehemently anti-German and unanimously happy about his policy.[247] He was aware that he needed this broad support to maintain the *non belligeranza* policy. Therefore, he skilfully tried to maintain and, if possible, expand the coalition. He promoted Badoglio's son Mario, who was a member of the diplomatic corps, to consul general of Tangier, and at events and receptions he courted the financial and industrial sectors.[248]

In light of Italy's disastrous economic and military situation, Ciano never saw a realistic chance of winning a war on Germany's side.[249] Domestically, he feared that the people would revolt against the regime if Italy entered the war, as "many sections of Italian society remained sceptical, if not hostile towards war on Germany's side."[250] This move would have threatened his position at a time when he was on the cusp of becoming Italy's most important politician.[251] In the autumn and winter months of 1939–40, Ciano reached the zenith of his power. Not only did he surpass other fascist hierarchs, but for the first time ever, he also managed to step out of Mussolini's shadow. Because of Mussolini's absence and indecisiveness as he struggled to find support for his bellicose plans, Ciano was able to push through his own plans without interference. Moreover, the *Duce*'s absence made it easier for Ciano to dominate the narrative of international politics in general and German aggression in particular.

Ciano's new position of power was most evident in the cabinet reshuffle of 31 October 1939.[252] As a result, most ministerial posts were now in the hands of people who were close to Ciano and sympathetic to or even supportive of the *non belligeranza* policy.[253] After the cabinet reshuffle, Ciano immediately tried to persuade new ministers like Giovanni Host-Venturi (minister of communications), Renato Ricci (minister of corporations), and Raffaelo Riccardi (minister for exchanges and currencies) of the German "betrayal" and win them over to his side.[254]

In addition, Mussolini replaced Alberto Pariani with Rodolfo Graziani as the army's chief of general staff before also relieving the former of his post as state secretary in the War Ministry, where he was replaced by one of Ciano's protégés, Ubaldo Soddu. General Giuseppe Valle, chief of staff of the air force, was forced out in favour of Francesco Pricolo.[255] These changes, however, can only partly be explained by Mussolini's desire to reassure his German audience by firing senior military figures for their apparent failure to prepare Italy for war.[256] The navy chief of staff, Domenico Cavagnari, a close friend of the Cianos and an ardent supporter of the non-belligerent policy, remained in his post. Thus, the changes must be seen rather as another victory for Ciano in pushing aside opponents of the non-belligerence policy. Thanks to these changes, Ciano and the Foreign Ministry were able to dictate "the official position of the Italian Wehrmacht leadership." As a consequence, the Italian Supreme Command did not want "to get in touch with the relevant German authorities for joint preparatory work for a possible future joint war."[257]

Despite his solid position, Ciano was concerned about the unstable mood of the *Duce*, whom he accused of losing touch with reality.[258] Mussolini feared that his prestige among the Italian people would plummet. "The Italians," he told Ciano, "after having heard my warlike propaganda for eighteen years, cannot understand how I can become the herald of peace, now that Europe is on fire."[259] The *Duce*, perhaps unintentionally, confessed to Ciano that his policy of constant mobilization had led him into a dead end from which he could hardly escape – but from which he did not particularly want to escape, as the propaganda machinery continued to spread Italy's alleged bellicosity over the radio and the press.[260]

"The battle that I have to fight with him is hard," Ciano wrote in his diary, "but I must fight to the end. Otherwise it will mean the ruin of the country, the ruin of Fascism, and the ruin of the *Duce* himself."[261] His only intention was to "fight like a lion to preserve peace for the Italian people."[262] Even though his entry must be taken with a grain of salt, his priorities during these days are especially revealing: first, he cared about Italy and the Italians; second about fascism; and only third about the *Duce*. His former unconditional adoration of Mussolini had given way to a more realistic assessment of the situation.[263]

The Scapegoat

Ultimately, the attempts to keep Italy out of the war failed. On the evening of 10 June 1940, Mussolini appeared on the balcony of the *Palazzo Venezia*, accompanied by leading fascists including Ciano, to announce Italy's entry into the war. The crowd, with the exception of the party's claqueurs, accepted Mussolini's speech without exaggerated enthusiasm.[264] Finally, the *Duce* had his war and could lead the Italian troops as self-appointed *condottiere*. But what were the domestic reasons for the failure of the *non belligeranza* policy? And what were the consequences for Ciano?

Guerri, who otherwise is very uncritical of Ciano, accuses him of not provoking a split from Germany after the cabinet reshuffle in October 1939.[265] In his sweeping criticism, however, he forgets one important point: Mussolini and Ciano were merely representatives of various political, military, and social groups, both of whom were dependent on domestic political alliances to enforce their policies. Ciano's support was crumbling rapidly by early 1940, thanks to a combination of German military successes, Allied losses, and a new confrontation between Rome and London. Ciano's protégés Alfieri, Pavolini, and Muti joined the interventionists' camp, while others such as Thaon de Revel, Anfuso, intelligence officer Sante Emanuele, and Soddu, who were closely aligned with the armaments industry, withdrew their support.[266] The heterogeneous alliance of war opponents dissolved because there was no consensus on the future of Italy; what previously united them was merely their objection to entering the war on the side of Berlin when they doubted a German victory. As happened so often in the history of fascism, coalitions were formed and defined by a "negative" attribution (being against) and not by a "positive" one (being for).

Ciano had tried to win Mussolini over, adhering to the principle that "constant dripping wears the stone." But there is no evidence that Ciano was ready to provoke an open conflict with the *Duce*. After the October reshuffle, Ciano felt so powerful that he assumed Mussolini would follow his lead without protest.[267] By the time he realized in the spring of 1940 that the *Duce* had completely different ideas, his own position had eroded. He categorically ruled out a coup against Mussolini, as he did not see any chance of it succeeding.[268] Ciano's failure, however, must be seen as a failure of the entire opposition. None of those who continued to support the *non belligeranza* policy despite Germany's successes – including Grandi, Bottai, and the monarchy – were willing to challenge the *Duce*.

In March 1940 Mussolini returned to the political arena and immediately launched a public attack on Ciano's previous opposition to the war.[269] At the same time, Ciano's name appeared only sporadically in the Italian press, and once again Italy was flooded with rumours of his removal.[270] In his own notes, Ciano justified his attitude and tried to downplay the conflict between himself and the *Duce*, insisting that his policy had only served the "fatherland and the Duce." But his priorities once again betrayed him: while he pledged his allegiance to Mussolini, the Italian nation was again more important to him. Yet, he remained passive and did not consider resigning; instead he fatalistically commented on the rumours about his dismissal with a biblical reference: "The Lord gives, the Lord takes!"[271]

To increase his chances of remaining in office, however, Ciano gradually let himself be drawn in by the enthusiasm of the interventionists.[272] A good example of his changed attitude and his attempt to rebrand himself as a supporter of the war was a belligerent speech he gave on 16 May 1940 in Milan. In addition to the speech's content, the staging of the event spoke a clear language: Ciano wore his militia uniform, while before him hung a banner with the sign of the fascist group *Disperata*.[273]

A striking example of Ciano's dependence on Mussolini and his fear of being removed from office had already occurred in April 1940. Ciano wrote in his diary on 12 April: "I go to bed with a very bad flu and remain there until Saturday the twentieth."[274] The pages of the following six days are torn out, and 19 April is crossed out. We can only speculate about the reasons why these pages were removed and what – if anything – was written on them. It could be possible that Ciano expressed his criticism and frustration with the *Duce*'s warlike policy, since the issue of Italian intervention culminated in a rift between Ciano and Mussolini that was only resolved on 20 April.[275] US Ambassador William Phillips was surprised that on 22 April Ciano urged him not to believe rumours of a falling out between himself and the *Duce*. Phillips assumed that the *Duce* had decided to enter the war in light of Germany's victories and that Ciano, who rejected such a move, did not have the courage to challenge his father-in-law and therefore deliberately called in sick to avoid a conflict.[276] A few days later, Ciano noted that Rome was full of rumours about his absence and that there was talk of a "diplomatic illness." He did not refute these insinuations.[277]

Although Ciano remained at the Foreign Ministry, the rumours of growing discord between him and Mussolini could not be silenced.[278] The vehemence with which Ciano denied these disputes proves that he was aware of his fragile position in the regime. Any rumours of a conflict between him and the *Duce* made him vulnerable to his rivals. Ciano's dependency benefitted and suited Mussolini very well, and he was unwilling to end it quickly. He told Muti and Buffarini Guidi – two of Ciano's prominent critics at the time – that Ciano still had his full confidence. Despite this assurance, there is no evidence that he defended his battered foreign minister in public.[279]

Even after Italy's entry into the war, Ciano remained in office – a decision that many of his colleagues and friends criticized, seeing Ciano's behaviour as proof that he loved the power and glamour of his office too much.[280] Today, one is inclined to follow this interpretation, particularly as Ciano himself did not discuss his motives in his diary. Even the typical justification that he stayed in office to prevent worse – an argument that many of his colleagues at home and abroad voiced in similar situations – does not appear.[281] However, it would be too simplistic to accept Ciano's obsession with power or his kinship with Mussolini as his only motivations. First, it should not be forgotten that the resignation of a minister in Italian political culture, especially under fascism, was very rare.[282] On 10 June 1940 no other minister or secretary of state who had previously opposed Italy's entry into the war resigned. Officially, only one person decided the actual appointment and dismissal of a minister and a state secretary: Benito Mussolini.[283] Yes, Ciano could have shown moral greatness, but he preferred to withdraw from the political intrigues of Rome and joined his bomber squadron in Pisa.[284]

Second, we must take into account Ciano's upbringing. Although his father had often been absent due to his military obligations, he nevertheless significantly shaped Galeazzo's childhood. In the following years, Ciano was also drawn towards strong, male personalities. Of course, Benito Mussolini and Adolf Hitler were among them, but Winston Churchill also fascinated him.[285] Ciano was no exception in his admiration of charismatic figures; it was a trait typical of his generation.[286]

Third, the accusation of political opportunism must be examined further. Despite his position, Ciano always remained an exception within the regime – a problem he did not seem to understand. When he entered politics in 1933, he was a newcomer to the fascist ruling class. His own age cohort had placed its hopes in him to break up the old structures of the system. At the same time, he had no intention of promoting the extensive fascistization of state and society, primarily focusing instead on eliminating potential rivals and strengthening his own power. The generational conflict within the fascist regime took on a new dynamic when, with the 1942 appointment of the twenty-six-year-old party secretary Vidussoni, an even younger generation of fascists entered the arena. As a consequence, Ciano's legitimacy sustained a direct hit because he was no longer the youngest member of the fascist elite and could no longer claim to be spearheading the reform movement. Ciano therefore shifted direction and demanded a return to the party's beginnings. Although he counted himself now among the old guard, he was never actually one of them.[287] The moment had passed Ciano by, and he was left holding an untenable middle ground: too old to claim the legitimacy of a reformer, he was also too young to lay effective claim to traditionalism and the founding generation.

The *non belligeranza* policy had enabled a coalition between former competitors; however, the alliance between the old guard and Ciano was short-lived and did not survive Italy's entry into the Second World War. Ciano's sudden after the fact public endorsement of the war was interpreted as a sign of his chameleon-like behaviour and unreliability. Moreover, the coalition suffered a severe blow on 28 June 1940 when Italo Balbo's aircraft was mistaken for a British bomber and shot down by Italian air defences near Tobruk. In view of the former tensions between Balbo and Ciano, rumours, which have since been refuted, quickly circulated that the friendly fire was not accidental.[288] However, these insinuations neglect the fact that the relationship between Ciano and Balbo had improved since the summer of 1939. Although Balbo was still a rival of Ciano due to his popularity among the people, their collaboration during the *non belligeranza* period brought them closer. Ciano acknowledged that Balbo was one of the few people who was convinced of the true need for the *non belligeranza* policy until the end. Thus, Ciano's grief over Balbo's death should be regarded as sincere, especially since his statements at the time were not exaggerated.[289]

The end of the *non belligeranza* policy was a clear sign that Ciano's position within the regime was in jeopardy. To regain his former influence, he sought close contact with war enthusiasts around Mussolini. When he tried to remove people who had supported the *non belligeranza* policy, they attacked him because of his rapid about-face.[290] Ciano saw another opportunity in Mussolini's increasingly aggressive stance towards Greece in the summer of 1940, when the *Duce* threatened to occupy the Ionian Islands after it became known that Greece served as a retreat for the British navy.[291] Ciano began to promote and plan military action against Athens because he predicted a quick and easy victory that would win back Mussolini's favour.[292]

But when the Greek campaign, which began on 28 October 1940, fell apart, Ciano realized that the public blamed him for the disaster.[293] He tried to absolve himself by shifting blame with the argument that an invasion of Greece would never have been possible without the *Duce*'s consent. He even claimed that he had not said a single word at the crucial meeting on 15 October 1940 and that he had confidential information about the weaknesses of the Greece military – both statements were actually close to the truth.[294] But though Ciano also possessed information to the contrary, he chose to believe what he wanted to hear – thus, repeating the mistake that he had accused Mussolini of making when Italy entered the war.[295] The general staff also played a part in the decision to invade Greece. Internal disputes and rivalries as well as the desire for personal gain dominated the day-to-day business, preventing a united opposition on the part of army leadership and ultimately allowing the opportunistic attitude within the government to prevail.[296]

Ciano's supporters dwindled, though he could still count on a few. Giovanni Ansaldo, editor of *Il Telegrafo*, repeatedly stressed that Ciano was against the war and that he had no sympathy for Germany.[297] A certain Principessa Y. also stated that Ciano did not want war and that his first concern had always been his country.[298] The most prominent fascist who sided with Ciano was Roberto Farinacci, who launched a smear campaign against the chief of staff, Pietro Badoglio. Farinacci's obvious attempt to ally himself with Ciano and potentially rescue his own position was reflected in the writing and subsequent publication of Farinacci's hagiography of Costanzo Ciano. His harsh attacks against Badoglio proved counterproductive, however, as they were perceived by the population as unfounded defamation.[299]

All these attempts to justify Ciano's actions were undermined by rumours that Ciano had described the Greek campaign as his "small war."[300] At the same time, there was widespread speculation in Italy about his wealth, corruption, and fraud; about his links with the Freemasons and the Jews; or about his affairs with other women. The accusation that Ciano was enriching himself to the detriment of the Italian people was particularly serious at a time when the ordinary population lacked such basic things as bread.[301] "Whether or not these rumours are true," German Ambassador Mackensen said, "they bear witness to the fact that the role of Ciano in Italy is considered to be over."[302] Obviously, Ciano served as an outlet for the Italian people to vent their anger.[303] The irony becomes apparent when one considers Ciano's notes. He was concerned about the food shortage in Italy and initiated plans to bring it under control. The *Duce*, on the other hand, was indifferent to the suffering of his countrymen. Rather, he philosophized about whether the bad conditions would finally make the Italians a hard, warlike people.[304]

Ciano faced hostility from the army as well.[305] Facing off with the army, Ciano suddenly found support from Mussolini, but it was not earnest, nor did it signal Ciano's return to his good graces. Mussolini used the conflict between Ciano and the army leadership to remove key figures from the officer corps who had been sceptical of the war. The most prominent victim of these purges was Badoglio, who was forced to resign on 26 November 1940 and was succeeded by General Ugo Cavallero.[306] Rumours circulated that Cavallero was appointed only because of his good relationship with Ciano. More salaciously, there was speculation that Ciano had had an affair with Cavallero's daughter. It seemed the only logical explanation for Cavallero's appointment, given his desultory military skills and unpopularity with other officers and the public.[307]

Officers and parts of the population saw in Cavallero's appointment an important victory for Ciano over his rivals.[308] Ciano's reticent reaction to Cavallero's promotion and his growing criticism of him may therefore come as a surprise. As early as November 1940, he wrote that the only reason for Cavallero's appointment was his unbroken and unrealistic optimism. Beginning in the late summer of 1941, Ciano considered Cavallero a "greedy person," a liar, and a powerful rival when it came to the *Duce*'s favour. In October 1941 Ciano noted that a "bad wind" came from Cavallero, who promised the *Duce* ninety-six well-equipped divisions, although Cavallero knew perfectly well that he could not marshal even a third of that figure. Ciano described him as a slave of Germany and criticized Cavallero's plea to end the parallel war, a scenario that Ciano was determined to prevent.[309] In the wake of the Greek debacle, the *Duce* agreed with Cavallero's assessment and took advantage of the situation to appoint new military officers, none of whom looked favourably upon Ciano. General Alfredo Guzzoni in Albania was replaced by Soddu, whom Ciano despised for abandoning the *non belligeranza* policy. By far the most obvious indication of Ciano's weakened position was the removal of Cavagnari from his post as the navy's chief of staff and the appointment of Arturo Riccardi as his successor, a man who had already been a rival of Galeazzo's father.[310]

At the beginning of 1941, Ciano tried to escape public criticism by retiring to the golf course outside Rome.[311] Continuing speculation about his possible ousting and the fact that his name was rarely mentioned in the press further demonstrate the precariousness of his position.[312] Still, German diplomat Hasso von Etzdorf believed that Ciano would not face immediate dismissal because "the Duce is still strong enough to be able to afford Ciano."[313] The *Duce* indeed decided against firing his foreign minister. But it was not because he was too strong; rather, he needed his son-in-law as a valuable scapegoat whose presence enabled Mussolini to sidestep criticism and hatred from the people, the army, and other leading fascists for a war that Mussolini had always wanted and had actively sought.[314]

In early 1941 the *Duce* sent high-ranking government officials including Bottai, Pavolini, and Ciano to the front for several months. He justified this step by arguing that the politicians who had wanted the war against Greece must now prove they could lead it.[315] However, the actual role they had played in the decision to attack Greece was only of secondary importance; the *Duce* rather intended to restore his already compromised reputation by symbolically degrading politicians who were unpopular among the people.[316] He wanted to demonstrate that he took public discord seriously without suffering any of the consequences personally.[317] Many observers were surprised by Mussolini's move; the *New York Times* dubbed it a "strange form of 'voluntary and temporary' exile."[318] The secretary of the German embassy, Prince Otto II von Bismarck, came very close to the truth when he stated that Mussolini most likely wanted to show decisiveness, but at the same time avoid a change of the cabinet.[319]

Mussolini's professional distance from his son-in-law developed into open mistrust during the Greek fiasco. Farinacci, who had previously defended Ciano, reported that the *Duce* accused Muti and Ciano of causing the disaster in Greece.[320] While Mussolini apparently had no scruples about blaming him, Ciano was surprised by the *Duce*'s suspicion. He realized that he was no longer fully involved in and informed about all domestic and foreign policy decisions. The press was the only way for him to receive information about current political events and the course of the war. He, the foreign minister, was even excluded from important events, such as the Italian-Spanish talks in Bordighera.[321] The apparent suddenness with which Ciano fell from favour left its mark, and it finally dawned on him that Mussolini held him responsible for the disaster in Greece and thus for the end of the Italian dream of a parallel war. Again and again, he complained that he was wrongly stigmatized as the sole culprit of the Greek campaign, but to no avail.[322]

The deployment of leading ministers to the front also affected the dynamics within the fascist system of rule. Some contemporaries saw it as Mussolini's gravest mistake, because this step united the ministers against him. Some hierarchs, such as Pavolini, instead turned their anger on Ciano as they were convinced that their de facto exile was part of a cover-up by Mussolini. Ultimately, the departure of the ministers brought to the surface the internal conflicts that had been smouldering for years. A war of everyone against everyone had begun.[323]

After Ciano finished his front mission, he assured Princess Colonna in June 1941 that he was as powerful and influential as ever. This self-evaluation was contradicted by the fact that he was still not particularly well informed about political or military developments.[324] American journalist John T. Whitaker reported that the Germans had eliminated Ciano as a political figure and with him the *Palazzo Chigi* had lost all influence.[325] Furthermore, Ciano remained unpopular with the public, where rumours about his wealth and corruption continued to damage his reputation.[326] Even Ciano seemed uncertain about his own position. At the end of July, he took a sick leave from the *Palazzo Chigi* and went to Livorno for two months – ostensibly, for an urgent surgery. Although we do not possess any diary entries about this time, there are clues that Ciano used his illness as an excuse to escape the political turmoil in Rome. Among other things, the operation did not take place until the end of August – not exactly a sign of an acute illness. Filippo Anfuso also reported that the Italian foreign minister regularly attended parties and other social events during his time in Livorno, where he would openly insult the *Duce*.[327]

In September 1941 SS officer Eugen Dollmann noted that Ciano, "the tie-wearing sonnyboy who had to endure so much cheap German mockery," had become quieter, more thoughtful. He also mentioned Ciano's "profound internal and external changes." However, he reported that Ciano was "still the most controversial, passionately opposed, yet unshakably powerful figure next to the *Duce*."[328] Dollmann's assessment suggests that Ciano had apparently returned to the inner circle of power. How did that happen?

During his absence, representatives of the Catholic Church and the royal house along with such fascists as Bottai and Grandi formed a heterogeneous coalition in light of the worsening course of the war. Though initially reluctant, they became increasingly critical of Mussolini and sought Ciano's help once the latter had returned to Rome. In Ciano's presence, Bottai described the *Duce* as a true "tyrant," an "autodidact who had a bad teacher and was a very bad student," and expressed scepticism about the future of "state life in Italy."[329] In the summer of 1942, the Italian police obtained information that Ciano had met with potential conspirators, though their exact plans and intentions remained unknown. The group included Arpinati, Badoglio, Carboni, and Ciano's father's former rival, Augusto Turati.[330]

Apparently, the conspirators hoped that Ciano could still influence the *Duce* because of their familial connection. Ciano's reaction is both astonishing and revealing. In his diary, there is no indication that he repeated these explosive statements to Mussolini or that he defended the *Duce*. On the contrary, Ciano also accused Mussolini of having lost all contact with his people, though he mostly attacked domestic policy in general.[331] Ciano hesitated, kept a low profile, and did not dare step into the open. He tried to avoid being caught between Mussolini and his supporters, on the one hand, and the regime's critics, on the other. Perhaps he hoped to assume the role of a *peso determinante* (determining weight) within the ruling class to regain his former power.

Even in this period, it becomes clear that the alienation between Mussolini and Ciano was the culmination of many years of slow decay, a trend that began in 1938 and ended when Ciano lost all belief in the *Duce*'s supposed genius. Except for a brief note in March 1942, when Ciano described Mussolini as a "great statesman" for the last time, there was no longer any talk of Mussolini being infallible or of how he moved Ciano to tears. Instead, Ciano became extremely critical of Mussolini's actions, statements, and military views.[332] Beginning in the summer of 1942, foreigners also observed the increasing distance between Ciano and the *Duce*.[333] When Mussolini suffered from severe stomach cramps in early autumn 1942, however, Ciano was concerned about the *Duce*'s health.[334] His criticism of his former idol's political and military abilities stood in contrast to the personal attachment and made his relationship with Mussolini seem deeply ambiguous at the time.

The *Duce*'s declining health fuelled speculation about a possible change at the top of the Italian government. Rumours about Ciano's future, though he apparently believed that Italy had no future, circulated. At the time, the *Duce*'s sister, Edvige Mussolini, even stated her wish that Ciano take over the Ministry of the Interior – but he refused.[335] His refusal was due less to disinterest in domestic affairs, since he commented many times on the mood and events in Italy, and more to fear of interfering in the turmoil of domestic politics, which would have brought him into direct conflict with his biggest rival at the time, State Secretary Buffarini Guidi. It seems Ciano had significant doubts about challenging Buffarini Guidi, perhaps because he lacked the necessary support from within the ruling elite. Given the chaotic situation in Italy, the rumours, and the extremely fluid power structures within the constantly changing coalitions, it is understandable that Ciano acted extremely cautiously. There was also the fact that, if he chose to take over the Ministry of the Interior at this time, he would be replacing its current head minister, Mussolini. What, then, does it mean that the *Duce*'s sister approached Ciano with such an idea? The answer depends largely on Mussolini's knowledge of his sister's initiative. If he knew, he was obviously contemplating a secret cabinet reshuffle; if he did not know, one can assume that there was criticism of Mussolini even within his own family.

In the meantime, Mussolini became increasingly paranoid over his son-in-law's activities and his continuing absence from Rome. Apparently, he thought Ciano was organizing a coup against him. In mid-July 1942 he therefore ordered a reluctant Ciano to come back from Livorno to the Italian capital, once again triggering a host of conspiracy theories.[336] Bitterly disappointed, Ciano realized that Mussolini believed the rumours, and his criticism of the *Duce* consequently intensified. At the end of January 1943, he accused Mussolini of living in his own "fool's paradise," lulling "himself with many dangerous illusions," and only believing in the false optimism of General Cavallero.[337]

The ousting of Cavallero therefore became a top priority for Ciano. An opportunity arose when a group around General Vittorio Ambrosio complained about Cavallero's incompetence. Ciano immediately informed the *Duce* about the military's reservations.[338] What exactly he told Mussolini, and whether his report underscored the rumours about an alleged conspiracy against the *Duce*, remains unknown.[339] Nevertheless, to Germany's annoyance and Ciano's delight, Mussolini fired his chief of staff and appointed Ambrosio as his successor.[340] Ciano believed that he would have more influence over Ambrosio and his associate, General Giuseppe Castellano, but that was unfounded.[341]

The last chapter of Galeazzo Ciano's political career began on 5 February 1943, when he met Mussolini in the *Palazzo Venezia*. "The moment I entered the room," Ciano noted, "I perceived that he was very much embarrassed. I understood what he was prepared to tell me."[342] Thus did Ciano describe his removal from the Foreign Ministry. Although he stated in his notes that he was unsurprised by this move, there is no reference in his diary to support claims that he knew ahead of time. When Mussolini offered him several different posts, Ciano opted for the post of ambassador to the Holy See. Back in the *Palazzo Chigi*, he ordered the Italian envoy to the Vatican, Raffaele Guariglia, to initiate his accreditation.[343] Although he described his ousting as a "heavy blow," he understood that the new post was one of the most rewarding and least delicate tasks at the time, and that it also enabled him to leave the *Palazzo Chigi* with his head held high.[344] On 8 February 1943 Ciano officially handed over control of the Foreign Ministry and said goodbye to Mussolini.[345]

Even though fascist propaganda tried to portray Ciano's transfer to the embassy at the Holy See as unremarkable, many contemporary observers at home and abroad were surprised by its suddenness.[346] Although there were numerous rumours of personnel reshuffle, Mussolini seemed to have decided to remove Ciano at short notice.[347] Apparently, Ciano was amused by all the speculations regarding his dismissal. It was further proof, he explained, "that even behind the simplest and most natural processes the world must assume ever more complicated contexts."[348] Mussolini also refused to comment further on the changes within his cabinet. He merely stated that he did not care about private family relationships when the nation's interests were at stake.[349]

Meanwhile, a rumour persisted that the *Duce* wanted to prevent a coup in which Ciano was involved. In this context, the absence of the original pages for 1 and 2 February 1943 in Ciano's diary is significant. Hans Bernd Gisevius, former German vice consul in Zürich and officer of the *Ausland/Abwehr*, reported that the German *Abwehr* succeeded in intercepting and deciphering numerous telegrams from the US embassy in Bern. In one of these messages, dated 1 February 1943, the name Ciano appeared in a list of persons the Allies intended to recruit as potential collaborators. Hitler sent the list directly to Mussolini and shortly afterwards Ciano was dismissed.[350] At the beginning of February 1943, the Americans also obtained information that a plot against the *Duce* had been uncovered with the help of the Gestapo.[351] During this time, which was marked by alleged coups against the head of government, Mussolini apparently again turned to the old guard of fascists. He appointed Giuseppe Bastianini as state secretary in the Ministry of Foreign Affairs, and Carlo Scorza took over the PNF. These personnel decisions were intended to stabilize the regime; above all, however, they were signs that, after almost twenty-one years, the regime had failed to bring forward a new generation of competent fascist leaders.[352]

The Catholic and Monarchist

The negotiation of power between the three great players of Italian politics and society – the fascist regime, the monarchy, and the Catholic Church – represent yet another area of significant conflict during the fascist era. This diverse community of interests and its importance to the function of the Italian fascist system of rule has faded into the background due to the culturalist turn of recent research.[353] Although the influence of the king and the church on day-to-day politics had diminished since the early 1930s, both institutions – especially when we examine the public's sympathies and their influence on social structures – represented a constant danger to the totalitarian claims of fascist purists and to the position of the *Duce*.[354] They could look back on a traditional authority, which, though overshadowed by Mussolini's charisma since 1922, had never been abolished.

Furthermore, many members of the fascist regime were closely associated with these institutions due to their upbringing and political trajectories. For them, the further marginalization or abolition of both the church and the monarchy – as Mussolini repeatedly demanded – was not an option. On the contrary, for certain individuals the Catholic Church, with its transnational orientation, and the Italian royal family were stabilizing the regime and society, as they shared important interests such as the fight against communism and an expansionist foreign policy. Included in this group were key figures of the regime such as Luigi Federzoni, De Vecchi, and Giuseppe Volpi. Even Costanzo Ciano, who had pushed for the fascistization of central areas of the Italian economy, never questioned the power-sharing.[355] But how did his son Galeazzo behave towards the Vatican and the Royal House of Savoy?

Galeazzo Ciano was a devout Catholic and followed the traditional religious rites in his personal life. Ciano's devotion was seriously tested for the first time in 1937–38. Differences in opinion between the Vatican and the fascist regime emerged after the government adopted increasingly stringent anti-Semitic measures. The Vatican shared – albeit modestly – the criticism voiced by Western democracies and by Jewish associations and organizations.[356] Even if Ciano maintained that he was indifferent to the "Jewish question" and did not publicly reprimand the Vatican, his ministry either justified or outright denied the anti-Semitic campaign.[357] Another point of conflict developed when the Catholic Church expressed its concern about the German-Italian rapprochement in order to draw attention to the discrimination and persecution of Catholic dignitaries in the Third Reich. The PNF in turn accused the Catholic lay organization *Azione Cattolica* of fighting for the "communist cause." Although Ciano was irritated by the allegedly philo-communist attitude of the Catholic Church, he also expressed understanding of "the difficulties Germany is causing" the Vatican.[358] Instead of joining Mussolini's anti-Catholic tirades, he tried to mediate between the two sides and thus contributed to a temporary détente.[359]

Ciano's mediation efforts were evident when Pope Pius XI announced ahead of Hitler's May 1938 visit to Rome that he would leave the city for his summer residence, Castel Gandolfo. His public withdrawal served as a denunciation of the Nazi regime's actions against Catholic clergy in Germany. At the same time, he indirectly criticized the rapprochement with Berlin being actively pursued by Rome – and Ciano. Still, Ciano tried to exert a moderating influence over the church leader, as it was imperative that nothing should spoil Hitler's visit. In the end, he succeeded in convincing the Holy See to avoid giving the impression of a complete blockade, at least to the outside world. The Vatican agreed to the temporary surveillance of ecclesiastical institutions in Rome and kept the lights in the city on during Hitler's visit to maintain the fiction that the Vatican was continuing its day-to-day business.[360] Nonetheless, the pope and many other dignitaries left the Eternal City, and the Vatican museums were closed. The reactions in the Catholic community to the papal exodus were mixed. While some praised the pope's decision to retreat in protest, others had hoped that he would stand up to the "Antichrist" Hitler.[361]

While Mussolini threatened to "break a few bludgeons on the backsides of the priests" and to "revive Ghibelline Italy," Ciano repeatedly met with representatives of the Vatican to prevent substantial conflict between the regime and the church.[362] He emphasized the similarities between the Catholic Church and fascism, and tried to defuse possible points of contention.[363] Ciano thus became a prominent mediator between the government and the Vatican – a role he increasingly enjoyed. He was also the official envoy of the government at the ten-year anniversary of the Lateran Treaties (February 1939) and the accession of Pius XII to the throne of Peter (March 1939). Unlike Mussolini, who had refused to participate in either celebration, Ciano felt honoured by the invitations and saw them as confirmation of his efforts to reconcile the Vatican and the regime. Ciano also had a positive impression of the new church leader following his first audience with Pope Pius XII.[364]

Ciano sought particularly close contact with the Vatican during the time of *non belligeranza*. The pope and the Catholic clergy had repeatedly spoken against the war and supported Ciano's non-interventionist policy. On 21 December 1939 King Vittorio Emanuele III met with Pope Pius XII in the presence of Ciano, who wore his official uniform as foreign minister, thus publicly illustrating his close attachment to the royal house and traditional Italian foreign policy.[365] Although Ciano had not been directly involved in organizing the meeting, rumours that he was the actual architect of the get-together circulated.[366] Evidently, the Italian public assumed that Ciano was on good terms with the Royal House of Savoy and the Vatican because of his anti-German views and his policy of *non belligeranza*.[367]

Furthermore, in December 1939 the Catholic Church also attempted to publicly strengthen Ciano's position by awarding him the Order of the Golden Spur for his work in favour of the "noblest cause of peace." It is the second-highest honour a pope can bestow and was a clear sign that the church also realized the potential of political rituals and ceremonies. While Mussolini continued to attack the Catholic Church, calling it a "cancer that devours our national lives," Ciano was visibly proud of his award and subsequent recognition.[368]

Examination of the period from 1941 to 1943 further underlines the closeness of the Vatican-Ciano relationship. In April 1941 a dispute between Farinacci and the Vatican escalated and was exacerbated by Mussolini's plans to abolish Christmas. Frustrated with the continuous influence of the church in day-to-day life, the *Duce* claimed that Italy was not a religious nation and therefore did not need the Catholic Church.[369] Aldo Vidussoni's vicious attacks against the Vatican in 1942 were met with incomprehension on Ciano's part. "This is the result," Ciano stated, "of letting children play with matters of importance."[370] In autumn 1942 Farinacci, Buffarini Guidi, and Giovanni Preziosi launched another smear campaign against the Vatican when the American diplomat Myron Taylor met with the pope.[371] Apparently, the order had come down from Berlin to greet the American with a "solemn booing" and accuse him of advocating the bombardment of Rome. To Ciano, these accusations seemed eminently "foolish," "ridiculous," and "disgusting."[372]

Ciano was extremely indignant over such anti-Catholic outbursts. He continued to regularly attend church services and found validation for his belief that the Italian people sought refuge in the church.[373] In the conflict between the hardliners in the fascist regime and the Catholic Church, his sympathies were clearly with the Vatican. He described people such as Farinacci as "bunglers" and "pigs" when they ranted against the Vatican.[374] Whenever possible, he tried to stop attacks against the church and took the opportunity to strengthen his personal relationship with the Vatican, even if it brought him directly into conflict with Mussolini. For example, in the summer of 1942 when the *Duce* intended to arrest Giuseppe Dalla Torre, editor-in-chief of the Vatican newspaper *Osservatore Romano*, and ban the newspaper for articles critical of the regime, Ciano successfully argued against such a move. He was convinced that "today the prestige of the Church is extraordinarily great" and that such an anti-Catholic attack would ultimately only harm the regime.[375] Despite his earlier efforts, Ciano could not prevent the PNF from intensifying its aggression against the church at the turn of 1942–43, as the *Duce* promoted and partly initiated them.[376] The attacks against the Vatican not only illustrate the level of alienation between Mussolini and Ciano at the time, but also demonstrate Ciano's diminished influence within the regime.

When the Allies threatened to bomb Rome at the turn of 1942–43, Ciano once again sought to cooperate with the Vatican. Even if Ciano was sceptical about the Vatican's possible peace initiatives, both sides demanded the withdrawal of the German command from the city in order to declare Rome an "open city" and thus avoid the bombing of the capital.[377] Although the cooperation between Ciano and the Vatican did not prevent the bombing of Rome – the city was bombed for the first time on 19 July 1943 – it helped to delay the attack and eventually paved the way for the first declaration of Rome as an "open city" at the end of July 1943.[378] Although the church praised Ciano for his commitment, they also rejected his sweeping recriminations against the Allies as inappropriate and unjustified, given the presence of German troops in the city.[379]

On 12 January 1943 Ciano invited some confidants to the house of Isabelle Colonna. In addition to the hostess, Cardinal Giovanni Battista Montini, representing the Vatican, diplomat Leonardo Vitetti, and Cyprienne Del Drago, wife of diplomat Marcello Del Drago, were present. The conversation revolved around the war and the role of the church, with Ciano explicitly praising the Vatican's commitment to preventing the bombardment of Rome. Ciano also took the opportunity to present himself as a devout Catholic. He emphasized that Italy was a Catholic country and therefore every government should always maintain a good relationship with the church. He denounced the anti-Catholic polemics of the PNF and stressed that now was not the time for a "policy for the party, but only for the homeland."[380]

But was Ciano's respect for and devotion to the Vatican based on reciprocity? How did leaders of the Catholic Church perceive the *Duce*'s son-in-law? While existing documents from the 1930s and 1940s reflect at least a mutual respect, some unnamed employees of the Vatican were not pleased when Ciano was appointed ambassador to the Vatican in 1943. They criticized the fact that Rome changed ambassadors too often, and expressed fears that the Anglo-American countries would suspect the Holy See of cooperating with the fascist regime, which would in turn compromise the pope's ability to act as a future mediator.[381] On 17 July 1943 State Secretary for Foreign Affairs Bastianini visited Cardinal State Secretary Luigi Maglione on behalf of Mussolini. The conversation focused primarily on the question of who could take "our Italy" out of the Axis and the war as soon as the time was ripe.[382] Both sides agreed that only the *Duce* could do so, though they knew that the Allies were unwilling to negotiate with Mussolini or any other leading fascist.[383] Bastianini also expressed his gratitude for the cooperation of the Holy See and promised that, in the future, relations between the Vatican and Rome would no longer be conducted through Ambassador Ciano. He apparently noticed a certain distaste for Ciano among the

Vatican's representatives. Maglione in particular was not fond of Ciano and frequently wondered why Rome had sent "this boy to us" in the first place.[384]

As yet, scholars have ignored these critical voices from the Vatican; however, they reveal a more nuanced picture of relations between the fascist regime and the Vatican. Influential personalities within the Vatican, such as Maglione, increasingly distanced themselves from Ciano after he was deposed as foreign minister and transferred to the Vatican. Personal animosity, however, should not be regarded as the main reason for this distancing, given there is no evidence of it in previous years; rather, it was likely Ciano's diminished influence within the regime that made it prudent for these individuals to distance themselves from the former foreign minister. Instead of communicating through the *Duce*'s battered son-in-law, the Vatican now preferred direct contact with the Foreign Ministry.[385]

Let us now turn to Ciano's relationship with the royal family in general and King Vittorio Emanuele III in particular. Given the good relationship between Costanzo Ciano and the royal family, it is not surprising that his son's relationship with the monarchy was marked by mutual respect in the mid-1930s.[386] This relationship apparently changed after Hitler's visit in May 1938. The German delegation did not miss any opportunity to express its revulsion at the Italian monarchy; whether it was Joseph Goebbels, Rudolf Hess, or Heinrich Himmler, high-ranking Nazis believed that the Italian monarchy was a relic from a bygone age and had to be abolished.[387] While some fascist dignitaries were visibly irritated by the provocative and insensitive behaviour of the Germans towards an Italian state institution, Ciano agreed with their harsh criticism.[388] "The whole milieu," Ciano wrote, "is mouldy: a dynasty a thousand years old does not like the appearance of a revolutionary regime."[389]

Historians have often interpreted this statement as a clear indication that Ciano despised the royal family.[390] To support this interpretation, Renzo De Felice and others additionally reference the appointment of Mussolini as the first marshal and commander-in-chief of the Italian Army on equal terms with the king on 30 March 1938. To that effect, the Chamber of Deputies under President Costanzo Ciano passed the law, which was then submitted to the Senate without prior notice. Senate President Luigi Federzoni reacted with surprise and indignation, but ultimately did not stop the law – though it irreversibly eroded trust between the fascist regime and the monarchy.[391] In his 1967 memoirs, Federzoni blamed Galeazzo Ciano for this great affront to the monarchy.[392] But what was Galeazzo Ciano's actual role?

Unfortunately, the relevant pages in Ciano's diary are missing, and Federzoni's version should not be believed without reservation.[393] Nearly thirty years after the event, he tried to minimize his own role and that of Costanzo Ciano, whom – in contrast to Galeazzo – Federzoni held in high esteem. However, it is very likely that Federzoni's criticism was caused by Ciano's negative opinion of Federzoni, evidence of which we find in Ciano's diary.[394] In contrast to Federzoni, the Italian parliamentarian Luigi Gasparotto wrote in his diary that Galeazzo Ciano had tried in vain to dissuade his father from passing such a law.[395] Ultimately, the *Duce*'s promotion cannot be fully understood without taking into account international events. After the German annexation of Austria, the outbreak of war in Europe became more likely. When faced with such a scenario, the entire fascist regime – from the Cianos to Federzoni to Mussolini – wanted direct control over the army. Moreover, Hitler's visit to Rome was imminent, and it was out of the question for Mussolini to meet Hitler, the sole commander-in-chief of the German military, on less than equal footing.[396]

That leaves the issue of explaining Ciano's disparaging statements about the monarchy during and immediately after Hitler's visit. Given – as I will show in the chapter "The Diplomat" – his constant attempts to impress Hitler and the Germans, he must have been furious when he learned that the guests had formed a bad impression of the Italian royal family and thus maybe of Italy. This observation was most likely the main reason for his rage and anger, which we can only find in temporal proximity to Hitler's visit. So far, however, scholars have overlooked this connection between Ciano's determination to impress Hitler and his criticism of the monarchy.[397] Unlike Mussolini, Ciano's negative opinion cannot simply be equated with a fundamental rejection of the monarchy. This view is reinforced by noting that Ciano neither disagreed with the king's characterization of Hitler as "a mentally and physically degenerate man" nor agreed with the countless curses that the *Duce* piled on the monarchy.[398] Mussolini's behaviour shows a certain anger, frustration, and impotence that he was unable to get rid of the king. Sometimes he hoped that the king would simply die of old age; at other times he considered asking Hitler to help him eliminate all "anachronisms" after the war.[399]

Ciano's outburst about the monarchy also should not be linked to the monarchy's anti-German attitude. German-Italian rapprochement between 1936 and 1939 was one of the central topics of conversation between the king and Ciano. Vittorio Emanuele III repeatedly warned Ciano about the disloyalty of the Germans.[400] Even in February 1939 when the king criticized the regime's foreign policy and thus Ciano, whom he described as Hitler's "tool," Ciano kept quiet.[401] In light of an unstable national and international situation, the foreign minister wanted to avoid an open conflict with the royal family at all cost, as the monarchy still enjoyed great support in many Italian regions.[402] Instead, he sought to maintain the image of unity between the regime and the monarchy to prevent negative headlines about Italy's internal chaos. As in the case of the Vatican, he wanted to capitalize on the monarchy's prestige to stabilize the regime and ultimately his own position. He therefore supported the king's plan to honour Mussolini at the beginning of 1939. The *Duce*, however, thought this proposal was a "ridiculous" idea and rejected it.[403]

In August 1939 King Vittorio Emanuele III awarded Ciano the Supreme Order of the Most Holy Annunciation in recognition of the foreign minister's role in the conquest of Albania, even though he had been critical of the campaign.[404] Ciano was moved by this honour, which not only made him a cousin to the king but also elevated him to the company of fellow members of the order: Pietro Badoglio, Costanzo Ciano, Luigi Federzoni, and Emilio De Bono.[405] Awarding the order at exactly this time – it was four months after Albania's occupation – was a clever move by Vittorio Emanuele III, as he intended to strengthen the then anti-German group around Ciano and bind Ciano closer to the royal house before the outbreak of the Second World War.[406]

At the time, Ciano regarded the king's recognition as proof of his good relationship with the monarchy. As he did with the Vatican, he intended to leverage his contact with the monarchy as an asset in his struggle against the interventionists.[407] Royalists not only supported the *non belligeranza* but were even thinking of positioning King Vittorio Emanuele III against Mussolini. In March 1940 the king's minister, Pietro d'Acquarone, contacted Ciano and told him: "From one moment to the next there might be the need for intervention in order to turn things around."[408] Ciano, however, did not respond to the intrigue against Mussolini, as he was no longer convinced that it would be successful. When the king made this cautious attempt to organize resistance against Mussolini, the balance of power between non-interventionists and interventionists had long since shifted in favour of the latter group.[409] Nevertheless, it must be noted that there is no evidence Ciano shared the king's intentions with the *Duce*.

Ciano not only tolerated the existence of the monarchy but also promoted its influence, as he favoured the integration of the Italian royal family into the occupation administration of newly conquered territories. Many scholars today argue that, while an alliance existed between the fascist regime and the monarchy in Italy, the fascists refused to let this alliance expand into the new territories and colonies[410] – rendering Ciano's stance all the more meaningful. We get an initial view of Ciano's concept of a successful occupation policy by looking at his plans for the administration of Albania. On 12 April 1939 a Constituent Assembly confirmed the merging of the royal houses of Albania and Italy, and four days later entrusted Vittorio Emanuele III with the Albanian crown.[411] Historian Davide Rodogno argued that the transfer of the Albanian crown to the Italian monarch was only intended as a temporary solution, since the *Duce* was merely waiting for an opportunity to get rid of the "encrusted monarchy."[412]

However, this thesis is based on a teleological interpretation that focuses on the *Duce*'s totalitarian aspirations. Rodogno and others neglect the fact that the union between the Albanian and Italian royal houses was devised by Ciano and the Foreign Ministry, not Mussolini. Moreover, this procedure was not unique to Albania and therefore did not present an anomaly. Albania was instead a blueprint for the Foreign Ministry's occupation policy in the Balkans.[413] For example, Ciano pressured Ante Pavelić to accept Prince Aimone, Duke of Spoleto and a member of the Italian royal family of Savoy, as Croatia's new king.[414] Although Aimone had no idea of his new duties and – as he assured Ciano – felt uncomfortable with the scheme, he accepted the crown.[415] Ultimately, he only wielded nominal power over his new kingdom, which he never entered. Not only did he face the substantial risk of assassination, but he also lost the support of the fascist government when he sided with Croatian claims in Dalmatia against Rome. The latter stand shows that Aimone was never a "crowned governor of the fascist empire"[416] who merely followed orders from Rome. Rather, with the backing of the Quirinal Palace, he articulated his own ideas for the benefit of his territory.

Differences between Ciano and the royal family arose in the case of Montenegro. While Vittorio Emanuele III wanted to reintroduce the monarchy, Ciano wanted to appoint a high commissioner as in the province of Ljubljana.[417] Ciano was concerned that the restoration of the monarchy would fuel the expansionist claims of the Montenegrins and potentially have a negative impact on Albania, his "personal duchy."[418] Thus, his opposition was not so much directed against the monarchy as it was in favour of Albania. In the end, the king prevailed, and the Montenegrin crown was offered to the nephew of the Italian Queen Elena, Prince Michael of the House Petrović. Only when he refused was Ciano able to appoint his protégé Serafino Mazzolini as governor of Montenegro.[419]

Despite these tensions, there can be no doubt that Ciano wanted to integrate the newly conquered Balkan regions into the "imperial system" in order to stabilize the Italian Empire.[420] Although the direct influence of the monarchy on the actual occupation policy was initially limited, its integration nevertheless extended the fragile alliance between the Italian king and the fascist regime into the new territories. Ciano felt that the monarchy should use its reputation among the army, its international influence, and its royal networks to consolidate the Italian territories. He was also convinced that the Slavic peoples were more familiar with the monarchical form of government than the fascist one, which seemed to him yet another reason to integrate the royalty into the administration of the conquered areas.[421]

The Italian monarchy also repeatedly played a role in Ciano's dealings with Hungary. During the *non belligeranza* period, he proposed to the Hungarian foreign minister István Csáky that Budapest should give the Hungarian crown to a prince from the House of Savoy. Csáky would only agree to such an idea in the event that Germany attacked Hungary.[422] According to Ciano's diary, Hungarian Prime Minister Pál Teleki made a similar offer at the end of March 1940; this time, the only precondition was, so it seems, that Italy must stay out of the war.[423] Ciano's reaction to Teleki's proposal is not known, but it can be assumed that he refused it since Italy's entry into the war had already been decided. Two years later, a possible union between the Italian and Hungarian monarchies was again discussed. When István Horthy, the designated successor to the regent of Hungary, Miklós Horthy, died in a plane crash on 20 August 1942, the regent toyed with the idea of appointing his minor grandson Sharif István Horthy as his successor. In Ciano's opinion, this proposal was Horthy's last, desperate attempt to build his own dynasty in order to push back against the increasing influence of the Germans. Nevertheless, Ciano advised against such a step, which would unnecessarily provoke Berlin.[424] On the contrary, Ciano advocated another plan, which was to give the Crown of St. Stephen to King Vittorio Emanuele III. Not only would this proposal have extended the power of the Italian royal family and of Rome, but it would also have been directed against the Germans. However, Mussolini vetoed the idea because he feared the Italian crown would become too powerful, and he also did not want to strain relations with the Third Reich any further.[425]

These examples demonstrate that a collaborative relationship existed between Ciano and the royal house to maintain and, if possible, expand their respective influence. This collaboration became particularly clear when Italy stumbled from one military disaster to the next, and both Ciano and the royals tried to re-establish their previous contact. The first overture was made by Vittorio Emanuele III, who awarded Ciano the title of Count of Buccari in January 1942, thus remembering one of his father's great deeds during the First World War and indirectly reminding Galeazzo Ciano of the close contacts between his father and the monarchy.[426] When Amedeo, Duke of Aosta, died of tuberculosis and malaria in a British prison camp on 3 March 1942, a visibly saddened Ciano, unlike Mussolini, paid his respects to the royal family. He described the prince as a "noble figure" who, like himself, was against the war. He noted that the entire country was moved by honest sympathy for Amedeo, and he dismissed German proposals to propagandistically exploit the prince's death as tasteless.[427] Ciano interpreted the renewed interest of the monarchy as a confirmation that it acknowledged and supported his policy. Like the Vatican, the monarchy became a focal point for considerations to initiate a separate peace with the Western Allies in late 1942. When the king saw an opportunity in November 1942 to reach an agreement with the Western democracies, he asked Ciano to resume contact with Washington and London, no matter how thin.[428]

After the vote of the Fascist Grand Council in July 1943, however, the unstable foundation on which the previous alliance between Ciano and the royal family was based became apparent. While rumours persisted that Vittorio Emanuele III was helping Dino Grandi, among others, to escape, the new government – with the king's backing – placed Ciano under house arrest and intended to formally charge him one month later. The actions taken by the king were in this case guided by pure state reason, since it would have been a heavy burden on his reputation and Badoglio's government to simply ignore or even protect Mussolini's son-in-law. The Italian public still regarded Ciano as a symbol of a corrupt and reprehensible regime, even though he had opposed Mussolini in July 1943.[429] The king did not seem completely unhappy when he learned of Ciano's escape to Germany; he even hoped that Ciano would not return to Rome, thus implying that he did not want to be forced to take action against the *Duce*'s son-in-law.[430] As was the case with the Vatican, Ciano had overestimated his standing with the royal house and realized too late that, after he was dismissed as foreign minister, he was no longer of any value to the king.

The Fascist Oligarchy

Previous studies on Galeazzo Ciano have usually painted a straightforward image: his political career and ultimate fall were entirely dependent on Mussolini's whims and support. Without a doubt, the *Duce* played an important role in Ciano's career trajectory and duration, but it would be too simplistic to characterize Ciano solely as Mussolini's puppet. Ciano used a variety of resources to preserve and expand his position within the fascist elite, thereby trying to adapt to new situations. His behaviour sheds new light on the functioning of the fascist system of rule and forces us to rethink the political mechanism of Italian fascism.

An analysis of ever-changing alliances and networks among the fascist elite illustrates that Ciano's position and popularity were dependent on his work as a minister. After he restructured his ministries and instituted a strict hierarchical structure with him on top, he secured a prominent position in the public view. In this, Ciano suffered unintended consequences: whereas his successes were more often than not attributed to the *Duce*'s genius, failures and scandals were exclusively blamed on him.[431] Ciano had to be successful at all times in order to maintain his position and fully utilize his institutional ties as a power resource. In the world of fascism, success meant that he needed to be perceived as a person who constantly sought to change and negate the status quo. Yet, his support for the *non belligeranza* policy, his preference for traditional social models, and his adherence to the power compromises between the Catholic Church, the fascists, and the monarchy contradicted this image.

Within the alliance system Galeazzo Ciano formed a bridge between the *Duce* and the other ministers because of his personal connection to Mussolini. Officials tried to include him in their networks to indirectly increase their popularity with Mussolini, and Ciano in turn used the attention to further his own influence. Ciano ferociously defended this position, given that the *Duce* was initially the most important person in his network, the "sun around which Ciano's world revolved."[432]

Ciano's coalitions were usually not defined by common political goals, but by identifying and then excluding the "enemy." In almost every other fascist movement, personal rivalries were also far more decisive in the demarcation of factions than the dispute between radical and moderate fascists within the regime. This situation explains why Ciano formed temporary alliances with such a diverse group of people including Starace, Farinacci, Federzoni, Balbo, and Grandi.[433]

Ciano also represented a group of young newcomers, most of whom were born after 1900 and belonged to the so-called war youth generation. They naturally came into competition with the cadres of earlier phases of the fascist movement. The tension between different age cohorts was a conflict specific to Italian fascism and has so far only attracted a few scholars. Nevertheless, Ciano's life clearly illustrates that merely belonging to a common age cohort was insufficient to form a stable coalition of like-minded people. Although the peer group could and did play a role in forming alliances, common experiences were much more important in developing a generational sense of community.[434] Ciano's meteoric rise isolated him from his own age cohort. His career not only exposed him to experiences none of his peers could share, but it also influenced the direction of his ambitions and interests, which in turn pushed him even further from his cohort.

Ciano's behaviour towards the PNF was primarily conditioned by his personal desire for power. Although he was not a major player in the early phases of the fascist movement, he was attracted by some of the futurist and fascist slogans and promises in his teens. For career purposes, he would later exaggerate his fascist past when he began his political career, inventing an image of himself as an early and staunch fascist. The further his career progressed, the more strained his relationship with the PNF became. Ciano opposed excessive intervention by the party in state politics, and in times of conflict he sided with the state institutions because he perceived the party and its secretaries as competitors for his position. While the PNF indeed limited and sometimes threatened Ciano's influence, Ciano's case indicates that very close party affiliation was not a precondition for maintaining one's influence and power once in the regime's inner circle. To get rid of one of his main competitors, Ciano intended to bridge the existing polycratic structures between party and state by using personal networks to assert his dominance over the PNF. The case of General Secretary Ettore Muti reveals the limits of this plan. When Muti was appointed to the highest position in the party he gained substantial power, and his new direct access to Mussolini and other high-ranking fascists freed him from his dependency on Ciano.[435]

In addition, Ciano's contacts with the church and the monarchy further complicated his relationship with the PNF. While he regarded both institutions as central pillars of Italy's social and political landscape, the party's secretaries sought their destruction. Thanks to tradition, both institutions enjoyed great prestige among the Italian people and were able to reach even groups that were staunchly sceptical of fascism. Thus, collaboration with the church and the royal house would help stabilize the regime and Ciano's position. Moreover, any impression of domestic turmoil that could jeopardize the image of a strong, unified Italy was to be avoided. For both pragmatic and political reasons, he chose to oppose a "second fascist revolution" that would have endangered his position. The reluctance of fascists such as Ciano to break with the old elites was another reason why Mussolini failed to abolish the "citadel of Catholicism."[436]

Ciano's behaviour also sheds new light on the functioning of the fascist system as an entity. Historian Rainer Behring recently criticized scholars' tendency to portray Mussolini as the central figure of Italian fascism, who was single-handedly responsible for all foreign and domestic politics.[437] By contrast, numerous studies on the Third Reich have produced a much more nuanced picture of the Nazi political system. Today, National Socialism is widely understood as a polycratic system with both competing and collaborating state and party institutions. Adolf Hitler presided over this system as the monocratic point of reference, detached from the day-to-day quarrels, and used both the Nazi Party and the SS apparatus to keep the balance of power between state and party institutions fluid in order to defend his position. Ultimately, direct access to the dictator often defined the influence of groups and individuals. As a consequence, this institutional and personal rivalry, increased by the polycratic structure, would eventually lead to a radicalization of National Socialist policies, including the Holocaust, as each fraction tried to outdo the others.[438]

Although Mussolini undoubtedly held an internal position within the system, Ciano's situation illustrates that it would be too simplistic to interpret Italian fascism with the same approach as the Nazi regime. Like Hitler, Mussolini was the ideological point of reference for the regime.[439] But the *Duce* never created an agency that came even close to the power and influence of the German SS. Instead, he repeatedly strengthened state institutions to keep the party and its radical fringes as well as the local *ras* in check. This approach was also shown by the fact that he repeatedly presided over several ministries, unlike Hitler.[440] As a consequence, the PNF and its sub-organizations were weaker compared to their German counterparts, and the fascistization of state institutions – including the *Palazzo Chigi* under Ciano – often remained superficial.[441] Furthermore, the *Duce* and the party failed to break up local power structures, and Mussolini was unable to replace the bureaucracy that had developed since the nineteenth century with the party apparatus. In another contrast to Hitler, Mussolini also failed to make the civil servants, diplomats, and soldiers swear an oath only on his person.[442] He was always in competition with King Vittorio Emanuele III, who – like the Vatican – remained a player in the Italian power game. And last but not least, Mussolini's back-and-forth in political matters in public and behind closed doors, the discrepancy between his words and deeds, in short, his unpredictability made it nearly impossible to "work towards the *Duce*" as Rodogno implied in his studies.

As a result, Italian politics were shaped by a multitude of different actors and conflicts that were not limited by a mere party-state dichotomy. Mussolini tried to use the constant rivalry between ministers, party leaders, and traditional elites to strengthen his own position, but this strategy had only a moderate success. The crucial difference from the Third Reich was the sheer number and heterogeneity of the actors involved. Establishing effective control over all these groups was almost impossible. Nevertheless, Mussolini became directly and indirectly involved in the formation of alliances in order to block the formation of a powerful opposition and to obtain a supportive majority for his policies.[443] If the latter was lacking, he did not simply impose his will, but worked to gain the necessary majority. As soon as the *Duce* was sure of a majority, he implemented his policy. This finding calls into question the assumption that the *Duce* was the sole authority to shape domestic and foreign policy during this period.[444]

Galeazzo Ciano's life helps to illustrate Mussolini's various tactics. First, the *Duce* was fond of ministerial reshuffles and repeatedly used them to integrate a younger generation of fascists into the government and party hierarchy, beginning with Ciano and Vidussoni. He thereby created a new line of conflict – one between different generations.[445]

Second, the *Duce* was able to deflect any blame for the regime's failure onto other ministers or officials. As a result, his own charisma among the Italian public and the international partners did not suffer. Mussolini thus needed Ciano as a scapegoat, which can explain why he kept him in his government. Certainly, it was not out of affection.[446]

Third, Mussolini used the Italian rumour mill to discipline, hamstring, or frighten potential rivals. Historian Paul Corner has stressed the importance of rumours as a tool of the regime to discipline the public.[447] The rumours about Ciano's private life, his opulent lifestyle, and his various falls from Mussolini's grace demonstrate that they were also used to control the fascist elite. Ciano's diary indicates that Ciano and the *Duce* took these rumours seriously and that they influenced their actions. Consequently, the rumours' veracity was less important than their mere existence, which was enough to silence potential critics in a system dominated by competition, resentment, and arbitrariness.[448]

Instead of continuing to portray Mussolini as the almighty dictator in Italian fascism, future research should rather analyse the various groups at the centre of political power and their agendas. It was the influence of these alliances that decisively shaped the future and direction of Italian politics. Certainly, Mussolini had a unique position – after all, the propaganda constantly portrayed him as the "messiah," the almighty unifying element of the Italian nation. Indeed, his word and his support could sometimes shift the delicate balance of power. Yet, disputes such as those over the policy of *non belligeranza* highlight that Mussolini's ability to impose his will was not limitless. He too had to take into account the balance of power, as it was constituted by the ever-changing alliances between the various actors. If we accept that these different alliances wielded political power and possessed substantial agency, then we should reject the idea that Italian fascism was equivalent to a single-man dictatorship. The fascist system in Italy would instead be best described as an authoritarian regime with an oligarchic structure.[449]

Different factions of the state and party apparatus pursued their own interests and tried everything in their power to see them realized. Perhaps this oligarchic structure might be one reason why Fascist Italy acted in some political areas differently from the Third Reich, even though its rhetoric sometimes appeared at least as ferocious.[450] The military defeats in the winter of 1941–42 in particular weakened the home front, delegitimized the fascist regime and the party under Mussolini, and strengthened institutions like the monarchy, the church, and the military. This situation could explain why in some political areas, including racial and occupation policy – a topic I will explain in the next chapter – we can see evidence of what the German philosopher Ernst Bloch called the "simultaneity of the non-simultaneous":[451] while institutions like the church and the *Palazzo Chigi* tried to moderate affairs, others like the fascist party and the Ministry of the Interior pushed for a further radicalization of fascist policies. Instead of predominantly focusing on fascist discourses and debates, historians in future should rather analyse the political structure of the fascist dictatorship and how it influenced fascist policies. By doing so, scholars would move beyond the idea of Mussolini as the almighty dictator and be able to expose all the elements within the fascist regime and the Italian nation that often pursued and supported radical projects similar to those undertaken by Nazi Germany. We would also be able to better understand why and when those groups were unable to dominate fascist politics, and other less-radical elements were able to determine the course of action, without falling back on an apologetic characterization of Fascist Italy as "harmless" – a description that remains prominent today and is still used in the attempt to absolve the entire Italian nation of guilt.

3
The Diplomat

Italy's Role in the World

Basing their assessment primarily on the memoirs of Italian diplomats, scholars have long claimed that the Foreign Ministry and its diplomats had a moderating effect on the *Duce*. The *Palazzo Chigi* became a "hotbed of resistance" against Mussolini's expansionist foreign policy.[1] The differences between the *Duce* and Foreign Ministry's officials, however, were not as drastic as some diplomats have claimed. They in fact shared several of Mussolini's foreign policy objectives, including revision of the Paris Treaties as well as expansion in the Mediterranean and the Danube Basin. Beginning in the late nineteenth century, both diplomats and politicians did not rely only on the *peso determinante* strategy, which involved gaining geostrategic advantages by playing other European powers against each other, to achieve these goals. Politicians like Francesco Crispi preferred a military conflict that would reshape Europe, unite the still divided Italian nation, and create the "new Italian."[2]

Given Crispi's aggressive foreign policy, historians such as Richard Bosworth emphasize that Mussolini's seizure of power in 1922 did not lead to a radical break with more traditional Italian foreign policy goals. Moreover, they reject the claims by the likes of Denis Mack Smith and Gaetano Salvemini that the fascist regime acted without a solid plan of what it hoped to achieve in the realm of foreign policy. They do, however, stress that a certain pragmatism prevailed when it came to the question of how to achieve specific objectives.[3] Historians such as Davide Rodogno and Wolfgang Schieder have argued instead that Mussolini, whom they consider the key figure of Italian diplomacy, intended from the beginning to end the traditional friendship with the "bourgeois nation" of Great Britain and to wage war against the decadent Western countries in order to build a new empire. War should create the "new man" and establish a totalitarian state in Italy. This close link between domestic and foreign affairs is considered the key feature of a new, fascist foreign policy.[4]

Although Galeazzo Ciano was the only foreign minister in the fascist era who had formal diplomatic training, scholarly assessments of his actions are dominated by three simplistic narratives:[5] first, that he was merely an assistant in the implementation of the *Duce*'s will, one who shared Mussolini's worldview; second, that the *Palazzo Chigi* experienced its fascist period under Ciano, since he only sought close relationships with other fascist regimes and movements; third, that he was too young and possessed no diplomatic skills or concepts of his own. These narratives, however, prevent a balanced understanding of Italian foreign policy in the years 1936 to 1943. Specifically, they reinforce a deterministic, even fatalistic interpretation, which not only presents the Axis and the subsequent war against the Western powers as inevitable but also reaffirms the "one man alone" thesis of an all-powerful Mussolini, which indirectly absolves the Foreign Ministry and Ciano of any guilt.[6]

A closer examination of Ciano's worldviews and ideologies, however, reveals a different story. From the start he had his own goals and initially no moral restraints in pursuing them. To overcome the international isolation and precarious economic situation in which Italy found itself after the Ethiopian War, he sought international recognition for the Italian Empire and the end of the League of Nations' sanctions. In Ciano's opinion these were the key prerequisites for the establishment of an empire in the Mediterranean.[7] As such, before the Second World War he was particularly interested in obtaining French territories, including regions from the Italian border to the Rhone with the cities of Marseille, Nice, and Toulon; bridgeheads in Lyon, Valence, and Avignon; Corsica, Tunisia, and Djibouti; as well as the French naval bases in Algiers, Mers-el-Kebir, and Casablanca. Moreover, Beirut was to be declared a neutral zone, and Italy was to receive shares of the Suez Canal. Ciano was also interested in seizing Corfu.[8] However, he did not explicitly demand territories owned or controlled by Great Britain, such as Malta and Gibraltar, regions in the Middle East, or the former British crown jewel in the Mediterranean, Egypt. When it came to territories in the Balkans, he was more ambivalent. While he was in favour of an Italian protectorate in Albania for personal and strategic reasons, he was not an ardent supporter of annexing large parts of Yugoslavia.[9]

In the end, building a Mediterranean empire was only a partial victory for Ciano. In the spring of 1938, he confided to his diary: My "conception of the Fascist Empire is not ... static. We still must go on advancing."[10] This concept of dynamism, the idea that politics must always keep moving and deny the status quo, was a central paradigm of fascist thinking. But the word "still" suggests that Ciano somehow imagined a future scenario in which all his goals had been achieved. Such a point of saturation, however, contradicts fascist ideology that sees any standstill as a betrayal of fascist ideals.[11] But what kind of future did he have in mind?

Ciano never limited his ambitions solely to Europe. He repeatedly stressed that Italy must be represented on all continents and take its rightful place as a great power in the international community.[12] In April 1938 he even wanted to erect a new building for the Foreign Ministry at the *Piazza Barberini*, which was supposed to be worthy of the "role it will have to play – the Imperial Ministry."[13] In his thinking, everyone should witness and acknowledge the new Italian self-confidence. He thus echoed what Italians had been dreaming about since the nineteenth century. While the British Empire served as a contemporary inspiration, he legitimized his claims by looking to the past. He frequently mentioned famous expeditions to the Far East, like those of Marco Polo and Matteo Ricci, and repeatedly referred to the power and greatness of the Roman Empire, thus evoking the idea of the *Pax Romana*.[14]

Jewish-Italian historian Arnaldo Momigliano, who had to flee Fascist Italy in 1938, noted that the *Pax Romana* "is a simple formula for propaganda, but a difficult subject for research."[15] It was first proclaimed in 13 BC when Emperor Augustus and Agrippa returned from pacifying the provinces. In retrospect the term referred to two centuries of minimal Roman expansions and relative peacefulness, mostly defined by an absence of violence and war. During this time, the Roman Empire reached its peak territorial extent, and its population grew to 70 million people. Thus, the *Pax Romana* fit perfectly into the fascist rhetoric: "peace" was not secured by some form of compromise or signed agreement; rather, it was established through the sheer force and power of the Roman Empire and its army. Thus, it is hardly surprising that again and again fascists, including Ciano, referred to the *Pax Romana* in speeches, writings, art, architecture, and iconography. One of the most famous examples was the inauguration of the restored *Ara Pacis* on 28 September 1938. Ciano's personal belief in the rebirth of the Roman Empire and in the *Pax Romana* as a model for his new, saturated empire was deeply rooted in various ideologies, worldviews, and national stereotypes.[16] The most important ones included nationalism and irredentism, racism, as well as anti-communism.

Ciano's Worldview

Even Ciano's birthplace, Livorno, known as a multicultural, cosmopolitan city, was affected by the increasingly radical nationalism that spread across Europe in the late nineteenth century. The nationalist feeling in the city triggered an antipathy towards France and in particular its control over Corsica. The island, which had been a French territory since 1769, was a thorn in the self-perception of the irredentists, who regarded Corsica as a legitimate part of Italy.[17] Ciano's statements and notes reveal a strong nationalist conviction, an excessive and obsessive love for his country, which he shared with his father and which was strengthened by state propaganda during the First World War.[18] He was convinced that the Italian claims to Corsica were legitimate and believed in the validity of the irredentist movement, which gained increased momentum after the Great War due to the "mutilated victory" mythos.[19] "On a fine winter day," he wrote in 1938, "Corsica seems as though you could hold out your hand and touch it. Ours it is, one of the groups of our islands, inhabited by our people. They can't understand in Livorno why it has to belong to foreigners."[20]

Galeazzo Ciano never doubted that Italy had a right to expand. He was convinced that the future belonged to Italy and the other "young nations," including Japan, Germany, and the United States.[21] This belief should not be interpreted as a genuinely fascist element of his worldview, even if the concept of youth was a central component of fascism. The conviction that only "young" and "rising" nations were the true heirs to the empires of old and must claim their rightful place in the world originated in the late nineteenth century, when it dominated the global imperialism debate and was a central theme in Rudyard Kipling's poem "The White Man's Burden."[22] Therefore, it should come as no surprise that Kipling was among those admired by Italian fascists, including Ciano and Grandi.[23]

Ciano loved Kipling's poem for another reason: it called on the "white peoples" to civilize the inferior and poor peoples of the earth.[24] In Italy this form of cultural imperialism was a product of the racial discourse at the end of the nineteenth century, which was an essential part of the newly created nation-state's attempt to construct a new identity from scratch.[25] The Italians – the self-perceived heirs of the Roman Empire and the Renaissance – believed that it was their task to civilize peoples they deemed to be inferior. The terms "*italianità*" and "*romanità*" were repeatedly used to justify this claim.[26]

The largely unsuccessful colonial campaigns and the increasing nationalism led to a radicalization of this once supposedly philanthropic mission. In order to prove their racial superiority, the "civilizing mission" had to be carried out by all available means. Groups who resisted would be deported, interned, or killed in the name of modernization and progress. Given that the Italians deported hundreds of Libyan families to the Isole Tremiti in 1911, where they were knowingly exposed to starvation and illness, they should not be portrayed as latecomers to the European racial discourse, nor should their culturally connoted racism be misinterpreted as a more humane version.[27] However, it bore an important distinction from how the German National Socialists saw their new *Lebensraum*. Whereas in the Nazi ideology it was clear that millions of natives were to perish in order to make place for Germans, the original idea behind the Italian *spazio vitale* (living space) was more that of a multi-ethnic empire as long as the Italian dogmas dominated.[28]

In recent years, scholars have focused on a biological component of Italian racism.[29] Even though many fascists – among them countless radical anti-Semites like Giovanni Preziosi and Telesio Interlandi – propagated this form, it had by no means replaced the concepts of *romanità* and *italianità*, which appealed to liberals, nationalists, and fascists, including Bottai and Ciano.[30] The latter claimed that it was the Ethiopian conflict that had awakened his "true" racial consciousness.[31] As minister of press and propaganda at the time, Ciano was responsible for the first large-scale racist propaganda campaign against the Ethiopian people.[32] He boasted of freeing the "uncivilized" Ethiopians from the "yoke" of slavery in order to bring them progress and turn them into "civilized savages."[33] Italy, he proudly said, would force civilization upon them by dropping bombs and in so doing avenge the "shame of Adwa."[34] After the war he objected to any "mixing" between Italians and Africans so that the "Italian race ... retains its strong purity."[35] For Ciano, there was never a doubt that the "white" should rule and the "black" serve.[36]

In contrast to Mussolini, however, Ciano did not regard the "black race" as a serious threat because, in his opinion, the Italians were far superior.[37] He believed that the Italians were already "the most intelligent of all," even though he complained every now and then that Italians were only respected for their cultural achievements and not for their fighting skills – an odd complaint, given that he himself was not always convinced of Italy's military achievements and painfully recalled defeats in Larissa (1866) or Adwa (1898).[38]

Nevertheless, Ciano's comments illustrate that Italians were still haunted by their past failures, especially during the age of imperialism, which impelled them to prove their own feeling of superiority in military campaigns.[39] However, Ciano did not want to go as far as

Mussolini, who repeatedly spoke of the necessity to transform Italians into a "true people," a "Nordic people," through wars and deprivation.[40] Whenever the *Duce* reiterated these ideas, Ciano usually made no comment or even rejected them as misguided and dangerous.[41]

These diverging views reveal a significant difference between Mussolini and Ciano. The *Duce* was obsessed with racism and ultra-nationalism, shaped by a social-Darwinian understanding of international relations. The belief that the stronger nation had the right to rule over weaker nations without being bound to moral barriers was a core element of his fascist ideology.[42] He was convinced that only war could bring Italians new greatness. However, if they proved to be weak in conflicts, they had no right to exist after all and would perish.[43] Ciano did not share such an absolutist view. His nationalism was shaped by a more realistic pragmatism and a racial self-perception that, as will be explained, always drove him to look out for Italy's security.

But contrary to what Ciano said, his own understanding of race had already developed before the Ethiopian War and was not limited to a dichotomy between "civilized" Europeans and "barbaric" Africans. During the First World War, he was exposed to war propaganda that dehumanized Italy's enemies, including Germans and Austrians. Studies have shown that children in particular were receptive to this sort of propaganda, which formed and reaffirmed national stereotypes.[44] He spent his youth in multi-ethnic cities like Livorno and Venice, and after lived abroad between 1926 and 1933. Early on he thus came into contact with a variety of foreign cultures and people, which he met with curiosity but also tried to relate to his racial self-perception. As a result, he formed his own racial hierarchy, which included among others the Americans, British, French, Germans, Japanese, and Slavs.[45]

When Ciano talked about the French, he always spoke highly of their culture and history and emphasized the "Latin brotherhood" between the Italians and the French. On the day of the declaration of war against France in June 1940, Ciano thought the whole situation was confusing, irrational, and insane.[46] In the summer of 1940 he even wanted to come to France's rescue after the German Wehrmacht had crushed the French army.[47] But while he honoured a common ancestry, he was also convinced that the "French race" was in a state of decline. He stressed the superiority of the "Italian sister" and made derogatory remarks about the poor constitution of France, which had lost all its former glory and thus no longer had any right to its worldwide possessions.[48] Three factors in particular were responsible for Ciano's ambivalent attitude towards France: first, his upbringing in the francophobic environment of Livorno; second, his belief that France had cheated Italy of its rightful claims after the First World War; and third, his anti-communism, which I will discuss in more detail later.

Ciano often criticized the policies of the governments in London and accused the British of betraying Italy after the First World War. For him, Foreign Minister Anthony Eden in particular personified the British politician who denied the Italians their rightful claims and was also the sort to wage war against Italy. During the Ethiopian War, Ciano orchestrated with the help of Ambassador Grandi a merciless propaganda campaign against Eden, turning him into Italy's "Enemy No. 1."[49] This smear campaign was not only aimed at humiliating Eden; Ciano also sought to turn Britain into a common enemy in order to unite Italians behind the regime during the war. Ciano underestimated the far-reaching consequences of his campaign for British-Italian relations. Concerned US ambassador Breckinridge Long noted: "Every man, woman and child in Italy hates England today … [which] will place a permanent burden on international relations."[50]

Nevertheless, Ciano had no racial bias against Italy's long-standing ally, the British, nor against the Americans. He, unlike Mussolini, respected and almost admired their people.[51] His more positive attitude might be traced back to his anglophile mentor Daniele Varè and to his own father, who was fascinated by the power of the British Royal Navy.[52] Ciano himself admired the greatness of the British Empire and the strength of the Royal Navy. Shortly after Italy entered the Second World War, he acknowledged that the British navy still possessed the "aggressive ruthlessness of the captains and pirates of the seventeenth century."[53] Again and again, he was impressed by the pride, perseverance, tenacity, and determination of the "British race," ignoring the cheap anti-British propaganda that was being transmitted over the air and published in the Italian press during the Second World War.[54]

Ciano's relationship with nations that propagated a biological racism, such as Japan and Nazi Germany, was much more ambivalent, in part because their racial doctrines inevitably clashed with his ideas of *italianità* and *romanità*. Already as Italian consul general in Shanghai in the early 1930s, Ciano encountered the Japanese racial doctrine. As head of the diplomatic commission he witnessed the attack of Japanese forces on the Chinese city in early 1932. In its reports to the League of Nations, the commission blamed Tokyo for the brutal escalation of the conflict as well as for violating international law, and accused Japan of acts of terrorism and indiscriminate executions.[55]

Like many of his compatriots, Ciano mistrusted Tokyo's hegemonic and expansionist policy and was suspicious about Japan's belief in racial superiority.[56] As Japanese racism, which promoted a "Greater East Asia

Co-Prosperity Sphere" under Tokyo's leadership, was not only directed against Asians but also against the West, relations between Tokyo and Rome hit rock bottom when Italian racism became more and more popular in the wake of the Ethiopian conflict.[57] Although Ciano supported Tokyo's ascension to the Axis alliance because he was intrigued by Japan's military power, his distrust of the Japanese remained. In light of Japan's military successes at the turn of 1941–42, he predicted – in contrast to Mussolini – a terrible tragedy for the "white race" should they fail to stop the "yellow race."[58]

Ciano hardly identified with German culture and habits, claiming that the Germans and Italians are "drawn in opposite directions by race, culture, religion, and tastes."[59] Moreover – in contrast to English and French – he did not speak the German language.[60] He repeatedly denounced German racism, the "national formula" of the Nazis, and contrasted it with the Italian concept of *romanità* in order to illustrate the differences between National Socialists and Fascists.[61] He was convinced that the German racial theory posed a threat to the Italian nation, despite – or perhaps because of – his admiration for the achievements, strength, and power of the German people.[62] This fear of German hegemony and dominance surfaced every time Berlin's actions ran counter to Ciano's foreign policy interests, as happened with Dollfuß's murder in 1934, the annexation of Austria in 1938, and the occupation of Prague in 1939.[63] "But is it really a physical necessity for these Teutons," he wrote, "to exasperate the whole human race until its forms a coalition against them?"[64] That Ciano used the anachronism "Teutons," of all things, and thus invoked the Latin saying "*Furor Teutonicus*," spoke volumes. It stood for the unbridled, merciless aggression of the Germanic tribes who always threatened the civilized Roman Empire.[65]

Ciano, of course, was not the first person to resort to these images when criticizing the Germans. In fact, they can be traced back to the writings of Tacitus, including *Germania*, which was read by Ciano, thus illustrating the *longue durée* of these powerful stereotypes.[66] Moreover, the radicalization of the racial discourse in Italy since the late nineteenth century was a reaction to pseudo-scientific insinuations from Germany that the Italian race had lost its former purity through its connection with and influence from North Africa.[67] It culminated during the First World War – in which Ciano's father fought against the Central Powers – when Italian propaganda depicted the Germans as the barbaric Teutonic invaders and as snakes, while *Italia*, portrayed as a Roman warrior, defended Western civilization.[68]

Each time during the Second World War that Ciano received shocking descriptions of how Germans would daily massacre entire populations in their occupation zones, including children and women, he began to form an idea of what German barbarism looked like in the twentieth century.[69] When he personally advocated sending food to Greece to prevent the death of "some million innocent and unfortunate people,"[70] Hermann Göring had nothing but cynicism for Ciano's empathy.[71] As a result of German brutality, Ciano had little sympathy for the German population as a whole. In the spring of 1940, he indifferently predicted a storm from which "not a single German could save himself."[72] He also showed no pity when the number of bomber attacks against the Third Reich increased.[73]

Ciano's negative impression of the German people was mirrored in his opinion of high-ranking German politicians, including Hitler, Göring, and above all Ribbentrop. While he was at first ambivalent, oscillating between the extremes of "dazzler" and "genius," his antipathy towards German politicians significantly increased with the onset of the Second World War and stood in sharp contrast to the public displays of unity and friendship.[74] He criticized them as villains and traitors, questioned their military and political expertise, and called them liars and pigs.[75] He referred to German party leaders as notorious drunkards and cocky "plebeians," deliberately using a word that in ancient Rome described the uneducated, lower class.[76] The intense frictions and complaints against German politicians strengthened his negative stereotypes of the "German race" and vice versa; they are suggestive of an alliance that was defined more by rivalry than cooperation.[77]

Another integral part of the nineteenth century Italian racial discourse was the relationship between the Italians and the Slavic peoples. The Slavs were regarded as "inferior barbarians" and a major enemy that had conspired with the Habsburg Empire against the Italian nation.[78] In the early twentieth century, the resentment towards the Slavic population was further aggravated by a growing anti-communism among Italians.[79] The Slavs were identified as puppets of Moscow, promoting and spreading Bolshevism, which was considered a threat to the Italian nation due to its internationalist doctrine. The anti-Slavic feeling, combined with anti-communism, led to the bogeyman and neologism of *slavobolscevismo*, which was exploited by fascists even before they took control of Rome.[80]

The bogeyman of *slavobolscevismo* also appealed to Ciano, who never doubted that sooner or later the Slavs in the Balkans would have to be Italianized. In the tradition of Italian cultural racism, however, he expected a "peaceful assimilation" of the Slavic peoples without the use of force.[81] He even preferred the Slovenians living in Italy to the Germans in South Tyrol, since they were "quiet" and "modest."[82] Nevertheless, Ciano's impressions of Slavic politicians were shaped more by their political allegiance than by his racial stereotypes. While he advocated a ruthless war against Josip Broz Tito and his communist partisans, he regarded Prime Minister Milan Stojadinović as a true friend and trusted ally.[83]

Also illustrating Ciano's ambivalent relationship with the Slavs was his sympathy for the "great Polish race," which can be explained by several factors:[84] the Polish government had lifted the sanctions that were imposed against Italy during the Ethiopian War only a few days after Ciano's appointment; Poland's population was closely linked to the Italian nation by the Catholic faith; and anti-Bolshevism and belief in an authoritarian style of government were widespread in Poland.[85] Despite his sympathies for the Polish people, Ciano was hardly surprised when he heard about the tensions between the Germans and the Poles. He explained that the latter "inevitably contains all the elements of opposition towards Teutonic imperialism," such as "large nuclei of Jews."[86] But what was Ciano's relationship with Judaism?

Like many of his contemporaries, Ciano often used Jews as scapegoats and accused them of being anti-fascists. However, he also insisted that a Jewish problem did not exist in Italy.[87] Ciano apparently had not adopted the notion of radical anti-Semites who propagated the idea of a separate "Jewish race," a belief based on a biologically and racially connoted image of the "Eternal Jew," which had no strong traditional roots in Italy.[88] Even after the enactment of the Race Laws in November 1938, which included a pseudo-scientific, biological definition of the "Jewish race," Ciano did not change his opinion.[89] While religion and the ideology of Zionism, which he saw as a betrayal of Italian nationalism, remained his key criteria to criticize Jews, he always distinguished between "Italian" and "other" Jews in the years to come.[90]

Ciano's upbringing in Livorno and Venice might account for why he never adopted a biological anti-Semitism. Both cities had a prominent Jewish community that was integrated into the town's social life.[91] Moreover, none of his family members were known as anti-Semites, and Ciano's Catholic education and his mentor Varè might have strengthened his sectarian anti-Judaism.[92] And when we look at Ciano's close circle of friends and co-workers, we can find several people who were married to Jews or even Jews themselves, including Pecci-Blunt and Pietromarchi.[93] Thus, Ciano usually socialized in circles that did not support the physical elimination of "the Jew." His attitude towards the Jews was ambivalent: pragmatic-opportunistic and amoral in general, but under certain circumstances also tolerant and accepting. "Perhaps," he wrote in his diary, "Jews in small doses are necessary to society, just as yeast is necessary to bread."[94]

This form of sectarian anti-Judaism also prevailed among conservative Catholics, members of the royal house, and high-ranking diplomats.[95] Of course, there is the danger of minimizing or denying its terrible consequences for the Jewish community in Italy, especially when it is compared to the anti-Semitism of the Nazis. Yet, we must never forget that this form of anti-Judaism created in Italy a legal vacuum that made indiscriminate persecution possible and destroyed the political, economic, and social status of the Italian Jews.[96] Moreover, the discrimination and persecution of the Jewish population created bureaucratic preconditions such as lists of names, which would later facilitate the deportations and extermination of Jews in the areas under the control of the RSI.[97]

Similar to his antipathy towards Zionism, Ciano also rejected the ideology of communism due to its transnational character and thus its potential threat to the Italian nation.[98] His dislike of communism, however, ran much deeper and was personal. Ciano most likely inherited this attitude from his father and regarded communism as a threat to his social status, his lifestyle, and his wealth, in sum to everything he cherished. Even during his first years abroad, he displayed a strong opposition towards communism. When he was sent as embassy secretary to Beijing in May 1927, the city was in the hands of warlord Zhang Zuolin before being defeated by a war alliance led by Chiang Kai-Shek.[99] Ciano described the conflict between Zhang and Chiang as a completely unnecessary "trouble" (*bega*) and feared, like his superior Varè, that it would weaken the country and give the communists an opportunity to gain more influence in China.[100] In Italy, too, politicians and intellectuals were convinced of the necessity of supporting nationalist China to push back communism in the Far East. In their opinion Chiang Kai-Shek was the right man for this task, given his 1927 denunciation of the "First United Front" with Mao Zedong and his killing of thousands of communists in Shanghai.[101]

Although Ciano never mentioned the Chinese statesman in his diary, it nevertheless seems reasonable to assume that he shared the positive assessment of Chiang Kai-Shek as he pleaded for a closer relationship with nationalist China in the early 1930s.[102] While anti-communism initially offered a common ground for bilateral cooperation between China and Italy, it also led to its dissolution in 1937. Ciano tried to convince his former friend and mastermind of the Xi'an Incident (1936),[103] Zhang Xueliang, not to commit a real crime by forming a "Second United Front" with Mao Zedong in the face of Japanese aggression. His efforts were in vain, and so he offered a harsh verdict on Zhang Xueliang: he was a "man of very limited abilities ... a real bad guy."[104] When in August

1937 a Chinese delegation arrived in Rome and asked for military support, Ciano refused.[105] Instead, he sought a closer relationship to Tokyo and pushed to recognize the Japanese puppet regime in Nanjing under Wang Jingwei as the only legitimate government of China.[106]

Numerous other examples illustrate that anti-communism was a leitmotif of Ciano's diplomacy. Ciano – and not Mussolini – was the true *spiritus rector* of the Italian foreign policy directed against Moscow.[107] His negative verdict on the state of France was the result of socialist Léon Blum's election in June 1936 and the subsequent establishment of a government in Paris that was tolerated by the communists. The Popular Front government in France was, in Ciano's opinion, both a symbol and a consequence of French weakness. His negative assessment only changed when Édouard Daladier took office in Paris in April 1938.[108] His admiration for the British was also based on the fact that he thought the conservative establishment in the United Kingdom could be another ally against the communist world revolution.[109]

Moreover, for Ciano anti-communism was one of the central pillars of Italy's alliance with Japan and Germany.[110] He also sought to form Poland, Hungary, and Yugoslavia into a bulwark against Bolshevism, to be led by Italy. His belief that anti-communism was a common goal of all these countries blinded him to German military aggression against Poland, despite repeated warnings from Ambassador Bernardo Attolico.[111] A German attack against an anti-communist ally was beyond Ciano's imagination; therefore, his angry reaction to the signing of the Hitler-Stalin Pact and the German-Soviet Frontier Treaty should come as no surprise.[112] Even though he admitted that both treaties were "diplomatic masterpieces," he castigated the "monstrous union" as a betrayal of the united struggle against communism and as anti-Rome and anti-Catholic.[113] Despite his anti-communism, Ciano was sceptical about the success of Italy's military contribution to Operation Barbarossa. Nevertheless, publicly he legitimized it using stereotypical anti-communist propaganda, stating: "Not a problem of power politics is decided on this front, but the fate [of] three thousand years of occidental culture ... which Bolshevism has tried and still tries to eradicate in blind fury from the hearts of peoples and from history."[114]

Ciano's Foreign Policy Strategies

How, then, did Ciano intend to achieve his foreign policy goals given his own worldviews and belief in national stereotypes, and what did he view as obstacles to their successful conclusion? At the end of 1937 he wrote in his diary that "on the historical plane a conflict between Italy and Great Britain is inevitable"[115] in order to "break through the crust which is stifling the energy and the aspirations of the young nations."[116] Many scholars have used this statement and other anti-British and downright martial entries in his diary between October 1937 and February 1938 to argue that, like Mussolini, Ciano was only interested in a German-Italian military alliance to wage war against the "degenerated democracies."[117] Consequently, in this telling, Ciano's foreign policy was radically different from the diplomacy of his predecessors. Anyone suggesting otherwise has been accused of apologetic tendencies.[118] Yet, this interpretation has been clouded by a teleological explanation and an exclusively German-Italian focus.

Ciano's bellicose stance towards London makes the most sense when one considers the opposing views of Neville Chamberlain and Anthony Eden over the appropriate Italian policy. Ciano expected a British attack in the event that Eden succeeded in installing a new government in Westminster, a view that was supported by reports he received from his ambassador in London, Grandi.[119] In such a situation he could foresee only one solution – a pre-emptive strike against British positions, even if the chances of success were slim – as he was convinced that due to Italy's military and economic weakness a long war with London would prove fatal for Rome.[120] To avoid such a scenario in the first place, he tried everything in his power to strengthen Chamberlain's position and officially resumed negotiations with London immediately after Eden's resignation on 20 February 1938.[121] Even the British ambassador to the Vatican, Francis D'Arcy Osborne, congratulated Ciano and drank with him to Eden's resignation; and in the United States, Eden's resignation was seen as an important step towards European peace.[122] Thus, Ciano's martial statements in his diary must be interpreted against this political background. Scholars who view them as clear evidence of Ciano's alleged warlike policy against London disregard the historical context as well as Ciano's worldviews. But that still leaves us with the question of how Ciano intended to achieve his foreign policy goals.

Ciano's initial considerations focused around his attempts to isolate France internationally and thereby pressure Paris to hand over the territories he desired for Italy. Such a strategy would only work if Britain abandoned its partnership with Paris in favour of rapprochement with Italy. To convince the British government of the exclusivity of an alliance with Rome, Ciano torpedoed all German-British negotiations and sought rapprochement with Germany as leverage against London.[123] In his opinion, despite his distrust of the German people, Berlin was the logical choice for his strategy for several reasons: Italy and Germany were both "young" nations; they had both committed themselves to the struggle against communism; and they shared authoritarian political systems and an affinity for performative diplomacy. In addition, he was convinced that Berlin and Rome had different spheres of interest and any partnership between them would therefore be free of competitive strife.[124]

In this thinking, a close relationship with Germany was the easiest way to achieve his goals. He was looking for a *modus vivendi* with Berlin, a "parallelization" of German and Italian spheres of interest.[125] But Ciano opposed an exclusive and fundamental long-term military pact with Berlin, unlike Mussolini who was open to such an idea already in the summer of 1938. Not only did he refuse to propose such an alliance, but to the annoyance of Berlin and often against Mussolini's wishes, he rejected such offers from the Germans. He even considered the Pact of Steel, as I will argue, a temporary treaty with Berlin.[126] Several reasons for this behaviour, all deeply rooted in Ciano's personal worldview and national stereotypes, present themselves.

First, he feared as early as May 1936 that Germany was an autocratic and dangerous ally and that Italy would be only a "radiant second" at Berlin's side – which, of course, ran counter to his own perception of Italy's greatness.[127] Second, as recently as the annexation of Austria he realized that Berlin's geostrategic interests actually did impinge on his own goals, contrary to his original assumptions and German assurances. He recognized an alarming increase in German activities in many of the areas he considered to be within Italy's sphere, including the Balkans, South America, and South Tyrol. In addition, Berlin often kept Ciano in the dark about their plans and intentions, confirming the stereotypes Ciano harboured towards the Germans and, consequently, undermining any effort to establish trust.[128] Third, he feared that a military pact with Germany would forfeit Italy's autonomy, which Ciano – a believer in the *peso determinante* strategy – viewed as Rome's strength on the international stage. It would further push London closer to Paris, making it nearly impossible to isolate France, thus destroying his plan for "diplomatic expansion."[129]

To preserve Italy's autonomy from the Third Reich in the future, Ciano pursued a double strategy: First, he intended to sign bilateral treaties with other revisionist nations rather than integrate them into the Anti-Comintern Pact or the Pact of Steel.[130] Agreements with Poland, Hungary, Romania, Yugoslavia, and Spain were intended to build a "vertical" Axis and underpin the rapprochement with Germany. In his opinion, these treaties would protect against German hegemony in Europe and also function as an additional threat towards London and Paris.[131] Second, unlike Mussolini, who had long since turned away from the British, Ciano did not want to close the door on London.[132]

Not only did he admire the "British race," but London played an important role in his plan to build an Italian Empire. He wanted to convince the British, through a "strong and menacing" policy, that reconciliation with Italy even on his terms would be beneficial for London. He somehow had no doubt that this strategy would work. After all, how could London not prefer realpolitik to war?[133] Consequently, he considered the Gentleman's Agreement of 1937 and the Easter Agreement of 1938 as calculable and gratifying successes of his policy and as a way to strengthen the long-standing friendship with London.[134]

Parts of Ciano's early diplomatic strategy are reminiscent of his behaviour in domestic politics: ad hoc alliances with various groups were intended to secure, expand, and strengthen Italy's power, and these coalitions should be flexible in order to preserve Italy's freedom of manoeuvre in a dynamically changing world. Due to his racial self-perception, Ciano demanded that other states treat Rome in a non-condescending manner. After all, in his opinion a stable alliance could function only if it was formed between equal partners and based on mutual understanding, trust, and empathy.[135] While his thinking might have been successful domestically, given that the entire Italian political system operated according to similar rules, this strategy was problematic at the international level, especially on two fronts.

Ciano's Italian-centric worldview and overestimation of Italy's influence on the world stage blinded him to the plans and intentions of other states and led him to focus on individual, powerful nation-states, thus rejecting international organizations such as the League of Nations and treating smaller states and their representatives in a condescending manner.[136] The fact that the League of Nations offered smaller states the opportunity to express themselves on an equal basis and thus to have a say in politics was foreign to his understanding of power and race.[137] Moreover, during his time in Shanghai he realized first-hand that the League of Nations was unable to restrain aggressive imperialist powers like Japan.[138] Ciano's ideas more closely resemble the nineteenth century concept of a "concert of the great powers" than the reality of European diplomacy after the First World War. He evidently did not realize that smaller states were important for a successful *peso determinante* policy. As a result, his foreign policy was dominated by one paradigm: power.[139]

Moreover, Ciano's premise of a dynamic foreign policy also proved disastrous, because it would necessarily lead to armed conflict with the West, whose policies were committed to preserving the status quo. But Ciano was afraid of a military clash with the West – especially with an Anglo-American alliance – and hoped that it would never happen.[140]

Even if he did not theoretically rule out a war in November 1937, there is no convincing evidence that he was working towards one. Rather, he desired to avoid a prolonged conflict, mainly because he believed it would only put Italy's existence and his dream of an Italian Empire at risk. Thus, it should not come as a surprise that Ciano tried on many occasions, including the Ethiopian War, the Sudeten Crises, the invasion of Albania, and Germany's attack on Poland, to prevent a war against the West.[141] Ciano's chauvinistic arrogance, on the one hand, and his reluctance to start a military conflict, on the other, illustrate his dilemma. He was caught between the drive of his self-perception and the lack of available resources. Ciano knew that, after the Ethiopian War and the intervention in Spain, Italy lacked the economic, financial, and military means necessary to overcome the West in armed conflict.[142] Thus, he always needed to walk a thin line between putting enough pressure on the West to achieve Italian goals without risking the outbreak of an armed conflict. But how far would he go? And would he manoeuvre Italy into a position from which there was no turning back?

The meeting between Ciano, Hitler, and Ribbentrop on 11 and 12 August 1939 in Salzburg was a serious blow to Ciano's strategy. In light of the increasing tension between Germany and Poland, Ciano had travelled to Austria to discuss a "project for a world peace conference" and convince the Germans that "the outbreak of war at this time would be folly."[143] Yet, during the conversation, which according to Ciano took place in a tense and cold atmosphere, he finally had to acknowledge that the Germans were driven by an unwavering will to war and the "demon of destruction."[144] Ciano wrote in his diary that he realized "there is no longer anything that can be done ... [Hitler] has decided to strike and strike he will. All our arguments will not in the least avail to stop him."[145] This event was often described as Ciano's personal "Damascus experience." Consequently, the young minister apparently burned all bridges with Germany and committed himself to preserving European peace. This interpretation still dominates the Italian public remembrance and was, for example, dramatically depicted in the film *Mussolini and I*.[146] Conversely, some historians claimed that Ciano still unconditionally supported Mussolini's war policy against the West.[147] Neither of these judgments, however, do justice to Ciano's character.

Ciano skilfully used the talks in Salzburg – and the alleged betrayal of the Germans – to cover up his own naivety, while at the same time he avoided completely abandoning his foreign policy aims.[148] Documents reveal that he still intended to build a new Italian Empire without entering into an existentially threatening war against the West. Ciano thus found it necessary to adapt his strategy to fit the new circumstances.

He vehemently advocated a policy of *non belligeranza*, as he no longer regarded Germany as an asset but only as a danger to the Italian *spazio vitale*.[149] The concerns he had expressed in May 1936 now dominated his actions, and he focused on ways to achieve his goals with the help of the Western powers. His commitment to the *non belligeranza* policy, however, must not be misunderstood as a trend to pacifism. On the contrary, Ciano sought to provoke a revolution in Yugoslavia with the help of Croatian separatists in order to strengthen Italy's influence in the Balkans. Nevertheless, unlike Mussolini, he preferred to act with British and French consent.[150]

Furthermore, Ciano tried to separate Rome from Berlin to restore Italy's former "liberty ... which German hegemony would compromise for centuries."[151] Consequently, Ciano was intrigued when in September 1939 the Romanian foreign minister Grigore Gafencu proposed to him a Balkan Bloc led by Italy. He believed that such a pact would help him to achieve several of his objectives in one swoop. It would prevent a German and Soviet incursion into southeastern Europe and strengthen Italy's presence in the region. However, after German pressure, Mussolini completely abandoned any plans concerning the Balkan Bloc. By contrast, Ciano's attitude remained temperate, and he chose not to inform the Romanian foreign minister about the *Duce*'s abrupt turnaround.[152] He speculated that Gafencu might be able to persuade other states to support his ideas, which might induce Mussolini to change his opinion once again.[153] While Gafencu continued to negotiate with several states in the Balkans and the Danube regions, Ciano established closer ties with Hungary. In his opinion, Budapest was an ideal ally because the Hungarian government was staunchly anti-Bolshevik and anti-German.[154] Again, it should not come as a surprise that Germany did not approve of Hungarian-Italian rapprochement. Italy was soon forced to stand back and watch as Berlin used its economic power to block any further cooperation between Hungary and Italy.[155]

Ciano's behaviour during the phase of *non belligeranza* suggests a slight shift in his foreign policy strategy. Until then, strength and military power dominated his thinking and guided his actions. Both the West and the German Axis partner knew how important power was for Ciano, not least because he himself toyed with it again and again.[156] Thus, German diplomats were certain that he would rejoin the Axis camp should the military successes continue.[157] However, Ciano adhered to the *non belligeranza* policy longer than many members of the fascist elite, the army leadership, and even the Italian public.[158] While Ciano had to acknowledge the German successes, he still did not believe in a final victory for Berlin. He balked at reports about German victories and resisted the changing Italian opinion that favoured an interventionist stance.[159] Ciano's diary gives us at least some insights into his thoughts in this regard: He considered the "German race" the real danger to Italy and felt personally insulted, betrayed, and humiliated during the meeting in August 1939. He saw his worst stereotypes of the Germans confirmed and began to lash out against all the German traitors, calling them "sinister beings," "parvenus," and "drunkards."[160] Moreover, he was more attached to the Western lifestyle and appreciated the Western diplomats' willingness to negotiate, their honesty, and their sincerity. These traits he had once dismissed as weaknesses, but now he welcomed them as an antithesis to German lies and frauds.[161] In addition, family tragedies (the death of his father in June and the death of his beloved sister in October 1939) may have altered his character. Some of his confidants, such as Giuseppe Bottai, discovered a new side of Ciano, acknowledging that he had become "more intimate" and almost "lovable."[162] Even though Ciano was still fascinated by power and its use, his personal losses may have made him realize that he was no longer willing to pay any price.

Italy's entry into the war in June 1940 not only sealed the fate of Ciano's previous foreign policy strategy; it also decreased the influence of the Foreign Ministry and gave the general staff and the War Ministry more control. Even though Ciano's plans to establish an Italian Empire through "diplomatic expansion" had ultimately failed, he still wanted to establish Italy as a global player – and once again he sought to achieve this objective at the expense of France. This policy becomes clear when one looks at the Italian war aims of the summer of 1940, which were mainly written by Ciano and were explicitly directed against French and (some) British possessions.[163] He also tried to influence the regime's war policy by propagating attacks against French possessions such as Corsica and blocking attacks against British territories such as Malta.[164] Moreover, he never regarded Vichy France as an equal ally, but instead saw it as Rome's "vassal," which had no choice but to comply with Italy's demands.[165] Berlin, however, had other plans: as the relationship between Italy and Germany became more and more problematic, the Nazi regime sought to expand their alliance system by strengthening its ties to countries like Vichy France and Hungary. Thus, a further weakening of those countries was not in the interests of Berlin. Ciano feared that Vichy and other countries within the fascist cosmos could supersede Italy as Berlin's primary partner, which in turn would jeopardize Italy's chances for territorial expansion.[166]

During the first year of Italy's participation in the war, Ciano's mood changed almost daily. With each Axis victory, he hoped to create the long-desired *spazio vitale* and secure it through a peaceful compromise.

Despite these doses of optimism, Ciano still feared that the war would drag on, particularly if Washington became involved on behalf of the British.[167] Even in the first months of the war, Ciano persisted in viewing every failure and defeat as proof that his pessimism was justified. On 11 and 12 November 1940, the Royal Air Force launched a devastating attack on the port of Taranto, bombed the Albanian city of Durrës, and set its *Azienda Generale Italiana Petroli* (AGIP) plants on fire. It was by far the heaviest blow Britain had delivered against Italy and the first sign that the West still possessed considerable military strength after the French capitulation.[168]

Ciano's doubts were further reinforced during the terrible course of the Greek campaign.[169] Nevertheless, he again and again clung to positive reports from the front, hoping that the Axis might still be victorious and Italy could at least partially achieve its goals.[170] Beginning in the second half of 1941, however, his pessimism slowly outweighed his optimism, which he still voiced in the presence of ministerial colleagues, Italian deputies, senators, and allies.[171] After the United States entered the war, he suffered no illusions about the true balance of power between the Axis and the Allies. Especially after the Allies' victories in North and East Africa, he was convinced that Italy could no longer achieve its imperial ambitions and even predicted that Italy, the "Achilles' heel of the Axis," would become the "centre of attack by the Allies."[172] Now, even at official meetings of the Axis, he did not hold back his pessimism, and in January 1943 he fatalistically commented on the hopeless situation in his diary:[173] "I have the impression that the Axis is like a man who is trying to cover himself with a blanket that is too small. His head is cold if he wants to warm his feet, and his feet freeze if he wants to keep his head warm."[174]

Although such mood swings were hardly new, Ciano again adjusted his foreign policy strategy, deviating from his original objectives as he recognized the direct threat to Italy's security.[175] He renounced the creation of an Italian Empire in order to preserve Italy's national integrity. In contrast to a defiant *Duce*, Ciano had given up all hope of acquiring Italy's *spazio vitale*.[176] In the face of defeat, he had another more pressing question on his mind: How could an attack on Italy be prevented or at least delayed? In his search for an answer, he initially focused on the militant Arab and Indian independence movements in the British colonies. He wanted to help them build their own armies in order to put pressure on London, hoping that it might avert or delay an attack on Italy.[177] When this strategy failed, there was only one way for him to save his homeland from invasion: Italy had to end its alliance with Berlin and make a separate peace with the West.

While the search for a potential peace settlement occupied him during his last months as foreign minister and his time as ambassador to the Vatican, he began to subtly undermine the cooperation with Germany and other fascist regimes. Often in collaboration with diplomats and officers of the Royal Army, he attempted to assert Italian supremacy in the Balkans at the expense of the Germans and Croatians by advocating for a more moderate occupation policy and supporting arrangements with the Slovenes and the Serbs.[178] Moreover, Ciano stalled the handover of Italian Jews when German authorities demanded their extradition in the spring of 1942. In the second half of 1942 he also blocked the deportation of French Jews from Italian-occupied areas, although the Vichy government requested their transfer, and he extended the protection to Slavic Jews through a generous interpretation of who was entitled to Italian citizenship.[179] By recognizing the right of the Jews who lived in the annexed Balkan territories to Italian citizenship, Ciano in turn legitimized Italy's claim to these regions. Even though the motives of Ciano and his close associates are still debated, two conclusions are certain: First, the more moderate attitude towards the Jews demonstrated a break with Berlin, which pushed for the "Final Solution," while Rome might have hoped for "a sort of remission of sentence for good behavior"[180] after the Second World War. Second, Ciano's obstructionism did not escape the Germans' notice. The *Palazzo Chigi*'s intransigence prompted the German authorities to regard Ciano as the main opponent of the "Final Solution" on the Italian side.[181]

Diplomacy and Performance

Ciano initially intended to use ultimatums, intimidation, and threats, rooted in power and strength, to achieve his dream of an Italian Empire.[182] This idea derived from more than just his personal belief in Italian superiority; numerous examples of such a strategy's success were all around him, including how his father seized power in Livorno and the legendary "March on Rome." But given Italy's economic, financial, and military weakness and Ciano's initial reluctance to enter into inflexible military alliances, he had to find other means to implement his strategy of strength.

To solve this dilemma, he relied on a performative diplomacy to publicly construct Italy's strength and power – its military capabilities, its economic strength, its national unity behind the regime, and its solidarity and friendship with powerful allies, above all Germany. Historians Paul Baxa and Christian Goeschel have recently published groundbreaking studies on the role the performative dimension played in the relationship between Italy and Germany, which predominantly focus on the meetings between and the personalities of Benito Mussolini and Adolf Hitler.[183] A study of Ciano's performative foreign policy and how it related to Mussolini's strategy is still missing.

While many of Ciano's worldviews and theoretical considerations were rooted in the traditional Italian foreign policy of the nineteenth century, it was his love of parades, ceremonies, and festivities that radically distinguished him from his predecessors and replaced a more substantial form of diplomacy with a performative one. As an admirer of futuristic art and the potential of modern mass media, and as former minister of propaganda, Ciano was well versed in the potential advantages of performative politics.[184]

To guarantee that all major Italian news outlets would report on his trips and diplomacy in order to convince a national and international audience of Italy's strength – an essential prerequisite for a successful performative diplomacy – Ciano was always accompanied by an entourage of journalists. His close proximity to the journalists often allowed him to edit their reports, as he was less interested in a factual description of events than in the effect he could generate through them.[185] The performative foreign policy and the subsequent reporting also allowed him to capitalize on supposed results much faster, no matter how insignificant. The display of international successes enabled him, in turn, to sideline rivals, expand his own position of power in Italy, and satisfy this demand for recognition at home and abroad.[186]

Performative Foreign Policy in Peacetime

Ciano believed that Italy had only one option to break out of its international isolation: Germany.[187] In order to show the new solidarity and friendship between both countries to a national and international audience, Ciano took his first official trip abroad to Germany in October 1936, where he met several dignitaries of the Nazi regime, including Adolf Hitler, Hermann Göring, and Joachim von Ribbentrop.[188] The visit, the first official meeting between high-ranking officials of both countries after the end of the Ethiopian War, was an important milestone in the Italian-German rapprochement. It was Ciano's task to determine if Berlin was really the key for Italy to become a great power.

Ciano was greeted by an enthusiastic crowd and a colourful program, which was intended to convince him of Germany's unity and power. It included various parades, a wreath-laying ceremony at the German War Memorial (an unmissable sign that Italy and Germany had buried their past enmity), a performance by the Hitler Youth, and a show in Ciano's honour in the Berlin *Sportpalast*.[189] Ciano was particularly impressed when he visited the German Air Force in Gatow.[190] The Germans also wanted to flatter Ciano by showing their respect for the "Italian sense of pride" and emphasizing how important Rome was as a partner for Germany. Even small gestures, such as the performance of the opera *Don Giovanni* in Munich, were key to achieving this goal.[191] The German government spared no expense and effort to give their Italian guest a unique welcome, spending around 43,000 Reichsmarks just to decorate squares and streets in Munich.[192]

Ciano also believed in the power of symbols to showcase the special bond between the two nations. On his arrival he wore the uniform of the fascist militia, which not only expressed the importance of ideology and militarism in Italy but also underlined his own masculinity, his position within the regime, and his past as a *squadrista*. The militia uniform, which Ciano wore at all public events during his visit, was also intended to symbolize his proximity to militaristic Germany. But wearing the uniform of a paramilitary unit – a central characteristic of fascist movements[193] – also sent a clear message to the international audience. It publicly emphasized the similarity between Rome and Berlin in opposition to the Western democracies.

From the beginning of the Italian-German rapprochement, clothing played an important role. When Hitler visited Mussolini in 1934, the *Duce* complained that Hitler had shown up in a "wrinkled trench coat" instead of a military uniform.[194] When Mussolini and Ciano visited Germany three years later, Ciano explained to his staff that the Italian delegation "must look more Prussian than the Prussians" and had extra uniforms made for them.[195] He would wear either his fascist militia or his flying uniform to almost all public rallies with high-ranking members of the Nazi regime to underline his attachment to German militarism. Nevertheless, there is one important exception: when Ciano met Hitler and Ribbentrop in August 1939 and wanted to convince them of the necessity of peace, many published photographs also showed him in civilian dress (figure 7).[196] This unusual contrast to his other public appearances in the presence of German politicians reinforces the impression that he sought to express his opposition to the looming war through his choice of clothing.[197]

Ciano's trip to Germany in 1936 was the successful dress rehearsal for what would define the future relationship between Italy and Germany. Berlin used Ciano's visit to test various rituals and ceremonies that would eventually become key elements of the performative diplomacy between Rome and Berlin – and the effort definitely paid off. Ciano and Mussolini were deeply impressed and satisfied by the treatment

Figure 7. Joachim von Ribbentrop (left) and Galeazzo Ciano (right) at Castle Fuschl, August 1939. Ullstein Bild #00256990.

the young foreign minister had received. After hearing Ciano's report, the *Duce* was convinced that his instincts of pursuing a rapprochement with Berlin were right, and he immediately let the national and international public know by proclaiming the Rome-Berlin Axis in November. What was still missing, of course, was a face-to-face meeting between Hitler and Mussolini that would blot out the memory of the awkward meeting in Venice in 1934.

The opportunity occurred in September 1937 when Ciano and Mussolini went to Germany.[198] The visit was similar to Ciano's trip a few months earlier, but this time everything was even more magnificent. The streets and squares of Munich were decorated with Italian and German flags, and a triumphal arch with the M-emblem of the *Duce* had been erected at the Karlsplatz. Reich stage designer Benno von Arent had transformed Berlin into a theatre stage for over a month. In addition to talks with Hitler and officials of the Third Reich, the agenda for the trip was once again packed with many symbolic events, including wreath-laying ceremonies, numerous parades, the award of the Golden Great Cross of the German Eagle Order to Mussolini and Ciano, a visit to the Krupp factory in Essen, and observation of the German army's autumn manoeuvres in Mecklenburg.[199] The tight security measures made sure that jubilant people greeted them everywhere.[200]

The enormous effort made by the Germans paid dividends. Mussolini's long-time mistress Margherita Sarfatti was visibly shocked when she saw how pleased the *Duce* was after his return to Italy.[201] Also Ciano was once again overwhelmed by the reception, the cheering crowds, and the choreographies. He praised the unity of the German people and the Wehrmacht, and told the German ambassador Hassell that he was "extraordinarily impressed and that his expectations were far exceeded."[202] The Germans had apparently succeeded in creating "a new, emotional image: the friendship between the two dictators and their peoples."[203] At this point, everything that mattered for the Italian delegation and the German hosts was the display of friendship and unity between Italy and Germany to the world.[204]

Ciano's visit to Berlin in May 1939 for the signing of the Pact of Steel followed the established routine. Once again, the Germans went to great lengths to impress their Italian guest with a staging planned down to the last detail.[205] An exchange-student delegation from the Italian *Balilla* welcomed the guest, and Ribbentrop personally hosted a magnificent dinner gala in Ciano's honour.[206] But, evidently, the Germans did not meet their own expectations. Immediately after the visit, a dispute broke out between Goebbels and Ribbentrop, who accused the Ministry of Propaganda of mistakes and sloppiness.[207] Ciano, however, was not aware of any disagreements; on the contrary, he was impressed by the "spontaneous" and "great demonstration" in his honour and visibly enjoyed the cheering crowds.[208]

The Italian state visits to Germany were mirrored whenever high-ranking German officials came to Italy. For example, Göring's and Ribbentrop's visits to Rome between 1937 and 1939 followed the established pattern. Ciano, who often personally took over the organization of such visits, was anxious to entertain and impress his guests in different ways. The repertoire included performances by fascist youth groups, enthusiastic crowds, wreath-laying ceremonies, as well as magnificent evening banquets.[209] Ciano not only wanted to imitate what he had experienced in Germany; rather, he used every opportunity to outdo the Germans in order to convince them of Italy's greatness, stress the country's claims and goals, and convince foreign countries of the strength, solidarity, and friendship of the Axis. By doing so, however, he sometimes overstepped the mark into the grotesque and absurd. When Ribbentrop came to Italy in May 1939, Ciano served him the best French sparkling wine, though he labelled it as an Italian product.[210]

An excellent example of Ciano's strategy is Adolf Hitler's visit in the late spring of 1938. As early as November 1937 a committee was set up under Ciano's chairmanship to plan the details.[211] Hitler arrived on 3 May 1938 at Ostiense station in Rome, which had been massively rebuilt just for this occasion. His trip into the city took him past the pyramid of Caius Celsius, the Palatine, the Colosseum, the Via dell'Impero, the Quirinal Palace, and 300,000 cheering Romans. Extensive reconstruction had been carried out along the route so that Hitler did not form a negative impression of the capital.[212] Ciano intended to make the *Führer* aware of the historical legacy of the Roman Empire and by doing so stress Italy's aspirations for a new empire. Exercises with live ammunition by all three branches of the Italian military complemented the numerous parades and ceremonies by fascist organizations.[213] Since many German experts questioned the capability of the Italian armed forces, Ciano, and with him the Italian press, attached great importance to these exercises. Furthermore, Italian culture – from painting to architecture to music – was presented as the most important art of past and present during a separate visit to Florence, Hitler's favourite Italian city.[214] In order to ensure that everything went smoothly, a large contingent of Italian and German security forces was sent to the city. Individuals whose fascist convictions were not guaranteed were removed, and the local Jewish population was forced to leave Florence. Thus, it comes as no surprise that the remaining residents hailed and celebrated both dictators.[215]

Paul Baxa's analysis of fascist diplomacy demonstrates that, although no treaty was signed, once again the enormous effort had shown the whole world that the Axis continued to exist despite Italy's anger over Germany's annexation of Austria.[216] Nevertheless, he misses one important point: Ciano also used the visit to show that Italy was not a "junior partner" to Germany. By impressing his German guests, he wanted to convince them of the benefits and advantages of cooperation with Rome.[217] Additionally, the Italian people also had to be convinced of Italy's equal role within the Axis following Austria's *Anschluss*. This objective was symbolically reflected in the flagging of the streets and public buildings. While throughout the country an even number of German and Italian flags could be found, in South Tyrol mainly Italian flags were displayed.[218] It was a clear sign to the German delegation and to the Italians that the fascist regime regarded South Tyrol as an integral part of Italy.

It would, however, cement a teleological-deterministic interpretation of Ciano's foreign policy if we only examine his performative diplomacy through the Berlin-Rome lens. In fact, he used it in his dealings with other authoritarian regimes and with the Western democracies. Whenever Ciano met representatives of other authoritarian regimes, including Hungary and Poland, similar behavioural patterns can be observed. Whether it was Ciano's receptions in Budapest between 1936 and 1939 or his trip to Warsaw in 1939 – he was welcomed everywhere by large and enthusiastic crowds, received with great honours, and entertained to the best of his hosts' abilities.[219] In return, Ciano personally took care of the details of the ceremonial and entertainment programs when head of states or governments such as Admiral Horthy travelled to Italy.[220] Ciano usually wore his fascist militia or his aviator uniform during public meetings and receptions. These receptions were also intended to show the friendship with like-minded governments and demonstrate the unity and solidarity of a "vertical" Axis as well as its demands to a national and international audience.[221] However, Ciano did not only have Western democracies in mind. He also wanted to stress Rome's autonomous position within the fascist cosmos vis-à-vis Berlin and by doing so turn his idea of a "vertical" Axis into reality.

A special relationship existed between Ciano and the Yugoslav prime minister Milan Stojadinović. From the beginning, both were on good terms, which formed the basis of the Italian-Yugoslav rapprochement between 1937 and 1939.[222] Their meetings in Yugoslavia and Italy were intended to publicly display their intimate friendship and show the solidarity between their two peoples, an image that was repeatedly evoked in the Italian media.[223] A closer look reveals that Ciano and Stojadinović relied on similar rituals and symbolic gestures to those that played a key role in the relationship between Rome and Berlin.[224]

Nevertheless, there were also significant differences. While Ciano usually wore his military or militia uniform when he met with German politicians in public, he dressed in civilian clothes in Stojadinović's presence. This sartorial choice illustrates that he viewed the relationship with Yugoslavia as separate from Rome's dealings with Berlin and other authoritarian regimes. Moreover, Mussolini only played a secondary role in the rapprochement between Rome and Belgrade. He only met Stojadinović once, and while the talks were conducted in a friendly atmosphere, the *Duce* never expressed the same interest in his guest from Belgrade as Ciano did, suggesting Mussolini's focus on the Axis in contrast to Ciano's more flexible diplomacy. And last but not least, Ciano's demonstrations of solidarity and friendship were not just for show as with the Germans.

Stojadinović became Ciano's closest and most trusted ally in the Balkans. He wanted to back him at all costs and predicted that

Stojadinović would become the true dictator of Yugoslavia. In pursuit of this goal, Ciano was even prepared to negotiate a compromise for the Slovenes living in Italy.[225] He attached so much importance to his friendship with Stojadinović that he considered dividing Albania between Italy and Yugoslavia to consolidate Stojadinović's position at home.[226] He was proud that he had initiated a fundamental revision of Italian-Yugoslav relations and that Rome would replace Paris as Belgrade's closest partner in the future.[227] A good partnership would not only undermine the French security system in Europe; it would also prevent the expansion of German and communist influence in southeastern Europe.[228]

There are no words to describe Ciano's surprise and shock when Prince Regent Paul of Yugoslavia deposed Milan Stojadinović in early February 1939.[229] Stojadinović's authoritarian style and his inability to find a solution with the leader of the Croatian minority, Vladko Maček, were key factors in his expulsion.[230] Stojadinović was placed under house arrest, and Dragiša Cvetković was appointed as his successor. Ciano's Balkan policy, which was based entirely on his friendship with Stojadinović, thus collapsed, leading him to acknowledge that the "Yugoslavia card" had lost "90 per cent of its value."[231] He also feared that Berlin might benefit from the new power balance in the Balkans. To limit the negative consequences for Italy, he immediately contacted the Croatian minority and supported it with financial aid.[232]

Ciano also used performative diplomacy to display Italy's power on a global level. In his opinion, the perfect forum to do so was the Anti-Comintern Pact. He called the pact an "alliance of three military empires," a "pact of giants," which should replace the League of Nations with a new kind of international order.[233] His confidence in the pact was emphasized by Italy's subsequent withdrawal from the League of Nations, which happened relatively late when we consider Ciano's anti-League rhetoric;[234] additionally, a photograph taken after Italy officially joined the pact in Rome in November 1937 was subsequently published in the press (figure 8). It showed Ciano and the German as well as the Japanese delegates in bourgeois suits instead of military uniforms. This dress code was intended to support the public statement Ciano gave at the ceremony to the effect that Italy's sole aim is to protect peace and civilization against the communist threat.[235] The assertion that the Anti-Comintern Pact would not be toothless like the League of Nations was also captured in the same photograph: Benito Mussolini stood in the middle of the group as the symbolic centre of the alliance. He was also the only one who wore a military uniform to stress the belligerent nature of his regime and of the pact. Rome, the location

Figure 8. Italy joined the Anti-Comintern Pact in November 1937 (from left to right: Ulrich von Hassell, Joachim von Ribbentrop, Benito Mussolini, Masaaki Hotta, Galeazzo Ciano). AKG Images #192399.

of the ceremony, was also intended to emphasize the special role and position of Fascist Italy within the alliance, although Italy was in reality the economically and militarily weakest member of the alliance.

Also, in numerous meetings with representatives of the Western powers, Ciano used performative diplomacy, displaying Italy's self-importance and its willingness to fight – he wanted to force the West to give into his demands by constructing the image of a powerful and determined country.[236] One example that illustrates this behaviour is the run-up to the Munich Conference in 1938. On 13 September 1938 Chamberlain directly contacted Hitler in order to negotiate a peaceful solution to the Second Sudeten Crisis. Even though Rome harshly criticized Chamberlain's willingness to negotiate as a "liquidation of the English prestige," the Italian government could not deny the fact that a key issue in European affairs might be solved without Rome's participation. The *Duce* tried to strike back with martial rhetoric. He used the *Popolo d'Italia* to attack the government in Prague, called for the Sudeten Germans' right to self-determination by exactly restating Hitler's views, and gave orders to prepare for war.[237] Yet Mussolini never truly believed in the outbreak of a European war over the Sudetenland. The sabre rattling instead served the purpose of bringing Italy back to the negotiating table and putting pressure on the West by demonstrating his absolute faithfulness to his alliance with Hitler.[238]

Ciano helped to create this imaginary military build-up by encouraging the Hungarian government to exert additional pressure on Czechoslovakia and claiming that the Italians were awaiting the rising storm with calm and strength.[239] On 28 September he informed British Ambassador Perth that "hostilities are to begin today ... When I add that nevertheless the Duce has accepted Chamberlain's request and has proposed a delay of 24-hours, he bursts into a sobbing laugh and rushes off to his Embassy"[240] This episode highlights Ciano's character and is revealing about his approach to diplomacy. Although he possessed no specific information on how Paris and London would react should Germany attack, and although he knew that Rome was not prepared for a European war, he did not want to show any weakness. Consequently, he tried to create the image of a strong and determined Italian nation and therefore deliberately dramatized the situation in order to stress the importance of Italian intervention.[241] Before Ciano met Perth, he had learned that Berlin planned to attack Czechoslovakia on 1 October and not on 28 September, as he told the British ambassador.[242]

Yet, behind the scenes Ciano had begun to calm the situation in order to increase the chances for possible negotiations. He asked the Hungarians to moderate their behaviour shortly after he had incited them.[243] But in the end, it was the demonstration of friendship with Berlin and of power and strength, no matter how fictitious and constructed it was, that did produce Ciano's desired outcome: namely, Italy's return to the concert of great European powers after London officially asked Mussolini to act as mediator.[244] The subsequent newsreel by LUCE about the Munich Conference then highlighted that all the present powers had agreed on the *Duce*'s proposal, stressing the important role Mussolini and Italy had played during the negotiations.[245] Ciano and Mussolini can be seen dressed in their fascist militia uniforms, underlining once again their masculinity and Italy's fictitious readiness to fight and thus indirectly threatening the West.[246]

Another example occurred on 30 November 1938 when Ciano invited the new French ambassador in Rome, André François-Poncet, to attend one of his speeches in the Chamber of Deputies. In a *tour d'horizon*, Ciano, dressed in his militia uniform, glorified Italy's strength and loyalty to Germany and stressed that Italy, despite its peaceful politics during the Munich Conference, was capable of successfully confronting any military challenges.[247] When Ciano mentioned the "natural aspirations of Italy," his speech was interrupted by heckling. Numerous deputies stood and shouted, "Tunis, Djibouti, Corsica, Nice."[248] Most Italians welcomed the scandal, which is not surprising considering that these demands were not rooted in fascist megalomania but enjoyed broad social support in the national-conservative milieu.[249] The whole situation, which was orchestrated by Ciano, was reminiscent of a scandal in the League of Nations on 30 June 1936, when on Ciano's behalf Italian journalists had disrupted the speech of the Ethiopian Emperor Haile Selassie by singing fascists songs, shouting "Long live the *Duce*!" and blowing whistles.[250]

However, Ciano did not trust that the calls for "Tunis, Djibouti, Corsica, Nice" alone would cause storms of enthusiasm among the population. With the support of other ministries he organized anti-Italian protests in Tunis and Corsica to incite the Italians and unite them behind his demands.[251] Ciano hoped to generate consensus within Italy and wanted to show the Italians that the Axis would be beneficial not only for Germany but also for Italy's ambitions – after the Munich Conference he wanted to force Paris to accept a similar agreement in order to satisfy Italy's territorial claims.[252] An irritated François-Poncet and the government in Paris were outraged and felt vindicated in their worst fears. In January 1939 Daladier rushed to Corsica, Tunis, and Algeria to emphasize France's claim to these regions – by doing so, he showed that democrats were also aware of the importance of performative politics.[253]

In the spring of 1939 Ciano realized that his plans to isolate France through performative diplomacy had failed. Neither the Anti-Comintern Pact nor the ratification of the Easter Agreement had brought him closer to his goal. Chamberlain's profession of faith to France in February 1939 was a clear sign of his failure.[254] Ciano's continued desire to blackmail France, through a synchronized display of Italy's strength and solidarity with Berlin, into handing over its territories made him finally receptive to Ribbentrop's idea of a military pact. The subsequent negotiations ultimately led to the naive signing of the bilateral Pact of Steel in Berlin in May 1939 – an alliance that ran contrary to Ciano's previous policy.[255] After all his other strategies had failed, he was convinced that with such "an instrument we could get whatever we want."[256] While Italy's willingness to sign an offensive, military alliance was paramount for the German government, Ciano, for his part, trusted Germany's verbal assurance to not start a war for at least the next three years, but he did not insist on including this assurance in the text of the pact. Given Ciano's negative stereotypes towards Germans and his distrust of German politicians after they often kept him in the dark about their own intentions and actions, the omission was a very "recklessness incompatible with solid diplomatic practice."[257] Ciano, however, was unconcerned; he believed the Axis was now so strong that all their demands would be granted in a "peaceful" manner and all the other major European powers would seek to avoid an armed conflict.[258] He was also convinced that Italy needed at least nine to ten years before Rome could even think about engaging in another war. Thus, he substantially extended the *Duce*'s three-year peace period, making any concrete prediction impossible given that the Pact of Steel only ran for ten years.[259]

Furthermore, Ciano thought that London had only signed the Easter Agreement because they felt threatened by the Anti-Comintern Pact. So why should his strategy not work again?[260] Thus, for Ciano, the pact was a "unity of purpose" in order to achieve his foreign policy objectives, and he repeatedly referred to the peace period, an essential part of his entire thinking.[261] It should give him sufficient time to find a solution acceptable to all nations in Europe and thus prevent a European war.[262] A photograph taken immediately after the Pact of Steel was signed and published in the magazine *L'Illustrazione Italiana* seemed to unintentionally capture its contradictions and different expectations. Together with leading figures of the Nazi regime, Ciano stepped onto the balcony of the *Reichskanzlei* to be cheered by the crowd. He, Hitler, and Ribbentrop responded with the Roman salute – but the arms of Ciano and the two Germans pointed symbolically in different directions (figure 9).

The Pact of Steel put an end to Ciano's attempts to force French concessions solely with performative policy. While he still believed in his "diplomatic game," high-ranking diplomats in the Foreign Ministry did not share his naivety and optimism, predicting that Rome was now bound to Berlin "to the bitter end."[263] Why, then, had Ciano's performative foreign policy ultimately failed? Ciano and his staff invested great effort in order to create a "new" reality that reflected their own goals and self-perception, but the political rituals and stagings were not enough. To illustrate this failure, let us examine what effects his performative foreign policy had on the four most important target groups: the West, Berlin and other authoritarian states, the Italian public, and himself.

Ciano's main goal was to put pressure on the West by exhibiting the close friendship between Nazi Germany and Fascist Italy, symbolized by Hitler and Mussolini, and the conclusion of presumed earth-shattering agreements.[264] Reports in the Western press about Ciano's visit to Berlin in 1936 and about the spectacle of the signing of the Anti-Comintern

Figure 9. Joachim von Ribbentrop, Galeazzo Ciano, Adolf Hitler, and Hermann Göring (from left to right) on the balcony of the *Reichskanzlei*, 22 May 1939. *L'Illustrazione Italiana*, 28 May 1939, 1136.

Pact in Rome illustrate that they were only partially successful in their endeavours.[265] *The Times* noted: "[The pact's] architecture is of such extreme simplicity that one feels that the journalists in their eulogies are slightly embarrassed at having to make so much of it."[266]

The reaction of British politicians to Hitler's visit in May 1938 also reveals the weakness in Ciano's foreign policy strategy. Neville Chamberlain publicly described the Axis as fragile, since the state visit had not yielded any new results and had not led to the signing of any agreement.[267] Others, like French Prime Minister Daladier, might have taken Ciano's threats more seriously; however, they also refused to make any concessions. Daladier argued that, even if Paris were to give in, the "bandit" Mussolini would remain true to the Axis and only make more demands.[268] His reaction shows that Ciano's performative diplomacy had destroyed any trust that might have once existed between Rome and the West. Without mutual trust – "the belief that others will reciprocate" – Ciano's strategy of a "diplomatic expansion" was doomed.[269]

Ciano's biggest problem was that the publicly exhibited power of Italy and the friendship between Rome and Berlin were, until the Pact of Steel, unsupported by facts. The discrepancy between the performative and the programmatic dimensions of Ciano's foreign policy had a decisive impact on the success and failure of his strategy. The goal to persuade the West to make concessions predominantly based on a symbolic demonstration of power largely failed due to Italy's military and economic weakness and Ciano's unwillingness to sign far-reaching treaties. And indeed, the Western observers were unimpressed by Italy's military achievements or the signed agreements between Berlin and Rome.[270] Consequently, Ciano's politics always ran the risk of collapsing if Western countries reacted to Italy's threats not with appeasement, but with confrontation. But he believed that Britain and France would not ultimately defend their own interests by military force if necessary, one of his biggest misjudgments and one that was met with great astonishment in London.[271]

The German reaction to the visit to Italy in May 1938 illustrates that Ciano's performative politics had also reached their limits within the Axis alliance. The delegation in general and Adolf Hitler in particular were enthusiastic about the warm reception and friendly hospitality of the Italians.[272] Yet, as already mentioned, they attacked the Italian royal house, were angry about the Vatican's public aloofness, and expressed scepticism about the condition and usefulness of the Italian armed forces. The pompous ceremonies and military display did nothing to end the negative stereotypes that many high-ranking German officials still harboured towards the Italians. The "betrayal of 1915" served as a strong reminder to many Germans that one should never trust the Italians. Thus, Ciano's attempt to convince the Germans of Rome's friendship and of the power and effectiveness of Italy's army, and thereby establish Italy as an equal partner within the Axis, failed – a failure he did not realize at that time.[273]

Furthermore, Ciano's strategy of strength could only work if the image of a monolithic, harmonious, and strong Axis could be maintained, and that image needed to go beyond the much-publicized personal friendship between Mussolini and Hitler. Internal disputes and conflicts of interest had to be kept secret – otherwise outsiders might interpret them as signs of weaknesses in the alliance.[274] Germany's aggressive and autonomous policies, however, often opposed Ciano's own ideas – a dilemma that the Italian foreign minister repeatedly encountered. After the annexation of Austria, for example, Ciano desperately tried to maintain the appearance of normality. His reaction followed an inner logic according to which he had to convince himself that sticking with the Axis was more important than an independent Austria. With Germany's occupation of Prague, Ciano was once again forced to preserve the appearance of a unified Axis, even if it was – as he had to admit – "difficult to lie."[275] By doing so, Ciano wanted to avoid the fact that Italy was being perceived as a "little child" on the national and international stage.[276] But the opposite was the case: his attempts to justify the alliance made him a hostage of German ambitions. Moreover, his arguments were far from credible, which in turn damaged his prestige at home and abroad.[277]

While the regimes' propaganda machines were busy covering up these tensions by focusing on the seemingly harmonious friendship between the two dictators, it was Ciano himself who undermined these efforts. In conversations with his close advisors and even with foreigners he expressed his disdain and frustration about Germany's actions. Consequently, the tensions between Rome and Berlin were not just lurking under the surface; they were real and known to the Western governments, thus undermining the image of a strong, monolithic Axis.[278]

Performative diplomacy also did little to defuse existing conflicts within the fascist cosmos in Europe. On the contrary, Ciano's policy towards Hungary and Romania and their intractable disputes are a good example of this failure. While he was willing to take a neutral stance, both regimes used Ciano's visits to underline Rome's particular solidarity with their countries, thereby upsetting the other regime. Ciano was patently aware of this problem but did little to mitigate it.[279] Moreover, Berlin also distrusted Ciano's idea of a "vertical" Axis – and rightly so – and tried to undermine his efforts by offering better deals or by putting pressure on the governments in Budapest and Bucharest.[280] Germany certainly had more to offer: with its stronger economy and more powerful military, Berlin remained the preferred partner for the countries of Eastern Europe.[281]

Analysis of the Italian public's reaction reveals the further limits of Ciano's performative foreign policy. His intention was to accustom his own people to a partnership with Germany, or at least to demonstrate the necessity of such an alliance, and to depict Italians as a fearless and belligerent people. Uniting the public behind his foreign policy, however, was not just a way to strengthen the alliance; given that the regime deliberately included the masses in their performative diplomacy as a counter-model to the often-secret foreign policy of Western countries, it was an absolute necessity to win the public's blessing and support.[282] Police reports from the second half of the 1930s reveal a different picture. While many Italians disliked the Germans, did not support the martial rhetoric, and disdained the rapprochement with Berlin, they enthusiastically welcomed the British delegation in January 1939 and the rapprochement with London.[283]

Moreover, many Italians repeatedly criticized Ciano for the Axis policy. Mussolini might have been the public face of an idealized equal friendship with Berlin in general and Hitler in particular; yet, he stood aloof from all the bureaucratic dealings between the two countries.[284] It was Ciano who signed all the important treaties with Germany, including the Cultural Agreement (1938) and the Pact of Steel (1939). As a consequence, the *Duce* was spared the public's more damning criticism, and Ciano was blamed as the person responsible for Italy's inferior role within the Axis due to his weak negotiating skills. Thus, Ciano faced a double dilemma: Renouncing the friendship with Berlin would have undermined his as well as Mussolini's credibility. However, he also could not just go back to business as usual, because Italians complained that, while Germany achieved one success after the other thanks to Italy's support and solidarity, Rome had so far not benefitted from the Axis.[285] Ciano was well aware of this mood and drew a simple conclusion, which – as will be shown – once again thwarted his entire strategy. He had to show the Italian people that the alliance with Berlin was also good for Rome, and so his gaze turned to Albania.[286]

Ciano's character and worldview were another reason why his performative foreign policy proved problematic in the end. His vanity and arrogance were an open secret. Foreign politicians skilfully exploited his weakness for pomp and circumstances to impress, flatter, and thus cater to his overconfidence. Berlin in particular succeeded time and again in convincing him of the effectiveness of the Wehrmacht and the Luftwaffe. In light of his early successes, such as the end of the sanctions imposed by the League of Nations, he also felt validated in his overall decision to rely on the "German horse." Why then should he change his strategy? In his opinion there was no better way to achieve his foreign policy objectives than to continue as he had begun.[287] Ciano's self-confidence made him believe in his ability to mentor and advise foreign politicians. When he returned from Germany in October 1936, a confident Ciano told his colleagues: "My impressions are excellent … I found the Germans much more accommodating and 'malleable' than I had imagined."[288] Ignorant of Berlin's real intentions, he thought he could use the political, military, and economic power of the Third Reich to exert pressure on the West in support of Italy's interests. He failed to realize that his conception of an alliance with Berlin differed from Mussolini's and Germany's visions.

Germany was hardly the only country for which we observe this fatal delusion. Be it Great Britain, France, Hungary, Romania, or the United States, Ciano remained convinced that he could influence – at least partially – the domestic and foreign policies of these countries.[289] Especially towards representatives of supposedly weak states he displayed an arrogance that was met with incomprehension and criticism from many diplomats and politicians.[290] Ciano thought he was the new Talleyrand who, as Otto von Bismarck once did, could play with the great powers as if with marbles. He was initially convinced that no one could hold a candle to him, the *"intrigo diplomatico."*[291] That Ciano viewed diplomacy as a "game" is also apparent in his diary. When he met Ribbentrop in August 1939, he made a bet with the German foreign minister that Britain and France would intervene should Germany attack Poland. Ribbentrop wagered against it. Years later, Ciano complained that Ribbentrop had not paid his debts.[292]

Yet the performative policy never thwarted Ciano's own deep scepticism towards the "German race."[293] Even though he supported the rapprochement with Berlin and became one of the most important Italian faces of the Rome-Berlin friendship besides Mussolini, he never really trusted the Germans. While Mussolini kept the public appearance of unity and solidarity with Germany alive, it was Ciano who often got second thoughts as soon as he felt that his own ambitions and goals were in danger. Even the vaguest rumour was enough for him to shatter the fragile structure of the German-Italian friendship, which was based on costly and time-consuming performative diplomacy.

Performative Foreign Policy during the Second World War

Although the German attack on Poland revealed the failure of Ciano's performative strategy, he continued to adhere to it. On 1 September 1939 the Fascist Grand Council proclaimed the policy of *non belligeranza.* Mussolini was particularly pleased with this specially created monstrosity of a word, as it still expressed Italy's loyalty to Germany and emphasized that it was an "armed" peace. Ciano also insisted that Italy's stance must be described with this term and criticized everyone who spoke of "neutrality."[294] Even in his choice of words, the intention to demonstrate strength and solidarity with Berlin was discernible, though Italy had obviously not fulfilled its Pact of Steel obligations.[295]

Ciano now used political rituals and symbolic communication in order to keep Italy out of the war. While Mussolini still saw Paris and London as the real enemies, it was Ciano's declared aim to highlight his personal closeness to Great Britain and the United States, and to present himself as a prudent statesman.[296] While he torpedoed the German-Italian relationship, he tried to gain new trust from the West in order to obtain advantages, maybe even territorial ones, for Italy. In turn, this manoeuvring should have strengthened the position of the non-interventionists and would have ultimately allowed Italy to break away from the Axis. In his efforts he proved surprisingly creative. He supported the Finns against the Soviet Union to defend the "West" against "barbaric communism";[297] he advised Allied ambassadors on how best to fight the German air force;[298] he supported economic agreements with France and Great Britain, including for arms supplies, to minimize the negative consequences of the British naval blockade;[299] and he gave confidential information about German propaganda and the Italian government's internal affairs to the British ambassador.[300] Ciano also rescued Polish aristocrats, negotiated with the Polish exile government about arms supplies, and initially kept the Italian embassy in Warsaw open. These gestures were intended to highlight Poland's national integrity even after Germany had invaded the country.[301] In addition, the British appreciated that he sent Giuseppe Bastianini as a new ambassador to London and informed Belgium and the Netherlands in November 1939 about an imminent German attack.[302] Even with his decision to present an official declaration of war on 10 June 1940 to the British and French ambassadors, he demonstrated that he acted in accordance with international law – in contrast to Mussolini who did not care at all.[303]

Thanks to the support of the cabinet and the Italian establishment at the time, Ciano was able to carry out many of these actions in opposition to Mussolini's will or without informing him of the details.[304] And once again his choice of clothing mirrored his foreign policy strategy as can be seen in photographs taken by the American Carl Mydans for *LIFE Magazine* in April 1940 (figure 10). Ciano, renouncing any military pomp and fascist awards, was dressed in a bourgeois suit. He inspired confidence, trust, and sympathy and seemed serious and diligent.[305]

In this context, we must also look at Ciano's much-vaunted "speech of truth" to the *Camera dei Fasci e delle Corporazioni* on 16 December 1939. Since October he had been mulling over what to say. Although he wanted to keep the "form," he intended to "tell the truth and so widen the breach between ourselves and the Germans."[306] He worked closely with confidants in the *Palazzo Chigi* to gather compromising material against the Germans.[307] A month later he was very pleased with the complete manuscript of his "very insidious speech."[308] It was published in all major Italian newspapers, distributed with 100,000 copies throughout the country, and translated into eleven languages.[309] After his speech, Ciano was overwhelmed by a childlike joy. Although not everybody would "discern the subtle anti-German poison," he was convinced this speech was the "real funeral of the Axis."[310]

But Italy's entry into the Second World War once again demonstrates the failure of Ciano's performative foreign policy. What went wrong? By analysing the international and domestic reactions to his actions

Figure 10. Galeazzo Ciano in his office, May 1940. Ullstein Bild #04950985.

between August 1939 and June 1940, we can reveal his miscalculations. One of his biggest problems was that his previous foreign policy had significantly contributed to the alienation between Italy and the West. Thanks to Ciano's use of threats and blackmail, his arrogant and cynical demeanour, the occupation of Albania, and the signing of the Pact of Steel, Rome was perceived as an untrustworthy and unreliable player on the international stage.[311] When he began to support the *non belligeranza* policy and publicly turned away from Berlin, Western diplomats were understandably suspicious about his true motives.[312] They expected him to change his allegiance once again if he thought it would benefit him. "Count Ciano," a British diplomat wrote in September 1939, "is so thoroughly unreliable that one instinctively disbelieves everything he says."[313]

Only gradually did Ciano succeed in partially rebuilding his reputation thanks in part to three Western ambassadors who were based in Rome: William Phillips (United States), Percy Loraine (Great Britain), and André François-Poncet (France). During that period Ciano and Loraine met almost daily and sometimes conferred at night in Ciano's private apartment.[314] Loraine warned his superiors that the "slightest leakage" about his collusion with Ciano would "compromise not only Ciano's position, but also the hope, however slender, that in the end Italy will return to cooperation, even maybe in arms, with her former allies of 1915–18."[315] Even on 10 June 1940, the day of the Italian declaration of war, mutual respect and trust prevailed.[316]

One of the consequences of this shift, however, was that Western policymakers began to judge the Italian elite in a naive and simplistic black-and-white pattern, which over time determined their policy towards Rome. On the one side stood the "pro-German" Mussolini, on the other, the "pro-Allied" Ciano, who kept his country out of the war.[317] In their view, the West had to remain firm; ultimately, Berlin would make further mistakes, and Rome would be driven to break away from Germany and turn to London as had happened in 1915.[318] A January 1940 survey in Great Britain showed that 34 per cent of those questioned were convinced that Italy would enter the war on the side of the Allies. Only 5 per cent assumed that Italy would join the Third Reich.[319] "Many people," wrote Malaparte, "shared … the delusion that Count Galeazzo Ciano was the 'Anti-Mussolini,' the man to whom London and Washington looked expectantly."[320] Western diplomats and politicians did indeed hope that Ciano would be much more amenable to logical arguments than Mussolini and other fascists due to his social environment, his own interests, and his knowledge of the world. It was therefore not only Ciano who was, as Malaparte wrote, "secretly convinced that he was viewed with favor by English and American public opinion."[321]

While at first glance it might seem that finally Ciano's performative politics had worked, this view is unsupported by facts. Western observers only heard what they wanted to hear: namely, Ciano's moderating statements at a time when the *Duce* kept aloof from politics. When they assessed the situation in Italy, they totally ignored the fact that the *Duce* intervened more actively after he had returned to the political stage; they underestimated Mussolini's commitment to the Axis and his fear of losing his credibility should he renounce the friendship with Berlin; and they overlooked above all the increasing influence of the interventionists. And even when the signs clearly pointed to an Italian entry into the war, the Western majority still believed in the possibility of a diplomatic solution. When Italy finally joined Germany in the Second World War, this decision was solely blamed on Mussolini.[322] Western policymakers neither made any self-criticism nor acknowledged that they had ignored the many forces and factors that contributed to the failure of *non belligeranza*. Only a few people had a more nuanced view. One of them was US diplomat Pierrepont Moffat, who described the Italian situation with a simple formula: while the *Duce* was pro-German, Ciano was anti-German. However, he noted that – as the British thought – Ciano's anti-German attitude should not be automatically assumed to be pro-Allied.[323]

The different reactions to Ciano's speech in December 1939 also show that Ciano was unable to create his preferred "new" reality solely through political rituals. While his speech was mostly praised by Western diplomats and supporters of the *non belligeranza* policy, he was unable to sway his critics.[324] In Germany, the response was mixed. While the German ambassador Hans Georg von Mackensen initially tried to point out a pro-German tenor, Ribbentrop and Goebbels were furious.[325] The latter ordered the press to report only briefly on this "rather unfriendly and devious" speech.[326] He benefitted from an agreement in which Rome assured Berlin they would not live broadcast the speech on the radio.[327] Even though Ciano's speech had an undeniable anti-German character, this agreement ultimately undermined his intention to widen the gap between Germany and Italy.[328] Yes, he confirmed the Italian public's prejudices against the Germans and ensured that leading Nazi figures were upset.[329] However, since Ciano's speech was only partially distributed in the Third Reich, it could not undermine Italian-German relations in the long term.[330] Moreover, Ciano failed to openly attack Germany; his criticism was often hidden between the lines. For example, he focused on dismissing

German allegations, like Ribbentrop's claim that Ciano had told the Western Allies Italy would not intervene on the side of Germany before the outbreak of the Second World War, or once again stressed the peace period Italy associated with the Pact of Steel. However, all this criticism could only have been known to the astute or highly informed and was overshadowed by accusations against the West for pursuing a policy of isolation towards Germany and Italy.[331] The anti-German overtone, the "subtle anti-German poison" of which Ciano was so proud, vanished before it had a chance to work. Nevertheless, German officials saw the speech as proof that it was Ciano who had betrayed the Italian-German alliance.

Furthermore, Ciano also failed to strengthen the non-interventionist faction within the Italian population in the long run. At first the non-belligerence policy was supported by the majority of Italians due to various factors, including their animosity towards the Germans informed by a racial worldview, but also due to the continuous peace propaganda in the Italian media.[332] Moreover, Italy was portrayed as a strong and above all independent country that would be able to decide its own destiny regardless of Berlin's support – one could even argue that this portrayal was aimed at driving a wedge between the Rome-Berlin Axis after the regime spent years constructing it. The news media would, for example, usually argue that Ciano and Mussolini only met with German officials or travelled to Berlin after Germany had asked for a meeting.[333] Nevertheless, in the end Ciano's subtle sabotage of the Italian-German Axis was not enough to repress the effects Germany's seemingly easy victories over the Allied forces had on Italians' morale. Especially after Berlin's Scandinavian campaign, the public shifted towards an interventionist attitude that was immediately seized upon by Mussolini and his close supporters.[334]

After Italy entered the war, Ciano supported the creation of the Italian Empire by force of arms in order to achieve what he had not achieved through diplomacy. A closer look, nonetheless, reveals that performative diplomacy continued to play an important albeit different role in his strategy. On the one hand, the entire concept of a parallel war and occupation policy, which he supported, was symbolic in nature. According to this idea, Italy would wage its own war parallel to that of Germany to achieve its own goals. Thereby, it did not really matter that the fascist leadership had completely different ideas about the actual war goals; even Mussolini vacillated between several ideas.[335] It was more important to appease critics of the Third Reich among the population, the fascists, and the army and to gain their support for the war by stressing Italy's autonomy. Maintaining the illusion of a parallel war, the Italians refrained from any obligatory coordination of Italian-German armed forces from the start.[336] In the end, it was politically and militarily naive to believe in the feasibility of a parallel war, as this concept was based on three fundamental misconceptions: first, the assumption that the Allies would distinguish between the Axis partners; second, the expectation that Germany would entrust Italy with the Balkans and its raw materials; and third, the idea that the Italian army would be able to wage its own war.

Trapped in this self-deception, Rome failed to realize that Italy had been Berlin's "junior partner" for a while now. The German interference in Greece, which was announced at a meeting between Hitler, Mussolini, and Ciano in January 1941, was not the beginning by far of German hegemony within the Axis. But it only now dawned upon the public, the military, and the politicians in Italy with a brutality that many had not expected.[337] Many Italians were deeply shocked, which can partially explain the violent reactions against Ciano at that time. Ciano had consistently avoided personally asking the Third Reich for help because he wanted to maintain the appearance of a parallel war.[338] In the run-up to the January meeting, however, Ciano and Mussolini obviously expected that they had to request German aid, given the terrible news from the Greece campaign. Both insisted on secrecy. Photographers and journalists were excluded, and no crowds were present. In addition, no press release was published.[339] If Italy had to travel to Germany as a petitioner, Ciano and Mussolini at least wanted to prevent it from becoming public knowledge. However, as historian Christian Goeschel argues, the stark contrast to the past meetings was not easy to hide. "The encounter exposed the new and clear hierarchy between the two dictators ... Gone were the days when these meetings represented a new face-to-face diplomacy of two regimes making a New Order in Europe ... The myth of the dictatorial couple began to fade."[340]

Italy's entry into the Second World War not only affected Ciano's performative foreign policy; as several incidents show it also shattered his belief in its intrinsic value. At first, however, he believed that a public display of loyalty and support towards Berlin would be sufficient to sideline his critics and regain his former prominence. Photographs showed him clapping enthusiastically when Hitler finished his Reichstag speech in July 1940. And when the Wehrmacht gave him a tour of the Western Front, he posed smiling for the camera in a German *Kübelwagen* (analogous to the American jeep). Yet, Ciano's exaggerated efforts to reappear as a friend of the Germans seemed hollow and ultimately failed.[341] As a consequence, he seemed to become more and more critical of performative diplomacy's benefits in his dealings with Berlin.

When Ciano visited Berlin on 27 September 1940 to sign the Tripartite Pact, the Nazi leadership once again staged a glamorous reception to convince the guests of Germany's power, will, and unity. Sixteen thousand Wehrmacht and Waffen SS soldiers alone lined the way from Tempelhof Airport to Bellevue Castle, where Ciano was accommodated.[342] However, Ciano was unimpressed and observed a "cool atmosphere" in the city. Finally, he thought the German people had understood that the war would continue for a long time to come – something he had always predicted.[343]

When Hungary, Romania, and Slovakia joined the Tripartite Pact in November 1940, Italy's attack against Greece had cast yet another shadow over Berlin's opinion of Ciano. While Hitler defended Mussolini, Ciano became the main culprit for the disastrous campaign.[344] The aversion towards Ciano was also reflected in the lukewarm reception he received at the accession ceremony. While he could not yet figure out what the inclusion of the other countries meant for Italy's standing within the alliance, he was overall unenthusiastic about bringing them into the pact system. In his opinion, this step was only supposed to distract from Germany's failed conquest of Great Britain and would actually weaken the alliance.[345] Western observers shared Ciano's opinion and argued that the agreement should be interpreted as a propagandistic and psychological move meant to deter the United States from further helping London. US journalist William Shirer, like Ciano, doubted whether this tactic would be successful. Shirer's reaction illustrates that the West was not deceived by those political rituals and symbolic acts designed to highlight the strength and unity of the Axis.[346]

During the war, Ciano was repeatedly furious when officers and politicians spread false success stories in order to construct a strong and powerful Italy.[347] Ciano accused the naval leadership under Admiral Arturo Riccardi of turning every little thing – such as a British warship in a dry dock – into a major success: "This is equivalent to declaring that a man is probably slightly dead because he has gone to live near the cemetery. Clowns, tragic clowns."[348] And when in April 1941 Ugo Cavallero and Mussolini celebrated their triumph against Greece, Ciano was stunned and upset by how they asserted that only the blood of Italian soldiers had shattered the Greek armies.[349] He was convinced that the Italians would not believe such martial praise in light of all the bad news coming from the front, thus destroying the trust and confidence of the people in the fascist leadership. Ciano's damning criticism was shared by many of his close confidants such as Giovanni Ansaldo, editor-in-chief of *Il Telegrafo*.[350]

When at the turn of 1941–42 the Axis suffered heavy losses, Ciano saw an opportunity to again exert more influence on the foreign policy of his home country. He did not fatalistically give up, as some scholars and former diplomats have claimed, but devoted himself with the help of his staff to his new goal:[351] preserving the existence of Italy and thus of the "white civilization." In this situation, he once again fell back on his long-favoured performative foreign policy, though he abstained from pompous ceremonies and instead relied on less costly symbolic political rituals. Thereby, he mainly focused on supporting the declarations of independence for India and the Arab world while supporting the creation of an Arab and an Indian army. He sought to build trust with both in order to save Italy's sovereignty and drive a wedge between his country and Germany.

It was above all his subconscious fear of the "yellow race" that shaped Ciano's policy towards India in 1941 and 1942. Although he had no high hopes for the militant independence movement in India under Subhash Chandra Bose, he pressed Italy's allies to issue a declaration of independence for India in the summer of 1941.[352] The Japanese government refused to support this symbolic act, arguing that such a step would only make sense if the Tripartite Pact could actually aid a possible uprising. But Ciano was not convinced and suspected that the Japanese government wanted to distract and delay. He assumed that Tokyo sought to conquer India, thus echoing speculations that had been circulating in Indian nationalist circles for a while. Ciano's proposal for a declaration of independence was therefore designed to assure India that the Axis had no territorial ambitions in the country.[353]

In the spring of 1942, Ciano renewed his request. He wanted to torpedo the mission of Sir Stafford Cripps who in March 1942 travelled to India to win the country's unrestricted help in the Second World War.[354] At the same time, Tokyo threatened to invade India after Japanese troops had previously invaded Burma and the British were unable to guarantee India's defence.[355] In this context, Ciano's goal was two-fold: while he obviously wanted to put pressure on the British government, which had intensified its attacks against Italy, he also intended to position an independent India as a bulwark against Japanese ambitions. His attempt ultimately failed, mostly because Berlin and Tokyo blocked his proposal.[356] Ciano's enthusiasm for Indian independence waned in the summer of 1942 after the Americans stopped the Japanese advance at the Battle of Midway in June and later began their counteroffensive, meaning that the danger of a Japanese invasion of India was averted.[357]

In the spring of 1942, Ciano also pleaded for a declaration of independence for the Arab states in the Middle East and North Africa to tie up British troops in the region.[358] By doing so, he sought to win over the Arabs as allies and use them against London. However, Mussolini – with the backing of Berlin – consistently rejected such a declaration, as it would have undermined his plans for an Italian Empire in the Mediterranean.[359] Ciano and Mussolini's starkly opposing views revealed Ciano's changed strategy. Unlike the *Duce,* he was prepared to cede areas that were originally earmarked as part of the Italian *spazio vitale.* This behaviour was one of the first indications that he had abandoned the dream of establishing the Italian Empire. Ciano's shift becomes particularly clear when one compares his thinking in 1942 with that of 1940.

Back in the summer of 1940, Ciano gave orders to contact potential Egyptian revolutionary leaders and rekindle anti-British propaganda in the region.[360] But his behaviour towards Egyptian Prime Minister Ali Maher Pasha remained ambivalent. While he welcomed the prime minister's statement not to break off diplomatic relations with Italy, he failed to support a possible revolt in Egypt with money and material. The British proved less scrupulous. They deposed and interned Pasha without further ado. On 29 July 1940 Ciano instructed his staff to draw up a plan for the post-war order in the Middle East and North Africa. While the Ministry of Italian-Africa and the Army Command pleaded for military occupation, the Foreign Ministry preferred to secure political influence in countries such as Sudan, Egypt, Syria, and Iraq. The ministries all agreed not to issue an official declaration promising independence for the Arabs after the war as such a move would have jeopardized the dream of an empire in the Mediterranean.[361]

Parallel and Secret Diplomacy

Italy's diplomacy in general and its relationship to Germany in particular cannot be fully understood by only focusing on the performative dimension of foreign policy. Since the 1920s the fascist regime employed special envoys – sometimes in public, sometimes in secrecy – to further and strengthen Italy's power and standing in Europe and worldwide. These emissaries played a key role in the rapprochement of Italy and Germany, and were instrumental in building global networks and contacts with other fascists groups and movements.[362] While these new channels of communication were more unpredictable, unstable, and dependent on personal sympathies, they were also faster and more elastic than the time-consuming formalities that marked negotiations through official channels.[363]

When Ciano returned to Italy in 1933, he was no stranger to this personalized diplomacy. Although the Cianos were the youngest diplomatic couple in Shanghai, they quickly integrated into the diplomatic community. Their house, where they hosted lavish dinners and bridge evenings, became a popular watering hole for the city's upper class. Of course, Ciano was not acting altruistically; he had political aims in mind, as he was convinced that only a personalized style of diplomacy marked by emotional affection, loyalty, and trust would avoid laborious negotiations and bring the desired success.[364] Thus, similar to his behaviour in domestic affairs, Ciano adapted his diplomatic style to the traditions of China's political culture in which informal contacts took precedence over legal norms and administrative structures. This strategy paid off in China, where Ciano established good relationships with journalists like Henry Woodhead and such important personalities as Zhang Xueliang and British diplomat Sir Miles Lampson.[365] These informal contacts earned him the respect of Western and Chinese diplomats, politicians, and journalists, which persisted long after Ciano's departure.[366]

After Ciano returned to Italy in 1933, he immediately began to employ special envoys in consultation with the *Duce*, which in turn allowed him to become an architect of the Axis despite his personal antipathy towards German politicians. With a mandate from Ciano or Mussolini, these emissaries could hold preliminary summits, tackle problems, and try to find a solution ahead of official talks. This practice facilitated Ciano's ability to sign deals and agreements. Consequently, he was able to portray himself as a capable, dynamic minister with only Italy's best interests in mind and thus consolidate his standing and prestige in Italy.

On the German side, Prince Philipp of Hesse was one of the *Duce* and Ciano's most trusted contacts when it came to the fundamental and sensitive questions of German-Italian cooperation, including the German population in South Tyrol and the annexation of Austria.[367] In contrast to his opinions of the diplomats at Wilhelmstraße, Ciano viewed Hesse as a thoroughly likeable personality. The two first met in Kassel in 1936, where Hesse was able to convince Ciano of Germany's good intentions. Following these talks, the two developed a friendly relationship that lasted far into the Second World War.[368]

On the Italian side, Hesse's counterpart was Giuseppe Renzetti.[369] Mussolini had been accustomed to using Renzetti's services during State Secretary Fulvio Suvich's tenure at the Foreign Ministry, despite the latter's attempts to stop or at least restrict Renzetti's activities.[370] While as state secretary of press and propaganda Ciano initially supported Renzetti, the latter continued to act independently when Ciano headed the Foreign Ministry.[371] As Ciano grew increasingly sceptical of and irritated by German politics, Renzetti was still wholeheartedly committed to the Axis. Ciano rightly feared that Renzetti would use his excellent networks in Berlin to meddle in German-Italian relations without Ciano's blessing. He also accused Renzetti of sowing seeds of division between him and Berlin by discrediting the embassy secretary and his brother-in-law, Massimo Magistrati, in the presence of German officials.[372] Despite the tension between Renzetti and Ciano, the latter was able to recall Renzetti from Germany only in March 1941.[373]

Renzetti, however, was not an isolated case. Ciano also used personal emissaries in other countries to pursue a parallel, often-secret foreign policy as soon as he took over Mussolini's press office. He used this method to exert pressure on Western democracies and, if possible, more directly influence their policies, and to strengthen alliances within the fascist cosmos. First, Ciano sent press attachés to various Italian embassies, such as Amedeo Landini, who was Ciano's man in Paris. Landini not only maintained valuable contacts with leading journalists such as Pertinax,[374] but also wrote speeches for French deputies legitimizing Italy's plans in Ethiopia and sharply attacking possible sanctions.[375] Much to Ambassador Cerruti's displeasure, Landini informed Ciano in detail about the events in France in order to make Italian propaganda more effective.[376] An internal note to Ciano written by the Directorate-General for Propaganda in the summer of 1935 particularly praised Landini as "one of our best propaganda agents."[377] Even the British Foreign Office acknowledged that Italian propaganda in the French press was extremely effective at the time.[378]

Second, Ciano turned to Italians living abroad such as Italo Sulliotti, editor-in-chief of the French newspaper *Nuova Italia*. In consultation with Ciano and with his financial support, Sulliotti pursued a parallel diplomacy by negotiating with politicians and trying to establish contacts with philo-fascist movements in France. He also came into increasing conflict with Ambassador Cerruti, who continuously called for Sulliotti's dismissal – to no avail. It was not until January 1936 that the journalist's popularity declined when it was discovered that he had bribed French deputies. In response, the *Duce* recalled him to Rome.[379]

Third, Ciano tried to bribe sympathizers of the fascist regime abroad, including fascist or philo-fascist politicians, parties, and organizations, to support Italy's agenda. These sympathizers included Sir Oswald Mosley's British Union of Fascists; the French groups *Action française*, under Léon Daudet, and the *Parti populaire français*, under Jacques Doriot; Paul Hoornaert's Belgian *Légion Nationale*; and the Croatian *Ustaša*, under Ante Pavelić.[380] The support of fascist movements in Europe, however, continued even after Ciano's tenure as minister of press and propaganda ended. He recycled this strategy as foreign minister, paying close attention to ensure that all contacts would now run solely through his ministry. Due to Italy's lack of resources, he repeatedly asked Berlin to co-finance foreign groups, including the Belgian Rexists under the leadership of the young journalist Leon Degrelle. The encirclement and threat against France by fascist powers and movements was another piece of Ciano's plan to isolate Paris and thereby realize Italy's demands.[381]

Fourth, in his attempt to control foreign fascist movements while he was minister of press and propaganda, Ciano also used Eugenio Coselschi's *Comitati d'Azione per l'Universalità di Roma* (CAUR). Coselschi's plan, initially supported by Mussolini, had been to create a "fascist international" with Rome at its centre. In October 1934 he invited several European leaders of fascist and far-right movements to Montreux, Switzerland, to begin his – in the end unsuccessful – project. While he continuously clashed with the Foreign Ministry under Suvich, he was supported by Ciano. For Ciano, cooperation with the CAUR offered an opportunity to pursue a parallel foreign policy, to position himself against his rival Suvich, and to spread fascist propaganda at a time when the propaganda institutions were still in their infancy.[382]

After Ciano was appointed foreign minister, however, he banned Coselschi's activities and cut off his support. He would no longer tolerate the CAUR's activism and did not want to have an organization outside his jurisdiction meddling in the delicate matter of maintaining contacts with fascist movements.[383] Moreover, with the proclamation of the Axis in November 1936, the fascist regime had rejected at least for now the idea of a multilateral "fascist international" with somewhat of an anti-German bias in favour of a bilateral cooperation with Berlin. "I can't believe that you," wrote a bitterly disappointed Coselschi to Ciano, "who has always shown me so much friendship, will now bring me into such a situation."[384]

Despite the official subordination of the CAUR under the Ministry of Popular Culture in September 1937, Coselschi continued to insist on the CAUR's uniqueness. It was all the more important for him since, at the turn of the year 1937–38, numerous organizations at home and abroad became more and more active. In addition to Ruggero Zangrandi, who wanted to set up a fascist youth movement in Europe, the International Anti-Semitic Conference in Erfurt attracted Italians, including the intellectuals Julius Evola and Alberto Luchini, who were originally involved in the CAUR.[385]

Coselschi thought he still possessed one trump card in order to convince Ciano of the CAUR's importance: Ciano's anti-communism. He argued that the CAUR was the only capable organization battling Bolshevism; in his view, the Anti-Comintern Pact was a cheap imitation. To prove his point, he founded the magazine *Antibolscevismo* and assured Ciano of its popularity at home and abroad.[386] All his efforts were in vain: for Ciano, the Anti-Comintern Pact should not only replace the League of Nations; it should also play a similar role to what Coselschi had always had in mind for his "fascist international." After Italy joined the Anti-Comintern Pact, the CAUR declined further into a mere propaganda tool, spreading not only anti-communist but increasingly anti-Semitic messages. On 20 September 1939 the CAUR were finally dissolved.[387]

And fifth, Ciano repeatedly relied on the services of leading figures of the Italian regime who had well-developed connections with foreign statesmen and politicians due to their personal or professional interests. In contrast to the other strategies, he also used this last approach to improve Italy's relations with the West. One example of such a connection is industrialist Alberto Pirelli, who was in good standing with the British establishment and, through direct contact with the Italian embassy in London, promoted an understanding between the British and the Italians.[388]

In addition, Ciano turned to members of the aristocracy, including those working at his ministry such as Del Drago and Pietromarchi. Ciano's relationship with Prince Umberto, son of Vittorio Emanuele III, also strengthened his connection to Philipp of Hesse, who in turn was married to Umberto's sister, Mafalda of Savoy. Through Umberto's wife, Marie José of Belgium, whom Ciano considered an honourable person due to her aversion to Germany, Ciano warned the Belgians of an imminent German attack in November 1939. Moreover, his contacts with Roman aristocrats such as Galeazzo Di Bagno and Isabelle Colonna proved helpful time and again.[389] The close relationship between Ciano and Colonna even led to rumours that the foreign minister was personally involved with the princess.[390] Whether this insinuation was true or mere rumour, it is certain that the *Palazzo Colonna* was indeed a place where Ciano met with Western diplomats undisturbed.[391]

Although the Western states were not pleased with Ciano's parallel diplomacy, they drew two conclusions from it: first, that it was essential to be on good, personal terms with Ciano; and second, due to the tense official bilateral relations, any diplomatic breakthrough could only be achieved by secretly contacting Ciano.[392] By trying to adopt Ciano's form of diplomacy, though, the Western statesmen theoretically not only violated Woodrow Wilson's fourteen points; they also became ensnared in a strategy that had so far brought little success in their dealings with Italy, as the failure of the Hoare-Laval Pact in 1935 showed.[393] Nevertheless, several examples illustrate that the West continued to use special envoys in their attempts to work with Ciano.

British Prime Minister Neville Chamberlain turned to Adrian Dingli, an employee of the Italian embassy in London, who had excellent contacts among the conservative circles of Sir Joseph Ball and Sir Robert Vansittart. Without the knowledge of Anthony Eden, his sceptical foreign minister, Chamberlain asked Dingli to travel to Rome and explore possibilities for an understanding between the two countries. The emissary met with Ciano for the first time on 16 July 1937. Ciano initially signalled his willingness to talk, provided that London officially approached Rome. However, the talks were prematurely cancelled because of an intensification of the Spanish Civil War.[394] In April 1940 Dingli contacted Ciano again in the hope of keeping Italy out of the war. However, Ciano was not enthusiastic about meeting Dingli, as Rome's entry into the war had already been decided.[395]

When the bilateral relations between Italy and Great Britain reached a low point at the turn of 1937–38, Neville Chamberlain also sent his sister-in-law, Lady Ivy Chamberlain, to Rome.[396] Diplomats in the United States and Great Britain strongly criticized this move and saw it as an obvious and deliberate repudiation of Eden.[397] Ciano also was sceptical and critical of Lady Chamberlain, accusing her of being unpatriotic. Two explanations for his reaction present themselves. First, he wanted to publicly reduce London to the position of supplicant and refused to engage in informal talks. And second, as I have already pointed out, he strongly believed that women should usually stay out of politics. Therefore, he may have interpreted Lady Chamberlain's visit to Rome as a sign of London's weakness and desperation.[398]

Paris also thought that secret negotiations with Ciano might lead to a breakthrough in French-Italian relations. When in the spring of 1939 Italy tended more and more to the Axis, Paris attempted to solve some of the disputed territorial issues by contacting Ciano directly. On behalf of Daladier and Foreign Minister Bonnet, Paul Baudouin, the French director general of the *Banque d'Indochine* and supporter of the far-right *Action française*, met Ciano in February 1939 without informing Ambassador François-Poncet. Ciano demanded that Paris must officially approach the Italian government in order to begin negotiations about the cession of French territories. The talks ultimately failed when the French journalist Pertinax published a report about Baudouin's secret negotiations, provoking a massive outcry among the French public. Paris was forced to deny the truth of the article and immediately stopped all negotiations.[399] Echoing Mussolini's notion, Ciano felt himself vindicated at that time: it was indeed impossible to conduct successful negotiations with the democracies. One month later Ciano learned that Ribbentrop, whom he had reluctantly informed about his talks with Baudouin on behalf of the *Duce*, had passed the information on to Pertinax.[400]

Scholars still debate the seriousness of the Italian dialogue with Great Britain and France. What is missing from this discussion is a differentiation between Mussolini's and Ciano's attitudes. The *Duce*, obsessed with the German-Italian Axis, did not attach great value to a possible rapprochement with the Western powers. For him, it did not matter whether Paris and London were willing to negotiate about a few territories because he intended to conquer these territories through war anyway.[401] Ciano, however, had different goals. He wanted to present the negotiations with the West as a victory for Italy, a clear demonstration of Italy's power, and an indication that it was the West and not Rome that asked for friendship – a narrative that was also prominent in the fascist press whenever official talks with Western countries took place.[402] While it would have been a humiliation for London and Paris, almost a "trip to Canossa," Ciano could have portrayed the negotiations as a success for his foreign policy strategy and used it to preserve Rome's autonomy. As a consequence, Ciano always rejected secret negotiations with the West – they had to be conducted in the public eye. Ciano's arrogance and hubris upset even the British politicians, who in general were not averse to coming to terms with Rome. Thus, even if he was not strictly against talks with the West, Ciano can be accused of provoking the end of the secret negotiations even before they had really started.[403]

Despite these negative experiences, the United States sent Sumner Welles as a special envoy to Europe during the *non belligeranza* period.[404] On 25 February 1940 the American envoy and his delegation arrived in Naples. This time the negotiations were not conducted in secrecy. There was much speculation as to why Roosevelt sent Welles, who was not a specialist in European affairs. It is possible that the US president wanted to facilitate negotiations by stressing the personal connections between Italians and Americans, since Welles was related to Ciano's confidante Del Drago. And indeed, it was Del Drago who, at Ciano's initiative, personally greeted the US delegation at the port and drove Welles to Rome in Ciano's private car.[405]

Welles's memoirs give the impression that the US strategy seemed to work, as his report about the trip was mostly positive.[406] Ciano was also impressed by the US envoy and praised him as "a man of dignity, an American distinguished in appearance and in manner."[407] Ciano hoped to build trust and sympathy with the American envoy as this meeting may have been, after all, his last chance to keep Italy out of the war.[408] He was dismayed, however, when he realized that the *Duce* disliked Welles, and in any event Mussolini's negative judgment doomed Welles's mission from the start.[409]

Beginning in 1942 personal contacts and secret diplomacy again played a role in Ciano's dealings with the Allies when he considered the possibility of a separate peace with the West. His diary contains only fragmentary clues, which break off with the end of his notes in February 1943. The argument, however, that Ciano only used his notes to construct an alibi for the impending defeat of Italy is not convincing. Two reasons especially present themselves. First, his notes are too vague to convince readers of his pacifism; and second, the diary shows numerous gaps, especially in the summer and autumn months of 1942. According to many rumours, it was exactly in this time period when Ciano solidified his contacts with the Western Allies. Thus, a removal of these pages would only have weakened his alibi. The lack of entries in this period can therefore be interpreted either as a sign that Ciano was afraid these notes might fall into the wrong hands or as confirmation that nothing significant happened despite all the speculation.[410]

Yet, the frequency with which the *Palazzo Chigi* and Ciano were associated with Italian peace proposals should rather be seen as an indication that he was indeed considering such a possibility.[411] In addition to Ciano's diary, other memoirs and diaries and numerous archival records testify to Ciano's pacifist leanings.[412] Moreover, since the appointment of D'Ajeta in April 1942, all of Ciano's closest collaborators – including Vitetti, Del Drago, and Carboni – had personal or familial relations in Anglo-American countries.[413] Considering his understanding of diplomacy, Ciano might have believed they would be helpful in negotiations with the West. But even if there were signs that Ciano was thinking about a separate peace, his actions reveal that his plans often did not go beyond the initial stage or were not motivated by anything other than personnel changes in his ministry.

Ciano hesitated, was not wholeheartedly behind his case, and placed his hope in external help that never materialized. Just as the fortunes of war repeatedly changed in 1941–42, Ciano's considerations waffled between entering into a bargain with the West and continuing to fight. Only when the military situation became desperate at the end of 1942 did Ciano become more serious in his attempts to remove Italy from the war. This very back-and-forth confirmed the negative impressions held by possible negotiators that Ciano should not be trusted. But this policy in fact typified Ciano's approach to diplomacy: he wanted to keep all options open, which is most likely why he decided to become ambassador to the Holy See in the spring of 1943. The post allowed him to remain in Rome, close to the political events, yet removed from the intrigues and internal conflicts of the regime.[414]

The ongoing losses sustained by German and Italian troops and the superiority of the Allies made Ciano doubt the chances of successful peace negotiations. "We have the choice," Ciano told Pirelli in October 1942, "between a compromise peace and defeat. The opponent has the choice between a compromise peace and victory. So why should we believe that Roosevelt and Churchill don't want to achieve everything?"[415] Today, we might dismiss this logic as an excuse not to talk to the Allies in the first place. However, it once again illustrates Ciano's understanding of power and strength. In his opinion, there was no obvious reason why a nation should give away a total victory – a fascist government, one could conclude from his argument, would not have done so. Indeed, the British were not eager to make peace with Italy and refused to negotiate with Mussolini or any other fascist leader.[416] London's attitude was another reason why Ciano's peace initiatives were only lukewarm at the beginning. However, one fact is certain: until the end of 1942 Ciano was not ready to act independently of the *Duce*; he wanted to start his peace offers with Mussolini, not without him.[417]

Blackmail, Terror, and War

Ciano rejected the idea of a great war against the Western powers while he did not shy away from violence and war in general. However, they had to offer a quick and relatively inexpensive way for Italy to expand its empire or at least its influence, as is illustrated by Italian intervention in the Spanish Civil War (1936–39) and the occupation of Albania in April 1939. Both examples provide significant insight into the connection between Ciano's political standing in Italy and his foreign policy, his ideas about the creation and administration of an Italian *spazio vitale*, and his previously described performative foreign policy, his strategies, tactics, and worldviews.

The Spanish Civil War

Immediately after the outbreak of the Spanish Civil War on 17 July 1936, Francisco Franco requested material help from Rome.[418] Whereas Mussolini and the head of the *Servizio Informazione Militare* (SIM), Mario

Roatta, rejected Franco's request, Ciano wanted to support the nationalists as he was convinced that it was of utmost importance to assist Franco.[419] He possessed information that Catholic churches had been desecrated by followers of the Republic, Italian citizens were in danger, and the government in Madrid had already asked Paris for help.[420] On 27 July he announced that planes were ready to take off for Melilla on 30 July.[421] Many scholars have speculated that Ciano was acting on his own without Mussolini's approval.[422] Such autonomous action seems very unlikely, given Ciano's devotion to Mussolini at the time. Nevertheless, Ciano still closely observed the developments in Spain and evaluated the chances of a successful intervention without informing the *Duce* in any detail. He was one of the driving forces in Rome who wanted Italy to intervene in the civil war on Franco's behalf.[423]

In the end, the *Duce* gave in to Ciano's urging. Reports from Italian diplomats and military and intelligence experts had assured that small but effective support would suffice to decide the conflict in favour of the nationalists.[424] France, although willing to help the Spanish Republic, was inhibited by Britain.[425] The counsellor of the Italian embassy in London, Vitetti, possessed reliable information that Great Britain would rather support the rebels than the current government.[426] Several other diplomats reported that the Soviet Union did not intend to interfere in the conflict and that Berlin was supporting Franco's uprising. While German aid increased Franco's chances of victory, Ciano feared that Berlin's presence in Spain would lead to a subsequent reduction of Italy's influence in the Mediterranean.[427] However, the claim that Rome only became involved in Spain after Germany pressured the Italians to do so is a fabrication that former fascists spread after the Second World War.[428]

Ciano's decision to help the insurgents was thus indispensably linked to the realistic chances of the rebel's victory.[429] It would be wrong to accuse him of carelessness in his decision-making simply because the civil war dragged on for three years.[430] However, consumed by the prospect of a quick and easy victory, Ciano did not consider the possibility of a long conflict and its consequences. In addition to economic and political benefits, Ciano and the *Duce* anticipated geostrategic advantages in the case of a nationalist victory.[431] Three other factors also played a role in Ciano's thinking. First, the Spanish Civil War was a manifestation of the ideological conflict between fascism and communism. Even when faced with the death of many Italians in Spain, Ciano did not question the decision to intervene since it was "our culture and our revolution" that was being defended on the Iberian Peninsula. Moreover, Ciano realized that the anti-communist card was useful in obtaining moral support from the Catholic Church and the conservative establishment of Europe at large.[432] Second, Ciano feared that, with the current government in Madrid, another Popular Front regime in addition to the one in France could hold power in the Mediterranean region.[433] The anti-French element of Italian interference was reflected in the Spanish-Italian Friendship Treaty of November 1936, in which Franco pledged to prevent any transfer of troops between France and North Africa.[434] Finally, personal motives such as vanity, the pursuit of fame, prestige, and recognition played a role for Ciano, as did his own expectations and those of the public that the interests of Fascist Italy would always be forcefully communicated to the outside world.[435]

Mussolini also intended to promote the formation of a fascist regime in Madrid and to fascistize Spanish society.[436] Ciano, too, apparently harboured such ambitious plans, even though he set other priorities for the time being. For him, it was much more important to re-establish the monarchy in Madrid. He argued that, since the fascist movement in Spain was far too insignificant, only a restoration could provide the peace and stability that the country so urgently needed.[437] Unlike Mussolini, Ciano viewed the monarchy as a strong ally, and his desire to restore the monarchy also shaped his initial dealings with Franco. In February 1937 he appointed Roberto Cantalupo, a staunch monarchist, as the first Italian ambassador to Franco.[438] At the beginning of March, Roberto Farinacci visited Franco on a "delicate mission." On Ciano's orders, he was supposed to convince the *Caudillo* to enthrone a prince from the Italian royal family of Savoy, namely Amedeo, Duke of Aosta, as the new Spanish king. Then it would have been easy for the Italian government to decisively influence domestic politics in Spain, including the fascistization of Spanish society. Although Farinacci's mission failed and a scandal erupted between him and Cantalupo, who was not privy to the plans of the *ras*, it exemplifies Ciano's sense of purpose, which he had internalized since his time as minister of propaganda.[439]

The Italian intervention did not start well. Of the original twelve aircraft, only nine reached their destination.[440] With the advent of Italian support for the insurgents, the French government, with British backing, proposed the creation of a Non-Intervention Committee (NIC) to prevent escalation of the conflict. This committee, set up in London on 15 August 1936, was intended to ensure that no foreign power intervened in the civil war and that the integrity of Spanish territory was preserved.[441] As was already clear from Ciano's attitude towards the League of Nations, international bodies did not deter him from pursuing a policy that would propel Italy to greatness. For this reason, he instructed the Italian representative on the committee, Ambassador Grandi, to sabotage its work by means of diplomatic tricks and subterfuge.[442]

While the committee was debating, Italian deliveries of weaponry to Franco continued uninterrupted.[443] Contrary to Ciano's hopes the nationalists failed to secure a rapid victory, and the longer the conflict lasted, the more he and the fascist regime depended on Franco's success. Failure would have meant a serious setback for Italy at the international level and a bitter defeat for Ciano personally, especially after the *Duce* had appointed him to lead the Spanish campaign.[444] For the *Duce*, Machiavellian considerations played a role in giving Ciano a free hand in Spain. Should the nationalists win with Italian support, he knew that the success would ultimately be credited to him. Should they lose, however, he could easily blame Ciano, who publicly staged himself as the mastermind behind Italian intervention.[445] The disastrous defeat in Guadalajara (March 1937), the "Caporetto in Spain," proved the efficacy of Mussolini's strategy as Ciano was solely blamed for the fiasco.[446] Therefore, the *Duce* took on no personal risk by participating in the civil war, but a defeat for the nationalists would have cast doubt on Ciano's abilities and intensified accusations of nepotism against him. Consequently, the conflict in Spain became Ciano's personal prestige project.

Knowing that he was doomed to win in Spain, Ciano did everything he could to help Franco. Even when the *Duce* contemplated retreat after devastating defeats, Ciano defended the intervention.[447] He not only had to fight Mussolini's moodiness but also resistance from the army and members of the fascist regime. One of his main opponents was Federico Baistrocchi, army chief of staff and state secretary in the Ministry of War. In October 1936 Ciano was able to remove him in favour of Alberto Pariani. Pariani made no secret of his philo-German attitude, which would come in handy when coordinating Italian and German intervention in Spain.[448] At the same time, Baistrocchi's removal allowed Ciano to settle a score from the Ethiopian War, when Baistrocchi had tried to initiate legal proceedings against Ciano's friend Zenone Benini on grounds of a lack of discipline.[449]

Baistrocchi was, however, no exception. Other people also became victims of Ciano's zeal, people he accused of being insufficiently committed to Franco's victory. This reshuffling was particularly evident in his unconventional personnel decisions as to who should lead the Italian voluntary troops in Spain – the *Corpo di Truppe Volontarie* (CTV). When Franco suffered a defeat at the gates of Madrid in November 1936, Mussolini and Ciano decided to send Italian soldiers to Spain. Their number grew rapidly to 47,000 men, 20,000 of whom belonged to the regular Italian army.[450] Mussolini initially entrusted the CTV to General Roatta. After the defeat in Guadalajara, Ciano replaced Roatta with General Mario Berti. But Berti could not meet the high expectations either, so Ciano relieved him of his duties in October 1938 and installed General Gastone Gambara as his successor.[451] If the dismissals of the commanders show similar motives and patterns to those we already observed when Baistrocchi was ousted, the case of Gambara illustrated that the opposite could also happen. Ciano was so pleased with Gambara's work that he actively supported the general's promotion well into the Second World War.[452]

London in particular criticized the deployment of Italian soldiers to Spain. In the NIC heated arguments between the British and Italians erupted, and Britain issued numerous sharp protest notes. Ciano justified the participation of Italian soldiers and militias as a "voluntary and spontaneous" expression of a widespread anti-communist feeling among Italian youth. In addition, he threatened to send more "volunteers" if London did not stop Paris from helping the Spanish Republic, hoping that this threat alone would have the desired effect. But still, unlike Mussolini, Ciano acted cautiously in 1937 and did not want to force the British government – and Neville Chamberlain in particular – into action and potentially provoke an escalation of the conflict through an uncontrolled deployment of Italians. That is why he always paid close attention to how many Italian fighters were actually in Spain.[453]

In order to be able to monitor the campaigns in Spain, Ciano created the *Ufficio Spagna* under Luca Pietromarchi, which also controlled the interactions with the Germans, in particular with the military attaché at the German embassy in Rome, Major General Enno von Rintelen.[454] Through this office Ciano also had direct contact with the Italian commanders in Spain, neatly circumventing the Italian general staff. This arrangement allowed him to intervene not only in personnel issues but also in strategic and tactical planning.[455] He had Italian submarines patrolling to stop supply and troop transports for the Spanish Republic. In the summer of 1937 alone, seven transport ships were sunk. Ciano was "very satisfied" and optimistic that the transports would soon stop. He even considered using poison gas as the last resort to win the civil war.[456]

Ciano's influence was also evident when Franco's troops conquered Santander. In August 1937 he ordered Italian troops to cut off the city from the local water supply and launch the final assault while Britain and the Soviet Union were distracted by the conflict between China and Japan. In collaboration with the Japanese government, Ciano agreed to maintain pressure on Moscow both in Asia and Spain to ultimately prevent effective Soviet intervention in both conflicts. After Santander was taken, Ciano was relieved and particularly proud of the praise he received from the *Duce*.[457]

Of course, whenever nationalist troops achieved a victory with Italy's support a well-staged celebration was in order. It was an excellent opportunity to publicly show the world the power of Italian fascism. Therefore, Ciano sent many war correspondents to Spain with the task of highlighting the successes of the Italian soldiers and spreading anti-Bolshevik propaganda.[458] He was particularly interested in inserting stories and news featuring the "glorious" role of the Italians in the German press. He hoped both to improve Italy's image with the German public and to convince the Nazi leaders of the strength of Italy's army and the advantages of an alliance with Rome.[459]

Ciano not only manipulated the NIC, interfered in the course of the war, and deposed critics (or, in his opinion, incompetent military personnel), but he also tried to stop any form of aid for the Spanish Republic, including the large number of volunteers who fought in the "International Brigades."[460] Italian anti-fascists supported the Spanish Republic, offering living proof that Italy was not a nation united behind the *Duce*, as Italian propaganda trumpeted. Among the most prominent activists were the brothers Nello and Carlo Rosselli, who lived in exile in Paris, the "capital of anti-fascism." As co-founders of the anti-fascist group *Giustizia e Libertà*, they recruited volunteers for the International Brigades, fought with the Republic, and had preached against Fascist Italy for years.[461] Thanks to an excellent network of informers in Paris, the government in Rome was well informed about their actions and commitment.[462] On 9 June 1937 the Rosselli brothers were killed by members of the secret French right-wing extremist organization *Cagoule*. The Italian government and media immediately put the blame for the murders on disputes within the anti-fascist milieu. However, a member of the *Cagoule* later testified before a court that the murders had been ordered by Sante Emanuele, head of the Italian secret service's counterintelligence department of the SIM. An agent provocateur at the Italian embassy in Paris acted as an intermediary between the SIM and *Cagoule*.[463]

Today, this claim by the French extremist seems very likely true. To what extent high-ranking officials of the fascist regime such as then head of the SIM, Roatta, or the *Duce* were involved in the assassination plot is still debated. There are numerous clues that Ciano himself was pulling the strings in the background, as Emanuele and Vittorio Cerruti testified under oath in September 1944.[464] But we should be cautious in taking these statements at face value as both Emanuele and Cerruti were directly or indirectly involved in the murder of the Rosselli brothers. Did they blame a deceased person in order to obtain a sentence reduction? We do not possess any written documents from the summer of 1937 to verify their claims. The relevant pages in Ciano's diary are also missing.[465] But their testimony is not the only indication that Ciano was very likely involved – two additional reasons present themselves. First, the Rosselli murders dovetail with Ciano's unscrupulous attempts to end the Spanish Civil War as quickly as possible by any available means. Second, Ciano employed Sante Emanuele to remove unwelcome critics at least one other time. In the summer of 1938, he hired Emanuele to kidnap his former superior at the newspaper *L'Impero*, Emilio Settimelli, who had fallen from grace because he criticized the fascist regime.[466] Even though there are no further remarks about the "Settimelli case" in Ciano's diary, the Italian security apparatus soon caught up with the dissident journalist and sentenced him to several years of exile.[467]

Despite Ciano's attempts to end the conflict quickly, it soon developed into a long war of attrition. Wishing to protect himself from increasing criticism he began to look for other parties outside his commanders whom he could blame. In particular, he aimed his anger at the Spanish and Franco himself. He accused Spanish diplomats in Franco's service of a pro-British attitude and criticized Franco's army as having "no momentum and no rush" to end the campaign.[468] Moreover, he accused Franco of passivity and inability, in his opinion typical signs of Spanish negligence and weak leadership.[469] He did not realize that both the contacts with British diplomats and the delaying tactics were part of Franco's strategy.[470]

From the very beginning, Ciano, who believed in the racial superiority of the Italians, viewed the Italian relationship with Spain as that of a teacher and student, respectively. He publicly lectured Spanish politicians and officers, Franco included.[471] Thus, the relationship between Rome and Franco was confrontational from the outset. One reason for this stance was that Franco, Mussolini, and Ciano did not pursue common goals; rather, their cooperation was mostly based on shared resentments: anti-communism and an opposition to French hegemony in the Mediterranean. Paul Preston offered an apt assessment of the Spanish-Italian cooperation in those years: "In the last resort, [the relationship] ... was one of give and take in which the Duce had given, and the Caudillo had taken."[472]

When on 26 January 1939 Barcelona surrendered, the situation in Spain finally turned in favour of the nationalists. According to Mussolini, Franco's victory in the Catalan capital was a milestone in creating the new Europe.[473] Above all the capture of the city meant that an end to the civil war was in sight and Italy would be freed from its costly commitment to Franco. Franco's troops finally conquered Madrid on 28 March 1939, officially ending the war. "Madrid has fallen," Ciano wrote in his diary. "The war is over. It is a new formidable victory for Fascism, perhaps the greatest one so far."[474] Franco's victory was indeed a prestigious win for fascist movements throughout Europe and increased the pressure on Paris. The danger of French encirclement by fascist powers loomed, despite Britain's assurances of solidarity.

In the summer of 1939, Ciano visited Spain at the invitation of then Spanish minister of the interior Ramón Serrano Suñer and tried to showcase Italy's power and strength.[475] The journey was supposed to be a personal triumphal march for Ciano, who sought to reap the rewards for his support of Franco's cause. Therefore, one thing was certain: Ciano needed to get to Spain as soon as possible in order to demonstrate that Franco owed his victory above all to Ciano and Italy.[476] Despite his self-centred narcissism, Ciano knew that he was deeply indebted to one of his employees, Luca Pietromarchi, the director of the *Ufficio Spagna*. Ciano therefore insisted that Pietromarchi accompany him on his journey so that he also could enjoy Spanish gratitude. Ciano's gesture, as well as his commitment to seeing Pietromarchi amply rewarded for his work, underlines once again Ciano's respect for Pietromarchi.[477]

On 10 July 1939 the Italian delegation arrived in Barcelona and continued by plane to Madrid. Ciano, dressed in his aviator uniform, and his companions were given a solemn reception, and he was welcomed by the political dignitaries of the new Spain, including Franco.[478] Franco praised and thanked Mussolini in a way that convinced Ciano that Franco was completely taken with the *Duce*'s personality.[479] Nevertheless, the Spaniards also made it very clear that Ciano was only a guest in their country. The journalist Signoretti described how a sobered Ciano reacted with injured pride to the distanced behaviour of Spanish politicians. Ciano had given himself the illusion, Signoretti continued, that he would be celebrated as the "great protector of the new Spanish nation," as "Franco's Hidalgo."[480] In the end, Ciano was unable to make any real progress in the diplomatic field. Despite the publicly displayed "brotherhood" between Fascist Italy and Francoist Spain, he was unable to bring Spain closer to the Axis, as he had originally intended.[481]

The Occupation of Albania

Italian governments persistently showed a strong interest in Albania and attempted to expand their influence into this region, particularly for geostrategic reasons and control of Albania's raw materials.

Ciano continued this policy as soon as he took over the *Palazzo Chigi* by (unsuccessfully) using his aristocratic contacts and by supporting Italy's economic and financial penetration of Albania.[482] When Ciano ordered the expansion of the embassy building in Tirana in August 1937, he displayed Italian self-perception for all to see. Taking the premises of the British High Commission in Cairo as a model, Ciano argued that the new embassy building must "emphasize our predominance" in the country.[483]

In April 1938 Ciano concluded that, in light of the German annexation of Austria, only the territorial conquest of Albania was acceptable. He convinced the *Duce* of his plans and proposed a radical solution:[484] inciting a revolution against the Albanian king, Ahmet Zog, and then occupying Albania in order to protect Italian interests, or so the official justification would claim. With this scenario in mind, Ciano began to intensify the pro-Italian propaganda in Albania, which was increasingly directed against the Albanian royal family. He ordered the delivery of large quantities of grain to the poor in Albania and made a generous monetary donation to those in need. Although the latter was Ciano's official wedding present to King Zog and the Hungarian Countess Geraldine Apponyi de Nagy-Appony, he deliberately dedicated the money to those who had the most reason to despise the current regime in Tirana.[485]

However, in addition to international developments, the situation in Albania began to slowly turn against Italy. As the country's budget slowly stabilized, Albania's financial dependence on Italy moved towards an end, and King Zog tried to free himself from the tightening noose. He established closer contacts with Western states and dismissed his minister of economic affairs, Jak Koçi. Koçi – a friend of Rome with strong Italian roots – was largely responsible for giving Italian companies great influence in Albania.[486]

After losing his local confidante, who had to flee to Italy, and after the ousting of Stojadinović in February 1939, Ciano discussed the next steps with Francesco Jacomoni, then head of the Italian legation in Tirana. With the backing of Mussolini both agreed that they had to start the invasion in early April in order to avoid further complications.[487] Koçi even agreed to assassinate King Zog for ten million lire, and Italian companies began to buy up coastal areas in consultation with Ciano to facilitate the potential landing of Italian troops in these areas.[488] Thus, the course was set for the assassination of the king and the Italian occupation – a change of heart was hardly possible considering the loss of prestige it would incur.

After the German occupation of Prague, Ciano pushed for even faster action as he feared that Berlin would continue to move southeast and jeopardize Italy's plans for Albania. He therefore made it clear to Ambassador Mackensen that he expected Germany to show the same lack of interest in the Balkans as Italy did in Czechoslovakia. After all, Albania was an Italian "family affair."[489] Even Ribbentrop's personal confirmation that Berlin had no interests in the region did not completely reassure Ciano.[490] The occupation of Albania was for Ciano primarily a response to Germany's actions in Austria and Prague; Mussolini, on the other hand, regarded the conquest of Albania as an anti-British and anti-French manoeuvre. Thus, he put the plans for the conquest of Albania on hold after his initial anger over the invasion of Prague had calmed. Reluctantly, Ciano obeyed the orders for now and publicly announced that Italy had no ambitions in Albania.[491]

On 24 March Ciano officially resumed talks with King Zog and made him a new proposal for future bilateral relations. However, this offer was more of an ultimatum, a demand for Tirana's surrender, than a serious basis for negotiations. Ciano was nevertheless convinced that Zog would accept it. After all, Zog's wife was expecting a child, and Ciano presumed that the monarch would not want to put his pregnant wife at risk.[492] This logic once again demonstrates the calculating cynicism of which Ciano was capable in pursuit of a goal. But it also reveals that Ciano hoped until the end that Zog would surrender in order to avoid a military conflict. Diplomatic manoeuvres, threats, and coercion were Ciano's weapons of choice in the pursuit of new territories, not an open war that could escalate. Ciano therefore approached the Albanian envoy in Rome, Zef Serreqi, and asked him to convince King Zog to accept the Italian ultimatum. To motivate Serreqi further Ciano gave him a "tip" of 15,000 lire and promised a place in Italian schools for his relatives.[493]

Ciano was all the more disappointed when Zog, instead of accepting the ultimatum, requested new negotiations. For a moment he was unsure what to do; he was still not ready to fire the "first shot," which might incite a major European conflagration.[494] Yet Ciano had also manoeuvred himself into a dead end. Further talks would buy Zog valuable time and signal that Italy had yielded to a weaker country. In this situation, the *Duce* once again changed his mind. After Franco had conquered Madrid, he pushed for an invasion of Albania to happen sooner rather than later. The previous German successes in Austria and Czechoslovakia combined with Franco's victory in the Spanish Civil War put Mussolini under increasing pressure. As the self-proclaimed founder of fascism, he had to show the world and his own people that Italy was also able to achieve a victory. He ordered Ciano to "take the conquest plans for Albania out of the drawer."[495] When Ciano was finally informed by his secret service that London was not prepared to risk a war over Albania, he gave the orders to resume military preparations, though without informing the armed forces about the exact terms of the invasion.[496]

Italian diplomats in Rome and Albania still stuck to their denial: no, a landing of Italian troops was not planned. Ciano and Jacomoni, enamoured of their own cunning, were certain that nobody suspected their real plans. As Ciano noted, you can tell diplomats anything you want.[497] Although Ciano's assessment might hold true for some foreign ministers and members of the embassies in Rome, foreign diplomats in Albania were much better informed and much more suspicious about Italy's behaviour. That is why Ciano also ordered the Italian secret service to block British communication channels between Albania, London, and Rome.[498] To Hugh G. Grant, US consul in Tirana, all the lies, obfuscations, and intrigues were reminiscent of Shakespeare's play *The Comedy of Errors*.[499]

In the meantime, Ciano took over planning for the invasion. He had to abandon his first idea to send Ettore Muti to Tirana to provoke anti-Italian uprisings because the Albanian capital was on high alert.[500] Instead, he focused on creating a diplomatic environment favourable for the imminent invasion by putting increased pressure on the government in Belgrade. To avoid interference from Yugoslavia, he continued to support the Croatian separatists and successfully asked the Hungarian government to mobilize its troops on the border with Yugoslavia.[501] On 4 April Mussolini convened his cabinet in Rome for a meeting at which Ciano informed the ministers of the imminent invasion.[502]

Unfortunately, it is nearly impossible to accurately reconstruct Ciano's next moves, as his own diary proves to be untrustworthy. He wrote his notes on several pages, stuck on additional notes, and repeatedly changed individual passages – this mishmash alone makes it hard to extract a precise chronological order.[503] In addition, the content is rife with inconsistencies. For example, on 4 April he wrote that the *Duce* had set King Zog an ultimatum valid until noon on Thursday, 6 April. A day later, following a request from the Albanian king to give him more time, Mussolini set a new ultimatum: Thursday, 6 April, noon.[504] However, Bottai reported that it was already clear on the evening of 4 April that the invasion of Albania would begin at 4:30 am on Friday, 7 April.[505] One cannot help but suspect that Ciano used his diary to record his own version of the truth, like his story about the situation of Italian citizens in Albania, which Grant called the "official excuse" for Italy's invasion.[506] In this respect, Ciano had noted that the situation for the Italians in Albania was deteriorating sharply, which is why Rome had been pushed into sending two warships to Vlora and Durrës to evacuate those affected.[507]

On the evening of 6 April, King Zog and the Albanian parliament rejected the Italian ultimatum. At the same time, they signalled their willingness to negotiate new conditions. Once again, the Albanian regime sought to buy time, hoping to improve the country's defences and to remove the royal family from the country.[508] While diplomatic skirmishes continued, Italians continued their preparations and began to evacuate their citizens from Albania under the protection of airplanes. Ciano hoped that the planes would demonstrate Rome's military power and might lead to a domestic uprising against the king. According to information he received from Tirana, his strategy seemed to work, as people were filled with horror when they saw the aircrafts.[509] The report by the American consul Grant reads quite differently. Anti-Italian demonstrations took place on the streets, and the people demanded mobilization and armament. "The scene," Grant continued, "recalled to my mind a student demonstration in a typical American university on the eve of a big football game."[510]

On 7 April 1939 Ciano boarded his plane at six in the morning to witness the conquest of Albania. Visibly pleased with the development of the invasion, Ciano returned to Rome and informed a delighted Mussolini. Their joy proved premature. The Italian commanding officer, General Alfredo Guzzoni, had to halt the advance and negotiate with representatives of King Zog due to insufficient military planning. Ciano was outraged by the general's allegedly unauthorized actions.[511] He feared losing valuable time and urged a resolute advance to take the capital, Tirana, because there, he wrote in his diary, Albanian "bandits" allegedly not only plundered the royal palace but also threatened the Italian legation.[512] Once again, Grant's report raises doubts about the accuracy of Ciano's notes. "It may be revealed one of these days," Grant noted, "that the so-called 'night of terror' in Tirana and the looting of the Palace was a part of the carefully planned Italian plot, cunningly designed to discredit the King and establish a pretext for the alleged necessity of bringing in Italian troops to quell the rioting."[513]

On Saturday, 8 April about 300 Italian aircraft carrying about 1,000 Italian soldiers landed in Tirana and secured the airport of the Albanian capital. In mid-morning Ciano arrived in Tirana, accompanied by members of the Ministry of Propaganda and several journalists.[514] He promised the Albanian parliamentarians that Rome would respect Albania's independence and "guarantee the political, social, and civil development of the Albanian people."[515] Immediately after his arrival, Ciano started a pro-Italian propaganda campaign. He promised 10,000 poor

Albanian children a holiday in an Italian coastal region and personally distributed money to Albanian politicians and the poor.[516] Ciano also ordered the release of "political prisoners."[517] According to Italian sources, 12 Italians were killed and 43 injured throughout the operation. These low figures were quickly questioned. According to today's estimates, more than 700 Italian soldiers died during the invasion of Albania.[518]

Congratulations from Germany and Hungary aside, international reactions were largely negative. Western criticism was directed primarily against Ciano who had portrayed himself as the mastermind of this plot. The American consul Grant pointed out to his government that Ciano's speech to the Chamber of Deputies on 15 April contained so many untruths about the Italian invasion and the whereabouts of the Albanian queen that he and his colleagues were forced to publish a correction.[519] In addition, Washington protested against Italy's "totalitarian tactics" and did not establish formal relations with the new Albanian foreign minister, who was regarded as Ciano's puppet.[520]

Ciano, however, was pleased to notice that London accepted the annexation of Albania without any fuss. To London's surprise, Ciano put a totally different spin on Britain's conciliatory approach.[521] He argued that London obviously had no interest in following the Easter Agreement of April 1938, in which Italy and Britain had committed themselves to maintaining the status quo in the Mediterranean. By occupying Albania, Rome had violated the agreement. If London had insisted on compliance with the agreement, London should have intervened – ergo, he accused the British government of not being serious about the Easter Agreement. Ciano's condescending attitude, his smugness, and his arrogance all caused great discontent and anger in London. A British diplomat was astounded by Ciano's "logic ... We behaved well over Albania, where Signor Mussolini shook our confidence in the Agreement, so the Italians must ask us whether we still attach importance to it; Fascist logic with a vengeance."[522]

The continued deployment of Italian troops to Albania did nothing to ease British-Italian tensions. By mid-May about 75,000 Italian soldiers and more than 200 tanks were stationed in the country. Athens reacted by improving its defences and mobilizing troops.[523] Although neither Greece nor Britain feared an immediate attack, London demanded immediate assurance of Greece's territorial integrity from Ciano.[524] The threat to Greece as well as public pressure finally led the British government to reconsider their policy towards Fascist Italy. As a consequence, London signed a defence treaty with Greece and Turkey, which committed them to maintaining the status quo.[525]

Ciano considered the conquest of Albania a personal success, though he failed to recognize the high price he had paid for the victory. He had lost all credibility with both the British and the Americans.[526] Ciano had been so proud of his improved British-Italian relations in the course of the Easter Agreement, but he then jeopardized that progress with his policy in Albania. At the end of May 1939 Ciano acknowledged that the "British-Italian agreement is dead."[527] Neither he nor the British Ambassador Loraine saw any chance to improve relations in a timely manner.[528] This deadlock was also reflected in Ambassador Dino Grandi's recall from London; Ciano initially chose not to appoint any successor.[529]

Guerri claimed that after the occupation of Albania Ciano was considering withdrawing Italy from the Axis.[530] But such a step would only have resulted in Italy's isolation, given Rome's strained relations with the West at that time. Moreover, the conquest of Albania was clearly intended to demonstrate to the Italian public the benefits of being part of the Axis. Besides, Ciano seemed unconcerned about Italy's reputation in the West. He had more power and prestige in Italy than ever before – what could go possibly wrong? It was not until the end of April 1939 that his convictions were shattered when Bernardo Attolico indicated that Germany's invasion of Poland was imminent. Could this be true? Had Ribbentrop not claimed less than a year ago that Berlin would accept the "Polish Corridor ... for an indefinite period of time?"[531] If Attolico was right, then Ciano had no illusions about the future: "That would mean war."[532]

While relations between Rome and the West were at a low point and Ciano was concerned about Germany's intentions, he began to implement his long-planned political ideas for Albania.[533] A Council of Regency was formed, and a Constituent Assembly was convened on 12 April, which confirmed the royal personal union between Albania and Italy. Ciano wanted to demonstrate that the Italian presence in Albania was not a hostile takeover but had been initiated by the Albanians themselves. Therefore, Rome did not formally annex the country, though the Italian press was instructed to no longer speak of an "Albanian state."[534] Once again Ciano had too much confidence in his own cunning. The American consul Grant never doubted the inferior status of the Albanian protectorate and exposed the Council of Regency and the Constituent Assembly as a farce, revealing that their members had been bribed by Italy.[535]

On 13 April Ciano established the State Secretariat for Albania within the Foreign Ministry under the leadership of Zenone Benini. With a budget of 490 million lire, the new office was responsible for political, economic, and administrative matters.[536] Francesco Jacomoni, who was promoted to the rank of viceroy, took over the coordination on the spot.[537] Ciano even tried to exercise control over the Albanian Fascist Party, which was officially under the jurisdiction of Achille Starace. With Ciano's backing, Piero Parini, who had previously been responsible for the *fasci all'estero* in the Foreign Ministry, became the new party leader in Albania.[538] In sum, these measures enabled Ciano to personally control the future developments in Albania.

At the end of April, the newly formed Albanian cabinet under Prime Minister Shefqet Bej Vërlaci conferred on Mussolini the title "Albania's first honorary citizen" and on Ciano the title "Tirana's honorary citizen." Ciano, the official statement read, had become a close confidante to the Albanian people in a "historic hour."[539] Furthermore, the Roman salute was introduced for all state officials; fascist party organizations such as *Dopolavoro* were created; and key functionary positions in Albania were occupied by Italians.[540] The Albanian gendarmerie and army were integrated into the corresponding Italian institutions, and in mid-May the *Palazzo Chigi* took over the Albanian Foreign Ministry.[541] Ciano also brought the media and propaganda landscape under Italian supervision in order to spread Italian culture in Albania.[542] Moreover, the school system was redesigned according to the Italian model, and the teaching materials were adapted to the Italian ones in order to educate the Albanian youth in the ethos of the fascist regime. In addition, Ciano was careful to secure the goodwill of the Albanian ministers by showering them with offices and titles.[543]

The *Palazzo Chigi* under Ciano also urged the Albanians to pass anti-Jewish laws similar to those adopted in Italy.[544] It was a further step in Italy's gradual takeover of Albania, with which Ciano hoped to secure the continuous support of Albanian nationalists. Since the summer of 1938 they had been trying to discriminate against Jews and close the country's borders to Jewish refugees.[545] Although Italian diplomats on the ground expressed serious doubts about the necessity of anti-Jewish measures, the *Palazzo Chigi* nevertheless revised a first draft of an Albanian race law in order to prevent differing "Jewish policies" in Albania and Italy.[546] Ciano and the *Palazzo Chigi*'s ambiguous attitude towards the Jews was also evident in Jacomoni's attempt to quickly expel all foreign Jews from the country. It was neither possible to implement this measure in the short term nor was Ciano willing to grant the Jews a temporary right of residence in Italy as put forward by Jacomoni.[547] Little is known today about the fate of the Jews in Albania from the outbreak of the war and beyond. The available information suggests that, whereas the expulsion of the Jews remained extremely difficult, many Jews actually fled to Albania or were deported there by Italian authorities and finally interned.[548]

The Italians also took over the Albanian economy. After the establishment of the Albanian-Italian customs union, corporatism and Italian economic law were introduced, and the lira became the sole means of payment in 1941. These measures allowed Italian companies such as the AGIP to acquire monopolies over economic sectors and resources. In order to increase production in Albania and export more raw materials to Italy, a massive expansion of the country's infrastructure was planned, including 1,400 kilometres of new roads and improved water and electricity supplies.[549]

Italy's takeover of the state institutions of Albania was only the prelude to Ciano's more far-reaching plans.[550] He wanted to bring thousands of Italians to Albania without, however, driving the Albanians out of their territory; he wanted to build Italian villages, construct public buildings, and Italianize Albanian towns and communities. The Albanian port city of Saranda was renamed Porto Edda in honour of his wife.[551] Several streets and squares in the capital Tirana also received new names such as Benito Mussolini, Vittorio Emanuele, and Costanzo and Galeazzo Ciano.[552] In addition, pompous ceremonies and events continuously reminded the Albanian people who was now in charge.[553]

Again, and again, Ciano assured those who would listen that everything had been done for the benefit of Albania. The Italians, he argued, were aware of their responsibility to lead the Albanian people into a "new order" and to "new greatness."[554] Ciano's policy in Albania exemplifies some of his key ideas of what constituted an appropriate occupation policy:[555] Italianization of the native population, society, and politics; coordination with the Italian state; involvement of the Italian crown; economic penetration; and the bribery of influential personalities in order to secure their cooperation – and all of it should happen under the direction, control, and coordination of the Foreign Ministry. This ideal assumed that the majority of Albanians would comply with Italian rule – a fundamental misconception rooted in Ciano's belief in Italian racial and cultural superiority.

Shortly after the Italian takeover the first Albanian resistance groups formed. Neither Ciano nor Jacomoni were concerned about this development. In their arrogance they even dismissed the seriousness of an attempt to assassinate King Vittorio Emanuele III during his visit in early summer 1941. Ciano was confident that the Albanian people supported rule by Rome and had no doubt that they would see Italianization as he did: a blessing for all inferior races.[556] He regarded the expansion of Albanian territory after the conquest of Yugoslavia and Greece in particular as a stroke of genius. He thought that making Rome a champion of Albanian nationalism would only increase Italy's popularity among the Albanians.[557] In October 1940 the fascist government even unveiled a statue of Albanian national hero Skanderbeg on the *Piazza Albania* in Rome in the presence of Ciano and Mussolini.[558] Ciano did not realize that attempts to fascistize and Italianize Albania had already failed. The attempts to introduce an "artificial model" based on Italian doctrine cost Rome valuable support and sympathy from the Albanians.[559] Moreover, the Italian rulers were incapable of managing the disastrous living conditions and food shortages.[560]

The dissolution of the State Secretariat for Albania in August 1941 strengthened Jacomoni's position, who capitalized on his new power by requesting the replacement of Prime Minister Vërlaci with the nationalist Mustafa Kruja in November 1941. He hoped that this move would secure the support of the people in the face of growing resistance. Personal motivations cannot be ruled out either, as the relationship between Jacomoni and Vërlaci was far from friendly. Ciano was sceptical at first but capitulated when the *Duce* approved the plan. Kruja's appointment was a further sign of Ciano's decreasing influence within the larger fascist regime. Until this point, he had mostly decided Albania's destiny on his own, and the *Duce* had let him do it.[561]

Despite Jacomoni's unshakable optimism, the new prime minister failed to calm the situation in Albania. But Ciano continued to blindly trust the positive reports sent by the Italian viceroy in Tirana.[562] In the summer of 1942, Ciano informed the Senate Committee on Foreign Affairs about the situation in Albania. He drew a utopian image of a pacified country that stood in direct contrast to the rest of Europe. He obviously chose not to address the manifold problems in Albania, given that the report was mainly about solidifying his legacy.[563]

Only a few months later Ciano received a worrying report on covert British operations in Albania. To his mind, the new information confirmed what he and Jacomoni had always suspected. The uprisings in "his duchy" were not the product of Italy's policies but merely the result of the machinations of external forces.[564] Both men failed to realize that the disastrous living conditions in the country had ultimately enabled communists to build a united front against the Italians, which included various resistance groups ranging from the Zogists to the nationalists. Under joint leadership and with a unified strategy, the new Albanian opposition at the turn of 1942–43 posed a much more serious threat to Rome than ever before.[565]

The more the resistance against the Italians grew, the more important military counterinsurgency strategies became. As a result the civil authorities and thus the Foreign Ministry under Ciano increasingly lost their influence to their military counterparts – a phenomenon we can observe in all Italian-occupied areas.[566] In early 1943 the reports from Tirana left no doubt that the Albanians were striving for freedom from the Italian yoke. Ciano desperately tried to get the *Duce*'s approval to remove Jacomoni, because he thought the viceroy was incapable of defeating the rebels, and to deploy more troops to Albania.[567] His earlier premise of the need to concentrate soldiers in Italy to protect his homeland was suddenly forgotten when his beloved Albania was in danger.[568] "Only force will win," Ciano wrote, "though it is not to be used in the beginning, at least we should show that it is there."[569] Even in the face of open revolution, he hoped, as he had so often done during his time as foreign minister, that a show of power alone would suffice to avoid a military clash. In light of a crumbling empire and looming defeat, this view bordered on naivety and was rooted in despair, not conviction. When Mussolini offered Jacomoni's post to Ciano, he declined. He argued that he could not shoot and hang those to whom he had promised brotherhood and equal rights. It was only after Ciano's ousting as foreign minister that the *Duce* appointed the retired General Alberto Pariani as Jacomoni's successor.[570]

Assessing Fascist Italy's Foreign Diplomacy

The character of Italian foreign policy during the fascist era is still the subject of numerous debates. These discussions focus not only on Mussolini's supposed omnipotence in the political decision-making process, but also on questions of continuity and inconsistency in Italian diplomacy. Previous studies on Rome's foreign policy exhibit three major shortcomings. First, they predominantly deal with the Italian-German partnership, while Italy's relations with other states are either ignored or tainted by apologetic tendencies.[571] Second, Mussolini is often portrayed as the all-knowing mastermind behind Italian diplomacy. As a result, inconsistencies and contradictions like the *non belligeranza* policy and his martial rhetoric are interpreted as components of Mussolini's "master plan."[572] Third, many scholars only deal with Italy's foreign policy up to June 1940, when the country entered the Second World War. However, Italian diplomats continued to pursue specific goals and tried to influence the course of events – not always unsuccessfully.[573]

Recently, scholars have increased our knowledge of Italian foreign policy during the fascist era by deconstructing the meaning and consequences of the performative dimension of the bilateral relations between Rome and Berlin. The focus, however, has remained mostly on the two dictators and how they dominated the direction of their countries' foreign policy. An in-depth analysis of Galeazzo Ciano's performative and substantial diplomacy, including its areas of overlap and its reciprocal influences, enables us to expand on those studies and offer a more nuanced assessment of Italy's foreign policy. Such a multifaceted examination forces us to look behind the publicly constructed solidarity of the Axis and allows us to reveal its cracks, which then helps us better understand the dynamic that lead to Italy's entry into the Second World War.

Rome's foreign policy was much more heterogeneous than has previously been assumed. Several factions tried to influence the fate of the country on an international level, with Benito Mussolini and Galeazzo Ciano representing two different foreign policy schools. For Mussolini, life was defined by constant struggle. Heavily influenced by social-Darwinism and a follower of Georges Sorel's philosophy of the virtue of violence, he regarded war as men's essential purpose in life. It was through war that he intended to revolutionize Italian society and politics, break the "shackles" in the Mediterranean, build an empire, and create the "new man" in battle. Mussolini felt that the regime should break with traditional strategies such as the *peso determinante* and pursue a truly fascist foreign policy to realize those goals.[574]

Ciano's strategy deviated decisively from the *Duce*'s. His worldview was rooted in the chauvinistic and racist sense of superiority that emerged in nineteenth-century Italy – a fact that should not come as a surprise given his socialization, education, and the influence of his first mentors. Racism, irredentism, and imperialism, as well as the desire to be recognized as a great power, were key elements of his worldview. Nevertheless, when Ciano was at the centre of power nothing remained of the revolutionary spirit he possessed when he was attracted by the futurists as a student. Now, it was not Ciano's goal to start another revolution in Italy or to form the "new man" through a war with the Western democracies, as both would have endangered his position within the existing regime. Rather, in line with the traditional politics of the nineteenth-century great powers, Ciano wanted to create an empire in the Mediterranean and thus raise Italy to their level of standing. Such ideas fit into a more general discourse focused on the universality of the fascist idea in the early 1930s. Intellectuals of a younger generation believed that fascism had global validity and that Italian culture could serve as an engine for the civilization of colonial territories. This belief in a civilizing mission was rooted in the conviction that the Italians were the heirs of the Roman Empire and the Renaissance. Therefore, imperialism was justified through constant references to ancient Rome with the ultimate aim of recreating the *Pax Romana*.

Ciano's foreign policy may have been cynical and marked by arrogance; he may have succumbed to the pageantry of parades, ceremonies, and performative acts that blinded him to the broader contexts; and he may have become a victim of his own arrogance and naivety; but an ultimate confrontation with the Western powers was not among his goals. He probably had an early inkling that his ideas did not fully align with Mussolini's, but it was only in the spring of 1940, when the *Duce* decided to enter the Second World War, that he became fully aware of the depth of divide. Until then, Ciano had freely influenced Italian foreign policy, sometimes against Mussolini's preferences – or at least not always with Mussolini's unqualified approval. For as long as he had the support of the majority of fascist leaders, the royal house, the Vatican, industry, and above all the army leadership, he could assert himself against the *Duce*'s war plans and radical fascists, as the phase of *non belligeranza* impressively proves.

Despite their different understandings, Rome's relationship with Berlin was an important factor for both Ciano and Mussolini. There is no doubt that a personal bond existed between the *Duce* and Hitler, and that the propaganda machine deliberately used it to further the image of friendship between Berlin and Rome. This image became so convincing that both dictators found "themselves stuck with each other until war's bitter end."[575] Ciano was instrumental in creating and maintaining this image for a long time, which in turn gained political momentum of its own and offered no way out unless the dictators chose to forfeit their credibility. According to Goeschel, the "potent performance … usually succeeded in obscuring the long-standing tensions and mistrust between the two countries."[576] While the tendency of current research to focus on Hitler and Mussolini supports this argument, Ciano's role in the Axis relationship, however, reveals the limits of the performative diplomacy.

Ciano's ultimate goal was to create a new international reality by using a performative diplomacy to conjure the image of a strong and powerful Italy – mostly because the country lacked military, financial, and economic resources. In light of Italy's apparent weaknesses Ciano relied on the power of performance to bolster Italy's international standing. In particular, the degree of performance and its importance set him apart from his predecessors. It was not just a so-called new *tono fascista* that shaped Ciano's foreign policy, as some historians have suggested. Even Francesco Crispi's rhetoric was not far behind many martial fascist statements.[577] Much more important were the public demonstrations of power, the military parades, and the oaths of loyalty between the Axis powers, all of which were intended to conceal Italy's underlying weaknesses.

The publicly displayed friendship with Berlin was an important part of Ciano's strategy to construct Italy's power; however, Ciano himself was living proof of the mistrust and rivalry between Rome and Berlin as he would not hide his dislike of the Germans. This attitude meant that the misunderstandings, tensions, and rivalry were not only present behind the scenes, but were out in the open for everyone to see. As a consequence, Western politicians and diplomats did not fully buy the notion of a powerful Italy and an unbreakable friendship between Italians and Germans that extended beyond their leaders. Ciano's failure to also convince the Italian people, and himself for that matter, further undermined his entire strategy.

Consequently, Ciano's intended message proved futile, and the West was not ready to comply with his demands. It was therefore as consistent as it was reckless when Ciano escalated his strategy in the spring of 1939. He formed a military alliance with Berlin, closely linking Italy's fate with that of Germany and thus forfeiting his autonomy. At the time, he did not realize the full scope of this step, as he was still under the illusion that he could control Berlin. His naivety in these months does not excuse the fact that he played a decisive role in radicalizing and destabilizing the international order by bringing about the Pact of Steel, which Ciano regarded as the crucial tool for exerting pressure on the West to meet all his demands "peacefully."

When assessing Ciano's decision to finally enter into a military treaty with Berlin, we should not forget that the *Duce* was already willing to sign such an agreement in the summer of 1938. While Mussolini repeatedly stressed that the friendship between Germans and Italians existed in their hearts and thus did not require a formalized treaty, it seems that he himself was not so sure that it was true.[578] In opposition to the vast majority of Italians, including Ciano, he intended to sign a treaty with Germany early on, giving the performative friendship a substantial basis.

Despite Ciano jeopardizing the image of an unassailable Axis alliance, Mussolini and Hitler were determined to keep it alive and even enforce it during the war, when the cracks became more and more obvious.[579] The fear of losing credibility as well as geostrategic and ideological reasons played a vital role in this decision. The case of Ciano, however, reveals another reason why preservation of image was at all possible: Even before the August 1939 meeting, the Germans were increasingly suspicious of Ciano's real intentions and his commitment to the alliance. Eventually he would become the scapegoat for all the problems and tensions within the Italian-German alliance. Such tactics mirror those used in the Italian domestic sphere. Mussolini was always at a distance from criticism directed against the regime; the blame thus fell on the ministers and Ciano in particular, who were derided as incompetent and selfish. In addition to Ciano's criticism of Germans, his restructuring of the *Palazzo Chigi* put him at the centre of Italian diplomacy, a position he underscored by signing all the important treaties with Berlin. This central position in turn made him a better target for those seeking to pass the blame for diplomatic weaknesses and failures.

The case of Ciano demonstrates that the *Duce* was not perceived as being solely in charge of Italy's foreign policy.[580] Ciano played an essential role in the construction of the Rome-Berlin friendship, which officially began with the pomp and circumstance surrounding his visit to Germany in 1936. The fact that Ciano and other high-ranking officials of both countries would thereafter be received in a similar fashion strengthened the image of a deep and abiding friendship, not just between the two leaders but also between the peoples. This image was further supported by the reception given to members of the "second guard" of Italian and German leadership, including Ciano, who visited the other country more or less in equal numbers and frequency. These exchanges gave the impression that Italy and Germany were equal partners within the Axis, though Mussolini's frequent trips to Germany undermined such impressions by suggesting it was actually Hitler who called the shots.[581]

In addition, examining Ciano's actions reveals that Italy's performative diplomacy was not restricted to the Rome-Berlin Axis. It was an integral part of Ciano's approach to democratic and authoritarian countries alike – though his intentions varied accordingly. While such an extravagant diplomatic style was largely foreign to democratic governments and diplomats, the Third Reich and other authoritarian regimes such as Hungary, Romania, Yugoslavia, and Franco's Spain realized its significance when they wanted to establish good relations with Ciano and therefore Italy.[582] These governments also used a performative approach to foreign policy to highlight their power and importance and to construct an alliance system, the latter of which was based less on treaties, ideological similarities, and interests and more on a sense of communal belonging. Even the Axis had "no common strategy, let alone common war aims."[583]

The alliances between various authoritarian and fascist regimes mirror what historian Sven Reichardt has observed about the Italian fascist movement in general: it was held together "neither [by] a common … interest nor a consistent ideology, but above all [by] a … feeling."[584] Scholars have argued that this heterogeneity and the lack of a definite common ground would eventually lead to various conflicts within the fascist movement and between state and party institutions, resulting in a radicalization of domestic and racial politics. If there is a strong similarity between the domestic fascist system of rule and the bi- and multilateral relationships between different fascist movements and regimes, then this heterogeneity, a form of a polycratic structure of international relations, can also help us to understand the dynamic of radicalization on an international level. The constant struggle for dominance between Rome and Berlin within the fascist cosmos and the attempts by other movements and regimes to become close to either government should be considered as a driving force in the radicalization of international relations in future research.

The question arises as to why Ciano, despite his personal affinity for Great Britain, eventually turned to Germany and other authoritarian regimes. How important was his ideological proximity to German National Socialism or to other movements that formed the fascist cosmos in Europe? Ciano's own worldview and National Socialism had only a few similarities, such as anti-communism and belief in the power of "young nations." Yet, Ciano recognized the dangers inherent in National Socialist ideology early on. German racism, the German population in South Tyrol, and Berlin's expansion into southeastern Europe all threatened key Italian interests. From the outset, Ciano had few illusions that Italy would ever cease to be a subordinate partner in any alliance with Berlin.

Why, then, did he personally push for rapprochement with Germany between 1936 and 1939? In addition to the strategic role Nazi Germany occupied within the Italy-Great Britain-Germany triangle, we also have to look at Ciano's domestic standing, which depended predominantly on his ability to produce good results. This objective could be more frequently and quickly achieved in dealings with authoritarian governments that, like Ciano, also relied more on a performative foreign policy. Lengthy, complicated, and sometimes frustrating negotiations with the West stood in the way of this goal. In addition to performative politics, personal relationships were key for Ciano when it came to achieving results quickly.[585] The multilayered nature of Nazi rule, especially in foreign policy, meant that the German-Italian rapprochement could be negotiated at a personal level, either through Hitler or through selected emissaries. While unpredictable and unstable, these new channels were also faster and more elastic than the time-consuming formalities that marked negotiations with democracies, whose governments were always accountable to a critical public.[586] If all that matters is the result, it makes sense that Ciano would have pursued a diplomatic path that allowed him to produce more results at a faster pace. It should therefore come as no surprise that those regimes who also favoured performative diplomacy and personal relationships became the target of Ciano's ambitions. Such commonalities drove the rapprochement between Berlin and Rome despite the icy personal relationship between Joachim von Ribbentrop and Galeazzo Ciano.

The examination of Ciano's performative and substantial foreign policy and how it affected the radicalization of European international affairs in the interwar period points to an underlying theme that has so far not received the necessary attention of scholars studying Rome's diplomacy: the issue of trust and distrust. Trust rests on the credibility and predictability of future actions – or, as Niklas Luhmann argued, "to show trust is to anticipate the future. It is to behave as though the future was certain."[587] Trust in international relations can be established and maintained through both substantial and performative diplomacy. The latter, however, is especially helpful in overcoming potential mistrust.[588] Scholars of international relations usually distinguish between "strategic trust," referring to cooperation that derives from the belief that others' interests encapsulate one's own, and "moralistic trust," based on honesty and integrity, emotions and feelings, which reflect traits of the trustee rather than the situation.[589]

What does this understanding of "trust" mean for Italy's foreign policy under Ciano? Given his negative attitude towards the Germans, his cooperation with Berlin was primarily based on "strategic trust" and his belief that Italy could only achieve its goals by working with Germany. The public displays of friendship through ceremonies, uniforms, glorious receptions, military parades, and the awarding of medals – in short, pomp and circumstance – helped to gloss over major political differences in the short term and convince Ciano of the strategic advantages offered by an alliance with Germany. However, such displays were never strong enough to mitigate Ciano's deep racial biases and mistrust towards the German people and politicians.[590] Moreover, strategic trust works best if both countries have a similar goal; in the Italian and German case, however, no such goal existed. A closer look reveals that their aims were often contradictory – as the situation in the Balkans illustrates. The longer Ciano was in charge of the *Palazzo Chigi*, the more he realized that he was unable to predict any of the Germans' moves and that Germany would ultimately not reciprocate Italy's support and goodwill.[591] Eventually, Ciano's "strategic trust" was replaced by a "moralistic mistrust," whereas for Mussolini Germany remained the only possible ally capable of fulfilling his dream of a fascist Italian Empire.

The diverse concepts of Italy's diplomacy – itself a result of the polycratic structure of Italian foreign policy[592] – meant that Italy's goals and actions were increasingly unpredictable. This unreliability in turn had a negative impact on Rome's relations with its fascist, authoritarian, and democratic neighbours. Ciano ignored the erosion of Italy's credibility until it was too late; his symbolic acts during the non-belligerence period, intended to re-establish trust with the West, were both only partially effective in achieving this goal and harmful to the constructed trust with Berlin.

Ultimately, Ciano failed to establish a solid form of trust with either democratic or authoritarian governments. Such trust, however, was essential to his theory of foreign policy, rooted as it was in the traditional strategy of *peso determinante*. Due to Rome's ongoing unpredictability, arrogance, and impudence, none of the major powers on either side were inclined to enter into an equal partnership – and why should they, given Italy's lack of the necessary financial, economic, and military resources?[593] Thus, Italy remained in a predominantly self-inflicted isolation following the Ethiopian War, despite the appearance of close collaboration with Hitler's Germany. As we have seen in this chapter, the appearance of friendship was based on ceremonial and performative gestures, and not on the more enduring trust characteristic of substantial diplomacy.

4
The Successor

The Deputy *Duce*

Whether in North Africa or Greece, in the Balkans or the Middle East, in the Pacific region or Latin America, disputes over jurisdiction and direction between Berlin, Rome, and Tokyo erupted everywhere beginning in 1942. Not only did the dream of an Italian parallel war need to give way to reality, but Germany determined the military and political actions of the Axis.[1] The disastrous course of the war, the loss of Italian colonies, the danger of an imminent attack against Italy, and the desperate living conditions in the country intensified expressions of displeasure against the *Duce* and led to the formation of the first opposition groups, including members of the fascist and military elite, industrialists, diplomats, and members of the royal house and the Vatican.[2]

Speculation about a plot against Benito Mussolini and possible peace talks with the Allies gained new impetus in the spring of 1943 when Ciano was sacked as foreign minister and transferred to the Vatican.[3] After the landing of the Allies in Sicily and the first bombardment of Rome in mid-July 1943, discussions about a possible separate peace treaty gained new momentum, and the search for a possible heir to the *Duce* intensified. Despite being considered by many contemporaries to be Mussolini's de facto heir, even Ciano never became the *Duce*'s successor. But why did Ciano and other members of the Fascist Grand Council fail in their bids to become the new rulers of Italy? Why were Mussolini and other fascist dictators reluctant to designate an heir? Using Galeazzo Ciano as a case study, this section touches on the crucial issue of succession in fascist Italy and in any fascist movement or government.

Other scholars have dismissed the successor issue as a non-issue stemming from Mussolini's wish to not elevate a potential rival and undermine his own charisma, but this argument is misleading for several reasons. Namely, it espouses a false understanding of both the mechanisms of fascist rule in Italy and the concept of charismatic authority. First, as I have argued before, even though Mussolini ruled for over two decades and wielded immense power, he was far from the almighty dictator historiography has often portrayed him. Second, charismatic authority is not something a leader just possesses; rather, it is an attribute given to him by the people. Thus, Mussolini himself was not in total control of his charismatic aura, which could at any time be challenged by a rival deemed more worthy by the people. Furthermore, if we accept the deterministic argument, we would wrongly accept that the *Duce* never wanted to name a successor and that fascism in Italy would have died with him. This thesis, however, is contradicted by the mandate he gave to the Grand Council to choose a successor, the fascist doctrine with its emphasis on youth, and Mussolini's attempts to build his family dynasty. And last but not least, strict adherence to this argument means we would be unable to clearly understand the manifold factors that determined why nobody from within the fascist hierarchy was able to take over in Rome and later Salò once the *Duce* was deposed in the summer of 1943.

According to his wife Edda Ciano, "it was Ciano's ambition to become the head of state one day. Who doesn't dream of success in life? And what other position should he have aspired to since he was already Foreign Minister?"[4] Grandi called Ciano the "deputy dictator," and in 1938 Bottai mentioned Ciano's "tireless work" towards the creation of his own successor myth.[5] Foreign observers such as Goebbels, Himmler, and Gafencu regarded Ciano as the "second man" in Italy and stated that "Ciano believed he is the *Duce*'s deputy."[6] The residents of Ciano's hometown Livorno were convinced that Mussolini would officially name Ciano as his successor.[7] And when the *Duce* appointed many friends and close collaborators of Ciano as ministers and party officials in October 1939, even the most sceptical observer was convinced that Ciano would be designated heir to the regime.[8] British diplomats saw him as the natural successor, even though they stressed that Ciano "would … be a total failure."[9]

While many contemporaries were convinced that Ciano was to follow the *Duce*, Ciano denied all rumours and never commented publicly on his ambitions. Even in his diary there is not a single reference to such intentions. How can we explain this discrepancy between external attribution and the missing self-testimonies? And if Ciano wanted to succeed Mussolini, did he realize the importance of charisma as a power resource? Did he try to construct a profile similar to Mussolini's? When analysing Ciano's demeanour, the intent behind it, and how the Italian people and the fascist hierarchy reacted to it, three different perspectives must be examined: First, how did he act in the public sphere and what impression did he create in public? Second, did he direct events so as to put himself in the limelight of public attention, and if so, how did he organize these events and what symbols did he use? And finally, how did contemporaries view and react to Ciano?

Many stories recount Ciano's attempts to imitate his father-in-law's gestures, facial expressions, and idioms as early as 1933 and thus actively construct his own successor image.[10] During his first years as foreign minister he also used the international stage to present himself as Italy's second man by imitating the *Duce* in rhetoric and gestures.[11] Apparently, he believed that by presenting himself like Mussolini he would enjoy a similar personal charisma among the fascists and the rest of the Italian population. Numerous published photographs and released video footage verify these efforts. One of the most memorable examples is a photographic portrait by Ghitta Carrell taken in 1936: Ciano appears in a frontal shot, dressed in a white suite, his arms folded across his chest. He furrows his brow, presses his lips together, and pushes his chin forward – easily one of the most recognizable of Mussolini's poses for photographs (figure 11).[12] In the mid- and late 1930s – at least until the outbreak of the Second World War – many more photographs were distributed in which Ciano clearly imitated Mussolini's distinctive expression.[13]

In his endeavours, Ciano benefitted from the fact that he oversaw the regime's propaganda institutions for three years. As soon as he took over Mussolini's press office, he used the position for his own purposes by staging events that promoted his image as one of the most important figures in the regime. For instance, he distributed photographs that showed the royal family, Mussolini, and himself to Italian newspapers, diplomatic missions, the Italian tourist association *Ente Nazionale Italiana per il Turismo*, and the *fasci all'estero*, while pictures of other fascist hierarchs were rarely seen.[14]

One reason for the relative paucity of such images is that the fascist press did not feature them. In one of his directives Ciano argued that in fascism it is not the person who matters but the function he performs within the system. The individual, he continued, had to immerse himself totally in the system. There was no space for personal vanity.[15] Ciano, of course, did not come up with this doctrine on his own, but rather echoed traditional fascist notions of the relationship between the individual and the system.[16] Consequently, he instructed the press to

Figure 11. Galeazzo Ciano, portrait by Ghitta Carrell, 1936. Ullstein Bild #00310982.

report on prominent figures of the regime and society in moderation. Where his own persona was concerned, however, he threw caution to the wind. He used his good connections to journalists like Signoretti to promote himself and made sure that the press praised his "heroic deeds" in Ethiopia; it was only after he learned that British diplomats and the public were disgusted by these reports did he instruct his deputy to avoid mentioning his name.[17]

Did Ciano primarily seek to use the media to raise his prestige at the expense of others? There is certainly some truth to this assumption. But cynical self-interest can explain only part of the picture. When the press reported about the *Duce,* Ciano also asked the editors to occasionally restrain themselves.[18] He wanted to avoid portraying the people and achievements of the regime in such an exaggerated way that they became unbelievable. This caution was a reaction to letters in which often-anonymous writers argued that the frequently overblown reporting would only harm the true essence of fascism.[19] Given the constant reminders that Mussolini would be the "messiah of the fatherland," it is clear that the press did not adhere to this strategy too strictly.

Even after he left the Ministry of Press and Propaganda, Ciano continued to meddle in its affairs. Well aware of the importance of propaganda for his own prestige and to ensure that he received top billing, Ciano made certain that the ministry was led by close friends such as Dino Alfieri or Alessandro Pavolini; his ongoing influence was so well known that it earned Alfieri the sobriquet of "Ciano's jester."[20] In 1938, for example, he ordered the press to show him and Mussolini together as often as possible.[21] It is therefore hardly surprising that the frequency with which the media reported on Ciano was used to evaluate the degree of power he possessed within the regime. Ciano's continuous intervention in other ministries and party organizations was interpreted by contemporary observers such as Ulrich von Hassell, the German ambassador in Rome, as a clear sign of Ciano's ambition to be recognized as Mussolini's sole legitimate heir.[22]

State visits and ceremonies were important to the Italian regime's diplomatic efforts, but, as mentioned earlier, they also boosted Ciano's self-esteem, a weakness his counterparts abroad were quick to exploit. Nearly every statesmen and politician in the authoritarian states had studied Ciano's character extensively. They flattered him, catered to him, and thus reinforced his overblown self-confidence. King Zog, for example, organized a soccer match and several other large-scale events in Ciano's honour. His guest was pleased with the courtesy and attention, which he interpreted as appropriate recognition for his position as the second most important man in Italy.[23] At their first official meeting in October 1936, Hitler gave Ciano a signed copy of *Mein Kampf*, and understood that pomp and flattery would pay dividends in dealing with Ciano. "To say that Hitler," wrote Anfuso, "was with Ciano sugar and honey is too little; in his sober uniform of a night porter of a hotel, he met the Italian minister and caressed his hands ... The interpreter Schmidt poured on Ciano rivers of Hitlerian eloquence."[24]

One thing was certain: if one could use Ciano's vanity and narcissism to one's advantage; if one were able to confirm Ciano's own belief that he was the second most important man in Italy; if one were able to flatter him, then bilateral relations would be much easier.[25] A member of the German Ministry of Propaganda made this fact clear when a journalist asked him if Ciano actually was a great man: "Not at all, but for our purposes he has to believe that we think he is."[26] Ciano never grasped this strategy for what it was; instead, he allowed himself to be flattered and interpreted the various flourishes as proof of his own importance. His arrogant remarks about personalities he met on his travels and his behaviour as though he were superior suggests that he regarded himself as the second most powerful man in Fascist Italy, right behind the *Duce*. Indeed, whenever diplomats called him Mussolini's successor, he displayed an almost childlike joy and made no attempt to deny it.[27]

When Ciano visited other countries, he invested heavily in pompous ceremonies more appropriate for a head of government like Mussolini or a head of state like the king of Italy. An example of this pomp is a newsreel by the state broadcaster LUCE when Ciano visited Albania in August 1939. Thousands of Albanians cheered while Ciano publicly inspected the "marvellous" work that was done under Italian rule. One of the first and most memorable scenes shows Ciano standing in his car, waving, while passing beneath a sign proclaiming "The King of Italy and Albania."[28] In the absence of King Vittorio Emanuele III and Mussolini, the meticulous detailing in this scene implies that Ciano wanted to be perceived – at least by the Albanian people – as an Italian political personality on the same level as the king and the *Duce*. This perception was strengthened by a photograph in Italian journals that showed an enthusiastic crowd in Tirana holding up banners with his name that clearly outnumbered similar signs with Mussolini's or the king's name on them.[29] Obviously Ciano enjoyed the attention of the people and the fact that the Albanian dignitaries waited for him. He proudly noted in his diary that the Albanians apparently asked him to personally become the country's head of state – a generous offer that he, of course, magnanimously refused.[30]

Unfortunately, there is little information about how Ciano personally reacted to ceremonies and receptions in Italy. In his diary he only sporadically describes domestic public appearances and fails to give much insight into his personal views on these events and what conclusions he hoped the audience to draw from them.[31] When Ciano supported a policy of non-intervention after the outbreak of the Second World War, he obviously enjoyed the ensuing public support, but he nevertheless made sure that his increased popularity would not be interpreted as an affront to the *Duce*.[32] When his name was shouted as often as Mussolini's during events in Livorno and Florence, he insisted that people should only hail the *Duce*, turning false modesty to his advantage.[33] According to his diary he paid particular attention to the audience's reaction when he gave a speech in front of the parliament or the Grand Council. Mussolini's praise and the recognition of various ministers, senators, and representatives were everything he longed for.[34]

In the 1930s a self-confident Ciano tried to establish himself as the successor of the *Duce* on every occasion he thought suitable. Yet, despite the public cultivation of that image and the private praise he received from Mussolini, the *Duce* never officially named him as heir. There exists no written or oral evidence that Mussolini even contemplated handing over the Italian fascist regime to Galeazzo Ciano at any point.[35] Mussolini's reluctance to publicly acknowledge Ciano did not go unnoticed. Writer Ugo Ojetti stated that Ciano was living under the "illusion" that he would become Mussolini's successor.[36] Additionally, the cabinet reshuffle of October 1939 that strengthened Ciano's standing within the regime was only provisional in nature; in order to focus on improving his poor health, Mussolini opted to temporarily leave the government in the hands of a family member.[37] When the disagreements between Mussolini and Ciano over domestic and foreign affairs escalated, the *Duce* attempted to curtail Ciano's power.[38] Though Ciano's ambitions to be Mussolini's heir declined during the war, the question arises as to why he was never able to convince his father-in-law to name him the official successor.[39] Several answers – some of which have already been discussed in detail in other chapters – suggest themselves.

First, the *Duce* was obsessed with youth. Information about his real age was censored and suppressed. It was not encouraged to mention his children and even more so his grandchildren. Mussolini's decision to shave his head was an attempt to conceal his greying and thinning hair. Naturally, any public discussion about a potential successor to the *Duce* was banned because it would have touched upon the issue of Mussolini's age and health.[40]

Second, Ciano always remained an exception within the regime despite his personal proximity to Mussolini. Many members of the older generation, those who participated in the "March on Rome," followed Ciano's career with a mix of envy, scepticism, and disapproval. They saw Ciano as Mussolini's willing pawn to limit their influence. Because Ciano refused to promote a "second fascist revolution" that might have endangered his own career, the younger generation of fascists likewise turned against him. For many radical fascists, Ciano represented the dark side of the regime and of Italian society: he was accused of nepotism and corruption, being friends with the Roman nobility, embracing bourgeois culture, and supporting the king and the Vatican.

Third, a reputation for competency might have compensated for other deficiencies, but there too Ciano struggled. He suffered from a reputation as an incompetent upstart and became a scapegoat for the regime's failures. His rapid career advancement was attributed solely to his marrying Mussolini's daughter. Ciano was never able to convince the public that he was anything other than the *Duce*'s son-in-law. Even the constant praise for his deeds and accomplishments that he received in the media and the various photographs that showed him at work in his ministry were not enough.[41] The insinuation of nepotism, which was a key element of the hated patronage system that dominated liberal Italy, was a shadow from which Ciano never escaped. Italian public opinion focused on his allegedly luxurious lifestyle when the nation was suffering, accused him of corruption, and most damningly, claimed that he would try to steal Mussolini's victories if given the opportunity.[42] Ciano seemed not to realize that the Italian public despised him or that he was – in Goebbel's assessment of Italian opinion – the devil.[43] He failed to achieve one of the essential aspects of a charismatic leadership: to appear as a "man of the people."

Fourth, Mussolini did not protect his son-in-law from public criticism as he, among other things, refused to rectify numerous rumours about Ciano's possible dismissal. He instead turned these rumours into a tool of governance because it was politically convenient for Mussolini to turn Ciano into a scapegoat.[44] According to Paul Corner, Mussolini's ability to blame other people for the failures of the regime explains why he was able to govern Italy for twenty-one years, despite many broken promises and military disasters. The Italian public clung to the image of the "good Mussolini" who stood against the egotistical, corrupt, power-hungry, and incapable fascist elite that Ciano personified so well.[45]

And fifth, Ciano's attempts to imitate the *Duce* like no other of his colleagues proved disastrous.[46] One of his biggest miscalculations was that he thought he could win people over by convincing them of his abilities. But he did not realize that his behaviour was more damaging than helpful.[47] In numerous letters found in the Italian archives and memoirs, contemporaries convey their irritation or even disgust with Ciano's imitation of the *Duce*, pointing out that he was exactly the opposite of Mussolini. They accused him of having a weak, nasal, and feminine voice and of not being eloquent and photogenic; they criticized his "morbid" walk and his nervousness in front of public audiences.[48]

Analysis of the surviving visual records verifies some of the accusations against Ciano, suggesting that they were not merely the work of envious rivals. Mussolini was a masterful speaker, knowing exactly when and for how long to pause; Ciano's pauses, however, sounded awkward and constrained. Whereas Mussolini spoke without notes, Ciano often read from his notes, as in his speech after the signing of the Pact of Steel in 1939. While the *Duce* had a loud, strong voice, Ciano's voice was weak and high-pitched.[49] Some astute individuals in the propaganda department must have realized these deficits because there are very few clips of Ciano giving a speech. Even Carrell's 1936 photograph reveals a flaw: in this and all other portraits the viewer is able to catch Ciano's gaze. By contrast, there are many photographs and paintings of Mussolini where it is nearly impossible to catch his glance. He glares into the distance, implying his detachment from the viewer, from the rest of the people, and from the profane world, giving the impression that only he knew what lay in the nation's future.[50]

Mussolini's facial expressions, rhetoric, and gestures, all of which so inspired his Italian listeners, created a physical foundation for his charismatic authority. Ciano, on the other hand, only confused large segments of the public by appearing grotesque, even ridiculous. This difference is hardly surprising: Mussolini was a skilful performer and orator, a fact even his opponents acknowledged.[51] At the time, however, the discrepancy between Ciano's and Mussolini's prestige was also a product of the regime's propaganda, which Ciano himself helped to create and direct. The *Duce* was made into a godlike idol, the "new Augustus," the "messiah of the fatherland," "the Motor of the Century," "the Supreme Saviour of the Roman Sky" – in short, he was a "total genius."[52] Ciano failed to realize that he could not construct or enforce his own charismatic authority by merely imitating Mussolini. Ciano did not grasp that propaganda built upon and extended charisma rather than the reverse; it was something the population bestowed from below instead of accepting it as delivered from on high. One anonymous person expressed this sentiment in a letter to the *Duce*: "We want you, Mussolini, not Ciano … We have the right to choose a successor, and we don't want the new *Duce* chosen for us."[53]

Historian Mimmo Franzinelli has argued the reverse, that in fact Ciano was more charismatic than Mussolini because he was more photogenic and looked attractive and handsome in whatever clothes he wore – something the *Duce* held against his son-in-law. Ciano's picture also appeared on the cover of many glossy magazines – though this telling neglects the fact that he and his allies were the ones who put him on those covers.[54] While Franzinelli's simplifying equation of "good looks" and charisma is misleading, he does unintentionally hint at another important point. Apparently, Ciano not only tried to portray himself as the "deputy" *Duce* in public; he also sought recognition as a member of the establishment.

Ciano's appearance as a *bon vivant* actually undermined his reputation among committed fascists. It suggested that he enjoyed the bourgeois lifestyle and that he quickly adapted to elite social milieus – milieus that Mussolini and fascist hardliners boasted they would eliminate in the first place. Ciano felt at home in these circles, and numerous testimonies, photographs, and videos illustrate that Ciano adopted the habitus of his upper-class friends and sought to be perceived as part of the *grande bourgeoisie* or even the nobility. He hosted and attended gala events during the Second World War like the Biennale in Venice; he enjoyed driving around in sport cars;[55] he frequented luxurious restaurants on the Via Veneto; he vacationed in Ostia and on the beaches of Viareggio, a posh seaside resort in Tuscany (see Figure 5);[56] and he was known as an art enthusiast who posed – almost narcissistically – in front of the sculptures (Figure 12) and paintings in his ministries (one of them even showed his father).[57] His repeated efforts to be immortalized in paintings and busts in order to construct his own dynasty have already been noted. Hunting trips were part of his regular schedule whenever he went abroad or welcomed foreign dignitaries to Italy.[58] Although hunting had lost its former exclusivity as a noble privilege after the First World War, it had become a status symbol for a new elite, which combined the aristocracy and the new wealthy bourgeoisie.[59] And the repeated references to him in the Italian press as "Count Ciano" would – maybe unintentionally – strengthen the impression of his close links to the aristocracy, at least in the perception of radical fascists.[60]

Ciano's elitist demeanour, which demanded time and money, stood in strong contrast not only to Mussolini, who conspicuously disrespected the arts and was always careful to be perceived as an ordinary "man of the people,"[61] but also to his father, Costanzo Ciano. According to Roberto Farinacci, Ciano's father had no interest in literature, art, or culture, because he invested all his "drive" into his military career

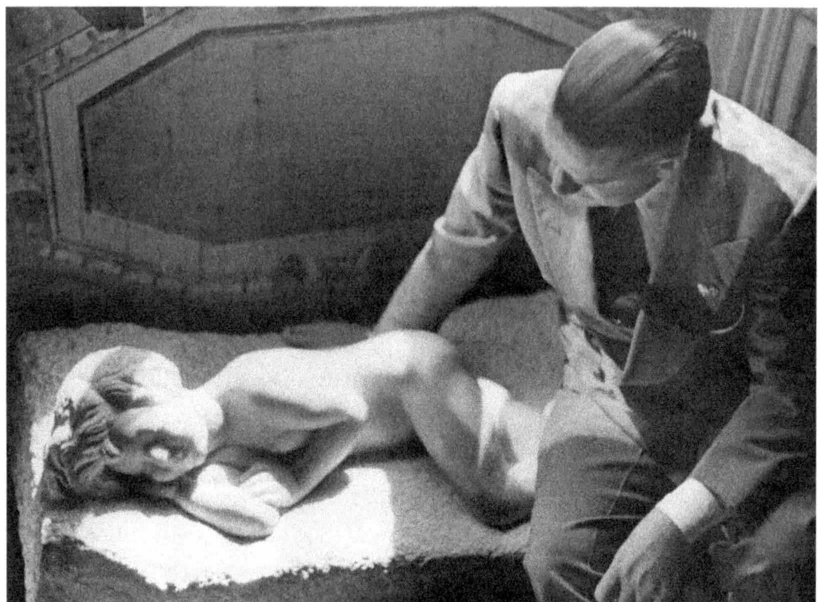

Figure 12. Galeazzo Ciano beside a contemporary marble sculpture in his office at the *Palazzo Chigi* in Rome, 1940. Ullstein Bild #01082584.

and the betterment of Italy.[62] Among staunch fascists art and culture were not only seen as feminine – the futurists had previously expressed contempt for museums and libraries – but a waste of time.[63] A charismatic leader was expected to sacrifice himself for the state, so distractions such as vacations, art, and culture had no place in his life. It is no coincidence that virtually no pictures of Mussolini vacationing were made public and that he put great value on being regarded as a man of the people. Ciano's obvious love for the elitist milieu and art, however, implied a distance from the ordinary Italian people; in fact, it was reported that he deliberately avoided or at least did not directly seek proximity to ordinary people.[64]

In sum, Ciano was unable to construct a convincing image as a charismatic fascist leader à la Mussolini. The reactions to his demeanour show that his own personality was not persuasive and that he did not receive any legitimacy from below. There are two main reasons for this failure to capture elite and popular opinion. First, according to Weber, charismatic authority is zero sum. Anyone who aspired to become a recognized charismatic leader had to compete with and challenge the charismatic authority of the *Duce* should Mussolini fail to nominate his successor and step down.[65] Second, Ciano's self-staging could only work if the potential target group – in this case the Italian people and the fascist elite – believed him suited to the role. At the same time, he wanted to be seen as a member of the Italian establishment, yet he failed to realize that his public image as a fascist "new man" and as a member of the bourgeois elite contradicted one another in crucial ways. Whereas Mussolini represented the ideal fascist man, Ciano was viewed as a symbol of the aristocracy and elite bourgeoisie, the arch-enemies of fascism. This perception, of course, damaged his reputation among radical fascists, and he was unable to convince both the Italian people and fellow members of the Grand Council that he was capable of leading Fascist Italy.

Fascist Masculinities: Ciano versus Mussolini

Ciano's failure to construct a viable image of himself as the rightful heir to Mussolini is also obvious when considering two of the main characteristics associated with the "new fascist man": athleticism and combat prowess. The "new men" were to be physically superior to everyone else, regardless if they were athletes during peace time or soldiers in war. The fascists celebrated an ideal of masculinity that emphasized the power and strength of the Italian race. A youthful and above all athletic body, as it was idealized during the Renaissance period – Michelangelo's David should be mentioned here – was the inspiration for the "new man." Thereby, art and iconography played an important role for the fascist regime in propagating this image of masculinity. Even today we can see the fifty-nine heroic statues of male athletes that line the *Stadio dei Marmi*, part of the Olympic site in Rome that was created between 1928 and 1932.[66]

From the beginning, the fascists expended enormous effort to improve sports and physical education. They reacted against what they saw as Italians' apparent physical weakness as revealed during the First World War.[67] Sports education served the many purposes of building strong Italians, fostering comradeship and discipline, and highlighting the masculinity of the athletes.[68] Party Secretary Achille Starace insisted that the fascist hierarchs must publicly practice sports to demonstrate their physical superiority over the politicians in democratic countries.[69] The triumphs of Italian athletes at international events were presented as evidence of Italian supremacy and used to boost Italian national pride.[70] "The fascist regime," Patrizia Dogliani states, "made Italy one of the first modern nations to understand how to use sport as a means of political propaganda."[71] As head of fascist

Figure 13. Benito Mussolini swimming in the Adriatic, 1930s. Ullstein Bild #01075973.

propaganda, Galeazzo Ciano himself played an essential part in creating the image of the *Duce* as Italy's "number one" athlete. As a pilot, racer, swimmer, rider, gymnast, or skier, Mussolini was Italy's top athlete who – almost nonchalantly – triumphed over the forces of nature such as water and cold (figure 13).[72] Fascist propaganda used numerous photographs and video footage of Mussolini to propagate this image, thus highlighting that a fascist leader in Italy was expected to be both athletic and energetic.[73]

In a similar fashion, Mussolini provided the model for the perfect Italian soldier. Like many other fascist hierarchs, such as Farinacci and Balbo, he had participated in the First World War. His widely circulated wartime memoir, *Il mio Diario di Guerra*, was published in 1923 and later translated into several languages.[74] During the 1930s and 1940s, he usually wore his fascist uniform in public. Moreover, many photographs and much video footage portrayed him as a common soldier or a military leader, and showed him giving speeches atop tanks.[75] In 1937 the *Duce* was photographed wielding the "Sword of Islam" on horseback, and in November 1938 a statue depicting Mussolini as a *condottieri* of the Renaissance period, the "Sword of Islam" raised high, was dedicated in Tripoli.[76] Even though many of these pictures and newsreels were retouched, they helped to construct the image of Mussolini as the "first soldier" of the nation. The message was simple: in a war, Mussolini would be the first in the front line and would lead the Italian nation to glory and a new and better future.[77]

A comparison with Adolf Hitler illustrates how important it must have been for Mussolini to be identified as the "number one" athlete and soldier. While the *Duce* attached considerable importance to being perceived as a sports spectator and military strategist as well as an active athlete and soldier, Hitler acted within the more passive of the two spheres – for example, as a spectator during the Olympic Games in 1936 or as a strategist in the *Führer*'s headquarters. This difference between the two most prominent European fascist leaders demonstrated a peculiar Italian characteristic associated with the legitimacy of the fascist leader in Italy. Although similar ideals of masculinity played a crucial role in both regimes, most members of the ruling elite in Nazi Germany did not bother trying to fulfil them – apart from Heinrich Himmler, who trained publicly for the SS sports badge. Mussolini had to impress through his physical prowess, which became more difficult and less convincing as he aged, in order to compensate for the Italian lack of self-confidence.[78] Hitler's appearance, on the other hand, met an almost eschatological desire for a transcendent leader in Germany.[79] Following in Mussolini's footsteps, Ciano thus needed to perform as both a passive and active athlete and soldier.

How did Galeazzo Ciano compare to these central virtues of the "new man?"[80] If his imitation of Mussolini as a statesman was a failure, could he at least present himself as the incarnation of the "new man"? Playing the role of a sports fan came naturally enough to Ciano, who went to many events ranging from soccer matches to car races. In this regard, Ciano also had a strong family pedigree: his father, as described earlier, had realized the importance of sport in enhancing his and his family's prestige. Galeazzo Ciano became engaged with furthering his own physical development at an early age and participated in various sports.[81] As a diplomat in China, he spent his free time playing tennis, riding, and practicing fencing – sports that were particularly popular in the upper class.[82] He also became interested in what Daniele Varè would later call his "true love": car racing.[83]

Despite Ciano's evident enthusiasm for sports, there are not many published images or film clips that show him as an active athlete.

Figure 14. Galeazzo Ciano at the beach of Ostia, 1938. *Illustrierter Beobachter*, 11 August 1938, Aufnahme: Weltbild, in IfZ, Presseausschnittssammlung: Ciano, Galeazzo.

Moreover, most of these photographs were not published in Italian but rather in foreign newspapers.[84] What could account for this absence, especially given the importance of presenting oneself as a sportsman? The *Duce* already occupied the place as the "number one" athlete, and so every image that showed an athletic Ciano would eventually be compared to Mussolini. In this regard, Ciano's problem appears obvious. Whereas Mussolini might appear to swim stoically, ski downhill without a shirt, impervious to the cold, or ride a horse without use of the reins, Ciano always appeared to struggle. Images of Ciano swimming show his eyes and mouth wide open, gasping for air; while rowing, he grimaces and bites his lip in the act of physical exertion (figure 14). He consistently appears exhausted and – most importantly – not in control. Mussolini, by contrast, seemed to endure physical hardship without difficulty and master any activity with ease – a perfect embodiment of the ideal "new man" and leader.

One explanation for the paucity of images might be that Ciano realized his disadvantage, and so few were taken. To be sure, Edda Ciano admitted that her husband was not a very good athlete.[85] Still, Ciano understood the importance of appearing young and sportive. Thus, he cultivated his athleticism indirectly. One of the best examples of this

Figure 15. Galeazzo Ciano (right) and Dino Alfieri (left) near the beach of Ostia, August 1938. *Illustrierter Beobachter*, 11 August 1938, Aufnahme: Weltbild, in IfZ, Presseausschnittssammlung: Ciano, Galeazzo.

strategy is a picture taken in 1938 that showed him and then minister of popular culture Dino Alfieri at the beach (figure 15). Whereas Alfieri is getting out of a car, Ciano straddles a bicycle. Even though we cannot see Ciano in motion, the picture nonetheless gives the impression of sporting prowess by contrasting Ciano cycling with Alfieri driving. Moreover, it emphasized Ciano's proximity to the people because cycling was one of the most popular sports in Italy.[86]

If we look closer at the photograph, there are a number of problems. Ciano, the person who is supposed to personify the fit "new man," is noticeably flabbier than Alfieri. Furthermore, Alfieri's suit suggests that he was working, whereas the sandal-wearing Ciano confirms the perception of his perpetual vacationing, a message reinforced by his footwear, which was ill-suited to athletic cycling but ideal for a vacation day at the beach. The latter was also alluded to by the caption in the German magazine.[87] Moreover, despite its general popular appeal, cycling was not embraced by fascist elites. It was rather perceived as an individualistic sport, associated with pre-1914 bourgeois modernity. Notably, the *Duce* did not attend cycling events, and there are no known photographs of Mussolini cycling.[88]

A photograph from 1933 offers yet another example in which Ciano's athleticism is implied (figure 16). It shows him and Mussolini together with Austrian Chancellor Engelbert Dollfuß at the beach of Riccione. In contrast to Dollfuß, who is dressed in a suit with a button-up shirt and a tie, the Italians wear swimming trunks. Thus, the picture indicates that Mussolini and Ciano have either just gone swimming or are about to dive in. Moreover, the display of the naked torso strongly emphasizes Ciano and Mussolini's "virility and athleticism whilst demonstrating ... [their] accessibility."[89] The contrast to the well-dressed authoritarian Dollfuß illustrates, once again, that blatant demonstrations of athleticism were apparently a distinctive feature of Italian fascist leadership. Nevertheless, the photograph was also bad for Ciano's image. Mussolini looks determined, and the forced perspective makes him look larger and more powerful than the other two men. Ciano, by contrast, looks awkward and lanky.[90]

Ciano also failed in comparison to Mussolini in trying to be the ideal athlete in that Ciano's favourite sport was golf. Although he discovered his love for golf relatively late in life, he obviously had talent and spent much of his free time at the Acquasanta Golf Club near Rome.[91] In fact, golf fascinated some other prominent fascists as well. Giuseppe Bottai was also a member of Acquasanta, and Giuseppe Volpi founded a club near Venice with the help of American industrialist Henry Ford.[92] The fascists tried to promote golf as a typically fascist sport. Marcello Cirillo, president of the *Federazione Italiana del Golf*, stated that golf was fascist and thus totalitarian because it demanded concentration and discipline. This promotional endeavour, however, proved unconvincing. Golf was ill-suited for demonstrating such fascist virtues as comradeship or courage, physical fitness by displaying a naked torso, or will power to overcome fatigue. Furthermore, expensive club membership fees meant that golf was accessible only to the elite and foreign diplomats, thus failing to become a sport of the people.[93] In fact, the general secretary of the fascist party, Aldo Vidussoni, wanted

Figure 16. Galeazzo Ciano, Engelbert Dollfuß, and Benito Mussolini (from left to right) on the beach of Riccione, August 1933. AKG Images #5014707.

to ban golf as un-fascist and close all clubs in 1942. Ciano, however, intervened.[94]

According to historian Richard Bosworth, high-ranking fascists who endorsed the elitist Anglo-American sport golf resisted "the Fascist boast of totalitarianism" and thus "saved Italians from too direct an involvement in some of the tragedies and horrors of the 20th century's age of violence."[95] Even though Bosworth might have overdrawn the relationship between golf and the fascist regime, it is nevertheless true that the sport was inconsistent with the ideal of the "new man." Golf represented wealth and aristocratic Anglo-American flair. Rather than burnish Ciano's credibility through sports, his preference for the game seemed to confirm all the pre-existing prejudices against him: that he was a wealthy snob, an aristocrat who was also a close friend of many Anglo-Americans.

Reviewing his skills as a soldier, Ciano faced one crucial disadvantage. When Italy entered the First World War, Ciano was twelve years old and lived with his family in Venice. The city was under a strict military administration, and the constant air strikes created a tense atmosphere of violence and death. The fact that Ciano was too young to participate in the war but experienced its direct consequences closely affected him and many other Italians of the same generation – it was a "piercing thorn of missed opportunity."[96] In contrast to many other prominent fascists such as Mussolini, Balbo, and Farinacci, Ciano had yet to prove both his skill as a soldier and his willingness to self-sacrifice for the good of the nation, something that had helped to make his father's reputation and the family's status.[97]

His first chance to remedy this weakness came during the Ethiopian War. He was well aware that he could not remain in Rome while potential rivals like Farinacci and Starace joined the armed forces.[98] To the applause of the fascist press, he obtained his pilot's licence in November 1934, and on 1 August 1935 he enthusiastically volunteered for the Italian Air Force before the war against Ethiopia broke out.[99] On 25 August 1935 over 200,000 Italians cheered and wished him well when he left the city of Naples for Asmara on the ship *Saturnia*.[100] His departure to East Africa, which was recorded by LUCE as a newsreel, also brought Ciano his first-ever headlining photograph in the magazine *L'Illustrazione Italiana*.[101] Even notoriously critical journalists such as Alberto Moravia praised Ciano for his widely publicized enrolment.[102]

Thus, the war in East Africa offered him the perfect opportunity to follow in his father's footsteps for heroism, glory, and honour.[103] Ciano was aware that his participation in the war was expected by the public and the fascist elite. Thirteen years after the fascist takeover, courage, honour, and heroism were still regarded as prerequisites for acceptance into the inner circle of the fascist leadership.

His decision to join the air force in 1935 was a clever political decision. The Ethiopians did not have an air force, and their air defence was poor.[104] Furthermore, flying, the conquering of the air, had long fascinated proponents of the far right, including Hermann Göring and Charles Lindbergh. Mussolini regarded flying as something typically fascist, and many prominent figures of the regime, ranging from the sons of Mussolini, to Farinacci, to Balbo, obtained a flying licence. The envy of his peers and the competition, especially with Balbo, may have been additional incentives for Ciano to make his name as an aviator.[105]

As soon as Ciano arrived at the headquarters of the Italian armed forces, he took command of the 15th bomber squadron. He named it *La Disperata* to highlight his own enthusiasm for the fascist cause. The name referred to Gabriele D'Annunzio's personal guard under Guido Keller during the occupation of Fiume in 1919–20 and to several fascist combat groups that were active during the early 1920s.[106] Ciano was

Figure 17. Galeazzo Ciano as a fighter pilot, Ethiopia, 1935.
Ullstein Bild # 01087852

accompanied by Alessandro Pavolini, then a war correspondent for the *Corriere della Sera*. In 1937 Pavolini published his widely acclaimed book, *Disperata*, in which he extensively described Ciano's heroic war efforts.[107] Unlike other fascists, Ciano did not personally publicize his war experience, though he had an offer from publisher Arnaldo Mondadori.[108] He wanted to make sure that, on the surface, a neutral party was responsible for reporting his heroic deeds in order to make them even more convincing. Obviously, Ciano had noticed how important D'Annunzio's work was for the construction of his father's charismatic aura during the First World War.[109] Rumours that he would have preferred to take his long-time journalist friend Orio Vergani along, though the latter suffered from fear of flying, were later denied by Vergani himself.[110] And indeed, it seems unlikely that Ciano would hire a lesser-known journalist, especially since Pavolini's reputation as an objective and well-respected reporter would be more beneficial to furthering Ciano's prestige.[111] In addition, an army of journalists ensured that reports of Ciano's deeds in the war and his photographs featured regularly in the Italian newspapers (figure 17). There can be no doubt:

Ciano wanted the Italian – and the international – public to be constantly confronted with the image of a "combative minister."[112]

To prove his worthiness, Ciano was eager to fly in the first assault against enemy lines. During the fighting, Ciano's squadron suffered relatively high losses. Ciano's plane was first hit by an enemy salvo on 14 October on its way from Mekelle to Amba Alagi; it was hit again on two more missions. Whenever his plane was hit by enemy fire, he proudly presented the bullet holes to the press to underscore his own commitment. After the war, Ciano never got tired of referring to his damaged bomber and even kept a model of his plane in his office, complete with the bullet holes (figure 18). Pictures of the plane were also included in Pavolini's book, and years later Ciano told the Greek king George II about his experience in the war, which was recounted by US Ambassador MacVeagh:[113] "Count Ciano ... boasted of his courage and seemed to think that because his plane in Ethiopia had received two bullets through the wing he was the bravest of the brave. 'In telling me this he got up and walked about thumping his breast,' said the king, and added, 'I couldn't help thinking of Tarzan of the Apes.'"[114]

On 24 November 1935 Ciano received his first medal, and the national and international press were full of praises, as were his co-workers at home.[115] However, he knew that he had to remain in East Africa until the end of the campaign in order to return to Italy as a hero.[116] A "fascist soldier," he wrote two years later, was not allowed to ever show any signs of indifference and apathy.[117] His moment came on 30 April 1936 when he flew – together with Ettore Muti and Alessandro Pavolini – on a raid to Addis Ababa, then still in enemy hands. He intended to land at the airport, take prisoners, question them about the city's defences, and then return to his troops. In remembrance of his father's deeds during the First World War, it should now be his turn for his personal *beffa*.[118] But due to air defences, he had to abort his plans, returning to base after making a few circles over the city.[119] Mussolini sent a telegram to his son-in-law congratulating him on his "extremely bold action," and the Italian press extensively praised Ciano's heroism and compared it to his father's deeds.[120] He even earned his second silver medal for bravery, although his actions did not have any military value. On his return to Italy on 17 May 1936, fascist propaganda celebrated Ciano as a war hero, and Pavolini called him the best example of a "fierce man."[121]

After the Ethiopian War, Ciano proudly wore the uniforms of the fascist militia and the Italian Air Force to emphasize his masculinity and military commitment.[122] He sometimes even expressed a deep longing for military action. When Bruno Mussolini rejoined the air force during

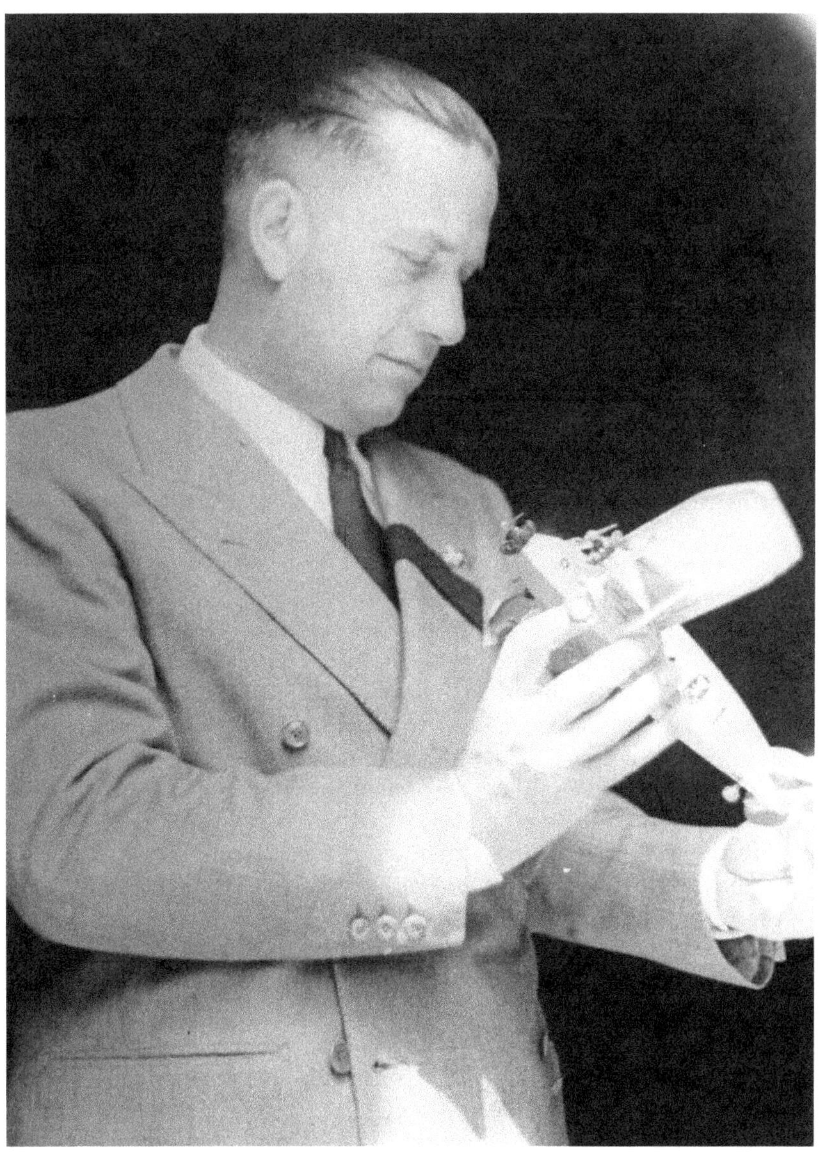

Figure 18. Galeazzo Ciano with the replica of the fighter plane he flew as squadron captain during the Ethiopian War, 1940. Ullstein Bild #01082597.

the Sudeten Crisis in September 1937, a jealous Ciano noted that he felt "nostalgia for the war."[123]

Another chance to present himself as a capable and daring warrior materialized for Ciano after Italy entered the Second World War. He joined a bomber squadron stationed near Livorno,[124] because – as he noted – he wanted "to fight where I was born and where my father rests in eternal sleep."[125] As mentioned earlier, the decision to go to the front was motivated by hopes of regaining his position in the fascist regime after he lost the battle for the *non belligeranza* policy against Mussolini and radical fascists. After all, what better way to prove his worthiness and loyalty then by fighting as a voluntary soldier? During the first days, and following Franco-British bombing of Turin and the Ligurian coast that killed twenty-four people, he purportedly flew missions against the French naval port Toulon and the cities of Calvi and Borgo.[126] After bombing Toulon on 13 June, Ciano supposedly called his wife and told her about his experience:

> I have tasted again in full the intoxication of being a flyer. It is magnificent, soothing, indescribable! … I led my flock in an impeccable manner in the skies over Toulon, where we carried out a real slaughter … On the way back … I saw a ship that proceeded placidly and majestically from north toward the south-southwest. I point my Zeiss. British flag. Imagine my orgasm! … I look down at the indicator, in the hope that some bomb, after the raid on Toulon, still remained, on the undercarriage. But no! … I had to renounce the greatest coup of my flying career. Imagine my anger.[127]

Had Ciano lost all his scepticism about the war within a few days and succumbed to an inner desire to go into battle? Did he know that the secret service was intercepting his calls and thus chose to demonstrate his loyalty to Mussolini? Or did he seek to feign heroism to his wife who had described Ciano's policy of *non belligeranza* as a disgrace for Italy?

Without reliable documents recounting the phone call – it is based solely on an anecdote described by Duilio Susmel – or confirming Ciano's participation in the raid against Toulon, it is difficult to find a definite answer. There are, however, strong indications that he did not participate in the Toulon episode at all.[128] The press did not report on Ciano's participation in the bombardment of Toulon, and Giovanni Ansaldo noted on 13 June that Ciano had not yet participated in any attack.[129] In his own diary, Ciano only mentioned his missions against Calvi and Borgo, as well as a reconnaissance mission in the region of Nice. The diary's pages from 12 to 14 June are crossed out, which makes it unlikely that he subsequently redacted them. It seems improbable that Ciano would fail to mention his "magnificent" experience. Nevertheless, presuming the phone call actually happened, it is clear that Ciano had a great desire to refashion himself as a patriotic fascist and a worthy pilot. We also know that Mussolini was pleased with Ciano's decision to go to the front and that he preferred to have Ciano as a soldier rather than a minister.[130]

Ciano also participated in Italy's initial attack on Greece in the fall of 1940. He once again joined the air force to – in the words of General Quirino Armellini – "lead his [own] war."[131] He volunteered mainly because he was convinced that the invasion would be simple and Italy would secure a quick victory.[132] On 1 November he flew his first mission against Thessaloniki, an attack that failed miserably.[133] Even in his diary he refused to acknowledge the failure of the mission, instead describing it as "decent." He also mentioned that he engaged two Greek fighters and was, according to his own diary, not very keen to get into a similar situation any time soon.[134] This comment did not sound like a soldier who would never hesitate to sacrifice himself for the fascist cause. Once again, the Italian public was regularly informed about his activities, thanks to extensive reports and numerous images.[135] However, when Mussolini forced several ministers including Ciano to return to the disastrous Greek campaign in January 1941, the Italian press remained silent. Except a small note about his departure, there were no reports about Ciano's potential heroic missions against the Greek forces.[136]

Given all of Ciano's efforts to construct the image of a successful and daring pilot, the crucial question remains: Did the Italian public and the fascist hierarchy believe it? Four reasons present themselves to explain why his endeavours were ultimately unsuccessful. First, his own underlying scepticism about the Ethiopia campaign – a scepticism that would become a driving force in his support for the *non belligeranza* policy in 1939 – undermined his image as a brave soldier. Despite his publicly displayed bravery and enthusiasm, Ciano was concerned about the outcome of the Ethiopian War and pleaded for a diplomatic solution as early as November 1935.[137] People like Bottai and Pavolini were surprised by Ciano's anxiety. Aldo Borelli, editor-in-chief of the *Corriere della Sera*, suggested that it might be best if Ciano returned to Italy.[138]

And indeed, Ciano took Borelli's suggestion to heart, and on 13 December he returned to Italy for several weeks.[139] It is hardly coincidental, however, that his pessimistic statements about the war and his leave happened soon after his plane was hit by enemy fire for the first time.[140] "Death is our Lover" was a line in *La Disperata*'s own song. But Ciano was not eager to accept his lover's embrace.[141] Hoping to forestall rumours of his cowardice, Pavolini later released an official and at least somewhat plausible explanation: Ciano had to return to Italy in order to undergo nose surgery in the spring of 1936.[142] Ciano had already suffered similar symptoms in China and had a penchant for being a hypochondriac; he often withdrew from public life at the first signs of discomfort.[143] Reports of the attending physician and recovery wishes lend some credibility to the claim.[144]

Most of Ciano's biographers took Pavolini's explanation for granted. Nevertheless, scepticism is justified as to whether nasal trouble was really the decisive reason for Ciano's return. Pavolini's telegrams to Ciano, which he wrote around Christmas 1935, indicate that the surgery was not planned from the beginning. In addition to Christmas greetings and a short reporting about the "very picturesque" bombing of Arciagli, Pavolini looked forward to Ciano's return before New Year's Eve.[145] Moreover, the treatment only took place in January, over a month after Ciano's return home, undermining the claim that it was urgently needed. It seems that surgery was not the reason for Ciano's return home, but rather a welcome opportunity to extend his stay in Italy.[146] This official explanation for why Ciano stayed away from the fighting, however, also damaged his image, because the "new man" was not allowed to show any weakness and certainly no symptoms of illness. That was also the reason why Mussolini's diseases were never reported publicly.[147]

Second, Ciano used his time in Italy to attend important national events such as the *Giornata della Fede* and to be promoted to the Fascist Grand Council. Instead of helping his comrades in East Africa, he was more interested in advancing his own political career. Most of Ciano's companions were irritated by his pessimism about the war, and then minister for colonies, Alessandro Lessona, harshly attacked him for his defeatism. He called Ciano a bad soldier, a friend of the British, and an anti-fascist.[148]

Ciano became more sceptical, defeatist even, during the Greek campaign as soon as he realized how dangerous his military service was. Close friends noted how Ciano appeared more pensive and had lost his zest for life after encountering the Greek fighters.[149] Indeed, Ciano was reluctant to rejoin the air force when Mussolini sent him to Bari at the beginning of 1941. "This time," he noted, "it's harder for me to say goodbye, although I have a certain amount of practice in saying goodbye. No premonition. Only little conviction and therefore even less enthusiasm. All the comrades who have been forcibly volunteered think like me."[150] His initial hesitation soon turned into frustration and anxiety, especially after hearing false rumours about his own "accidental death."[151] The combination of his pessimistic statements and his egotistical behaviour contradicted the fascist ideal of a soldier, who was supposed to be willing to sacrifice himself at any time.[152]

Third, Ciano did not embrace the idea of fighting a fascist war in East Africa, meaning a war that would create the "new men" and initiate a "second revolution" at home. In this regard he differed from fascists such as Oreste Bonomi, Bottai, Pavolini, and Renato Ricci.[153] Ciano joined the army for personal and egotistical reasons. If anything, he perceived the Ethiopian endeavour in traditional imperialistic terms. He wanted to take revenge for Italy's defeat in Adwa in 1896 and to "civilize" the "barbaric" Ethiopians by force. This objective is illustrated not only by his own public statements but also by personal accounts written before and during the campaign. Ciano was ready – in the words of his favourite poet Rudyard Kipling – to take up the "white man's burden."[154]

And fourth, as in sports, where he had to compete unsuccessfully against Mussolini, another fascist already occupied the position of the top pilot: Italo Balbo. Among other accomplishments, Balbo had made the difficult flight across the Atlantic in the summer of 1933 and landed at Chicago's World Exhibition. The Italian was triumphantly received in the American city, and even today there is a monument to his deed and his name adorns Broadway in New York. Thanks to these actions, Balbo became one of the most famous fascist personalities after Mussolini, especially on an international level. Balbo was thus already known worldwide as the Italian "hero of flying" before Ciano even acquired his pilot's licence.[155]

These four points led many Italians to question press and media reports about Ciano's heroism and fighting skills. The persistence with which Ciano sought to present himself as a soldier led to an almost instinctive rejection on the part of the population. In 1935–36 the public doubted the official explanation for Ciano's presence in Italy during the Ethiopian War and called him a coward.[156] During the Second World War, stories quickly circulated that he did not live the life of an ordinary soldier.[157] And indeed, he took up his own quarters and did not stay with his comrades. He also surrounded himself with numerous close associates from the Foreign Ministry in order to continue conducting diplomatic business while away from Rome.[158] Such special treatment was criticized even by those who usually supported him, such as Giovanni Ansaldo. Rumours also circulated that he was a coward who would prefer to play golf instead of participating in the military campaign against Greece and who chose to stay in a luxury hotel suite with bodyguards.[159] While the Italian public was suffering because of the war – a war, the public was convinced, for which Ciano bore full responsibility – he enjoyed a luxurious life. Once again Ciano acted clumsily and failed to put these allegations to rest, but rather added new fuel to the rumours. He indeed kept quarters in a former luxury hotel and continued to insist that he not be addressed as an ordinary *Colonello*, but as Italy's foreign minister and thus by the title of *Excellenza*.[160] The campaign in Greece, his sojourn in Bari, and the consequent loss of his position in Italy marked the low point in Galeazzo Ciano's career.

The Undecided One

When the Allies landed in Sicily in the summer of 1943 and Rome was bombed, leading fascists like Giuseppe Bottai and Dino Grandi demanded that Mussolini convene the Fascist Grand Council to discuss the grave situation. Ciano, too, was concerned about the consequences of the Allied offensive. On 13 July he told Giovanni Ansaldo that Vittorio Emanuele III would most likely depose Mussolini. Then the *Duce* would flee to Germany, while the king would justify his actions by citing domestic political reasons. Thereafter, he would appoint as Mussolini's successor a general, who would move to disarm the Wehrmacht soldiers stationed in Italy and remove Italy from the war. Meanwhile, as his speculations suggest, Ciano himself tried to keep to the sidelines.[161] It is therefore hardly surprising that he initially reacted with extreme caution when Bottai and Grandi approached him with their plan to convene the Grand Council. He first pretended to have a fever, once again using an ostensible illness to avoid being dragged into political intrigues and forced to pick a side. Even when Mussolini tried to talk to him on 20 July, he ducked the meeting, pretending to be ill; a day before, however, he had actually conferred with Bottai.[162]

After a meeting near San Fermo between Mussolini and Hitler on 19 July failed to produce any new results, the *Duce* finally gave in to Bottai's demands and ordered the acting PNF secretary, Carlo Scorza, to call for a meeting of the Grand Council on 24 July.[163] Mussolini's decision triggered frantic action on the part of Bottai and Grandi, as they had not yet discussed the details of the meeting or what they wanted to achieve. They prepared two different petitions and presented them to Ciano, Vittorio Cini (minister of communications), and Zenone Benini (minister of public works). The first petition allowed Mussolini to keep political control but revoked his supreme military command and handed it over to the king; in the second version, the king would have assumed both military and political leadership of the country.

While Cini and Benini pleaded for the more radical solution and promised that Justice Minister Alfredo De Marsico would also support such a petition, Ciano initially expressed little optimism. He feared that the *Duce* could still win over any sceptics. It appears that even in the summer of 1943 Ciano's respect for Mussolini's charismatic aura remained strong. After careful consideration he finally agreed to support the first petition.[164] Ignoring Ciano's early hesitation, other historians have claimed that he decisively helped to draft the text of the petition, despite the absence of any empirical documents that support such a hypothesis.[165] It is undisputed, however, that over the next few days he tried – albeit cautiously – to find new allies for the first petition.

On 23 July he returned to his old workplace, the *Palazzo Chigi*, for the first time in three months. He visited State Secretary Giuseppe Bastianini to sound out his attitude towards the forthcoming meeting of the Grand Council and ultimately received positive signals.[166] Especially after the talks near San Fermo had failed, Bastianini had joined the growing opposition within the fascist regime.[167] Ciano also informed Dino Alfieri about the petition, presenting it as the only way to save Italy from German domination. Still, he chose not to reveal any details, but instead apparently filled Alfieri's ears with empty phrases and vague excuses.[168] Such behaviour was perfectly in line with his actions at that time, though it should be kept in mind that, like Bottai and Grandi, he had only vague ideas as to what would happen during and after the meeting. This lack of a detailed plan is also illustrated by the numerous, sometimes contradictory, rumours concerning who might serve in a new cabinet. According to Benini, Ciano thought about replacing Mussolini with a triumvirate consisting of himself as chairman, Bottai as interior minister, and Grandi as foreign minister. Their first task would be to drive the Germans out of Italy and then to prevent an American occupation. Those plans nevertheless stood in contrast to scenarios put forth by Pirelli and others.[169] While high-ranking fascists agreed to submit a petition, apparently there was no consensus as to what should happen after the Grand Council meeting, and no binding agreements were made or even discussed. Neglecting this part of the plan proved to be fatal for the internal opposition.[170]

As the day of the Grand Council meeting approached, Mussolini's wife, Rachele, and his mistress, Claretta, became nervous. Both urged the *Duce* not to attend the council. They had information about a possible coup d'état against him, carried out by none other than his son-in-law Ciano. Although their story was supported by State Secretary for the Interior Guido Buffarini Guidi, Mussolini attended anyway.[171] The meeting that took place from 24 to 25 July is mentioned by almost all of the participants and contemporary observers in their diaries and memoirs. The *Duce* opened the meeting with a chaotic two-hour-long monologue.

Afterwards, fascist hierarchs such as Emilio De Bono, Roberto Farinacci, Giuseppe Bottai, and Dino Grandi commented on the state of affairs.[172] At the end of his speech, Grandi put forward the petition and concluded his remarks by saying that the "supporters" must be loyal to the "boss," but the "boss" must also be loyal to his "supporters."[173] Grandi's implicit accusation that Mussolini had violated this agreement was hardly subtle. The accusation was extremely dangerous to Mussolini's charismatic authority, since charismatic leadership only works when the aura is ascribed to the leader from "below." Grandi's speech indicated that some members of the Grand Council were willing to revoke Mussolini's charismatic authority in a crisis situation.

Ciano spoke next, primarily attacking Germany in complement to Grandi and Bottai's focus on domestic issues, and scholars often portray this speech as the greatest, most consequential moment in his life. Finally, he had summoned the courage to challenge the *Duce* and confront him with his own arguments. Ciano's behaviour was all the more courageous, or so the dominant narrative holds, because he was only seven metres away from the *Duce* and was sitting between Roberto Farinacci and Enzo Emilio Galbiati.[174] In his memoirs from 1959, Giuseppe Bastianini praised Ciano's speech, which he delivered with unusual clarity and conviction. Ciano gave the impression that he feared nothing and no one, and ended his speech with the exclamation: "Long live Italy! Italy above all others!"[175]

Contemporary descriptions of the meeting, such as the one Bottai wrote down in his diary, paint a different, less heroic, and more credible picture. In his speech, Ciano not only called for a continuation of the war, but also repeatedly accused Berlin of treason. He argued that Germany was solely responsible for Italy's catastrophic situation, and he uttered not a single word of criticism against Mussolini.[176] On the contrary, Ciano even tried to indirectly protect the *Duce* (and himself) by claiming that Mussolini directed him to sign the Pact of Steel to restrain German belligerence. Ciano also made obviously false statements; for instance, he claimed that only Berlin wanted an alliance with Rome and that the Italian regime knew nothing of the attack on Belgium. The *Duce*'s own intentions to reach a military agreement with Berlin in 1938 and Ciano's knowledge of German plans to attack Belgium, which he had personally relayed on to the Belgian crown, were suddenly forgotten.[177]

At the end of the meeting, Grandi's first petition was put to the vote. By the time Ciano gave his approval, several people had already signed, and a rejection had become very unlikely.[178] In the end, nineteen members of the council voted in favour of Grandi's petition and seven rejected it. Only Farinacci and Senate President Giacomo Suardo, who had tried to mediate between the different factions, abstained from voting.[179] In one fell swoop, the majority of the fascist elite had deprived Mussolini of his charismatic authority and thus destroyed one of the key pillars that braced the fascist regime.[180]

A seemingly stoic *Duce* accepted the result and returned to the Villa Torlonia.[181] Despite the willingness of the fascist militia to take action against the "conspirators," Mussolini did not order their arrest or even arrange for his own security. Apart from health problems and a depressive mood, the *Duce*'s lethargic behaviour might also have been a way for him not to publicly show emotions and thus – according to fascist doctrine – weakness. Instead, he tried to suggest normality and therefore began 25 July with his usual routine. Until the end, he continued to believe that performative actions, the attempt to create a different reality, would enable his political survival.

During his audience with King Vittorio Emanuele III, however, the monarch told Mussolini that he had relieved him of all his duties and appointed Marshal Pietro Badoglio as his successor. The king used Grandi's petition as a *carte blanche* to deprive Mussolini of both his military and political power. After the royal audience, Mussolini was arrested by the *Carabinieri* and ultimately imprisoned in a sanatorium on the Gran Sasso.[182] To the surprise of the royal house and Badoglio, neither the fascist party nor the fascist militia intervened on Mussolini's behalf.[183]

The members of the Fascist Grand Council learned of Mussolini's arrest and Badoglio's appointment only belatedly, as communication channels were cut off and a state of emergency had been declared.[184] In this atmosphere, Grandi gradually realized that he had failed to preserve the power of the moderate fascists. While he initially intended to legitimize a transitional but still fascist government by way of the Chamber of Fasci and Corporations, the royal house and the military opposition had reconciled their mutual interests and seized the opportunity to finally break with the fascist system. Grandi became aware of his failure on the day after the meeting when he arrived to discuss details with the minister of the royal court, d'Acquarone.[185] Members of the fascist opposition were outraged by the monarch's actions and accused him of betraying the people who brought Mussolini down. They claimed that the military and the monarchy just used the vote of the Grand Council as a means of legitimizing their plan to depose Mussolini and the fascist system.[186]

But what exactly was Ciano's role in these crucial events? And in what ways – if at all – did it affect his public image? Since the summer of

1942, Ciano had been in contact with various individuals and circles who favoured some kind of change at the centre of government. Yet, he was never really the driving force; rather, various groups contacted him, some for advice and some to force his cooperation. Ciano was, after all, still a key figure in the regime, even if his former influence and power had diminished, and the only member of the inner circle who possessed a private channel to the head of government. Such a channel might have made it easier to reorganize the regime with Mussolini's cooperation, rather than without him. Indeed, most plans for a government reshuffle, which were discussed until the spring of 1943, did not speak of a violent removal of the *Duce*. They instead favoured a solution "with Mussolini." Even in July 1943, not everyone who supported Grandi's petition seemed to have intended to arrest Mussolini.[187]

Ciano's kinship with Mussolini also had the effect of making some conspirators reluctant to inform him about the details – a reluctance that was reinforced by Ciano's reputation for inconsistent and unreliable behaviour. Moreover, there seemed to exist a deep, mutual distrust among all conspirators, not just in relation to Ciano. Mussolini's years of playing various individuals and factions against each other had weakened the cohesion of the internal opposition in 1943. Carboni would later claim that, of all people, only Ciano acted in good faith and for the good of his country, and that he did not realize everybody, especially the army and the royal family, intended to use him.[188] Ciano's opportunism in a tense situation like the one in the summer of 1943 is best viewed as political naivety – or at least as a sign of chronic indecision. Only after the meeting of the Grand Council did he realize that he was never part of the conspirators' inner circle.[189]

After the meeting, Ciano ordered the police to bring Edda Ciano and his three children, who were in Livorno, to Rome.[190] Uncertain of how events were unfolding and whether the *Duce* had ordered their arrest, he waited in his house and desperately tried to obtain useful information.[191] Like many other fascists who voted for Grandi's petition, Ciano was surprised by the subsequent events and the decisive action taken by the king. Unlike Grandi or Bottai, however, he underestimated the possible consequences and waited idly while the two leading opponents went into hiding in Rome or left the country without his knowledge.[192]

Ciano put the affairs of the Italian embassy in the Vatican into the hands of embassy counsellor Blasco D'Ajeta and retired to his private residence in Rome. On 31 July he announced his official resignation, but at the same time offered to help and support the new regime under Badoglio if need should arise.[193] The new government declined his offer, since neither the Badoglio government nor the Vatican wanted to collaborate with someone who was on the Allied list of potential war criminals, and placed the Cianos under house arrest. This measure did not significantly restrict Ciano's day-to-day life, and close friends and former colleagues tried in vain to persuade Ciano to immediately flee the country.[194]

Today, it is difficult to determine why Ciano did not immediately follow their advice. Of course, it might be that he simply underestimated the danger of the situation and hoped that his contacts with the crown, the nobility, and the church would protect him.[195] Overall, however, his behaviour should not surprise the attentive observer; his failure to act after the Grand Council meeting was similar to many of his previous actions: the indecisive Ciano hesitated – it seems he was a person overwhelmed by the events and did not want to make a decision he might (or might not) regret later.

Meanwhile, his situation worsened by the day, beset on the one side by the threat of retaliation from remaining supporters of the *Duce* or the Germans and on the other by pressure from the new government under Badoglio.[196] But only after Ettore Muti, former party secretary, was shot by partisans on 24 August 1943 did Ciano act.[197] He decided to flee the country with his family. In hindsight, it seems grotesquely naive that he asked German authorities for help, though he knew that high-ranking personalities of the Third Reich like Goebbels and Ribbentrop were hostile to him. Perhaps he overestimated his value to the new government at a time when Mussolini was still in custody. Perhaps he thought that only the Germans were capable of bringing him and his family safely out of Italy, because his wife had already established contact with Dollmann and worked on an escape plan.[198] Or maybe we should believe Ciano himself, who stated that for the benefit of his children he had to grasp at every straw, no matter how small, that offered a chance to escape.[199]

The flight of the Ciano family on 27 August 1943 caused a public outcry.[200] Wild speculation about Ciano's whereabouts and the circumstances of his escape circulated at home and abroad.[201] Had the Badoglio government permitted or even supported the escape through a deliberate lack of security?[202] Did Vittorio Emanuele III not want to arrest a bearer of the Annunciation Order and thus a "cousin of the king"? Or did the new regime aid Ciano's escape in return for his vote during the meeting of the Grand Council?[203] While Italian security forces searched in vain for Ciano, the Badoglio government confiscated the family's assets and initiated an investigation against Arturo and Alessandro Ciano for illegal profiteering.[204] The new foreign minister, Raffaele Guariglia, began the first of several purges in his ministry. Many people – the exact number is not known – who had been admitted to the diplomatic service in recent years without the usual examination procedure were dismissed. Ciano and Grandi were officially dismissed as ambassadors, and both were expelled from the diplomatic service.[205] Crucially, Blasco Lanza D'Ajeta, one of Ciano's closest confidants, was unaffected by the reshuffle. Guariglia sent him to Lisbon to contact the Allies and explore possibilities for a separate peace. In the Portuguese capital, D'Ajeta met British Ambassador Sir Ronald Campbell on 4 August 1943 and laid the foundation for the Italian armistice of 3 September 1943.[206]

Ultimately, we return to the question of whether Ciano's hesitant behaviour affected his reputation and his potential charismatic authority – and thus, his chances to follow in Mussolini's footsteps. In the weeks spanning July and August 1943, when Italy's future was decided, rumours filled the streets and squares of a capital dominated by manic activity. The royal house, the Vatican, senior army officers, and leading fascists struggled to find a way out of the crisis that had been brewing under the surface for months but was thrust into the open by the Allied invasion of Sicily. And Ciano was but one figure at the centre of the events. Even though he appeared to have a realistic grasp of the situation, he was indecisive and hesitant.[207] Instead of spearheading a fascist reform movement, he preferred to keep a low profile. By doing so, however, he missed another opportunity – his last – to present himself as a true (fascist) leader. Unlike Benito Mussolini, who had taken his chance during the crisis of the early 1920s and seized control of the fascist movement, Ciano remained a prisoner to his own wait-and-see attitude. He thus proved that he lacked yet another central quality of a charismatic leader: determination.

Ciano's reluctance – but also the indecisive behaviour of other high-ranking fascists like Grandi or Bottai – enabled Vittorio Emanuele III to act. The king's intervention was especially damaging to Ciano's prospects in that, as early as November 1942, the king made it clear that he never considered Ciano an alternative to the *Duce*. He acknowledged Ciano's energy, but doubted his "seriousness" and feared that Edda Ciano would stab her husband in the back and switch her support to Mussolini. Moreover, he was convinced that Ciano had no political and social support and was too young. By the summer of 1943, youth, held by fascists in such high regard, was no longer seen as an asset in a potential leader. Experience and reliability, qualities that Pietro Badoglio embodied, were much more important.[208]

Ciano's actions – or rather inaction – in the first half of 1943 were not isolated cases; rather, his indecision in the face of a crisis was a constant theme in his life. With very few exceptions, such as the non-belligerence policy, Ciano tended to hesitate when faced with a new situation or called in sick. Usually he kept a low profile, hiding behind his father and later behind Mussolini. Even his support for *non belligeranza* and thus his refusal to enter Italy into a military conflict – often cited as one of his best political decisions – can be interpreted as signs of cowardice and indecision according to the fascist doctrine and thus undermined his potential authority in a fascist state. Neither as minister for propaganda nor as foreign minister did he take on risky initiatives, openly oppose the official policies of the regime, or publicly assume responsibility for political decisions – even if he sometimes pushed for the implementation of certain plans, such as the invasion of Albania or the interference in the Spanish Civil War. Ciano preferred to write criticisms in his diary rather than express them in public or in conversation with the object of his criticism. Finally, he repeatedly stressed that only the *Duce* possessed the power to make political decisions; but as a henchman of the head of government, he could hardly construct the image of a determined politician, a visionary who would not shy away from doing what he thought was right.

That a charismatic leader in a fascist system of rule could never afford to give the slightest sign of indecision was something Benito Mussolini himself had to learn the hard way. His lethargy after the meeting of the Grand Council in July 1943 led to astonishment, even criticism of his leadership capabilities. Even close confidants, devout followers, and his German ally doubted whether the *Duce* still possessed the "infallible will" that had once distinguished him.[209] A sacrifice, then, was necessary for Mussolini to restore the public's faith in him, and his son-in-law fit the bill.

The "Good Fascist"

After the meeting of the Grand Council, Ciano and Antonino Tringali Casanova, the president of the special courts, supposedly engaged in a lively debate. The latter predicted that the "young man" would "pay for this betrayal with blood." Ciano replied that he regretted that he had to vote the way he did, "but I cannot betray my homeland as you do."[210] This brief anecdote shows two different narratives about how Ciano's behaviour was judged in the aftermath of the Grand Council meeting. Even though the narratives were contradictory, they both circulated around the theme of betrayal. On the one hand, the vote for Grandi's petition was interpreted as a betrayal of the *Duce* and thus of fascism; in Ciano's case, it was also a betrayal of his father-in-law and thus of a family member.[211] On the other hand, Ciano and his supporters argued that not signing the petition would have doomed the country and thus been a betrayal of their beloved homeland. These two narratives, however, did not suddenly emerge in the summer of 1943; instead, they were rooted in Ciano's previous public image as well as his failed attempts to portray himself as Mussolini's successor and a "new man," and thus were already part of the debates about the future of the *Duce*, fascism, and the country, all of which became more urgent at the turn of 1942–43.

For months Mussolini had suspected that Ciano might betray him in order to take power for himself. In June 1943, just a month before the meeting of the Grand Council, the *Duce* was irritated that Ciano had informed the king – but not him – of a conversation he had with Cardinal Luigi Maglione. In that meeting Maglione apparently had told Ciano that the Allies had no reservations about a reign by Vittorio Emanuele III. Hearing this, Mussolini suspected that Ciano sought to position the king against him and ordered his son-in-law to be surveilled.[212] Thus, Ciano's vote in the Grand Council may have disappointed the *Duce*, but he may not have necessarily been surprised.

Foreign observers had likewise taken notice of the growing opposition within the fascist elite towards Mussolini. The Allies tried to exploit the growing discontent by intensifying their propaganda campaign, which painted the picture of the "innocent Italians" who did not want to go to war in the first place and Benito Mussolini who was solely blamed for the war.[213] The political and diplomatic decision-makers in Berlin, however, were surprised by the suddenness of Mussolini's fall.[214] After the vote, nobody in the *Führer*'s headquarters had a clear picture of what was going on in Rome. Did Mussolini resign? Was he still alive? Who was to blame? Rumours flew fast and thick in Germany, but the truth remained elusive.[215]

On 26 July 1943 Ambassador Mackensen was told to compile a list of thirty persons who were considered notorious opponents of the German regime – with this order the search for the traitors of Italian fascism had begun.[216] Mackensen dutifully reported that only Vittorio Cerruti, Dino Grandi, Fulvio Suvich, Giuseppe Volpi, and Galeazzo Ciano fell into this category.[217] The name Ciano may come as a surprise, as Mackensen had thus far protected him from accusations.[218] Perhaps the German ambassador was trying to protect himself, since he too had been taken by surprise and had not accurately informed Berlin about possible consequences of the Grand Council meeting.[219] This rationale would also explain why he was so eager to send additional telegrams to his superiors in which he mentioned new names like General Ambrosio, Isabelle Colonna, Admiral Riccardi, and General Roatta.[220] These lists laid the foundation for possible future arrests carried out by the German secret service in Italy.[221]

When Galeazzo Ciano and his family arrived in Munich aboard a JU-52 on 29 August, leading Nazis and fascists were for quite some time convinced that he had betrayed Mussolini and Italian fascism.[222] The Cianos were first housed under the name Blank in a villa near Oberallmannshausen. Himmler's *Reichssicherheitshauptamt* (RSHA; Reich Main Security Office) took care of the accommodation, including all the expenses. Himmler and the Cianos tried to maintain a cordial relationship in public; while both parties pursued their own interests, they knew that they needed one another in order to achieve their objectives. Whereas Ciano needed Himmler in order to flee to Spain or Latin America, Himmler wanted to obtain Ciano's diary since there were numerous rumours that it incriminated Ribbentrop in the eyes of Hitler.[223] The diary, however, was beyond Ciano's reach because he had entrusted it to his mother, Carolina, in Ponte a Moriano before he left Italy.[224] Nevertheless, he offered the diary to the RSHA in return for a quick escape from Germany.

Himmler deeply mistrusted the Ciano family. He ordered their surveillance in an "appropriate and cautious manner" and wanted to be informed about the behaviour of the "female guest" in particular.[225] In addition, Himmler's friend, the writer Hanns Johst, regularly notified him about the behaviour of the Cianos. In numerous letters Johst complained about Galeazzo's allegedly outrageous appearance and made it more than clear what fate he hoped would befall the former Italian foreign minister: "It will be saved what must be saved for reasons of sentimentality, and it will fall what is ripe. They'll have to separate them from him if they want to save the children for an honest life."[226]

While his neighbour wished for him to die, Ciano seemed to take little offence at Johst's behaviour or at the fact that his departure from Germany was repeatedly delayed. This attitude suddenly changed when Mussolini was liberated by a German commando under Otto Skorzeny on 12 September, brought to Munich, and accommodated with his family in Castle Hirschberg near Lake Starnberg. Edda Ciano immediately visited her father and urged him to see Galeazzo. She wanted to give her husband an opportunity to explain to the *Duce* what role he had played at the meeting of the Grand Council and to refute the accusation that he had committed a double betrayal of both the *Duce* of Fascist Italy and a family member. The meeting eventually took place in Munich in the presence of Rachele Mussolini and Edda Ciano. Ciano tried to justify his vote in the Grand Council and attacked Grandi, Bottai, Badoglio, and Cavallero, whom he accused of being the real traitors. As

Ciano told it, he had been a victim of ignorance and had never wanted to replace Mussolini or see him imprisoned. He even offered to serve in a new government or the Italian army as proof of his unshakable loyalty to the *Duce*.[227]

Apparently, Ciano played the role of the naive dupe who had fallen victim to a conspiracy quite convincingly.[228] It seemed that Mussolini believed his son-in-law, and even Ciano thought he had persuaded the *Duce*.[229] Yet, he made several misjudgments. He believed that the *Duce*'s presumed forgiveness was only due to his own significance. He still thought that he was one of the most influential personalities in Italy, one whom Mussolini could not just cast aside. He also failed to realize that the *Duce* no longer possessed his former power within the fascist system; not only did Grandi's petition severely damage Mussolini's charismatic authority, but the *Duce*'s hesitant action after the meeting did nothing to restore it. As a consequence, Mussolini's control over the heterogeneous fascist elite was severely shaken, and more than before he was subject to shifting positions and alliances within the elite. When Ciano's personal rivals such as Alessandro Pavolini and Buffarini Guidi arrived at the *Führer*'s headquarters, the *Duce* was increasingly convinced of his son-in-law's guilt and equally certain that the traitors of July 1943 had to be punished.[230] Lastly, loyal fascists were never really concerned with Ciano as a person; rather, they were interested in punishing the "traitors" of the old regime – and such an accusation could no longer be settled privately between son-in-law and father-in-law.

That Ciano was in a precarious situation became more and more apparent on 18 September when Mussolini gave a radio address in Munich, which was also transmitted to Italy. The *Duce* promised the establishment of the *Repubblica Sociale Italiana* (RSI), a "new order," and announced that all the traitors from the July meeting would be eliminated.[231] Moreover, Mussolini, who reignited fascism in northern and central Italy with the help of the Germans and his supporters, Interior Minister Buffarini Guidi and Party Secretary Pavolini, increasingly distanced himself from Ciano. In October he wrote a letter to Claretta Petacci in which he claimed that Ciano would be the most hated man in Italy, and rightfully so.[232] His estrangement from his son-in-law was evident even in his word choice, no longer referring to him as "Galeazzo," as he had done in most private letters, but rather as "Count Ciano." Using the title "Count" also stressed Ciano's proximity to the aristocracy and thus presented him as an opponent of fascism.[233] The often-cited story that Mussolini had forgiven his son-in-law for good must be seen as an attempt to portray the *Duce* in a humane light and was nothing more than a fairy tale.[234] Ciano realized that, with Mussolini's return to the political stage, the question of his future became increasingly urgent. But resignation and indecision set in when his escape plans failed, and he realized the hopelessness of his situation – a typical behaviour for Ciano. He "gets his raving fits every day," Hanns Johst wrote, "curses his German dungeon, sometimes wants to kill his guards, sometimes himself. Sometimes he declares war on us, sometimes his love."[235]

On 19 October 1943 Ciano was handed over to Mussolini and extradited to the RSI. Immediately after his arrival in Verona, he was arrested and held in Scalzi prison. On 11 November 1943 the government of the RSI established by decree a special court to convict the traitors of July 1943.[236] The law was written by Buffarini Guidi and Justice Minister Antonino Tringali Casanova – the same Casanova who had already predicted Ciano's death.[237] Rudolf Rahn, the German plenipotentiary to the RSI, assumed that the trial would end with a death sentence for Ciano, because the court's members were known as fascist hardliners and critics of Ciano.[238] The investigating magistrate, Vincenzo Cersosimo, began his interview with Ciano on 14 December. The former foreign minister apparently was not only surprised by the accusation of high treason, but also angry and horrified. He firmly rejected all allegations made against him and stressed that he was the only one present at the meeting who pleaded for a continuation of the war. Ciano's hearing was officially concluded on 29 December 1943.[239]

The trial, in which nineteen people in total were accused of high treason, began on 8 January 1944 (figure 19), but the Salò regime was only able to arrest Galeazzo Ciano, Emilio De Bono, Carlo Pareschi, Giovanni Marinelli, Luciano Gottardi, and Tullio Cianetti. The remaining accused – Giuseppe Bottai, Giuseppe Bastianini, Edmondo Rossoni, Alberto De' Stefani, Umberto Albini, Annio Bignardi, Giovanni Balella, Luigi Federzoni, Giacomo Acerbo, Dino Grandi, Dino Alfieri, Cesare Maria De Vecchi, and Alfredo De Marsico – were tried in absentia.[240] During the trial, Ciano took over his own defence. He tried to present himself as the victim of a conspiracy and also as Mussolini's liberator.[241] He argued that, as soon as he had credible information about the whereabouts of the *Duce*, he passed it on to an unnamed "foreign power." This simple strategy of suggesting that Mussolini was only freed thanks to the information he gave to the Germans came to naught when the Germans denied they had received such information from Ciano.[242] Ciano then took a different tack, now claiming that he had not committed an act of betrayal, but had simply made a mistake. He claimed that he had not expected or anticipated Mussolini's fall and had had no knowledge about Badoglio's and the king's plans.[243] The problem with his new strategy, however, was that mistakes, ignorance, and emotions were signs of weakness according to fascist doctrine – and that weakness, once again, contradicted the fascist image of masculinity and could therefore neither be accepted nor tolerated in the new RSI regime. Thus, even in the last weeks of his life, he confirmed the negative image fascist radicals had of him rather than countered it.

On 10 January the special court dealt more intensively with the alleged masterminds of the conspiracy: former chief of general staff Ugo Cavallero, Pietro Badoglio, and King Vittorio Emanuele III. All three were accused of using the dissatisfied members of the Fascist Grand Council to take revenge and stage a coup against Mussolini. The names Dino Grandi and Giuseppe Bottai were mentioned, but the name Galeazzo Ciano was notably missing.[244] At the end of the day, the verdicts were announced. All of those tried in absentia and also Ciano, De Bono, Pareschi, Marinelli, and Gottardi were sentenced to death, with only Cianetti receiving thirty years in prison.[245] The execution of the sentence was scheduled for the next morning. In its official communiqué, the fascist government of Salò was anxious to present the sentences as the result of an orderly and fair trial for high treason to undermine any suspicion that it was an act of revenge.

The evening before the execution was as dramatic as the circumstances leading up to it. Hoping to escape death, the convicts decided to submit a plea for clemency to Mussolini. Apparently, Ciano had to be persuaded to sign the petition.[246] Whether it was personal pride or simply resignation that made Ciano hesitate is not known; however, the numerous farewell letters he wrote to his wife and children as well as to close friends like Vitetti make the latter more likely. He confided to Vitetti that he could "die light-heartedly, for he was certain of God's judgment."[247] In the end, Pavolini intercepted the request for clemency, and it was not even passed on to the *Duce*.[248]

According to Zenone Benini, who had been arrested by RSI security forces and had been imprisoned at Scalzi since 30 November, Ciano was full of hatred for the Germans in the last hours of his life. Berlin, however, had information that Ciano was particularly angry with Mussolini and more ambivalent towards the Germans.[249] In this context, a diary entry by Joseph Goebbels is of particular interest:

> Ciano confessed ... that he had received the Belgian envoy on behalf of the *Duce* the day before our Western offensive to inform him that the German Wehrmacht intended to break into France via Belgium the next morning. If this is true, the Duce is not only an unfaithful ally, but a traitor ... This was the last straw for the Führer. Mussolini is now essentially finished for him. He no longer has any personal relations or friendship with him.[250]

Figure 19. Galeazzo Ciano (fourth from left) during the Verona trial, 1944. Photograph taken from the image in NA, WO 204/6090.

The timing of Ciano's confession suggests that he sought to discredit Mussolini with the Germans and sow distrust between Berlin and the *Duce* as a way of retaliating against Mussolini who had refused to save him. Goebbel's diary entry seems to confirm that he succeeded in his endeavour and that it was Ciano who hammered another nail into the coffin of the friendship between the two dictators, which had so far – at least publicly – survived all the tensions between the two nations.

In addition to his vengeful attempt to drive a wedge between Mussolini and Hitler, the fatalist Ciano also concerned himself with salvaging his own reputation and then wrecking Mussolini's in his final weeks. By the end of 1943, Ciano had given up all hope. Edda's attempts to free him had failed, and Mussolini had made it unmistakably clear that kinship would not affect politics. Otherwise, according to the *Duce*, politics would be only one big lie.[251] Ciano's letters to the Italian king and Winston Churchill, in which he tried to justify his political actions, offer a clear insight into his mood before and during the trial. It is hardly surprising that in both letters he blamed Mussolini alone for Italy's entry into the war and its downfall. In doing so, he tried to distance himself from the *Duce*, portraying himself more as the "anti-Mussolini" than the most likely successor of his former idol.[252] Although Ciano had given up all hope of survival, he had not given up the fight as to how the world would judge him. The foreword to his diary, which he wrote in the form of a political will on 23 December 1943, can be viewed in the same way. If the letters were primarily directed against Mussolini, he used the diary preface to justify his own peaceful diplomacy and to blame Germany and Joachim von Ribbentrop for the outbreak of the Second World War.[253]

On 11 January 1944 at 9:30 am the death sentence was carried out by firing squad (figure 20).[254] As with so much else in his life, the manner of Ciano's death developed into a heated debate between his opponents and friends. While former enemies and Western propaganda claimed that Ciano died like a coward, his followers argued that Ciano faced his own death heroically and courageously.[255] Still, even some opponents like Sergio Panunzio, who had often criticized Ciano's character, were reluctant to say anything bad about someone who had so courageously looked his death in the eye.[256]

In the wake of the execution, many questions emerged. Who was responsible for the death of Ciano, who had for years been considered the *Duce*'s most likely successor? Did Mussolini really give the order to execute his own son-in-law? Ciano's former associate Renato Prunas was shocked when he heard about the execution; the entire procedure was so "un-Italian" and so uncharacteristic for the *Duce* as well.[257] But if not the *Duce*, then who was responsible?

In Italy, one narrative spread quickly: the Germans were not only aware of the shooting, but they had pressured the regime in Salò to carry it out.[258] Did not the German consul in Florence, Gerhard Wolf, already announce on 8 November that Ciano definitely would be shot?[259] In his book *Il Carcere degli Scalzi*, Zenone Benini in particular argued that Ciano's fate had been predetermined.[260] Mussolini, too, repeatedly referred to the "German hand," since he maintained that he was wholeheartedly convinced of his son-in-law's innocence.[261] Moreover, the rumour was spread that the Germans would never have accepted a pardon for Ciano. To prove their point, proponents of this thesis reiterated that Ciano was guarded by Germans and that an SS agent was present at the execution site to check whether the person shot was really the former foreign minister.[262]

What is certain is that Mussolini was extremely clever in portraying himself as the real victim of Ciano's death.[263] In a letter to his lover Petacci, he referred to his poor health and spoke cautiously about the trial he "expects."[264] After the execution, he told Serafino Mazzolini that

Figure 20. Monsignore Giuseppe Chiot gives the last blessing to the executed Galeazzo Ciano, 1944. Photograph taken from the image in NA, WO 204/6090.

he was living through the greatest tragedy imaginable in human life: his son-in-law sentenced to death and his daughter on the run. Mazzolini wrote in his diary that the *Duce*'s drama could be sensed in every word.[265] One year later, Mussolini described the day of Ciano's execution as a "dramatic day for me."[266] The *Duce*'s letter to Carolina Ciano outdid all other forms of self-denial. In a self-pitying manner he wrote that the death of her son was extremely sad for him and that without Ciano he was very lonely.[267] The *Duce*, however, was not alone in the negation and trivialization of his own role in Ciano's execution. Rachele Mussolini also claimed in her memoirs that machinery had been set in motion that could not be stopped. She insisted that all remaining fascists longed for justice and desired only appropriate punishment for those who had brought down the regime.[268] In this assertion, she elided the fact that she had demanded Ciano's execution.[269]

The Germans denied all involvement in Ciano's execution, and to date there is no convincing evidence suggesting otherwise. On the contrary, there are numerous indications that Berlin kept its distance. Ribbentrop declared on behalf of Hitler that the Verona trial was an Italian matter, and he told Rahn that the German authorities had to stay out of it.[270] In addition, several leading Nazis, including Goebbels, were surprised by the death sentence against Ciano, having obviously expected him to be spared.[271] Even the initial report on the court's decision reflected this expectation. It stated that Ciano – and not Cianetti, as was really the case – had been sentenced to thirty years imprisonment.[272] Thus, the portrayal of the RSI as a weak state and the trial in Verona and the death sentences as the work of the Germans must be seen as part of the constructed Italian public remembrance in the style of the "good Italian" and the "bad German."[273] Nevertheless, moral pressure from Berlin should not be ruled out. As with Italy's entry into the war, orders were not required; discreet indications at the right time and in the right situation were sufficient to influence the Italian decision.[274] The fascist government in Salò assumed that a pardon for Ciano would not have been received positively in Berlin.[275]

Ciano's execution by firing squad can be interpreted as a symbolic political act. The trial and execution were not so much about killing Ciano as they were about eliminating what he stood for and thus setting a course for the future of the RSI. For many fascists, Ciano had embodied the "bourgeois face"[276] of fascism. Given Ciano's previously described politics and habitus, he personified in their minds the compromises of power between the fascist state, the church, and the monarchy, all of which were blamed for Mussolini's deposition. During the trial Ciano did nothing to refute this negative impression; rather, his public appearance and behaviour confirmed the negative image radical fascists already had of him. It was therefore necessary for the RSI government to establish a clear break with the old regime.[277] In a very cynical way, one could argue that only Ciano's sacrifice – though he never became Mussolini's successor – made it possible to create and legitimize the RSI, the successor state to the previous Fascist Italy. Richard Bosworth argues that Ciano's former protégés, such as Alessandro Pavolini, were especially keen to make a show of their break from Ciano and fervently demanded his trial and execution. The execution was a clear sign that the time of compromises was over and that a "new order" would reign in Salò.[278] There was good reason, after all, for the court's sobriquet, the "Revolution Court."[279]

Nevertheless, it must be stressed that the rift between Ciano and people like Pavolini or Buffarini Guidi did not centre solely on Mussolini's fall. Rather, the beginning of alienation can be seen as early as the Greek campaign in 1940–41. Ciano's role in deposing Mussolini along with the establishment of the RSI finally offered such individuals an opportunity to publicly demonstrate their break with Ciano. Moreover, it was up to Pavolini as secretary of the *Partito Fascista Repubblicano* (PFR) to inspire a new generation of fascists – thus a clear break with the old regime and a tough stance against the conspirators of 25 July 1943 seemed appropriate for political and tactical reasons. Most leading members of the PFR also supported Ciano's execution and, by extension, a strict crackdown on the traitors of fascism and the revolutionary idea.[280]

Mussolini's decision to ultimately join forces with the hardliners must likewise be understood in this context. The execution of his son-in-law offered him an opportunity to restore his reputation as an uncompromising, charismatic leader and by doing so sideline potential rivals and regain his room to manoeuvre. Moreover, given his radio speech on 18 September, his credibility was at stake should he grant Ciano clemency. Thus, if he wanted to regain respect among the ruling class of the RSI and of Germany, a pardon was never an option. Mussolini was buttressed in his view by none other than his mistress Claretta Petacci.[281] The *Duce*, as Bosworth put it, sent Ciano to his death in order to restore his damaged charismatic authority.[282] The reactions of the RSI's fascist movement and in Berlin showed that Mussolini's calculation was at least temporarily successful: Ciano's execution impressed the members of the PFR and replenished the *Duce*'s domestic prestige. In turn, Goebbels noted with satisfaction in his diary: "It speaks absolutely for Mussolini to have the traitors of fascism executed." The *Duce* "doesn't seem to be quite the sick and used-up man we've seen so far."[283]

It is therefore not surprising that the German diplomat Rahn met a completely calm and composed *Duce* on the day of Ciano's execution.[284] That Mussolini remained in the background throughout the entire process was due less to a "deeper cowardice"[285] than to a cool, calculating strategy. It was the only way for Mussolini to simultaneously carry out the death sentences against the traitors and publicly present himself as an understanding father-in-law who regretted Ciano's unfortunate death. In a conversation with Mazzolini immediately after the execution, Mussolini said that the trial and the verdict were the result of a pure state reason – which might have been the *Duce*'s only honest statement regarding Ciano's death. Mazzolini himself, who began his career under Ciano, summed up the fatalistic attitude of many of his contemporaries who continued to remain loyal to Mussolini by lamenting: "What a very sad hour! Old and trusted friends have been killed. But if the fatherland orders such an act for his salvation, then we will endure this pain as well."[286]

When we contextualize Mussolini's behaviour within the broader issue of succession in a fascist regime, we can draw two conclusions. First, the typical traits of a charismatic leader such as making decisions in a perceived crisis situation were still key to becoming the head of a (new) fascist regime. To become his own successor, Mussolini once again had to portray himself as the fearless and assertive leader. Second, however, the fact that the *Duce* was his own successor highlights the failure of the Italian fascist system to produce a suitable heir. With Mussolini's charismatic authority tarnished by the vote of the Grand Council and his subsequent inaction in the face of a crisis, it would never have been easier for other radical fascists to present a new leader. However, the *Duce* was still needed as he was the sole figure able to enforce the bond between the regime, its people, and the German ally. Even the new RSI was unable to solve the problem of succession.

The international and domestic reactions to Ciano's trial and execution were mixed. In Germany, the execution was welcomed as the only way to keep fascism alive in Italy. "Now," Goebbels stated, "fascism at least morally has a basis from which it can work again."[287] Leaders in Berlin tried to benefit from the execution in Verona on two other fronts. First, Hitler used the trial as an instrument to deter potential conspirators within his own ranks.[288] Second, the regime used it to intimidate other allied countries such as Hungary and Romania, which were considering leaving the war. The immediate reaction from Budapest nonetheless revealed that this strategy was only partially successful.[289] Although the public and politicians in Hungary were shocked by Ciano's death, at the request of Baron György Prónay on 18 January 1944 they honoured Ciano, who had "tragically departed from life."[290] In addition, the leader of the Spanish fascist party, José Luis de Arrese, publicly criticized the execution and claimed it happened on Berlin's order.[291]

The Western press reserved prominent first-page placement for their reports on the trial and subsequent execution. The *New York Times* aptly summed up a basic mood in the press stating: "They rightly deserved their fate, but it is one of the ironies of history that they should have died, not for crimes they committed, but for crimes they did not commit."[292] Former US ambassador Phillips criticized Ciano's vanity and volatility, but otherwise expressed a positive opinion of the former foreign minister. However, he also was undecided about the role of the *Duce* and the Germans in the execution of Ciano: "It shows ... either the remorselessness and brutality of Mussolini or the fact that he has lost control of everything and that the sentence was carried out by German orders."[293] Even though Phillips did not offer a final verdict as to who was ultimately responsible for Ciano's execution, he nevertheless tended to assume that the Germans might have pushed for it out of revenge as they disliked Ciano.

The majority of Italians, both within the RSI and within the territories under Badoglio, did not react to the execution the way the regime in Salò had hoped. It did not take long for the victims and Ciano in particular to become martyrs for the fatherland, even though the public had previously demanded their blood. In the public's view, was not Germany behind the execution? And besides, how could Mussolini give his (silent) blessing to the shooting of a family member?[294] The intention of the tribunal and RSI's leadership to brand Ciano as a traitor to fascism and thus to Italy had failed. Apparently, Mussolini was not surprised by the change of public opinion and claimed that he had foreseen it. His claim, however, is hardly convincing. Just as there was no doubt that Ciano was unpopular in Italy before his execution, there is also no evidence that Mussolini was alerted to the dramatic change in mood.[295] Rather, Mussolini tried desperately to defend the nimbus of an infallible politician and statesman. In a typically opportunistic manner, he even attempted to exploit Ciano's death for his benefit at the expense of the Badoglio government by declaring that the accusations of corruption against Ciano were simply a lie.[296] Suddenly, Mussolini, the judge over Ciano's life, acted in complete distortion of the facts as a defender of his son-in-law's reputation and at the same time attempted to both justify and conceal his own culpability.

Even though Ciano never convinced his accusers and adversaries, his interpretation of the events – Mussolini was solely responsible, the Germans had been a faithless ally and betrayed Italy, and the Italians were generally blameless – would eventually come to dominate public memory about Italy's participation in the Second World War, in large part thanks to his posthumously published diary.[297] In this respect Hanns Johst proved prescient when he urged Himmler not to offer Ciano any kind of platform. He warned that one must never give this "guy the slightest publicity, he would know how to use it very cleverly against us, and Badoglio would have one more great Italian."[298]

On 10 January 1946 the first English-language edition of Ciano's diary from 1939 to 1943 was published. "A modern Machiavelli," the publisher Doubleday advertised, "tells the inside story of war makers at work and play"; and a critic of the *New York Herald Tribune* described it as "one of the most incisive, indiscreet, and revealing commentaries ever left by the foreign minister of a great power."[299] The diary sparked a great deal of discussion after its publication. Even though some commentators were disappointed with its actual content, they still agreed that Ciano was finally getting back at Mussolini, the man who killed him.[300] Literary critic Charles Poore hoped that the diary would also help "to convict a number of the former friends of Ciano."[301]

In his Ciano biography, Eugenio Di Rienzo tries to unmask how the diary was instrumental in constructing Ciano's imagine as the "good fascist" at Mussolini's expense. He argues that there never existed a dispute between them and that Ciano altered his diary in order to create a peace alibi for himself. Consequently, he questions the historical authenticity of the entire diary. Di Rienzo's criticism misses the point. It was not so much the diary itself but the selective reading of the diary by politicians, scholars, and intellectuals alike, as well as the absence of a critical edition of the diary, that allowed for a posthumous glorification of Ciano's opposition to Mussolini while ignoring his deep involvement within the regime.

An early case in point of this selective and deliberate (mis)interpretation of the diary occurred during the Nuremberg Trials. Prosecutors repeatedly used the diary in their indictment against the former German foreign minister Joachim von Ribbentrop and cross-referenced it with other official records, giving it additional authenticity.[302] Ribbentrop along with other contemporaries cast doubt on the veracity of the diary, accusing Ciano of having repeatedly altered it.[303] Ribbentrop was at least partially right, because Ciano did not actually write the words "We want war" on 12 August 1939, as the prosecutors in the trial implied. Ciano only added them retrospectively in December 1943, when he was imprisoned in Verona. Ribbentrop's defence strategy did not work: on 1 October 1946 Geoffrey Lawrence, chairman of the International Military Court in Nuremberg, announced the death sentence against Ribbentrop, which was carried out two weeks later.

The instrumentalization of the diary during the Nuremberg Trials already showed that Ciano and with him the Italian nation would not have been successful in claiming a status of victimhood after the Second World War if it were not for the Allies. Another example illustrates how the commanding officers of the Allied occupying army in Italy also quickly recognized the propagandistic value of the Verona trial after the end of the Second World War. They intended to use the preface to Ciano's diary and also pictures from the trial and the execution of the former Italian foreign minister (see Figures 19 and 20)[304] to depict Ciano as a martyr and Mussolini as a heartless tyrant who had the father of his grandchildren executed. The photograph of Ciano at the dock, for example, was well suited for that purpose; in it, he is the only person wearing a light-coloured jacket, and he sits directly under the incoming light. Moreover, after September 1945 the image of the executed Ciano may have evoked associations with the last scenes of Roberto Rossellini's film *Roma città aperta* in that the priest who supported the Italian *resistenza* in Rome was also shot while tied to a chair.[305] This analogy would have placed Ciano in the circle of the resistance who fought against the German occupation – gone was the image of Ciano as the fascist pretender and born was the image of the "good fascist," or even the anti-fascist.

Galeazzo Ciano was first buried in a cemetery in Verona, but his last journey began on 4 April 1944. After a service in Verona, the coffin with his body was brought to Livorno accompanied by a policeman who wrote a detailed report on the transfer for the Ministry of the Interior. Ciano was buried in Livorno next to his father on 5 April 1944.[306] The only member of the Ciano family who was present at the funeral mass was Gino Ciano.[307] Edda Ciano was still in Switzerland at that time, having escaped there on 9 January 1944 with the help of her friend Emilio Pucci; her three children had already safely arrived in Switzerland at the end of 1943.[308] She was extradited by the Swiss authorities to the Allies in Italy on 30 August 1945, where she was first interned on the island of Lipari.[309] She apparently never forgave her father for having her husband "murdered."[310] Three months later, an Italian court sentenced her to two years in police custody. The judges found that she only had to answer for "moral complicity" in the fascist regime. Apparently, there was insufficient evidence to prove that she had any direct involvement in the crimes committed by her father's regime.

After just one year in prison, she enjoyed the general amnesty pronounced by the minister of justice, Palmiro Togliatti, and subsequently lived in Rome and Lipari. She received a monthly pension of $140 financed from her confiscated property.[311] However, she never saw the money she had received from the Americans for photographing her husband's diary.[312] It had been transferred to a US bank account, which in turn was frozen by the Americans after Edda Ciano was classified as an accomplice of the fascist regime.[313] In 1976 she had an extensive interview published in which she described her role in fascism, often in euphemistic and less self-critical words, and explained her relationship with Galeazzo Ciano and Benito Mussolini. Edda Ciano died on 8 April 1995, aged eighty-four years, in a hospital in Rome. She was buried in Livorno next to her husband.[314] Her youngest son, Marzio Ciano, had already died in a motorcycle accident two years before her interview.[315] Her daughter, Raimonda Ciano, died on 25 May 1998 in Rome, and Edda's eldest son, Fabrizio Ciano, who published his memoirs entitled *Quando il nonno fece fucilare papà* in 1991, died on 8 April 2008 in San José, Costa Rica. His passing marked the death of the last family member who had personally known Galeazzo Ciano, Count of Cortellazzo and Buccari, the "Fascist pretender."

Succession and Struggle in Fascism

The search for Benito Mussolini's potential political heir had preoccupied the Italian fascist regime since the 1920s. As early as the Matteotti crisis in 1924 and following numerous attacks on his person, the *Duce* was forced to think about a potential successor. His pick was not one of the more powerful and prominent fascists like Balbo and Grandi, whose intentions and ambitions he distrusted; it was none other than Galeazzo Ciano's father, Costanzo.[316]

There can be no doubt that his designation as Mussolini's successor would have been the highest honour Costanzo Ciano could have ever received – the only problem is that the alleged internal memorandum in which the *Duce* appointed him heir seemingly does not exist. The only clues we have are several popular rumours and Galeazzo Ciano's diary. According to Galeazzo's notes, Mussolini told his son-in-law in July 1939 that he had appointed Costanzo as his successor in November 1926, and gave him the relevant document.[317] However, such a record has not yet been found in the archives. Additionally, the nature of the source itself – Ciano's diary – and the fact that Costanzo Ciano was already dead should raise some red flags. It is possible that Mussolini pretended to have named Costanzo Ciano as his successor in order to secure his son-in-law's continued loyalty at a time when they were at odds over Italy's future foreign policy and the *Duce*'s obsession with the Axis was highly criticized by the rest of the fascist ruling class.[318]

Even so, regardless of the missing evidence it is doubtful whether Costanzo Ciano could have successfully filled the role of Mussolini's heir, as he did not possess anything close to the *Duce*'s personal presence and prestige on a national level. The Fascist Grand Council, which was supposed to draw up a list of potential successors, also failed to agree on any candidates.[319] Rather than concrete plans, numerous rumours circulated about possible succession arrangements, especially with the beginning of the Second World War. Much speculation centred on Galeazzo Ciano, who did little to refute it. On the contrary, at the end of December 1942 Ciano himself seemed to have raised his own name as a potential successor.[320] The rumours and hesitancy of the actors involved ultimately revealed a major dilemma for the opposition leaders, because as a result they were unable to form a strong alliance against Mussolini and his loyal followers. This uncertainty stemmed from years of mistrust among members of the fascist elite, which undermined any effective cooperation.

What conclusions can we draw from the regime's inability to find a suitable successor among the fascist elite? How do the questions of succession and the role that charismatic authority played force us to rethink our understanding of the fascist system of rule? According to recent historiography, the collapse of the Italian army and the looming Allied invasion alone brought an end to the fascist regime in Italy. Following this logic, one could presume that, without the catastrophic course of the war, a fascist system might have survived past 1945.[321] My examination of Ciano's life illustrates that, while it is true that the events of summer 1943 prompted the Grand Council and Vittorio Emanuele III to act, the fall of Mussolini and the collapse of the regime cannot be explained by external pressure alone. The absence of a suitable heir not only indicates signs of collapse from within; it also highlights the importance of a charismatic leader for the survival of the fascist regime. Such an individual's charisma and not the fascist party or other fascist institutions built the existential bond between the regime and the people.[322]

Corruption, nepotism, mismanagement, and the poor conduct of the war meant that even before the Grand Council vote in July 1943 the regime's days were numbered.[323] These factors also heavily undermined Mussolini's charismatic authority. It had long been possible for Mussolini to blame leading fascists such as Ciano for the failures of the regime, but during the 1930s and especially after the entry into the Second World War, the *Duce*'s aura gradually tarnished, thanks also to his involvement with the Petacci family.[324] Ciano noted in September 1941 that "the real misery of our people is due to a lack of food, fats, eggs, et cetera. But this aspect of the situation is not the one that disturbs the Duce [and the party]."[325] Facing this emergency, segments of the Italian populace started to question the regime. This unrest was not yet an irreversible step away from Mussolini and fascism, but the mere fact that serious questions were raised testifies to the weakening of the *Duce*'s prestige.[326]

The regime's reliance on Mussolini's charisma to create a unifying bond between the people and the fascist movement was becoming dangerous. At the time, only two solutions seemed possible to save the fascist system: either re-establish Mussolini's charisma or create a new charismatic leader.[327] In this respect it is instructive to return to Weber's analysis of charismatic authority, because he argued that there exist several options for appointing a new charismatic leader. These include an individual being designated by the original leader or by qualified staff, hereditary charisma, office charisma, and revelation.[328] Thus, the often-cited argument that there was no successor simply because Mussolini never appointed one neglects the complex mechanics of charismatic rule that allow for the naming of a successor through means other than direct appointment. Moreover, the power of the Grand Council to name a potential successor also shows that the fascists were aware of this problem and were making plans with a new generation of fascist leaders. Yet, Galeazzo Ciano, the individual who was perhaps best positioned to secure the role of successor, failed to do so. His inability to muster sufficient charismatic authority and invent an image for himself as a believable charismatic fascist leader was central to that failure and must be explained in greater detail.

Although Ciano invested a great deal of time and money in presenting himself as a reflection of Mussolini, he failed to follow in the footsteps of his former idol and turn his own charisma into a power resource. Ciano did not realize that he could not construct or enforce his own charismatic authority through mere imitation of Mussolini's facial expressions and demeanour; on the contrary, the imitation undermined his authority because he paled in comparison to the *Duce*. Ciano struggled to grasp that charismatic authority was built upon a populist appeal from below and not conferred by a higher authority from above. So he played at being a member of the old establishment while trying to build charisma within a movement that was revolutionary (that is, anti-establishment) at its core. A charismatic leader was expected to sacrifice himself for the state – distractions such as vacations, art, and culture had no place in the life of such a self-abnegating figure. Consequently, whereas Mussolini represented the ideal fascist man and ignored such distractions, Ciano became a symbol of the aristocracy and elite bourgeoisie – an image that was also carried by the Italian press, which would repeatedly refer to him as "Count."[329] This image, of course, damaged his reputation among radical fascists, and he failed to convince both the Italian people and his fellow members of the Grand Council that he was capable of leading Fascist Italy. Furthermore, his often-ridiculous attempts to present himself as a successful athlete and soldier did not sway an already critical public. Even his young age, which according to fascist ideology would have helped legitimatize his rule, did not work to his benefit. His behaviour in the summer of 1943 in particular illustrates that he lacked the crucial attributes usually associated with youth: courage, physical power, determination, and, above all, willpower.[330]

Ciano and his failure to become Mussolini's official heir created a dilemma for the entire fascist government. Faced with the problem of succession, intellectuals turned to the Catholic Church and the papacy as a potential model for solving the issue. They argued that the leader's charisma would eventually transfer to the regime's institutions, rendering it unnecessary for each successor to possess comparable degrees of charisma.[331] Mussolini's work might then be continued by a new "aristocracy of fascism."[332] These considerations, however, faced three major problems: First, Mussolini never accepted another strong personality next to him. He used rumours and cabinet reshuffles to ensure he remained unrivalled. But he failed to transfer his personal charisma to the institutions of the fascist state as some intellectuals thought should happen.[333] Second, the assumption that a system based on a single charismatic figure for decades could transform itself into a traditional system within a generation was risky. Unlike Mussolini, the pope's and the king's legitimacy was "based on the sanctity of ancient ('ever-existing') orders and lords' power."[334] Third, intellectuals knew that their ideas could only work if no other institution competed with the fascist state in terms of history and prestige, particularly during the transitional phase. Mussolini remained in competition with the traditional authority of the Italian monarchy and the Catholic Church until the end, his eroding charisma no match for the enduring legacies of throne and altar. Despite his pompous rhetoric, the *Duce* was unable to end the "uneasy but effective collaboration with traditional elites"[335] who had helped him to gain power in 1922.

When in the summer of 1943 a new crisis broke out, calls for political change grew louder. Segments of the Italian public, traditional elites, and some fascists lost confidence in Mussolini. The *Duce* appeared physically and mentally weak, was rarely seen in public, and his "mission" of creating an Italian *spazio vitale* visibly crumbled under the enemies' bombs – indeed, the very existence of Italy was at stake. By questioning Mussolini's competence and withdrawing their support for the *Duce*, the Grand Council effectively disputed Mussolini's charismatic authority. Yet, because the leader's charisma was a central pillar of the regime's stability, their move against him undermined the entire system. Under such circumstances, fascism could not continue. It remains doubtful as to whether a new fascist leader – or leaders – could have been appointed at this critical juncture given the previous failure to find a suitable solution for a post-Mussolini era. The case of Galeazzo Ciano and his failure to be selected to succeed the *Duce* illustrates the unlikelihood of any such solution to the crisis succeeding in 1943.

When a suitable successor to Mussolini failed to emerge from the fascist ranks, the monarchy under Vittorio Emanuele III stepped forward and took charge of the government. The king was hardly a charismatic, energetic leader with his diminutive five-foot stature and slender, frail build, but he represented an institution of traditional authority that was backed by both the Catholic Church – the "guarantor of mass consensus" (Enzo Collotti) – and the military high command. The monarch could, in sum, promise a more stable and predictable future. He was therefore able to invoke monarchical tradition and the petition of the Grand Council as a mandate to lead the country once again.

The events of July 1943 illustrate the failure of Mussolini and the radical fringe within the fascist party to impose an enduring totalitarian system in Italy. Despite twenty-one years of fascist rule based on Mussolini's charisma, the king never lost his traditional office's authority. Though it required a crisis to push Mussolini aside, Vittorio Emanuele III wielded considerable political influence during the years of fascist rule. The *Duce* was correct when he closed the session of the Grand Council with the words, "Gentlemen, you have initiated the crisis of the regime,"[336] though the conditions of the crisis, for which he held significant responsibility, had been building since the 1930s.

But was the problem of succession only present in Italy? How did other European fascists cope with it? A look at similar regimes and movements – or at least movements and governments that at one point flirted with fascism – reveals striking parallels to the Italian case. The list of fascist movements and regimes that were unable to successfully transfer power from their founders to possible successors is lengthy: Arthur Fonjallaz in Switzerland (*Schweizerische Faschistische Bewegung*), Ante Pavelić in Croatia (*Ustaša*), Sir Oswald Mosley in Great Britain (British Union of Fascists), Ferenc Szálasi in Hungary (*Nyilaskeresztes Párt*), Eoin O'Duffy in Ireland (National Corporate Party), Jacques Doriot in France (*Parti populaire français*), Corneliu Zelea Codreanu in Romania (*Garda de fier*), and José Antonio Primo de Riviera in Spain (*Falange*).[337] All these men founded fascist groups and became their undisputed and only leaders. With each leader's death, execution, withdrawal, or arrest, their movements were unable to produce a capable successor and ceased to exist. There is no question that the course of the Second World War and the horrors committed in the name of fascism certainly delegitimized the ideology and accelerated the demise of fascist movements. But the fact that both before and during the war none of the movements was able to successfully hand over the leadership to a second generation suggests once again that the war was not the only factor weakening these movements.

Of course, the essence of the respective charismatic authority differed from country to country as the comparison between Mussolini and Hitler illustrates. Just imitating another charismatic leader would have undermined the ultranationalist appeal of the leader, while specific national traditions and cultures shaped the people's expectations in their charismatic figure. Nevertheless, there is no denying that in fascism the leader formed the bond between regime, party, and people. The failure to find an alternative that could successfully replace the leader's aura reveals that succession was an issue inherent to every fascist movement, one that, once again, exposes a fundamental crack in the totalitarian facade of the fascist experiment.[338]

The regimes and movements not only failed to find an individual who could succeed the charismatic leader; they also failed to create a new leadership cadre that would wield enough prestige and influence to carry the fascist system after the demise of their founder and leader; and they failed to establish a totalitarian state in which a single party wielded absolute power. The charismatic leader's symbolic importance – independent of his actual political power – was, in the end, a ticking time bomb for the survival of fascism itself. This fact set the political system of fascism apart from military, monarchical, and communist authoritarian regimes of the twentieth century, which also heavily relied on leaders with a charismatic authority.[339] Compared to those dictatorships, fascism remained at its core a "one generation" system. Generation thus becomes another important lens that can further our understanding of fascism, one I want to turn to in the following epilogue.

Epilogue:
A Man of His Time

Galeazzo Ciano's place in Italian collective memory remains ambivalent. Some consider him a naive and spoilt upstart who lacked political skill and wisdom. Others highlight his opposition to the Germans and the war, thus illustrating that Ciano's efforts to shape his posthumous self-image were at least partially successful. Common to most of these assessments, however, is that he is not considered a fascist, even though he served the regime for a total of eighteen years. Giordano Bruno Guerri, author of the first comprehensive Ciano biography, denied that his protagonist had any affinity for fascism. The French historian Michel Ostenc titled his biography *Ciano. Un conservateur face à Hitler et Mussolini*; and Zenone Benini described Ciano as a "democratic intellectual" whose mistake was to idolize a dictator.[1] Bosworth's verdict is more nuanced, describing Ciano as the face of "bourgeois fascism"; but by doing so he combined two terms that, according to fascist self-perception, are mutually exclusive.[2] Lastly, Galeazzo Ciano himself told Daniele Varè that he was a "convinced fascist" only between 1936 and 1938.[3]

My study of Galeazzo Ciano has focused on four aspects of his life and work that reveal the limits of the "totalitarian experiment" in Italy. By doing so, the study also exposes Ciano's multifaceted character, as he often changed his appearance and adapted his self-image to specific circumstances ranging from Ciano the diplomat, the athlete, and the aristocrat to Ciano the fascist, the soldier, or Mussolini's successor. The diversity of Ciano's self-images shows that it would be overly simplistic and misleading for our understanding of the fascist system to label Ciano with seemingly apodictic categories such as "fascist" and "conservative"; rather these images illustrate that fascism never lost its heterogeneous character, offering a wide range of people the chance to participate and benefit from the regime's policies. But what does

Ciano's case tell us about the functioning of fascist systems in general and Italian fascism in particular? How does Ciano fit into the history of Italian fascism and the European interwar period? In short, who was Galeazzo Ciano, Count of Cortellazzo and Buccari, whom the American diplomat Sumner Welles described so accurately as a "creature of his times"?[4]

Born in Livorno in 1903, Galeazzo Ciano belonged to the so-called war youth generation. While we possess numerous detailed studies that deal with this age cohort during the Third Reich, comparable studies on their Italian counterparts are largely missing.[5] Ulrich Herbert and Michael Wildt emphasize that common experiences during childhood and adolescence formed a generation-specific sense of belonging in Germany that transcended social and political boundaries.[6] For example, this "uncompromising generation" was too young to participate in the First World War, but old enough to comprehend the war's impacts. This "piercing thorn of a missed opportunity" resulted in a desire to prove themselves in another military conflict, often imagining it as a game or an exciting adventure.[7] Other life-changing experiences occurred in the early 1920s, when many of this generation attended universities. Hyperinflation, the occupation regime, and the "diktat peace" of Versailles discredited moderate politicians as "*Erfüllungspolitiker*" ("fulfilment politicians") and extended further to the entire bourgeois social order.[8] As a consequence, the war youth sought to overcome the "crisis of classical modernity" (Detlev Peukert) by supporting new sociopolitical models that centred on strong leadership and authority.[9] The war youth were convinced that they were destined to shape their nation's future and waited for their chance to finally "actively intervene."[10]

Galeazzo Ciano's life reveals many similarities with Germany's "uncompromising generation," including his admiration of strong male personalities, his zeal for action, and his experience during the First World War, when he saw first-hand the war's destruction in Venice and was exposed to nationalistic propaganda despite being too young to participate. These experiences resulted in his wish to prove himself in a military conflict, his anticipation of the Ethiopian campaign, his use of hunting metaphors when describing his combat missions, and his efforts to create one of his multiple self-images: Ciano as the pilot and soldier – hardly an exception within his age cohort.[11] In addition, Ciano believed in youth as a historical force, which would eventually draw him towards the futurist and fascist movements in the 1920s. When political violence plunged Italy into chaos, both movements promised social and political advancement for the war youth. Thus, it should not come as a surprise that this generation would make up a considerable proportion of the Blackshirts.

However, different national developments in the 1920s and early 1930s exposed Galeazzo Ciano to experiences that would eventually set him apart from the German war youth generation. When Germany was hit by hyperinflation and political chaos, both of which were exploited by the far right to discredit traditional bourgeois society, the Italian fascists were already in power. Thus, it was harder for them to include these economic crises in propaganda designed to bolster their anti-bourgeois and anti-capitalist program and to entice Ciano's age cohort.[12]

The career of his father, who joined the fascist movement in 1921 and was instrumental in the fascist takeover in Livorno, also demonstrated that many leading proponents of the "fascist revolution" were unwilling to break with core principles of Italy's traditional political culture. In order to secure and eventually increase his family's social and political status on a local and national level, Costanzo Ciano embraced means that were deeply rooted in and associated with the political culture of Italy's liberal era, including corruption, bribery, nepotism, and clientelism. While the German war youth and the Italian radical fascists despised the traditional political culture and the bourgeois lifestyle, Costanzo Ciano's behaviour and success showed Galeazzo the benefits of the "old system" and what he could achieve by putting its tools to good use.

And indeed, Galeazzo Ciano would follow his father's example. On numerous occasions he promoted another of his multiple self-images: Ciano as a member of the bourgeoisie or even the aristocracy. His study of law and his diplomatic training brought him into close contact with the upper-middle classes and the nobility, allowing him to build personal connections with the Roman establishment. While Mussolini continued his attacks against the establishment, Ciano saw his contacts in the nobility as a confirmation of his social status and wealth. Moreover, he also made sure that his children would be exposed to bourgeois values and family models. Thus, the Cianos exemplified the hypocrisy of the fascist movement, which had set out to end – but ultimately strengthened – the "vices" of liberal Italy such as nepotism, corruption, regionalism, and individualism.

Ciano's career also exposed him to influences and experiences that set him apart from other members of his peer group. By the age of thirty he had already risen to the centre of power, and by thirty-three he was one of the most important ministers of the regime. While Ciano continued his career, many members of the war youth, such as Asvero Gravelli (born in 1902), and war children, such as Ruggero Zangrandi (born in 1915), were demanding a "second revolution" and thought that Ciano would use his power to push for it in order to save Italian fascism from becoming an ordinary dictatorship.

Ciano would indeed use the fascist pomp and circumstance to portray himself (with Mussolini's blessing) as a dynamic young fascist – another of his multiple selves. However, he was never willing to endanger his own social and political position, and thus would – especially behind the scenes – oppose key projects such as the "total" fascistization of society and the waging of a war that threatened Italy's very existence. In the end, the power of political rituals and symbolic communication was not enough to conceal that he preferred to defend the status quo once he was in power. As a consequence, Ciano lost the image of the young and dynamic fascist, and members of an even younger generation of fascists such as Aldo Vidussoni began to reach the upper echelons of power.

The contradictions between reality and demands for constant change not only undermined Ciano's position, but also eroded the consensus between the fascist elite, the *Duce*, and the Italian public. Such contradictions epitomize the dilemma for a fascist regime once it seizes power: either the regime continues its "revolutionary duty" in order to maintain the appearance of dynamism and strength, or it attempts to consolidate the power it has gained and thus creates and defends a new status quo. In the latter case, however, the regime would cease to be genuinely fascist and turn into an ordinary authoritarian system of rule.[13]

Ciano's loss of his image as the young fascist exemplifies that he never was in total control of how he was perceived in public. Rather, his own images were constantly challenged, scrutinized, and contrasted with other negative public perceptions of Ciano as the incompetent upstart or the traitor to fascism. To counter these negative images and therefore defend his position against internal rivals, Ciano used a variety of tactics, both subtle and overt. Certainly, his proximity to the *Duce* was important for him, but it also lent credibility to accusations of nepotism. Moreover, tying his fate to that of his father-in-law eroded his ability to separate and grow his influence outside of Mussolini's sphere, which made him vulnerable to the intrigues within the Mussolini family. Ciano's closeness to Mussolini became less beneficial and more burdensome over time.

As a consequence, Ciano consciously cultivated other power resources, drawing on his father's reputation, his personal networks, and the institutional power of the ministries he headed. In addition, he established close contacts with the Catholic Church and the monarchy and defended both institutions against attacks from Mussolini and radical fascists. Unfortunately, such tactics made it easy for Ciano's opponents to denounce him as a defender of the old, traditional political culture. Thus, by looking for alternate roles and allies Ciano would ultimately further weaken his reputation among the core fascists.

The fluid, often unstable compromises of power between the three major actors – the fascists, the church, and the monarchy – gave "fascist rule its characteristic mixture of feverish activism and lack of structure."[14] Ciano personified these compromises in his constantly changing public self-images. To further complicate matters, the fascist elite itself was anything but homogeneous. Scholars often distinguish between proponents of an "extremist party fascism" and a "monarchical state fascism of the nationalists" (Wolfgang Schieder); others use terms such as "radical fascists" and "moderate fascists" to describe these internal factions.

My study provides us with an even more nuanced insight into these conflicts and contradictions. It illustrates how these divisions between "moderate" and "radical" fascists were often transcended by other factors in order to build short-lived alliances, including economic, regional, and family interests as well as political-ideological convictions, institutional ties, religious beliefs, personal sympathies, and one's generational cohort. These various lines of conflict are, once again, mirrored in Ciano's own career and his efforts to construct different images of himself according to specific circumstances and times.

By doing so, Ciano hoped to form ad hoc alliances with various groups within the upper echelons of power in order to maintain and defend his influence. While his opportunistic behaviour eventually undermined his reputation as a trustworthy actor, it did not help that Mussolini actively sought to destroy any long-lasting alliances between the various groups within the regime's elite. Yet, due to the multitude of actors – the fascist regional *ras*, the church, the royal house, the armed forces – even the *Duce* was not able to exert total control. The magnitude and diversity of actors who could influence political decisions through coalitions is reminiscent of an oligarchic system, which is also typically characterized by very low rates of personnel turnover. We see evidence of this feature in the history of the fascist regime. Leading personalities of the early 1920s, such as Grandi, Bottai, Farinacci, and Scorza, still held influential positions within the regime in 1943.

The continuity of personnel highlights the regime's failure to create a new fascist elite. This problem, however, did not appear out of the blue;

it was already apparent at the local level in the early 1930s.[15] In contrast to the Third Reich, where a loyal and committed war youth generation spearheaded the implementation of National Socialist doctrine, a comparable group seemed to be missing in Italy. Yet, the inclusion of members of a younger age cohort was imperative for the regime's survival, as the leadership had to ensure that the transfer of power to members of the war children – and thus to those who had been indoctrinated solely in fascist youth organizations – would be carried out smoothly. And once again, Ciano's career and his failure to construct a convincing image of himself as the "new man" and "Mussolini's heir" exemplify this dilemma. Long regarded as the leader of the fascists' "next generation," he was only interested in this kind of aura if it benefitted him and dropped any fascist zeal for revolution as soon as he reached the upper echelons of power.

Galeazzo Ciano's life and his many, constantly shifting self-images – some he created and others attributed to him – proves that inflexible categories such as "fascist" and "conservative" do not do his complex character justice. In addition, he did not fit into Wildt's "uncompromising generation." Apart from the sometimes justified criticism of this generational model, Ciano's example illustrates that the war youth's experiences were shaped by various national peculiarities, thus resulting in a very heterogeneous "European war youth generation."[16]

In addition, Ciano's biography reveals the diversity of the Italian war youth. Due to different regional and political experiences, the development of a generation-specific feeling of community was already complicated; it was further hindered after the fascist takeover in 1922 when the concept of "nation" superseded that of "age cohort" in forming a common generational identity. Ciano's evolving allegiances expose the fragility of ideas of specific generational belonging. At first, he saw himself as part of a younger generation demanding more political power and change. Then, beginning in the late 1930s – and especially after the death of his father – he showed an emotional attachment to the older fascists and the lifestyle and worldview of the upper-middle classes and the aristocracy.

Galeazzo Ciano's biography illuminates the contradictions of the fascist regime on an individual level. Despite his initial affinity for the movement, he is an excellent example of the limits of the "totalitarian experiment" in Italy. On the one hand, he belonged to the age cohort that was to safeguard the continuation of the fascist system. But on the other hand, his rapid career advancement made him an exception in his peer group. Instead of dedicating himself to a permanent "fascist revolution," he succumbed to the temptations of power. His actions, which included both traditional and fascist elements, were devoted to defending himself and his position. Whether Galeazzo Ciano was an exception in this respect or whether his life may be representative of fascism's "lost generation" – the age cohort that was supposed to take over the fascist regime but, due to their socialization and integration into the state apparatus, lacked fascism's revolutionary zeal – can only be clarified by further biographical and prosopographical works.

Analysing Galeazzo Ciano through the lens of a modern political biography using a broad selection of different sources has helped debunk several "urban legends" concerning him and his family. More importantly, however, it demonstrates the relevance of engaging with the lives and work of leading figures of the fascist regime other than Mussolini. Only this larger study will help us gain a better understanding of the dynamics of the fascist dictatorship on a personal, social, transnational, and cultural level. This group includes, in addition to the ministers, the secretaries-general of the PNF, the heads of the secret services (for example, Arturo Bocchini), the members of the Grand Council, the officers of the royal army (for example, Pietro Badoglio, Rodolfo Graziani, and Mario Roatta), members of the royal house and Italian nobility (for example, Isabelle Colonna), and leading industrialists (for example, Alberto Pirelli).[17]

Their memoirs and autobiographies, which were published and promoted after the Second World War as they supported Italy's policy of public remembrance and the narrative of "victimhood," in addition to scholars' focus on the life and work of Benito Mussolini reduced these figures into "people who merely took orders and executed [his] will."[18] The scholarly obsession with the *Duce*, combined with the state-directed – and Allied-tolerated – amnesia concerning everything that happened before Mussolini's deposition in 1943, helped many civil servants and officers to continue their careers after the Second World War and to whitewash their own involvement in the fascist regime and its attendant crimes. The question of whom to blame for the atrocities and suppression had – also thanks to the biased reading of Ciano's diary – already been answered: Mussolini and the Germans. As a consequence, many historians studying Fascist Italy shied away from looking into the political structures of the fascist regime or engaging with leading figures of the regime, which would have complicated such simplistic narrative.[19]

For years, it was assumed that the political history of Fascist Italy had been thoroughly and critically examined, when that was not really the case. Italy's archival landscape with its restrictive rules and outdated or missing finding aids did nothing to remedy this state of research. While this situation resulted in fascinating and insightful studies on the cultural history of Fascist Italy, particularly in Anglo-American literature, a systematic discussion of the political structure of fascist rule, a debate that dominated the historiography on Nazi Germany for decades, is still largely missing. Yet, without a serious discussion on the *Duce*'s position, the interdependence between various forms of rule, or the existence of polycratic and – as I have suggested in my book – oligarchic elements within fascist rule, scholars unintentionally have far too often ceded the overall narrative to the earlier approaches that primarily tried to rescue Italy's reputation.

Although we can see a recent trend in the historiography on Italian fascism where scholars have begun to question the value of the post-war memoirs of leading fascists and examine more thoroughly their role within the regime, well-researched and methodologically innovative monographs on this circle of people are still largely missing. But as this study has shown, biographical and prosopographical studies on the Italian elite during the fascist era can force us to rethink fascist rule's "everyday execution."[20] Studies of this type are essential to examining and evaluating the contradictions, the complexity, and the vacillations of fascist domestic and foreign politics – in short, what Robert Paxton described as "lack of structure."

Chronology

Year	Date	Galeazzo Ciano's Biographical Data	Date	Important Events
1903	18.3.	Birth of Galeazzo Ciano		
1914			28.6.	Assassination of Archduke Franz Ferdinand
1915			26.4.	Treaty of London
			23.5.	Italy declares war on Austria-Hungary
1916			27.8.	Italy declares war on Germany
1917			24–27.10.	Battle of Caporetto
1918			10–11.2.	*Beffa di Buccari*
			4.11.	Battle of Vittorio Veneto ends
1919			12.9.	Occupation of Fiume begins
			18.9.	Paris Peace Conference begins
1920			29.12.	Occupation of Fiume ends
1922			2.8.	Fascist "takeover" in Livorno
			27.10.	"March on Rome"
			30.10.	First government of Benito Mussolini
			15.12.	Fascist Grand Council
1921		Ciano begins his law studies at Sapienza University in Rome (until 1924)		
1923	June	Premiere of Ciano's drama *La felicità di Amleto*		

Year	Date	Galeazzo Ciano's Biographical Data	Date	Important Events
1924			6.4.	General election
	17.7.	Premiere of Ciano's comedy *Er fonno d'oro*	10.6.	Murder of Giacomo Matteotti
1925		Joins diplomatic service vice consul in Rio de Janeiro	1.12.	Locarno Treaties
1926		2nd embassy secretary in Buenos Aires	4.4.	Youth organization *Balilla* founded
1927	May	Transfer to the embassy in Beijing		
1929			11.2.	Lateran Treaties
1930	24.4.	Marriage to Edda Mussolini		
	12.9.	Transfer to Shanghai		
1931	1.10.	Birth of Fabrizio Ciano		
1932	3.2.	First session of the League of Nations' commission in Shanghai under the chairmanship of Ciano		
1933	12.6.	Participates at the London Economic Conference		
	1.8.	Appointment as head of the USCG		
	12.12.	Birth of Raimonda Ciano		
1934			17.3.	Rome Protocols
	10.9.	Appointment as state secretary of press and propaganda	14–15.6.	Hitler visits Venice
			25.7.	Murder of Dollfuß
1935			14.4.	Final Declaration of the Stresa Conference
	25.6.	Appointment as minister of press and propaganda	16.5.	*Mostra d'arte italiana* begins in Paris
	24.8.	Departs to Ethiopia		
	13.12.	Returns to Italy		

Year	Date	Galeazzo Ciano's Biographical Data	Date	Important Events
1936	7.2.	Returns to Ethiopia		
	7.5.	Returns to Italy	5.5.	Occupation of Addis Ababa
	11.6.	Appointment as foreign minister	9.5.	Proclamation of the Italian Empire
			17.7.	Spanish Civil War begins
	20–24.10.	Ciano visits Germany	1.11.	Mussolini proclaims Axis
1937			2.1.	Gentleman's Agreement
			8–23.3.	Battle of Guadalajara
	24.9.	Ciano and Mussolini visit Germany	9.6.	Rosselli brothers murdered
			14.9.	Nyon Conference
	18.12.	Birth of Marzio Ciano	6.11.	Italy joins Anti-Comintern Pact
1938			20.2.	Eden resigns
			13.3.	Annexation of Austria
			16.4.	Easter Agreement
			3.5.	Hitler visits Italy
			30.9.	Munich Agreement
1939			11–12.1.	Chamberlain and Halifax visit Rome
	6–7.5.	Ciano and Ribbentrop meet in Milan	15.3.	German occupation of Prague
			7.4.	Italian occupation of Albania
			22.5.	Pact of Steel signed
	11–12.8.	Meeting between Ciano, Hitler, and Ribbentrop in Salzburg	24.8.	German-Soviet Non-Aggression Pact
			1.9.	German invasion of Poland
			21.10.	South Tyrol Option signed
			1.11.	Beginning of "Ciano's Cabinet"
1940			24.2.	German-Italian Economic Agreement
	11.6.	Joins squadron in Pisa	10.6.	Italy enters the Second World War
			27.9.	Tripartite Pact
			28.10.	Italy attacks Greece
1941	26.1.	Joins squadron in Bari		
			19.5.	Italian army surrenders in Ethiopia
			22.6.	Operation Barbarossa begins
			7.12.	Attack on Pearl Harbor
			11.12.	Italy declares war on the United States
1942			21.6.	Occupation of Tobruk

Year	Date	Galeazzo Ciano's Biographical Data	Date	Important Events
1943			14–24.1.	Casablanca Conference
	8.2.	Appointment as ambassador to the Vatican	24–25.7.	Meeting of the Grand Council; arrest of Mussolini; Badoglio new head of government
	29.8.	Flees to Germany and arrives in Munich	3.9.	Armistice between Italy and Allies
			12.9.	Mussolini rescued by Germans
	19.10.	Arrest in Verona	29.12.	Trial against Ciano begins
1944	9.1.	Edda Ciano flees to Switzerland		
	11.1.	Execution of Galeazzo Ciano		

Abbreviations

AGIP	Azienda Generale Italiana Petroli
ANIC	Azienda Nazionale Idrogenazione Combustibili
CAUR	Comitati d'Azione Universalità di Roma
CTV	Corpo di Truppe Volontarie
DGAT	Direzione Generale degli Affari Transoceanici
DGP	Direzione Generale per la Propaganda
DGSE	Direzione Generale per la Stampa Estera
DGSI	Direzione Generale per la Stampa Italiana
EIAR	Ente Italiano per le Audizioni Radiofoniche
EUR	Esposizione Universale di Roma 1942
FIAT	Fabbrica Italiana Automobili Torino
GUF	Gruppi Universitari Fascisti
LUCE	L'Unione Cinematografica Educativa
MAS	Motoscafo Armato Silurante
NIC	Non-Intervention Committee
PFR	Partito Fascista Repubblicano
PNF	Partito Nazionale Fascista
PSI	Partito Socialista Italiano
RSHA	Reichssicherheitshauptamt
RSI	Repubblica Sociale Italiana
SIM	Servizio Informazioni Militare
SS	Schutzstaffel
UCFE	Ufficio Centrale per i Fasci all'Estero
UD	Unione Democratico
URI	Unione Radiofonica Italiana
USCG	Ufficio Stampa del Capo del Governo

Notes

Introduction

1 The following stories are speculative.
2 Lettera (Torino) a Mussolini (Roma), 16 October 1936, in ACS, SPD, Categgio, b. 115. All translations, unless otherwise attributed, are by the author.
3 Feldkommandostelle an Reichsmarschall Göring, 20 September 1943, in BArch, NS19, AZ 912, 14.
4 Based on Robert Paxton's and Richard Griffin's seminal works on fascism, I consider the presence of the following characteristics as a litmus test for the fascist character of politics, politicians, and ideas: the utopian rebirth of a powerful nation under the auspices of extreme nationalism; the creation of a strong "new man" and a new society through social engineering; a populist movement centred on a (charismatic) leader; and violent support by paramilitary units. See Griffin, "Palingenetischer Ultranationalismus," 17, 24, and 32; Paxton, *Anatomy of Fascism*, 218–19. For further definitions of fascism, see Bauerkämper, *Faschismus in Europa*, 13–46; Ben-Ghiat, "Italian Fascism"; Griffin, *Nature of Fascism*; Kallis, *Fascist Ideology*; Mann, *Fascists*; Payne, *History of Fascism*, 441–95.
5 For a short overview of Ciano's life, see the chronology in the appendix.
6 See Amendola, *Una scelta della vita*, 98; Vergani, *Ciano*, 13–14; Guerri, *Galeazzo Ciano*, 74–7; Susmel, *Vita sbagliata*, 10–24.
7 See Verbale di Cessazione dal Servizio, 8 September 1930, in ASMAE, Ambasciata Santa Sede, b. 4, fasc. 11, sotto 2; Ciano, *Mia Vita*, 39; Susmel, *Vita sbagliata*, 27. Rare film material of Ciano's stay in Shanghai can be found in Edda e Galeazzo Ciano in Shanghai, in ASL, Documentari, D065203. The dates of Ciano's assignments remain vague because Ciano's personal file from the Italian Foreign Ministry is missing. According to the finding aid, his personal files should be under ASMAE,

Archivio del Personale, Serie I: Diplomatici e Consoli, b. 33, fasc. 120, I C/96.

8 Bonsaver, *Censorship*, 108; Montefusco, *L'ordinamento*, 9–10.

9 See Mallet, "Fascist Foreign Policy," 178–9; Michaelis, "Conte Galeazzo Ciano," 141–2; Petersen, *Hitler-Mussolini*, 461–6.

10 Riall, "Shallow End," 376.

11 See Riall, *Garibaldi*; Szöllösi-Janze, *Fritz Haber*. For the modern political biography, see Bödeker, *Biographie schreiben*; Depkat, "The Challenges of Biography"; Etzemüller, "Die Form der 'Biographie'"; France and St. Clair, *Mapping Lives*; Lässig, "Toward a Biographical Turn?"; Leckie, "Biography Matters"; LeGoff, "Wie schreibt man eine Biographie"; Riall, "Shallow End"; Rotberg, "Biography and Historiography"; Szöllösi-Janze, "Lebens-Geschichte."

12 Di Rienzo, *Ciano*; Guerri, *Galeazzo Ciano*; Innocenti, *Ciano*; Moseley, *Mussolini's Shadow*; Ostenc, *Ciano*; Susmel, *Vita sbagliata*. In addition, two articles (Gilbert, "Ciano"; Michaelis, "Conte Galeazzo Ciano") and short chapters (see relevant chapters in Festorazzi, *Tutti gli uomini*; Innocenti, *Gerarchi;* Moriconi, *Uomini di Mussolini*; Secciani, *Gerarchi*) deal with Ciano. Guerri published his biography in its third edition with La nave di Teseo in 2019 without any revisions. He claims that there have been no fundamentally new findings since 1979, when his book was first published. This assessment, however, is more than astonishing given the new insights the latest research on fascism has provided.

13 For recent works in these fields, see, for example, Goeschel, *Mussolini and Hitler*; Hierro and Albanese, *Transnational Fascism*; McLean, *Mussolini's Children*; Ponzio, *Shaping the New Man*; Rodogno, *Fascism's European Empire*.

14 Examples of superficial biographies include Alessandri, *Diplomatico*; Canosa, *Farinacci*; Guerri, *Giuseppe Bottai*, *Italo Balbo*, *L'arcitaliano*, *D'Annunzio*, and *Filippo Tommaso Marinetti*; Nello, *Dino Grandi*; Segrè, *Italo Balbo*. One positive exception is Bosworth, *Claretta*. For criticism, see Dipper, "Italienische Zeitgeschichtsforschung"; Dogliani, *Fascismo degli italiani*, 347.

15 For recent studies on Mussolini, see Bosworth, *Mussolini*; Cardoza, *Benito Mussolini*; Chessa, *Dux*; Clark, *Mussolini*; Farrell, *Mussolini*; Finaldi, *Mussolini*; Hibbert, *Mussolini*; Morgan, *Fall of Mussolini*; Moseley, *Mussolini*; Schieder, *Mythos*; Woller, *Mussolini*.

16 For example, see Gerwarth, *Hitler's Hangman*; Herbert, *Best*; Longerich, *Heinrich Himmler*; Wildt, *Generation*.

17 Cited in Szöllösi-Janze, *Fritz Haber*, 13.

18 Riall, "Shallow End," 381.

19 LeGoff, "Wie schreibt man eine Biographie?" 105.

20 In this study, I follow Jonathan Hearn's thoughtful and critical deconstruction of Michel Foucault's non-hierarchical concept of power. See Hearn, *Theorizing Power*. See also Hörnqvist, *Risk*; Howarth, *Poststructuralism*; Kelly, *Foucault and Politics*; Lynch, "Foucault's Theory"; Taylor , *Michel Foucault*.
21 Szöllösi-Janze, "Lebens-Geschichte," 12.
22 See Weber, *Grundriss der Sozialökonomie*. For the criticism, see Eatwell, "Concept and Theory," 4; Gentile, "Mussolini's Charisma," 221.
23 Eatwell, "Concept and Theory," 6. For Mussolini, see Gentile, "Mussolini"; Gori, "Model of Masculinity," 32.
24 Eatwell, "Concept and Theory," 7–8.
25 Ibid., 11–13. See also Duggan, "Political Cults."
26 See Pinto, Eatwell, and Larsen, *Charisma and Fascism*.
27 Griffin, "Political Modernism," 31–2. For D'Annunzio, see Duggan, *Force of Destiny*, 376–7; Woodhouse, "Gabriele D'Annunzio."
28 See Corner, "Plebiscites"; Duggan, *Fascist Voices*, xx; Gentile, Corner, and Duggan, "Two New Books," 677–81.
29 For performance theory, see Fischer-Lichte, "Performance"; Jobs, *Welcome Home*; Martschukat and Patzold, "Geschichtswissenschaft"; Shepherd, *Cambridge Introduction*; Wulf and Zirfas, *Ikonologie des Performativen*.
30 For example, see Baxa, "Capturing the Fascist Moment"; Berezin, *Making the Fascist Self*; Falasca-Zamponi, *Fascist Spectacle*.
31 Jobs, *Welcome Home*, 14–23; Kertzer, *Ritual*, 78–9.
32 Cassirer, *Myth of the State*, 285; Jobs, *Welcome Home*, 33; Kertzer, *Ritual*, 119.
33 Riall, "Shallow End," 393.
34 See Osti Guerrazzi, "Das System Mussolini."
35 For the errors and inconsistencies, see Requests for information on certain people who will appear in a further volume of Ciano's Diary, 7 March 1951, in NA, FO 370/2175; Trevor-Roper, *Letters from Oxford*, 19–20; Hillgruber, *Hitlers Strategie*, 282n17; Hof, "Tagebücher"; Knox, *Mussolini Unleashed*, 291–3.
36 Smyth, *Secrets*, 76. The photographs can be found in LoC, Working Papers, Box 4 and Box 5; BSB, Mussolini Papers, Reel 5; NA, GFM 36/642–5.

For the years 1939 to 1943, I used the photographs of the diary from the UK National Archives (NA, GFM 36/642–5). For the years 1937–38, I used Ciano, *Ciano's Hidden Diaries*. In the following notes, I will refer to all entries from the diary as "Ciano Diary, Entry." The English translation of the diary is based on a careful comparison between the original photographs and the published English versions of the diaries. Possible issues and inconsistencies between the original and the translation are mentioned in the notes in this volume.

The original photographs of additional notes and documents written by Ciano, which were later published in Ciano, *L'Europa*, can be found in NARA, RG 242, T816, Reels 1–3.

37 For a more detailed analysis of the diary, see Hof, "Tagebücher"; Smyth, *Secrets*. For rumours about various versions of the diary, see Telegramma Scop (Madrid) alla Segreteria Particolare del Duce (Salò), 2 August 1944, in BSB, Mussolini Papers, Reel 453, Frame 029688/A-9; Monreale (Madrid) a Mazzolini (Salò), 15 August 1944, in ibid., Reel 1346, Frame 98639.

38 Martschukat and Patzold, "Geschichtswissenschaft," 27; Wulf and Zirfas, "Bild, Wahrnehmung und Phantasie," 29.

39 König, *Kooperation als Machtkampf*, 293–5.

40 Mack Smith, *Mussolini*, 128.

1. The Family

1 Ciano Diary, Entries 26.6.1939, 27.6.1939, and 28.6.1939.

2 For Ciano's admiration and remembrance of his father, see Ciano Diary, Entries 27.6.1940 and 11.11.1940; Whitaker, *We Cannot Escape History*, 62.

Ciano mentioned his father and his sister Maria in the diary (Ciano Diary, Entries 16.6.1939, 26–27.6.1939, 2.7.1939, 9.10.1939, 17–18.10.1939, 20–23.10.1939, 1.11.1940, and 27.6.1940). There are a few remarks about his wet nurse, his wife, and his children (Ciano Diary, Entries 12.9.1937, 20.9.1937, 1.10.1937, 16.10.1937, 24.10.1937, 18–19.12.1937, 12.6.1938, 9.10.1938, 25.7.1940, 25.9.1940, 9.5.1942, 27.12.1942, and 31.12.1942).

3 Ciano Diary, Entry 1.7.1939.

4 Szöllösi-Janze, *Fritz Haber*, 23.

5 Duggan, *Force of Destiny*, 312–17.

6 Hom, "Origins of Making Italy," 1–16; Patriarca, *Italian Vices*, 8.

7 Bosworth, *Mussolini's Italy*, 35.

8 Mazzoni, *Livorno*, VIII.

9 Cited in Santini, *Scoperta di Livorno*, 24–5.

10 Cited in Santini, *Scoperta di Livorno*, 20.

11 Abse, *Sovversivi e fascisti*, 2; Bosworth, *Mussolini's Italy*, 15.

12 James, *Italian Hours*, 431.

13 Abse, *Sovversivi e fascisti*, 2–3.

14 Altgeld et al., *Geschichte Italiens*, 341.

15 Ibid., 351–2.

16 For the history of the Orlando shipyard, see Ceccotti, *Fascismo a Livorno*, 243–53; Marchi and Cariello, *Cantiere F.lli Orlandi*, 13–180.

17 Abse, *Sovversivi e fascisti*, 3–4; Tomassini, "Grande guerra," 291–3.

18 Bonsaver, *Censorship*, 115.

19 This assessment was the result of a search of the library catalogues of the Biblioteca Nazionale Centrale di Roma and the Library of Congress, Washington, DC, on 15 May 2019. Several of these biographies are listed in the bibliography. For the documentary, see *L'eroe di Cortelazzo*, 1939, in ASL, Documentari, D063104.
20 See Kertzer and Hogan, *Family*, 7; Barbagli and Kertzer, "Introduzione," 15–16.
21 His brothers Alessandro, Arturo, and Gino Ciano also attended the academy.
22 Guerri, *Galeazzo Ciano*, 17–18; Querél, *Costanzo Ciano*, 40.
23 Ciano, *My Truth*, 53; Moseley, *Mussolini's Shadow*, 6–7.
24 Guerri, *Galeazzo Ciano*, 19.
25 Gestrich, *Geschichte der Familie*, 20; Kertzer and Hogan, *Family*, 174.
26 Farinacci, *Costanzo Ciano*, 20. For the Libyan War, see Childs, *Italo-Turkish Diplomacy*; Labanca, "Discorsi coloniali."
27 Duggan, *Force of Destiny*, 323–35; Hof, "'Legionaries of Civilization,'" 137–8.
28 Scarabello, *Martirio di Venezia*, Vol. 2, 359. For Italy's entry into the war, see Afflerbach, "Bündnispartner."
29 Bosworth, "Venice," 9.
30 See Bianchi, "Venezia nella Grande guerra," 360 and 386; Bosworth, *Mussolini's Italy*, 22–4.
31 Scarabello, *Martirio di Venezia*, Vol. 2, 250. In 1918 the Italian admiralty established the *Ispettorato e Comando Superiore MAS* under Costanzo Ciano (23 April 1918 to 16 May 1918). See Favre, *Marina*, 308–9.
32 For the Battle of Caporetto, see Labanca, *Caporetto*.
33 Farinacci, *Costanzo Ciano*, 38. Guerri (*Galeazzo Ciano*, 21) used Farinacci's story and ignored the other Italian warships.
34 Favre, *Marina*, 232–3.
35 D'Annunzio, *Diari di Guerra*, 472 and 481–4; Santini, *Costanzo Ciano*, 63–4.
36 Farinacci, *Costanzo Ciano*, 43.
37 He received a total of four medals of merit in silver and one in gold. For the demobilization, see Ceva, *Storia delle forze armate*, 183–5.
38 Moro, *Viribus Unitis*, 36. Many biographies, including Di Rienzo's *Ciano* (62), argue that Ciano himself rejected a promotion.
39 Santini, *Costanzo Ciano*, 87.
40 Farinacci, *Costanzo Ciano*, 194; De Felice, *Mussolini il fascista*, Vol. 1, 81.
41 A total of 42 air strikes were carried out against the city, killing 52 people and injuring 84. Between November 1917 and April 1918, about 70,000 inhabitants (approximately 73 per cent of the population) left the city. Citizens who either could not afford to flee or who worked in the public service and in the army stayed. See Bianchi, "Venezia nella Grande

Guerra," 363–7; Bosworth, *Italian Venice*, 95–7; Bregantin, Fantina, and Mondini, *Venezia Treviso e Padova*, 17–21 and 35.

42 Querél, *Costanzo Ciano*, 104. Socialism and communism were particularly embraced by sailors – the strikes in Germany at the end of the First World War are just one example. Consequently, navy officers regarded these ideologies as a threat to military discipline. For the mistreatment of war veterans, see Mondini, *Politica delle armi*, 23.

43 Farinacci, *Costanzo Ciano*, 54–5; Fiorentino, *Un uomo d'azione*, 121.

44 Woller, *Geschichte Italiens*, 80.

45 For the occupation of Fiume, see Vogel-Walter, *D'Annunzio*, 131–54.

46 See "D'Annunzio Idol of Army at Fiume," *New York Times*, 10 October 1919, 1; "D'Annunzio Threat to Blow up Fiume," *New York Times*, 9 May 1920, 2; Duggan, *Force of Destiny*, 410–19; Samuels, *Machiavelli's Children*, 162–3. For the avant-garde theatre, see Fischer-Lichte, "Grenzgänge," 291–300.

47 Farinacci, *Costanzo Ciano*, 61–2; Guerri, *Galeazzo Ciano*, 31–2.

48 Abse, "Rise of Fascism," 61. For irredentism, see Reichman and Golan, "Irredentism."

49 D'Avila, *Vita eroica*, 25.

50 Griffin, "Political Modernism," 32.

51 Bosworth, *Mussolini*, 122. See also Franzinelli, *Fascismo anno zero*.

52 See Reichardt, *Faschistische Kampfbünde*, 595; Roberts, "Myth, Style, Substance," 12; Woller, *Geschichte Italiens*, 88.

53 Abse, *Sovversivi e fascisti*, 249; Levy, "Fascism," 101; Sluga, *Problem of Trieste*, 39.

54 Tomassini, "Grande guerra," 252.

55 Abse, *Sovversivi e fascisti*, 253.

56 Ceccotti, *Fascismo a Livorno*, 63–6; Di Giovanni, *Periodici Livornesi*, 1. Pedani's foreign policy goal corresponded with the sometimes more vague "Fascist Manifesto" of June 1919 ("Fasci Italiani di combattimento," *Il Popolo d'Italia*, 6 June 1919, 1).

57 Woller, *Geschichte Italiens*, 88.

58 Mazzoni, *Livorno*, 11–13.

59 The local section of the PSI was founded in 1893 under the leadership of Giuseppe Emanuele Modigliani, brother of the famous painter Amedeo Modigliani. See Abse, *Sovversivi e fascisti*, 4–5; Tomassini, "Grande guerra," 274.

Throughout Italy, the clashes between fascists and socialists during the *bienno rosso* (1919 to 1922) claimed between 3,000 and 4,000 lives. See Woller, *Geschichte Italiens*, 90–1.

60 Tomassini, "Grande guerra," 253.

61 Woller, *Geschichte Italiens*, 85. For the strikes, see Abse, *Sovversivi e fascisti*, 6–8; De Grand, *Hunchback's Tailor*, 234–5.

62 Querél, *Costanzo Ciano*, 108–9; Mazzoni, *Livorno*, 15.
63 In his biography of Galeazzo Ciano, Di Rienzo (*Ciano*, 73) claims without proof that Costanzo Ciano only joined the *fascio* to avoid a civil war in his hometown.
64 Abse, "Rise of Fascism," 72.
65 Farinacci, *Costanzo Ciano*, 65.
66 Abse, *Sovversivi e fascisti*, 257–8. Amendola (*Una scelta della vita*, 71) pointed out that many Italians joined the fascists hoping to maintain their status.
67 For Ciano's campaign, see Querél, *Costanzo Ciano*, 114; Ceccotti, *Fascismo a Livorno*, 86.
68 See Ceccotti, *Fascismo a Livorno*, 25–6; Mazzoni, *Livorno*, 16–18.
69 De Felice, *Mussolini il fascista*, Vol. 1, 92; De Grand, *Hunchback's Tailor*, 242.
70 Abse, "Rise of Fascism," 74–6; Mazzoni, *Livorno*, 22–3.
71 Querél, *Costanzo Ciano*, 119; Mazzoni, *Livorno*, 4.
72 See *L'eroe di Cortelazzo*, 1939, in ASL, Documentari, D063104; Farinacci, *Costanzo Ciano*, 48. He wore a militia uniform at the anniversary of the "March on Rome" and when he welcomed the returning soldiers from Ethiopia in 1936. Pictures and video recordings of Costanzo Ciano can be found in the Archivio Cinematografico of the Istituto Nazionale Luce at https://www.archivioluce.com/archivio-cinematografico-2/.
73 Abse, *Sovversivi e fascisti*, 253–8; Mazzoni, *Livorno*, 19–21.
74 Chiurico, *Storia della rivoluzione*, 190; Mazzoni, *Livorno*, 13.
75 Abse, "Rise of Fascism," 76; Tomassini, "Grande guerra," 280–1. See also Corner, "Everyday Fascism," 197; Gentile, "Problem of the Party," 252.
76 Snowden, *Fascist Revolution*, 154–5.
77 Mazzoni, *Livorno*, 27–8.
78 Querél, *Costanzo Ciano*, 122–3.
79 Ceccotti, *Fascismo a Livorno*, 118.
80 Snowden, *Fascist Revolution*, 155.
81 Abse, "Rise of Fascism," 61 and 80–1.
82 Farinacci, *Costanzo Ciano*, 10.
83 Ibid., 46; Di Rienzo, *Ciano*, 63.
84 Farinacci, *Costanzo Ciano*, 53, 64, and 183. See also *L'eroe di Cortelazzo*, 1939, in ASL, Documentari, D063104.
85 "Costanzo Ciano Lauded," *New York Times*, 15 May 1939, 8; Susmel, *Vita sbagliata*, 18–19. See also Sarfatti, *My Fault*, 148.
86 Farinacci, *Costanzo Ciano*, 71.
87 Ciano, *My Truth*, 96; Mazzoni, *Livorno*, 116.
88 Ciano Diary, Entries 30.6.1939 and 28.11.1939.
89 See circular letter (velina; 27 June 1939), in Tranfaglia, *Stampa*, 115; "Il miliardo di Casa Ciano," *La Nuova Stampa*, 14 August 1945, 1; Guerri, *Galeazzo Ciano*, 846–7.

90 See Ciano Diary, Entry 10.2.1940; "Costanzo Ciano austeramente celebrato a Livorno," *La Stampa*, 28 June 1941, 2; "Rito funebre a Livorno," *La Stampa*, 28 June 1943, 4. In May 1941, when Rome and the Independent State of Croatia discussed borders, Ciano took a conciliatory stance in order to avoid further tensions with Croatia. However, he demanded to annex the Bay of Buccari to preserve his father's memory. See Ciano Diary, Entries 29.4.1941 and 7.5.1941.

91 Ciano Diary, Entry 1.7.1939.

92 Mazzoni, *Livorno*, 113–14.

93 See "Persone illustri: Arturo Dazzi," *Carrara Online*, accessed 12 April 2020, https://www.carraraonline.com/arturo-dazzi.html.

94 Ciano Diary, Entry 2.7.1939.

95 See Gentile, *Sacralization of Politics*.

96 Ciano Diary, Entries 27.2.1940 and 18.10.1941; Ciano in Albania visita cantieri edili, 23 August 1939, in ASL, Giornale Luce, B1572. In 1926 Livorno began to build a magnificent sea promenade in Costanzo Ciano's honour, the *Terrazza Costanzo Ciano*, which also epitomized his attachment to the sea – the place that had earned him so much fame during the First World War. Today, the promenade is named after the composer Pietro Mascagni. See Matteoni, "Città e architettura," 35; Mazzoni, *Livorno*, 184.

97 Ciano Diary, Entry 23.3.1940; velina (1 July 1939), in Tranfaglia, *Stampa*, 116.

98 Ciano Diary, Entry 29.12.1940; L'inaugurazione a Cortellazzo del villaggio di pescatori, 3 January 1941, in ASL, Giornale Luce, C0106.

99 Ciano Diary, Entries 15.9.1940 and 16.11.1941; *L'Illustrazione Italiana*, 22 September 1940, cover; Getty Images #901518902. Another statue was erected in Ravenna in 1942. See L'inaugurazione a Ravenna di un monumento all'eroe di Buccari, 17 July 1942, in ASL, Giornale Luce, C026302.

100 L'inaugurazione del monumento all'eroe di Cortellazzo e di Buccari, 23 September 1940, in ASL, Giornale Luce, C0077; L'inaugurazione del monumento all'eroe di Buccari, 20 November 1941, in ASL, Giornale Luce, C0198; "Costanzo Ciano," *La Stampa*, 28 June 1941, 2; "La Dominante inaugura il monumento all'eroe di Buccari," *La Stampa*, 17 November 1941, 6. For Ciano's hero status, see *L'Illustrazione Italiana*, 6 July 1941, 6; and 5 July 1942, 13.

101 See "Galeazzo Ciano a Livorno," *La Stampa*, 12 February 1940, 1; D'Avila, *Vita eroica*, 11; Farinacci, *Costanzo Ciano*, 206–9.

102 Eisenstadt and Roniger, *Patrons*, 211–12.

103 Ibid., 211–13.

104 Bastianini, *Uomini, cose, fatti*, 236; Ward Price, *Führer und Duce*, 258.

105 Cancogni, *Storia dello squadrismo*, 163; De Felice, *Mussolini il fascista*, Vol. 1, 372–4.
106 Cited in Woller, *Geschichte Italiens*, 92–3. For the "March on Rome," see Albanese, *Mussolinis Marsch auf Rom*.
107 De Felice, *Mussolini il fascista*, Vol. 2.1, 386–7.
108 Bosworth, "Dictators Strong or Weak," 267–9.
109 For the glorification, see Farinacci, *Costanzo Ciano*, 84–5, 111–14, and 123–6.
110 De Felice, *Mussolini il fascista*, Vol. 2.1, 86–98. For Ciano's opposition, see Di Rienzo, *Ciano*, 76; Gentile, "Problem of the Party," 253–4; Lewis, *Latin Fascist Elites*, 19–22.
111 D'Avila, *Vita eroica*, 52; Querél, *Costanzo Ciano*, 154. Mussolini suggested making Ciano a permanent member of the Fascist Grand Council in January 1929. See "Der Große Rat," *Dolomiten*, 23 January 1929, 1. Moseley (*Mussolini's Shadow*, 7) and Susmel (*Vita sbagliata*, 21) claim that Costanzo Ciano became a permanent member in 1923.
112 De Grazia, *Culture of Consent*, 136–7.
113 For example, see Di Rienzo, *Ciano*; Guerri, *Galeazzo Ciano*.
114 See Duggan, *Force of Destiny*, 310–19; Eisenstadt and Roniger, *Patrons*, 205 and 226.
115 Eisenstadt and Roniger, *Patrons*, 48–9 and 211–14; Piattoni, "Clientelism," 2 and 6; Warner, "Mass Parties," 129.
116 Corner, "Everyday Fascism," 196; Eisenstadt and Roniger, *Patrons*, 239–40.
117 Bosworth, *Mussolini's Italy*, 154.
118 Ceccotti, *Fascismo a Livorno*, 134; Mazzoni, *Livorno*, 131–40.
119 For the family's role in general, see Eisenstadt and Roniger, *Patrons*, 230; Levi, "Famiglia e parentela," 313.
120 Barbagli and Kertzer, "Introduzione," 21.
121 Mazzoni, *Livorno*, 128–9 and 155.
122 Piattoni, "Clientelism," 11.
123 Commissione Reale per gli Accertamenti degli Indebiti Arricchimenti, 28 August 1943, in ACS, MI, DGPS, b. 298, fasc. Ciano, Alessandro; Casali and Cattaruzza, *Sotto i mari*, 190; Mazzoni, *Livorno*, 124; Mori, "Materiali, temi e ipotesi," 186–95.
124 Zamagni, "Rich in a Late Industrialiser," 147–50.
125 Casali and Cattaruzza, *Sotto i mari*, 132–3, 176–9.
126 Mazzoni, *Livorno*, 119.
127 Casali and Cattaruzza, *Sotto i mari*, 187–90.
128 Ceccotti, *Fascismo a Livorno*, 221; Mazzoni, *Livorno*, 69.
129 Matteoni, "Città e architettura," 39, 47, and 52.
130 See Castronovo, *Giovanni Agnelli*, 341–5; Santini, *Costanzo Ciano*, 163–4.

131 Cited in Ceccotti, *Fascismo a Livorno*, 181.

132 Ceccotti, *Fascismo a Livorno*, 187. Guido Buffarini Guidi was *ras* of Pisa. As secretary of state in the Ministry of the Interior, he became one of Galeazzo's fiercest opponents. To what extent this episode contributed to the hostility, however, remains unclear. See Mazzoni, *Livorno*, 67.

133 Mazzoni, *Livorno*, 171 and 210.

134 Ciano Diary, Entry 29.6.1939.

135 Matteoni, "Città e architettura," 54–69; Mazzoni, *Livorno*, 169; Nuovo ospedale a Livorno, November 1931, in ASL, Giornale Luce, A0879.

136 Matteoni, "Città e architettura," 59–62.

137 See "La Storia dell'A.S. Livorno Calcio," A.S. Livorno Calcio, accessed 4 October 2020, https://www.livornocalcio.it/storia/.

138 See *R.a.c.i.*, 28 July 1929, 2; La Coppa Ciano, August 1931, in ASL, Giornale Luce, A0828; *L'Auto Italiana*, 10–20 August 1933, 43; La grande gare, 1933, in ASL, Giornale Luce, B0311; XIV Coppa Ciano a Livorno, July 1934, in ibid., B0508; Coppa Ciano di automobilismo, 5 August 1936, in ibid., B0933; La Coppa Ciano, 10 August 1938, in ibid., B1352.

139 Di Rienzo, *Ciano*, 87; Mazzoni, *Livorno*, 203–6.

140 Di Giovanni, *Periodici Livornesi*, 170.

141 See Telegramma Mussolini (Roma) a Prefettura (Torino), 29 November 1926, in USHMM, RG 40.005, Reel 1, Frame 0000780; Lettera Studio Avocati Erizzo (Genova) a Commissione Centrale per le asseguazioni al confino (Roma), no date, in ibid., Frame 0000775–6.

142 See Telegram Phillips (Rome) to Hull (Washington), 12 March 1940, in NARA, RG 59, CDF, Box 2950, File 740.00119EW/274; "Italian Comment," *Washington Post*, 4 July 1940, 9; Ansaldo, *Giornalista*, 87 and 123.

143 Ciano Diary, Entries 10.11.1937 and 1.11.1938; Bojano, *Wake of the Goose Step*, 76 and 91; Viani, *"Il Telegrafo,"* 44–8.

144 De Grazia, *Culture of Consent*, 136.

145 Ciano Diary, Entries 26.6.1939, 30.6.1939, and 1.7.1939; Telegram Loraine (Rome) to FO (London), 28 June 1939, in NA, FO 371/23786, R5324/1/22, 110; "L'omaggio del Re e del Duce," *La Stampa*, 28 June 1939, 1.

146 "State Rites Today for Count Ciano," *New York Times*, 28 June 1939, 27; Bottai, *Diario*, 150–1.

147 Ciano Diary, Entry 2.7.1939.

148 Sarfatti, *My Fault*, 147; Viani, *"Il Telegrafo,"* 78–9.

149 For Galeazzo's absence at the *Coppa Ciano*, see Ciano Diary, Entries 10.8.1938 and 2.8.1939; La Coppa Ciano, 10 August 1938, in ASL, Giornale Luce, B1352; Coppa automobilistica Ciano, 2 August 1939, in ibid., B1559. Whenever Galeazzo attended the *Coppa Ciano*, his father Costanzo remained the centre of attention. See Ciano Diary, Entry 12.9.1937; *R.a.c.i.*, 26 July 1934, 12; La Coppa Ciano di automobilismo, 1935, in ASL,

Giornale Luce, B072703; *R.a.c.i.*, 19 July 1936, 11; 15° Gran Premio d'Italia, 15 September 1937, in ASL, Giornale Luce, B116706.

In addition, the Archivio Luce and Getty Images databases only contain pictures and videos of Galeazzo Ciano in Livorno when he was there for his father's funeral and for Serrano Suñer's visit in 1942 (as of 21 August 2019).

For Galeazzo's attendance at soccer matches, see ASL, Codice Foto, A00019837; L'incontro di calcio Roma-Lazio, 12 October 1936, in ASL, Giornale Luce, B0977; L'incontro di calcio Roma-Genova a Testaccio, December 1936, in ibid., B1001.

150 Mazzoni, *Livorno*, 231.

151 Ciano Diary, Entries 19.10.1941 and 31.5.1942.

152 For Galeazzo Ciano's time in Livorno in 1942, see chapter two.

153 Ciano Diary, Entries 30.6.1939 and 23.5.1941; Ansaldo, *Giornalista*, 315–16.

154 Mazzoni, *Livorno*, 140. In his diary Ciano mentioned Ajello on 6 June 1938, 24 July 1938, and 23 October 1942.

155 Casali and Cattaruzza, *Sotto i mari*, 192–4.

156 Gooch, *Mussolini and His Generals*, 219–21. For the Italian navy under fascism, see De Ninno, *Fascisti sul mare*.

157 Ciano's mother is only mentioned twice in his diary. See Ciano Diary, Entries 1.1.1941 and 23.5.1941. Ciano met his uncles at the funerals of Costanzo and Maria Ciano. See "L'estremo salute di Livorno," *La Stampa*, 24 October 1939, 1.

158 Rapporto, Roma, 20 December 1941, in ACS, MI, DGPS, b. 298, fasc. Ciano, Alessandro.

159 Casali and Cattaruzza, *Sotto i mari*, 206.

160 See "L'ammiraglio Arturo Ciano morto improvvisamente," *La Stampa*, 31 August 1943, 1; Sarfatti, *My Fault*, 148n9–10.

161 Levi, "Famiglia e parentela," 313.

162 Amendola, *Una scelta della vita*, 98.

163 Bosworth, *Mussolini*, 219.

164 Note by Nobel, 7 July 1939, in NA, FO 371/23826, R5522.

165 Sarfatti, *My Fault*, 167–8; Mazzoni, *Livorno*, 123; Di Rienzo, *Ciano*, 61.

166 Koon, *Believe, Obey, Fight*, 155.

167 Fisher, "Futurism and Radio," 232.

168 Bosworth, *Mussolini's Italy*, 219; Santini, *Costanzo Ciano*, 151–4.

169 "Mussolini Talks by Phone to Relatives in Shanghai," *New York Times*, 13 November 1932, E7.

170 Ciano Diary, Entry 20.12.1937.

171 Montroni, "Aristocracy and Professions," 274.

172 Scarantino, *"L'Impero,"* 67; Vergani, *Ciano*, 13–17.

173 "Le Memorie di Mimy Aylmer," *Epoca*, 7 December 1958, 77; Vergani, *Ciano*, 21–2.

174 Moseley, *Mussolini's Shadow*, 9; Smith, *Imperial Designs*, 119.

175 Karst, "Deutschland," 29; Nattermann, "Politische Beobachtung," 311.

176 For Costanzo Ciano's aristocratic title, see D'Avila, *Vita eroica*, 51; Jocteau, "Nobili del fascismo," 699–700; Sarfatti, *My Fault*, 147. To date, Ciano biographers, including Di Rienzo (*Ciano*, 59), Guerri (*Galeazzo Ciano*, 66), and Ostenc (*Ciano*, 6), wrongly claim that Costanzo received his title in 1925.

177 In his memoirs, *Uomini, cose, fatti*, Bastianini did not mention his support. For the friendship, see Bastianini, *Uomini, cose, fatti*, 227.

178 Di Rienzo (*Ciano*, 203), Guerri (*Galeazzo Ciano*, 63), and Santini (*Costanzo Ciano*, 149) all claim that Costanzo Ciano did not help his son out of "pride."

179 Ducci, *Bella gioventù*, 29; Scarabello, *Martirio di Venezia*, 428. Cavagnari also met Galeazzo Ciano when the latter was stationed in Shanghai in 1932. See ASL, Codice Foto, A00035809.

180 Ciano Diary, Entry 2.5.1940. For Cavagnari's role during the *non belligeranza*, see Entry 27.9.1939; Salerno, *Vital Crossroads*, 200–9.

181 Rapporto, Roma, 9 July 1942, in ACS, MI, DGPS, b. 22A, fasc. 2.

182 Ciano Diary, Entries 16.10.1941, 13.5.1942, and 24.9.1942.

183 De Vecchi, *Quadrumviro*, 166.

184 See Ciano Diary, Entries 15.11.1940, 27.11.1940, and 28.11.1940.

185 Guerri, *Galeazzo Ciano*, 113.

186 De Vecchi, *Tra Papa, Duce e Re*, 83.

187 Ibid., 137.

188 See Klein, *Geschichte Chinas*, 110–12.

189 For Ciano's friendship with Oliver, see Lettera Ciano (Pechino) a Maria Rosa Oliver (Buenos Aires), 6 April 1928, in Mudd Library, Maria Rosa Oliver Papers, Box 3, Folder 4, Series 2a; Guerri, *Galeazzo Ciano*, 67–9.

For Ciano's friendship with Helfand, see Ciano Diary, Entries 8.9.1937, 10.8.1938, and 14.7.1940; Borstendoerfer, *Graf Ciano*, 38–9 and 51–2; Telegram N. Charles (Rome) to Nichols (London), 24 August 1938, in NA, FO 371/22432, R7282/281/22; Telegram N. Charles (Rome) to Nichols (London), 17 November 1939, in NA, FO 371/23799, R10445/9/22, 11–15; Telegramm SS-Brigadeführer (Berlin) an Luther (Berlin), 2 August 1940, in PAAA, Inland II, R101084, Fiche 2795, 283980–1; Phillips Diary, Entry 14.9.1939, in Houghton Library, William Phillips, Box 10/20, Folder 9. For Leon Helfand's life, see the documents in NA, KV 2/2681.

190 Amendola, *Una scelta della vita*, 97–8 and 109.

191 It is possible that Amendola meant Tito Zaniboni, who attempted an attack on 4 November 1925 when Ciano was still in Rome.

192 See Bonsaver, *Censorship*, 223; De Grand, "Curzio Malaparte," 75–87; Guerri, *Italo Balbo*, 279–81; Parlato, *Sinistra fascista*, 8 and 31–2. See also Pardini, *Curzio Malaparte*.
193 Malaparte, *Kaputt*, 611.
194 Letter Malaparte (Capri) to Loraine (London), 14 June 1947, in NA, FO 1011/214.
195 Querél, *Costanzo Ciano*, 30; Guerri, *Galeazzo Ciano*, 75.
196 Agnelli, *Matrosenkleider*, 158; Ciano, *My Truth*, 70.
197 Lettera Anfuso (Shanghai) a Ciano (Roma), 6 February 1934, in ACS, MCP, Gabinetto, b. 8, fasc. 33, 26–30.
198 Lettera Ciano (Roma) a Ricci (Roma), 4 June 1935, in ACS, MCP, Gabinetto, b. 56, fasc. 350; Lettera Ricci (Roma) a Ciano (Roma), 7 June 1935, in ibid.
199 Lettera Ciano (Roma) a Valle (Roma), 19 August 1935, in ACS, MCP, Gabinetto, b. 10, fasc. 32.
200 Lettera Ciano (Roma) a On. Le Capo Compartimento Ferrovie dello Stato (Napoli), 8 April 1938, in ACS, MI, DGPS, b. 22A, fasc. 1.
201 Ciano Diary, Entry 18.4.1939. For Benini's relationship with the Ciano family, see Entry 14.9.1937; Benini, *Carcere degli Scalzi*, 155.
202 Nelson Page, *L'Americano*, 134–6; Bosworth, *Whispering City*, 171–2.
203 Other exceptions were Filippo Cremonesi, the last elected mayor of Rome before he was made governor in January 1926, and Giovanni Orgera, who was governor of Rome under German occupation between January and June 1944.
204 Musella, "Professionals in Politics," 320.
205 Cardoza, "Long Goodbye," 349.
206 Montroni, "Aristocracy and Professions," 256–8; Wasson, *Aristocracy*, 157–8.
207 Cerruti, *Frau eines Botschafters*, 290; Ciano, *My Truth*, 87–8.
208 For Ciano's nobility, see Vergani, *Ciano*, 13–14; Susmel, *Vita sbagliata*, 24.
209 Malatesta, "Introduction," 21–2; Musella, "Professionals in Politics," 317.
210 De Begnac, *Palazzo Venezia*, 572–4; Sarfatti, *My Fault*, 151.
211 For Ciano's love of golf and hunting, see chapter four.
212 See Ciano Diary, Entries 15.12.1937 and 14.2.1942; "Il principe Gian Giacomo Borghese lascia il Governatorato," *Capitolium* 9, 1943, in ASC, ID 1621; Amicucci, *600 giorni*, 84; Knigge, *Dilemma eines Diplomaten*, 18.

A list of Ciano's close friends can be found in ACS, MI, DGPS, b. 298, fasc. Ciano, Galeazzo. It also contains the names of the following aristocrats: Baron Edmondo Sanjust di Teulada; Count Cesarino Celani; Count Leonardo di Casalino; Prince Alessandro Torlonia; Duchess Antonia Laurenzana Gaetani.
213 Ciano Diary, Entries 21.2.1938 and 2.3.1938; Ciano, *My Truth*, 89–92.

214 Malaparte, *Kaputt*, 573.
215 Ibid., 572.
216 See Ciano Diary, Entries 13.11.1937, 14.12.1937, 10.7.1938, and 14.11.1938; Telegramm Mackensen (Rom) an AA (Berlin), 23 August 1940, in PAAA, Inland II, R101084, Fiche 2795, 283993; Malaparte, *Kaputt*, 572–3. For the anti-bourgeois campaign, see Patriarca, *Italian Vices*, 143.
217 Malaparte, *Kaputt*, 575.
218 Ibid., 573.
219 Brian Parshall, "Finding aid for the Anna Laetitia Pecci-Blunt collection of maps of Rome, circa 1550–1883," Online Archive of California (OAC), accessed 11 April 2020, http://www.oac.cdlib.org/findaid/ark:/13030/tf8k40065c/entire_text/. For Rome's reconstruction, see Baxa, *Roads and Ruins*.
220 Navarra, *Memorie*, 156–7. An entry in William Phillips's diary shows, however, that Ciano continued to meet Pecci-Blunt. See Phillips Diary, Entry 4.12.1939, in Houghton Library, William Phillips, Box 11/22, Folder 6.
For anti-Semitism in Fascist Italy, see Galimi, "'New Racist Man'"; Knox, "Faschistische Italien"; Wong, *Race*; Wood, *Defying Evil*; Zuccotti, *Italians*.
221 Ciano Diary, Entry 4.6.1938; Bosworth, "Per necessità famigliare," 375–6.
222 Ciano Diary, Entry 11.11.1938.
223 For Mussolini's criticism against the bourgeoisie, see Ciano Diary, Entries 13.11.1937, 10.7.1938, 14.11.1938, 10.8.1940, 7.1.1941, 27.9.1941, and 8.5.1942; Woller, *Mussolini*, 162–3.
224 Mussolini, *My Life*, 121; Nelson Page, *L'Americano*, 566; Bosworth, *Claretta*, 62.
225 Aktennotiz, 8 January 1941, in PAAA, Botschaft in Rom – Geheimakten, 97.
226 Ciano Diary, Entry 24.5.1939.
227 Bottai, *Diario*, 167. Ciano criticized the bourgeoisie in November 1937 (Ciano Diary, Entry 13.11.1937). His criticism must be interpreted in the context of Rome's tense relations with Great Britain (see chapter three) and not as a fundamental rejection of the bourgeoisie.
228 Ciano Diary, Entry 10.8.1940. See also Patriarca, *Italian Vices*, 143–4.
229 Ciano Diary, Entry 22.10.1939.
230 Ciano Diary, Entry 8.5.1942.
231 Ibid.
232 Agnelli, *Matrosenkleider*, 158; Bastianini, *Uomini, cose, fatti*, 245.
233 Bojano, *Wake of the Goose Step*, 101.
234 Rapporto, Roma, 25 August 1943, in ACS, MI, DGPS, b. 298, fasc. Ciano, Galeazzo.
235 Guerri, *Galeazzo Ciano*, 88; Susmel, *Vita sbagliata*, 29–32; Ward Price, *Führer und Duce*, 257.

236 "The Reburial of Sun Yat-Sen," *The Times*, 3 June 1929, 15; Varè, *Lachende Diplomat*, 459–65. Many biographers, including Di Rienzo (*Ciano*, 214), claim that Ciano was recalled at the end of the year.
237 Ciano, *My Truth*, 55–9; Guerri, *Galeazzo Ciano*, 87.
238 Vergani, *Ciano*, 30. De Vecchi (*Quadrumviro*, 135) claimed that Galeazzo had asked his father to contact him in order to initiate Ciano's recall. Thus, he indirectly confirmed that Costanzo played a crucial role. However, given Varè's diary entries, it seems very unlikely that Galeazzo himself took the initiative. See Varè, *Lachende Diplomat*, 489.
239 See "Rome Flocks to See Mussolini Wedding," *New York Times*, 25 April 1930, 1; Ciano, *My Truth*, 55; Ciano, *Quando il nonno*, 28; Di Rienzo, *Ciano*, 258; Sarfatti, *My Fault*, 153; Schad, *Sie liebten den Führer*, 83–5.
240 Ciano, *My Truth*, 60; Moseley, *Mussolini's Shadow*, 1.
241 De Vecchi, *Tra Papa, Duce e Re*, 83.
242 See Bosworth, *Mussolini*, 209; Cereghino and Fasanella, *Carte Segrete*, 156–9. The surveillance continued after the wedding. See the documents in ACS, MI, DGPS, b. 22A, fasc. 1.
243 Moseley, *Mussolini's Shadow*, 10–13.
244 De Grazia, *How Fascism Ruled Women*, 128; Kertzer and Hogan, *Family*, 137 and 177.
245 "Il Duce's Daughter Married to Count," *Washington Post*, 25 April 1930, 3; De Vecchi, *Tra Papa, Duce e Re*, 115–16 and 133.
246 Lettera Francesco Borgongini Duca (Roma) a Eugenio Pacelli (Vaticano), 23 April 1930, in USHMM, RG 76.002, A, Italia.
247 Sottosegretario di Stato Giunta (Roma), 20 March 1930, in BSB, Mussolini Papers, Reel 456, Frame 029647/A; "Edda Mussolini to Be Wed Today," *New York Times*, 24 April 1930, 9.
248 See "Edda Mussolini to Wed Son of Father's Aide," *New York Times*, 16 February 1930, 25; "Il Duce's Daughter Married to Count," *Washington Post*, 25 April 1930, 3; "Rome Flocks to See Mussolini Wedding," *New York Times*, 25 April 1930, 1; A Roma le nozze di Edda Mussolini con Galeazzo Ciano, April 1930, in ASL, Giornale Luce, A0566;
249 See "The Royal Bride Sees Prince Lead Review," *New York Times*, 10 January 1930, 5; "Rome Wedding Festivities Military Review," *The Times*, 10 January 1930, 12; "The Royal Wedding Celebration in Rome," *Manchester Guardian*, 13 January 1930, 10.
250 Innocenti, *Gerarchi*, 14; Mazzoni, *Livorno*, 129.
251 See Durchhardt, "Dynastische Heirat."
252 Sarfatti, *My Fault*, 126.
253 De Vecchi, *Tra Papa, Duce e Re*, 84.
254 Ibid., 84–5.
255 Cited in Mazzoni, *Livorno*, 130. See also Di Rienzo, *Ciano*, 262–3.

256 For photographs, see *Illustrierter Beobachter*, 11 August 1938; *La Rivista Illustrata del Popolo d'Italia*, February 1937, 64.

257 Guerri (*Galeazzo Ciano*, 741) claims that Galeazzo's portrait has been lost. According to Cristallini ("De Chirico's Disregarded E42 Invitation," 184), the painting is privately owned. Pictures of the busts can be found in ASL, Codice Foto, A00069762–5 and A00069773–4. Amerigo Bartoli also made a painting of Ciano. See Ciano Diary, Entry 19.11.1941. Photographs of Messina's busts and Edda's portrait were published in *L'Illustrazione Italiana*, 17 January 1937, 57; and 10 May 1942, 450.

258 Cristallini, "De Chirico's Disregarded E42 Invitation," 183–5.

259 See "La costituzione del Ministero per la Stampa e la Propaganda," *Il Popolo d'Italia*, 26 June 1935; Die italienische Presse zum neuen Ministerium für Presse und Propaganda, Rom, 26 June 1935, in BArch, R4902, AZ 4879; Telegram Kirk (Rome) to Hull (Washington), 28 June 1935, in NARA, RG 59, M1423, Reel 4, File 865.002/189.

260 Lettera a Mussolini, C. Ciano e Starace, 26 June 1935, in ACS, MCP, Gabinetto, b. 5. See also Di Rienzo, *Ciano*, 356.

261 For criticism, see Lettera, Commenti del pubblico a Stresa, 24 April 1935, in ACS, MCP, Gabinetto, b. 5; Lettera (Torino) a Mussolini (Roma), 16 October 1936, in ACS, SPD, Carteggio, b. 115; Lettera a Duce, 31 June 1937, in ibid.; Bojano, *Wake of the Goose Step*, 36; Lampson, *Politics and Diplomacy*, 272; Duggan, *Fascist Voices*, 328; Spaulding, *Lisa Sergio*, 77. For praise, see Telegram Kirk (Rome) to Hull (Washington), 12 June 1936, in NARA, RG 59, M1423, Reel 4, File 865.002/203, 3; "Il conte Galeazzo Ciano agli Esteri," *La Stampa*, 10 June 1936, 1; Ward Price, *Führer und Duce*, 259.

262 See Rapporto, Roma, 26 May 1939, in ACS, MI, DGPS, b. 22A, fasc. 1; Rapporto, Roma, 24 August 1939, in ibid.; Ojetti, *Taccuini*, 518.

263 See Meldung, Berlin, 18 December 1940, in BArch, R58, AZ 9486, Frame 790023; Telegram Campbell (Belgrade) to FO (London), 4 February 1941, in NA, FO 371/29924, R823/28/22, 257; Memorandum on Italian Morale, London, 5 March 1941, in NA, FO 371/29925, R2011/28/22, 123; Caviglia, *Diario*, 337; Di Rienzo, *Ciano*, 1170–1.

264 Talbot, *Censorship*, 28.

265 Telegram Perth (Rome) to Ingram (London), 11 June 1938, in NA, FO 371/22412, R5593/281/2, 2.

266 Duggan, *Fascist Voices*, 328.

267 Ginsborg, *Family Politics*, 173; Willson, "Introduction," 6–11.

268 Gestrich, *Geschichte der Familie*, 6–9.

269 Farinacci, *Costanzo Ciano*, 210.

270 Ginsborg, *Family Politics*, 175; Patriarca, *Italian Vices*, 136; Willson, "Women in Mussolini's Italy," 208. For the demographic campaign, see Ipsen, *Dictating Demography*.

271 See Benadusi, "Borghesi in Uniform," 29.
272 Corner, "Women in Fascist Italy," 51; Dogliani, *Fascismo degli italiani*, 118–19; Gundle, "Film Stars," 323.
273 De Grazia, *How Fascism Ruled Women*, 220–1; Willson, "Women in Mussolini's Italy," 204–7.
274 Dogliani, "Propaganda and Youth," 187–9; Ponzio, *Shaping the New Man*, 152–70.
275 Gestrich, *Geschichte der Familie*, 8 and 36. For youth education, see McLean, *Mussolini's Children*; Ponzio, *Shaping the New Man*.
276 For the Goebbels family, see Longerich, *Goebbels*.
277 "Shanghai Post to Ciano," *New York Times*, 23 June 1930, 8; Ciano, *Mia Vita*, 36–9.
278 Lu, *Beyond the Neon Lights*, 27–8.
279 Huxley, *Jesting Pilate*, 241.
280 Wakeman, *Policing Shanghai*, 9.
281 Sergeant, *Shanghai*, 2.
282 Lu, *Beyond the Neon Lights*, 27.
283 Ciano, *My Truth*, 104 and 152; Guerri, *Amore fascista*, 76.
284 Ciano, *Mia Vita*, 39–40.
285 Ducci, *Bella gioventù*, 144.
286 Bericht Depaoli mit Sendung 38, Rom, 14 December 1940, in BArch, R58, AZ 9478, Frame 050252–3; Rapporto, Roma, 20 June 1942, in ACS, MI, DGPS, b. 298, fasc. Ciano, Galeazzo; Mussolini, *Il duce*, 79; Di Rienzo, *Ciano*, 252–315; Gundle, "Film Stars," 332; Spaulding, *Lisa Sergio*, 83–4.
287 Ciano, *My Truth*, 81–2.
288 Telegramm Bergen (Rom) an AA (Berlin), 4 May 1943, in PAAA, Geheime Reichssachen, R61177, 2; Ginsborg, *Family Politics*, 168.
289 Ciano, *Mia Vita*, 44.
290 Bosworth, *Claretta*, 33; Innocenti, *Gerarchi*, 26–7.
291 Berenson, *Rumour and Reflection*, 319. The anecdote, however, is misleading as Ciano had already been foreign minister for two years before Mackensen was appointed as ambassador.
292 Pro-Memoria, Roma, 15 February 1940, in ACS, MI, DGPS, b. 22A, fasc. 1; Nelson Page, *L'Americano*, 505.
293 Malaparte, *Kaputt*, 569.
294 Moffat Diary, Entry 19.3.1940, in FDR Library, Sumner Welles Papers, Box 211, Folder: Moffat Diary, 1937–1941, 52. See also Phillips Diary, Entry 28.9.1936, in Houghton Library, William Phillips, Box 6/11, Folder 5; Conversation John F. Montgomery with Baron Apor, Budapest, 3 January 1939, in Frank, *Discussing Hitler*, 223.
295 Telegram Kennedy (London) to Hull (Washington), 17 March 1939, in NARA, RG 59, M1423, Reel 2, File 865.00/1805.

296 Telegram Perth (Rome) to Cadogan (London), 24 March 1939, in NA, FO 371/22797, R2098/9/22, 311.

297 See Schellenberg, *Aufzeichnungen*, 41–2; Di Rienzo, *Ciano*, 290.

298 Italian Diplomat and German Women, Bern, 23 October 1943, in NARA, RG 84, Entry 3208, Box 8, Folder 707. A similar rumour circulated about Veronika von Clemm. See Rapporto, Roma, 1 September 1940, in ACS, MI, DGPS, b. 22A, fasc. 1, 3; Knigge, *Dilemma eines Diplomaten*, 13.

299 Malaparte, *Kaputt*, 581.

300 Rapporto, Roma, 12 March 1943, in ACS, MI, DGPS, b. 22A, fasc. 2, 1; Malaparte, *Kaputt*, 451; Sarfatti, *My Fault*, 139. The regime regarded Cortina D'Ampezzo as a "refuge" for Jews. See Ministero dell'Interno (Roma), 5 October 1939, in USHMM, RG 40.004, Reel 64, Frame 125881.

301 Information about Edda Ciano's life can be found in Guerri, *Amore fascista*; Schad, *Sie liebten den Führer*, 78–112; Spinosa, *Edda*. However, due to their limited source material and their descriptive nature, these studies do not do justice to Edda's prominence.

302 Ciano, *My Truth*, 110. See also "Italy Hears Swiss Ousted Edda Ciano," *New York Times*, 10 June 1945, 6; "Fascism Fades as Edda Ciano Turns Tide with Italy," *Washington Post*, 19 August 1947, B5; Oven, *Mit Goebbels bis zum Ende*, 173.

303 Ciano, *My Truth*, 73 and 111–12.

304 Cerruti, *Frau eines Botschafters*, 290–2.

305 See Ullstein Bild #00162798; Mussolini, *Il duce*, 76; Moseley, *Mussolini's Shadow*, 11; Schad, *Sie liebten den Führer*, 89.

306 Rapporto, Brescia, 21 September 1941, in ACS, MI, DGPS, b. 298, fasc. Ciano, Galeazzo; Sarfatti, *My Fault*, 154.

307 Lettera Edda Ciano (Capri) a Sebastiani (Roma), 4 July 1933, in ACS, MI, DGPS, b. 298, fasc. Ciano, Galeazzo; Guerri, *Amore fascista*, 77–9.

308 Goebbels, *Tagebücher*, Part I, Vol. 3.1, Entries 8.6.1936 and 9.6.1936, 100–2. After Mussolini's fall, Goebbels claimed that Edda was not the *Duce*'s daughter and a Jew. See Part I, Vol. 9, Entry 23.9.1943, 557–92.

309 Ciano Diary, Entry 20.9.1937. If Galeazzo did indeed try to make his wife adapt to the fascist conventions – as claimed by Mussolini (*Il duce*, 79), Ciano (*My Truth*, 80), and Guerri (*Amore fascista*, 94–5) – his efforts failed.

310 Eisenstadt and Roniger, *Patrons*, 212.

311 Sarfatti, *My Fault*, 139–43; Bosworth, *Mussolini*, 209.

312 De Grazia, *How Fascism Ruled Women*, 273; Gundle, "Film Stars," 323.

313 Cited in Galassi, *Pressepolitik*, 455.

314 "Fascism Fades as Edda Ciano Turns Tide with Italy," *Washington Post*, 19 August 1947, B5; Mussolini, *Il duce*, 78.

315 Le Chef du Département des Finances et des Douanes, E. Nobs, au Chef du Département de Justice et Police, ed. von Steiger, Bern, 20 January 1944, in DDS, Vol. 15, Doc. 41, Annexe II, 108.

316 Ciano, *My Truth*, 115.
317 "500 Italians Feted on Visit to Berlin," *New York Times*, 3 June 1936, 14.
318 Sir E. Phipps (Berlin) to Foreign Office (London), 2 July 1936, in DBFP, Series II, Vol. XV, Doc. 400, 547.
319 Goebbels, *Tagebücher*, Part I, Vol. 3.2, Entry 8.6.1936, 100–1.
320 Goebbels, *Tagebücher*, Part I, Vol. 3.2, Entries 10.6.1936 and 11.6.1936, 102–4; Suvich, *Memorie*, 28–32 and 72. High-ranking Nazis regarded Suvich as an enemy of Germany. See Goebbels, *Tagebücher*, Part I, Vol. 2.3, Entry 4.6.1934, 194–200.
321 Sir E. Phipps (Berlin) to Mr. Eden (London), 12 June 1936, in DBFP, Series II, Vol. XVI, Doc. 363, 502. See also M. François-Poncet, Ambassadeur de France à Berlin, à M. Delbos, Ministre des Affaires Étragères, Berlin, 6 June 1936, in DDF, Serie 2, Vol. II, Doc. 278, 435–6. In July, Galeazzo thanked Goebbels for the friendly reception of his wife. See Goebbels, *Tagebücher*, Part I, Vol. 3.2, Entry 3.7.1936, 122–3.
322 Ciano, *My Truth*, 116.
323 Ciano Diary, Entries 1.5.1942 and 18.5.1942; Telegramma Anfuso (Roma) a Alfieri (Berlino), 21 September 1941, in ASMAE, Gabinetto, Serie I, b. 438; Rapporto, Roma, 10 August 1942, in ACS, MI, DGPS, b. 22A, fasc. 1; Goebbels, *Tagebücher*, Part II, Vol. 4, Entries 4.5.1942, 231–7 and 8.5.1942, 254–60.
324 Brief Edda Ciano Mussolini an Heinrich Himmler, 2 September 1943, in BArch, NS19, AZ 912, 6; Ciano, *My Truth*, 119 and 169.
325 Ciano Diary, Entry 10.5.1940.
326 Ciano Diary, Entries 7.9.1937, 15.9.1937, and 11.11.1938.
327 Ciano Diary, Entries 10.5.1940 and 2.8.1942.
328 See Rapporto, Roma, 17 February 1941, in ACS, MI, DGPS, b. 298, fasc. Ciano, Galeazzo; Rapporto, Roma, 12 August 1942, in ibid., b. 22A, fasc. 1. See also Barnes, *British Fascist*, 80; Cerruti, *Frau eines Botschafters*, 286–7.
329 For the *Giornata della Fede*, see Terhoeven, *Liebespfand fürs Vaterland*. In contrast to Terhoeven, Bonsaver (*Censorship*, 116) convincingly shows that the publisher Mondadori had the idea for the *Giornata della Fede*.
330 *L'Illustrazione Italiana*, 29 December 1935, 1305–6; Ginsborg, *Family Politics*, 211.
331 Ciano Diary, Entry 17.10.1940; Ciano, *My Truth*, 69.
332 De Grazia, *How Fascism Ruled Women*, 224.
333 Telegram Phillips (Rome) to Welles (Washington), 21 March 1941, in NARA, RG 59, LM142, Reel 3, File 865.00/1954, 4; Ansaldo, *Giornalista*, 293–4. The relevant passages are missing from Ciano's diary.
334 Schönberger, "Mütterliche Heldinnen," 112.
335 Ibid., 121; Di Rienzo, *Ciano*, 248; La Torre, Bellotti, and Sironi, "Sample of Italian Fascist Colonialism," 174. Members of the aristocracy working for

the Red Cross featured widely in magazines; see *L'Illustrazione Italiana*, 27 December 1942, 638; *La Stampa*, 1 October 1939, 1.

336 Bosworth, "Per necessità famigliare," 369.

337 Ciano, *My Truth*, 82–3.

338 See Ciano Diary, Entries 19.12.1937 and 21.6.1940; Ansaldo, *Giornalista*, 140.

339 Telegramma Mussolini (Roma) a Edda Mussolini Ciano (Shanghai), 6 October 1931, in ACS, SPD, Autografi, b. 15.

340 Ciano Diary, Entry 21.6.1940. It was not uncommon for Mussolini to attribute symbolic meanings to first names. The name of his son Romano was supposed to remind people of *romanità* and thus of the Roman Empire of old. See Bosworth, *Claretta*, 54.

341 Pietromarchi, *Diari e le agende*, 227.

342 Agnelli, *Matrosenkleider*, 112; Ciano, *My Truth*, 83.

343 Ciano, *Quando il nonno*, 36.

344 Ciano, *My Truth*, 82–3; Sarfatti, *My Fault*, 148.

345 Ciano Diary, Entry 28.6.1939.

346 Ciano Diary, Entries 16.10.1937 and 24.10.1937.

347 Ciano Diary, Entry 28.11.1937.

348 Gestrich, *Geschichte der Familie*, 39.

349 See Ciano Diary, Entries 26.1.1938, 9.10.1939, and 5.4.1942; Telegramma Bocchini (Roma) a Commissario P.S. (Orvieto), 9 June 1935, in ACS, MI, DGPS, b. 22A, fasc. 1; Petacci, *Mussolini Segreto*, 57.

350 Ciano Diary, Entry 16.10.1937; Ciano, *Quando il nonno*, 33–6; Bosworth, *Claretta*, 18.

351 L'inizio dell'anno scolastico, 20 October 1937, in ASL, Giornale Luce, B1187; *L'Illustrazione Italiana*, 24 October 1937, 1307.

352 Additional images can be found in *Illustrierter Beobachter*, 15 October 1938; Ullstein Bild #01084760.

353 Getty Images #3162210. Another photograph of this series can be found at Alamy Stock Photos, ID 2AX23F3.

354 Gestrich, *Geschichte der Familie*, 38.

355 Kertzer and Hogan, *Family*, 143.

356 Ciano Diary, Entries 3.7.1939 and 24.10.1939.

357 The telegrams can be found in ACS, SPD, Autografi, b. 15 and BSB, Mussolini Papers, Reel 456, Frames 029658/A, 029668/A, and 029675/A.

358 Ciano Diary, Entry 1.7.1939.

359 Sarfatti, *My Fault*, 140.

360 Ginsborg, *Family Politics*, 168–9. See also Bojano, *Wake of the Goose Step*, 56; Mussolini, *Il duce*, 75; Ward Price, *Führer und Duce*, 250–1.

361 Anfuso, *Rom – Berlin*, 286; Bosworth, *Claretta*, 165.

362 Ginsborg, *Family Politics*, 167. Dario Pater appears in Ciano's diary for the first time in 1938. See Ciano Diary, Entry 11.8.1938.

363 Bosworth, *Claretta*, 154.
364 Ciano Diary, Entries 16.5.1941, 26.5.1941, 31.5.1941, and 8.7.1942.
365 Ciano Diary, Entry 29.3.1941.
366 Navarra, *Memorie*, 89; Innocenti, *Gerarchi*, 15.
367 Ciano Diary, Entries 16.5.1941, 3.6.1941, and 4.6.1941.
368 Ortona, *Diplomazia*, 242.
369 Dollmann, Aufzeichnungen für Botschafter Mackensen, Rom, 16 July 1942, in PAAA, Mackensen, 7, 440344; Dollmann, Aufzeichnungen für Botschafter Mackensen, Rom, 18 July 1942, in ibid., 440345.
370 Oven, *Mit Goebbels bis zum Ende*, 173; Sarfatti, *My Fault*, 143–4.
371 Bosworth, *Claretta*, 26.
372 Duggan, *Fascist Voices*, 217–18.
373 Bosworth, "Per necessità famigliare," 368–9.
374 Petacci, *Mussolini Segreto*, 59.
375 Ciano Diary, Entry 26.5.1941.
376 Rapporto, Roma, 4 February 1941, in ACS, MI, DGPS, b. 22A, fasc. 1.
377 Ciano Diary, Entries 29.3.1942, 13.4.1942, 24.4.1942, and 2.6.1942.
378 Ciano Diary, Entry 21.6.1942; Senise, *Quando ero capo della polizia*, 154–6; Bosworth, *Claretta*, 164. Buffarini Guidi also collaborated with the Petacci family on other occasions. See Ciano Diary, Entries 24.12.1941 and 27.4.1942.
379 Ciano Diary, Entries 22.1.1942, 8.7.1942, and 6.8.1942. The *Banca Nazionale del Lavoro* collaborated with Farinacci, Bottai, Rossoni, and the Cianos, which is why the Petacci family targeted the bank. See Bosworth, *Mussolini*, 227.
380 Ciano Diary, Entry 8.7.1942.
381 Bosworth, *Claretta*, 169–70.
382 Ciano Diary, Entry 8.1.1943.
383 See Vermerk, Berlin, 6 June 1941, in BArch, R58, AZ 9486, Frame 790608; "Edda Ciano Holds Mussolini Weak," *New York Times*, 21 September 1945, 12; Armellini, *Diario*, 267; Ciano, *My Truth*, 25 and 182; Bosworth, *Claretta*, 112.
384 Bosworth, "Per necessità famigliare." See also Canali and Volpini, *Mussolini e i ladri di regime*; Giovannini and Palla, *Fascismo dalle mani sporche*. The book *Tangentopoli Nera* by Cereghino and Fasanella also deals with corruption during fascism. However, the source base is rather thin, and the analysis is not integrated into broader questions of fascist historiography.
385 Ciano Diary, Entries 2.6.1939 and 5.6.1942.
386 Ciano, *Quando il nonno*, 58–9; Guerri, *Galeazzo Ciano*, 848–9.
387 According to Ciano, he owned four houses in Rome, worth approximately five million lire, and three-quarters of the newspaper *Il Telegrafo*.

In his bank accounts he had 1,400,000 lire. He also held shares of the following companies: *Montecatini* (2000); *Romana Elettricità* (1400); ANIC (1000); *Valdarno* (1000); *Metallurgica* (1000); AMIATA (700); ILVA (500); *Terni* (500); *Navigazione Generale* (300); and IMI (100). See Lettera Ciano (Roma) a Badoglio (Roma), 23 August 1943, in NA, GFM 36/431, 082148–7.

388 Prefettura di Lucca al Ministero dell'Interno, 1 September 1943, in ACS, MI, DGPS, b. 22A, fasc. 1; Prefettura di Vicenza al Ministero dell'Interno, 10 September 1943, in ibid., b. 298, fasc. Ciano, Galeazzo.

389 Rapporto, Milano, 5 November 1943, in ACS, MI, DGPS, b. 298, fasc. Ciano, Galeazzo; Rapporto, Milano, 24 August 1943, in ibid.; Moraglia, Questura di Livorno, 5 April 1944, in ibid.

390 See Rapporto, Lucca, 25 February 1944, in ACS, MI, DGPS, b. 298, fasc. Ciano, Galeazzo; "114 Ciano Apartments Seized," *New York Times*, 24 March 1945, 7.

391 Casali and Cattaruzza, *Sotto i mari*, 179.

392 Ciano Diary, Entries 30.9.1942 and 31.10.1942; Telegram Harrison (Bern) to Hull (Washington), 9 February 1943, in NARA, RG 84, Entry 3207, Box 86. At the same time, Ciano also adopted a positive attitude towards Switzerland. See Le Chef du Service des Intérêts étrangers de la Légation de Suisse à Roma, M. de Stoutz, au Chef du Département politique, M. Pilet-Golaz, Rome, 29 July 1942, in DDS, Vol. 14, 714–5.

In 1945, the Americans investigated life insurance policies that Ciano allegedly had taken out in Switzerland – to no avail. See Safehaven Report #9722, Bern, 4 May 1945, in NARA, RG 226, Entry 19, Box 130; Safehaven Report #9810, Bern, 24 May 1945, in ibid., Box 131; Safehaven Report #11657, Bern, 11 June 1945, in ibid., Box 158.

393 Pro-Memoria, Genova, 27 October 1939, in ACS, MI, DGPS, b. 22A, fasc. 1; Rapporto, 27 August 1941, in ibid., b. 298, fasc. Ciano, Galeazzo; Rapporto, 30 August 1941, in ibid. b. 298, fasc. Ciano, Galeazzo; Aufzeichnung, Rom, no date, in BArch, R58, AZ 9482, Frame 410361; "Ciano Is Described as Gaining Wealth," *New York Times*, 2 June 1942, 4; Duggan, *Fascist Voices*, 328.

394 Rapporto, Roma, 3 October 1942, in ACS, MI, DGPS, b. 22A, fasc. 1; Telegramm Mackensen (Rom) an Freiherr von Doernberg (Berlin), 10 February 1943, in PAAA, Büro des Staatssekretärs, R29638, Fiche 538, 123896; Pietromarchi, *Diari e le agende*, 90.

Moreover, it seems likely that the Badoglio government exaggerated the estimates in the course of the investigation in order to highlight the corruption of the fascist regime. See Le Ministre de suisse à Rome, P. Vieli au Chef de la Division des Affaires étrangères du Département politique, P. Bonna, 8 September 1943, in DDS, Vol. 15, Doc. 1, 1–2.

395 Pro-Memoria, Genova, 27 October 1939, in ACS, MI, DGPS, b. 22A, fasc. 1; Bericht von Weidmann über Italienreise September 1941, in BArch, R58, AZ 9480, Frame 180106; La confisca dei beni del Partito Fascista e delle fortune improvvise, Milano, 9 August 1943, in ACS, MI, DGPS, b. 298, fasc. Ciano, Galeazzo; Denunzia contro Galeazzo Ciano, Roma, 5 September 1943, in ibid., fasc. 2; Oven, *Mit Goebbels bis zum Ende*, 174.

396 See Telegram Loraine (Rome) to Cadogan (London), 26 June 1939, in NA, FO 371/23798, R5632/9/22, 200; Telegram Butler (Berne) to Nichols (London), Situation in Italy, 24 October 1939, in NA, FO 371/23798, R9847/9/22, 327–8.

397 Telegramma Cini a Ciano, Roma, 27 January 1940, in ACS, Ente Autonomo EUR, b. 39, fasc. 26.

398 Cerruti, *Frau eines Botschafters*, 290.

399 For the "white telephone" films, see Forgacs, "Fascism and Italian Cinema"; Gundle, *Mussolini's Dream Factory*, 75; Hay, *Popular Film Culture*; Landy, *Fascism in Film*, 230–4.

400 See velina (22 March 1934), in Tranfaglia, *Stampa*, 173; velina (31 May 1934), in Tranfaglia, *Stampa*, 174; Sarfatti, *My Fault*, 151–2.

401 "La dottrina del fascismo," in Mussolini, *Opera Omnia*, Vol. XXXIV, 119–21.

402 Gentile, Corner, and Duggan, "Two New Books"; Schieder, *Italienische Faschismus*.

403 Griffin, "Political Modernism," 30. For Szálasi, see Rady, "Ferenc Szálasi." For Francetić, see Yeomans, "'For Us, Beloved Commander.'"

404 Eisenstadt and Roniger, *Patrons*, 241 and 254.

405 Piattoni, "Clientelism," 124.

406 Ibid., 19.

407 See Corner, "Everyday Fascism," 196–8 and 209; Gentile, "Problem of the Party," 261–5; Mazzoni, *Livorno*, 130.

408 Michaelis's judgment, which classified Costanzo Ciano as an insignificant figure of the regime, can no longer be upheld. See Michaelis, "Conte Galeazzo Ciano," 117.

409 Ciano, *My Truth*, 96; Mazzoni, *Livorno*, 116.

410 Cited in Mazzoni, *Livorno*, 129.

411 Cited in Wasson, *Aristocracy*, 112.

412 Bosworth, *Claretta*, 61–2.

413 Ginsborg, *Family Politics*, 208–9.

414 Ibid., 174.

415 De Grand, "Cracks in the Facade."

416 Bosworth, "Dictators Strong or Weak," 272; Ginsborg, *Family Politics*, 224–5.

417 Cited in Goeschel, "Parallel History?" 618.

2. The Politician

1 Mussolini, *Opera Omnia*, Vol. III, 190; Painter, *Mussolini's Rome*, 2.
2 Varè, *Lachende Diplomat*, 277; Bosworth, *Mussolini's Italy*, 15–16.
3 Garzarelli, "*Parleremo al mondo*," 30–1.
4 Appunti circa il "Reichsministerium fuer Volksaufklärung und Propaganda," in ACS, PCM, f. 1.1./2, b. 2219; Di Rienzo, *Ciano*, 367–71; Williams, *Mussolini's Propaganda*, 9.
5 Kennedy, *The Times*, 81; Magistrati, *Prologo del dramma*, 44; Goeschel, *Mussolini and Hitler*, 37–59.
6 Bonsaver, *Censorship*, 109. For the failure of the Hitler-Mussolini meeting, see Der Botschafter in Rom von Hassell an das Auswärtige Amt, Rom, 21.6.1934, in ADAP, Serie C, Vol. III, 1, Doc. 26, 61–5; Cerruti, *Frau eines Botschafters*, 186; Kirkpatrick, *Mussolini*, 278–83.
7 His predecessor Polverelli and Bottai shared this opinion. See Bonsaver, *Censorship*, 108; Hoffend, *Kultur-Achse*, 75.
8 Il Duce visita la nuova sede dell'Ufficio Stampa del Capo del Governo, July 1934, in ASL, Giornale Luce, B050404; Nelson Page, *L'Americano*, 446.
9 Ferrara and Giannetto, "Introduzione," 29–30.
10 MacDonald, "Radio Bari," 195; Marzano, "'Guerra delle onde,'" 6.
11 Giancarlo Vallauri, a graduate of the *Accademia Navale di Livorno*, headed the EIAR from November 1934.
12 Galassi, *Pressepolitik*, 416.
13 Relazione a S.E. il Sottosegretario di Stato sulla attività della DGSE, in ACS, MCP, Reports, b. 1, 006452; Garzarelli, "*Parleremo al mondo*," 34.
14 Canosa, *Voce del Duce*, 56 and 71–84; Galassi, *Pressepolitik*, 430–6; Talbot, *Censorship*, 43–6.
15 Der Propaganda-Haushalt vor dem italienischen Senat, Rom, 22 May 1936, in Barch, R4902, AZ 4879.
16 ASL, Codice Foto, A00065476; Nelson Page, *L'Americano*, 439–48.
17 Rapporto Personale nei riguardi del Cons. Gen. Emanuele Grazzi, 4 February 1936, in ACS, MCP, Gabinetto, b. 10, fasc. 85, 10.
18 "Morto l'editore Gherardo Casini," *Corriere della Sera*, 8 July 1994, 31; Hoffend, *Kultur-Achse*, 41.
19 Siebers, *Mussolinis Medienmacht*, 59–60.
20 Reich, "Mussolini at the Movies," 10.
21 *L'Amministrazione Centrale*, Vol. 1, 60.
22 On 24 September 1936, the *Ispettorato per il Teatro* was transformed into a directorate-general. See Montefusco, *L'ordinamento*, 11.
23 See De Peppo, Appunto, Roma, 11 January 1935, in ACS, MCP, DGSP, b. 61, fasc. 1934; Telegramma Sanseverino (Roma) a Ministero delle Corporazioni (Roma), 17 March 34, in ibid.; "Il Sottosegretario Ciano riceve

personalità straniere della cinematografia," *Il Popolo d'Italia*, 1 March 1935, 3; Galassi, *Pressepolitik*, 402–5; Garzarelli, "*Parleremo al mondo*," 24–8; Hay, *Popular Film*, 70 ; Ricci, *Cinema and Fascism*, 70.

24 Williams, *Mussolini's Propaganda*, 9.

25 Bonsaver, *Censorship*, 110.

26 Galassi, *Pressepolitik*, 417.

27 Vergani, *Ciano*, 39.

28 Lettera Bonomi (Roma) a Ciano (Asmara), no date, in ACS, MCP, Gabinetto, b. 10, fasc. 82, 38.

29 Telegramma De Peppo (Roma) a Ciano (Asmara), 11 September 1935, in ACS, MCP, Gabinetto, b. 10, fasc. 87, 1.

30 Talbot, *Censorship*, 82–4.

31 Nelson Page, *L'Americano*, 440.

32 Koon, *Believe, Obey, Fight*, 159.

33 For example, see the sections "The Son of a Hero," "The Fascist Family," "The Fascist," and chapter four. For the literature on the regime's cultural policy, see, for example, Arthurs, *Excavating Modernity*; Baxa, *Roads and Ruins*; Bonsaver, *Censorship*; De Grazia, *Culture of Consent*; Forgacs and Gundle, *Mass Culture*; Mattioli and Steinacher, *Für den Faschismus bauen*; Painter, *Mussolini's Rome*; Reich and Garofalo, *Re-viewing Fascism*; Ricci, *Cinema and Fascism*; Talbot, *Censorship*

34 Orsini, "Diplomazia," 319; "Italy to Shift 35 in Foreign Service," *New York Times*, 16 October 1936, 16.

35 Phillips Diary, Entry 25.9.1936, in Houghton Library, William Phillips, Box 6/11, Folder 5; Schmidt, *Statist*, 551.

36 Bastianini, *Uomini, cose, fatti*, 232; Luciolli, *Palazzo Chigi*, 5–6.

37 Telegram Phillips (Rome) to Hull (Washington), 20 September 1939, in NARA, RG 59, M1423, Reel 6, File 865.021/34.

38 Orsini, "Diplomazia," 314.

39 Cerruti, *Frau eines Botschafters*, 288; Nelson Page, *L'Americano*, 489.

40 Telegram Harrison (Bern) to Hull (Washington), 13 February 1943, in NARA, RG 59, CDF, Box 1878, File 701.6566A/8; Pietromarchi, *Diari e le agende*, 76.

41 Luciolli, *Palazzo Chigi*, 54–5; Meldung, Berlin, 22 November 1940, in BArch, R58, AZ 9486, Frame 790148–9. For example, in May 1940 Ciano withheld information from the *Duce*. See Ciano Diary, Entry 12.5.1940.

42 See Telegram Phillips (Rome) to Welles (Washington), 21 March 1941, in NARA, RG 59, LM142, Reel 3, File 865.00/1954, 5; Telegram Phillips (Rome) to Welles (Washington), 20 May 1941, in ibid., File 865.00/1958.

43 Ciano Diary, Entry 10.3.1942; Nelson Page, *L'Americano*, 644–5.

44 Telegramm Mackensen (Rom) an AA (Berlin), 14 November 1941, in PAAA, Geheime Reichssachen, R61140, 125–8; Rapporto, Roma, 1 September 1940, in ACS, MI, DGPS, b 22A, fasc. 1.

45 Officials, 22 October 1943, in NARA, RG 84, Entry 3208, Box 12, Folder 800, 3.
46 Orsini, "Diplomazia," 325.
47 Luciolli, *Palazzo Chigi*, 55–6. During Ciano's tenure, the total number of employees at the *Palazzo Chigi* increased. See Vermerk, no date, in PAAA, Botschaft in Rom, 815b.
48 For other subdivisions, see Orsini, "Diplomazia," 321; *L'Amministrazione Centrale*, Vol. 1, 165–6.
49 For the Italian intervention, see chapter three.
50 See Telegramm Mackensen (Rom) an AA (Berlin), 16 November 1942, in PAAA, Geheime Reichssachen, R61140, 290–1; Pietromarchi, *Diari e le agende*, 14 and 224; Orsini, "Diplomazia," 321. Without convincing evidence, Burgwyn ("Mussolini's Troika," 299–300) claims that Pietromarchi was a "long standing fascist."
51 Ciano Diary, Entry 1.12.1939, 367; Pietromarchi, *Diari e le agende*, 373n42; Mallett, "Anglo-Italian War," 151–2.
52 Pietromarchi, *Diari e le agende*, 454.
53 Orsini, "Diplomazia," 321; *L'Amministrazione Centrale*, Vol. 1, 180.
54 Rodogno, *Fascism's European Empire*, 115; Pietromarchi, *Diari e le agende*, 19.
55 For a more detailed description of the various directorates-general, see Hof, *Galeazzo Ciano*, 169–70; *L'Amministrazione Centrale*, Vol. 1, 166–71.
56 Borzoni, *Renato Prunas*, 129; Luciolli, *Palazzo Chigi*, 54.
57 *L'Amministrazione Centrale*, Vol. 1, 168–9.
58 Borzoni, *Renato Prunas*, 130–3; Samarani, "Historical Turning Point," 593.
59 A small *Direzione Generale Affari Politici, Commerciali e Privati di Africa, America, Asia e Australia* had existed from 1920 to 1932. See *L'Amministrazione Centrale*, Vol. 1, 113–14 and 145.
60 See Luciolli, *Palazzo Chigi*, 6; Ojetti, *Taccuini*, 564.
61 Nelson Page, *L'Americano*, 477.
62 See Eden, *Memoiren*, Vol. 1, 258; Jones, *Diary*, 370; Nicolson, *Diaries*, 247; Mills, "Sir Joseph Ball," 301–2.
63 Serra, "Italy," 309–12.
64 Vergani, *Ciano*, 53–5.
65 Nelson Page, *L'Americano*, 472–3.
66 For Cerruti's withdrawal from Paris in 1937 as a reaction to the absence of a French ambassador in Rome, see Bottai, *Diario*, 120.
67 Michaelis, "Conte Galeazzo Ciano," 135.
68 Magistrati, *Prologo del dramma*, 91.
69 Ciano Diary, Entry 21.11.1937. See also Entry 16.11.1937.
70 Suvich, *Memorie*, 31.

71 Orsini, "Diplomazia," 323–4. Di Rienzo (*Ciano*) and Guerri (*Galeazzo Ciano*), however, still use these memoirs uncritically.

72 See Legge n862: Ordinamento della carriera diplomatico-consolare, 2.6.1927, in *Gazzetta Ufficiale del Regno d'Italia*, n. 136, 13.6.1927, 2390–2. After the reform it was up to the selection committee to pass a final verdict as to whether the applicant possessed the "right morality" and the "correct political behaviour." As part of the reform, Grandi filled 120 posts with new recruits. See Karst, "Deutschland," 30; Serra, "Italy," 311. For the history of the *Palazzo Chigi* under Grandi, see Orsini, "Diplomazia," 290–307.

For the UCFE, see Cassels, "Fascism for Export," 707–11; De Caprariis, "'Fascism for Export'?" 151–83; Gentile, "Fasci italiani," 95–115.

73 Serra, "Italy," 302.

74 Other friends included Franco Bellia, Candido Bigliardi, Raffaele Boscarelli, Casto Caruso, Alessandro Marieni, and Antonio Venturini. See Ciano Diary, Entry 23.4.1942; Report Diego, Diplomats, Bern, 22 October 1943, in NARA, RG 84, Entry 3208, Box 12; Ciano, *My Truth*, 193; Susmel, *Vita sbagliata*, 29.

75 Magistrati, *Prologo del dramma*, 127 and 136; Borzoni, *Renato Prunas*, 436. An early photograph shows Ciano in the middle of his most trusted collaborators (Pietromarchi, Bastianini, Buti, De Peppo, and Anfuso), all of them wearing civilian dress. See Ullstein Bild #01082613.

76 For Germany, see Hürter, "German Foreign Office," 82–4.

77 Rossi, *Mussolini e il diplomatico*, 398–9. Emanuele Grazzi briefly joined the RSI. However, he was relieved of all posts just a couple of weeks later due to trust issues. See Di Rienzo, *Ciano*, 1120.

78 These aspects will be discussed in chapter three, "The Diplomat."

79 Ciano Diary, Entry 21.11.1937.

80 Telegram Phillips (Rome) to Hull (Washington), 19 August 1938, in NARA, RG 59, M1423, Reel 1, File 865.00/1772; Sarfatti, *Jews in Mussolini's Italy*, 155.

81 Ciano Diary, Entries 1.8.1938 and 8.8.1938.

82 The reference to La Pera's letter can be found in Lettera Ciano (Roma) a Buffarini Guidi (Roma), 17 August 1938, in USHMM, RG 40.004, Reel 64, Frame 126037. One year later, another request was sent. See Dispaccio Direzione Generale Demografia e Razza a tutti i ministeri, Roma, 11 August 1939, in ibid., Frame 125964.

83 Lettera Ciano (Roma) a Buffarini Guidi (Roma), 17 August 1938, in USHMM, RG 40.004, Reel 64, Frame 126037.

84 Lettera Buffarini Guidi a tutti i ministeri, Roma, 31 March 1939, in USHMM, RG 40.004, Reel 64, Frame 125968; Telegramma Vidau (Roma) a

Ministero dell'Interno, Direzione Generale Demografia e Razza (Roma), 13 April 1939, in ibid., Frame 125967.

85 The circular is mentioned in Telegramma Crolla (Londra) a Ministero degli Affari Esteri (Roma), 16 December 1938, in USHMM, RG 40.002, Reel 1, Frame 1297–8.

86 Telegramma Rotini (Liverpool) all'Ambasciata Londra, 24 January 1939, in USHMM, RG 40.002, Reel 1, Frame 1291.

87 Telegramma Crolla (Londra) a Ministero degli Affari Esteri (Roma), 25 January 1939, in USHMM, RG 40.002, Reel 1, Frame 1290.

88 See Telegramma Vinci (Budapest) a Ciano (Roma), 9 April 1938, in USHMM, RG 40.002, Reel 5, Frame 8999–9001; Lettera Ciano (Roma) a Lantini (Roma), 2 May 1938, in ibid., Frame 9008; Telegramma Vitetti (Roma) a Ministero dell'Interno (Roma), 18 August 1938, in USHMM, RG 40.004, Reel 55, Frame 110286–7.

89 Unfortunately, even with the help of the archival staff, I was not able to locate these documents. They should be in ASMAE, Archivio del Personale, Serie I: Comune, b. 121, fasc. 500. See also Hof, "Widerwillige Helfer?" 201–2.

90 Ciano Diary, Entries 24.4.1940, 26.4.1940, and 27.4.1940; Goeschel, *Mussolini and Hitler*, 180.

91 Orsini, "Diplomazia," 323.

92 See Telegram Steinhardt (Moscow) to Hull (Washington), 9 February 1941, in NARA, RG 59, LM142, Reel 3, File 865.00/1935; Telegram Phillips (Rome) to Welles (Washington), 21 March 1941, in ibid., File 865.00/1954, 5; Telegram Phillips (Rome) to Hull (Washington), 20 June 1940, in FDR Library, PSF, Box 42; Telegram Phillips (Rome) to Hull (Washington), 28 April 1941, in ibid.

93 Bach and Breuer, *Faschismus als Bewegung*, 330.

94 Dogliani, "Propaganda and Youth," 187; Giansanti, *Generazione littoria*, 53–76; La Rovere, *Storia dei GUF*, 38–59.

95 Koon, *Believe, Obey, Fight*, 184–5. For Marinetti, see Guerri, *Filippo Tommaso Marinetti*; Ialongo, *Filippo Tommaso Marinetti*.

96 See Benini, *Carcere degli Scalzi*, 38–9; De Vecchi, *Quadrumviro*, 55; Lessona, *Memorie*, 332; Di Rienzo, *Ciano*, 173; Guerri, *Galeazzo Ciano*, 48–9; Michaelis, "Conte Galeazzo Ciano," 120; Moseley, *Mussolini's Shadow*, 8–9; Susmel, *Vita sbagliata*, 18.

97 Guerri, *Galeazzo Ciano*, 45.

98 Mazzoni, *Livorno*, 26n4.

99 Mann, *Fascists*, 29; Reichardt, *Faschistische Kampfbünde*, 364.

100 Pavolini, *Disperata*, 58; Ceccotti, *Fascismo a Livorno*, 271. See also "S.E. Galeazzo Ciano aviatore," *La Stampa*, 1 November 1934, 1.

101 Signoretti, "*La Stampa*," 88.

102 Vergani, *Ciano*, 16; De Begnac, *Palazzo Venezia*, 582; Santini, *Costanzo Ciano*, 123–5.
103 Chiantera-Stutte, *Avantgarde*, 101–2.
104 Amendola, *Una scelta della vita*, 98; Scarantino, "*L'Impero*," 67.
105 However, Di Rienzo (*Ciano*, 177), Guerri (*Galeazzo Ciano*, 52), Moseley, (*Mussolini's Shadow*, 9), and Ostenc (*Ciano*, 7) all claim that Ciano had worked for *Il Mondo*. For the anecdote, see Nelson Page, *L'Americano*, 531.
106 The stories were titled "L'inaugurazione," "Andarci a piedi," "La paura del buio," "Trovarsi nella vita," "Signore, si uccida!" and "L'attesa della fortuna." The comedy was titled "Er fonno d'oro." See Guerri, *Galeazzo Ciano*, 55–7.
107 "Mimy Aylmer tra Umberto di Savoia e Galeazzo Ciano," *Epoca*, 23 November 1958, 68–9; "Le Memorie di Mimy Aylmer," *Epoca*, 7 December 1958, 77. Aylmer's memoirs should be treated with caution, as some dates are either inaccurate or given in the wrong context.
108 The view that his failure as a writer marked his character is put forward by Boothe (*Europe in Spring*, 56–8), Di Rienzo (*Ciano*, 190), and Guerri (*Galeazzo Ciano*, 47).
109 Vergani, *Quando Gabriele*, XXII and 16–18; Chiantera-Stutte, *Avantgarde*, 131.
110 Mosse, "Political Culture," 259. For Futurism, see Adamson, "Culture of Italian Fascism"; Berghaus, *Futurism and Politics;* Griffin, "Multiplication of Man"; Strauven, "Futurist Poetics"; Versari, "Futurists Machine Art."
111 Cited in Guerri, *Galeazzo Ciano*, 55. Ciano also used the motif of the "superhuman" in his work *La felicità di Amleto*. See Guerri, *Galeazzo Ciano*, 56.
112 The "death wish" or early premonition theory is advanced by Guerri (*Galeazzo Ciano*, 54–5).
113 See Ciano Diary, Entries 3.10.1941 and 28.8.1942.
114 Marchicelli, *Futurism*, 112. For the connection between futurism and fascism, see Aragno, "Futurismus"; Mosse, "Political Culture."
115 Vergani, *Quando Gabriele*, 17. For the Matteotti crisis, see Bosworth, *Mussolini*, 199–200.
116 Letter Malaparte (Napoli) to Loraine (London), 14 June 1947, in NA, FO 1011/214, 1–2; Guerri, *Malaparte illustrato*, 60.
117 Federzoni, *Italia di ieri*, 103; Bosworth, *Mussolini*, 202.
118 De Grand, "Curzio Malaparte," 83.
119 Berghaus, *Futurism and Politics*, 196; Parlato, *Sinistra fascista*, 8; Susmel, *Vita sbagliata*, 24.
120 Bosworth, *Mussolini's Italy*, 213; Chiantera-Stutte, *Avantgarde*, 124; Santoro, *Roberto Farinacci*, 180–6.
121 "Le memorie di Mimy Aylmer," *Epoca*, 30 November 1958, 77.
122 Santoro, *Roberto Farinacci*, 176.

123 See Bastianini, *Uomini, cose, fatti*, 238; D'Avila, *Vita eroica*, 40; De Vecchi, *Quadrumviro*, 95; Mussolini, *My life*, 70; Vergani, *Ciano*, 21; Mazzoni, *Livorno*, 117.
124 Scarantino, "*L'Impero*," 67.
125 "Le memorie di Mimy Aylmer," *Epoca*, 30 November 1958, 74.
126 Chiantera-Stutte, *Avantgarde*, 126; Scarantino, "*L'Impero*," 67.
127 See the telegrams in ACS, SPD, Autografi, b. 15; and in BSB, Mussolini Papers, Reel 456, Frame 029658/A and Frame 029675/A.
128 The erosion of the liberal-democratic system began with the establishment of the Fascist Grand Council and the reform of the electoral law in July 1923. See Bosworth, *Mussolini*, 181; Sørensen, "Dual State," 31–4.
129 Cited in Woller, *Geschichte Italiens*, 141. See also Barnes, *Universal Aspects*, xxvii.
130 Lettera Mussolini (Roma) a Edda Ciano (Shanghai), 22 September 1932, in BSB, Mussolini Papers, Reel 456, Frame 029677/A.
131 De Caprariis, "'Fascism for Export'?" 158.
132 Trento, "Fasci in Brasile," 152–4.
133 See Aliano, "Identity in Transatlantic Play"; Gentile, "L'emigrazione italiana," 384–9; Trento, "Viaggiatori d'era fascista"; Zanatta, "Fasci in Argentina."
134 De Caprariis, "Fasci italiani all'estero," 6–7.
135 Ciano rarely mentioned the foreign *fasci*. See Lettera Ciano (Pechino) a Maria Rosa Oliver (Buenos Aires), 6 April 1928, in Mudd Library, Maria Rosa Oliver Papers, Box 3, Folder 4, Series 2a.
136 Guerri (*Galeazzo Ciano*, 69–70) claims that Ciano did not become involved with the *fasci* because he was not interested in fascism.
137 Cassels, "Fascism for Export," 708.
138 For the ill will, see Smith, *Imperial Designs*, 120.
139 De Caprariis, "'Fascism for Export'?" 163–4.
140 Smith, *Imperial Designs*, 114. France was suspicions about Ciano's activities. See M. Baudet, Chargé d'Affaires de France a Nankin, à M. Wilden, Ministre de France à Pékin, Nankin, 17 July 1933, in DDF, Serie 1, Vol. IV, 13.
141 Il Sottosegretario agli Esteri, Fani, al Ministro degli Esteri, Grandi, a Ginevra, Roma, 24 September 1931, in DDI, Serie 7, Vol. XI, Doc. 27, 40–1; Promemoria della Direzione Generale America, Asia ed Australia per il Ministro degli Esteri, Grandi, Roma, 9 October 1931, in ibid., Doc. 45, 82–4.
142 Galassi, *Pressepolitik*, 412.
143 Borstendoerfer, *Graf Ciano*, 40.
144 Galassi, *Pressepolitik*, 561.
145 For sports coverage, see velina (24 October 1933), velina (22 March 1934), velina (30 January 1934), and velina (16 November 1934), in Tranfaglia, *Stampa*, 172–5; velina (28 June 1935), in Cassero, *Veline del Duce*, 16;

Dogliani, "Sport and Fascism," 327–32. For the demographic campaign, see velina (22 March 1934), velina (31 May 1934), and velina (5 February 1935), in Tranfaglia, *Stampa*, 91 and 173–4.

146 For language, see velina (18 September 1933) and velina (2 April 1934), in Tranfaglia, *Stampa*, 172–3.

147 See velina (9 August 1933), in Tranfaglia, *Stampa*, 105; Galassi, *Pressepolitik*, 454; Talbot, *Censorship*, 82–6. For censorship, see Bonsaver, *Censorship*, 94–111; Forgacs and Gundle, *Mass Culture*, 225.

148 See Forgacs and Gundle, *Mass Culture*, 208; Hay, *Popular Film*, 70; Ricci, *Cinema and Fascism*, 68; Wilson, *Puccini Problem*, 185–93. For Italy's influence on the Cairo Opera, see the documents in ACS, MCP, DGSP, b. 61, fasc. 1934.

149 Ansaldo, *Giornalista*, 105; Bottai, *Diario*, 102; De Grand, "Mussolini's Follies," 140–1; Gentile, "Problem of the Party," 265.

150 "Italian Sovereignty over Ethiopia," *The Times*, 18 May 1936, 13; "Ciano Made a General," *New York Times*, 22 October 1936, 6.

151 Guerri, *Galeazzo Ciano*, 233. For his participation in Florence, see ASL, Codice Fotografico, A00066983 (6 October 1936); *L'Illustrazione Italiana*, 11 October 1936, cover.

152 For Starace's pro-German attitude, see Politischer Bericht Hassell (Rom) an AA (Berlin), 8 October 1937, in PAAA, Botschaft in Rom, 709b.

153 Ciano Diary, Entry 29.6.1938; Telegramm Deutsches Konsulat (San Remo) an Deutsche Botschaft (Rom), 25 June 1938, in PAAA, Botschaft in Rom, 709b; Sir R. Glyn (London) to Mr. Ingram (London), 28 July 1938, in NA, FO 371/22432, R6678/281/22, 126.

154 Ciano Diary, Entry 24.10.1938.

155 Ciano Diary, Entries 5.12.1938, 9.12.1938, and 26.12.1938.

156 Initially, Starace praised the *non belligeranza* policy. See Ciano Diary, Entry 1.9.1939. For the criticism, see Entries 27.8.1939 and 4.10.1939.

157 Ciano Diary, Entry 13.9.1939.

158 Senise, *Quando ero capo della polizia*, 38–9.

159 Ciano Diary, Entry 22.9.1939.

160 See Ciano Diary, Entry 4.10.1939. For the relationship between Muti and the Cianos, see Telegram Reed (Rome) to Hull (Washington), 13 November 1939, in NARA, RG 59, M1423, Reel 2, File 865.00/1868; Questura di Roma a Capo della Polizia (Roma), 28.8.1943, in ACS, MI, DGPS, b. 22A, fasc. 2.

161 Ciano Diary, Entry 4.10.1939.

162 Ciano Diary, Entry 30.10.1939. See also Cianetti, *Memorie*, 313; Nelson Page, *L'Americano*, 578.

163 See Betrachtungen über die politische Situation Italiens 1935–1941, in PAAA, Dienststelle Ribbentrop, R27160, 274951; Meldung, Berlin, 22 October 1940, in BArch, R58, AZ 9486, Frame 790148–9.

164 Ciano Diary, Entry 16.1.1940; Telegram Charles (Rome) to Nichols (London), 17 November 1939, in NA, FO 371/23799, R10445/9/22; Die Lage Italiens im Dezember 1941, no date, in PAAA, Inland II, R101084, Fiche 2796, E050148.
165 Ciano Diary, Entry 29.12.1939; Ansaldo, *Giornalista*, 214. Early on, Giovanni Ansaldo feared that Muti would be corrupted by power and break away from Ciano. However, Ciano did not share his concerns. See Ansaldo, *Giornalista*, 198–9 and 206–8. The reason why Ciano did not benefit from Muti's tenure as party secretary had more to do with the shifting power relations within the regime and less with Muti's alleged incompetence as Di Rienzo (*Ciano*, 154) argues.
166 See Telegram Charles (Rome) to Nichols (London), 21 November 1939, in NA, FO 371/23799, R10662/9/22; Graziani, *Ho difeso la patria*, 187.
167 Ciano Diary, Entry 19.1.1940; Letter Loraine (n.l.) to Murray (Edinburgh), 24 November 1943, in FO 1011/214; Pietromarchi, *Diari e le agende*, 421.
168 Ciano Diary, Entry 28.3.1940.
169 See Rapporto, Roma, 11 September 1940, in ACS, MI, DGPS, b. 22A, fasc. 1; Rapporto, Roma, 25 February 1941, in ibid.; Pietromarchi, *Diari e le agende*, 506; Nelson Page, *L'Americano*, 578.
170 Ciano Diary, Entry 4.10.1940; Bottai, *Diario*, 223–6.
171 Given that Serena was a member of the Ciano Cabinet and that Ciano was upset when Serena was dismissed (Ciano Diary, Entry 23.12.1941), we can assume that at least a neutral personal relationship existed between Ciano and Serena.
172 See Rapporto, Milano, 13 January 1942, in MI, DGPS, b. 22A, fasc. 2; Rossi, *Mussolini e il diplomatico*, 294–6.
173 See Die Lage Italiens im Dezember 1941, no date, in PAAA, Inland II, R101084, Fiche 2796, E050148; SS-Brigadeführer (Rom) an Luther (Berlin), 19 December 1940, in ibid., Fiche 2795, 284030–5.
174 Ribbentrop's attention to these reports is demonstrated by the numerous dossiers that the German foreign minister had filed on Ciano. See PAAA, Dienststelle Ribbentrop.
175 Bosworth, "Per necessità famigliare," 361–2.
176 Ciano Diary, Entry 27.12.1941. See also Entry 26.12.1941; Telegramm Bismarck (Rom) an AA (Berlin), 30 December 1941, in PAAA, Botschaft in Rom – Geheimakten, 124, E257542–5.
177 Ciano Diary, Entries 2.12.1941, 6.1.1942, 24.1.1942, 5.2.1942, 19.2.1942, and 28.3.1942; Goebbels, *Tagebücher*, Part II, Vol. 4, Entry 25.6.1942, 611–18.
178 Ciano Diary, Entry 27.12.1941.
179 Ciano Diary, Entry 22.3.1942. In the Italian publications, this entry only exists after the fifth edition. However, the wording is completely different from the original text (Ciano, *Diario, Volume Secondo*, 252.). It can be

assumed that the editors took the text from the first French edition and simply retranslated it.

Another assassination attempt against Ciano was planned in May 1942. See Ciano Diary, Entry 10.5.1942. For the anti-fascist groups, see Combined Intelligence Report No. 24, Lisbon, 25 May 1942, in USHMM, RG 59.006, Reel 19, Frame 60.

180 Ciano Diary, Entry 11.6.1941.

181 See Ciano Diary, Entry 2.4.1942; Serrano Suñer, *Zwischen Hendaye und Gibraltar*, 291.

182 Ciano Diary, Entry 26.2.1942.

183 In reaction to their experiences of exile and the Second World War, former radical fascists like Malaparte also moderated their views. See Telegram Hull (Washington) to Algiers, 30 November 1943, in NARA, RG 59, CDF, Box 5643, File 865.00/2232A; De Grand, "Curzio Malaparte," 87–8.

184 Ciano Diary, Entry 17.11.1942.

185 Ciano Diary, Entry 2.11.1942.

186 Paxton, *Anatomy of Fascism*, 23.

187 See Ciano Diary, Entry 26.8.1937; Letter Glyn (London) to Ingram (London), 28 July 1937, in NA, FO 371/22432, R6678/281/22; Telegram Charles (Rome) to Nichols (London), 29 August 1938, in ibid.; Telegram Phillips (Rome) to Hull (Washington), 23 December 1939, in NARA, RG 59, M1423, Reel 1, File 865.00/1789; Telegram Phillips (Rome) to Hull (Washington), 3 March 1939, in ibid., Reel 2, File 865.00/1803; Telegram Perth (Rome) to Cadogan (London), 24 March 1939, in NA, FO 371/22797, R2098/9/22, 310; Armellini, *Diario*, 166; Lessona, *Memorie*, 334–6.

188 Bosworth, "Per necessità famigliare," 373.

189 Kershaw, *Hitler*, Vol. 1, 27; Rodogno, "Fascism and War," 245.

190 Bach and Breuer, *Faschismus als Bewegung*, 320–30.

191 Woller, *Geschichte Italiens*, 104–15.

192 De Felice, *Mussolini il fascista*, Vol. 2.2, 554–8; Galassi, *Pressepolitik*, 399; Talbot, *Censorship*, 80.

193 Telegramm Botschafter Hassell (Rom) an AA (Berlin), 3 May 1934, in PAAA, Botschaft in Rom, 709a.

194 Galassi, *Pressepolitik*, 419.

195 Der Botschafter in Rom von Hassell an das Auswärtige Amt, Rom, 7 January 1936, in ADAP, Serie C, Vol. IV, 2, Doc. 486, 958; Hassell, Aufzeichnung, 13 February 1936, in PAAA, Botschaft in Rom – Geheimakten, 40, D682440.

After the Second World War, Suvich was often praised for his alleged anti-German and peaceful policy. See Federzoni, *Italia di ieri*, 213; De Felice, *Jews in Fascist Italy*, 169; Di Rienzo, *Ciano*, 420; Goeschel, *Mussolini and Hitler*, 45. Contemporaries, however, were less flattering and described Suvich as a cold and calculating man. See Telegram Phillips (Rome) to Dunn (Washington), 24 June 1936, in NARA, RG 59, M1423, Reel 4, File 865.002/206.

196 Cited in Moseley, *Mussolini's Shadow*, 21.

197 See Lettera Alfieri (Roma) a Ciano (Asmara), 3 November 1935, in ACS, MCP, Gabinetto, b. 8, fasc. 31; Der Propaganda-Haushalt vor dem italienischen Senat, Rom, 22 May 1936, in BArch, R4902, AZ 4879; "Le vittorie della civiltà fascista," *Corriere della Sera*, 21 May 1936, 1; "Il conte Galeazzo Ciano illustra al Senato," *La Stampa*, 23 May 1936, 1–2; Telegramm Hassell (Rom) an AA (Berlin), 27 November 1936, in PAAA, Botschaft in Rom, 709b.

Ciano's work as minister of propaganda also received international praise. Reichsführer SS, Leitheft: Italienische Presse, März 1937, in BArch, R58, AZ 1101; Telegramm Plessen (Rom) an AA (Berlin), Rom, 11 August 1936, in PAAA, Botschaft in Rom, 833a; Note by Mr. Thompson, Foreign Office, 7 October 1935, in DBFP, Series II, Vol. XV, Doc. 42, 48.

198 Galassi, *Pressepolitik*, 419.

199 Telegramm Hassell (Rom) an AA (Berlin), 18 February 1937, in PAAA, Botschaft in Rom – Geheimakten, 45, 4628512.

200 Vergani, *Ciano*, 39–40; Namier, *Europe in Decay*, 108.

201 Guariglia, *Ricordi*, 330; Susmel, *Vita sbagliata*, 51–2.

202 See Ciano Diary, Entries 27.11.1937, 11.12.1937, 19.12.1937, 10.3.1938, 3.6.1938, 28.6.1938, and 4.7.1938. Of course, Ciano was not the only person who admired the *Duce*. For other cabinet members, see Duggan, *Fascist Voices*, 236.

203 Ciano Diary, Entry 29.9.1938.

204 Cannistraro and Sullivan, *Il Duce's Other Woman*, 347.

205 Bosworth, "Dictators Strong or Weak," 269.

206 Bonsaver, *Censorship*, 109.

207 Griffin, "Europe for the Europeans," 141–2; Ledeen, *Universal Fascism*, 42–3.

208 De Grand, "Mussolini's Follies," 136.

209 Ledeen, *Universal Fascism*, 72–5.

210 Dogliani, "Propaganda and Youth," 186; La Rovere, "Fascist Groups," 460–1; Mann, *Fascists*, 87.

211 Ledeen, *Universal Fascism*, 71.

212 Cited in Ledeen, *Universal Fascism*, 29.

213 Cited in Ledeen, *Universal Fascism*, 107. See also Nelson Page, *L'Americano*, 460.

214 Zangrandi, *Lungo viaggio*, 146; Bonsaver, *Censorship*, 145 and 156.

215 This reasoning and motivation on the part of Mussolini is put forward by Grandi (*Mio Paese*, 410–14).

216 Bastianini, *Uomini, cose, fatti*, 245; Federzoni, *Italia di ieri*, 159.
217 Telegram Phillips (Washington) to Child (Chicago), 21 July 1933, in FDR Library, POF, 233, Box 1; Telegram Roosevelt (Washington) to Victor Emanuel III (Rome), 21 July 1933, in ibid.; Letter Taylor (St. Louis) to Long (Rome), 7 August 1933, in LoC, Breckinridge Long Papers, Box 106; Long Diary, Entry 20.3.1935, in ibid., Box 4.
218 Kennedy, *The Times*, 113.
219 Ciano Dairy, Entries 26.8.1937 and 31.8.1937.
220 Politischer Bericht Hassell (Rom) an AA (Berlin), 31 January 1936, in PAAA, Botschaft in Rom – Geheimakten, 40, D682416–9.
221 Ciano Diary, Entry 5.9.1937; Ducci, *Bella gioventù*, 144.
222 Ciano Diary, Entries 2.11.1937, 14.12.1937, 15.12.1937, and 23.6.1938.
223 Ciano Diary, Entry 14.12.1937. There is no evidence in Ciano's diary that he informed Mussolini about Balbo's earlier criticism.
224 Politischer Bericht Hassell (Rom) an AA (Berlin), 8 October 1937, in PAAA, Botschaft in Rom, 709b; Letter Charles (Rome) to Nichols (London), 24 August 1938, in FO 371/22432, R472/8/38.
225 Canosa, *Farinacci*, 265; Guerri, *Italo Balbo*, 338.
226 Ciano Diary, Entry 26.10.1938; Arielli, *Fascist Italy*, 150.
227 See Eden, *Memoiren*, Vol. 1, 258; Jones, *Diary*, 370; Nicolson, *Diaries*, 247; Mills, "Sir Joseph Ball," 301–2.
228 Grandi never mentioned Ciano's instructions but repeatedly stated that he acted on his own initiative. See Telegram Mr. Eden (London) to Perth (Rome), 19 January 1938, in USHMM, RG 59.022, Reel 3, 13; Grandi, *Mio Paese*, 429–32. For Ciano's instructions, see Ortona, *Diplomazia*, 32; Mills, "Sir Joseph Ball," 298.
229 Ciano Diary, Entries 16.10.1937, 9.2.1938, and 27.5.1938; Grandi, *Mio Paese*, 412.
230 Telegram Perth (Rome) to Cadogan (London), 28 January 1938, in NA, FO 371/22402, R871/23/22.
231 See Aufzeichnungen für Botschaftsrat, Rom, 2 June 1938, in PAAA, Botschaft in Rom, 709b; Telegram Knox (Budapest) to FO (London), 23 March 1939, in NA, FO 371/22796, R1924/9/22; Telegram Phillips (Rome) to Hull (Washington), 27 September 1941, in NARA, RG 59, LM142, Reel 3, File 865.00/1970.
232 For the gradual improvement of the relationship between Ciano and Grandi in 1939, see Ciano Diary, Entries 6.1.1939, 2.7.1939, and 28.11.1939.
233 The press would also spread this image. See "Il discorso di Galeazzo Ciano," *La Stampa*, 16 October 1936, 1.
234 See Ciano Diary, Entries 21.4.1938 and 14.3.1939 to 19.3.1939; Telegram Perth (Rome) to Cadogan (London), 24 March 1939, in NA, FO 371/22797, R2098/9/22, 309–15; Der Deutsche Geschäftsträger in Rom

an das Auswärtige Amt, Telegramm, Rom, 12 March 1938, in ADAP, Serie D, Vol. I, Doc. 361, 476; Pietromarchi, *Diari e le agende*, 265.

235 Aufzeichnung des Botschafters in Rom, 24 March 1939, in ADAP, Serie D, Vol. VI, Doc. 87, 85–9; Bottai, *Diario*, 144.

236 Ciano Diary, Entry 17.3.1938.

237 Ciano Diary, Entries 9.2.1939 and 14.3.1939; Weizsäcker, Aufzeichnungen, Berlin, 31 March 1939, in PAAA, Mackensen, 2, 64474–6.

238 Ciano Diary, Entry 15.3.1939. For the annexation of Albania, see chapter three.

239 See Ciano Diary, Entries 7.4.1939 and 9.4.1939; See Rapporto, Roma, 24 August 1939, in ACS, MI, DGPS, b. 22A, fasc. 1; Rapporto, Roma, 26 May 1939, in ibid.; Ojetti, *Taccuini*, 518.

240 See Telegram Phillips (Rome) to Hull (Washington), 24 February 1939, in NARA, RG 59, M1423, Reel 1, File 865.00/1884; Telegram Knox (Budapest) to FO (London), 22 March 1939, in NA, FO 371/22796, R1924/9/22, 275–6.

241 Ciano Diary, Entries 11.8.1939 and 12.8.1939; Caviglia, *Diario*, 225; Schmidt, *Statist*, 438–40; Weizsäcker, *Erinnerungen*, 246.

242 Ciano Diary, Entry 15.8.1939.

243 Ciano Diary, Entry 27.8.1939. See also Report, 21 December 1939, in NA, GFM 33/791, 440250.

244 Ciano Diary, Entry 15.8.1939.

245 Ansaldo, *Giornalista*, 196.

246 Ciano Diary, Entries 1.9.1939, 7.11.1939, and 14.12.1939; Telegram Loraine (Rome) to Cadogan (London), 13 October 1939, in NA, FO 1011/204; Rapporto, Roma, 13 November 1939, in ACS, MI, DGPS, b. 22A, fasc. 1; Telegramma Federzoni (Roma) a Ciano (Roma), 16 December 1939, in ACS, Archivi Federzoni, b. 3; Telegram Phillips (Bern) to Hull (Washington), 31 March 1940, in NARA, RG 59, CDF, Box 2950, File 740.00119EW/304; Carboni, *Memorie*, 12–14; Grandi, *Mio Paese*, 557; Pietromarchi, *Diari e le agende*, 234, 337, and 373n28; Pirelli, *Taccuini*, 229–33; Ortona, *Diplomazia*, 73; Rossi, *Mussolini e il diplomatico*, 250.

247 See Ciano Diary, Entries 14.8.1939, 2.9.1939, and 13.9.1939; Telegram Phillips (Rome) to Hull (Washington), 6 September 1939, in FDR Library, PSF, Box 42; Rapporto, Roma, 25 January 1940, in ACS, MI, DGPS, b. 22A, fasc. 1; Pietromarchi, *Diari e le agende*, 385.

248 Ciano Diary, Entry 3.1.1940; Pietromarchi, *Diari e le agende*, 347.

249 See chapter three.

250 Goeschel, *Mussolini and Hitler*, 166.

251 Rapporto, Roma, 4 October 1939, in ACS, MI, DGPS, b. 22A, fasc. 1; Goebbels, *Tagebücher*, Part I, Vol. 7, Entry 22.11.1939, 204–6.

252 For potential reasons for the cabinet reshuffle, see Telegram Mackensen (Rom) an AA (Berlin), 1 November 1939, in PAAA, Botschaft in Rom,

709d; Telegram Reed (Rome) to Hull (Washington), 3 November 1939, in NARA, RG 59, M1423, Reel 2, File 865.00/186.

253 Ciano Diary, Entry 19.10.1939.

254 Ciano Diary, Entry 2.12.1939; Cianetti, *Memorie*, 300–2.

255 Ciano Diary, Entries 16.10.1939 and 27.10.1939; Telegram Bullitt (Paris) to Hull (Washington), 31 October 1939, in NARA, RG 59, M1423, Reel 2, File 865.00/1857; Telegramm Plessen (Rom) an AA (Berlin), in PAAA, Botschaft in Rom, 709d.

256 This reason is the main one given by Goeschel (*Mussolini and Hitler*, 167).

257 Cited in König, *Kooperation als Machtkampf*, 21.

258 Ciano Diary, Entries 4.9.1939, 20.11.1939, and 3.12.1939.

259 Ciano Diary, Entry 9.10.1939. See also Entry 3.12.1939; Bottai, *Diario*, 161; Ojetti, *Taccuini*, 530; Schreiber, "Politische und militärische Entwicklung," 9.

260 Armellini, *Diario*, 175; Goeschel, *Mussolini and Hitler*, 180.

261 Ciano Diary, Entry 4.9.1939. Ciano, using the parable of "Bertoldo's Tree," interpreted Mussolini's reluctance to name an exact date for Italy's entry into the war as a sign that Italy would never enter the conflict. See Ciano Diary, Entries 16.3.1940 and 18.3.1940; Ansaldo, *Giornalista*, 225–26.

262 Ciano Diary, Entry 30.9.1939.

263 Carboni, *Memorie*, 142 and 379.

264 Ciano Diary, Entry 10.6.1940; Bottai, *Diario*, 193.

265 Guerri, *Galeazzo Ciano*, 634.

266 See Ciano Diary, Entry 1.3.1940; SD des RFSS Polte (Wien) an RSHA Amt VI (Berlin), 9 May 1940, in BArch, R58, AZ 9483, Frame 500002; Letter Loraine (London) to Murray (Edinburgh), 24 November 1943, in NA, FO 1011/214; Carboni, *Memorie*, 54–5 and 59; Graziani, *Ho difeso la patria*, 187.

267 For example, on the evening of 7 December 1939, Ciano explained the *non belligeranza* policy to the Grand Council. He later wrote that his speech had made a great impression and even Mussolini had liked it. Ciano, however, missed the fundamental differences with Mussolini's subsequent speech. See Ciano Diary, Entry 7 8.12.1939; Bottai, *Diario*, 169.

268 See Ortona, *Diplomazia*, 83.

269 Ciano Diary, Entry 29.2.1940; Anfuso, *Rom – Berlin*, 109.

270 See Rapporto, Roma, 18 March 1940, in ACS, MI, DGPS, b. 22A, fasc. 1; Rapporto, Roma, 25 April 1940, in ibid.; Telegram Phillips (Rome) to Hull (Washington), 11 April 1940, in NARA, RG 59, M982, Reel 18, File 740.0011/2091; Rossi, *Mussolini e il diplomatico*, 261.

In April and May Ciano avoided the public and went to Albania to escape from Rome. See Telegram Loraine (Rome) to FO (London), 19 May 1940, in NA, FO 371/24868, R6153/6153/90.

271 Ciano Diary, Entry 31.3.1940.

272 Ansaldo, *Giornalista*, 234; Signoretti, "*La Stampa*," 194–5. In April and May, Ansaldo announced in the newspaper *Il Telegrafo* the imminent entry into the war. See Telegram Phillips (Rome) to Hull (Washington), 16 April 1940, in NARA, RG 59, M982, Reel 18, File 740.0011/2255; Telegram Phillips (Rome) to Hull (Washington), 1 May 1940, in ibid., Reel 21, File 740.0011/3212.

273 See "Italian War Move Indicated by Ciano," *New York Times*, 20 May 1940, 1; *L'Illustrazione Italiana*, 26 May 1940, 764.

274 Ciano Diary, Entry 12.4.1940. For Ciano's absence, see Telegram Phillips (Rome) to Hull (Washington), 10 April 1940, in NARA, RG 59, M982, Reel 19, File 740.0011/2348; Telegram Phillips (Rome) to Hull (Washington), 18 April 1940, in ibid., File 740.0011/2322;

275 According to the British Foreign Office, Ciano called in sick on 13 April following a dispute with Mussolini. In addition, the Americans had information that Hitler pressured Mussolini to enter the war on the same day. See Telegram Bullitt (Angers) to Hull (Washington), 18 April 1940, in NARA, RG 59, CDF, Box 4368, File 740.0011/2320; Telegram Bucknell (Geneva) to Hull (Washington), 22 April 1939, in ibid., File 765.00/146; Telegram Nichols (London) to Osborne (Vatican), 6 May 1940, in NA, FO 1011/210.

276 Phillips Diary, Entry 22 April 1940, in Houghton Library, William Phillips, 12/25, Folder 5.

277 Ciano Diary, Entry 20.4.1940. For the rumours, see Telegram Phillips (Rome) to Hull (Washington), 19 April 1940, in FDR Library, PSF, Box 42; Rapporto, Roma, 25 April 1940, in ACS, MI, DGPS, Roma, b. 22A, fasc. 1; Telegramm Mackensen (Rom) an AA (Berlin), 26 April 1940, in PAAA, Botschaft in Rom – Geheimakten, 74, E086899–901.

278 See SD des Reichsführers SS an den SD Leitabschnitt Berlin, 11 June 1940, in BArch, R58, AZ 9478, Frame 090022; Mr. Myron Taylor, Personal Representative of the President to Pope Pius XII to President Roosevelt, Rome, 30 April 1940, in FRUS, 1940, Vol. II, 692–3.

279 Ciano Diary, Entry 20.4.1940; Ansaldo, *Giornalista*, 235.

280 Ansaldo, *Giornalista*, 230; Malaparte, *Kaputt*, 612; Moseley, *Mussolini's Shadow*, 105.

281 "Suvich Explains Service to Ciano," *New York Times*, 30 January 1945, 5.

282 Ward Price, *Führer und Duce*, 314.

283 Telegramm Plessen (Rom) an AA (Berlin), 1 November 1939, in PAAA, Botschaft in Rom, 709d.

284 Guerri, *Galeazzo Ciano*, 681.

285 See Ciano Diary, Entry 20.8.1940; Bottai, *Diario*, 210–17; Pirelli, *Taccuini*, 310–11; Shirer, *Berlin Diary*, 458; Moseley, *Mussolini's Shadow*, 110.

286 Eatwell, "Concept and Theory," 13.

287 Ciano Diary, Entry 26.2.1942.
288 Cerruti, *Frau eines Botschafters*, 304; Phillips Diary, Entry 1.7.1940, in Houghton Library, William Phillips, Box 12/24, Folder 6; Guerri, *Galeazzo Ciano*, 678–81.
289 Ciano Diary, Entries 14.2.1940, 1.6.1940, 2.6.1940, and 29.6.1940; Le nonce en Italie Borgongini Duca au cardinal Maglione, Rome, 29 June 1940, in ADSS, Vol. IV, Doc. 12, 71–2.
290 Carboni, *Memorie*, 105.
291 Ciano Diary, Entries 3.7.1940 and 5.7.1940; Bottai, *Diario*, 219; Aufzeichnung über die Unterredung zwischen dem Führer und dem Grafen Ciano, 7.7.1940, in Hillgruber, *Staatsmänner und Diplomaten*, Vol. 1, 158.
292 Niederschrift, Italienische Kriegsführung, 4 December 1940, in PAAA, Botschaft in Rom – Geheimakten, 87, 481762. It seems unlikely that Ciano had to convince Mussolini to attack Greece as Moseley (*Mussolini's Shadow*, 114) claims. According to Ciano's diary, Mussolini supported an operation against Greece. See Ciano Diary, Entry 5.7.1940.
293 For the campaign in Greece, see Ciano Diary, Entries 22.10.1940 and 27.10.1940; Armellini, *Diario*, 128; König, *Kooperation als Machtkampf*, 34; Sadkovich, "Italo-Greek War." For the criticism, see Di Rienzo, *Ciano*, 1161–7.
294 Conversation John F. Montgomery with Mr. De Kanya, Budapest, 18.12.1940, in Frank, *Discussing Hitler*, 332; Armellini, *Diario*, 158. According to the stenographic report, Ciano spoke three times. See Visconti Prasca, *Io ho aggredito Grecia*, 201–7.
295 For the warnings, see Amè, *Guerra segreta*, 25; Bastianini, *Uomini, cosi, fatti*, 258; Grazzi, *Principio della fine*; Guariglia, *Ricordi*, 477–8. However, we should be cautious about taking some of those warnings at face value as they were voiced in memoirs published after the Second World War.
296 For example, see Pricolo's bypassing of Badoglio in Ciano Diary, Entry 22.10.1940.
297 Rapporto, Genova, 19 February 1941, in ACS, MI, DGSP, b. 22A, fasc. 1.
298 Ojetti, *Taccuini*, 554. It is very likely that the princess was Isabelle Colonna.
299 See Fiske, Military Attaché Report, Rome, 16 December 1940, in FDR Library, Harry L. Hopkins Papers, Box 189, Folder VI, Doc. 121; Telegramm SS-Brigadeführer (Berlin) an Luther (Berlin), 19 December 1940, in PAAA, Inland II, R101084, Fiche 2795, 284030–5; Telegram Kirk (Rome) to Welles (Washington), 23 December 1940, in FDR Library, Sumner Welles Papers, Box 70; Goebbels, *Tagebücher*, Part I, Vol. 9, Entry 16.12.1940, 55.
300 Telegram Hoare (Madrid) to FO (London), 11 March 1941, in NA, FO 371/29926, R2639/28/22, 23–24; Conversation John F. Montgomery with Mr. De Kanya, Budapest, 18.12.1940, in Frank, *Discussing Hitler*, 332.

301 Pro-memoria per Il Duce, 19 November 1940, in BSB, Mussolini Papers, Reel 453, Frame 028264; Telegramm SS-Brigadeführer (Berlin) an Luther (Berlin), 19 December 1940, in PAAA, Inland II, R101084, Fiche 2795, 284030–5; SD des RSFS SS (Klagenfurt) an RSHA (Berlin), 15 January 1941, in BArch, R58, AZ 9486; Verschlusssache für Geschäftsträger persönlich (Sonderzug), 15 February 1941, in PAAA, Geheime Reichssachen, R61140; Rapporto, Roma, 15 February 1941, in ACS, MI, DGPS, b 22A, fasc. 1.

302 RSHA, Amt VI E, Berlin, 6 February 1941, in BArch, R58, AZ 9478, Frame 160274–5.

303 See Rapporto, 20 December 1940, in ACS, MI, DGPS, b 22A, fasc. 1; Rapporto, Roma, 25 December 1940, in ibid.; Rapporto, Roma, 12 January 1941, in ibid.; Memorandum on Italian Morale, London, 5 March 1941, in NA, FO 371/29925, R2011/28/22; Goebbels, *Tagebücher*, Part I, Vol. 9, Entries 14.12.1940, 16.12.1941, 23.12.1940, 14.2.1941, 51, 55, 65, and 142.

304 Ciano Diary, Entries 24.12.1940, 22.9.1941, 2.12.1941, 15.2.1942, 24.2.1942, and 5.4.1942; Il Ministro degli Esteri, Ciano, al Presidente del Consiglio e Ministro degli Esteri Ungherese Bardossy, in DDI, Serie 9, Vol. VIII, Doc. 278, 310–11. For the food shortage in Italy, see Combined Intelligence Report No. 13, Lisbon, 7 January 1942, in USHMM, RG 59.006, Reel 19, Frame 8; Combined Intelligence Report No. 26, Lisbon, 2 June 1942, in ibid., 65–6.

305 See Vermerk, Berlin, 12 March 1941, in BArch, R58, AZ 9486, 790338–9; Ortona, *Diplomazia*, 111.

306 Armellini, *Diario*, 193; Rintelen, "Mussolinis Parallelkrieg," 35.

307 See Vermerk, Berlin, 16 January 1941, in USHMM, RG 11.001M.01, Reel 12; SD des Reichsführers SS an den SD Leitabschnitt, Berlin, 26 June 1941, in BArch, R58, AZ 9478; Memorandum on Italian Morale, London, 18 July 1941, in NA, FO 371/29928, R7196/28/22, 156–9; Rapporto, Roma, 3 July 1942, in ACS, MCP, Gabinetto, b. 181, fasc. Lazzotti; Armellini, *Diario*, 188 and 268.

308 Italienische Kriegsführung 1940, Rom, 4 December 1940, in PAAA, Botschaft in Rom – Geheimakten, 87, 481759; Der Kampf um Ciano, 9 December 1940, in BArch, R58, AZ 9486, 795369; Report (Italy), Bern, 21 January 1943, in NARA, RG 84, Entry 3208, Box 11, Folder 800, 2.

309 For Ciano's negative remarks about Cavallero, see Ciano Diary, Entries 18.11.1941, 8.12.1941, 21.1.1942, 13.2.1942, 6.3.1942, 27.3.1942, 16.5.1942, 31.5.1942, 6.6.1942, 11.6.1942, 22.7.1942, 4.11.1942, and 23.11.1942.

310 Ciano Diary, Entry 27.10.1939; Rapporto, Roma, 10 December 1940, in ACS, MI, DGPS, b. 22A, fasc. 1; Rintelen, "Mussolinis Parallelkrieg," 36–7. Apparently, Ciano prevented an earlier dismissal of Cavagnari. See Rapporto, Roma, 19 December 1940, in ACS, MI, DGPS, b. 22A,

fasc. 1; Mackensen, Aufzeichnungen, Rom, 8 December 1940, in PAAA, Botschaft in Rom – Geheimakten, 87, 481768.

311 Telegram from Hoare, Madrid, 1 January 1941, in NA, FO 371/29924, R130/28/22, 55.

312 See Die Stimmung in Italien, 9 December 1940, in BArch, R58, AZ 9486, 795365–6; Der Kampf um Ciano, 9 December 1940, in ibid., 795369; Telegram Kirk (Rome) to Welles (Washington), 15 December 1940, in FDR Library, PSF, Box, 41; SS-Brigadeführer (Rom) an Luther (Berlin), 19 December 1940, in PAAA, Inland II, R101084, Fiche 2795, 284030–5; Rapporto, Roma, 13 May 1941, in ACS, MI, DGPS, b. 22 A, fasc. 1; Armellini, *Diario*, 173, 203, and 209; Ortona, *Diplomazia*, 135; Rossi, *Mussolini e il diplomatico*, 309.

313 Halder, *Kriegstagebuch*, Vol. 2, 235.

314 An das Reichssicherheitshauptamt, Amt VI, 24 March 1941, in BArch, R58, AZ 9478, 1068; "Exodus from Rome," *New York Times*, 29 January 1941, 16; Ortona, *Diplomazia*, 121; Duggan, *Fascist Voices*, 358.

Some contemporaries believed that Edda or the Germans protected Ciano. See Eindrücke meiner Italienreise vom 29. Juni bis 7. Juli 1941, 11 August 1941, in BArch, R58, AZ 9483, 555387; Telegram Campbell (Belgrade) to FO (London), 4 February 1941, in NA, FO 371/29924, R823/28/22, 257; Caviglia, *Diario*, 337.

315 Ciano Diary, Entry 8.1.1941.

316 Memorandum on Italian Morale, London 1 April 1941, in NA, FO 371/29926, R3498/28/22, 80–1; Statements by Signor Remo Aliotti on the Situation in Italy, 11 April 1941, in NA, FO 371/29927, R4568/28/22, 58–60; Goebbels, *Tagebücher*, Part I, Vol. 9, Entry 13.2.1941, 140.

317 Rapporto Il Conte Ciano al fronte, Milano, 2 February 1941, in ACS, MI, DGPS, b. 22A, fasc. 1; Telegramm für Geschäftsträger persönlich (Sonderzug), 15 February 1941, in PAAA, Geheime Reichssachen, R61140, 66–8.

318 "2 More Ministers to Fight for Italy," *New York Times*, 29 January 1941, 2. See also "Ciano Sent to War," *New York Times*, 28 January 1941; "Duce Orders Ciano to Duty on Bomber," *Washington Post*, 28 January 1941, 1; Hassell, *Vom andern Deutschland*, 159.

319 Telegram Bismarck (Rom) an AA (Berlin), 29 January 1941, in PAAA, Botschaft in Rom – Geheimakten, 97, 481053–60.

320 Ciano Diary, Entry 14.11.1940. It is possible that Farinacci merely passed on rumours and deliberately (mis-)informed Ciano of Mussolini's mistrust in order to increase the tension between the two.

321 See Memorandum on Italian Morale, London, 5 March 1941, in NA, FO 371/29925, R2011/28/22, 122–3; RSHA, Amt VI E: Bericht über Italien, Berlin, 6 February 1941, in BArch, R58, AZ 9478, 160274–5; Alfieri, *Dictators*, 195–6; Rossi, *Mussolini e il diplomatico*, 312; Ortona, *Diplomazia*, 132.

322 Telegramm für Geschäftsträger persönlich (Sonderzug), 15 February 1941, in PAAA, Geheime Reichssachen, R61140, 66–7.

323 Ibid; Alarmierende Nachrichten aus Italien, no date, in BArch, R58, AZ 472; Anfuso, *Rom – Berlin*, 144–5; Burgwyn, *Mussolini Warlord*, 69–70.

324 Telegram Phillips (Rome) to Welles (Washington), 10 June 1941, in NARA, RG59, LM142, Reel 3, File 865.00/1966; Phillips Diary, Entry 16.5.1941, in Houghton Library, William Phillips, Box 13/26, Folder 4.

325 Cited in Telegram Kirkpatrick (London) to FO (London), 17 July 1941, in NA, FO 371/29928, R7157/28/22, 142–5.

326 Letter Phillips (Rome) to Welles (Washington), 10 June 1941, in NARA, RG 59, LM142, Reel 3, File 865.00/1966.

327 Anfuso, *Rom – Berlin*, 191–2. Anfuso described Ciano's illness as partly real, partly "political in nature." The information about Ciano's health was contradictory. Whereas Ciano spoke in his diary of a sore throat, the German authorities reported a kidney inflammation, and Mazzolini reported a nervous breakdown. See Ciano Diary, Entry 22.9.1941; Aufzeichnungen des Gesandten Schmidt (Büro RAM), Berlin, 13 September 1941, in ADAP, Serie D, Vol. XIII, Doc. 308, 399n17; Rossi, *Mussolini e il diplomatico*, 349–50.

328 Dollmann, Bericht, Rom, 5 September 1941, in BArch, NS19, AZ 3001.

329 Ciano Diary, Entries 17.5.1941, 21.5.1941, 8.6.1941, 21.10.1941, and 22.9.1942.

330 Ciano Diary, Entry 13.5.1942; Mr. Savery, British Embassy to Poland, London, 17 June 1942, in FO 371/33219, R4025/3/22, 48–53; Rapporto, Roma, 9 July 1942, in ACS, MI, DGPS, b. 22A, fasc. 2; Carboni, *Memorie*, 139–46.

331 Ciano Diary, Entries 30.5.1941, 4.10.1941, and 22.10.1941. Only once did Ciano reject Bottai's criticism. See Entry 3.6.1942.

332 Ciano Diary, Entries 17.11.1941, 7.3.1942, and 11.3.1942.

333 See Mr. Savery, British Embassy to Poland, London, 17 June 1942, in NA, FO 371/33219, R4025/3/22, 48–53; Dixon, Foreign Office Minutes, London, 17 July 1942, in ibid., R4691/3/22, 76–9.

334 Ciano Diary, Entries 8.8.1942, 26.9.1942, 13.10.1942, and 26.10.1942. Edda Ciano sent her husband a letter expressing concern about her father's health. See NA, GFM 36/645, 623–6.

335 Ciano Diary, Entries 24.9.1942 and 29.10.1942; Ortona, *Diplomazia*, 173. D'Ajeta denied rumours that Ciano would take over the Ministry of the Interior. See Telegramm Mackensen (Rom) an AA (Berlin), 26 October 1942, in PAAA, Botschaft in Rom – Geheimakten, 124, E257639–41.

336 Dollmann, Aufzeichnungen für Mackensen, Rom, 16 July 1942, in PAAA, Mackensen, 7, 440344.

In Livorno, Ciano met, for example, with Serrano Suñer. See Japanese Minister (Madrid) to Foreign Ministry (Tokyo), 10 July 1942, in NA, HW

1/733, No. 733; Japanese Minister (Madrid) to Foreign Ministry (Tokyo), 10 July 1942, in NA, HW 1/752, No. 734; Japanese Ambassador, Rome, Reports Interview with Ciano, 14 June 1942, in NA, HW 1/645, No. 105538; Spanish and Italian Foreign Ministers to Meet: Report from Japanese Minister, Madrid, 16 June 1942, in NA, HW 1/654, No. 105633.

337 Ciano Diary, Entries 29.12.1942 and 15.1.1943. Since it was Buffarini Guidi who informed Ciano about Mussolini's distrust, it might be possible that Buffarini Guidi deliberately launched false reports in order to increase the mistrust between Mussolini and Ciano.

338 Ciano Diary, Entries 20.1.1943, 22.1.1943, and 27.1.1943.

339 Rachele Mussolini mentioned a conspiracy in *My Life*, 117–18.

340 Ciano Diary, Entry 30.1.1943. Aufzeichnungen für Mackensen, Rom, 3 November 1943, in PAAA, Botschaft in Rom – Geheimakten, 125, E257883–4; Bericht Dollmanns über die Reise des RFM Göring nach Italien, Rom, December 1942, in BArch, NS19, AZ 1697, 3–4; Di Rienzo, *Ciano*, 1317.

341 Carboni, *Memorie*, 196; Zangrandi, *1943*, 56; Guerri, *Galeazzo Ciano*, 779.

342 Ciano Diary, Entry 5.2.1943; Pirelli, *Taccuini*, 455.

343 Notes de Mgr Montini, Vatican, 6 February 1943, in ADSS, Vol. VII, Doc. 105, 218–19.

344 Ciano Diary, Entry 5.2.1943; Lettera Ciano a Mussolini, Roma, 7 February 1943, in ACS, SPD, Carteggio, b. 115.

345 Ciano Diary, Entry 8.2.1943.

346 Telegramm Wüster (Berlin) an AM (Berlin), 11 February 1943, in PAAA, Inland II, R101085, Fiche 2798; "Italy Names Ciano Envoy to Vatican," *New York Times*, 8 February 1943, 3; Alfieri, *Dictators*, 193.

347 Telegramm Mackensen (Rom) an AA (Berlin), 6 February 1943, in PAAA, Büro des Staatssekretärs, R29638, Fiche 538, 123891.

348 Cited in Telegramm Mackensen (Rom) an Ribbentrop (Berlin), 18 February 1943, in PAAA, Büro des Staatssekretärs, R29638, Fiche 538, 123962.

349 Ortona, *Diplomazia*, 203.

350 See Letter Gisevius to Dulles, 24 January 1949, in NARA, RG 226, Entry 190C, Box 9, Folder 123, 22–3; Memorandum Dulles, Bern, Secret, 14 April 1943, in ibid., Box 10, Folder 162, 1; Document 1–17, Telegram 729, 1 February 1943, in Petersen, *From Hitler's Doorstep*, 35–6.

A message from Bern had already been intercepted on 9 January. See Telegramm Weizsäcker (Berlin) an Botschaft (Bern), 27 January 1943, in PAAA, Geheime Reichssachen, R61140, 327–30.

351 Telegram Steinhardt (Ankara) to Hull (Washington), 13 February 1943, in NARA, RG 59, LM142, Reel 3, File 865.00/2035.

352 Telegramm Ehrlich (Rom) an den Gauleiter der Auslands-Organisation der NSDAP (Berlin), 22 December 1942, in BArch, NS19, AZ 1880.

353 See Gentile, "Faschismus," 93–4; Gentile, "Mussolini," 124. For criticism against the dominance of cultural studies, see Bosworth, "Per necessità famigliare," 357; Paxton, "Kultur und Zivilgesellschaft," 35–7.

354 Bosworth (*Whispering City*, 180–2) emphasized that, in the 1920s and 1930s, Catholic ceremonies often attracted more visitors and onlookers than the festivals of the regime.

355 For Costanzo Ciano's close relationship to the monarchy, see Ciano Diary, Entry 1.7.1939; De Felice, *Mussolini, il fascista*, Vol. 2.1, 97–8; Santini, *Costanzo Ciano*, 97; Tobia, "Milite ignote," 619–25.

356 See Telegramma Ciano (Roma) a On. Presidenza del Consiglio (Roma), 10 October 1938, in USHMM, RG 40.004, Reel 61, Frame 119542–4.

For recent scholarship about the Vatican's attitude towards the "Jewish question," see Ceci, *Vatican and Mussolini's Italy*; Moro, *Chiesa e lo sterminio*; Ostermann, *Zwischen Hitler und Mussolini*.

357 Telegramma Rocco (Roma) a Grandi (Londra), 22 December 1936, in USHMM, RG 40.002, Reel 1, Frame 431; Telegramma Ciano (Roma) a Grandi (Londra), 24 December 1936, in ibid., Frame 430; Telegram Phillips (Rome) to Hull (Washington), 29 July 1938, in LoC, Hull Papers, Reel 16.

358 Ciano Diary, Entry 4.1.1938. For the Vatican's concerns, see Memorandum a Montini, Roma, 10 May 1938, in USHMM, RG 76.002, C.

359 Ciano Diary, Entries 24.12.1937, 4.1.1938, and 5.1.1938; Der Botschafter in Rom an das Auswärtige Amt, Telegramm, 9 April 1937, in ADAP, Serie D, Vol. III, Doc. 242, 227.

360 Appunto, Roma, 28 March 1938, in USHMM, RG 76.001, Reel 68, Frame 9; Appunto, Roma, 1 April 1938, in ibid., Frame 10; Burgwyn, *Italian Foreign Policy*, 174.

361 Lettera M.C., 28 April 1938, in USHMM, RG 76.001, Reel 68, Frame 28; Baxa, "Capturing the Fascist Moment," 238.

362 Ciano Diary, Entries 24.12.1937, 8.8.1938, and 14.12.1938.

363 Ciano Diary, Entry 22.8.1938. He usually only criticized the Catholic Church on Mussolini's behalf. See Entry 20.7.1939.

364 Ciano Diary, Entries 2.1.1939, 5.2.1939, 9.2.1939, 10.2.1939, 12.2.1939, 2.3.1939, 12.3.1939, and 18.3.1939.

365 "La visita di sovrani d'Italia al papa," *La Stampa*, 22 December 1939, 1.

366 See Rapporto, Roma, 25 January 1940, in ACS, MI, DGPS, b. 22A, fasc. 1; Betrachtungen über die politische Situation Italiens 1935–1941, in PAAA, Dienststelle Ribbentrop, R27160, 274945.

367 Rapporto, Roma, 12 November 1939, in ACS, MI, DGPS, b. 22A, fasc. 1. Despite overlapping interests, the anti-clerical attitude of the royal house prevented a strong alliance that could have threatened Mussolini's reign. See Ciano Diary, Entry 11.4.1939; De Grand, "Cracks in the Facade," 523.

368 Ciano Diary, Entries 18.12.1939, 21.12.1939, 27.12.1939, and 12.5.1940.
369 Ciano Diary, Entry 22.12.1941. Already in December 1940 Ciano did intervene when the *Duce* wanted to abolish St. Joseph's Day. See Entries 2.12.1940 and 5.12.1940.
370 Ciano Diary, Entry 22.2.1942.
371 Le nonce en Italie Borgongini Duca au cardinal Maglione, Rome, 18 November 1942, in ADSS, Vol. VII, Doc. 21, 100–2.
372 Ciano Diary, Entries 25.9.1942 and 18.11.1942. The *Duce* was apparently considering arresting Myron Taylor. See Entry 26.10.1942.
373 See Ciano Diary, Entries 12.5.1940, 22.12.1941, 25.12.1941, and 5.4.1942.
374 See Le nonce en Italie Borgongini Duca au cardinal Maglione, Rome, 28 April 1941, in ADSS, Vol. IV, Doc. 330, 470–1; Notes de Mgr Tardini, Vatican, 4 June 1941, in ibid., Doc. 387, 530–1; Le nonce en Italie Borgongini Duca au cardinal Maglione, Rome, 20 November 1942, in ADSS, Vol. VII, Doc. 27, 109–10.
375 Ciano Diary, Entries 12.6.1942 and 4.11.1942.
376 Ciano Diary, Entry 18.11.1942.
377 Ciano Diary, Entries 5.12.1942, 12.12.1942, and 24.12.1942; Le nonce en Italie Borgongini Duca au cardinal Maglione, Rome, 18 November 1942, in ADSS, Vol. VII, Doc. 21, 100–2; Pirelli, *Taccuini*, 411.
378 Ciano Diary, Entries 30.12.1942 and 2.1.1943; Notes du Cardinal Maglione, 3 June 1943, in ADSS, Vol. VII, Doc. 226, 400–1. For the first bombing, see Baldoli and Knapp, *Forgotten Blitzes*, 204–7; Overy, *Bombenkrieg*, 752–4.
379 Ciano Diary, Entry 12.1.1943; L'Ambassade d'Italie à la Secréteirerie d'Etat, Rome, 7 July 1943, in ADSS, Vol. VII, Doc. 279, 468–71. For the criticism against Ciano, see La Secrétairerie à l'Ambassade d'Italie, Vatican, 23 July 1943, in ibid., Doc. 311, 517–19.
380 Notes de Mgr Montini, Vatican, 12 January 1943, in ADSS, Vol. VII, Doc. 88, 185–9. See also Ciano Diary, Entry 12.1.1943.
381 Notes de Mgr Montini, Vatican, 6 February 1943, in ADSS, Vol. VII, Doc. 105, 218–19; Pirelli, *Taccuini*, 408.
382 Caviglia, *Diario*, 399; Plehwe, *Schicksalsstunden*, 222.
383 Le délégué apostolique à Washington Cicognani au cardinal Maglione, Washington, 25 June 1943, in ADSS, Vol. VII, Doc. 265, 450; Di Rienzo, *Ciano*, 1393–9.
384 Ortona, *Diplomazia*, 252.
385 Given that the Vatican only opened its archive on the papacy of Pius XII in March 2020, these findings must be regarded as preliminary.
386 Ciano Diary, Entry 31.8.1937.
387 Goebbels, *Tagebücher*, Part I, Vol. 5, Entry 6.5.1938, 288–90; Baxa, "Capturing the Fascist Moment," 239.

388 Federzoni, *Italia di ieri*, 235.
389 Ciano Diary, Entry 4.5.1938. See also Entry 2.4.1938; Bottai, *Diario*, 124.
390 De Felice (*Mussolini il duce*, Vol. 3.2, 39–43), Di Rienzo (*Ciano*, 134), and Guerri (*Galeazzo Ciano*, 434–5) all claim Ciano despised the royal family.
391 Ciano Diary, Entry 6.4.1938. For press reports, see USHMM, RG 76.002, B.
392 Federzoni, *Italia di ieri*, 166–77.
393 According to Susmel (*Vita sbagliata*, 92–3), Ciano destroyed these entries in order to erase the prominent role he played in that episode. Di Rienzo (*Ciano*, 133) follows Susmel's interpretation. However, because we do not possess the original diary entries, it remains pure speculation whether they were removed and, if so, who removed them.
394 Ciano Diary, Entry 26.8.1937. For Federzoni's criticism of Ciano, see Federzoni, *Italia di ieri*, 163.
395 Duggan, *Fascist Voices*, 299–300.
396 Sullivan, "'Where One Man,'" 124.
397 There are no other entries in Ciano's diaries that suggest a fundamental rejection of the monarchy.
398 Ciano Diary, Entries 7.5.1939, 18.6.1938, and 17.7.1938.
399 Ciano Diary, Entries 17.7.1938, 3.6.1939, 12.5.1940, and 6.6.1940.
400 Ciano Diary, Entries 7.1.1938, 5.3.1938, and 20.10.1938.
401 Ciano Diary, Entry 20.3.1939; Asst. Military Attaché Sumner Waite, Rome, 10 February 1939, in FDR Library, Harry L. Hopkins Papers, Box 188, Folder Volume III – Italy, Doc. 61.
402 Ciano Diary, Entry 15.6.1939. The royal family regularly featured in Italian journals and was thus a constant element of public discourse, cementing their prominent position within Italian politics and society. See the editions of *L'Illustrazione Italiana* in the 1930s and 1940s.
403 Ciano Diary, Entry 24.3.1939.
404 Telegram Bullitt (Paris) to Hull (Washington), 6 May 1939, in NARA, RG 59, M1423, Reel 1, File 865.00/1817.
405 Mazzoni, *Livorno*, 132.
406 Rapporto, Roma, 24 August 1939, in ACS, MI, DGPS, b. 22A, fasc. 1.
407 Ciano Diary, Entries 13.12.1939, 22.2.1940, and 5.3.1940.
408 Ciano Diary, Entry 14.3.1940. There is some indication that during the Sudeten Crisis in 1938 an alliance between the royal house and the conservative elite attempted a coup against Mussolini to avoid a war. See Sullivan, "'Where One Man,'" 128.
409 After the war, the royal family used this episode to mitigate its own role during fascism. See "King Sought Il Duce Ouster in 1940 Magazine Reports," *Washington Post*, 17 July 1966, A16.
410 De Grand, "Mussolini's Follies," 138.
411 Ciano Diary, Entries 9.4.1939 and 16.4.1939. For more details, see chapter three.

412 Rodogno, *Fascism's European Empire*, 57–8.
413 Telegramm Bismarck (Rom) an AA (Berlin), 24 December 1941, in PAAA, Botschaft in Rom – Geheimakten, 108, E247458.
414 Lettera al Poglavnik di Croazia, Pavelić, Zagrabia, Roma, 30.4.1941, in Ciano, *L'Europa*, 656–7. Ciano's idea to unite the Italian and Croatian royal houses existed long before the Second World War. See Ciano Diary, Entries 9.3.1939, 17.3.1939, 19.3.1939, 30.3.1939, and 21.1.1940; Di Rienzo, *Ciano*, 543.
415 Ciano Diary, Entry 14.5.1941.
416 Ibid.
417 Cavallero, *Comando Supremo*, 88.
418 Ciano Diary, Entries 28.4.1941 and 26.5.1941.
419 Burgwyn, *Empire*, 42.
420 Ciano Diary, Entry 15.12.1941.
421 Ciano Diary, Entry 16.2.1942; Visconti Prasca, *Io ho aggredito*, 13.
422 Telegram Kirkpatrick (London) to Loraine (Rome), 13 March 1940, in NA, FO 1011/210.
423 Ciano Diary, Entry 24.3.1940. This issue had already been considered in January. See Entry 13.1.1940.
424 Ciano Diary, Entry 26.8.1942; Il Ministro a Budapest, Anfuso, al Ministro degli Esteri, Ciano, Budapest, 22 August 1942, in DDI, Serie 9, Vol. IX, Doc. 60, 68–9.
425 Anfuso, *Rom – Berlin*, 207–8.
426 Ciano Diary, Entries 15.10.1941, 20.1.1942, and 7.2.1942. In contrast to popular belief and the available biographies, including Di Rienzo's *Ciano* (59), the title "Count of Buccari" was never awarded to Galeazzo's father Costanzo. See Jocteau, "I nobili del fascismo," 700, and the newspaper articles on Galeazzo and Costanzo Ciano in *Corriere della Sera*, *Il Popolo d'Italia*, and *La Stampa*.
427 Ciano Diary, Entries 3.3.1942, 4.3.1942, 11.3.1942, and 11.10.1942.
428 Ciano Diary, Entry 19.11.1942.
429 Carboni, *Memorie*, 239.
430 Telegramm Moellhausen (Rom) an AA (Berlin), 1 October 1943, in PAAA, Inland II, R101086, Fiche 2802, E411537.
431 Bastianini, *Uomini, cose, fatti*, 238.
432 "Missing Ciano Notes on Munich," *Washington Post*, 2 August 1953, B6.
433 Signoretti, "*La Stampa*," 107.
434 Jureit, *Generationenforschung*, 82.
435 These personal networks and their importance for overcoming the polycratic system have been studied for the Third Reich. See Reichardt and Seibel, "Radikalität und Stabilität," 10–12.
436 Bosworth, *Mussolini*, 239.
437 Behring, "Italien im Spiegel," 361–2.

438 See Kershaw, *Hitlers Macht*; Kuller, "'Kämpfende Verwaltung,'" 230–3. For the radicalization in Germany as a consequence of the system of rule there, see Reichardt and Seibel, "Radikalität und Stabilität"; Seibel, "Staatsstruktur und Massenmord."

439 Ruck, "Führerabsolutismus," 45.

440 Paxton, "Fünf Stadien des Faschismus," 76.

441 See also Levy, "Fascism," 111. Mann (*Fascists*, 14) also stated that the polycratic system, the rivalry between state and party institutions, was less developed in Italy than in Germany.

442 Kuller, "'Kämpfende Verwaltung,'" 229 and 238; De Grand, "Cracks in the Facade," 520–6.

443 Bosworth, *Mussolini*, 173.

444 Bosworth, "Dictators Strong or Weak," 264–5.

445 Telegramm Plessen (Rom) an AA (Berlin), 1 November 1939, in PAAA, Botschaft in Rom, 709d.

446 Telegram British Embassy (Rome) to Halifax (London), 27 December 1938, in NA, FO 371/22796, R36/118/38; Duggan, *Fascist Voices*, 297.

447 Corner, "Italian Fascism," 331.

448 As yet, there is no study on whether Mussolini or other leading fascists deliberately launched misinformation as an instrument of rule. However, we do have studies in this regard for socialist and communist regimes. See Schilling, "Mächtige Signale." For rumours in politics and society, see Allport and Postman, "Analysis of Rumor."

449 In 1911 Robert Michels, syndicalist and since 1928 member of the PNF, published a study on the tendencies of democracies and socialist parties to transform into oligarchic structures. See Michels, *Soziologie des Parteiwesens*. His approaches – especially since they also combine ideas of charismatic leadership and repeatedly refer to the situation in Italy – could offer new insights into the Italian fascist system given Mussolini's career in the socialist party. In particular, Michels emphasized the dominant belief in Italy that political destiny should be in the hands of a minority, and he argued that the "single dictatorship ... does not differ significantly in its effects from the dictatorship of a group of oligarchs" (372). It should also be noted that Michels's definition of the "fascist elite" was basically similar to the oligarchic structures he defined. See Hacke, "Selbsttäuschung aus Enttäuschung."

Germans used terms like "oligarchy" or "plutocracy" to describe the power and corruption of Ciano, his friends, and his confidantes. See Betrachtungen über die politische Situation Italiens, 1935–1941, in PAAA, Dienststelle Ribbentrop, R27160, 274914–79; Goebbels, *Tagebücher*, Part II, Vol. 1, Entry 20.7.1941, 98. Emilio Gentile also occasionally used the term "oligarchy" to emphasize the privileges of all PNF members. See Gentile, "Fascism in Power,"168–7.

450 See, for example, Bosworth, "Dictators Strong or Weak"; Hof, "Widerwillige Helfer?"

451 Bloch, *Erbschaft dieser Zeit*, 104.

3. The Diplomat

1 See Burgwyn, *Italian Foreign Policy*, 1–56; Gooch, "Re-Conquest and Suppression," 1007–21; Mattioli, "Vergessenen Kolonialverbrechen," 212; Woller, *Geschichte Italiens*, 131–6. Di Rienzo (*Ciano*, 471) still follows this interpretation.

2 Cassels, "Fascist Foreign Policy," 257–63; Duggan, *Force of Destiny*, 326–32.

3 For example, see Azzi, "Historiography," 187–8; Bosworth, *Italy the Least of the Great Powers*; Burgwyn, "Diplomacy," 321–32; Karst, "Deutschland," 31–2; Petersen, "Außenpolitik des faschistischen Italiens," 419–20; Schreiber, "Politische und militärische Entwicklung," 106–111.

4 For example, see Behring, "Italien im Spiegel," 361–2; De Grand, "Mussolini's Follies," 129; Erlich, "Periphery and Youth," 394–5; Mallett, *Italian Navy*, 205 and 216; Rodogno, "Fascism and War"; Schieder, *Italienische Faschismus*.

5 See Phillips Diary, Entries 10.4.1940 and 22.4.1940, in Houghton Library, William Phillips, Box 12/23, Folder 3 and 5; Library and Archives Canada, Diaries of William Lyon Mackenzie King, Entries 23.4.1940 and 24.4.1940; Telegram Kirk (Rome) to Hull (Washington), 17 December 1940, in FDR Library, PSF, Box 41; Ciano, *My Truth*, 154; Guariglia, *Ricordi*, 328; Rintelen, *Mussolini*, 40; Burgwyn, "Diplomacy," 324; Di Rienzo, *Ciano*, 469; Guerri, *Galeazzo Ciano*, 267 and 391; Innocenti, *Gerarchi*, 16–17; Michaelis, "Conte Galeazzo Ciano," 116 and 145; Petersen, "Außenpolitik des faschistischen Italien," 419.

6 The "one man alone" theory was first voiced by Churchill on 27 July 1943. See Goeschel, *Mussolini and Hitler*, 252.

7 For the sanctions, see Burgwyn, *Italian Foreign Policy*, 125–6.

8 See Ciano Diary, Entries 1.11.1937, 14.11.1938, 19.3.1939, and 14.6.1939; Aufzeichnung, Rom, 9 June 1934, in PAAA, Botschaft in Rom – Geheimakten, 12, 5–6; Lettera Ciano (Roma) a Grandi (Londra), 14 November 1938, in ASMAE, Carte Grandi, b. 43 fasc. 107; Deutsche Botschaft (Rom) an AA (Berlin), 1 December 1938, in PAAA, Botschaft in Rom, 809c, 2; Telegram Perth (Rome) to Halifax (London), 27 December 1938, in NA, FO 371/22796, R36/118/38, 115.

9 See Iuso, "Politica destabilizzante."

10 Ciano Diary, Entry 12.2.1938. The word *ancora* ("still") is missing in the English version. See Ciano, *Ciano's Hidden Diaries*, 74.

11 Gentile, "Faschismus," 94–5.
12 Ciano, *Außenpolitik Italiens*, 38–43.
13 Ciano Diary, Entry 4.4.1938. See also Entry 11.4.1938.
14 See Ciano Diary, Entry 20.11.1937; Bottai, *Diario*, 60–1; De Giorgi, "Shadow of Marco Polo," 582. Ciano repeatedly used words like "imperial" and "empire." See Ciano Diary, Entries 1.11.1937, 13.4.1938, and 14.4.1938; "Il discorso di Galeazzo Ciano," *La Stampa*, 16 October 1936, 1; Ansaldo, *Giornalista*, 129.
15 Momigliano, "Peace of the Ara Pacis," 228.
16 Hof, "Narratives of 'True Peace.'"
17 Ciano Diary, Entry 11.5.1939.
18 See Ciano Diary, Entries 4.9.1939, 30.9.1939, and 31.3.1940; "Le memorie di Mimy Aylmer," *Epoca*, 30 November 1958, 77; "Mimy Aylmer tra Umberto di Savoia e Galeazzo Ciano," *Epoca*, 23 November 1958, 69; Bianchi, *Crescere in tempo di guerra*; Di Rienzo, *Ciano*, 207.
19 Ciano Diary, Entries 12.5.1938, 8.12.1938, 5.5.1940, 4.6.1940, 24.9.1940, and 25.10.1940; Telegram Perth (Rome) to Halifax (London), 27 December 1938, in NA, FO 371/22796, R36/118/38, 111–16; Ansaldo, *Giornalista*, 255.
20 Ciano Diary, Entry 6.6.1938.
21 Ciano Diary, Entry 6.11.1937; Ciano, *Außenpolitik Italiens*, 38; Aufzeichnung, Rom, 9 June 1934, in PAAA, Botschaft in Rom – Geheimakten, 12, 12.
22 Wolpert, "Rudyard Kipling," 35–6.
23 See documents in ASMAE, Carte Grandi, b. 43, fasc. 105; velina (2 January 1936) and velina (26 May 1936), in Tranfaglia, *Stampa*, 294; Varè, *Two Impostors*, 241. British avant-gardists like Kipling and journalists like Vladimir Poliakoff supported Italy's claims in Ethiopia. See Ciano Diary, Entry 4.9.1937; Letter Milner (London) to Grandi (London), 1 June 1936, in ASMAE, Carte Grandi, b. 43, fasc. 105; Kennedy, *The Times*, 79–80; Firchow, "Faschismus"; Poliakoff, *Europe*, 49.
24 Wolpert, "Rudyard Kipling," 35–6.
25 See Gordon, "Race," 315; Kallis, *Fascism and Genocide*, 64–70.
26 Siebers, *Mussolinis Medienmacht*, 93.
27 De Grand, "Mussolini's Follies," 142. Schneider (*Mussolini in Afrika*, 261) characterized the Italians as late starters in the race discourse.
28 Mann, *Dunkle Seite der Demokratie*, 453.
29 Sarfatti, *Jews in Mussolini's Italy*, 113 and 131–5.
30 Visser, "Fascist Doctrine," 17–18. For Interlandi, see Michaelis, "Mussolini's Unofficial Mouthpiece." For Bottai, see Hoffend, *Kultur-Achse*, 406–19.
31 Telegramm Hassell (Rom) an AA (Berlin), 29 May 1936, in PAAA, Rundfunkpolitische Abteilung, R122638, E529616; The Ambassador in Italy

(Phillips) to the Secretary of State, Rome, 29 July 1938, in FRUS, 1938, Vol. II, 587–8.

32 See Articolo sulla schiavitù in Etiopia, Cairo, 5 October 1935, in ACS, MCP, DGSP, b. 61, fasc. 1935; Telegramma Alessandria a Ministero per la Stampa e Propaganda, 7.12.1935, in ibid.; Talbot, *Censorship*, 117.

33 See Ciano, Testo del discorso, Asmara, 1 November 1935, in ACS, MCP, Gabinetto, b. 17. Italy's alleged fight against "slavery" was an integral part of fascist propaganda. See Baravelli, *L'ultimo baluardo*; "Italy's Note to League," *The Times*, 1 July 1936, 16.

34 Guerri, *Galeazzo Ciano*, 189. For Adwa, see Gooch, *Army, State and Society*, 36; De Grand, "Mussolini's Follies," 129.

35 Cited in Schneider, *Mussolini in Afrika*, 150. See also velina (26 May 1936), in Tranfaglia, *Stampa*, 149; Siebers, *Mussolinis Medienmacht*, 65.

36 Ciano Diary, Entry 8.1.1938; Bosworth, *Mussolini*, 307; De Grand, "Mussolini's Follies," 142.

37 For Mussolini, see Del Boca, "Yperit-Regen," 50; Duggan, *Fascist Voices*, 286; Sarfatti, *Jews in Mussolini's Italy*, 53.

38 Ciano Diary, Entries 25.2.1939, 19.12.1939, and 10.11.1940.

39 Hof, "Extreme Violence," 69–75.

40 Ciano Diary, Entries 13.11.1937, 10.7.1938, 29.1.1940, 7.2.1940, 21.6.1940, 11.7.1940, 10.1.1941, and 7.3.1942.

41 Ciano Diary, Entries 12.12.1940, 24.12.1940, and 5.1.1941.

42 Paxton, *Anatomy of Fascism*, 220.

43 Cassels, "Fascist Foreign Policy," 265.

44 See Bianchi, *Crescere in tempo di guerra*; Row, "Mobilizing the Nation."

45 For Ciano's mostly positive opinion about Argentinians and Chinese, see Lettera Ciano (Pechino) a Maria Rosa Oliver (Buenos Aires), 6 April 1928, in Mudd Library, Maria Rosa Oliver Papers, Box 3, Folder 4, Series 2a. His negative comments about Argentina in January 1938 (Ciano Diary, Entry 30.1.1938) should not be interpreted as a fundamental dislike of Argentina and of his racial bias (see Di Rienzo, *Ciano*, 209; Guerri, *Galeazzo Ciano*, 66–7). They must be seen in relation to Attilio Biseo and Bruno Mussolini's flight from Rome to South America in February 1938 and the possibility of anti-fascist demonstrations should they land in Buenos Aires.

46 Ciano Diary, Entries 9.6.1940 and 10.6.1940. French diplomats and politicians also referred to the "Latin brotherhood" in order to improve relations with Rome. Ciano, however, reacted irritated, claiming to have the sole right to interpret what was "Latin" and what was not. See Ciano Diary, Entry 12.2.1938.

Another example is the *Mostra d'arte italiana* (16 May to 22 July 1935) in Paris. While the French perceived the exhibition as an expression of "Latin friendship," Ciano saw it as a means of propaganda. In the heart of the French capital, Italy's importance for Western culture was highlighted by works of famous artists (for example, Michelangelo, Leonardo da Vinci) and by Italian celebrities attending the opening event, including Bottai and Ciano. See M. Laval, Ministre des Affaires Étrangères, a General Denain, Ministre de l'Air, Paris, 2 May 1935, in DDF, Serie 1, Vol. X, Doc. 287, 459n1, 460; "Italy's Finest Art on Exhibit in Paris," *New York Times*, 17 May 1935, 19; "La grande Esposizione d'arte italiana a Parigi," *Popolo d'Italia*, 17 May 1935, 1.

47 Ciano Diary, Entries 3.9.1939 and 8.6.1940; Bastianini, *Uomini, cose, fatti*, 257; Guariglia, *Ricordi*, 772. Apparently, Ciano already prophesized in October 1937 that Italy and France would have to protect civilization against Nazi Germany in the future. See Bottai, *Diario*, 120; Moseley, *Mussolini's Shadow*, 37.

48 See Telegramm Hassell (Rom) an Auswärtiges Amt (Berlin), 13 May 1937, in PAAA, Botschaft in Rom, 674b; Pirelli, *Taccuini*, 179–80.

49 See Loraine Diary, Entry 12.8.1935, in NA, FO 1011/245; L'Ambasciatore a Londra, Grandi, al Capo del Governo e Ministro degli Esteri, Mussolini, Londra, 17 August 1935, in DDI, Series 8, Vol. I, Doc. 765, 777–82; Eden, *Memoiren*, Vol. 1, 258; Mallett, "Fascist Foreign Policy," 164–7; Thorpe, *Eden*, 159.

50 Telegram Long (Rome) to Roosevelt (Washington), 6 September 1935, in FDR Library, PSF, Box 41, 1.

51 See Ciano Diary, Entries 9.2.1938, 25.8.1938, 17.5.1939, 10.5.1940, 8.11.1941, 11.12.1941, 27.12.1941, and 30.4.1942; Pirelli, *Taccuini*, 327, 348–51, and 373. Ciano's respect for the United States was also reflected in the attention he gave the American public before and during the Ethiopian War. See Telegramma Alfieri (Roma) a Ciano (Asmara), 27 October 1935, in ACS, MCP, Gabinetto, b. 17; Ciano, Testo del discorso, Asmara, 1.11.1935, in ibid.; "Il ministro volontario in Africa parla al popolo americano," *Corriere della Sera*, 8 September 1935, 1; "Speech of Ciano to American People," *The Times*, 9 September 1935.

For Mussolini's negative verdicts, see Ciano Diary, Entries 3.9.1937, 14.9.1937, 23.5.1938, 12.9.1938, and 29.9.1938; Bottai, *Diario*, 292; Federzoni, *Italia di ieri*, 34; Burgwyn, *Mussolini Warlord*, 103.

52 Di Rienzo, *Ciano*, 119; Santini, *Costanzo Ciano*, 152.

53 See Ciano Diary, Entries 19.2.1940, 10.5.1940, and 4.7.1940; Telegram Phillips (Rome) to Hull (Washington), 11 April 1940, in NARA, RG 59, M982, Reel 18, File 740.0011/2091; Namier, *Europe in Decay*, 116–17.

54 See Ciano Diary, Entries 13.10.1939, 18.1.1940, 7.6.1940, and 4.7.1940; velina (26 May 1936), in Tranfaglia, *Stampa*, 149; Bottai, *Diario*, 62 and 95. For the propaganda, see *L'illustrazione Italiana*, 18 August 1940, cover and 239–71.

55 See reports in ASMAE, Affari Politici, Cina, b. 11; Telegram Wilson (Geneva) to Hull (Washington), 7 February 1932, in NARA, RG 59, M976, Reel 65, File 793.94 Commission/77; Telegram Gilbert (Geneva) to Hull (Washington), 9 February 1932, in ibid., File 793.94 Commission/90; Telegram Gilbert (Geneva) to Hull (Washington) 7 March 1932, in NARA, RG 59, M976, Reel 65, File 793.94 Commission/133; Mr. Brenan (Shanghai) to Mr. Holman (Beijing), 14.2.1932, in DBFP, II, Vol. IX, Doc. 448, 482–3.

Information about his activities can be found in NARA, RG 59, M976, Reels 65 and 83; NARA, RG 59, LM63, Reels 63 and 66–8; ASMAE, Affari Politici, Cina, b. 11; Thorne, *Limits of Foreign Policy*, 202–72.

56 Il Ministro a Shanghai, Ciano, al Capo del Governo e Ministro degli Esteri, Mussolini, Shanghai, 19 November 1932, in DDI, Serie 7, Vol. XII, Doc. 441, 558–9.

57 See L'Ambasciatore a Tokio, Auriti, al Capo del Governo e Ministro degli Esteri, Mussolini, Tokio, 5 June 1935, in DDI, Serie 8, Vol. I, Doc. 338, 345; Del Boca, "Yperit-Regen," 50; Ishida, "Racisms Compared," 383–4.

58 Ciano Diary, Entries 20.2.1942, 24.2.1942, 10.3.1942, 15.3.1942, and 11.4.1942.

59 Ciano Diary, Entries 29.9.1937, 23.10.1937, 8.9.1939, and 1.11.1941.

60 Varè, *Two Impostors*, 89–91; Ward Price, *Führer und Duce*, 258.

61 Ciano Diary, Entry 20.11.1937; Burgwyn, *Italian Foreign Policy*, 98; Visser, "Fascist Doctrine," 12.

62 See Ciano Diary, Entries 1.9.1939 and 30.8.1942; Telegramm Hassell (Rom) an AA (Berlin), 29 May 1936, in PAAA, Rundfunkpolitische Abteilung, R122638, E529616; velina (5 February 1935), in Tranfaglia, *Stampa*, 91; Whitaker, *We Cannot Escape History*, 59–62. For Ciano's fears, see Ciano Diary, Entries 13.3.1938 and 21.4.1938; Memorandum by Jay Pierrepont Moffat, 2 June 1938, in NARA, RG 59, LM192, Reel 7, File 762.65/464.

63 Ciano Diary, Entry 15.3.1939; Telegram Bullitt (Paris) to Hull (Washington), 30 March 1939, in NARA, RG 59, M982, Reel 1, File 740.00/709; Burgwyn, *Italian Foreign Policy*, 98; Viani, "*Il Telegrafo*," 71.

Contemporaries and scholars have claimed that Ciano approved the *Anschluss* of Austria (see Anfuso, *Rom – Berlin*, 21; Goebbels, *Tagebücher*, Part I, Vol. 3, 2, Entries 10.6.1936 and 12.6.1936, 102–4; Pietromarchi, *Diari e le agende*, 93n27). However, Ciano's attitude was more complex. As minister of propaganda, he used the Austrian question to attack Suvich; yet, as soon as he was foreign minister, he changed course. Now he wanted to delay the inevitable *Anschluss* as long as possible. See Ciano Diary, Entries 24.11.1937 and 11.2.1938; Brief Hassell (Rom) an Göring (Berlin), 30 January 1937, in PAAA, Botschaft in Rom – Geheimakten, 45, 462829–31; Der Botschafter in Rom von Hassell an das Auswärtige Amt, Rom, 18 June 1936, in ADAP, Serie C, Vol. V, 2, Doc. 381, 595; Deutsch-italienisches

Protokoll, Berlin, 23 October 1936, in ibid., Doc. 624, 1057; Der Botschafter in Rom von Hassell an das Auswärtige Amt, Telegramm, 24 April 1937, in ibid., Vol. VI, 2, Doc. 333, 720–2; Le Ministre de Suisse à Vienne, M. Jaeger, au Chef du Départment politique, G. Motta, Wien, 18 February 1938, in DDS, Vol. 12, Doc. 210, 464.

64 Ciano Diary, Entry 18.4.1938.

65 See also Ciano Diary, Entries 25.2.1939, 18.3.1939, and 20.9.1939.

66 Ciano Diary, Entry 18.3.1938. For the importance of stereotypes in Italian society, see Goeschel, "Parallel History," 615–16.

67 Kallis, *Fascism and Genocide*, 64.

68 Row, "Mobilizing the Nation," 147 and 153.

69 See Ciano Diary, Entries 4.1.2.1939, 12.12.1939, 17.1.1940, 25.4.1941, 25.11.1941, and 27.5.1942; Telegram Loraine (Rome) to Halifax (London), 5 December 1939, in FO 1011/66; Il Capo del Servizio Informazioni Militari, Amè, al Ministro degli Esteri, Ciano, 14 March 1942, in DDI, Serie 9, Vol. VIII, Doc. 369, 413–14; Colloquio del Conte Ciano col Führer, col Marsciallo Göring e col Ministro degli Affari Esteri Ribbentrop, 24.-27.11.1941, in Ciano, *L'Europa*, 693.

70 Ciano Diary, Entries 26.1.1942 and 16.3.1942. Ciano was worried that the Allies would blame Italy for the famine. See Aide Memoire, 3 October 1942, in FDR Library, Sumner Welles Papers, Box 85.

71 Colloqui del Conte Ciano col Führer, col Maresciallo Göring e col Ministro degli Affari Esteri von Ribbentrop, 24.11.1941, in Ciano, *L'Europa*, 692–3. See also Aly and Heim, *Vordenker der Vernichtung*, 365.

72 Ciano Diary, Entry 27.3.1940.

73 Ciano Diary, Entries 1.5.1942 and 2.5.1942.

74 For Hitler, see Ciano Diary, Entries 19.3.1939, 8.9.1939, 1.10.1939, 20.1.1941, 5.5.1941, 25.10.1941, 21.12.1941, 29.4.1942, and 19.12.1942; Ciano, *My Truth*, 119; Vergani, *Ciano*, 36; Moseley, *Mussolini's Shadow*, 15 and 29.

For Göring, see Ciano Diary, Entries 17.4.1938, 20.4.1938, 28.10.1938, 2.10.1939, 6.2.1940, 23.4.1940, 20.7.1940, 28.1.1941, 1.6.1941, 2.2.1942, and 4.2.1942; Burgwyn, *Italian Foreign Policy*, 153; Rintelen, *Mussolini*, 26–7; Susmel, *Vita sbagliata*, 66.

For Ribbentrop, see Ciano Diary, Entries 5.2.1938, 6.5.1938, 23.10.1938, 21.8.1939, 28.8.1939, 25.9.1939, 28.9.1939, 5.10.1939, 26.10.1939, 7.11.1939, 2.1.1940, 9.4.1940, 27.4.1940, 4.12.1940, 13.5.1941, and 29.4.1942; Telegram Rendel (Sofia) to Strang (London), 20 October 1939, in NA, FO 371/23810, R9517/57/22, 319–322; Il Ministro degli Esteri, Ciano, all'Ambasciatore a Berlin, Attolico, Roma, 8 November 1939, in DDI, Serie 9, Vol. II, Doc. 144, 104–5; Telegramm Mackensen (Rom) an Ribbentrop (Berlin), 5 February 1943, in PAAA, Büro des Staatssekretärs, R29638, Fiche 538; Telegramm Ciano (Vatikan) an Ribbentrop (Berlin), 20 March 1943, in ibid.,

Fiche 540; Ciano, *Mia Vita*, 57; Ribbentrop, *Zwischen London und Moskau*, 290; Weizsäcker, *Erinnerungen*, 160; Welles, *Time for Decision*, 80 and 136–7; Bloch, *Ribbentrop*, 140–1.

According to Baldur von Schirach, he had a good relationship with Ciano. See Telegram Phillips (Rome) to Hull (Washington), 2 October 1936, in NARA, RG 59, LM192, Reel 6, File 762.65/226; Schirach, *Ich glaubte an Hitler*, 224.

75 Ciano Diary, Entries 17.1.1941 and 2.6.1941; Ciano, *My Truth*, 174. Ciano also did not believe Berlin's official statements about Rudolf Hess's flight to Great Britain. See Ciano Diary, Entries 12.5.1941 and 15.5.1941.

76 Ciano Diary, Entries 5.12.1939, 26.2.1940, 19.3.1942, 25.9.1942, and 27.10.1942.

77 König, *Kooperation als Machtkampf*.

78 Gobetti, "Royal Army's Betrayal?" 105; Reichman and Golan, "Irredentism," 57

79 Gooch, *Mussolini and his Generals*, 13.

80 Mussolini, *Scritti politici*, 196; Troha, "Ethnopolitische Flurbereinigungen," 60.

81 Ciano Diary, Entries 29.4.1941 and 13.5.1941. For the Italianization policy, see Entry 18.5.1941; documents in ASMAE, Gabinetto, b. 1507, fasc. AG Croazia 54; Telegramm Bismarck (Rom) an AA (Berlin), 24 December 1941, in PAAA, Botschaft in Rom – Geheimakten, 108, E247457–9.

82 Ciano Diary, Entry 24.2.1938.

83 During the Second World War, Ciano opposed plans by PNF secretary Vidussoni to have all Slovenes shot. See Ciano Diary, Entry 5.1.1942.

84 Ciano Diary, Entry 21.1.1940.

85 See Ciano Diary, Entries 24.3.1938, 25.2.1939, 30.3.1939, 15.5.1939, and 14.8.1939; Colloquio con l'ambasciata di Polonia, Roma, 27.6.1936, in Ciano, *L'Europa*, 26–7; Telegramm Hassell (Rom) an AA (Berlin), 14 May 1937, in PAAA, Botschaft in Rom, 674b, 2; Telegram Perth (Rome) to Halifax (London), 18 March 1939, in NA, FO 371/22439, R3116/1105/22; Telegram Loraine (Rome) to Halifax (London), 5 December 1939, in FO 1011/66; Ciano, *Außenpolitik Italiens*, 29.

86 Ciano Diary, Entry 25.2.1939.

87 See Ciano Diary, Entries 3.12.1937, 29.12.1937, 6.2.1938, 10.2.1938, 28.3.1938, 23.4.1938, 21.6.1938, 24.7.1938, and 6.12.1938; Ansaldo, *Giornalista*, 142.

88 Gordon, "Race," 299; Kallis, *Fascism and Genocide*, 29; Moses, "Empire," 34; Steinberg, *All or Nothing*, 220–35.

89 Sarfatti, *Jews in Mussolini's Italy*, 138.

90 See Ciano Diary, Entry 11.11.1938; Telegramma Ciano (Roma) a Attolico (Berlino) in ASMAE, Affari Politici, Germania, b. 46, fasc. Antisemitismo, 4022.

91 Sarfatti, *Jews in Mussolini's Italy*, 26.
92 Notiz, Bern, 6 October 1944, in USHMM, RG 58.003, Reel 18; Ansaldo, *Giornalista*, 143; Varè, *Two Impostors*, 177–8; Maryks, "*Pouring Jewish Water*," 135–9.
93 See Ciano Diary, Entry 11.11.1938; Lista, in USHMM, RG 40.002, Reel 4, Frame 5999–6000; Bericht Depaoli mit Sendung 37, Rom, 11 December 1941, in BArch, R58, AZ 9478, 050270. Pietromarchi was married to Emma Zuccari, a Trieste native of Jewish faith. See Pietromarchi, *Diari e le agende*, 14–16.
94 Ciano Diary, Entry 3.12.1937.
95 Michaelis, "Attitude of the Fascist Regime," 21.
96 See Capristo, "Exclusion of Jews"; Finzi, "Damage to Italian Culture"; Nidam-Orvieto, "Impact of Anti-Jewish Legislation"; Stille, "Double Blind"; Toscano, "Italian Jewish Identity."
97 See Levis Sullam, *Italian Executioners*; Schlemmer and Woller, "Italienische Faschismus," 195.
98 For the fascist belief that transnational ideologies pose a threat to the Italian nation, see Mann, *Fascists*, 35; Paxton, "Fünf Stadien des Faschismus," 59.
99 Varè, *Lachende Diplomat*, 436; Smith, *Imperial Designs*, 114.
100 Lettera Ciano (Pechino) a Maria Rosa Oliver (Buenos Aires), 6 April 1928, in Mudd Library, Maria Rosa Oliver Papers, Box 3, Folder 4, Series 2a; Varè, *Lachende Diplomat*, 369–70.
101 Varè, *Lachende Diplomat*, 441 and 582; De Giorgi, "Shadow of Marco Polo," 579.
102 See Il Ministro a Shanghai, Ciano, al Capo del Governo e Ministro degli Esteri, Mussolini, Shanghai, 19 November 1932, in DDI, Serie 7, Vol. XII, Doc. 441, 558–9; "Italy Aids China in Air," *New York Times*, 28 April 1935, 21; Ferrante, "Missione Aeronautica;" Smith, *Imperial Designs*, 122.
103 On 12 December 1936, officers under the leadership of Zhang Xueliang mutinied and imprisoned Chiang Kai-Shek for two weeks. The exact circumstances of the incident are controversial. However, it resulted in the formation of a "Second United Front" between nationalists and communists against Japanese aggression.
104 Cited in Guerri, *Amore fascista*, 80–1.
105 Ciano Diary, Entry 23.8.1937.
106 L'Ambasciatore a Shanghai, Taliani, al Ministro degli Esteri, Ciano, Shanghai, 31 January 1940, in DDI, Serie 9, Vol. III, Doc. 237, 199.
107 Schreiber, "Politische und militärische Entwicklung," 12. Ciano entered the Soviet embassy in Rome for the first time in November 1940, when the Italian attack on Greece collapsed. See Ciano Diary, Entry 7.11.1940.

In addition, Mussolini sought a separate peace with Moscow as soon as the Axis was forced onto the defensive. See Di Rienzo, *Ciano*, 1504.

108 Blum was also disliked by other Italian diplomats, including Grandi, Suvich, and Cerruti. See Collotti, *Fascismo e politica*, 280–6.

109 Ibid., 292. For the British conservatives, see Messerschmidt, "Außenpolitik und Kriegsvorbereitung," 682–3.

110 See Summary of Dispatch No. 3165 from American Embassy in Berlin, 24 December 1936, in FDR Library, PSF, Box 32, Folder: William E. Dodd; Ciano, *Außenpolitik Italiens*, 42; Ishida, "Racism Compared," 386.

111 Ciano Diary, Entries 6 16.4.1939, 19.7.1939, and 21.7.1939.

112 See Ciano Diary, Entries 8.12.1938 and 21.8.1939; Sir P. Loraine (Rome) to Viscount Halifax (London), 1 September 1939, in DBFP, Series III, Vol. VII, No. 677, 491; SD des Reichsführer SS an den SD Leitabschnitt Berlin, 11 June 1940, in BArch, R58, AZ 9478, 090022; Mackensen, Bemerkungen zu den deutsch-italienischen Beziehungen, Rom, 3 January 1940, in PAAA, Mackensen, 7, 440272–3; Bottai, *Diario*, 164–5; Ojetti, *Taccuini*, 540.

Although Ciano had only been informed of the Hitler-Stalin Pact on 21 August, the first reports of a possible agreement between Berlin and Moscow had already been received in Rome in June. However, Ciano ignored them since he considered a rapprochement between the Soviet Union and Germany impossible. See Telegramma Internonciature Apostolique The Hague a Maglione (Roma), 17 June 1939, in USHMM, RG 76.002, B, 75; Magistrati, *Prologo del dramma*, 24; Sullivan, "'Where One Man,'" 132–3.

113 Ciano Diary, Entries 26.9.1939 and 28.12.1939; Telegram Phillips (Rome) to Hull (Washington), 22 August 1939 in NARA, RG 59, M982, Reel 8, File 740.00/2101.

114 "Rundfunkansprache des italienischen Außenministers," *Völkischer Beobachter*, 11 September 1941. See also Le Ministre de Suisse à Rome, P. Ruegger, au Chef du Département politique, M. Pilet-Golaz, Rome, 24 June 1941, in DDS, Vol. 14, Doc. 64, 200; "La lotta contro il bolscevismo," *La Stampa*, 12 September 1941, 1. The participation was supported by the Catholic Church. See Goeschel, *Mussolini and Hitler*, 216.

For the scepticism, see Ciano Diary, Entries 10.10.1941, 11.10.1942, and 24.3.1942; Phillips Diary, Entry 12.9.1941, in Houghton Library, William Phillips, Box 14/27, Folder 7.

115 Ciano Diary, Entry 12.12.1937.

116 Ciano Diary, Entry 6.11.1937.

117 For Ciano's actions, see Arielli, *Fascist Italy*, 84; MacDonald, "Radio Bari," 200–4. For the scholarship, see Burgwyn, "Diplomacy," 318; Mallet, *The Italian Navy*, 2. For Ciano's anti-British statements, see Ciano Diary, Entries 1.11.1937, 6.11.1937, 22.11.1937, 12.12.1937, 19.12.1937, 3.1.1938, 20.1.1938, and 14.2.1938; Telegram Perth (London) to FO (London), 3

January 1938, in NA, FO 371/22402, R67/23/22; Telegram (Geneva) to FO (London), 31 January 1938, in NA, FO 371/22437, R932/899/22.

118 Burgwyn, *Mussolini Warlord*, 7; Mallett, "Fascist Foreign Policy," 185.

119 Ciano Diary, Entries 22.12.1937, 23.12.1937, 3.2.1938, and 19.2.1938; Di Rienzo, *Ciano*, 645.

120 See Ciano Diary, Entries 16.9.1937, 24.12.1937, 1.2.1938, 6.2.1938, and 14.2.1938.

121 For Ciano's outreach to London starting November 1937, see Ciano Diary, Entry 19.2.1938; Ministerialdirektor von Weizsäcker an Botschafter von Hassell, Berlin, 22 November 1937, in ADAP, Serie D, Vol. 1, Doc. 34, 59; Der Deutsche Botschafter in Rom an das Auswärtige Amt, Telegramm, 4 December 1937, in ibid., Doc. 62, 83; Lettera del Conte Ciano all'Ambasciatore a Londra, Grandi, Roma, 16 February 1938, in DDI, Serie 8, Vol. VIII, 191; Cooper, *Old Men Forget*, 214–15; Pirelli, *Taccuini*, 204; Mills, "Sir Joseph Ball," 300.

122 Ciano Diary, Entry 21.2.1938; Telegram Phillips (Rome) to Hull (Washington), 24 February 1938, in LoC, Cordell Hull Papers, Reel 16.

123 See Colloquio col ministro von Neurath, Berlino, 21.10.1936, in Ciano, *L'Europa*, 88; Colloquio col Führer, Berchtesgaden, 24.10.1936, in ibid., 97; Telegramma Grandi (London) a Ciano (Roma), 5 November 1936, in ASMAE, Carte Grandi, b. 43, fasc. 107; Telegramm Bülow-Schwante (Berlin) an Weizsäcker (Berlin), 22 September 1937, in PAAA, Geheime Reichssachen, R61140, 14–16; Gafencu, *Last Days*, 156; Rintelen, *Mussolini*, 15; Messerschmidt, "Außenpolitik und Kriegsvorbereitung," 610–11; Thorpe, *Eden*, 180.

As early as the 1920s, contemporaries observed a deterioration in Franco-Italian relations. See D'Abernon, *Botschafter der Zeitenwende*, 291.

124 In October 1936, Ciano told a less than enthusiastic Hermann Göring that the Mediterranean belonged to Italy, while Germany could expand into Northern Europe. See Aufzeichnungen über die Begegnung zwischen dem Generalobersten Göring und dem italienischen Außenminister Graf Ciano, Budapest, 13 October 1936, in ADAP, Serie C, Vol. V, 2, Doc. 600, 1008–9.

125 See Ciano Diary, Entry 29.9.1937; Telegram Dodd (Berlin) to Hull (Washington), 15 October 1936, in NARA, RG 59, LM192, Reel 6, File 762.65/238; Bottai, *Diario*, 120; Ciano, *Außenpolitik Italiens*, 16.

126 Ciano Diary, Entries 5.5.1938 and 12.5.1938; Der Reichsminister des Auswärtigen Freiherr von Neurath, an Ministerialdirektor Freiherr von Weizsäcker, Leinfelden, 31 July 1937, in ADAP, Serie C, Vol. VI, 2, Doc. 502, 1047; Rintelen, *Mussolini*, 44–51; Weizsäcker, *Erinnerungen*, 158–9; Burgwyn, *Italian Foreign Policy*, 175; Watt, "Hitler's Visit," 28.

For Mussolini's flirtation with a military Italian-German alliance in 1938 and Ciano's objection, see Ciano Diary, Entries 27.6.1938, 11.7.1938, 15.7.1938, 10.9.1938, 30.9.1938, 27.10.1938, 28.10.1938, 29.10.1938, and 1.1.1939; Telegram Raber (Rome) to Hull (Washington), 15 July 1938, in NARA, RG 59, LM192, Reel 7, File 762.65/478; Gafencu, *Last Days*, 156; Watt, "Rome-Berlin Axis," 536.

Ciano was only willing to sign a "pact of mutual respect," which would have preserved Austria's autonomy. Berlin brusquely declined. See Ciano Diary, Entries 30.4.1938 and 1.5.1938; Aufzeichnungen des Reichsministers des Auswärtigen Freiherr von Neurath, Berlin, 7 July 1937, in ADAP, Serie C, Vol. IV, 2, Doc. 453, 955; Der Botschafter in Rom an Ministerialdirektor Freiherr von Weizsäcker, Rom, 29 July 1937, in ibid., Doc. 499, 1032–5.

127 Pirelli, *Taccuini*, 179. This opinion was shared by Ciano's close advisor Ansaldo. See Ansaldo, *Giornalista*, 125–6; Viani, "*Il Telegrafo*," 77.

128 For example, see Ciano Diary, Entries 3.4.1938, 17.3.1938, 21.4.1938, 19.8.1938, 5.9.1938, 1.12.1938, 15.3.1938, and 17.3.1939; Telegramma Ciano (Roma) a Attolico (Berlino), 23 March 1938, in ASMAE, Affari Politici, Germania, b. 46, fasc. Alto Adige; Telegramma Ciano (Roma) a Magistrati (Berlino), 20 April 1938, in ibid.; Der Deutsche Botschafter in Rom an das Auswärtige Amt, 22 April 1938, in ADAP, Serie D, Vol. I, Doc. 749, 883–6; Telegramm Mackensen (Rom) an AA (Berlin), 3 May 1939, in PAAA, Botschaft in Rom – Geheimakten, 52, 465224–7; Telegramm Mackensen (Rom) an AA (Berlin), 17 March 1939, in ibid., 465300–3; Pietromarchi, *Diari e le agende*, 265.

129 For the continuation of the *peso determinante* policy under Ciano, see Ciano Diary, Entry 16.3.1939; König, *Kooperation als Machtkampf*, 327; Schreiber, "Politische und militärische Entwicklung," 100. Diplomats such as Grandi and Pietromarchi also preferred the *peso determinante* strategy and did not want to risk a rift between Italy and Britain. See Pietromarchi, *Diari e le agende*, 155; Gilbert, "Ciano," 513; Rodogno, "Fascism and War," 243.

130 Ciano Diary, Entries 5.10.1938 and 18.8.1939.

131 Ciano Diary, Entries 9.3.1938 and 20.12.1938; Der Gesandte in Belgrad von Heeren an das Auswärtige Amt, Belgrad, 8 March 1937, in ADAP, Serie C, Vol. VI.1, Doc. 254, 544–5; Ciano, *Außenpolitik Italiens*, 16; Rintelen, *Mussolini*, 30; Viani, "*Il Telegrafo*," 84.

132 Ciano Diary, Entry 9.9.1937; Moffat Diary, Entry 31.8.1937, in Houghton Library, Jay Pierrepont Moffat, Vol. 39.

133 Ciano Diary, Entry 29.8.1938; Pirelli, *Taccuini*, 180.

134 16 aprile 1938 L'accordo di Pasqua, 20 April 1938, in ASL, Giornale Luce, B129108.

135 Ciano Diary, Entries 10.4.1938, 12.4.1938, and 13.4.1938; Ciano, *Außenpolitik Italiens*, 17.

136 See Ciano Diary, Entries 14.2.1938 and 13.12.1941; Telegramm Mackensen (Rom) an AA (Berlin), 28 November 1938, in PAAA, Botschaft in Rom – Geheimakten, 51, 464890–1; Colloquio con l'Ambasciatore di Turchia, Roma, 15.6.1936, in Ciano, *L'Europa*, 21; Ciano, *Außenpolitik Italiens*, 7–8; Bastianini, *Uomini, cose, fatti*, 238; Magistrati, *Prologo del dramma*, 113.

137 See Colloquio con l'Ambasciata di Gran Bretagna, Roma, 30.6.1936, in Ciano, *L'Europa*, 29; Il Ministro degli Esteri, Ciano, all'Ambasciatore a Buenos Aires, Arlotta, Roma, 14 June 1936, in DDI, Serie 8, Vol. IV, Doc. 261, 316; Il Ministro degli Esteri, Ciano, all'Ambasciatore a Bruxelles et. al., in ibid., Doc. 352, 401.

138 Despite the establishment of the Lytton Commission by the League of Nations on 21 November 1931 to investigate Japan's invasion of China, Tokyo attacked Shanghai in early 1932. See the documents in DBFP, II, Vol. IX; Hell, *Mandschurei-Konflikt*; Woodhead, *Current Comment*, 31.

139 See Le Vicomte Davignon, Ministre de Belgique à Berlin, à M. Spaak, Ministre des Affaires Étrangères, Berlin, 13 November 1936, in DDB, Vol. 4, Doc. 169, 431; Goebbels, *Tagebücher*, Part I, Vol. 4, Entry 15.5.1937, 139–40.

140 Memorandum of Conversation, 19 December 1939, in LoC, Breckinridge Long Papers, Box 208; Phillips Diary, Entry 15.1.1940, in Houghton Library, William Phillips, Box 11/22, Folder 2; Armellini, *Diario*, 15; Bottai, *Diario*, 221.

Even in the summer of 1939 Ciano believed in a "peaceful solution." See Ciano Diary, Entries 4.8.1939, 6.8.1939, 9.8.1939, and 10.8.1939; Letter Loraine (Rome) to Cadogan (London), 6 July 1939, in NA, FO 1011/204; Telegram Phillips (Rome) to Hull (Washington), 22 July 1939, in NARA, RG 59, M982, Reel 7, File 740.00/1942.

141 See Ciano Diary, Entries 25.8.1938 and 17.5.1939; Sir P. Loraine to Viscount Halifax, Rome, 2 September 1939, in DBFP, Series III, Vol. VII, Doc. 711, 508; Minute Sir P. Loraine, Rome, 2 September 1939, in ibid., Doc. 731, 520–1; Sir P. Loraine to Viscount Halifax, Rome, 2 September 1939, in ibid., Doc. 739, 523–4; Reynaud, *Thick of the Fight*, 235–7.

142 See Ciano Diary, Entries 16.9.1937, 29.4.1939, 2.5.1939, and 2.6.1939; Favagrossa, *Perché perdemmo la guerra*.

143 Ciano Diary, Entries 6.8.1939 and 9.8.1939.

144 Ciano Diary, Entry 11.8.1939.

145 Ciano Diary, Entry, 12.8.1939.

146 *Mussolini and I*, directed by Alberto Negrin; Guariglia, *Ricordi*, 330–1; Rintelen, *Mussolini*, 102.

147 Pietromarchi, *Diari e le agende*, 326.

148 Ciano immediately informed Western ambassadors and journalists about his version of the events. See Telegram Loraine (Rome) to FO (London), 22 August 1939, in NA, FO 1011/66; Telegram Loraine (Rome) to Cadogan (London), 23 August 1939, in NA, FO 371/23827, R6472/269/G, 164; Telegram Phillips (Rome) to Hull (Washington), 18 August 1939, in NARA, RG 59, M1423, Reel 2, File 865.00/1843; Telegram Phillips (Rome) to Hull (Washington), 17 August 1939, in FDR Library, PSF, Box 22; Bonnet, *Vor der Katastrophe*, 249; Pirelli, *Taccuini*, 226; Whitaker, *We Cannot Escape History*, 61.

149 See Ciano Diary, Entries 17.8.1939 and 31.12.1939; Telegramm Reichsminister der Finanzen (Rom) an Reichsministerium des Äußeren (Berlin), 23 August 1939, in BArch, R2, AZ 24243, Fiche 1, 10; Goebbels, *Tagebücher*, Part I, Vol. 7, Entry 21.10.1939, 162; Colloquio fra il Ministro degli Esteri del Reich e il Duce in presenza del Conte Ciano e dell'Ambasciatore von Mackensen, Roma, 10.3.1940, in Ciano, *L'Europa*, 512–27; Mallett, *Mussolini*, 210–11; Salerno, *Vital Crossroads*, 145.

150 For these plans, see Ciano Diary, Entries 5.9.1939, 20.9.1939, 12.10.1939, 26.12.1939, 21.1.1940, and 22.1.1940.

151 Ciano Diary, Entry 5.3.1940.

152 "Italy Is Passing for Balkan Bloc," *New York Times*, 9 September 1939. Ciano used economic arguments to convince Mussolini and the Germans of the pact's benefits. See Ciano Diary, Entries 5.9.1939 and 28.9.1939; Marzari, "Italian-led Balkan Bloc," 771–4.

153 Sullivan, "'Where One Man,'" 143.

154 See Colloqui col Ministro degli Affari Esteri di Ungheria Conte Csáky, Venezia, 6–7 gennaio 1940, in Ciano, *L'Europa*, 501–4; "Csaky Ends Italian Visit Abruptly," *New York Times*, 8 January 1940, 1; Rossi, *Mussolini e il diplomatico*, 235.

155 Il Ministro degli Esteri, Ciano, al Capo del Governo, Mussolini, Venezia, 6–7 January 1940, in DDI, Serie 9, Vol. III, Doc. 44, 29–31; Moffat Diary, Entry 27.2.1940, in FDR Library, Sumner Welles Papers, Box 211, Folder: Moffat Diary; Goebbels, *Tagebücher*, Part I, Vol. 7, Entry 9.1.1940, 264.

Ciano's attempt to conduct a foreign policy independent of Berlin was not limited to Europe. In January 1940 he intended to recognize Wang Jingwei's puppet regime in Nanjing, hoping that his personal relations with Wang would make Rome Nanjing's preferred European partner. However, his plan was suppressed, and Germany and Italy eventually recognized Wang in July 1941. See Il Ministro degli Esteri, Ciano, a Wang Ching-Wei, Roma, 10 January 1940, in DDI, Serie 9, Vol. III, Doc. 71, 51; L'Ambasciatore a Shanghai, Taliani, al Ministro degli Esteri, Ciano, Shanghai, 5 March 1940, in ibid., Doc. 452, 386–7; Il Ministro degli Esteri, Ciano, all'Ambasciatore a Berlino, Attolico, Roma, 30 March 1940, in ibid., Doc. 652, 560–1.

156 See Ciano Diary, Entry 10.5.1940; Telegram Phillips (Rome) to Hull (Washington), 11 April 1940, in NARA, RG 59, M982, Reel 18, File 740.0011/2091; Bonnet, *Vor der Katastrophe*, 315; Reynaud, *Thick of the Fight*, 398.

157 Mackensen, Aufzeichnungen, Rom, 14 December 1939, in PAAA, Mackensen, 7, 440254.

158 See Ciano Diary, Entry 3.5.1940. Ciano got used to the idea of a "short" war in mid-May. See Entry 14.5.1940. But even then, Joseph Goebbels called Ciano a "retarding element" that prevented Italy's entry into the war. See Goebbels, *Tagebücher*, Part I, Vol. 8, Entry 29.5.1940, 142.

159 See Ciano Diary, Entry 10.4.1940; Telegram Biddle (Warsaw) to Hull (Washington), 16 April 1940, in NARA, RG 59, M982, Reel 18, File 740.0011EW/2246; Telegram Kennedy (London) to Hull (Washington), 26 April 1940, in ibid., Reel 19, File 740.0011EW/2497.

160 Ciano Diary, Entries 28.9.1939, 5.10.1939, and 5.12.1939.

161 Ciano Diary, Entries 13.8.1939, 17.8.1939, 28.8.1939, 30.8.1939, and 12.9.1939.

162 Bottai, *Diario*, 150–1. For Ciano's affection for his sister, see "Vivo cordoglio per la morte della contessa Magistrati-Ciano," *La Stampa*, 23 October 1939, 4.

163 Ciano Diary, Entry 21.5.1940; Colloquio con il Ministro degli Esteri del Reich von Ribbentrop, Monaco, 19.6.1940, in Ciano, *L'Europa*, 562–5; Colloquio del Conte Ciano col Führer, Berlino, 7.7.1940, in ibid., 572; Meissner, *Staatssekretär*, 546–7; Arielli, *Fascist Italy*, 167.

164 Cavallero, *Comando Supremo*, 63. Malta has always been a target of Italian expansionism, but Rome was always hesitant to attack. See Telegram Phillips (Rome) to Hull (Washington), 21.5.1940, in NARA, RG 59, M982, Reel 20, File 740.0011/2855 2/28. For Ciano's attitude, see Ciano Diary, Entries 22.4.1942, 12.5.1942, 31.5.1942, and 20.6.1942; Carboni, *Memorie*, 133–7.

165 See Ciano Diary, Entries 4.10.1940, 24.10.1941, 9.6.1941, 18.11.1941, 29.12.1941, 30.12.1941, 1.1.1942, 20.1.1942, and 15.2.1942; Il Ministro degli Esteri, Ciano, all'Ambasciatore a Berlino, Alfieri, Roma, 17 May 1941, in DDI, Serie 9, Vol. VII, Doc. 123, 119; "'Hands off' at Vichy Covers Italy's Policy," *New York Times*, 20 April 1942, 4; Pirelli, *Taccuini*, 280–2 and 320; Weizsäcker, *Weizsäcker-Papiere*, 220; Burgwyn, *Mussolini Warlord*, 128–33.

166 See Goeschel, *Mussolini and Hitler*, 227.

167 Ciano Diary, Entries 20.5.1940, 1.6.1940, and 24.6.1940; Le Ministre de Suisse à Rome, P. Ruegger, au Chef du Départment politique, M. Pilet-Golaz, Rom, 16 July 1940, in DDS, Vol. 13, Doc. 341, 831; Guerri, *Giuseppe Bottai*, 298; Pirelli, *Taccuini*, 249.

168 Ciano Diary, Entry 12.11.1940; Rintelen, "Mussolinis Parallelkrieg," 25–6.

169 Ortona, *Diplomazia*, 109; König, *Kooperation als Machtkampf*, 35.

170 For Ciano's isolated sparks of optimism in that time period, see Ciano Diary, Entries 22.12.1940, 27.11.1941, and 24.6.1942.

171 See Ciano Diary, Entries 20.7.1941 and 26.9.1941; Telegram Tittmann (Rome) to Hull (Washington), 9 April 1941, in NARA, RG 59, LM110, Reel 2, File 765.94/155; Telegramm Mackensen (Rom) an AA (Berlin), 8 November 1941, in PAAA, Botschaft in Rom – Geheimakten, 119, E249742–5; Japanese Ambassador (Rome), Reports Ciano's Account of Visit to Germany, 16 November 1941, in NA, HW 1/217, No. 097773; Japanese Ambassador (Rome), Reports Interview with Ciano, 14 June 1942, in NA, HW 1/645, No. 105538; Japanese Ambassador (Rome) to Foreign Ministry (Tokyo), 1 December 1942, in NA, HW 1/1189, No. 730; Il Ministero degli Esteri, Ciano, ai membri della Commissione Affari Esteri del Senato, Roma, 30 May 1942, in DDI, Serie 9, Vol. XIII, 626–42; Rossi, *Mussolini e il diplomatico*, 350.

Ciano also hoped to preserve Argentina's neutrality by spreading his calculated optimism because he regarded the country as an important ally against the United States. See Il Ministro degli Esteri, Ciano, all'Ambasciatore a Buenos Aires, Boscarelli, 6 May 1941, in DDI, Serie 9, Vol. VII, Doc. 62, 58; Argentine Ambassador (Rome) to Ministry for Foreign Affairs (Buenos Aires), 3 August 1942, in NA, HW 1/816, No. 65; Finchelstein, *Transatlantic Fascism*, 36–7.

172 Ciano Diary, Entries 1.11.1942, 8.11.1942, 17. 11.1942, and 30.11.1942.

173 Ciano Diary, Entry 12.11.1942; Telegram Japanese Ambassador (Rome) to Foreign Minister (Tokyo), 5 December 1942, in NA, HW 1/1189, No. 730; Telegram Argentine Ambassador (Rome) to Minister for Foreign Affairs (Buenos Aires), 3 August 1942, in NA, HW 1/816, No. 65; Schmidt, *Statist*, 553.

174 Ciano Diary, Entry 6.1.1943.

175 Ciano Diary, Entry 9.10.1942.

176 Telegram Squire (Geneva) to Hull (Washington), 23 June 1942, in NARA, RG 84, Entry 3208, Box 6, 3.

177 Appunto per il Duce, 6 November 1941, in ASMAE, Affari Politici, Iraq, b. 18, fasc. 2; Telegramma Anfuso (Berlino) a Ministero degli Affari Esteri (Roma), 2 December 1941, in ibid.; Appunto per L'Eccellenza il Ministro, 17 May 1942, in ibid.; Cenno riassuntivo sulla costituzione e funzionamento del centro militare A, Roma, 15 June 1942, in ibid.; Il Ministro degli Esteri, Ciano, al Capo di Stato Maggiore Generale, Cavallero, Roma, 17 March 1942, in DDI, Serie 9, Vol. VIII, Doc. 374, 418–19.

Ciano and the Germans fundamentally disagreed about the right strategies. See Ciano Diary, Entry 26.7.1942; Telegramma D'Ajeta (Roma) a Alfieri (Berlino), 18 May 1942, in ASMAE, Affari Politici, Iraq, b. 18, fasc. 2;

Missione Berlino – Promemoria N. 8, 26 May 1942, in ibid.; Il Ministro degli Esteri, Ciano, all'Ambasciatore a Berlino, Alfieri, 18 May 1942, in DDI, Serie 9, Vol. VIII, Doc. 549, 597; Burgwyn, *Mussolini Warlord*, 103; Krusenstjern, "*Dass es Sinn hat zu sterben*," 430–3.

178 See Ciano Diary, Entries 29.4.1941 and 22.1.1942; Convorbire cu Domnul Lorcovici, Ministrul de Externe al Croatiei, Berlin, 27 November 1941, in USHMM, RG 25.004, Reel 34, File 40040–41; Il Comandante della Seconda Armata, Roatta, al Capo di Stato Maggiore dell'Esercito, Ambrosio, e al Ministro degli Esteri, Ciano, 6 March 1942, in DDI, Serie 9, Vol. VIII, Doc. 345, 384–7; Hof, "'Legionaries of Civilization,'" 105–6; Jareb, "NDH's Relations;" Trifković, "Rivalry between Germany and Italy."

179 See Telegramm Luther (Berlin) an Deutsche Botschaft (Rom), 17 September 1942, in PAAA, Inland II, R100872, Fiche 2242, E401609–10; Comando Superiore Forze Armate al Comando del V. Corpo d'Armata et al., 17 October 1942, in USHMM, RG 40.014, Fiche 1; Nota Verbale, Roma, 26 October 1942, in USHMM, RG 40.002, Reel 6, Frame 10116; Ministero degli Affari Esteri (Roma) a Comando Supremo (Roma), 17 November 1942, in ibid., 10067–7; Ufficio Collegamento col Comando 2° Armata a R. Ministero dell'Interno et al., no date, in ibid., 10350–2.

For the "Jewish policy," see the documents in USHMM, RG 40.002, Reels 2 and 3; USHMM, RG 40.004, Reels 2, 26, 50–6, 61–5. For anti-Semitism in Vichy, see Caron, *Path to Vichy*; Marrus and Paxton, *Vichy France*.

180 Steinberg, *All or Nothing*, 169.

181 Telegram Ribière (Nice) to Secretary-General for the Police, 14.1.1943, in Poliakov and Sabille, *Jews under the Italian Occupation*, Doc. 2, 54. See also Telegramm Kasche (Agram) an Deutsche Botschaft in Rom, 20.10.1942, in *Judenverfolgung in Italien*, 99. For a discussion about the "Jewish policy" of the *Palazzo Chigi*, see Bernhard, "The Great Divide"; Hof, "Widerwillige Helfer"; Lagos, "Agony"; Nattermann, "Humanitäres Prinzip."

182 See Telegram Phillips (Rome) to Hull (Washington), 5 January 1938, in FDR Library, PSF, Box 21, 2; Pirelli, *Taccuini*, 179–80.

183 See Baxa, "Capturing the Fascist Moment"; Goeschel, *Mussolini and Hitler*.

184 For the importance of modern mass media for a performative diplomacy, see Goeschel, *Mussolini and Hitler*, 294.

185 These journalists included Virginio Gayda (*Giornale d'Italia*), Raffaele Mauri and Orio Vergani (both *Corriere della Sera*), Giovanni Ansaldo (*Il Telegrafo*), and Alfredo Signoretti (*La Stampa*). See Ansaldo, *Giornalista*; Signoretti, "*La Stampa*," 157; Viani, "*Il Telegrafo*," 77.

186 Telegram Perth (Rome) to Cadogan (London), 28 January 1938, in NA, FO 371/22402, R871/23/22.

187 German diplomats also acknowledged that Italy's isolation could bring the two countries together. See Politischer Bericht Hassell (Rom) an AA

(Berlin), 2 January 1936, in PAAA, Botschaft in Rom, 674a; Petersen, "Vorspiel zu 'Stahlpakt,'" 48.

188 Telegramm Lorenz (Berlin) an Deutsche Botschaft (Rom), 29 September 1936, in PAAA, Botschaft in Rom, 696a; Telegramm Hassell (Rom) an AA (Berlin), 12 October 1936, in ibid.; Aufzeichnungen des Reichsministers des Auswärtigen Freiherr von Neurath, Berlin, 30 September 1936, in ADAP, Serie C, Vol. V, 2, Doc. 562, 770–1; Colloquio col Führer, Berchtesgaden, 24.10.1936, in Ciano, *L'Europa*, 94–5; Petersen, *Hitler-Mussolini*, 491–2.

Ciano's first trip abroad actually led him to Budapest where he attended the funeral of Hungarian Prime Minister Gyula Gömbös who died on 6 October 1936. See "Goemboes Funeral Held in Budapest," *New York Times*, 11 October 1936, 39; Cornelius, *Hungary in World War II*, 55–6; Zeidler, *Gyula Gömbös*, 133–4.

189 Visita di Ciano a Berlino, 28 October 1936, in ASL, Giornale Luce, B097905; "Ciano Welcomed with Great Pomp," *New York Times*, 21 October 1936, 6; "Ciano Made a General," *New York Times*, 22 October 1936, 6; Dodd, *Ambassador Dodd's Diary*, 359; Signoretti, "*La Stampa*," 158–9.

190 "Graf Ciano Gast des Ministerpräsidenten Generaloberst Göring," *Völkischer Beobachter*, 24 October 1936, 7.

191 Magistrati, *Prologo del dramma*, 127–9.

192 Der Staatssekretär und Chef der Präsidialkanzlei an den stellvertretenden Gauleiter München-Oberbayern der NSDAP, Berlin, 16 February 1937, in BArch, R 55, AZ 512.

193 Mann, *Fascists*, 8 and 13.

194 Schieder, *Italienische Faschismus*, 77–8.

195 Cited in Bender, *Hitler Albums*, 9. See also Ciano Diary, Entries 27.8.1937 and 23.9.1939.

196 For Ciano's appearance, see the photographs in Getty Images, #548865665, #545966569, and #545975785; *Berliner Illustrierte Zeitung* 34, 24 August 1939; *L'Illustrazione Italiana*, 20 August 1939, 301; *Washington Post*, 12 August 1939, 5.

197 Ciano once again displayed his opposition to the war when he went to Berlin in the fall of 1939. At the train station in Rome he was wearing civilian clothes and accompanied by his wife and his son Fabrizio. See *L'Illustrazione Italiana*, 8 October 1939, 533.

198 Goeschel, "Staging Friendship," 160. The article provides a detailed description of the visit.

199 See "Munich's Packed for Il Duce's Visit," *New York Times*, 25 September 1937, 9; *L'Illustrazione Italiana*, 3 October 1937; Goebbels, *Tagebücher*, Part I, Vol. 4, Entry 24.8.1937, 277–80; Magistrati, *L'Italia a Berlino*, 66–83; Bender, *Hitler Albums*, 24–50 and 75; Michels, *Ideologie und Propaganda*, 162.

For the award, see Telegram Phillips (Rome) to Hull (Washington), 11 June 1937, in NARA, RG 59, LM192, Reel 6, File 762.65/323; Der Botschafter in Rom an das Auswärtige Amt, Rom, 25 May 1937, in ADAP, Serie C, Vol. VI, 2, Doc. 385, 834; Il viaggio del Duce in Germania, 1937, in ASL, Documentari, D025302.

The awarding of medals was another key element of performative diplomacy as it publicly emphasized the solidarity of countries and statesmen. For the bestowal of medals, see Ciano Diary, Entries 12.7.1938, 3.6.1939, 6.2.1940, 23.4.1940, 28.1.1942, and 10.1.1943; Rintelen, *Mussolini*, 26–7.

200 Goeschel, "Staging Friendship," 159.

201 Cited in Burgwyn, *Italian Foreign Policy*, 157. See also Duggan, *Fascist Voices*, 282; Goeschel, "Staging Friendship," 168.

202 Hassell, Aufzeichnung, Rom, 7 October 1937, in PAAA, Geheime Reichssachen, R61140, 28–31. See also Ciano Diary, Entry 24.9.1937; Anfuso, *Rom – Berlin*, 54.

203 Goeschel, "Staging Friendship," 168.

204 Ibid., 150 and 162.

205 "Reich Hails Ciano: Pact Signing Today," *New York Times*, 22 May 1939, 3; Goebbels, *Tagebücher*, Part I, Vol. 6, Entries 11.5.1939 and 17.5.1939, 344–5 and 350; Henderson, *Fehlschlag einer Mission*, 267. For the exact procedure and the German press reports, see documents in BArch, R901, AZ 60417.

206 Ciano Diary, Entry 23.5.1939, 356–7; *L'Illustrazione Italiana*, 28 May 1939, 1137–9; Getty Images #548865673 and #545726339.

207 Goebbels, *Tagebücher*, Part I, Vol. 6, Entries 1.6.1939 and 4.6.1939, 363–4 and 367–8.

208 Ciano Diary, Entry 21.5.1939.

209 Telegramm Kirk (Rome) to Hull (Washington), 17 February 1937, in NARA, RG 59, LM192, Reel 6, File 762.65/286; La visita di Goering a Roma, 20 January 1937, in ASL, Giornale Luce, B102705; Il maresciallo Goering visita Roma, 19 April 1939, in ibid. B149901.

210 Ciano Diary, Entry 3.5.1939; Rapporto, Milano, 30 June 1939, in ACS, MI, DGPS, b. 22 A, fasc. 1.

211 Ciano Diary, Entries 10.11.1937 and 15.11.1937; Luciolli, *Palazzo Chigi*, 45; Goeschel, *Mussolini and Hitler*, 97.

212 "Mussolini Greets Hitler in a Resplendent Rome," *New York Times*, 4 May 1938, 1. According to American information, 400 million lire were spent on the visit. See G2-Report, Paine, no date, in FDR Library, Harry L. Hopkins Papers, Box 188.

213 Telegram Phillips (Rome) to Hull (Washington), 13 May 1938, in NARA, RG 59, LM192, Reel 6, File 762.65/450; Ciano, *Quando il nonno*, 44.

214 Baxa, "Capturing the Fascist Moment," 230–4.

215 Telegram Putnam (Florence) to Phillips (Rome), 21 May 1938, in NARA, RG 59, LM192, Reel 7, File 762.65/461. Ciano had visited Florence in February to check the preparations for Hitler's visit. See Ciano Diary, Entry 27.2.1938. The removal and strict surveillance of German exiles and Jews were carried out in all of Italy. See Per la visita di Hitler a Roma, Roma, 17 January 1938, in USHMM, RG 40.004, Reel 50, Frame 98973.

216 Baxa, "Capturing the Fascist Moment," 227–9. See also Watt, "Rome-Berlin Axis," 521.

217 See Telegram Phillips (Rome) to Hull (Washington), 12 May 1938, in NARA, RG 59, LM192, Reel 6, File 762.65/450.

218 Baxa, "Capturing the Fascist Moment," 230–1.

219 For Hungary, see Ciano Diary, Entry 9.1.1938; Colloqui con Schuschnigg, Schmidt, Horthy, Darány e Kánya, Vienna-Budapest, 9–16.11.1936, in Ciano, *L'Europa*, 110; "Ciano Is Welcomed by Budapest Fete," *New York Times*, 14 November 1936, 7; Magistrati, *Prologo del dramma*, 140. For Poland, see Ciano Diary, Entries 26.2.1939 and 27.2.1939. For Romania, see Gafencu, *Last Days*, 156.

220 Ciano Diary, Entry 5.12.1937; Der Botschafter in Wien von Papen an das Auswärtige Amt, Telegramm, 30 November 1936, in ADAP, Serie C, Vol. VI, 1, Doc. 65, 128–9; "300,000 Acclaim Horthy in Rome," *New York Times*, 25 November 1936, 8.

221 See *L'Illustrazione Italiana* 11, 13 March 1938, cover and 337; Getty Images, #3352803, #541786943, #141557457, and #167639782.

222 Ciano Diary, Entry 5.12.1937; Djokić, "'Leader' or 'Devil'?" 155.

223 See, for example, *L'Illustrazione Italiana*, 1 May 1938, 645–96.

224 See Belgrado – La visita di Ciano, 22 April 1937, in ASL, Giornale Luce, B1082; La visita del primo ministro iugoslava, 15 December 1937, in ibid., B1219; L'incontro Ciano- Stojadinovic, 25 January 1939, in ibid., B1448; *L'Illustrazione Italiana*, 28 March 1937, 315; 4 April 1937, 330; 2 May 1937, 449; 12 December 1937, cover and 1521; 19 December 1937, 1549 and 1655; 22 January 1939, 114; and 29 January 1939, 188–9.

225 Aufzeichnungen des Vortragenden Legationsrates von Twardowski, Berlin, 30 April 1937, in ADAP, Serie C, Vol. IV, 1, Doc. 348, 754–5.

226 Ciano Diary, Entries 8.1.1939, 15.1.1939, and 19.1.1939; Pietromarchi, *Diari e le agende*, 254.

227 Colloquio col Presidente del Consiglio di Jugoslavia Stoiadinovic, Belgrado, 26.3.1937, in Ciano, *L'Europa*, 160–2.

228 See Ciano Diary, Entries 6.12.1938 and 24.1.1939; Aufzeichnungen von Reichsminister von Neurath, 21 October 1936, in PAAA, Botschaft in Rom – Geheimakten, 42, D682798.

229 Even a couple of days later Ciano had no clear picture of what had happened. See Ciano Diary, Entry 4.2.1939; Mackensen, Aktenvermerk, Rom,

7 February 1939, in PAAA, Mackensen, 7, 440171–2. After Stojadinović's removal, Ciano maintained friendly relations with him, thus proving that their mutual admiration was not only based on political factors. See Ciano Diary, Entry 25.6.1940.

230 Djokić, "'Leader' or 'Devil'?" 155–6.

231 Ciano Diary, Entry 7.2.1939.

232 See Ciano Diary, Entries 19.3.1939, 5.4.1939, and 26.5.1939.

233 Ciano Diary, Entries 1.11.1937 and 9.11.1937.

234 In May 1936, Ciano announced that Italy would leave the League of Nations. See Telegramm Kampenhoevener (Berlin) an Botschaft (Rom), no date, in PAAA, Botschaft in Rom, 674b; Telegramma Magistrati (Berlino) a Ciano (Roma), 28 December 1938, in ASMAE, Affari Politici, Italia, b. 50, fasc. 3; Pirelli, *Taccuini*, 180.

235 "Triple Pact Signed," *The Times*, 8 November 1937, 12.

236 Telegramm Hassell (Rom) an AA (Berlin), 13 May 1937, in PAAA, Botschaft in Rom, 674b; Telegram Phillips (Rome) to Hull (Washington), 20 January 1939, in FDR Library, PSF, Box 22. State receptions of Western politicians were often prepared as meticulously as the visits of politicians from authoritarian states. See Telegramm Mackensen (Rom) an AA (Berlin), 12 January 1939, in PAAA, Botschaft in Rom – Geheimakten, 52, 465144–7.

237 Ciano Diary, Entries 14.9.1938, 17.9.1938, 25.9.1939, and 29.9.1938; Goeschel, *Mussolini and Hitler*, 135.

238 Burgwyn, *Italian Foreign Policy*, 178.

239 Ciano Diary, Entries 19.9.1938, 20.9.1938, and 25.9.1938; Telegramm Mackensen (Rom) an AA (Berlin), 26 September 1938, in PAAA, Botschaft in Rom – Geheimakten, 50, 464525–7; Military Preparations: Mr. Gascoigne (Budapest) to Viscount Halifax, 18 September 1938, in DBFP, Series III, Vol. III, Doc. 9, 5–6; Sir G. Knox (Budapest) to Viscount Halifax, 21 September 1938, in ibid., Doc. 16, 11; Strang, "War and Peace," 167–8.

240 Ciano Diary, Entry 28.9.1938

241 See Ciano Diary, Entry 27.9.1938; Der Deutsche Botschafter in Rom an das Auswärtige Amt, Telegramm, 15 September 1938, in ADAP, Serie D, Vol. II, Doc. 494, 642; Pietromarchi, *Diari e le agende*, 191.

242 Burgwyn, *Italian Foreign Policy*, 179; Goeschel, *Mussolini and Hitler*, 138.

243 Der Botschafter in Rom an das Auswärtige Amt, Telegramm, 26 September 1938, in ADAP, Serie D, Vol. II, Doc. 627, 764.

244 Ciano Diary, Entry 28.9.1938.

245 L'atto conclusivo del "convegno a quattro" di Monaco, 5 October 1938, in ASL, Giornale Luce, B1386. For Italy's role during the conference, see Dogliani, "Faschistische Italien"; Woller, "Mythos der Moderation."

246 Getty Images #52017051, #545973691, and #545972341. Whenever Ciano wanted to stress Italy's military power, he wore his militia or his pilot

uniform in the presence of Western diplomats and statesmen. See Phillips Diary, Entry 7.4.1939, in Houghton Library, William Phillips, Box 10/19, Folder 2; *L'Illustrazione Italiana*, 15 January 1939, 70–1; Shirer, *Berlin Diary*, 156; Stafford, "Chamberlain-Halifax Visit."

247 Telegram Perth (Rome) to Halifax (London), 2 December 1938, in NA, FO 371/22439, R9699/899/22; *L'Illustrazione Italiana*, 4 December 1938, 947.

248 Deutsche Botschaft (Rom) an AA (Berlin), 1 December 1938, in PAAA, Botschaft in Rom, 809c, 2; Telegram Perth (Rome) to Halifax (London), 27 December 1938, in NA, FO 371/22796, R36/118/38, 115; Coulondré, *Von Moskau nach Berlin*, 337.

249 See Mackensen, Aufzeichnungen, Rom, 1 December 1938, in PAAA, Mackensen, 1, 64394; Telegram Perth (Rome) to Halifax (London), 2 December 1938, in NA, FO 371/22439, R9699/899/22, 6; "Bonnet Asks Italy to Explain Stand," *New York Times*, 2 December 1938, 1; Pietromarchi, *Diari e le agende*, 213; Guariglia, *Ricordi*, 371; Magistrati, *Prologo del dramma*, 41; Reynaud, *Thick of the Fight*, 148; Shirer, *Berlin Diary*, 154.

250 See Conseil Fédéral, Procès-verbal de la séance du 10 juillet 1936, 2 July 1936, in DDS, Vol. 11, Doc. 264, 772–6; Il Ministro degli Esteri, Ciano, al Capo del Governo, Mussolini, Roma, 30 June 1936, in DDI, Serie 8, Vol. IV, Doc. 413, 468; "Italy's Note to League," *The Times*, 1 July 1936, 16; Signoretti, "*La Stampa*," 95.

251 Ciano Diary, Entry 4.12.1938.

252 Ciano Diary, Entry 2.12.1938.

253 Deutsche Botschaft (Rom) an AA (Berlin), 1 December 1938, in PAAA, Botschaft in Rom, 809c, 3; Shorrock, *From Ally to Enemy*, 249.

254 Brunetta, *Tragedia*, 56–8; Shorrock, *From Ally to Enemy*, 251.

255 Even in the spring of 1939 Ciano, unlike Mussolini, showed little enthusiasm for these ideas. See Telegram Phillips (Rome) to Hull (Washington), 10 March 1939, in NARA, RG 59, CDF, Box 4355, File 762.94/299. But when Japan hesitated to join such an alliance, Ciano tended towards a pact between Rome and Berlin. See Ciano Diary, Entry 8.2.1939 and 3.3.1939.

256 Ciano Diary, Entry 12.1.1939. See also Telegram Hoare (Bucharest) to Sargent (London), 13 January 1939, in NA, FO 371/23784, R581/1/22, 147.

257 König, *Freundschafts- und Bündnispakt*, n10. See also Ciano Diary, Entry 13.5.1939; Goebbels, *Tagebücher*, Part I, Vol. 6, Entry 8.5.1939, 341–2.

258 See Ciano Diary, Entry 12.1.1939; Telegram Hoare (Bucharest) to FO (London), 9 February 1939, in NA, FO 371/23886, R1109/443/92, 34–5; Telegram Loraine (Rome) to FO (London), 11 May 1939, in NA, FO 371/23808, R3926/57/22; Telegram Bullitt (Paris) to Hull (Washington), 28 June 1939, in NARA, RG 59, CDF, Box 4248, File 741.61/734.

259 See Ciano Diary, Entry 13.5.1939; Freundschafts- und Bündnispakt zwischen Deutschland und Italien vom 22. Mai 1939, Art. VII.

260 Chamberlain, *Neville Chamberlain Diary*, 352–3.
261 Ciano Diary, Entry 24.5.1939.
262 Shortly after the signing of the pact, Ciano urged the Polish Ambassador Wieniawa-Długoszowski to exercise a moderating influence in Warsaw. He was anxious to find a diplomatic solution and argued that Warsaw must compromise in order to prevent a European war, which would destroy Poland. See Ciano Diary, Entry 15.5.1939; Telegram Loraine (Rome) to FO (London), 11 May 1939, in NA, FO 371/23808, R3926/57/22, 147–9; Telegram Phillips (Rome) to Hull (Washington), 17 May 1939, in NARA, RG59, LM192, Reel 7, File 762.65/594; Telegram Phillips (Rome) to Hull (Washington), 25 May 1939, in ibid., M982, Reel 6, File 740.00/1593.
263 Pietromarchi, *Diari e le agende*, 301.
264 Watt, "Rome-Berlin Axis," 530.
265 Presseausschnittsammlung zu deutsch-italienischen Besprechungen vom 21. bis 24. Oktober 1936, in Barch, R901, AZ 60322; "Italo-German Relations," *The Times*, 26 October 1936, 14.
266 "Triple Pact Signed," *The Times*, 8 November 1937, 12; Der Deutsche Botschafter in Rom an das Auswärtige Amt, 10 November 1937, in ADAP, Serie D, Vol. I, Doc. 18.
267 Aufzeichnung des Unterstaatssekretärs Woermann, Berlin, 25 May 1938, in ADAP, Serie D, Vol. I, Doc. 772, 913.
268 Telegram Bullitt (Paris) to Hull (Washington), 6 May 1939, in NARA, RG 59, M982, Reel 4, File 740.00/1355.
269 Rathbun, "Trust," 689.
270 See Telegram Bullitt (Paris) to Hull (Washington), 9 August 1938, in NARA, RG 59, CDF, Box 4200, File 740.00EW/461; Telegram Perth (Rome) to FO (London), 17 December 1938, in NA, FO 371/22439, R10058/899/22, 67–8; Telegram Phillips (Rome) to Hull (Washington), 6 July 1939, in NARA, RG 59, M1423, Reel 9, File 865.20/202; Paine, Italy's lack of essential war materials, Rome, 26 March 1938, in FDR Library, Harry L. Hopkins Papers, Box 188; Welles, *Time for Decision*, 83.
271 Telegram Knox (Budapest) to Sargent (London), 13 January 1939, in NA, FO 371/23784, R581/1/22, 147.
272 Telegram Phillips (Rome) to Hull (Washington), 12 May 1938, in NARA, RG 59, LM192, Reel 6, File 762.65/450, 11.
273 Aufzeichnung des Unterstaatssekretärs Woermann, Berlin, 25 May 1938, in ADAP, Serie D, Vol. I, Doc. 772, 913; Aufzeichnung des Reichsaußenministers von Ribbentrop, Berlin, 31 May 1938, in ibid., Doc. 774, 914–15; Luciolli, *Palazzo Chigi*, 46; Meissner, *Staatssekretär*, 430; Watt, "Hitler's Visit," 30.
274 Ciano Diary, Entry 7.10.1937.
275 Ciano Diary, Entry 17.3.1939.

276 Phillips Diary, Entries 9.5.1939 and 24.5.1939, in Houghton Library, William Phillips, Box 10/19, Folder 7–8; Burgwyn, *Italian Foreign Policy*, 173; Rodogno, *Fascism's European Empire*, 21.

277 Carboni, *Memorie*, 6–7.

278 For example, see Telegram Phillips (Rome) to Hull (Washington), 18 February 1938, in NARA, RG 59, LM192, Reel 4, File 762.63/479; Italy and the European Situation, London, 25 March 1939, in FO 371/23886, R2028/443/92; Telegram Kirk (Berlin) to Hull (Washington), 14 September 1939, in NARA, RG 59, LM192, Reel 7, File 762.65/683.

279 See Ciano Diary, Entry 10.3.1942; Il Capo di Gabinetto, Lanza D'Ajeta, al Ministro a Budapest, Anfuso, Roma, 15 January 1942, in DDI, Serie 9, Vol. VIII, Doc. 153, 148; Il Ministro degli Esteri, Ciano, al Ministro a Bucarest, Bova Scoppa, Budapest, 17 January 1942, in ibid., Doc. 166, 169–70; Lipski, *Diplomat in Berlin*, 273.

Even after the Second Vienna Award in August 1940, the disputes between Romania and Hungary strained the Axis alliance. See Ciano Diary, Entry 11.5.1942; the documents in USHMM, RG 25.020*01.

280 Ciano also esteemed foreign politicians when they explicitly criticized Germany. He always saw this situation as an opportunity to bind them closer to Rome and thus strengthen Italy's position vis-à-vis Berlin. For Horthy and Gafencu, see Ciano Diary, Entries 30.4.1939, 1.5.1939, 2.5.1939, 10.7.1941, and 24.1.1942; Il Ministro degli Esteri, Ciano, al Capo del Governo, Mussolini, Roma, 19 January 1942, in DDI, Serie 9, Vol. VIII, Doc. 176, 179–82. For Serrano Suñer, see Ciano Diary, Entries 5.6.1939 and 7.6.1939. Ciano only began to reconcile with Ion Antonescu – and thus with Romania – when Antonescu criticized Germany at the turn of 1942–43. As a sign of good will, Ciano wanted to hand over Horia Sima, the leader of the Iron Guard, to Antonescu. See Ciano Diary, Entries 26.11.1942 and 26.12.1942.

281 See Cornelius, *Hungary in World War II*, 71; Szöllösi-Janze, *Pfeilkreuzlerbewegung*, 97.

282 For including the masses as a new element of fascist diplomacy, see Goeschel, *Mussolini and Hitler*, 9–12.

283 See Ciano Diary, Entry, 13.11.1937; Goeschel, "Staging Friendship," 165; Goeschel, *Mussolini and Hitler*, 137 and 148. Moreover, it was also known in London and Paris that the German people were suspicious of the Italians.

284 Goeschel, *Mussolini and Hitler*, 145. For criticism of Ciano, see Mazzoni, *Livorno*, 231.

285 See Telegram Phillips (Rome) to Hull (Washington), 20 December 1937, in NARA, RG 59, CDF, Box 4090, File 711.652/163; Corner, "Everyday Fascism," 218.

286 Ciano Diary, Entries 14.3.1939 and 15.3.1939; Weizsäcker, Aufzeichnungen, Berlin, 31 March 1939, in PAAA, Mackensen, 2, 64474–6.

287 Ciano, *Außenpolitik Italiens*, 3 and 42.

288 Susmel, *Vita sbagliata*, 66. See also Bottai, *Diario*, 120; Carboni, *Memorie*, 6–7.

289 See Ciano Diary, Entry 11.1.1938; Colloqui con il Presidente del Consiglio d'Ungheria Darányi e il Ministri degli Esteri, Kánya, Budapest, 19–22.5.1937, in Ciano, *L'Europa*, 182–3.

290 See, for example, Ciano Diary, Entries 11.11.1937, 20.4.1939, 11.11.1940, 25.4.1941, and 15.6.1941.

291 Amicucci, *600 giorni*, 83–4; Bastianini, *Uomini, cose, fatti*, 239.

292 See Ciano Diary, Entries 14.10.1937, 11.1.1940, and 14.1.1941.

293 Ciano Diary, Entry 29.9.1937; Goeschel, *Mussolini and Hitler*, 89. Even before his trip to Germany in 1937, he was sceptical about German-Italian relations. See Bottai, *Diario*, 120.

294 See Il Ministro degli Esteri, Ciano, all'Ambasciatore a Madrid, Gambara, Roma, 7 October 1939, in DDI, Serie 9, Vol. I, Doc. 644, 400.

295 König, *Kooperation als Machtkampf*, 20; Steiner, *Triumph of the Dark*, 1010–11.

296 Ciano's first attempts to this effect – albeit still vague and cautious – can be traced back to the spring of 1939. See Ciano Diary, Entry 23.2.1939; Ortona, *Diplomazia*, 56; "Ciano Sees Trend to Peace in Fair," *New York Times*, 13 March 1939, 14. For Mussolini's opinion, see Goeschel, *Mussolini and Hitler*, 168.

297 See Ciano Diary, Entry 4.12.1939; Mackensen, Bemerkungen zu den deutsch-italienischen Beziehungen, Rom, 3 January 1940, in PAAA, Mackensen, 7, 440273; "Rome Press Lends Sympathy to Finns," *New York Times*, 30 November 1939, 7; Ansaldo, *Giornalista*, 210–11; Colville, *Fringes of Power*, 61; Hassell, *Vom andern Deutschland*, 105. The importance of the Finnish-Soviet war for Ciano has largely been ignored. For exceptions, see Goeschel, *Mussolini and Hitler*, 168; Schreiber, "Politische und militärische Entwicklung," 12–14.

298 See Telegram Loraine (Rome) to FO (London), 6 September 1939, in NA, FO 371/23786, R7170/1/22, 337–8; Letter War Office (London) to Nichols (London), 17 September 1939, in NA, FO 371/23787, R7782/1/22, 19–23; L'Ambasciatore di Gran Bretagna a Roma, Loraine, al Ministro degli Esteri, Ciano, Roma, 20 March 1940, in DDI, Serie 9, Vol. III, Doc. 597, 523.

299 For the blockade, see Ciano Diary, Entries 2.12.1939, 5.12.1939, 20.12.1939, 26.12.1939, 29.12.1939, 15.1.1940, and 18.1.1940; Long Diary, Entry 6.3.1940, in LoC, Breckinridge Long Papers, 192; Telegram Loraine (Rome) to Commander-in-Chief, 15 December 1939, in FO 1011/205; Letter Loraine (Rome) to Halifax (London), 29 December 1939, in NA, FO

1011/66; Telegram Charles (Rome) to FO (London), 17 November 1939, in NA, FO 371/23788, R10346/1/22, 4–6.

For the negotiations, see Ciano Diary, Entry 8.2.1940; documents in NA, FO 371/23788 and FO 371/23828; L'Ambasciata di Gran Bretagna a Roma, al Ministro degli Esteri, Ciano, Roma, 16 January 1940, in DDI, Serie 9, Vol. III, Doc. 144, 118–23; Bonnet, *Vor der Katastrophe*, 314; Dalton, *Fateful Years*, 330–1; Pietromarchi, *Diari e le agende*, 373n42 , 382, 384, and 398; Mallett, "Anglo-Italian War"; Salerno, *Vital Crossroads*, 161–8.

300 See Telegram Loraine (Rome) to FO (London), 10 October 1939, in NA, FO 371/23787, R8650/1/22; Telegram Loraine (Rome) to FO (London), 1 December 1939, in NA, FO 371/23788, R10948/1/22; Telegram Loraine (Rome) to FO (London), 1 December 1939, in NA, FO 371/23799, R10899/9/22, 31–2.

301 Ciano Diary, Entry 19.9.1939; Mr. Makins, Foreign Office Minutes, London, 2 February 1940, in USHMM, RG 59.006, Reel 9, Frame 472–3; Telegram Mr. Mackenzie (Air Ministry, London) to Mr. Makins (FO, London), 13 February 1940, in ibid.; Welles, *Times for Decision*, 81.

302 See Ciano Diary, Entries 26.12.1939, 30.12.1939, 2.1.1940, 9.1.1940, and 16.1.1940; Memorandum, 27 December 1939, in NA, FO 371/23828, R12021; Le Comte de Kerchove, Ambassadeur de Belgique à Rome, à Spaak, Ministre des Affaires Étrangères, Rome, 3 January 1940, in DDB, Vol. 5, Doc. 208, 446–50; Pietromarchi, *Diari e le agende*, 406–7; Pirelli, *Tacccuini*, 255.

303 Ciano Diary, Entry 30.5.1940.

304 For Mussolini's opposition, see Ciano Diary, Entry 14.1.1940. To date, scholars have argued that Mussolini allowed Ciano to warn Belgium and the Netherlands in January 1940 (see Di Rienzo, *Ciano*, 900; Goeschel, *Mussolini and Hitler*, 172). However, Ciano had already received information on 11 and 19 November 1939 about a German attack on the Low Countries, which was dismissed by Mussolini. In his *Memoiren eines Europäers*, Paul Henri Spaak wrote that Ciano had informed his government in November (46). If this detail is correct, Ciano seems to have acted without Mussolini's consent. See Ciano Diary, Entry 11.11.1939; Il Ministro Consigliere a Berlino, Magistrati, al Ministro degli Esteri, Ciano, Berlino, 19 November 1939, in DDI, Serie 9, Vol. II, Doc. 265, 228; Phillips Diary, Entry 30.1.1940, in Houghton Library, William Phillips, Box 11/22, Folder 4.

305 See also Getty Images #50446475 and #50446471

306 Ciano Diary, Entry 26.10.1939.

307 Pietromarchi, *Diari e le agende*, 360.

308 Ciano Diary, Entry 27.11.1939.

309 Guerri, *Galeazzo Ciano*, 636–7. The text can be found in Ciano, *L'Italia di fronte al conflitto*.

310 Ciano Diary, Entries 16.12.1939 and 19.12.1939. See also Grandi, *Mio Paese*, 557.

311 See Telegram Kennedy (London) to Hull (Washington), 17 March 1939, in NARA, RG 59, M1423, Reel 2, File 865.00/1805; Telegram (Perth) to Cadogan (London), 24 March 1939, in NA, FO 371/22797, R2098/9/22, 308; Kirkpatrick, *Inner Circle*, 140–2.

312 Telegram Charles (Rome) to Nichols (London), 27 November 1939, in NA, FO 371/23799, R11034/9/22, 39.

313 Telegram Loraine (Rome) to FO (London), 1 September 1939, in NA, FO 371/23810, R7051/57/22. See also Telegram Perth (Rome) to FO (London), 11 March 1939, in NA, FO 371/23800, R1640/10/22.

314 Ciano Diary, Entries 13.9.1939 and 31.1.1940; Telegram Loraine (Rome) to Halifax (London), 5 December 1939, in NA, FO 1011/66; Il Ministro degli Esteri, Ciano, al Capo del Governo, Mussolini, Roma, 16 September 1939, in DDI, Serie 9, Vol. I, Doc. 250, 153; Sir P. Loraine (Rome) to Viscount Halifax, Rome, 1 September 1939, in DBFP, Series III, Vol. VII, No. 653, 481; Bottai, *Diario*, 162; Colville, *Fringes of Power*, 49; Ortona, *Diplomazia*, 71; Pietromarchi, *Diari e le agende*, 332. See also the documents in NA, FO 1011/205.

315 Telegram Loraine (Rome) to Halifax (London), 13 September 1939, in NA, FO 1011/66. During the *non belligeranza* period, the British Foreign Office was afraid that official contacts could jeopardize Ciano's position and thus did not invite him to London. See Telegram Loraine (London) to Nichols (London), 3 November 1939, in NA, FO 371/23787, R9756/1/22, 296–304; Telegram Loraine (Rome) to Halifax (London), 20 January 1940, in NA, FO 1011/67.

316 Ciano Diary, Entry 10.6.1940; Loraine Diary, Entry 10.6.1940, in NA, FO 1011/246; Bottai, *Diario*, 193.

317 See Taylor, First Audience, Rome, 27 February 1940, in LoC, Myron Charles Taylor Papers, Box 1; Telegram Phillips (Rome) to Hull (Washington), 29 and 30 March 1940, in NARA, RG 59, LM142, Reel 3, File 865.00/1892–3; Diary of William Mackenzie King, Entry 5.4.1940, in Library and Archives Canada; Letter Loraine (Rome) to Halifax (London), 18 December 1939, in NA, FO 1011/66; Colville, *Fringes of Power*, 61. Ciano explicitly informed Western diplomats of Mussolini's pro-German attitude. See Telegram Phillips (Rome) to Hull (Washington), 13 March 1940, in NARA, RG 59, LM194, Reel 3, File 762.65/817.

318 Letter Loraine (Rome) to Halifax (London), 22 January 1940, in NA, FO 1011/67; Telegram Phillips (Rome) to Hull (Washington), 27 February 1940, in FDR Library, PSF, Box 3.

319 Gallup, *Gallup International Public Opinion Poll*, 29.

320 Malaparte, *Kaputt*, 578.

321 Vansittart, *Mist Procession*, 503.

322 See European Review, Week of April 4 to April 11, Washington, 19 April 1940, in NARA, RG 59, M982, Reel 19, File 740.0011/2384; Phillips, Memorandum, Rome, 2 May 1940, in ibid., File 740.0011/2691–2/7; Telegram Phillips (Rome) to Hull (Washington), 10 April 1940, in ibid., Reel 18, File 740.0011/2073; Nicolson, *Diaries*, 82; Colville, *Fringes of Power*, 88 and 142; Gellman, *Secret Affairs*, 183.

323 Moffat Diary, Entry 25.2.1940, in FDR Library, Sumner Welles Papers, Box 211, Folder: Moffat Diary. Warnings were also sent by US diplomats Alexander C. Kirk and William C. Bullitt. See Telegram Bullitt (Paris) to Roosevelt and Hull (Washington), 29 May 1940, in NARA, RG 59, M982, Reel 20, File 740.0011/2855 14/28; Kirk, Memorandum, 17 June 1940, in FDR Library, Sumner Welles Papers, Box 61, 2–4.

324 For a positive reaction, see Telegram Loraine (Rome) to FO (London), 16 December 1939, in NA. FO 371/23788, R11636/1/22, 205–9; Ortona, *Diplomazia*, 73. The American press was more sceptical. See "Germany's Moves Defended by Ciano," *New York Times*, 17 December 1939, 1; "Ciano Gives the Case Away," *New York Times*, 18 December 1939, 22.
Radical fascists like Giovanni Preziosi harshly criticized the speech. See Lettera Preziosi a Duce, no date, in USHMM, RG 40.005, Reel 7, 088551–64.

325 Mackensen, Aufzeichnungen, Rom, 21 December 1939, in PAAA, Mackensen, 7, 440262; Phillips Diary, Entry 20.12.1939, in Houghton Library, William Phillips, Box 11/21, Folder 10; Goebbels, *Tagebücher*, Part I, Vol. 7, Entry 17.12.1939, 234–5; Schmidt, *Statist*, 474–5.

326 Goebbels, *Tagebücher*, Part I, Vol. 7, Entry 18.12.1939, 235. For the German public's negative impression of Italy, see Der Reichsführer SS und Chef der Deutschen Polizei, III, Berlin, 15.11.1939, in BArch, R58, AZ 144, Fiche 3, 3. It is therefore hardly surprising that the few comments about the speech in the German press were mostly positive. See "Berlin Welcomes Ciano's Address," *New York Times*, 17 December 1939, 38.

327 Pietromarchi, *Diari e le agende*, 373.

328 Ciano Diary, Entry 18.12.1939, 374.

329 Bottai, *Diario*, 172. Italian diplomats in Germany tried to downplay the anti-German statements. See Aufzeichnungen Staatssekretär, Berlin, 21 December 1939, in PAAA, Akten des Ministerbüros, R29830, 233448; Aufzeichnungen des Staatssekretärs, Berlin, 23 December 1939, in ibid., 233449.

330 Hassell, *Vom andern Deutschland*, 100.

331 See Ciano, *L'Italia di fronte al conflitto*.

332 Too often it is forgotten that, besides the regime's martial rhetoric, newspapers used the peace premises to describe but also justify the partnership with Berlin. See *L'Illustrazione Italiana*, 14 May 1939, 974.

333 See "Il conte Ciano a Berlino su invito del Governo Tedesco," *La Stampa*, 1 October 1939, 1.
334 Goeschel, *Mussolini and Hitler*, 180–3.
335 See Ciano Diary, Entry 13.5.1940; Il Capo del Governo, Mussolini, al Re Vittorio Emanuele III et al., Roma, 31 March 1940, in DDI, Serie 9, Vol. III, Doc. 669, 576–9; Riunione presso il Capo del Governo, Mussolini, Palazzo Venezia, 29 May 1940, in ibid., Vol. IV, Doc. 642, 495–7; Arielli, *Fascist Italy*, 143; Rodogno, *Fascism's European Empire*, 116 and 220–2; Schreiber, "Politische und militärische Entwicklung," 87.
336 Burgwyn, *Mussolini Warlord*, 40; König, *Kooperation als Machtkampf*, 31; Schreiber, "Politische und militärische Entwicklung," 49.
337 See Telegram Phillips (Rome) to Hull (Washington), 25 August 1938, in NARA, RG 59, CDF, Box 4200, File 740.00/456; Burgwyn, *Mussolini Warlord*, 70–3; König, *Kooperation als Machtkampf*, 49.
338 Ciano Diary, Entry 4.12.1940; Aufzeichnung über die Unterredung zwischen dem Führer und dem italienischen Botschafter Alfieri, Berlin, 8.12.1940, in Hillgruber, *Staatsmänner und Diplomaten*, Vol. 1, 401.
339 Telegramm Mackensen (Rom) an AA (Berlin), 16 January 1941, in PAAA, Mackensen, 5, 65209–10; Goeschel, *Mussolini and Hitler*, 203.
340 Goeschel, *Mussolini and Hitler*, 204.
341 See Aufzeichnung über die Unterredung zwischen dem Führer und dem Grafen Ciano, Berlin, 7.7.1940, in Hillgruber, *Staatsmänner und Diplomaten*, Vol. 1, 150–62; "Italian War Move Indicated by Ciano," *New York Times*, 20 May 1940, 1; *L'Illustrazione Italiana*, 21 July 1940, 96, and 28 July 1940, 113; Armellini, *Diario*, 7; Nelson Page, *L'Americano*, 586; Pietromarchi, *Diari e le agende*, 439; Rossi, *Mussolini e il diplomatico*, 271; Shirer, *Berlin Diary*, 458.
342 Polizeipräsidium Berlin Nr. 1, 27 September 1940, in BArch, R19, AZ 432.
343 Ciano Diary, Entries 19.9.1940 and 27.9.1940. Goeschel (*Mussolini and Hitler*, 190) argues that the ceremonies once again strengthened the image of the Axis. However, Ciano's assessment shows that even high-ranking politicians of the alliance did not believe in it.
344 For Hitler's defense of Mussolini, see Goeschel, *Mussolini and Hitler*, 195–205
345 Ciano Diary, Entry 20.11.1940. Nevertheless, Ciano appreciated that at the official ceremony Ribbentrop welcomed him first and that he was sitting on the right side of the German foreign minister. He interpreted this protocol as a sign of Italy's importance within the alliance. See Ciano Diary, Entry 22.11.1940; Patto Anticomintern, December 1940, in ASL, Giornale Luce, C0202. See also Goeschel, *Mussolini and Hitler*, 193–4.
346 Shirer, *Berlin Diary*, 532–6; Hull, Memorandum of Conversation, 30 September 1940, in LoC, Cordell Hull Papers, Reel 30.

347 Ciano Diary, Entry 15.7.1941.

348 Ciano Diary, Entry 10.11.1941. See also Burgwyn, *Mussolini Warlord*, 110–11; König, *Kooperation als Machtkampf*, 85.

349 Ciano Diary, Entry 30.4.1941; König, *Kooperation als Machtkampf*, 69–70.

350 Burgwyn, *Mussolini Warlord*, 83–4.

351 Luciolli (*Palazzo Chigi*, 102–3) and Guerri (*Galeazzo Ciano*, 733,747) claimed erroneously that Ciano simply gave up at this point.

352 Ciano, however, was never convinced of Bose's plans. He was not sure how much credit he could "give this young man" – a clear sign of Ciano's arrogance, since Bose was six years older than him. See Ciano Diary, Entry 6.6.1941; L'Ambasciatore a Tokio, Indelli, al Ministro degli Esteri, Ciano, Tokio, 14 August 1942, in DDI, Serie 9, Vol. IX, Doc. 36, 50–1.

353 Il Ministro degli Esteri, Ciano, all'Ambasciatore a Berlino, Roma, 11 January 1942, in DDI, Serie 9, Vol. VIII, Doc. 125, 119–20.

354 Aufzeichnung des Staatssekretärs z. b. V. im Auswärtigen Amt Keppler, Abschrift, 21 March 1942, in ADAP, Serie E, Vol. II, Doc. 60, 102–3; Italian Minister, Kabul, Reports Success of Axis Propaganda in India, 16 June 1942, in NA, HW 1/654, No. 105617.

355 Ciano Diary, Entry 6.4.1942.

356 Ciano Diary, Entries 3.5.1942 and 4.5.1942.

357 Ciano Diary, Entry 10.8.1942; Il Capo di Gabinetto, Lanza D'Ajeta, all'Ambasciatore a Berlino, Alfieri, Roma, 11 August 1942, in DDI, Serie 9, Vol. IX, Doc. 33, 48–9; L'Ambasciatore a Tokio, Indelli, al Ministro degli Esteri, Ciano, Tokio, 14 August 1942, in ibid., Doc. 36, 50–1.

358 See Ciano Diary, Entries 10.2.1942, 18.2.1942, 26.6.1942, 28.6.1942, 2.7.1942, and 6.7.1942.

359 See Telegramma Anfuso (Berlino) a Ciano (Roma), 17 January 1942, in ASMAE, Serie Affari Politici, Iraq, b. 18, fasc. 1; Telegramma Raschid Ali el Gailani (Roma) a Ciano (Roma), 15 February 1942, in ibid.; Telegramma Raschid Ali el Gailani (Roma) a Ciano (Roma), 31 March 1942, in ibid.; Arab Independence, 16 May 1942, in NA, HW 1/573, No. 104477; Arab Independence, 17 May 1942, in NA, HW 1/575, No. 104512.

In mid-April, Tokyo proposed a joint declaration of independence for India and Arabia. Given the *Duce*'s well-known territorial ambitions in the Mediterranean, Mussolini rejected the proposal. Thus, the seriousness of Japan's offer must be viewed with scepticism. See Ciano Diary, Entry 14.4.1942.

360 See Telegram Fish (Cairo) to Hull (Washington), 22 September 1940, in NARA, RG 59, M982, Reel 36, File 740.0011/6570.

361 Rossi, *Mussolini e il diplomatico*, 278–83; Arielli, *Fascist Italy*, 177, 184, and 188; Morsy, "Britain's Wartime Policy," 64–72.

362 These emissaries could also include family members. See Schieder, "Italienische Experiment"; Sullivan, "Little Brother," 90–7. For example,

Mussolini had always shown a strong interest in Spain's domestic affairs. He maintained close contact with Miguel Primo de Rivera and supported right-wing extremist groups during the Spanish Republic. See Bosworth, *Mussolini*, 315; Esenwein and Shubert, *Spain at War*, 196; Preston, "Italy and Spain," 151.

363 Reichardt and Seibel, "Radikalität und Stabilität," 16.

364 Ciano, *Mia Vita*, 45.

365 Ciano, *My Truth*, 74 and 101–3; Suvich, *Memorie*, 199; Lampson, *Politics and Diplomacy*, 147; De Giorgi, "Shadow of Marco Polo," 573.

366 Mr. Charles Jorge (Fareham) to Eden (London), 14 October 1941, in NA, FO 371/29930, R9168/28/22, 64–7.

367 For Hesse's role, see Knigge, *Philipp von Hessen*. Other leading Nazi officials who played an important role in the rapprochement between Rome and Berlin included Hermann Göring and Hans Frank. See Aufzeichnung Rom, 23 September 1936, in ADAP, Serie C, Vol. V, Doc. 553, 929–32; Colloquio tra il Duce e il Ministro Frank, Roma, 23.9.1936, in Ciano, *L'Europa*, 74–81.

368 See Ciano Diary, Entries 20.4.1938, 18.2.1938, 11.7.1938, 2.9.1938, 6–7.9.1938, 10.9.1938, 25.9.1938, and 28.10.1938; Knigge, *Phillip von Hessen*, 15–19 and 28–30.

369 See Falanga, *Mussolinis Vorposten*; Schieder, "Faschismus im politischen Transfer"; Whealey, "Mussolini's Ideological Diplomacy," 435.

370 Bosworth, *Mussolini*, 270–1.

371 Il Maggiore Renzetti al Sottosegretario per la Stampa e la Propaganda, Ciano, Berlino, 21 June 1935, in DDI, Serie 8, Vol. I, Doc. 419, 438–41; Michaelis, "Conte Galeazzo Ciano," 119.

372 Ciano Diary, Entry 23.10.1937. For Renzetti's reputation among Germans, see Goebbels, *Tagebücher*, Part I, Vol. 3/2, Entry 6.10.1936, 204–5, and Entry 17.12.1936, 294–5.

373 Goebbels, *Tagebücher*, Part I, Vol. 9, Entry 21.3.1941, 197–9.

374 Pertinax was the alias of French journalist André Géraud.

375 Foxlee, *Albert Camus*, 207.

376 Documents can be found in ACS, MCP, Reports, b. 1. For the tensions between Landini and Cerruti, see Telegramma Landini (Paris) a Luciano (Roma), 14 July 1935, in ibid., 008583.

377 Appunto per S.E. il Ministro, Roma, 10 July 1935, in ACS, MCP, Reports, b. 1, 008581.

378 Note by Mr. Thompson, Foreign Office, 7 October 1935, in DBFP, Series II, Vol. XV, Doc. 42, 48–9.

379 Garzarelli, *"Parleremo al mondo,"* 131–6.

380 See Ciano Diary, Entries 2.9.1937, 20.3.1939, 2.4.1939, and 26.5.1939; Telegramma Ciano (Roma) a Bocchini (Roma), 23 March 1935, in ACS,

MCP, Gabinetto, b. 93; Telegramma Coselschi (Roma) a Ciano (Roma), 25 March 1935, in ibid.; Ciano, Appunto per il Duce, Roma, 5 November 1935, in ibid., b. 9, fasc. 67; Gobetti, "Da Marsiglia a Zagabria"; Goldstein, "Ante Pavelić," 85–6; Love, "'What's the Big Idea?'" 453–6.

381 See Ciano Diary, Entries 8.9.1937 and 25.8.1938; Gesandtschaftsrat Bräuer (Brüssel) an den Gesandten Freiherr von Richthofen (z. Z. Berlin), 6 September 1936, in ADAP, Serie C, Vol. V, 2, Doc. 527, 879–81; Goebbels, *Tagebücher*, Part I, Vol. 3.2, Entries 10.10.1936 and 22.10.1936, 208–9 and 221–2; Reynaud, *Thick of the Fight*, 146.

382 For the CAUR, see Borejsza, *Il fascismo*, 139–65; Cuzzi, *L'internazionale*; Hof, "Faschistische Internationale"; Longo, "Tentative."

383 See Telegramma De Peppo (Roma) a Ministero della Stampa e della Propaganda (Roma), 1 October 1936, in ASMAE, Gabinetto, b. 810; Telegramma Cerruti a Ciano, 3 February 1937, in ibid.; Cuzzi, *L'internazionale*, 381.

384 Lettera Coselschi (Roma) a Ciano (Roma), 11 February 1937, in ASMAE, Gabinetto, b. 810.

385 See Ruggero Zangrandi, Memoriale sulla necessità della fondazione di un istituto per il Fascismo Universale, no date, in ASMAE, Gabinetto, b. 810; Telegramma Alfieri (Berlino) a Ciano (Roma), 17 September 1937, in ibid.; Appunto per l'Ufficio, 21 October 1937, in ibid.; Zangrandi, *Il lungo viaggio*, 145.

386 Lettera Coselschi (Roma) a Ciano (Roma), 7 September 1937, in ASMAE, Gabinetto, b. 810, 2; Appunto Coselschi (Roma) per De Peppo (Roma), 9 December 1937, in ibid.

387 Cuzzi, *L'internazionale*, 351–3.

388 Ortona, *Diplomazia*, 72.

389 Ciano Diary, Entries 18.11.1939, 30.12.1939, 22.2.1940, and 11.11.1940

390 See Ducci, *Bella gioventù*, 145–6; Nelson Page, *L'Americano*, 477–8.

391 Ciano Diary, Entry 18.2.1940.

392 Telegram Loraine (Rome) to Halifax (London), 13 September 1939, in NA, FO 1011/66.

393 To end the Ethiopian War, London and Paris intended to give Ogaden and Tigray to Italy and, in return, offer the Ethiopian Empire access to the sea. On 9 December 1935 the plan was leaked to the press and caused a storm of indignation among the British and French public. See Steiner, *Triumph of the Dark*, 125.

394 Ciano Diary, Entries 15.9.1937, 18.9.1937, and 19.9.1937; Mills, "Sir Joseph Ball," 282–90. Dingli was also sent to Rome to discuss the Italian anti-Semitic laws. See Letter Cohen (London) to Dingli (London), 13 October 1938, in USHMM, RG 40.002, Reel 1, Frame 1004–5.

395 See Ciano Diary, Entries 5.4.1940 and 7.4.1940; Mills, "Sir Joseph Ball," 312.

396 Ivy Chamberlain was the widow of the former British foreign minister Austen Chamberlain, who initially had a good relationship with Mussolini. London hoped that this relationship would allow her to hold successful talks with the Italian government. See Edwards, "Austen Chamberlain-Mussolini Meetings."

397 See Telegram Perth (Rome) to FO (London), Anglo-Italian Relations, 17.2.1938, in NA, FO 371/22403, R1615/23/22; Harvey, *Diplomatic Diaries*, 86; Ortona, *Diplomazia*, 41; Self, *Neville Chamberlain*, 283–4.

398 Ciano Diary, Entries 1.1.1938 and 17.2.1938.

399 Shorrock, *From Ally to Enemy*, 255.

400 Ciano Diary, Entries 3.2.1939, 6.2.1939, and 18.3.1939; Telegramm Mackensen (Rom) an Ribbentrop (Berlin), 4 February 1939, in PAAA, Mackensen, 2, 64410–3; Coulondré, *Von Moskau nach Berlin*, 341.

401 Ciano Diary, Entry 6.2.1939; Botschafter von Mackensen an Reichsminister von Ribbentrop, 4 February 1939, in ADAP, Serie D, VI, Doc. 447, 500–1; Il Ministro degli Esteri, Ciano, all'Ambasciata a Parigi, Guariglia, Roma, 28 March 1940, in DDI, Serie 9, Vol. III, Doc. 636, 548.

402 One example was the Nyon Conference in September 1937. Although the conference was a diplomatic victory for Eden, Ciano tried to turn it into a defeat for London. See Ciano Diary, Entries 15.9.1937, 18.9.1937, and 19.9.1937. For the press, see "L'interesse di Londra per i colloqui di Roma," *La Stampa*, 30 March 1938, 1; "La Francia," *La Stampa*, 17 April 1938, 3.

403 Telegram Loraine (Rome) to FO (London), 2 June 1939, in NA, FO 371/23785, R4604/1/22, 193.

404 For Welles's trip, see documents in the FDR Library, Sumner Welles Papers, Box 156; Michael N. Wibel, "A Strange Odyssey: The Sumner Welles Mission to Europe," in FDR Library, Barbara Gellman Papers, Box 2; Telegram Phillips (Rome) to Hull (Washington), 3 March 1940, in LoC, Cordell Hull Papers, Reel 19; Rofe, *Franklin Roosevelt's Foreign Policy*.

405 Autobiography of Mathilda Welles, in FDR Library, Sumner Welles Papers, Box 20, Folder 4, 77–8; Moffat Diary, Entry 25.2.1940, in ibid., Box 211, Folder: Moffat Diary; Telegram Phillips (Rome) to Hull (Washington), 1 March 1940, in LoC, Cordell Hull Papers, Reel 19.

406 See Welles, *Time for Decision*, 78–89; Phillips Diary, Entry 26.2.1940, in Houghton Library, William Phillips, Box 11/22, Folder 8.

407 Ciano Diary, Entry 26.2.1940.

408 L'Ambasciatore a Berlino, Attolico, al Ministro degli Esteri, Ciano, Berlino, 12 February 1940, in DDI, Serie 9, Vol. III, Doc. 293, 248–9; L'Ambasciatore a Berlino, Attolico, al Ministro degli Esteri, Ciano, Berlino, 24 February 1940, in ibid., Doc. 375, 317.

409 L'Ambasciatore a Berlino, Attolico, al Ministro degli Esteri, Ciano, Berlino, 24 February 1940, in DDI, Serie 9, Vol. III, Doc. 375, 317; Gellman, *Secret Affairs*, 176–8; Guerri, *Galeazzo Ciano*, 641.

410 British Foreign Office, Desire of prominent Italians for a separate peace, London, 13 September 1941, in NA, FO 371/29929, R8371/28/22.

411 See Ciano Diary, Entry 19.11.1942; Le nonce en Italie Borgongini Duca au cardinal Maglione, Roma, 18 November 1942, in ADSS, Vol. VII, Doc. 21, 100–2.

412 Ciano Diary, Entries 22.12.1942, 19.1.1943, 20.1.1943, 28.1.1943, and 29.1.1943; Dollmann, Aufzeichnungen für Mackensen, Rom, 18 July 1942, in PAAA, Mackensen, 7, 440345; Telegram Sholes (Basel) to Harrison (Bern), Count Ciano and Peace, 11 January 1943, in NARA, RG 84, Entry 3208, Box 11, Folder 800; Ministero della Cultura Popolare, Ispettorato per la Radiodiffusione e la Televisione, Roma, 18 February 1943, in ACS, MCP, Gabinetto, b. 143, fasc. Segreteria Particolare del Duce; Telegram Pratt (Geneva) to Dulles (Bern), 24 January 1949, in NARA, RG 226, Entry 190C, Box 11; Paraphrase, 29 September 1943, in NARA, RG 84, Entry 3208, Box 8, Folder 707; Pirelli, *Taccuini*, 342 and 393; Linsenmeyer, "Italian Peace Feelers," 650.

For Dino Grandi's peace initiatives, see Italien Peace Overtures: Report from Japanese Consul-General (Vienna) to Foreign Ministry (Tokyo), 12 January 1943, in NA, HW 12/284, No. 113012.

413 Ciano Diary, Entry 31.5.1942; Anfuso, *Rome – Berlin*, 244.

414 Ciano Diary, Entry 5.2.1943; Benini, *Carcere degli Scalzi*, 40; Mussolini, *My Life*, 118.

415 Pirelli, *Taccuini*, 349.

416 Telegram McCloy (Washington) to Admiral Leahy, 1 October 1943, in FDR Library, PMF, Box 34.

417 Carboni, *Memorie*, 144; Pirelli, *Taccuini*, 373.

418 A wide range of studies deal with the international reaction to the Spanish Civil War, including Edwards, *British Government*; Leitz, *Economic Relations*; Podmore, *Britain, Italy, Germany*; Preston and Balfour, *Spain and the Great Powers*; Rodrigo, *Guerra fascista*; Viñas, "Internationale Kontext."

419 See L'Ufficiale addetto al Consolato Generale a Tangeri, Luccardi, al Ministero della Guerra, 19 July 1936, in DDI, Serie 8, Vol. IV, Doc. 569, 639–40; Il Capo del Servizio Informazioni Militare, Roatta, all'Ufficiale addetto al Consolato Generale a Tangeri, Luccardi, 21 July 1936, in ibid., Doc. 582–3, 651; L'Ufficiale addetto al Consolato Generale a Tangeri, Luccardi, al Ministero della Guerra, 23 July 1936, in ibid., Doc. 597, 664; Il Ministro degli Esteri, Ciano, al Console Generale a Tangeri, De Rossi, 24 July 1936, in ibid., Doc. 611, 687; Bosworth, *Mussolini*, 317; Preston, "Italy and Spain," 152–3.

420 Il consigliere dell'Ambasciata a Madrid, de Ciutiis, al Ministro degli Esteri, Ciano, Madrid, 21 July 1936, in DDI, Serie 8, Vol. IV, Doc. 581, 650–1; L'Ambasciatore a Parigi, Cerruti, al Ministro degli Esteri, Ciano, Paris, 22 July 1936, in ibid., Doc. 589, 656–7; Il Ministro degli Esteri, Ciano, al Console Generale a Tangeri, De Rossi, Roma, 24 July 1936, in ibid., Doc. 612, 687; Colloquio con l'Ambasciatore di Spagna, Roma, 22.7.1936, in Ciano, *L'Europa*, 39–40.

421 Il Ministro degli Esteri, Ciano, al Console Generale a Tangeri, De Rossi, Roma, 27 July 1936, in DDI, Serie 8, Vol. IV, Doc. 630, 705; Il Ministro degli Esteri, Ciano, al Console Generale a Tangeri, De Rossi, Roma, 29 July 1936, in ibid., 714.

422 Viñas, "Internationale Kontext," 199–200.

423 Collotti, *Fascismo*, 291.

424 Preston, "Italy and Spain," 155.

425 Il Servizio Informazioni Militare al Ministro degli Esteri, Appunto, 27 July 1936, in DDI, Serie 8, Vol. IV, Doc. 634, 707.

426 See Il Ministro degli Esteri, Ciano, all'Incaricato d'Affari a Londra, Vitetti, Roma, 27 July 1936, in DDI, Serie 8, Vol. IV, Doc. 633, 707; Il Ministro degli Esteri, Ciano, all'incaricato d'affari a Londra, Vitetti, Roma, 30 July 1936, in ibid., 719–20; L'incaricato d'affari a Londra, Vitetti, al Ministro degli Esteri, Ciano, Londra, 29 July 1936, in ibid., Doc. 670, 736–7; Jones, *Diary*, 240.

427 Cantalupo, *Fu la Spagna*, 65–6; Preston, "Italy and Spain," 153–54.

428 See Grandi, *Mio Paese*, 419.

429 Viñas, "Internationale Kontext," 201.

430 See Susmel, *Vita sbagliata*, 61.

431 Memorandum by Mr. Eden on Spain and the Balearic Islands, 14 December 1936, in DBFP, Series II, Vol. XVII, 677–84; Viñas, "Internationale Kontext," 200–2.

432 Ciano Diary, Entry 29.10.1937; Ciano, *Außenpolitik Italiens*, 11; Guariglia, *Ricordi*, 325; Collotti, *Fascismo*, 292. For the attitude of the Catholic Church and the conservatives in Europe, see Kent, "Vatican"; Moradiellos, "Gentle General."

433 Magistrati, *Prologo del dramma*, 113.

434 Der Botschafter in Rom an das Auswärtige Amt, Rom, 27 November 1936, in ADAP, Serie D, Vol. III, Doc. 130, 121; Preston, "Italy and Spain," 162.

435 Guerri, *Galeazzo Ciano*, 327.

436 Pietromarchi, *Diari e le agende*, 132n83.

437 Ciano Diary, Entry 14.11.1937.

438 See Pietromarchi, *Diari e le agende*, 85. Even during the Second World War, Ciano was convinced that a monarchic restoration would be the best

solution for Spain. See Ciano Diary, Entry 12.6.1942; Der Botschafter in Madrid von Stohrer an das Auswärtige Amt, Telegramm, 16 June 1942, in ADAP, Serie E, Vol. II, Doc. 301, 513.

439 Canosa, *Farinacci*, 239–44; Guerri, *Galeazzo Ciano*, 348–9. Whether Ciano indeed sent Farinacci to Spain in order to fascistize the country must be viewed critically, since this narrative is only based on Farinacci's own account. See Collotti, *Fascismo*, 299; Heiberg, "Mussolini," 61–6.

440 Preston, *Franco*, 157–8.

441 For the NIC, see Viñas, "Internationale Kontext."

442 Der Botschafter in Rom an das Auswärtige Amt, Rom, 8 February 1937, in ADAP. Serie D, Vol. III, Doc. 220, 205–6; Der Botschafter in Rom an das Auswärtige Amt, Rom, 5 March 1937, in ibid., Doc. 227, 211–12; Collotti, *Fascismo*, 298.

443 Viñas, "Internationale Kontext," 206.

444 Preston, "Italy and Spain," 157 and 162.

445 Der Botschafter in Rom an das Auswärtige Amt, Rom, 10 March 1937, in ADAP, Serie D, Vol. III, Doc. 229, 212–13.

446 Der Botschafter in Rom an das Auswärtige Amt, Rom, 29 March 1937, in ADAP, Serie D, Vol. III, Doc. 238, 223; Grandi, *Mio Paese*, 422; Pietromarchi, *Diari e le agende*, 167–70 and 241. For Guadalajara, see Coverdale, "Battle of Guadalajara"; D'Alessandro, *Guadalajara 1937*.

447 Ciano Diary, Entry 23.8.1937; Phillips Diary, Entry 22.4.1937, in Houghton Library, William Phillips, Box 7/13, Folder 1; Jones, *Diary*, 337.

448 Preston, "Italy and Spain," 164–5.

449 See Lettera a S. E. Baistrocchi, Roma, no date, in ACS, MCP, Gabinetto, b. 17, fasc. 223; Susmel, *Vita sbagliata*, 61.

450 Preston, "Italy and Spain," 165–8.

451 Ciano Diary, Entry 24.10.1938; Pietromarchi, *Diari e le agende*, 75n19.

452 Ciano Diary, Entries 4.1.1939, 7.1.1939, 27.1.1939, and 3.2.1942; Armellini, *Diario*, 77; Pietromarchi, *Diari e le agende*, 252.

453 Ciano Diary, Entries 30.8.1937, 5.10.1937, 8.10.1937, and 19.3.1938; Preston, "Italy and Spain," 170.

454 Ducci, *Bella gioventù*, 142; Rintelen, *Mussolini*, 17; Pietromarchi, *Diari e le agende*, 232.

455 Ciano Diary, Entry 26.8.1937.

456 Telegramm Plessen (Rom) an AA (Berlin), 16 August 1937, in PAAA, Botschaft in Rom – Geheimakten, 47, 463447; Der Botschafter in Rom an das Auswärtige Amt, Rom, 17 March 1937, in ADAP, Serie D, Vol. III, Doc. 230, 213; Der Reichsaußenminister des Auswärtigen an die Botschaft in Rom, Nürnberg, 12 September 1937, in ibid., Doc. 418, 375–6.

457 Ciano Diary, Entries 23.8.1937 and 30.8.1937; Der Botschafter in Rom von Hassell an das Auswärtige Amt, Rom, 7 July 1937, in ADAP, Serie C, Vol.

VI, 1, Doc. 452, 954; Telegramm Plessen (Rom) an AA (Berlin), 16 August 1937, in PAAA, Botschaft in Rom – Geheimakten, 47, 463447.

458 See Burdett, "Italian War-Correspondents"; Burdett, *Journeys through Fascism*, 148–71.

459 Aufzeichnung des Reichsministers des Auswärtigen, Berlin, 13 January 1937, in ADAP, Serie D, Vol. III, Doc. 200, 188–9.

460 For the "International Brigades," see Viñas, "Internationale Kontext," 229–32.

461 Pugliese, "Death in Exile," 307–9.

462 See Ciano Diary, Entry 4.2.1938.

463 Pugliese, "Death in Exile," 312–17.

464 "Ciano Ordered Rosselli Murders," *New York Times*, 24 September 1944, 1 and 27; Pugliese, "Death in Exile," 317.

465 The only reference to the *Cagoule* that can be found in Ciano's diary is a mention in the 16 September 1937 entry. Ciano commented on bombing attacks carried out by the *Cagoule* on 11 September in Paris: "The Duce is worried that the French police may be on the track of the authors of the Paris outrages. Em[manuele] tells me it is impossible. In any case, it's nothing to do with us. They are Frenchmen in the service of Met." See Ciano Diary, Entry 16.9.1937. Because the original entries are lost, it is impossible to figure out who "Met" was. The English version of the diary does not mention "Met" at all. See Ciano, *Ciano's Hidden Diaries*, 13.

466 Ciano Diary, Entries 28.5.1938 and 11.6.1938; Telegramma Landini (Parigi) a Ciano (Roma), 10 June 1938, in BSB, Mussolini Papers, Reel 453, Frame 028233; Telegramma Landini (Parigi) a Ciano (Roma), 22 June 1938, in ibid., Frame 028234.

467 In the fall of 1942, Settimelli's wife successfully asked the *Duce* to pardon her husband. See Lettera Settimelli (Roma) a Mussolini (Roma), 24 October 1942, in BSB, Mussolini Papers, Reel 453, Frame 028285.

468 See Ciano Diary, Entries 26.11.1937, 23.12.1937, and 27.12.1937; Der Botschafter in Rom an das Auswärtige Amt, Rom, 20 December 1937, in ADAP, Serie D, Vol. III, Doc. 489, 454; Ansaldo, *Giornalista*, 133.

469 For Ciano's (and Mussolini's) criticism of Franco, see Ciano Diary, Entries 6.2.1938, 3.9.1938, 20.9.1938, 26.9.1938, and 8.1.1939; Telegramm Mackensen (Rom) an AA (Berlin), 26 September 1938, in PAAA, Botschaft Rom – Geheimakten, 50, 464525–7. For Ciano's negative judgment of Serrano Suñer, see Ciano Diary, Entry 4.9.1942. It may have influenced Serrano Suñer's own memoirs, published in 1947. See Serrano Suñer, *Zwischen Hendaye und Gibraltar*, 283–5.

470 Viñas, "Internationale Kontext," 282.

471 Der Botschafter in Rom an das Auswärtige Amt, Rom, 7 July 1937, in ADAP, Serie D, Vol. III, Doc. 385, 339–40; Preston, *Franco*, 285–6.

472 Preston, "Italy and Spain," 176.
473 Ibid., 174.
474 Ciano Diary, Entry 28.3.1939.
475 See Ciano Diary, Entry 23.6.1939; *L'Illustrazione Italiana*, 16 July 1939, cover and 85–94; Di Febo, "Riti e propaganda," 247.
476 Ciano Diary, Entry 21.4.1939; Telegram Perth (Rome) to FO (London), 10 February 1939, in NA, FO 371/24116, W2489/5/41.
477 Pietromarchi, *Diari e le agende*, 309 and 320.
478 Ibid., 314; Telegram Mr. Yencken (San Sebastian) to Halifax (London), 19 July 1939, in USHMM, RG 59.022, Reel 1, Frames 104–6. "Ciano Is Pleased with Spanish Visit," *New York Times*, 16 July 1939, 19; "Italy Woos Spain with Ciano Visit," *Washington Post*, 16 July 1939, B7; Di Febo, "Riti e propaganda," 256–60.
479 Ciano did not mention the trip in his diary. However, after his return he wrote a report to the *Duce* (Colloquio col Generalissimo Franco, 19.7.1939, in Ciano, *L'Europa*, 439–46). The report is less a description of the real events, but rather Ciano's version of the journey to please Mussolini, who was indeed extremely satisfied with Franco's praise. See Ciano Diary, Entry 19.7.1939.
480 Signoretti, "*La Stampa*," 163.
481 See Telegram Mr. Yencken (San Sebastian) to Halifax (London), 20 July 1939, in USHMM, RG 59.022, Reel 1, Frame 107; "Ciano Wins Friends, Little Else in Spain," *New York Times*, 16 July 1939, 57; Di Febo, "Riti e propaganda;" Preston, *Franco*, 334–6.
482 See Ciano Diary, Entry 25.8.1937; Telegram Grant (Tirana) to Hull (Washington), 4 August 1937, in NARA, RG 59, M1211, Reel 9, File 875.00/491; Telegram Grant (Tirana) to Hull (Washington), 25 February 1939, in ibid., File 875.00/501, 7; Bojano, *Wake of the Goose Step*, 95; Fischer, *Albania at War*, 5–6.
483 Ciano Diary, Entry 30.8.1937.
484 Ciano Diary, Entries 28.4.1938, 30.4.1938, and 10.5.1938; Jacomoni, *Politica dell'Italia*, 78–80.
485 See Appunto, Roma, no date, in ASMAE, Affari Politici, Albania, b. 82, fasc. 12; Telegramma Jacomoni (Tirana) a Ministero degli Affari Esteri (Roma), 18 April 1938, in ibid., fasc. 13; Telegramma Ciano (Roma) a R. Legazione (Tirana), 20 May 1938, in ibid., fasc. 12; Appunto, Roma, 13 June 1938, in ibid., fasc. 18.
486 R. Legazione (Tirana) a Ciano (Roma), 6 June 1938, in ASMAE, Affari Politici, Albania, b. 82, fasc. 12; Telegramma Jacomoni (Tirana) a Ciano (Roma), 9 October 1938, in ibid., fasc. 28.
487 Ciano Diary, Entries 27.10.1938 and 3.12.1938. Koçi is not mentioned in the English version of the diary. See Ciano, *Ciano's Hidden Diaries*, 184.

See also Ciano Diary, Entries 5.2.1939, 8.2.1939, and 10.2.1939; Telegram Grant (Tirana) to Hull (Washington), 25 February 1939, in NARA, RG 59, M1211, Reel 9, File 875.00/501, 2–3.

488 See Ciano Diary, Entries 16.10.1938 and 19.10.1938; Ufficio Albania, Appunto, Roma, 14 January 1939, in ASMAE, Affari Politici, Albania, b. 82, fasc. 20.

489 Ciano Diary, Entries 11.2.1939, 3.3.1939, 15.3.1939, and 19.5.1939; Anfuso, *Rom – Berlin*, 98; Carboni, *Memorie*, 10.

Telegramm Pannwitz (Tirana) an Weizsäcker (Berlin), 27 June 1938, in PAAA, Botschaft in Rom – Geheimakten, 50, 464452–7; Telegramma Ciano (Roma) a R. Ambasciata (Berlino), 23 May 1938, in ASMAE, Affari Politici, Albania, b. 82, fasc. 24.1; Telegramma R. Ambasciata (Berlino) a Ciano (Roma), 2 June 1938, in ibid.; Der Botschafter in Rom an das Auswärtige Amt, 17 March 1939, in ADAP, Serie D, Vol. VI., Doc. 15, 12–13; Der Botschafter in Rom an das Auswärtige Amt, 20 March 1939, in ibid., Doc. 45, 40. See also Telegramma Babuscio Rizzo (Tirana) a Ciano (Roma), 22 September 1938, in ASMAE, Affari Politici, Albania, b. 82, fasc. 7; Telegramma Jacomoni (Tirana) a Ciano (Roma), 15 December 1938, in ibid.

490 See Telegramm Mackensen (Rom) an AA (Berlin), 10 February 1939, in PAAA, Botschaft in Rom – Geheimakten, 52, 465276–7; Mackensen, Aktenvermerk, Rom, 11 February 1939, in ibid., 465278–9; Brief Ribbentrop (Berlin) an Ciano (Rom), 20 March 1939, in PAAA, Mackensen, 3, 65629–31; Ribbentrop (Berlin) an sämtliche Reichsministerien (Berlin), 25 March 1939, in PAAA, Botschaft in Rom – Geheimakten, 52, 465135–6.

491 Ciano Diary, Entry 17.3.1939; Telegramm Mackensen (Rom) an AA (Berlin), 17 March 1939, in PAAA, Botschaft in Rom – Geheimakten, 52, 465303; Miller, "Dark Waters," 295–99.

492 Ciano Diary, Entry 25.3.1939.

493 Ciano Diary, Entry 1.4.1939; Telegram Grant (Tirana) to Hull (Washington), 24 May 1939, in NARA, RG 59, M1211, Reel 9, File 875.00/520, 36; Telegramma Legazione di Italia (Tirana) a Ciano (Roma), 9 October 1938, in ASMAE, Affari Politici, Albania, b. 82.

According to the *Reichssicherheitshauptamt*, Ciano paid a total of 19 million lire to Albanian officers and politicians. See RSHA, Amt IV E, Bericht, Berlin, 6 February 1941, in BArch, R58, AZ 9478, 160275.

494 Ciano Diary, Entry 31.3.1939.

495 Ciano Diary, Entries 23.3.1939 and 29.3.1939.

496 Fischer, *Albania at War*, 23.

497 Ciano Diary, Entries 3.4.1939 and 4.4.1939.

498 Ciano Diary, Entry 6.4.1939; Miller, "Dark Waters," 297.

499 Telegram Grant (Tirana) to Hull (Washington), 24 May 1939, in NARA, RG 59, M1211, Reel 9, File 875.00/520, 13.

500 Ciano Diary, Entries 2.4.1939 and 3.4.1939.
501 Ciano Diary, Entries 2.4.1939 and 5.4.1939; Miller, "Dark Waters," 296.
502 Bottai, *Diario*, 144–5.
503 The editors of the published versions of the diary contributed to the confusion, because they arbitrarily decided the date on which Ciano wrote his notes. For example, 6 April is very short in the English version. See Ciano, *Ciano Diaries*, 60–1.
504 Ciano Diary, Entries 4.4.1939 and 5.4.1939.
505 Bottai, *Diario*, 145.
506 Telegram Phillips (Rome) to Hull (Washington) and Appendix, 10 April 1939, in NARA, RG 59, M982, Reel 2, File 740.00/757. See also Telegram Grant (Tirana) to Hull (Washington), 24 May 1939, in NARA, RG 59, M1211, Reel 9, File 875.00/520, 7–10 and 19.
507 Ciano Diary, Entries 4.4.1939 and 5.4.1939.
508 King Zog fled to England and spent the war years in London. See Fischer, *Albania at War*, 105–6.
509 Ciano Diary, Entry 6.4.1939; Telegram Grant (Tirana) to Hull (Washington), 24 May 1939, in NARA, RG 59, M1211, Reel 9, File 875.00/520, 31.
510 Telegram Grant (Tirana) to Hull (Washington), 24 May 1939, in NARA, RG 59, M1211, Reel 9, File 875.00/520, 25–6.
511 Petacci, *Verso il disastro*, 95–7; Fischer, *Albania at War*, 22.
512 Ciano Diary, Entry 7.4.1939.
513 Telegram Grant (Tirana) to Hull (Washington), 24 May 1939, in NARA, RG 59, M1211, Reel 9, File 875.00/520, 34.
514 Nelson Page, *L'Americano*, 561; "Albania Held Firm in Hands of Italy," *New York Times*, 10 April 1939, 3.
515 Ciano Diary, Entry 8.4.1939. See also Telegram Grant (Tirana) to Hull (Washington), 24 May 1939, in NARA, RG 59, M1211, Reel 9, File 875.00/520, 35.
516 Telegram Grant (Tirana) to Hull (Washington), 24 May 1939, in NARA, RG 59, M1211, Reel 9, File 875.00/520, 37 and 59.
517 Ciano Diary, Entry 8.4.1939.
518 See Telegram Grant (Tirana) to Hull (Washington), 24 May 1939, in NARA, RG 59, M1211, Reel 9, File 875.00/520, 43; Fischer, *Albania at War*, 22.
519 Fischer, *Albania at War*, 36 and 56–7.
520 Ibid., 63. Telegram Phillips (Rome) to Hull (Washington), 14.4.1939, in FDR Library, PSF, Box 42; Hull, Memorandum, no date, in LoC, Cordell Hull Papers, Reel 28; "Attack on Albania Assailed by Hull," *New York Times*, 9 April 1939, 34.
521 Ciano Diary, Entries 6.4.1939 and 9.4.1939.
522 Telegram Loraine (Rome) to FO (London), 2 June 1939, in NA, FO 371/23785, R4604/1/22, 193.

523 Telegram Phillips (Rome) to Hull (Washington) and Appendix, 10 April 1939, in NARA, RG 59, M982, Reel 2, File 740.00/757. Athens' fears were not completely unfounded. In May 1939 Ciano wrote that all infrastructure measures in Albania were solely directed towards the Greek border. See Ciano Diary, Entry 12.5.1939.

524 Telegram Grant (Tirana) to Hull (Washington), 24 May 1939, in NARA, RG 59, M1211, Reel 9, File 875.00/520, 65; Petacci, *Verso il disastro*, 103.

525 Telegram FO (London) to Perth (Rome), 9 April 1939, in NA, FO 371/23785, R2502/1/22, 17–19.

526 Telegram Davies (London) to Jebb (London), 18 April 1939, in NA, FO 371/23785, R3002/1/22, 59.

527 Ciano Diary, Entry 28.5.1939.

528 Ciano Diary, Entry 1.6.1939.

529 Mills, "Sir Joseph Ball," 311.

530 Guerri, *Galeazzo Ciano*, 534.

531 Ciano Diary, Entry 6.5.1938. See also Entries 16.4.1939, 19.7.1939, and 21.7.1939.

532 Ciano Diary, Entry 20.4.1939.

533 For his plans, see Ciano Diary, Entries 26.3.1928, 10.8.1938, 11.8.1938, and 25.11.1938.

534 Ciano Diary, Entries 9.4.1939 and 16.4.1939; velina (12 April 1939), in Tranfaglia, *Stampa*, 254.

535 See Telegram Grant (Tirana) to Hull (Washington), 24 May 1939, in NARA, RG 59, RG 59, M1211, Reel 9, File 875.00/520, 37.

536 Ciano Diary, Entries 13.4.1939 and 21.4.1939; Ciano, La nuova Albania, 1941, in ACS, MCP, Gabinetto, b. 17, fasc. 223, 5.

537 "Jacomoni Is Named 'Viceroy' of Albania," *New York Times*, 22 April 1939, 23; Visconti Prasca, *Io ho aggredito*, 13.

538 See Ciano Diary, Entries 21.9.1937, 23.9.1937, and 6.1.1938; Hassell, Aufzeichnung, Rom, 7 October 1937, in PAAA, Geheime Reichssachen, R61140, 31; Politischer Bericht Hassell (Rom) an AA (Berlin), 17 October 1937, in PAAA, Botschaft in Rom, 709b.

539 Telegram Grant (Tirana) to Hull (Washington), 24 April 1939, in NARA, RG 59, RG 59, M1211, Reel 9, File 875.00/503.

540 Ibid; Ciano, La nuova Albania, 1941, in ACS, MCP, Gabinetto, b. 17, fasc. 223, 5.

541 Telegram Grant (Tirana) to Hull (Washington), 1 June 1939, in NARA, RG 59, RG 59, M1211, Reel 9, File 875.00/515; Telegram Grant (Tirana) to Hull (Washington), 9 May 1939, in ibid., File 875.00/508.

542 Ciano, La nuova Albania, 1941, in ACS, MCP, Gabinetto, b. 17, fasc. 223, 5.

543 Ciano Diary, Entries 2–3.6.1939.

544 Appunto per la Direzione Generale Affari Generali Ufficio IV, Roma, 26 May 1939, in ASMAE, Affari Politici, Albania, b. 82: fasc. Ebrei in Albania; Appunto per il Sottosegretariato per gli Affari Albanesi, Roma, 2 June 1939, in ibid.
545 Lettera Camera di Commercio (Tirana) a Ministro dell'Economia Nazionale (Tirana), 9 September 1938, in ASMAE, Affari Politici, Albania, b. 82: fasc. Ebrei in Albania. For German and Austrian Jews fleeing to Albania, see Report Italy and the Jewish Problem, 4 January 1939, in USHMM, RG 59.006, Reel 9, Frame 455–7.
546 Telegramma Ministero degli Affari Esteri (Roma) a Jacomoni (Tirana), 15 May 1939, in ASMAE, Sottosegretariato, b. 13. For the doubts, see Telegramma Babuscio Rizzo (Tirana) a Ministero degli Affari Esteri (Roma), 3 December 1938, in USHMM, RG 40.002, Reel 1, Frame 1588; Telegramma Babuscio Rizzo (Tirana) a Ministero degli Affari Esteri (Roma), 26 January 1939, in ASMAE, Affari Politici, Albania, b. 82: fasc. Ebrei in Albania; Telegramma Babuscio Rizzo (Tirana) a Ministero della Cultura Popolare (Roma), 2 February 1939, in ibid.
547 See Telegramma Jacomoni (Tirana) a Ministero degli Affari Esteri (Roma), 8 June 1939, in ASMAE, Sottosegretariato, b. 13; Telegramma Ciano (Roma) a Jacomoni (Tirana), 15 June 1939, in ibid.; Telegramma Jacomoni (Tirana) a Ministero degli Affari Esteri (Roma), 2 August 1939, in ibid.; Telegramma Benini (Roma) a Jacomoni (Tirana), 9 August 1939, in ibid.
548 See Telegramma Luogotenenza Generale in Albania (Tirana) a Presidenza del Consiglio dei Ministri (Roma), 30 August 1940, in USHMM, RG 79.001, Box 1, Folder 2; Telegramma Travaglio (Tirana) al Comando Superiore CC.RR. (Tirana), 2 February 1941, in ibid., Box 2, Folder 9; Telegramma Luogotenenza Generale in Albania (Tirana) al Comando Superiore Forze Armate Albania (Tirana), 8 August 1941, in ibid., Box 1, Folder 2. For the most recent study on the Jews in Albania, see Heim et al., *Verfolgung und Ermordung*, 687–742.
549 Ciano Diary, Entry 27.7.1939; Ciano, La nuova Albania, 1941, in ACS, MCP, Gabinetto, b. 17, fasc. 223, 6–10.
550 Badoglio, *Italien im Zweiten Weltkrieg*, 16.
551 Ciano Diary, Entries 25.8.1937, 26.4.1939, 13.6.1939, and 30.1.1940; Telegram Phillips (Rome) to Hull (Washington), 9 June 1939, in NARA, M1211, Reel 9, File 875.00/522; Rodogno, *Fascism's European Empire*, 58; Anfuso, *Rom – Berlin*, 97.
552 Vermerk, 17 March 1941, in USHMM, RG 11.001, Reel 12; "Jacomoni Is Named 'Viceroy' of Albania," *New York Times*, 22 April 1939, 23.
553 Telegram Grant (Tirana) to Hull (Washington), 25 April 1939, in NARA, RG 59, RG 59, M1211, Reel 9, File 875.00/504; Ciano in Albania visita cantieri edili, 23 August 1939, in ASL, Giornale Luce, B1572.

554 Ciano, La nuova Albania, 1941, in ACS, MCP, Gabinetto, b. 17, fasc. 223.

555 Albania has always been regarded as Ciano's personal "duchy" and can therefore be used to analyse Ciano's ideas about an efficient occupation policy. See Badoglio, *Italien und der Zweite Weltkrieg*, 16; Bastianini, *Uomini, cose, fatti*, 240; Cerruti, *Frau eines Botschafters*, 290.

556 Ciano Diary, Entries 30.1.1940, 23.5.1940, 10.5.1941, and 17.5.1941. For the situation in Albania, see Telegram Phillips (Rome) to Hull (Washington), 13 August 1941, in NARA, RG 59, M1211, Reel 15, File 875.00/534; Pirelli, *Taccuini*, 295–9; Neuwirth, *Widerstand*, 246.

557 Burgwyn, *Mussolini Warlord*, 80. Before the war Ciano intended to give the Greek Ciamura to Albania in order to calm "Albanian nationalism" and gain sympathy with the Albanian people. See Ciano Diary, Entry 22.5.1940; Burgwyn, *Mussolini Warlord*, 36–7. After the conquest of Greece, however, the Germans blocked his plan.

558 *L'Illustrazione Italiana*, 3 November 1940, 662.

559 Visconti Prasca, *Io ho aggredito*, 13. Even Ciano identified the "feudal structure" as an insurmountable obstacle for his politics. See Ciano Diary, Entry 16.2.1942.

560 Neuwirth, *Widerstand*, 246.

561 Ciano Diary, Entries 11.11.1941, 19.12.1941, 23.12.1941, and 16.2.1942; Villari, "Failed Experiment," 165–6. In the Italian edition of Ciano's diary, De Felice added words that are not in the original. De Felice wrote: "Kruja is not popular with the Albanians because of his nationalism." See Ciano, *Diario 1937–1943*, 561.

562 Ciano Diary, Entries 2.3.1942, 21.4.1942, and 1.9.1942.

563 Telegramm Mackensen (Rom) an AA (Berlin), 24 June 1942, in PAAA, Geheime Reichssachen, R61140, 223–4. For the speech, see Il Ministro degli Esteri, Ciano, ai membri della Commissione Affari Esteri del Senato, Roma, 30 May 1942, in DDI, Serie 9, Vol. VIII, Doc. 573, 626–42.

564 Ciano Diary, Entry 1.9.1942.

565 Neuwirth, *Widerstand*, 246–7.

566 Numerous documents on Italian occupation policy in the Balkans can be found in USHMM, RG 49.006, Reel 1 to 15 and USHMM, RG 49.002*01, *02 and *03. See also Adeli, "From Jasenovac to Yugoslavism"; Gobetti, "Royal Army's Betrayal?"; Hof, "'Legionaries of Civilization'"; Rodogno, *Fascism's European Empire*; Verna, "Notes on Italian Rule."

567 Ciano Diary, Entries 18.1.1943, 21.1.1943, and 1.2.1943. Already in September 1942 he voiced concerns about a lack of armed forces, but Jacomoni continued to provide optimistic reports about the internal situation in Albania. See Entries 9.9.1942 and 13.12.1942.

568 Ciano Diary, Entry 24.3.1942.

569 Ciano Diary, Entry 21.1.1943.

570 Ciano Diary, Entry 5.2.1943.
571 For example, see the works by Quartararo cited in the bibliography. See also Burgwyn, "Diplomacy," 318. For criticism, see Goeschel, "Parallel History," 626–9.
572 See Behring, "Italien im Spiegel," 361.
573 For example, see Burgwyn, *Italian Foreign Policy*; Collotti, *Fascismo*; Guerri, *Galeazzo Ciano*; Mallett, *Italian Navy*.
574 Messerschmidt, "Außenpolitik und Kriegsvorbereitung," 620; Rodogno, "Fascism and War," 239; Schieder, *Italienische Faschismus*, 75–7.
575 Goeschel, *Mussolini and Hitler*, 294–5.
576 Ibid., 6.
577 Nattermann, "Politische Beobachtung." For Crispi, see Duggan, *Force of Destiny*, 323–37.
578 Goeschel, "Staging Friendship," 169.
579 Goeschel, *Mussolini and Hitler*, 6 and 165.
580 As argued by Goeschel, *Mussolini and Hitler*, 155
581 Ibid., 186.
582 For the democracies, see Hoare, *Gesandter*, 117.
583 Goeschel, *Mussolini and Hitler*, 163.
584 Reichardt, *Faschistische Kampfbünde*, 595. See also Roberts, "Myth, Style, Substance," 12.
585 See also Gilbert, "Ciano," 524–5.
586 Reichardt and Seibel, "Radikalität und Stabilität," 16.
587 Cited in Klimke, Kreis, and Ostermann, "Introduction," 3.
588 Ibid., 4.
589 Rathbun, "Trust," 690–1.
590 So far, this understanding has only been highlighted for German-Italian relations. See Watt, "Rome-Berlin Axis," 521.
591 Rathbun, "Trust," 689.
592 Pietromarchi, *Diari e le agende*, 391.
593 Schreiber, "Politische und militärische Entwicklung," 100. This strategy failed, not only, as König (*Kooperation als Machtkampf*, 327) claims, when the Second World War broke out, but already in the second half of the 1930s.

4. The Successor

1 Italian Situation: Report from Mexican Chargé in Rome, 7 November 1941, in NA, HW 1/196, No. 097395.
2 Anti-Mussolini Intrigues in Italy, 9 December 1942, in NA, FO 371/33221, R8809/3/22.
3 See Dixon, Foreign Office Minute, 6 February 1943, in NA, FO 371/37262, R1180/242/22, 119–29; Telegram Harrison (Bern) to Hull (Washington),

13 February 1943, in NARA, RG 59, CDF, Box 1878, File 701.6566A/8; Telegram Matthews (London) to Hull (Washington), 18 February 1943, in ibid., File 701.6566A/10; Japanese Minister, the Vatican, Reports Conversation with Ciano, 17 July 1943, in NA, HW 1/1846, No. 120126; "Lettera Clara a Mussolini," Maggio 1943, in Mussolini, *A Clara*, 169n3; Agnelli, *Matrosenkleider*, 144; Pirelli, *Taccuini*, 432.

4 Edda, *My Truth*, 24.

5 Bottai, *Diario*, 121–2.

6 See Telegramm Hassell (Rom) an AA (Berlin), 18 February 1937, in PAAA, Botschaft in Rom – Geheimakten, 45, 462851–2; "Ciano Is Expected to Succeeded il Duce," *New York Times*, 8 October 1936; "Ciano Understudies a Role as Dictator," *New York Times*, 17 January 1937, 23; Goebbels, *Tagebücher*, Part I, Vol. 5, Entries 2.5.1938 and 6.5.1938, 282–3 and 288–90; Gafencu, *Last Days*, 156.

7 Rapporto, Livorno, 15 July 1938, in ACS, MI, DGPS, b. 22A, fasc.1.

8 Telegram Reed (Rome) to Hull (Washington), 13 November 1939, in NARA, M1423, Reel 2, File 865.00/1868; Telegram Charles (Rome) to FO (London), 17 November 1939, in NA, FO 371/23799, R10445/9/22, 11–15; Ansaldo, *Giornalista*, 207; Lessona, *Memorie*, 240; Nelson Page, *L'Americano*, 575; Valori, *Il fascista*, 262.

9 Telegram Campbell (Paris) to Sargent (London), 15 November 1939, in NA, FO 371/23810, R10372/37/22, 363. See also Telegram Perth (Rome) to Ingram (London), 11 June 1938, in NA, FO 371/22431, R5593/281/22, 2; Phillips Diary, Entry 20.10.1936, in Houghton Library, William Phillips, Box 6/11, Folder 7.

10 For example, see "Italy Hails Duce's Son-in-Law," *Washington Post*, 6 December 1938, B6; Borstendoerfer, *Graf Ciano*, 27; Sarfatti, *My Fault*, 155; Ward Price, *Führer und Duce*, 260; Namier, *Europe in Decay*, 116–17; Maugeri, *From the Ashes*, 89.

11 See Fischer, *Albania at War*, 8–9.

12 See also "Favored Son-in-Law of Premier Mussolini Conforms to Il Duce's Ideas of a Successor," *Washington Post*, 11 October 1936.

13 For example, see Getty Images #2669406 and #141557443; *La Domenica del Corriere*, 38, 23 September 1934, 5; *L'Illustrazione Italiana*, 12 June 1938, 978.

14 See Telegramma De Peppo (Roma) a R. Legazione d'Italia (Cairo), 25 April 1934, in ACS, MCP, DGSP, b. 61, fasc. 1934; Telegramma De Peppo (Roma) a R. Legazione d'Italia (Bulkeley), 7 July 1934, in ibid.; Telegramma De Peppo (Roma) a R. Legazione d'Italia (Buenos Aires), 26 January 1935, in ibid., b. 5, fasc. Materiale di propaganda per l'Argentina; Telegramma Ciano (Roma) a Sahab Refaat Almas (Roma), 26 December 1935, in ibid., b. 61, fasc. 1935.

15 Velina (7 August 1933), in Tranfaglia, *Stampa*, 105.
16 Paxton, "Fünf Stadien des Faschismus," 61.
17 Velina (5 November 1935), in Tranfaglia, *Stampa*, 109; Benini, *Carcere degli Scalzi*, 52; Guerri, *Galeazzo Ciano*, 195.
18 For example, see velina (2 March 1934), in Tranfaglia, *Stampa*, 138.
19 Lettera, 12 January 1935, in ACS, MCP, Gabinetto, b. 5.
20 Nelson Page, *L'Americano*, 487, 553–5, and 606,
21 Rapporto, Roma, 15 April 1938, in ACS, MI, DGPS, b. 22A, fasc.1. For example, see *L'Illustrazione Italiana*, 22 May 1938, 831; *L'Illustrazione Italiana*, 24 July 1938, cover.
22 Ojetti, *Taccuini*, 549; Gilbert, "Ciano," 520–1.
23 "Zog and Ciano Confer," *New York Times*, 1 May 1937, 1; "Albanians Greet Ciano," *New York Times*, 29 April 1937, 7; Jacomoni, *Politica dell'Italia*, 64–5.
24 Moseley, *Mussolini's Shadow*, 29–30; Ullstein Bild #00067374.
25 Der Botschafter in Rom von Hassell an das Auswärtige Amt, Rom, 21 June 1935, in ADAP, Serie C, Vol. IV, 1, Doc. 164, 331–3; "Private Lives in a Crisis," *LIFE*, 11 September 1939, 68–9; Michaelis, "Conte Galeazzo Ciano," 135.
26 Susmel, *Vita sbagliata*, 65.
27 Telegram Perth (Rome) to Foreign Office (London), 25.6.1938, in NA, FO 371/22412, R5856/281/22, 107.
28 See La visita di Ciano, 19 April 1939, in ASL, Giornale Luce, B1496; Galeazzo Ciano a Tirana, 23 August 1939, in NA, FO 371/22412, B1571; Ciano in Albania, 23 August 1939, in ibid., B1572.
29 *La Rivista Illustrata del Popolo d'Italia*, December 1939, 70.
30 Ciano Diary, Entry 12.4.1939.
31 Ciano Diary, Entries 29.4.1938 and 29.5.1938. Diplomats had no doubts, however, that these events were meant to build Ciano up as Mussolini's successor. See Phillips Diary, Entry 20.10.1936, in Houghton Library, William Phillips, Box 6/11, Folder 7.
32 See Ciano Diary, Entry 13.9.1939; Telegram Phillips (Rome) to Hull (Washington), 6 September 1939, in FDR Library, PSF, Box 42; Telegram Campbell (Paris) to Sargent (London), 15 November 1939, in NA, FO 371/23810, R10372/57/22; Telegram Charles (Rome) to Nichols (London), 27 November 1939, in NA, FO 371/23799, R11034/9/22.
33 Velina (6 November 1939), in Tranfaglia, *Stampa*, 140.
34 Ciano Diary, Entries 13.12.1937, 8.10.1938, and 9.10.1938.
35 Koon, *Believe, Obey, Fight*, 18.
36 Ojetti, *Taccuini*, 503
37 For Mussolini's health, see Foreign Office Minutes, 23 September 1939, in NA, FO 371/23814, R7954/79/22; Nobel, Foreign Office Minutes, 6 October 1939, in ibid., R8637/179/22.

38 Rapporto, Roma, 1 August 1940, in ACS, MI, DGPS, b. 22A, fasc. 1; Ortona, *Diplomazia*, 135.
39 Navarra, *Memorie*, 151. Ciano's declining ambitions were reflected by him avoiding the public. See Ciano Diary, Entry 3.1.1942.
40 For Mussolini's obsession with youth, see Koon, *Believe, Obey, Fight*, 16; Spackman, *Fascist Virilities*, 2.
41 See Getty Images #541055145, #541055505, #541055687, and #541072505; Ullstein Bild #01082580.
42 For example, see Rapporto, Roma, 26 February 1939, in ACS, MI, DGPS, b. 22A, fasc. 1; Rapporto, 26 May 1939, in ibid.
43 Di Rienzo, *Ciano*, 1349–54.
44 Telegram Perth (Rome) to Halifax (London), 27 December 1938, in NA, FO 371/22796, 114.
45 Corner, "Everyday Fascism," 217.
46 Although we still have almost no thoroughly researched academic biographies of any leading figures of the fascist regime, it seems that the other hierarchs did not attempt to imitate Mussolini with the same fervour.
47 Ciano, *My Truth*, 24; Vergani, *Ciano*, 42–3.
48 See Rapporto, 26 February 1939, in ACS, MI, DGPS, b. 22A, fasc. 1; Navarra, *Memorie*, 151; Moseley, *Mussolini's Shadow*, 22.
49 La firma del patto italo-tedesco, 1939, in ASL, Documentari, D007605. See also Discorso di Ciano a Palazzo Chigi, 11 November 1938, in ibid., D008202; Duggan, *Fascist Voices*, 236.
50 For example, see *L'Illustrazione Italiana*, 15 January 1939, cover; and 12 May 1939, cover; Getty Images #50713232, #79034346, #92423919, and #141551590. See also Antola, "Photographing Mussolini"; Pieri, "Portraits of the Duce."
51 Long Diary, Entry 7.12.1935, in LoC, Breckinridge Long Papers, Box 4; Gori, "Model of Masculinity," 37.
52 Bach and Breuer, *Faschismus als Bewegung*, 315; Woller, *Geschichte Italiens*, 104. For the cult of Mussolini, see Cicchino, *Il Duce*; Gundle, Duggan, and Pieri, *Cult of the Duce*; Luzzatto, *L'immagine del duce*.
53 Rapporto, Roma, 23 November 1939, in ACS, MI, DGPS, b. 22A, fasc. 1.
54 See Talbot, *Censorship*, 116.
55 For example, see Ciano Diary, Entry 28.8.1942; Getty Images #3400835.
56 His family was also shown vacationing in the posh ski resort Cortina D'Ampezzo. See *La Rivista Illustrata del Popolo d'Italia*, February 1937, 64.
57 Figure 12 shows Ciano in a civilian dress sitting next to a marble sculpture of a sleeping child. His body language suggests that he, the adult, protects the child. Since this photograph was taken in the Foreign Ministry at the time of the *non belligeranza* policy, the viewer may well have associated the sleeping child with the Italian nation: a young

and vulnerable nation destined for greatness, cared for by Ciano who was against entry into the war. See also Getty Images #541077035 and #541055137.

58 Ciano Diary, Entries 3.11.1938, 20.11.1938, 6.12.1938, 31.8.1940, 13.10.1941, 17.1.1942, and 27.8.1942; Telegram Tittmann (Rome) to Welles (Washington), 18 November 1941, in FDR Library, Sumner Welles Papers, Box 74; *L'Illustrazione Italiana*, 12 March 1939, 499.

59 Tacke, "'Nobilitierung' von Rehbock," 225–6.

60 For example, see the reports about Ciano in *Corriere della Sera*, *La Stampa*, *L'Illustrazione Italiana*, and *Il Popolo d'Italia*.

61 Ciano Diary, Entry 3.3.1940.

62 Santini, *Costanzo Ciano*, 34.

63 For the futurists, see Apollonio, *Futurist Manifestos*, 19–24.

64 Innocenti, *Gerarchi*, 16.

65 Michaelis, "Conte Galeazzo Ciano," 118.

66 For the fascist ideal of masculinity, see Benadusi, *Enemy of the "New Man,"* 14–21; Ben-Ghiat, "Unmaking the Fascist Man"; Dechert, *Star all'Italiana*; Gori, "Model of Masculinity," 39 and 49.

67 Dogliani, *Fascismo degli italiani*, 95 and 199.

68 Dogliani, "Sport and Fascism," 326–7.

69 Telegram Phillips (Rome) to Hull (Washington), 7 July 1938, in LoC, Cordell Hull Papers, Reel 16; *L'Illustrazione Italiana*, 10 July 1938, 41; and 30 July 1939, 176.

70 In 1934 and 1938 Italy became World Football Champion, and at the 1932 Olympics in Los Angeles the country took second place. Furthermore, the boxer Primo Carnera and the pilots Mazzotti and Lombardi gave Italy pride. Of course, reports and pictures about defeats were never published. See Bosworth, *Mussolini's Italy*, 229; Cante, "Propaganda und Fußball," 186–92; Dogliani, "Sport and Fascism," 327–31.

71 Dogliani, "Sport and Fascism," 332.

72 Ibid., 333; Gori, "Model of Masculinity," 43. For Mussolini as an athlete, see *L'Illustrazione Italiana Sportiva*, 3 December 1936; Ullstein Bild #00107283, #00108653, #00108654, #00112201, #00112202, and #00112205.

73 Bosworth, *Mussolini*, 209; Eatwell, "Concept and Theory," 9.

74 By 2015 there were five different editions of the book. See Bernhart, "Benito Mussolini," 357; Bosworth, "'Ich schreibe,'" 89.

75 For example, see *L'Illustrazione Italiana*, 22 September 1935, cover; Ullstein Bild #00109157, #00109055, #00096923, #00958735, #00107474, #1006732171, #00107233–5, #1012198255, #00112195, and #00112191.

76 *L'Illustrazione Italiana*, 13 November 1938, 866. For the 1937 photographs, see Getty Images #10440936 and #50793198. The publication of the photograph was part of Italy's anti-British and anti-Zionist propaganda at

the time. The "fascist empire wanted to show that it considered itself not only a European superpower but also a Muslim superpower." See Fränkischer Kurier, Italiens Islampolitik, 23 November 1938, in BArch, R901, AZ 60406, 1. See also Antola, "Photographing Mussolini," 185.

77 Just like Costanzo Ciano, the *Duce* embodied the ideal image of a fascist soldier. He initially admired General Field Marshal Erwin Rommel, whom he described as the ideal image of a fascist officer: daring and "always in his tank at the head of the attacking columns." See Ciano Diary, Entry 7.2.1942.

78 Schieder, *Italienische Faschismus*, 69.

79 See Bahro, *SS-Sport*, 105–6; Oelrich, "Hitler, Mussolini und der Sport."

80 Roberts, "Myth, Style, Substance," 4.

81 Ciano Diary, Entry 4.9.1938.

82 Lettera Ciano (Pechino) a Maria Rosa Oliver (Buenos Aires), 6 April 1928, in Mudd Library, Maria Rosa Oliver Papers, Box 3, Folder 4, Series 2a.

83 Varè, *Two Impostors*, 239; Ward Price, *Führer und Duce*, 260.

84 The databases of Getty Images, Ullstein Bild, Archivio LUCE, and leading Italian newspapers contained almost no images of Ciano playing sports.

85 Ciano, *My Truth*, 76–7.

86 Cardoza, "Making Italians," 364–6. One picture of the same photo series shows Ciano cycling (Getty Images, # 944566566). However, none of the major Italian or German newspapers and magazines published it.

87 "Begegnung am Strand ... wo Graf Ciano seine Urlaubstage verbringt" ["Encounter on the beach ... where Count Ciano spends his vacation"]," *Illustrierter Beobachter*, 32, 11 August 1938, 1.

88 Cardoza, "Making Italians," 367–69. For cycling during the fascist era, see also Foot, *Pedalare*, 52–70.

89 Antola, "Photographing Mussolini," 187.

90 Another photograph series in which Ciano's deficiencies in comparison to Mussolini are obvious was taken in February 1934. While Mussolini is always ahead of the group, hiking uphill on a snowy slope with no poles, Ciano uses a ski pole like his wife Edda (ASL, Codice Foto, A00052678). Moreover, another picture shows Ciano's failed attempts to ski: the snow on his dress and the skis' position suggest that he had just fallen down (ASL, Codice Foto, A00052689).

91 Pro-Memoria, Roma, 15 February 1940, in ACS, MI, DGPS, b. 22A, fasc. 1. See also Telegram Phillips (Rome) to Hull (Washington), 22 November 1939, in NARA, RG 59, M1423, Reel 2, File 865.00/1871; Barnes, *British Fascist*, 68; Ciano, *My Truth*, 76–7.

92 Agnelli, *Matrosenkleider*, 108.

93 Bosworth, "Golf," 348; Dogliani, "Sport and Fascism," 340.

94 Ciano Diary, Entry 8.5.1942.
95 Bosworth, "Golf," 352.
96 Jureit, *Generationenforschung*, 43–4. See also Ciano, *My Truth*, 52.
97 For the importance of participating in the First World War, see Bosworth, *Mussolini's Italy*, 79.
98 Guerri (*Galeazzo Ciano*, 194) and Cannistraro and Sullivan (*Il Duce's Other Woman*, 469) claimed that Ciano was not enthusiastic when he went to Ethiopia.
99 For example, see Rapporto, Firenze, 20 August 1935, in ACS, MI, DGPS, b22A, fasc. 1; Rapporto, Città del Vaticano, 22 August 1935, in ibid.; Galeazzo Ciano consegue il brevetto di pilota aviatore, 1936, in ASL, Giornale Luce, B056802; "Galeazzo Ciano ha brillantemente conseguito all'Aeroporto del Littorio il brevetto di pilota d'aeroplano," *Il Popolo d'Italia*, 1 November 1934, 1; "S.E. Galeazzo Ciano aviatore," *La Stampa*, 1 November 1934, 1; *L'Illustrazione Italiana*, 11 November 1934, 761; "Ciano a Cabinet Minister," *New York Times*, 4 October 1935, 3; Susmel, *Vita sbagliata*, 50.
100 "Seimila Camicie Nere salpano da Napoli per l'Africa Orientale," *Il Popolo d'Italia*, 25 August 1935; "5,000 Blackshirts Embarked," *The Times*, 26 August 1935, 10; De Bono, *Vorbereitungen*, 139–49; Nelson Page, *L'Americano*, 451.
101 See *L'Illustrazione Italiana*, 25 August 1935, 369; La partenza dei volontari per l'Africa Orientale, 28 August 1935, in ASL, Giornale Luce, B0737; Guerri, *Galeazzo Ciano*, 187.
102 Rapporto, Firenze, 20 August 1935, in ACS, MI, DGPS, b. 22A, fasc. 1; Talbot, *Censorship*, 96.
103 Susmel, *Vita sbagliata*, 50.
104 Rochat, *Guerre italiane*, 148–9.
105 For the relationship between fascism and aviation, see "Il Volo," in Mussolini, *Opera Omnia*, Vol. 15, 15–16; Bosworth, *Mussolini*, 142–3; Dogliani, "Sport and Fascism," 334–5; Esposito, *Mythische Moderne*.
106 De Bono, *Vorbereitungen*, 139–40; Pavolini, *Disperata*, 52–3; Vogel-Walter, *D'Annunzio*, 131–54.
107 Guerri, *Galeazzo Ciano*, 187–8; La partenza dei volontari per l'Africa Orientale, 1935, in ASL, Giornale Luce, B0740. For the reception of Pavolini's book, see "Disperata," *La Stampa*, 8 May 1937, 5.

A list of the December operations of Ciano's squadron can be found in Lettera Pavolini (Asmara) a Ciano (Roma), 20 December 1935, in ACS, MCP, Gabinetto, b. 10, fasc. 94, 31. According to that list, Ciano's unit did not use any poison gas. However, Del Boca ("Yperit-Regen," 48) and Cannistraro and Sullivan (*Il Duce's Other Woman*, 483–7) disagree. Nevertheless, it can be assumed that Ciano knew about the use of poison gas and war crimes, and that he participated in the bombing of civilians. See Letter National Liberty League of United States (New York) to Ciano (Rome), 4 January 1936, in ACS, MCP, Gabinetto, b. 17; Bottai, *Diario*, 102; Gentilli, "Storiografia aeronautica," 139–41; Duggan, *Fascist Voices*, 267.

108 Bonsaver, *Censorship*, 115.

109 For Ciano's judgment of D'Annunzio, see Ciano Diary, Entries 2.3.1938, 6.3.1938, and 17.8.1938.

110 See Guerri, *Galeazzo Ciano*, 187; Vergani, *Quando Gabriele*, XXI.

111 Bonsaver, *Censorship*, 142.

112 See "Il capitano Galeazzo Ciano," *Il Popolo d'Italia*, 16 October 1935, 1; and "In Africa orientale," 12 November 1935, 3; *L'Illustrazione Italiana*, 20 October 1935, 724 and 745; 10 May 1936, 811; and 12 July 1936, 55.

113 Pavolini, *Disperata*, 97.

114 MacVeagh, *Ambassador MacVeagh*, 121. See also "Disperata," *La Stampa*, 8 May 1937, 5; Ward Price, *Führer und Duce*, 260.

115 Telegramma Alfieri (Roma) a Ciano (Asmara), 20 November 1935, in ACS, MCP, Gabinetto, b. 47; Consegna di medaglie al valor militare, 24 December 1935, in ASL, Giornale Luce, B0803; "Count Ciano Decorated," *The Times*, 25 November 1935, 11; "Ciano's Plane Shot Down," *New York Times*, 19 November 1935, 1.

Already on 27 April he proudly informed his father that he would receive a medal. See Telegramma Ciano (Asmara) a Luciano (Roma), 27 April 1936, in ACS, MCP, Gabinetto, b. 17, fasc. 223.

116 Telegramma Ciano (Asmara) a Alfieri (Roma), 4 April 1936, in ACS, MCP, Gabinetto, b. 17, fasc. 223; Telegramma Ciano (Asmara) a Alfieri (Roma), 22 April 1936, in ibid.

117 Ciano Diary, Entry 1.6.1938.

118 "Man spricht von: Ciano," *Völkischer Beobachter*, 21 May 1939; Pavolini, *Disperata*, 288.

119 Susmel, *Vita sbagliata*, 53.

120 Telegramma Mussolini (Roma) a Ciano (Asmara), 3 May 1936, in ACS, SPD, Autografi, b. 16; "La 'beffa' di Galeazzo Ciano," *La Stampa*, 4 May 1936, 3; Guerri, *Galeazzo Ciano*, 206.

121 Pavolini, *Disperata*, 191. See also Il ritorno, 20 May 1936, in ASL, Giornale Luce, B0888; "Mussolini's Sons Return from War," *New York Times*, 18 May 1936, 11.

On 5 May, Italian troops conquered Addis Ababa, and four days later Mussolini proclaimed Italian rule over Ethiopia. However, the Italians never controlled the hinterland despite a brutal oppression that killed between 180,000 and 250,000 by 1941. See Telegramm Generalkonsul Richter (Addis Abeba) an AA (Berlin), 7 April 1937, in BArch, R43-II, AZ 1451b;

Poggiali, *Diario*, 179–84; De Grand, "Mussolini's Follies," 141; Woller, *Geschichte Italiens*, 149–50.

122 Although he did not participate in any combat during the occupation of Albania, Ciano posed in his uniform. See "Albania Held Firm in Hands of Italy," *New York Times*, 10 April 1939, 3; *L'Illustrazione Italiana*, 16 April 1939, cover.

123 Ciano Diary, Entries 9.9.1937 and 19.9.1937.

124 Ciano Diary, Entries 30.5.1940 and 11.6.1940; Telegram Phillips (Rome) to Hull (Washington), 7 June 1940, in NARA, RG 59, M982, Reel 20, File 740.0011/2855 20/28.

125 Ciano Diary, Entry 4.6.1940.

126 Ciano Diary, Entries 16.6.1940 and 17.6.1940.

127 Cited in Moseley, *Mussolini's Shadow*, 105–6.

128 Susmel, *Vita sbagliata*, 215–16.

129 Ansaldo, *Giornalista*, 256.

130 Ciano Diary, Entry 4.6.1940.

131 Armellini, *Diario*, 130.

132 Visconti Prasca, *Io ho aggredito*, 126–7.

133 Moseley, *Mussolini's Shadow*, 118.

134 Ciano Diary, Entry 1.11.1940.

135 Armellini, *Diario*, 223. While Getty Images #541055523 was published after the Greek campaign began on 6 November 1940, an exact date for the following pictures cannot be given: Getty Images #541050539, #541055093, and #541055117. See also "Ciano, Duce's Sons Reported on Raid," *Washington Post*, 7 November 1940, 8; "Promozioni negli atti gradi," *La Stampa*, 3 November 1940, 2.

136 For example, see "Ciano reassume il comando," *La Stampa*, 28 January 1941, 1; "Il ministro Ciano ha riassunto il comando," *Corriere della Sera*, 28 January 1941, 1. Pictures of Ciano as a pilot during the Greek campaign were occasionally published after Greek's surrender. See *L'Illustrazione Italiana*, 8 June 1941, 892.

137 Ciano Diary, Entries 19.11.1935 and 24.11.1935; Der Botschafter in Rom von Hassell an das Auswärtige Amt, Rom, 7 January 1936, in ADAP, Serie C, Vol. IV, 2, Doc. 486, 958.

138 Bottai, *Diario*, 57–9.

139 See Telegramma Alfieri (Roma) a Ciano (Montonave Vittoria), 15 December 1935, in ACS, MCP, Gabinetto, b. 47; "Lull on the War Front," *The Times*, 14 December 1935, 11; "Telegrams in Brief," *The Times*, 18 December 1935, 11; "Il ministro Ciano in Italia per un breve periodo," *Corriere della Sera*, 13 December 1935.

140 Guerri (*Galeazzo Ciano*, 196) argues that Ciano's low enthusiasm was the reason for his return. He neglects to mention that Ciano's lack of

euphoria stemmed from his fear of being shot down. Ciano even hoped that the Hoare-Laval Pact (1935) would bring an end to the fighting so he could return to Italy. See Varè, *Two Impostors*, 238.

141 See Bosworth, "War," 479; Pavolini, *Disperata*, 51.

142 Guerri, *Galeazzo Ciano*, 188–96.

143 For example, see Phillips Diary, Entry 4.4.1938, in Houghton Library, William Phillips, Box 8/16, Folder 1; Ciano, *My Truth*, 71.

144 See Telegramma Sebastiani (Roma) a Ciano (Firenze), no date, in ACS, SPD, Carteggio, b. 115.

145 Lettera Pavolini (Asmara) a Ciano (Roma), 20 December 1935, in ACS, MCP, Gabinetto, b. 10, fasc. 94; Lettera Pavolini (Asmara) a Ciano (Roma), 30 December 1935, in ibid.

146 Press reports released at the time of Ciano's departure from Ethiopia mentioned that he would return to Italy for a very short time due to matters concerning his ministry. See "Brevissimo ritorno di Galeazzo Ciano," *Il Popolo d'Italia*, 14 December 1935, 1.

147 Koon, *Believe, Obey, Fight*, 16; Spackman, *Fascist Virilities*, 3.

148 Lessona, *Memorie*, 239–41.

149 Ortona, *Diplomazia*, 109.

150 Ciano Diary, Entry 26.1.1942. See also Telegramm Bismarck (Rom) an AA (Berlin), 27 January 1941, in PAAA, Botschaft in Rom – Geheimakten, 97, 481048–50.

151 See Telegramm Botschaft Rom, 15 February 1941, in PAAA, Geheime Reichssachen, R61140, 65; SS-Brigadeführer an das AA, 27 January 1941, in PAAA, Inland II, R101084, Fiche 2796, 284070; Vermerk, 24 January 1941, in BArch, R58, AZ 9486, 790517; Ortona, *Diplomazia*, 132

152 See "S.E. Galeazzo Ciano membro del Gran Consiglio," *Il Popolo d'Italia*, 21 December 1935; "Il conte Galeazzo Ciano membro del Gran Consiglio," *Corriere della Sera*, 18 December 1935, 1; "Son-In-Law of Mussolini Named to Grand Council," *Washington Post*, 21 December 1935, 6.

153 See Telegramma Ciano (Roma) a Valle (Roma), 19 August 1935, in ACS, MCP, Gabinetto, b. 10, fasc. 82; Telegramma Alfieri (Roma) a Bonomi (Roma), 27 August 1935, in ibid.; Telegramma Bonomi (Roma) a Alfieri (Roma), 3 October 1935, in ibid.; Ducci, *Bella gioventù*, 83; De Grand, "Mussolini's Follies," 137.

154 For Ciano's statements, see Telegramma Alfieri (Roma) a Ciano (Asmara), 27 October 1935, in ACS, MCP, Gabinetto, b. 17; Ciano, Testo del discorso, Asmara, 1 November 1935, in ibid.

155 Telegram Taylor (Chicago) to Long (Rome), 7 August 1933, in LoC, Breckinridge Long Papers, Box 106; Letter Long (Washington) to Colonna (Washington), 8 August 1940, in ibid., Box 130; *L'Illustrazione Italiana*, 6 August 1933, 206–7; Dogliani, "Sport and Fascism," 335.

156 See Lettera, 24 January 1936, in BSB, Mussolini Papers, Reel 453, Frame 028389; Gli Aviatori Eroici d'Italia, no date, in ACS, SPD, Carteggio, b. 115.
157 Ortona, *Diplomazia*, 131; Oven, *Mit Goebbels bis zum Ende*, 174.
158 Telegramm Bismarck (Rom) an AA (Berlin), 27 January 1941, in PAAA, Botschaft in Rom – Geheimakten, 97, 481048–50; Telegram Phillips (Rome) to Hull (Washington), 28 January 1941, in NARA, RG59, M982, Reel 43, File 740.0011/7958; Le nonce en Italie Borgongini Duca au cardinal Maglione, Rome, 17 January 1941, in ADSS, Vol. IV, Doc. 237, 345–6; Ortona, *Diplomazia*, 127.
159 Rapporto, Bari, 22 February 1941, in ACS, MI, DGPS, b. 22A, fasc. 1; Rapporto, Roma, 13 May 1941, in ibid.; Commenti sulla posizione dell'Ecc. Ciano, Milano, 11 March 1941, in ibid., fasc. 2; Rapporto, Roma, 23 May 1941, in ibid., fasc. 1; Alfieri, *Dictators*, 196–7; Ansaldo, *Giornalista*, 257–8. Numerous other reports on Ciano's lifestyle in Bari can be found in ACS, MI, DGPS, b. 298. Armellini (*Diario*, 276) feared that the ministers would return to Rome triumphantly as "heroes." Then, according to the general, only an "intelligent epidemic" could save Italy.
160 Ansaldo, *Giornalista*, 295.
161 Ibid., 353–5. For Ciano's hesitant behaviour, see Telegram Harrison (Bern) to Hull (Washington), 13 February 1943, in NARA, RG 59, CDF, Box 1878, File 701.6566A/8; Memorandum for the President, 14 May 1943, in LoC, Myron Charles Taylor Papers, Box 2.
162 Bottai, *Diario*, 398–400; Lettera Segreteria Particolare al Duce, Roma, 17 July 1943, in BSB, Mussolini Papers, Reel 453, Frames 028511 and 028413; Lettera Segreteria Particolare al Duce, Roma, 20 July 1943, in ibid., Frame 028413. Anfuso (*Rom – Berlin*, 223) again spoke of a "political illness."
163 Telegram Harrison (Bern) to Hull (Washington), 10 August 1943, in NARA, RG 59, M982, Reel 167, File 30631; Deakin, *Brutale Freundschaft*, 550; Goeschel, *Mussolini and Hitler*, 246–8.
164 Bottai, *Diario*, 402–4; Bianchi, *25 luglio*, 468–72. For Grandi's lobbying work, see Memo on Col. Rossi's Account of Mussolini's Removal, no date, in NA, FO 660/379.
165 For example, the story that he helped draft the petition is claimed by Guerri (*Amore fascista*, 202–3).
166 Ortona, *Diplomazia*, 257.
167 Bosworth, *Mussolini*, 400.
168 Alfieri, *Dictators*, 279–81.
169 See Anfuso, *Rom – Berlin*, 229–31; Carboni, *Memorie*, 203; Pirelli, *Taccuini*, 449; Guerri, *Amore fascista*, 203–4; Rosen, "Viktor Emanuel III," 54.
170 Zangrandi, *1943*, 45
171 Buffarini Guidi, *Vera verità*, 104; Mussolini, *My Life*, 125–6; Bosworth, *Claretta*, 171.

172 Bosworth, *Mussolini*, 400–1.
173 Bottai, *Diario*, 412–15.
174 Alfieri, *Dictators*, 291; Guerri, *Galeazzo Ciano*, 826–29.
175 Bastianini, *Uomini, cose, fatti*, 261.
176 Ciano's hatred of Germany was also reflected in numerous anti-German comments he made during his time in the Vatican. See Rapporto, Vaticano, 21 May 1943, in BSB, Mussolini Papers, Reel 453, Frame 028409; Plehwe, *Als die Achse zerbrach*, 236–7.
177 Bottai, *Diario*, 404–21.
178 The exact time when Ciano cast his vote is disputed. According to Guerri (*Amore fascista*, 208–9), six people had already voted "yes" (De Bono, De Vecchi, Grandi, Rossoni, De' Stefani, and Albini), and only one person, Scorza, had voted "no." Therefore, three more definitive (Bottai, De Marsico, and Federzoni) and two very likely (Bastianini and Alfieri) "yes" votes could be expected. Including Ciano, that would have brought the number to twelve people who were expected to support Grandi's petition. In light of this count, we should not overestimate Ciano's courage when he voted "yes."
179 Bottai, *Diario*, 420–1; Woller, *Mussolini*, 268.
180 Gentile, "Mussolini," 114–23.
181 Mussolini, *My Life*, 126–7.
182 Bosworth, *Mussolini*, 401–2.
183 Rosen, "Viktor Emanuel III," 58.
184 Alfieri, *Dictators*, 292–4.
185 Rosen, "Viktor Emanuel III," 52–5 and 75–6; Telegramm Mackensen (Rom) an AM (Berlin), 27 July 1943, in PAAA, Büro des Staatssekretärs, R29640, 72463.
186 Bottai, *Diario*, 428–9; Carboni, *Memorie*, 201–3.
187 Bosworth, *Mussolini*, 400; Di Rienzo, *Ciano*, 1374.
188 Carboni, *Memorie*, 186–90.
189 Anfuso, *Rom – Berlin*, 220 and 229–31; Carboni, *Memorie*, 201–3.
190 Telegram Hoare (Madrid) to FO (London), 15 August 1943, in FDR Library, Harry L. Hopkins Papers, Box 160, Folder Italy; Guerri, *Galeazzo Ciano*, 838.
191 Guerri, *Amore fascista*, 210.
192 See Telegramm Ribbentrop (Berlin) an Botschaft (Lissabon), 27 August 1943, in PAAA, Inland II, R101085, Fiche 2801, E411503–4; Amicucci, *600 giorni*, 80.
193 Telegramm Weizsäcker (Vatikan) an AM (Berlin), 31 July 1943, in PAAA, Büro des Staatssekretärs, R29640, 72635; Notes du cardinal Maglione, Vatican, 31 July 1943, in ADSS, Vol. VII, Doc. 321, 533, Note 1.
194 Italian Crisis: Japanese Minister (Madrid), 29 July 1943, in NA, HW 12/290, No. 120572; Lettera Questura Roma a Senise, 28 August 1943, in

ACS, MI, DGPS, b. 22A, fasc. 2; Notes du cardinal Maglione, Vatican, 27 July 1943, in ADSS, Vol. VII, Doc. 316, 524–7; Agnelli, *Matrosenkleider*, 158.

195 Ortona, *Diplomazia*, 274.

196 Carboni, *Memorie*, 239; Senise, *Quando ero capo della polizia*, 227–8; Rosen, "Viktor Emanuel III," 53.

197 See Questura di Roma, 28 August 1943, in ACS, MI, DGPS, b. 22A, fasc. 2; Ciano, *Quando il nonno*, 71. Other fascists were also concerned about their own safety after Muti's assassination. See Bottai, *Diario*, 432–3.

198 Edda Ciano would later claim that they wanted to use Germany as a stopover to go to Spain or South America. She accused the Germans of betraying them by not letting them leave the country. The Germans, however, denied that such an arrangement ever existed. See Ciano, *My Truth*, 193; Guerri, *Galeazzo Ciano*, 852–3.

199 Varè, *Two Impostors*, 242.

200 See Commissariato di P.S. Flaminio a Regia Questura, Roma, 27 August 1943, in ACS, MI, DGPS, b. 22A, fasc. 2; Telegramma Senise (Roma) a Questori Regno, 31 January 1943, in ibid.; Telegram Harrison (Bern) to Hull (Washington), 31 August 1943, in NARA, RG 59, CDF, Box 5644, File 865.002/259; Ciano, *My Truth*, 196; Rossi, *Mussolini e il diplomatico*, 422.

201 See Rapporto, Roma, 3 September 1943, in ACS, MI, DGPS, b. 22A, fasc. 1; Telegramma Senise (Roma) a Questori Regno, 27 August 1943, in ibid., fasc. 2; Telegramma Senise (Roma) a Questori Regno, 28 August 1943, in ibid.; Telegramma Secreti (Siena) a Ministero dell'Interno (Roma), 30 August 1943, in ibid.; Telegramm Dieckhoff (Madrid) an Schellenberg (Berlin), 19 September 1943, in PAAA, Inland II, R101086, Fiche 2802, E411536; "Surrender of Ciano Is Reported in Italy," *New York Times*, 7 September 1943, 4; "Ciano's Recapture Reported by Italians," *New York Times*, 31 August 1943, 6.

202 Rapporto, Roma, 28 August 1943, in ACS, MI, DGPS, b. 22A, fasc. 1.

203 Galeazzo Ciano, Roma, 5 September 1943, in ACS, MI, DGPS, b. 22A, fasc. 2.

204 Prefettura di Pisa, 8 September 1943, in ACS, MI, DGPS,, b. 298; Lettera, Roma, 9 August 1943, in ACS, MI, DGPS, Cat. A1, 1943, b. 24.

205 Telegram Harrison (Bern) to State Department (Washington), 8 September 1943, in NARA, RG 84, Entry 3207, Box 86; Politischer Informationsdienst, Tagesbericht, 1 September 1943, in USHMM, RG 58.003, Reel 5, Frame 4.

206 Telegram Crocker (Lisbon) to Hull (Washington), no date, in NARA, RG 59, CDF, Box 5643, File 865.00/2236; Plehwe, *Schicksalsstunden*, 233. For the armistice, see Morgan, *Fall of Mussolini*, 93–126.

207 Even though Ciano's predictions on 13 July in the presence of Ansaldo came pretty close to what happened on 25 July, no documents prove that

Ciano knew what the king had in mind. According to Rosen ("Viktor Emanuel III," 52), the king only asked Badoglio to take over the government two days later.

208 Ducci, *Bella gioventù*, 176; Pirelli, *Taccuini*, 376.

209 Goebbels, *Tagebücher*, Part II, Vol. 9, Entry 23.9.1943, 557–92

210 Cited in Guerri, *Amore fascista*, 210.

211 Telegram Hoare (Madrid) to FO (London), 15 August 1943, in NA, FO 371/37264, R7427/242/22.

212 Ansaldo, *Giornalista*, 337, 348, and 350.

213 Focardi, "Italy's Amnesia," 10–11.

214 See documents in BArch, R58, AZ 187, Fiche 1–3; Telegramm R. Brandt (Berlin) an Wagner (Berlin), 19 July 1943, in PAAA, Inland II, R101085, Fiche 2799, 284203–3; Telegramm Mackensen (Rom) an AM (Berlin), 24 July 1943, in PAAA, Büro des Staatssekretärs, R29640, 72435–6; Hassell, *Vom andern Deutschland*, 288.

215 Goebbels, *Tagebücher*, Part II, Vol. 9, Entry 27.7.1943, 177. The German press blamed the Jews and Freemasons for Mussolini's fall. See Das Neue Europa vom 15.11.1943, in BArch, R4902, AZ 7464; "So sabotierten die Freimaurer die Arbeit des Duce," *Völkischer Beobachter*, 14 February 1944.

216 Telegramm Steengracht (Berlin) an Mackensen (Rom), 26 July 1943, in PAAA Büro des Staatssekretärs, R29640, 72486; Politischer Informationsdienst, 27 July 1943, in USHMM, RG 58.003, Reel 5, 4–5.

217 Telegramm Mackensen (Rom) an AM (Berlin), 27 July 1943, in PAAA, Büro des Staatssekretärs, R29640, 72495.

218 See Aufzeichnungen, Rom, 21 December 1939, in PAAA, Mackensen, 7, 440262; Di Rienzo, *Ciano*, 1382.

219 Knigge, *Dilemma eines Diplomaten*, 43; Villari, *Affari Esteri*, 113.

220 See Telegramm Mackensen (Rom) an AM (Berlin), 29 July 1943, in PAAA, Büro des Staatssekretärs, R29640, 72614; Telegramm Mackensen (Rom) an AM (Berlin), 30 July 1943, in ibid., 72626; Plehwe, *Als die Achse zerbrach*, 156–7.

221 Schellenberg, *Aufzeichnungen*, 300–1.

222 Ciano, *Mia Vita*, 77; Goebbels, *Tagebücher*, Part II, Vol. 9, Entry 14.8.1943, 246–70; Höttl, *Unternehmen Bernhard*, 141–50.

223 Telegram Young, Allied Force Headquarters, to Italian Archives Section, British Embassy (Rome), 18 January 1946, in NA, WO 204/12798; Höttl, *Unternehmen Bernhard*, 154. Since the summer of 1941 Ciano had attempted to establish contact with Himmler, because he knew about the rivalry between Himmler and Ribbentrop. See Telegramm Dollmann an Wolff, Rom, 16 February 1941, BArch, NS19, AZ 3840; Lettera Alfieri a Ciano, Berlino, 16 October 1942, in ACS, Archivi Alfieri, b. 6.

224 Telegram Kappler (Rome) to Berlin, 14 August 1943, in NA, HW 19/237, No. 5968; Smyth, *Secrets*, 1–19; Susmel, *Vita sbagliata*, 302–3.

225 See Fernschreiben SS Obersturmbannführer Brandt an SS Sturmbannführer Scheidler, Berlin, 2 September 1943, in BArch, NS19, AZ 912, 7–8; Fernschreiben SS Obersturmbannführer Brandt an SS Sturmbannführer Scheidler, Berlin, 10 September 1943, in ibid., 9.
226 Feldkommandostelle an Reichsmarschall Göring, 20 September 1943, in BArch, NS19, AZ 912, 15–16; Goebbels, *Tagebücher*, Part II, Vol. 9, Entry 23.9.1943, 274.
227 Hassell, *Vom andern Deutschland*, 298; Mussolini, *My Life*, 145–6.
228 It was to Ciano's advantage that his stories corresponded with the information the Germans had. See Moellhausen, *Gebrochene Achse*, 223.
229 Goebbels, *Tagebücher*, Part II, Vol. 9, Entry 23.9.1943, 557–92.
230 Amicucci, *600 giorni*, 81; Goebbels, *Tagebücher*, Part II, Vol. 9, Entry 27.7.1943, 177; Moellhausen, *Gebrochene Achse*, 224.
231 Bosworth, *Mussolini's Italy*, 506.
232 "Lettera Mussolini a Petacci, 10.10.1943," in Mussolini, *A Clara*, 76. Claretta Petacci also demanded the execution of the traitors. See Woller, *Mussolini*, 291.
233 Mussolini also used the title "count" when he replied to Serrano Suñer's letter in which the former Spanish foreign minister criticized Ciano's execution. See Di Rienzo, *Ciano*, 1781.
234 See Anfuso, *Rom – Berlin*, 260–2 and 284–5. Amicucci (*600 giorni*, 81) claimed that a reconciliation never happened.
235 Brief Hanns Johst (Oberallmannshausen) an Himmler (Berlin), 18 October 1943, in BArch, NS19, AZ 4046. For Ciano's suicidal thoughts, see Agnelli, *Matrosenkleider*, 180–1; Benini, *Carcere degli Scalzi*, 121; Schad, *Sie liebten den Führer*, 103.
236 Aufbau der italienischen Gerichtsbarkeit, Verona, 18 January 1944, in BArch, R70-Italien, AZ 15, 1214–15.
237 Telegramm Rahn an AM (Berlin), 27 October 1943, in PAAA, Inland II, R101086, Fiche 2803, E411588–90.
238 Deakin, *Brutale Freundschaft*, 721.
239 Moseley, *Mussolini's Shadow*, 24.
240 See Tribunale Speciale Straordinario, Verona, 30 December 1943, in NA, GFM 36/429. The documents and the interrogation protocols can be found in NA, GFM 37/429 to GFM 36/432.
241 Rossi, *Mussolini e il diplomatico*, 450.
242 Telegramm Kaltenbrunner, 9 January 1944, in PAAA, Inland II, R101087, Fiche 2804, 262447; Wagner, no date, in ibid., 262457; Cianetti, *Memorie*, 468.
243 "Germans Report Ciano, 4 Others Put to Death," *Washington Post*, 12 January 1944, 1; Moseley, *Mussolini's Shadow*, 226–7.
244 Telegramm Bock (Dienststelle Rahn) an Ribbentrop (Berlin), 10 January 1944, in PAAA, Büro des Staatssekretärs, R29645, Fiche 575, 71362–3.

245 Ibid., 71364; Buffarini Guidi, *Vera verità*, 104–6.
246 Der Befehlshaber der Sicherheitspolizei und des SD in Italien, 11 January 1944, in PAAA, Inland II, R101087, Fiche 2804, 26768.
247 Rossi, *Mussolini e il diplomatico*, 453.
248 Telegramm Rahn (Dienststelle Rahn) an Ribbentrop (Berlin), 14 January 1944, in PAAA, Büro des Staatssekretärs, R29645, Fiche 575, 71389–90.
249 Ibid.; Benini, *Carcere degli Scalzi*, 53.
250 Goebbels, *Tagebücher*, Part II, Vol. 11, Entry 25.1.1944, 158.
251 Rossi, *Mussolini e il diplomatico*, 445; Goebbels, *Tagebücher*, Part II, Vol. 9, Entry 23.9.1943, 567–8 and 572. For Edda's attempts to free Ciano, see Extract from 12th Army Group report of 18 June 45 on Hildegard Beetz, in NA, KV 2/412, 1; Telegram Kappler (Rome) to Hoettl (Berlin), 7.11.1943, in NA, HW 19/239, No. 8241; Benini, *Carcere degli Scalzi*, 79; Smyth, *Secrets*.
252 Churchill, *Second World War*, Vol. II, 115–16; Moseley, *Mussolini's Shadow*, 207–8.
253 Ciano's preface can be found in NA, GFM 36/645, Frames 696–701.
254 See Telegramm Rahn (Dienststelle Rahn) an Ribbentrop (Berlin), 11 January 1944, in PAAA, Büro des Staatssekretärs, R29645, Fiche 575, 71368–9; Der Befehlshaber der Sicherheitspolizei und des SD in Italien, 11 January 1944, in PAAA, Inland II, R101087, Fiche 2804, 267690; Benini, *Carcere degli Scalzi*, 118; Rossi, *Mussolini e il diplomatico*, 451; Cutler, "Three Careers," 517; Deakin, *Brutale Freundschaft*, 730–1.
255 For the negative reports, see "Cianos Execution Ordered Filmed by Mussolini," *Washington Post*, 27 June 1944, 1; Barnes, *British Fascist*, 132. For the positive verdicts, see Senise, *Quando ero capo della polizia*, 226.
256 Panunzio, "*Secondo Fascismo*," 181.
257 Letter Caccia (Rome) to MacMillan (Algiers), 16 January 1943, in NA, FO 660/368, R42/150/2, 1.
258 Harrison, Memorandum of Conversation with Italian Minister, Bern, 13 January 1944, in NARA, RG 84, Entry 3208, Box 16, Folder 800; Italian (Fascist) Executions: Report from Irish Minister, Rome, 18 January 1944, in NA, HW 12/296, No. 127248; "Dictator's Vengeance," *New York Times*, 12 January 1944, 22.
259 Berenson, *Rumour and Reflection*, 139. As early as October 1943 the American press stated that Ciano would receive the death sentence. See "Ciano's Execution Predicted," *New York Times*, 31 October 1943, 12. The Deutsche Nachrichtenbüro already reported the death sentences on 9 January. See Telegramm Rahn (Dienststelle Rahn) an Ribbentrop (Berlin), 10 January 1944, in PAAA, Büro des Staatssekretärs, R29645, Fiche 575, 71362–4.
260 See Benini, *Carcere degli Scalzi*, 88; Mussolini, *Il duce*, 82.

261 Di Rienzo, *Ciano*, 1725.

262 See Verantwortliche Vernehmung, Wolfsburg, 15 January 1968, in Landesarchiv Berlin, B Rep 057–01, Nr. 1223, Vol. 28, 4; Der Befehlshaber der Sicherheitspolizei und des SD in Italien, 11 January 1944, in PAAA, Inland II, R101087, Fiche 2804, 26769; Telegramm Kaltenbrunner an RAM, 13 January 1944, in ibid., 262454–5; Benini, *Cacere degli Scalzi*, 26 and 36; Moellhausen, *Gebrochene Achse*, 225.

263 See Eidgenössisches Politisches Department, Abteilung für Auswärtiges, Bern, 8 February 1944, in USHMM, RG 58.003, Reel 9, Frame 12; Oven, *Mit Goebbels bis zum Ende*, 172; Rahn, *Ruheloses Leben*, 251.

264 "Lettera Mussolini a Petacci," 7.1.1944, in Mussolini, *A Clara*, 92.

265 Rossi, *Mussolini e il diplomatico*, 450–4.

266 "Lettera Mussolini a Petacci," 10.1.1945, in Mussolini, *A Clara*, 348.

267 For the letter, see Susmel, *Vita sbagliata*, 361.

268 Mussolini, *My Life*, 152–4.

269 Amicucci, *600 giorni*, 81; Bosworth, *Mussolini*, 406.

270 Telegramm Reichsaußenminister von Ribbentrop (Sonderzug) an die Dienststelle Rahn, 26 December 1943, in ADAP, Serie E, Vol. VII, Doc. 147, 283.

271 Goebbels, *Tagebücher*, Part II, Vol. 11, Entry 4.1.1944, 46; Schellenberg, *Aufzeichnungen*, 302.

272 Telegramm Bock (Dienststelle Rahn) an Ribbentrop (Berlin), 10 January 1944, in PAAA, Büro des Staatssekretärs, R29645, Fiche 575, 71365.

273 Di Rienzo (*Ciano*, 1728–9) shows that this interpretation still circulates today in Italian historiography.

274 See Buffarini Guidi, *Vera verità*, 109; Goebbels, *Tagebücher*, Part II, Vol. 11, Entry 12.1.1944, 76.

275 Goebbels, *Tagebücher*, Part II, Vol. 11, Entry 12.1.1944, 74–8; Moellhausen, *Gebrochene Achse*, 226.

276 Armellini, *Diario*, 276; Innocenti, *Gerarchi*, 16.

277 Politischer Informationsdienst, Tagesbericht, 12–13 January 1944, in USHMM, RG 58.003, Reel 5, Frame 4.

278 Goebbels, *Tagebücher*, Part II, Vol. 10, Entry 19.12.1943, 498–506; Mussolini, *Due donne*, 17; Bosworth, *Mussolini's Italy*, 507–15; Deakin, *Brutale Freundschaft*, 727.

279 Eidgenössisches Politisches Department, Abteilung für Auswärtiges, Bern, 8 February 1944, in USHMM, RG 58.003, Reel 9, Frame 11.

280 See Fatta, "Verona," 387; Juso, *Processo di Verona*, 16; Innocenti, *Gerarchi*, 42. In particular, Edda Ciano (*My Truth*, 224–5) blamed Buffarini Guidi and Pavolini for her husband's death. In turn, Buffarini Guidi's son blamed Pavolini, who was killed in 1945. See Buffarini Guidi, *Vera verità*, 94–5. Di Rienzo (*Ciano*, 1705), however, seems to ignore these factors and claims that Pavolini had no reason to demand Ciano's execution.

281 Bosworth, *Claretta*, 17.
282 Bosworth, *Mussolini*, 16. See also "Ciano Condemned as Traitor," *New York Times*, 11 January 1944, 1; Goeschel, *Mussolini and Hitler*, 271.
283 Goebbels, *Tagebücher*, Part II, Vol. 11, Entry 12.1.1944, 75–6. See also Entry 22.1.1944, 139; Below, *Hitlers Adjutant*, 359.
284 Telegramm Rahn (Dienststelle Rahn) an Ribbentrop (Berlin), 14 January 1944, in PAAA, Büro des Staatssekretärs, R29645, Fiche 575, 71389–90.
285 Bosworth, *Mussolini*, 16.
286 Rossi, *Mussolini e il diplomatico*, 451.
287 Goebbels, *Tagebücher*, Part II, Vol. 11, Entry 12.1.1944, 76; Oven, *Mit Goebbels bis zum Ende*, 172.
288 "Dictator's Vengeance," *New York Times*, 12 January 1944, 22.
289 See Telegramm Kaltenbrunner an RAM, 13 January 1944, in PAAA, Inland II, R101087, Fiche 2804, 262454–5. For the negative reaction in Spain, see Telegram Hoare (Madrid) to MacMillan (Algiers), 20 January 1944, in NA, FO 660/368, R42/150/2, 3.
290 Das ungarische Oberhaus ehrt Ciano, 20 January 1944, in BArch, R8034-III, AZ 64, Bl. 16; Telegram Harrison (Bern) to Hull (Washington), 13 January 1943, in NARA, RG 84, Box 16, Folder 800.
291 Di Rienzo, *Ciano*, 1779.
292 "Dictator's Vengeance," *New York Times*, 12 January 1944, 22.
293 Phillips Diary, Entry 11.1.1944, in Houghton Library, William Phillips Diaries, Box 15/29, Folder 10. Churchill (*Second World War*, Vol. V, 438–9) claimed that Hitler was responsible for Ciano's execution.
294 See Telegramm Kaltenbrunner an RAM, Berlin, 13 January 1944, in PAAA, Inland II, R101087, Fiche 2804, 262454–5; Eidgenössisches Politisches Department, Abteilung für Auswärtiges, Bern, 8 February 1944, in USHMM, RG 58.003, Reel 9, Frame 11–12; Harrison, Memorandum of Conversation with Italian Minister, Bern, 13 January 1944, in NARA, RG 84, Entry 3208, Box 16, Folder 800; Italian (Fascist) Executions, 18 January 1944, in NA, HW 12/296, No. 127248; Goebbels, *Tagebücher*, Part II, Vol. 11, Entry 24.1.1944, 147–51.
295 Italian (Fascist) Executions, 18 January 1944, in NA, HW 12/296, No. 127248. There are isolated signs that the public regarded Ciano as anti-German and a pacifist as soon as he became ambassador in the Vatican. See Rapporto, Roma, 12 March 1943, in ACS, MI, DGPS, fasc. 22A, fasc. 2.
296 Rossi, *Mussolini e il diplomatico*, 463.
297 Focardi, *Falsche Freunde*, 51, 113–15, and 122–32.
298 Brief Hanns Johst (Oberallmannshausen) an Himmler (Berlin), 18 October 1943, in BArch, NS19, AZ 4046.
299 "Indiscretions of Mussolini's Son-in-Law," *New York Herald Tribune*, 13 January 1946.

300 "Missing Ciano Notes on Munich," *Washington Post*, 2 August 1953, B6; "Ciano's Apologia to History," *New York Times*, 13 January 1946, BR1.

301 "Books of Our Times," *New York Times*, 10 January 1946.

302 Telegram Dulles (Bern) to Donovan (Washington), 9 March 1945, in NARA, RG 226, Entry 134, Box 215, Folder 1345; Diary kept by Jackson, 27.4.–19.11.45, Entry 27.5.1945, in LoC, Robert Houghwout Jackson Papers, Reel 1; The General Secretary, International Military Tribunal, Nuremberg, 18 February 1946, in NA, FO 1019/15; Salter and Charlesworth, "Ribbentrop," 107.

303 Memorandum Dulles (Bern) to Shepardson (Washington), 19 January 1945, in NARA, RG 226, Entry 190C, Box 11, 1; Ribbentrop, *Zwischen London und Moskau*, 289. See also Anfuso, *Rom – Berlin*, 19; Dollmann, *Call Me Coward*, 33; Goebbels, *Tagebücher*, Part II, Vol. 9, Entry 23.9.1943, 572; Serrano Suñer, *Zwischen Hendaye und Gibraltar*, 286–7.

304 Telegram Edman to Barnes, 25 June 1945, in NA, WO 204/6090.

305 *Roma cittá aperta*, director: Roberto Rossellini.

306 Rossi, *Mussolini e il diplomatico*, 435.

307 Alfonso a Cosmin (Verona), 7 April 1944, in BSB, Mussolini Papers, Reel 456, Frame 029685/A.

308 For Edda's stay in Switzerland, see, for example, SCI Detachment Weimar, 14 June 1945, in CIA, FOIA, Special Collection, Beetz, Vol. 1_0062, 2; Vortrag von Dr. Heinrich Rothmund, St. Gallen, 31 January 1944, in USHMM, RG 58.003, Reel 82; Verantwortliche Vernehmung von Albin Franz Eisenkolb, Wiesbaden, 24 November 1959, in Landesarchiv NRW, NS-Verbrechen Nr. 3034, 46; Pucci Report, in NARA, RG 226, Entry 190C, Box 11, 5; Pucci Report, 1 October 1945, in NARA, RG 226, Entry 210, Box 111; Hof, "Tagebücher"; Smyth, *Secrets*.

309 "Swiss Deport Edda Ciano," *New York Times*, 31 August 1945, 11; "Ciano's Widow Headed for Internment," *Washington Post*, 1 September 1945, 5.

310 "Edda Ciano Holds Mussolini Weak," *New York Times*, 21 September 1945, 12; "The 'Mussolinids,'" *New York Times*, 20 September 1959, SM82.

311 "Ciano's Widow Given 2 Years as Pro-Fascist," *Washington Post*, 21 December 1945, 11.

312 See Telegram Dulles (Bern) to Buxton and Shepardson (Washington), 11 January 1945, in NARA, RG 226, Entry 190C, Box 11, 1; Memorandum Dulles (Bern) to Shepardson (Washington), 19 January 1945, in ibid., 5–6.

313 "U.S. Assets of Edda Ciano Taken Over," *Washington Post*, 3 August 1951, 3.

314 "Edda Ciano, 84, Daughter Disavowed Mussolini for Count," *New York Times*, 10 April 1995, B14.

315 "Marzio Ciano, a Grandson of Mussolini, Dies at 36," *New York Times*, 13 April 1974, 28. Marzio Ciano had two sons, Pietro Francesco (b. 1962) and

Lorenzo Ciano (b. 1965). Pietro is the father of the twins Carlo and Marzio Ciano, born in 2009.

316 "Mussolini Reported to Have Picked 'Heir,'" *New York Times*, 25 November 1930; "Admiral Ciano, 63, Head of Fascists," *New York Times*, 27 June 1939. Most monographs on Mussolini and Costanzo and Galeazzo Ciano repeat this narrative. See Di Rienzo, *Ciano*, 111–12; Guerri, *Galeazzo Ciano*, 89; Mazzoni, "Costanzo Ciano," 20.

317 Ciano Diary, Entry 3.7.1939. It should also be mentioned that Galeazzo Ciano was not in Italy in 1926.

318 Clark, *Mussolini*, 113.

319 De Felice, *Mussolini il fascista*, Vol. 2, 349; Morgan, *Fascism in Europe*, 133. In February 1938 the American consulate in Milan reported the existence of a list created by the Fascist Grand Council. It contained – in this order – the names Galeazzo Ciano, Starace, and Balbo. See Telegram Sholes (Milan) to Hull (Washington), 3 February 1938, in NARA, RG 59, M1423, Reel 5, File 865.002 Mussolini/214. According to Segrè (*Italo Balbo*, 368), De Vecchi and De Bono opposed Ciano.

320 Pirelli, *Taccuini*, 372–7 and 398.

321 Gentile, "Fascism in Power," 171–4; Gentile, Corner, and Duggan, "Two New Books," 679–80. Gentile, however, ignores the real possibility that a successful conduct of the war would have strengthened the myth of the *Duce* but not necessarily the prestige of the regime or the party, which had already suffered before Italy joined the war. See Auszüge a. d. Berichterstattung des MilAtt (Wehrmachtspropaganda) in dem Zeitraum v. 22.11.40 – 11.5.43: Die faschistische Partei, no date, in IfZ, MA 82, Vol. 6.

322 Italian Cabinet Changes, 9 February 1943, in NA, HW 12/285, No. 114022; Gentile, Corner, and Duggan, "Two New Books."

323 Corner, *The Fascist Party*, 8 and 274; Duggan, *Fascist Voices*, xx.

324 Duggan, *Fascist Voices*, 231–2. See also Bosworth, *Claretta*, 165; Corner, "Everyday Fascism," 218.

325 Ciano Diary, Entry 22.9.1941. For the party's failure to address the food shortage, see Entries 22.9.1941 and 23.10.1942.

326 See Ciano Diary, Entries 9.7.1941, 11.11.1942, and 23.11.1942. See also Politischer Bericht (Palermo) an Deutsche Botschaft (Rom), 30 October 1942, in PAAA, Botschaft in Rom – Geheimakten, 132.

327 See Telegram Hayes (Madrid) to Hull (Washington), 5 December 1942, in NARA, RG 59, M982, Reel 142, File 740.011EW/26287.

328 Weber, *Grundriss der Sozialökonomie*, 142–4.

329 For example, see *L'Illustrazione Italiana*, 30 May 1937, 567; "Il Discorso Ciano," *La Stampa*, 14 December 1939, 1, and other articles in *L'Illustrazione Italiana*, *La Stampa*, and *Il Popolo d'Italia*.

330 Jureit, *Generationenforschung*, 33.

331 Gentile, "Mussolini," 125.
332 Ward Price, *Führer und Duce*, 319.
333 Morgan, *Fascism in Europe*, 136.
334 Weber, *Grundriss der Sozialökonomie*, 130.
335 Paxton, *Anatomy of Fascism*, 219.
336 Guerri, *Amore fascista*, 209. See also Buffarini Guidi, *Vera verità*, 103.
337 See Goebbels, *Tagebücher*, Part I, Vol. 9, Entry 15.1.1941, 96; Hoare, *Gesandter*, 84; Deletant, "Ion Antonescu," 281–3; Fischer-Galati, "Codreanu," 110; Payne, *Fascism in Spain*, 310–61 and 380–1; Payne, "Franco," 60; Sánchez-Biosca, "Cinematic Image."
338 German sociologist Maurizio Bach argued that scholars should use the concept of charismatic authority more often to explain the demise of the fascist regime. Bach, "Mussolini und Hitler," 121.
339 Eatwell ("Universal Fascism," 37) stressed that charismatic leaders can often be found in authoritarian regimes. However, when we compare the authoritarian regime of Poland in the interwar period and that of Fascist Italy, there is a difference Eatwell did not elaborate: whereas an authoritarian regime continued in Poland after the death of Józef Piłsudski (see Mann, *Fascists*, 45–6), charismatic authority was necessary for the survival of the fascist system.

Epilogue: A Man of His Time

1 Benini, *Carcere degli Scalzi*, 41; Guerri, *Galeazzo Ciano*, 247; Ostenc, *Ciano*.
2 Bosworth, *Mussolini*, 397.
3 Varè, *Two Impostors*, 237.
4 Ciano, *Ciano Diaries*, xxxi.
5 One exception is Sven Reichardt's book *Faschistische Kampfbünde*. However, he only looks at the early phase of the fascist movement.
6 Herbert, *Best*, 49; Wildt, *Generation*, 848–9.
7 Wildt, *Generation*, 848. See also Jureit, *Generationenforschung*, 43–4; Herbert, *Best*, 43.
8 Wildt, *Generation*, 849.
9 Raithel, *Schwierige Spiel*, 549.
10 Herbert, *Best*, 44; Wildt, *Generation*, 27 and 855.
11 Alessandro Pavolini (b. 1903) and Vittorio Mussolini (b. 1916) described their experiences during the Ethiopian War in similar words. See Mussolini, *Bomben über Abessinien*, 134; Del Boca, "Yperit-Regen," 47–8. Guerri, *Galeazzo Ciano*, 192–3.
12 Paxton, "Fünf Stadien des Faschismus," 71.
13 Ibid., 77.
14 Ibid., 75.

15 Corner, "Everyday Fascism," 203.
16 Jureit, *Generationenforschung*, 46–7.
17 For one exception, see Conti, *Uomini di Mussolini*.
18 This assessment by Herbert (*Best*, 17) about the historiography on Nazi Germany before 1990 still applies today to the state of research on Italian fascism.
19 For Italy's victimhood narrative, see Battini, "Sins of Memory"; Focardi, "Italy's Amnesia"; Hof, "Of Italian Perpetrators."
20 Paxton, "Fünf Stadien des Faschismus," 79.

Bibliography

Archives

Archivio Centrale dello Stato, Rome (ACS)

Archivi di famiglie e di persone, Dino Alfieri (Archivi Alfieri), busta 6.
Archivi di famiglie e di persone, Luigi Federzoni (Archivi Federzoni), busta 3.
Ente Autonomo Esposizione Universale di Roma – Commissariato Generale per L'Esposizione Universale di Roma (Ente Autonomo EUR), busta 39.
Ministero della Cultura Popolare, Direzione Generale Servizi della Propaganda, Propaganda presso gli stati esteri (MCP, DGSP), busta 5, 61.
Ministero della Cultura Popolare, Gabinetto (MCP, Gabinetto), busta 5, 8–10, 17, 47, 56, 93, 143, 181.
Ministero della Cultura Popolare, Reports (MCP, Reports), busta 1.
Ministero dell'Interno, Direzione Generale Pubblica Sicurezza, Cat. A. 1 (MI, DGPS, Cat. A. 1), busta 24.
Ministero dell'Interno, Direzione Generale Pubblica Sicurezza – Divisione Polizia Politica, Fascicoli Personali, Serie A: 1927–1944 (MI, DGPS), busta 22A, 298.
Presidenza del Consiglio dei Ministri, Gabinetto, 1934–1936 (PCM), fasc. 1.1.2, n. 2219.
Segreteria particolare del Duce, Autografi del Duce – Carte della "cassetta di zinco" (SPD, Autografi), busta 15–16.
Segreteria particolare del Duce, Carteggio riservato (SPD, Carteggio), busta 115.

Archivio Storico Capitolino, Rome (ASC)

Archivio Storico Capitolino (website). Accessed 12 April 2020. http://www.archiviocapitolinorisorsedigitali.it.

Archivio Storico Luce, Rome (ASL)

Archivio Storico Luce (website). Accessed 12 April 2020. http://www.archivioluce.com.

Archivio Storico Ministero Affari Esteri, Rome (ASMAE)

Affari Politici 1931–1945 (Affari Politici).
- Albania, b. 82.
- Cina, b. 11.
- Germania, b. 46.
- Iraq, b. 18.
- Italia, b. 50.

Ambasciata di S.M. il Re d'Italia presso la Santa Sede (Ambasciata Santa Sede), b. 4.
Archivio del Personale, Serie I: Comune, b. 121.
Archivio del Personale, Serie I: Diplomatici e Consoli, b. 33.
Carte Dino Grandi (Carte Grandi), b. 43.
Gabinetto del Ministero e delle Segreteria Generale dal 1923 al 1943, Seconda Parte 1930–1943, Serie I: Gabinetto del Ministero (Gabinetto, Serie I), busta 438, 810.
Gabinetto del Ministero e delle Segreteria Generale dal 1923 al 1943, Seconda Parte 1930–1943, Serie V: Ufficio Armistizio Pace (Gabinetto, Serie V), busta 1507.
Sottosegretariato di Stato Affari Albanesi (Sottosegretariato), busta 13.

Bayerische Staatsbibliothek Munich (BSB)

Personal Papers of Benito Mussolini. Also Some Official Records of the Italian Foreign Office and the Ministry of Culture, 1922–1944 (Mussolini Papers). Reels 5, 453, 456, 1346.

Bundesarchiv Berlin-Lichterfelde (BArch)

NS19: Persönlicher Stab Reichsführer-SS, AZ 912, 1697, 1880, 3001, 3840, 4046.
R2: Reichsfinanzministerium, AZ 24243.
R19: Hauptamt Ordnungspolizei, AZ 432.
R43-II: Reichskanzlei ("Neue Reichskanzlei"), AZ 1451b.
R55: Reichsministerium für Volksaufklärung und Propaganda, AZ 512.
R58: Reichssicherheitshauptamt, AZ 144, 187, 472, 1101, 9478, 9480, 9482–3, 9486.
R70-Italien: Deutsche Polizeidienststellen in Italien, AZ 15.
R901: Büro des Reichsaußenministers, AZ 60322, 60406, 60417.

R4902: Deutsches Auslandswissenschaftliches Institut, AZ 4879, 7464.
R8034-III: Reichslandbund, Pressearchiv, Personalia, AZ 64.

Central Intelligence Agency, Freedom of Information Act Electronic Reading Room (CIA, FOIA)

Beetz, Hildegard. Special Collection. Nazi War Crimes Disclosure Act. Accessed 12 April 2020. https://www.cia.gov/library/readingroom/collection/nazi-war-crimes-disclosure-act.

Franklin D. Roosevelt Library and Museum, Hyde Park, NY (FDR Library)

Gellman, Barbara F. Papers. Box 2.
Hopkins, Harry L. Papers. Box 160, 188–9.
Roosevelt, Franklin D. Papers as President.
- President's Map Room File (PMF), Box 34.
- President's Official Files (POF), 233, Italy, Government of, Box 1.
- President's Secretary Files (PSF), Boxes 3, 21–2, 32, 41–2.

Welles, Benjamin Sumner. Papers. Boxes 20, 60–1, 70, 74, 85, 156, 211.

Houghton Library, Harvard University, Cambridge, MA (Houghton Library)

Moffat, Jay Pierrepont. (1896–1943). Diplomatic Papers. MS Am 1407, Box 39.
Phillips, William. (1878–1968). Diaries. MS Am 2232, Series III, Boxes 6–15.

Institut für Zeitgeschichte, Munich-Berlin (IfZ)

MA 82: Rintelen, Enno von, Vol. 6.
Presseausschnittsammlung: Ciano, Galeazzo.

Landesarchiv Berlin

B Rep 057–01, Nr. 1223, Vol. 28.

Landesarchiv Nordrhein-Westfalen, Abteilung Münster

NS-Verbrechen Nr. 3034.

Library and Archives Canada

Mackenzie King, William Lyon. Diaries of William Lyon Mackenzie King. Accessed 12 April 2020. https://www.bac-lac.gc.ca/eng/discover

/politics-government/prime-ministers/william-lyon-mackenzie-king/Pages/diaries-william-lyon-mackenzie-king.aspx.

Library of Congress, Washington, DC (LoC)

Hull, Cordell. Papers. Reels 16, 19, 28, 30.
Jackson, Robert Houghwout. Papers. Reel 1.
Ken McCormick Collection. Box 17.
Long, Samuel Miller Breckinridge. Papers. Boxes 4–5, 106, 192, 208.
Taylor, Myron Charles. Papers. Boxes 1–2.
Working Papers Relating to the Publication of the Ciano Diaries. Boxes 4–5.

National Archives, Kew, Richmond, UK (NA)

FO 370: Foreign Office: Library and the Research Department: General Correspondence from 1906: 2175.
FO 371: Foreign Office: Political Departments: General Correspondence from 1906–1966: 22402–3, 22412, 22431–2, 22437, 22439, 22796–7, 23784–8, 23798–800, 23808, 23810, 23814, 23826, 23828, 23886, 24116, 24868, 29924–30, 33219, 33221, 37262, 37264.
FO 660: Foreign Office and War Cabinet: Offices of Various Political Representatives, Second World War: Papers: 368, 379.
FO 1011: Loraine Papers, 66–7, 204–5, 210, 214, 245–6.
FO 1019: British War Crimes Executive, Nuremberg, and Court Contact Committee: Correspondence and Papers, 15.
GFM 33: Copies of Captured Records of the German, Italian, and Japanese Governments, German Foreign Ministry Archives, 791.
GFM 36: Copies of Captured Records of the German, Italian, and Japanese Governments, German War Documents Project: The Italian Collection (Captured Italian records): Photocopies and Reports.
– Subseries Ciano Papers, 642–5.
– Subseries Verona Trial, 429–32.
HW 1: Government Code and Cypher School: Signal Intelligence Passed to the Prime Minister, Messages and Correspondence, 1940–1945: 196, 217, 573, 575, 645, 654, 733, 752, 816, 1189, 1846.
HW 12: Government Code and Cypher School: Diplomatic Section and Predecessors: Decrypts of Intercepted Diplomatic Communications (BJ Series) 1919–1944: 284–5, 290, 296.
HW 19: Government Code and Cypher School: ISOS Section and ISK Section: Decrypts of German Secret Service: 237, 239.
KV 2: The Security Service: Personal (PF Series) Files: 412, 2681.

WO 204: War Office: Allied Forces, Mediterranean Theatre: Military Headquarters Papers, Second World War: 6090, 12798.

National Archives and Record Administration at College Park, Maryland, USA (NARA)

RG 59: Records of the Department of State.
- Central Decimal Files (CDF), 1930–1939: Boxes 4090, 4200, 4248, 4355, 4368.
- Central Decimal Files (CDF), 1940–1944: Boxes 1878, 2950, 5643–4.
- LM63: Records Relating to the Internal Affairs of China, 1930–1939: Reels 63, 66–8.
- LM110: Records Relating to Foreign Affairs of Italy, 1940–1944: Reel 2.
- LM142: Records Relating to the Internal Affairs of Italy, 1940–1944: Reel 3.
- LM192: Records Relating to Germany, Foreign Affairs, 1930–1939: Reels 6–7.
- LM194: Records Relating to Germany, Foreign Affairs, 1940–1944: Reel 3.
- M976: Records Relating to Political Relations between China and Japan, 1930–1939: Reels 65, 83.
- M982: Records Relating to World War II, 1939–1945: Reels 1–2, 6–8, 18–20, 36, 43, 142, 167.
- M1211: Records Relating to the Internal Affairs of Albania, 1910–1944: Reels 9, 15.
- M1423: Records Relating to the Internal Affairs of Italy, 1930–1939: Reels 1–2, 4, 6, 9.

RG 84: Records of the Department of State.
- Entry 3207: US Embassy and Legation, Bern, General Records, 1936–1942: Box 86.
- Entry 3208: US Embassy and Legation, Bern, Classified General Records, 1940–1964: Boxes 6, 8, 11–12, 16.

RG 226: Records of the Office of Strategic Service.
- Entry 19: Intelligence Reports ("XL" Series), 1941–1946: Box 130.
- Entry 134: Washington Registry Office Radio and Cable Files: Box 215.
- Entry 190C: Field Station Files: Boxes 9–11.
- Entry 210: Previously Withdrawn Materials: Box 111.
- M1642: Washington Director's Office Administrative Files 1941–1945: Reel 40.

RG 242: Foreign Records Seized Collection.
- T816: Papers of Count Ciano Received from the Department of State: Reels 1–3.

Politisches Archiv des Auswärtigen Amts, Berlin (PAAA)

Akten des Ministerbüros: R29830.
Botschaft in Rom (Quirinal): 674a, 674b, 696a, 709a, 709b, 709d, 809c, 815b, 833a.

Botschaft in Rom (Quirinal) – Geheimakten, 1920–1943: 12, 40, 42, 45, 47, 50–2, 74, 87, 97, 108, 119, 124–5, 132.
Büro des Staatssekretärs: R29638, R29640, R29645.
Dienststelle Ribbentrop: R27160.
Geheime Reichssachen der Politischen Abteilungen: R61140, R61177.
Inland II – geheim: R100872, R101084-R101087.
Nachlass Hans Georg von Mackensen (Mackensen): 1, 2–3, 7.
Rundfunkpolitische Abteilung/ Kult R 1939–1945: R122638.

Seeley G. Mudd Manuscript Library, Princeton University (Mudd Library)

Dulles, Allen W. Papers. Digital Files Series, 1939–1977.
Oliver, Maria Rosa. Papers. Box 3.

United States Holocaust Memorial Museum, Washington, DC (USHMM)

RG 11.001M.01: Records of the Reichssicherheitshauptamt, Berlin: Reel 12.
RG 25.004: Selected Records from Romanian Security Services, 1936–1948: Reel 34.
RG 25.020: Selected Records from the Romanian Diplomatic Missions, *01.
RG 40.002: Archivio Storico del Ministero degli Affari Esteri Records: Reels 1–6.
RG 40.004: Selected Records from the Archivio Centrale dello Stato 1938–1956: Reels 2, 26, 50–6, 61–4.
RG 40.005: Segreteria Particolare del Duce 1922–1943: Reels 1, 7.
RG 40.014: Records Relating to the Treatment of Jews by Italian and German Nationals during the Holocaust, 1941–1946: Fiches 1.
RG 49.002: Records Relating to the Occupation of Yugoslavia during World War II, *01, *02, *03.
RG 49.006: Selected Records from the Archives of the Military History Institute of the General Staff of the Armed Forces of Serbia and Montenegro, 1941–1944: Reels 1–15.
RG 58.003: Swiss Federal Archives Records, 1930–1950: Reels 5, 9, 18, 82.
RG 59.006: Foreign Office: Political Departments, General Correspondence, 1938–49: Reels 9, 19.
RG 59.022: Foreign Office: Confidential Correspondence, 1933–1945: Reels 1, 3.
RG 76.001: Selected Records from the Vatican Archives, 1865–1939: Reel 68.
RG 76.002: Additional Selected Records from the Vatican Archive Collections: A, B, C.
RG 79.001: Selected Records Pertaining to Jews in Albania 1912–1950: Boxes 1–2.

Published Primary Sources

Actes et documents du Saint Siège relatifs à la Seconde Guerre Mondiale (ADSS). Edited by Pierre Blet, Angelo Martini, Burkhart Schneider, and Robert A. Graham. 11 vols. Vatican: Liberia Ed. Vaticana, 1965–81.

– Vol. IV: *Le Saint Siège et la Guerre en Europe, Juin 1940–Juin 1941*. Vatican: Liberia Ed. Vaticana, 1967.

– Vol. VII: *Le Saint Siège et la Guerre Mondiale, November 1942–Décembre 1943*. Vatican: Liberia Ed. Vaticana, 1973.

Akten zur deutschen Auswärtigen Politik, 1918–1945 (ADAP), aus dem Archiv des Auswärtigen Amts. 75 vols. Göttingen: Vandenhoeck & Ruprecht, 1950–95.

– Serie C: 1933–1937, Vols. I–IV. Göttingen: Vandenhoeck & Ruprecht, 1971–81.

– Serie D: 1937–1941, Vols. I–XIII. Göttingen: Vandenhoeck & Ruprecht, 1950–70.

– Serie E: 1941–1945, Vols. I–VIII. Göttingen: Vandenhoeck & Ruprecht, 1969–79.

L'Amministrazione Centrale dall'Unità alla Repubblica. Le Strutture e i dirigenti. Edited by Guido Melis. 4 vols. Bologna: Il Mulino, 1992.

– Vol. 1: *Il Ministero degli affari esteri*. Edited by Vincenzo Pellegrini. Bologna: Il Mulino, 1992.

– Vol. 4: *Il Ministero della Cultura Popolare. Il Ministero delle Poste e Telegrafi.* Edited by Patrizia Ferrara and Marina Giannetto. Bologna: Il Mulino, 1992.

Apollonio, Umbro, ed. *Futurist Manifestos*. New York: Viking Press, 1973.

Cereghino, Mario José, and Giovanni Fasanella. *Le Carte Segrete del Duce. Tutte le rivelazioni su Mussolini e il fascismo conservate negli archivi inglesi*. Milan: Mondadori, 2014.

Ciano, Galeazzo. *Die Außenpolitik Italiens. Die Rede S. E. Galeazzo Ciano vor der Abgeordnetenkammer am 13. Mai 1937*. Rome: Ramo editoriale degli agricoltori, 1937.

– *L'Europa verso la Catastrofe. 184 Colloqui con Mussolini, Hitler, Franco, Chamberlain, Sumner Welles, Rustu Aras, Stoiadinovic, Göring, Zog, Francois-Poncets ecc. verbalizzati di Galeazzo Ciano con 40 documenti diplomatici inediti.* Milan: Mondadori, 1948.

– *L'Italia di fronte al conflitto. Discorso del conte Galeazzo Ciano, Ministro degli Affari Esteri, 16 dicembre 1939-XVIII, con appendice di documenti*. Milan: Istituto per gli Studi di Politica Internazionale, 1940.

I Documenti Diplomatici Italiani (DDI). Edited by Ministero degli Affari Esteri. 129 vols. Rome: Liberia dello Stato, 1952–2015.

– Serie 7: 1922–1935, Vols. X–XII. Rome: Liberia dello Stato, 1978, 1981, and 1987.

– Serie 8: 1935–1939, Vols. I–XIII. Rome: Liberia dello Stato, 1952–2001.
– Serie 9: 1939–1943, Vols. I–X. Rome: Liberia dello Stato, 1954–90.

Documents Diplomatiques Belges, 1920–1940; La Politique de sécurite extérieure (DDB). Edited by the Académie Royale de Belgique. 5 vols. Brussels: Académie Royal de Belgique, 1964–66.
– Vol. 4: *Période 1936–1937*. Brussels: Académie Royal de Belgique, 1965.
– Vol. 5: *Période 1938–1940*. Brussels: Académie Royal de Belgique, 1966.

Documents Diplomatiques Français, 1932–1939 (DDF). Edited by the Ministère des Affaires étrangères. 32 vols. Paris: Imprimerie Nationale, 1963–86.
– Serie 1: 1932–1935, Vols. IV–XIII. Paris: Imprimerie Nationale, 1968–84.
– Serie 2: 1936–1939, Vols. I–XIX. Paris: Imprimerie Nationale, 1963–86.

Documents Diplomatiques Suisses 1848–1945 (DDS). Edited by the Commission Nationale pour la Publication de Documents Diplomatiques Suisses. 16 vols. Bern: Chronos, 1979–97.
– Vol. 11: *1934–1936*. Bern: Chronos, 1989.
– Vol. 12: *1937–1938*. Bern: Chronos, 1994.
– Vol. 13: *1939–1940*. Bern: Chronos, 1991.
– Vol. 14: *1941–1943*. Bern: Chronos, 1997.
– Vol. 15: *1943–1945*. Bern: Chronos. 1992.

Documents on British Foreign Policy (DBFP), 1919–1939. 26 vols. London: H.M. Stationary Office, 1946–86.
– Series II: 1929–1938, Vols. XIV–XVII. Edited by Rohan Butler, J.P.T. Bury, M.E. Lambert, W.N. Medlicott, and Ernest L. Woodward. London: H.M. Stationary Office, 1976–79.
– Series III: 1938–1939, Vols. I–VIII. Edited by Rohan Butler, M.E. Lambert, Anne Orde, and Ernest L. Woodward. London: H.M. Stationary Office, 1949–55.

Ferrara, Patrizia, and Marina Giannetto. "Introduzione." In *L'Amministrazione Centrale dall'Unità alla Repubblica. Le Strutture e I dirigenti.* Vol. 4, *Il Ministero della Cultura Popolare. Il Ministero delle Poste e Telegrafi*, edited by Patrizia Ferrara and Marina Giannetto, 25–56. Bologna: Il Mulino, 1992.

Foreign Relations of the United States Papers, 1933–1945 (FRUS). 86 vols. Washington, DC: US Government Printing Office, 1949–69.
– 1938, Vol. II: *The British Commonwealth, Europe, Near East and Africa*. Edited by Matilda F. Axton, Rogers P. Churchill, N.O. Sappington, John G. Reid, Francis C. Prescott, Louis E. Gates, and Shirley L. Phillips. Washington, DC: US Government Printing Office, 1955.
– 1940, Vol. II: *General and Europe*. Edited by Matilda F. Axton and Shirley L. Phillips. Washington, DC: US Government Printing Office, 1957.

Frank, Tibor, ed. *Discussing Hitler: Advisers of U.S. Diplomacy in Central Europe, 1934–1941*. Budapest: Central European University Press, 2003.

Freundschafts- und Bündnispakt zwischen Deutschland und Italien vom 22. Mai 1939. Accessed 13 April 2020. http://www.1000dokumente.de/pdf/dok_0007_sta_de.pdf.

Gallup, George H., ed. *The Gallup International Public Opinion Poll, Great Britain: 1937–1975.* Vol. 1. New York: Random House, 1976.

Gazzetta Ufficiale del Regno d'Italia. No. 136. Rome: Liberia dello Stato, 1927.

Hillgruber, Andreas, ed. *Staatsmänner und Diplomaten bei Hitler. Vertrauliche Aufzeichnungen über Unterredungen mit Vertretern des Auslandes.* Vol. 1, *1939–1941*. Frankfurt a. Main: Bernard & Graefe, 1967.

Judenverfolgung in Italien, den italienisch besetzten Gebieten und in Nordafrika. Dokumentensammlung. Frankfurt a. Main: United Restitution Organization, 1962.

Mussolini, Benito. *Opera Omnia.* Edited by Edoardo Susmel and Duilio Susmel. 35 vols. Florence: La Fenice, 1951–62.

– *Scritti Politici.* Edited by Enzo Santarelli. Milan: Feltrinelli, 1979.

Petersen, Neal H., ed. *From Hitler's Doorstep: The Wartime Intelligence Reports of Allen Dulles, 1942–1945.* University Park: Pennsylvania State University Press, 1996.

Newspapers and Periodicals

L'Auto Italiana

Berliner Illustrierte

Corriere della Sera

Dolomiten

La Domenica del Corriere

Epoca

L'Illustrazione Italiana

L'Illustrazione Italiana Sportiva

Illustrierter Beobachter

LIFE

The Manchester Guardian

New York Herald Tribune

New York Times

La Nuova Stampa

Il Popolo d'Italia

R.a.c.i. Rivista mensile del real automobile club d'Italia

La Rivista Illustrata del Popolo d'Italia

La Stampa

The Times

Völkischer Beobachter

Washington Post

Movies

Mussolini and I. DVD. Directed by Alberto Negrin, 1985. Port Washington, NY: Koch Vision, 2003.

Roma città aperta. DVD. Directed by Roberto Rossellini, 1945. Paris: Studiocanal, 1999.

Autobiographies, Memoirs, and Diaries

Agnelli, Susanna. *Wir trugen immer Matrosenkleider*. 6th ed. Munich: Piper, 1997.

Alfieri, Dino. *Dictators Face to Face*. Westport: Greenwood Press, 1978.

Amè, Cesare. *Guerra Segreta in Italia 1940–1943*. Rome: Casini, 1954.

Amendola, Giorgio. *Una scelta di vita*. Milan: Rizzoli, 1976.

Amicucci, Ermanno. *I 600 giorni di Mussolini*. Rome: Faro, 1948.

Anfuso, Filippo. *Rom – Berlin in diplomatischem Spiegel*. Munich: Pohl, 1951.

Ansaldo, Giovanni. *Il giornalista di Ciano. Diari 1932–1943*. Edited by Giuseppe Marcenaro. Bologna: Il Mulino, 2000.

Armellini, Quirino. *Diario di Guerra. Nove mesi al Comando Supremo*. Milan: Garzanti, 1946.

Badoglio, Pietro. *Italien und der Zweite Weltkrieg*. Munich: List, 1947.

Barnes, James S. *A British Fascist in the Second World War: The Italian War Diary of James Strachey Barnes, 1943–45*. Edited by Claudia Baldoli and Brendan Fleming. London: Bloomsbury, 2014.

Bastianini, Giuseppe. *Uomini, cose, fatti. Memorie di un ambasciatore*. Milan: Vitagliani, 1959.

Below, Nicolaus von. *Als Hitlers Adjutant 1937–45*. Mainz: Hase & Koehler, 1980.

Benini, Zenone. *Carcere degli Scalzi*. Florence: Ponte alle grazie, 1994.

Berenson, Bernard. *Rumour and Reflection*. London: Constable, 1952.

Bojano, Filippo. *In the Wake of the Goose Step*. Chicago: Cassell, 1944.

Bonnet, Georges. *Vor der Katastrophe. Erinnerungen des französischen Außenministers*. Cologne: Greven, 1951.

Bottai, Giuseppe. *Diario 1935–1944*. Edited by Giordano Bruno Guerri. Milan: Rizzoli, 1989.

Buffarini Guidi, Glauco. *La vera verità. I documenti dell'archivio segreto del ministro degli interni Guido Buffarini Guidi dal 1938 al 1945*. Milan: Sugar, 1970.

Cantalupo, Roberto. *Fu la Spagna. Ambasciata presso Franco Febbraio – Aprile 1937*. Milan: Mondadori, 1948.

Carboni, Giacomo. *Memorie segrete, 1935–1948*. Florence: Parenti, 1955.

Cavallero, Ugo. *Comando Supremo. Diario 1940–43 del Capo di S.M.G.* Bologna: Cappelli, 1948.

Caviglia, Enrico. *Diario aprile 1925 – marzo 1945*. Rome: G. Casini, 1952.

Cerruti, Elisabetta. *Frau eines Botschafters*. Frankfurt a. Main: Scheffler, 1954.

Chamberlain, Neville. *The Neville Chamberlain Diary Letters*. Vol. 4, *The Downing Street Years, 1934–1940*, edited by Robert Self. Aldershot: Ashgate, 2005.

Churchill, Winston S. *The Second World War*. 6 vols. London: Houghton Mifflin Harcourt, 1954, 1967, 1968.

Cianetti, Tullio. *Memorie dal carcere di Verona*. Edited by Renzo De Felice. Milan: Rizzoli, 1983.

Ciano, Edda. *La mia vita. Intervisti di Domenico Olivieri*. Edited by Nicola Caracciolo. Milan: Mondadori, 1977.

– *My Truth as Told to Albert Zarca*. New York: Morrow, 1976.

Ciano, Fabrizio. *Quando il nonno fece fucilare papà*. Edited by Dino Cimagalli. Milan: Mondadori, 1991.

Ciano, Galeazzo. *The Ciano Diaries 1939–1943: The Complete, Unabridged Diaries of Count Galeazzo Ciano, Italian Minister for Foreign Affairs, 1936–1943*. Edited by Hugh Gibson. Garden City, NY: Simon Publications, 2001.

– *Ciano's Hidden Diaries 1937–1948*. Translated by Andreas Mayor. Introduction by Malcolm Muggeridge. New York: E.P. Dutton, 1953.

– *Diario, Volume Secondo 1941–1943*. Introduction by Ugo D'Andrea. 5th ed. Milan: Rizzoli, 1948.

– *Diario 1937–1943*. Edited by Renzo De Felice. Milan: Rizzoli, 1980.

Colville, John. *The Fringes of Power*. Guilford: Lyons Press, 2002.

Cooper, Duff. *Old Men Forget: The Autobiography*. London: Dutton, 1954.

Coulondré, Robert. *Von Moskau nach Berlin. Erinnerungen eines französischen Botschafters, 1936–1939*. Bonn: Athenäum-Verlag, 1950.

D'Abernon, Viscount. *Botschafter der Zeitenwende, Memoiren*. Vol. III, *Locarno (1924–1926)*. Leipzig: List, 1929.

Dalton, Hugh. *The Fateful Years: Memoires 1931–1945*. London: Muller, 1957.

D'Annunzio, Gabriele. *Diari di guerra 1914–1918*. Edited by Annamaria Andreoli. Milan: Mondadori, 2002.

De Vecchi, Cesare Maria. *Il quadrumviro scomodo. Il vero Mussolini nelle memorie del più monarchico dei fascisti*. Edited by Luigi Romersa. Milan: Mursia, 1983.

– *Tra Papa. Duce e Re. Il conflitto tra Chiesa cattolica e Stato fascista nel Diario 1930–1931 del primo ambasciatore del Regno d'Italia presso la Santa Sede*. Edited by Sandro Setta. Rome: Jouvence, 1998.

Dodd, William E. *Ambassador Dodd's Diary, 1933–1938*. Edited by William E. Dodd Jr. and Martha Dodd. New York: Harcourt, Brace, 1941.

Dollmann, Eugen. *Call Me Coward*. London: Kimber, 1956.

Ducci, Roberto. *La bella gioventù*. Bologna: Il Mulino, 1996.

Eden, Anthony. *Memoiren*. Vol. 1, *Angesichts der Diktatoren, 1923–1938*. Cologne: Kiepenheur & Witsch, 1962.

Favagrossa, Carlo. *Perché perdemmo la guerra: Mussolini e la produzione bellica*. Milan: Rizzoli, 1946.

Federzoni, Luigi. *Italia di ieri per la storia di domani*. Milan: Mondadori, 1967.

Gafencu, Grigore. *Last Days of Europe: A Diplomatic Journey in 1938*. New Haven, CT: Yale University Press, 1948.

Goebbels, Joseph. *Die Tagebücher von Joseph Goebbels*. Im Auftrag des Instituts für Zeitgeschichte und mit Unterstützung des Staatlichen Archivdienstes Russland. Edited by Elke Fröhlich. 24 vols. Munich: K.G. Saur, 1993–2006.

– Part I: Aufzeichnungen 1923–1941. Vols. 1–9. Munich: K.G. Saur, 1998–2006.

– Part II: Diktate 1941–1945. Vols. 1–15. Munich: K.G. Saur, 1993–96.

Grandi, Dino. *Il mio paese*. Edited by Renzo De Felice. Bologna: Il Mulino, 1985.

Graziani, Rodolfo. *Ho difeso la patria. Otto documenti fuori testo*. Milan: Garzanti, 1949.

Grazzi, Emanuele. *Il principio della fine: L'Impresa di Grecia*. Rome: Faro, 1945.

Guariglia, Raffaele. *Ricordi 1922–1946*. Naples: Edizioni scientifiche italiane, 1950.

Halder, Franz. *Kriegstagebuch. Tägliche Aufzeichnungen des Chefs des Generalstabes des Heeres 1939–1942*. Vol. 2, *Von der geplanten Landung in England bis zum Beginn des Ostfeldzuges (1.7.1940– 21.6.1941)*. Stuttgart: Kohlhammer, 1963.

Harvey, Oliver. *The Diplomatic Diaries of Oliver Harvey, 1937–1940*. Edited by John Harvey. New York: Collins, 1958.

Hassell, Ulrich von. *Vom andern Deutschland*. Frankfurt a. Main: Fischer, 1964.

Henderson, Nevile. *Fehlschlag einer Mission. Berlin 1937 bis 1939*. Zürich: Drei-Stern-Verlag, 1939.

Hoare, Samuel. *Gesandter in besonderer Mission*. Hamburg: Toth, 1949.

Höttl, Wilhelm. *Unternehmen Bernhard. Ein historischer Tatsachenbericht über die größte Geldfälschungsaktion aller Zeiten*. Wels: Verlag Welsermühl, 1955.

Huxley, Aldous. *Jesting Pilate: The Diary of a Journey*. London: Chatto & Windus, 1969.

Jacomoni di San Savino, Francesco. *La politica dell'Italia in Albania nella testimonianze del Luogotenente del Re Francesco Jacomoni di San Savino*. Bologna: Cappelli, 1965.

James, Henry. *Italian Hours*. New York: Horizon Press, 1968.

Jones, Thomas. *A Diary with Letters, 1931–1950*. London: Oxford University Press, 1954.

Kennedy, Aubrey L. *The Times and Appeasement: The Journals of A.L. Kennedy, 1932–1939*. Edited by Gordon Martel. Cambridge: Cambridge University Press, 2000.

Kirkpatrick, Ivone. *The Inner Circle*. London: Macmillan, 1959.

Lampson, Miles. *Politics and Diplomacy in Egypt: The Diaries of Sir Miles Lampson, 1935–1937*. Edited by M.E. Yapp. Oxford: Oxford University Press, 1997.

Lessona, Alessandro. *Memorie*. Florence: Sansoni, 1958.
Lipski, Jozef. *Diplomat in Berlin*. New York: Columbia University Press, 1968.
Luciolli, Mario. *Palazzo Chigi: anni roventi. Ricordi di vita diplomatica italiana dal 1933 al 1948*. Florence: Le Letter, 2011.
MacVeagh, Lincoln. *Ambassador MacVeagh Reports: Greece, 1933–1947*. Edited by John O. Iatrides. Princeton, NJ: Princeton University Press, 1980.
Magistrati, Massimo. *L'Italia a Berlino 1937–1939*. Milan: Mondadori, 1956.
– *Il prologo del dramma. Berlino 1934–1937*. Milan: Mursia, 1971.
Maugeri, Franco. *From the Ashes of Disgrace*. New York: Reynal & Hitchcock, 1948.
Meissner, Otto. *Staatssekretär unter Ebert – Hindenburg – Hitler. Der Schicksalsweg des deutschen Volkes von 1918 – 1945, wie ich ihn erlebte*. Hamburg: Hoffmann und Campe, 1950.
Moellhausen, Eitel F. *Die gebrochene Achse*. Altfeld: Alpha-Verlag, 1949.
Mussolini, Benito. *A Clara. Tutte le lettere a Clara Petacci 1943–1945*. Edited by Luisa Montevecchi. Milan: Mondadori, 2011.
Mussolini, Rachele. *My Life with Mussolini*. London: R. Hale, 1959.
Mussolini, Romano. *Il duce mio padre*. Milan: BUR, 2004.
Mussolini, Vittorio. *Bomben über Abessinien*. Munich: C.H. Beck Verlag, 1937.
– *Due donne nella tempesta*. Milan: Mondadori, 1961.
Navarra, Quinto. *Memorie del Cameriere di Mussolini*. Milan: Longanesi, 1972.
Nelson Page, Giorgio. *L'Americano di Roma*. Milan: Longanesi, 1950.
Nicolson, Harald. *Diaries and Letters, 1930–1939*. Edited by Nigel Nicolson. London: Collin, 1966.
Ojetti, Ugo. *I Taccuini 1914–1943*. Florence: Sansoni, 1954.
Ortona, Egidio. *Diplomazia di guerra. Diario 1937–1943*. Bologna: Il Mulino, 1993.
Oven, Wilfried von. *Mit Goebbels bis zum Ende*. Buenos Aires: Dürer, 1950.
Petacci, Claretta. *Mussolini Segreto. Diari 1932–1938*. Edited by Mauro Suttora. Milan: Rizzoli, 2009.
– *Verso il disastro. Mussolini in Guerra. Diari 1939–1940*. Edited by Mimmo Franzinelli. Milan: Rizzoli, 2011.
Pietromarchi, Luca. *I diari e le agende di Luca Pietromarchi (1938–1940). Politica estera del fascismo e vita quotidiana di un diplomatico romano del `900*. Edited by Ruth Nattermann. Rome: Viella, 2009.
Pirelli, Alberto. *Taccuini 1922/1943*. Edited by Donato Barbone. Bologna: Il Mulino, 1984.
Plehwe, Friedich-Karl von. *Als die Achse zerbrach. Das Ende des deutsch-italienischen Bündnisses im Zweiten Weltkrieg*. Wiesbaden: Limes Verlag, 1980.
– *Schicksalsstunden in Rom. Ende eines Bündnisses*. Berlin: Propyläen, 1967.
Poggiali, Ciro. *Diario AOI. 15 giugno 1936 – 4 ottobre 1937. Gli appunti segreti dell'inviato del "Corriere della Sera."* Milan: Longanesi, 1971.

Rahn, Rudolf. *Ruheloses Leben. Aufzeichnungen und Erinnerungen*. Düsseldorf: Diederichs, 1949.

Reynaud, Paul. *In the Thick of the Fight, 1930–1945*. New York: Simon and Schuster, 1955.

Ribbentrop, Joachim von. *Zwischen London und Moskau. Erinnerungen und letzte Aufzeichnungen*. Leoni am Starnberger See: Druffel-Verlag, 1953.

Rintelen, Enno von. *Mussolini als Bundesgenosse*. Tübingen: Wunderlich, 1951.

Rossi, Gianni Scipione. *Mussolini e il diplomatico. La vita e i diari di Serafino Mazzolini, un monarchico a Salò*. Soveria Mannelli: Rubbettino, 2005.

Sarfatti, Margherita Grassini. *My Fault: Mussolini as I Knew Him*. Edited by Brian R. Sullivan. New York: Enigma Books, 2014.

Schellenberg, Walter. *Aufzeichnungen*. Wiesbaden: Limes Verlag, 1979.

Schirach, Baldur von. *Ich glaubte an Hitler*. Hamburg: Mosaik-Verlag, 1967.

Schmidt, Paul. *Statist auf diplomatischer Bühne 1923–45. Erlebnisse des Chefdolmetschers im Auswärtigen Amt mit den Staatsmännern Europas*. Bonn: Athenäum-Verlag, 1949.

Senise, Carmine. *Quando ero capo della polizia, 1940–1943. Memorie di Carmine Senise*. Rome: Ruffolo, 1946.

Serrano Suñer, Ramón. *Zwischen Hendaye und Gibraltar. Feststellungen und Betrachtungen, angesichts einer Legende, über unsere Politik während zweier Kriege*. Zürich: Thomas-Verlag, 1948.

Shirer, William L. *Berlin Diary: The Journal of a Foreign Correspondent, 1934–1941*. New York: Alfred A. Knopf, 1942.

Signoretti, Alfredo. *"La Stampa" in camicia nera 1923–1943*. Rome: Volpe, 1968.

Spaak, Paul Henri. *Memoiren eines Europäers*. Hamburg: Hoffmann und Campe, 1969.

Suvich, Fulvio. *Memorie 1932–1936*. Edited by Gianfranco Bianchi. Milan: Rizzoli, 1984.

Trevor-Roper, Hughes. *Letters from Oxford: Hugh Trevor-Roper to Bernard Berenson*. Edited by Richard Davenport-Hines. London: Weidenfeld & Nicolson, 2006.

Valori, Aldo. *Il fascista che non amava il regime*. Edited by Valentina Tonelli Valori. Rome: Editori riuniti, 2003.

Vansittart, Robert. *The Mist Procession: The Autobiography of Lord Vansittart*. London: Hutchinson, 1958.

Varè, Daniele. *Der lachende Diplomat*. Berlin: Zsolnay, 1940.

– *The Two Impostors*. London: Murray, 1949.

Vergani, Orio. *Ciano. Una lunga confessione*. Milan: Longanesi, 1974.

– *Quando Gabriele s'innamorò di quella comica…* L'Aquila: Textus, 2005.

Villari, Luigi. *Affari Esteri 1943–1945*. Rome: Magi-Spinetti, 1948.

Visconti Prasca, Sebastiano. *Io ho aggredito Grecia*. Milan: Rizzoli, 1946.

Weizsäcker, Ernst von. *Erinnerungen*. Munich: List, 1950.

– *Die Weizsäcker-Papiere 1933–1950*. Edited by Leonidas E. Hill. Berlin: Propyläen, 1974.
Welles, Sumner. *The Time for Decision*. New York: Harper & Brothers, 1944.
Zangrandi, Ruggero. *Il lungo viaggio attraverso il fascismo. Contributo alla storia di una generazione*. Milan: Feltrinelli, 1962.
– *1943: 23 luglio – 8 settembre*. Milan: Feltrinelli, 1964.

Secondary Literature

Abse, Tobias. "The Rise of Fascism in an Industrial City: The Case of Livorno 1918–1922." In *Rethinking Italian Fascism: Capitalism, Populism and Culture*, edited by David Forgacs, 52–82. London: Lawrence and Wishart, 1986.
– *Sovversivi e fascisti a Livorno. Lotta politica e sociale (1918–1922)*. Milan: Angeli, 1989.
Adamson, Walter L. "The Culture of Italian Fascism and the Fascist Crisis of Modernity: The Case of Il Selvaggio." *Journal of Contemporary History* 30, no. 4 (1995): 555–75.
Adeli, Lisa M. "From Jasenovac to Yugoslavism: Ethnic Persecution in Croatia during World War II." PhD diss., University of Arizona, 2004.
Afflerbach, Holger. "Vom Bündnispartner zum Kriegsgegner. Ursachen und Folgen des italienischen Kriegseintritts im Mai 1915. " In *Der Kriegseinritt Italiens im Mai*, edited by Johannes Hürter and Gian Enrico Rusconi, 53–72. Munich: Oldenbourg, 2007.
Albanese, Giulia. *Mussolinis Marsch auf Rom. Die Kapitulation des liberalen Staates vor dem Faschismus*. Paderborn: Ferdinand Schöningh, 2015.
Alessandri, Giuseppe. *Il diplomatico. Dino Grandi*. Florence: Zella, 2007.
Aliano, David. "Identity in Transatlantic Play: Il Duce's National Project in Argentina." PhD diss., City University of New York, 2008.
Allport, Gordon W., and Leo Postman. "An Analysis of Rumor." *Public Opinion Quarterly* 10 (1946/47): 501–17.
Altgeld, Wolfgang, Thomas Frenz, Angelica Gernert, Michael Groblewski, and Rudolf Lill. *Geschichte Italiens*. 3rd ed. Stuttgart: Reclam, 2016.
Aly, Götz, and Susanne Heim. *Vordenker der Vernichtung. Auschwitz und die deutschen Pläne für eine neue europäische Ordnung*. Hamburg: Hoffmann und Campe, 1991.
Antola, Alessandra. "Photographing Mussolini." In *The Cult of the Duce: Mussolini and the Italians*, edited by Stephen Gundle, Christopher Duggan, and Giuliana Pieri, 178–92. Manchester: Manchester University Press, 2013.
Aragno, Piero. "Futurismus und Faschismus. Die italienische Avantgarde und die Revolution." In *Faschismus und Avantgarde*, edited by Reinhold Grimm and Jost Hermand, 83–91. Königstein: Athenäum, 1980.

Arielli, Nir. *Fascist Italy and the Middle East, 1933–1940*. Basingstoke, UK: Palgrave Macmillan, 2010.

Arthurs, Joshua. *Excavating Modernity: The Roman Past in Fascist Italy*. Ithaca, NY: Cornell University Press, 2012.

Azzi, Stephen Corrado. "The Historiography of Fascist Foreign Policy." *The Historical Journal* 36, no. 1 (1993): 187–203.

Bach, Maurizio. "Mussolini und Hitler als charismatische Führer. Was kann Max Webers Modell der charismatischen Herrschaft zur Erklärung der Dynamik faschistischer Bewegungen beitragen?" In *Der Faschismus in Europa. Wege der Forschung*, edited by Thomas Schlemmer and Hans Woller, 107–22. Munich: De Gruyter Oldenbourg, 2014.

Bach, Maurizio, and Stefan Breuer. *Faschismus als Bewegung und Regime. Italien und Deutschland im Vergleich*. Wiesbaden: VS Verlag für Sozialwissenschaften, 2010.

Bahro, Berno. *Der SS-Sport. Organisation – Funktion – Bedeutung*. Paderborn: Ferdinand Schöningh, 2013.

Baldoli, Claudia, and Andrew Knapp. *Forgotten Blitzes: France and Italy under Allied Air Attack, 1940–1945*. London: Continuum, 2012.

Baravelli, G.C. *L'ultimo baluardo della schiavitù. L'Abessinia*. Rome: Società editrice di Novissima, 1935.

Barbagli, Marzio, and David Kertzer. "Introduzione." In *Storia della famiglia italiana, 1750–1950*, edited by Marzio Barbagli and David Kertzer, 7–28. Bologna: Il Mulino, 1992.

Barnes, James S. *The Universal Aspects of Fascism*. London: Williams and Norgate, 1928.

Battini, Michele. "Sins of Memory: Reflections on the Lack of an Italian Nuremberg and the Administration of International Justice after 1945." *Journal of Modern Italian Studies* 9, no. 3 (2004): 349–62.

Bauerkämper, Arnd. *Der Faschismus in Europa 1918–1945*. Stuttgart: Reclam, 2006.

Baxa, Paul. "Capturing the Fascist Moment: Hitler's Visit to Italy in 1938 and the Radicalization of Fascist Italy." *Journal of Contemporary History* 42 (2007): 227–42.

– *Roads and Ruins: The Symbolic Landscape of Fascist Rome*. Toronto: University of Toronto Press 2010.

Behring, Rainer. "Italien im Spiegel der deutschsprachigen Zeitgeschichtsforschung. Ein Literaturbericht (2006–2013)." *Archiv für Sozialgeschichte* 54 (2014): 345–94.

Benadusi, Lorenzo. "Borghesi in Uniform: Masculinity, Militarism, and the Brutalization of Politics from the First World War to the Rise of Fascism." In *In the Society of Fascists: Acclamation, Acquiescence, and Agency in Mussolini's Italy*, edited by Giulia Albanese and Roberta Pergher, 29–48. London: Palgrave Macmillan, 2012.

– *The Enemy of the "New Man": Homosexuality in Fascist Italy*. Madison: University of Wisconsin Press, 2012.
Bender, Roger James. *The Hitler Albums: Mussolini's State Visit to Germany, September 25–29, 1937*. Palo Alto: R.J. Bender, 1970.
Ben-Ghiat, Ruth. "Italian Fascism and the Aesthetics of the 'Third Way.'" Special issue, *The Aesthetics of Fascism: Journal of Contemporary History* 31, no. 2 (1996): 293–316.
– "Unmaking the Fascist Man: Masculinity, Film and the Transition from Dictatorship." *Journal of Modern Italian Studies* 10, no. 3 (2005): 336–65.
Berezin, Mabel. *Making the Fascist Self: The Political Culture of Interwar Italy*. Ithaca, NY: Cornell University Press, 1997.
Berghaus, Günter. *Futurism and Politics: Between Anarchist Rebellion and Fascist Revolution, 1909–1944*. Providence: Berghahn Books, 1996.
Bernhard, Patrick. "The Great Divide? Notions of Racism in Fascist Italy and Nazi Germany: New Answers to an Old Problem." *Journal of Modern Italian Studies* 24, no. 1 (2019): 97–114.
Bernhart, Toni. "Benito Mussolini als Schriftsteller und seine Übersetzung ins Deutsche." In *Die akademische "Achse Berlin-Rom"? Der wissenschaftlich-kulturelle Austausch zwischen Italien und Deutschland 1920 bis 1945*, edited by Andrea Albrecht, Lutz Danneberg, and Simone De Angelis, 345–400. Berlin: De Gruyter Oldenbourg, 2017.
Bianchi, Bruna. *Crescere in tempo di guerra. Il lavoro e la protesta dei ragazzi in Italia 1915–1918*. Venice: Cafoscarina, 1995.
– "Venezia nella Grande guerra." In *Storia di Venezia. L'ottocento e il novecento*, edited by Mario Isnenghi and Stuart Woolf, 349–416. Rome: Istituto della Enciclopedia Italiana 2002.
Bianchi, Gianfranco. *25 luglio: crollo di un regime*. Milano: Mursia, 1964.
Bloch, Ernst. *Erbschaft dieser Zeit*. Frankfurt a. Main: Suhrkamp, 1973.
Bloch, Michael. *Ribbentrop*. London: Crown Publisher, 1992.
Bödeker, Hans Erich, ed. *Biographie schreiben*. Göttingen: Wallstein Verlag, 2003.
Bonsaver, Guido. *Censorship and Literature in Fascist Italy*. Toronto: University of Toronto Press, 2007.
Boothe, Clare. *Europe in the Spring*. New York: Alfred A. Knopf, 1941.
Borejsza, Jerzy W. *Il fascismo e l'Europa orientale. Dalla propaganda all'aggressione*. Bari: Laterza, 1981.
Borstendoerfer, Adolf. *Graf Ciano*. Buenos Aires: Editorial Cosmopolita, 1944.
Borzoni, Gianluca. *Renato Prunas diplomatico (1892–1951)*. Soveria Mannelli: Rubbettino, 2004.
Bosworth, R.J.B. *Claretta: Mussolini's Last Lover*. New Haven, CT: Yale University Press, 2017.
– "Dictators Strong or Weak: The Model of Benito Mussolini." In *The Oxford Handbook of Fascism*, edited by R.J.B. Bosworth, 259–75. Oxford: Oxford University Press 2009.

– "Golf and Italian Fascism." In *Science and Golf III: Proceedings of the 1998 World Scientific Congress of Golf*, edited by Martin R. Farrally and Alastair J. Cochran, 345–52. Leeds: Human Kinetics, 1999.

– "'Ich schreibe, um mich selbst neu zu schreiben.' Der Fall Benito Mussolini." In *Despoten dichten. Sprachkunst und Gewalt*, edited by Albrecht Koschorke, 67–94. Konstanz: Konstanz University Press, 2011.

– *Italian Venice: A History*. New Haven, CT: Yale University Press, 2014.

– *Italy the Least of the Great Powers: Italian Foreign Policy before the First World War*. Cambridge: Cambridge University Press 2009.

– *Mussolini*. New York: Arnold, 2002.

– *Mussolini's Italy: Life under the Dictatorship*. London: Penguin Books, 2005.

– "Per necessità famigliare: Hypocrisy and Corruption in Fascist Italy." *European History Quarterly* 30, no. 3 (2000): 357–87.

– "Venice between Fascism and International Tourism, 1911–45." *Modern Italy* 4, no. 1 (1999): 5–23.

– "War, Totalitarism and 'Deep Belief' in Fascist Italy, 1935–43." *European History Quarterly* 34, no. 3 (2004): 475–505.

– *Whispering City: Modern Rome and Its Histories*. New Haven, CT: Yale University Press, 2011.

Bregantin, Lisa, Livio Fantina, and Marco Mondini. *Venezia Treviso e Padova nella Grande Guerra*. Treviso: ISTRESCO, 2008.

Brunetta, Ernesto. *La Tragedia. La Società Italiana dal 1939 al 1939*. Milano: Mursia, 2006.

Burdett, Charles. "Italian War-Correspondents and the Spanish Civil War: Propaganda and Autobiography." In *Biographies and Autobiographies in Modern Italy: A Festschrift for John Woodhouse*, edited by Peter Hainsworth and Martin McLaughlin, 133–47. London: Legenda, 2007.

– *Journeys through Fascism: Italian Travel Writing between the Wars*. New York: Berghahn Books, 2007.

Burgwyn, H. James. "Diplomacy and World War: The (First) Axis of Evil." In *The Oxford Handbook of Fascism*, edited by R.J.B. Bosworth, 317–35. Oxford: Oxford University Press, 2009.

– *Empire on the Adriatic: Mussolini's Conquest of Yugoslavia, 1941–1943*. New York: Enigma Books, 2005.

– *Italian Foreign Policy in the Interwar Period, 1918–1940*. Westport: Praeger, 1997.

– "Mussolini's Troika in Occupied Yugoslavia: Fascist Commissars, 2nd Army, and Foreign Ministry." In *Die "Achse" im Krieg. Politik, Ideologie und Kriegsführung 1939–1945*, edited by Lutz Klinkhammer, Amedeo Osti Guerrazzi, and Thomas Schlemmer, 292–304. Paderborn: Ferdinand Schöningh, 2010.

– *Mussolini Warlord: Failed Dreams of Empire, 1940–1943*. New York: Enigma Books, 2012.

Canali, Mauro, and Clemente Volpini. *Mussolini e i ladri di regime: Gli Arricchimenti illeciti del fascismo*. Milan: Mondadori, 2019.

Cancogni, Manlio. *Storia dello squadrismo*. Milan: Longanesi, 1959.

Cannistraro, Philip V., and Brian R. Sullivan. *Il Duce's Other Woman: The Untold Story of Margherita Sarfatti, Benito Mussolini's Jewish Mistress, and How She Helped Him Come to Power*. New York: Morrow, 1993.

Canosa, Romano. *Farinacci. Il superfascista*. Milan: Mondadori, 2010.

– *La voce del Duce. L'agenzia Stefani: l'arma segreta di Mussolini*. Milan: Mondadori, 2002.

Cante, Diego. "Propaganda und Fußball. Sport und Politik in den Begegnungen zwischen den italienischen 'Azzuri' und den 'Weißen' aus Wien in der Zwischenkriegszeit." *zeitgeschichte* 26, no. 3 (1999): 184–202.

Capristo, Annalisa. "The Exclusion of Jews from Italian Academies." In *Jews in Italy under Fascist and Nazi Rule, 1922–1945*, edited by Joshua D. Zimmerman, 81–95. Cambridge: Cambridge University Press, 2005.

Cardoza, Anthony L. *Benito Mussolini: The First Fascist*. New York: Pearson Longman, 2006.

– "The Long Goodbye: The Landed Aristocracy in North-Western Italy, 1880–1930." *European History Quarterly* 23, no. 3 (1993): 323–58.

– "'Making Italians'? Cycling and National Identity in Italy: 1900–1950." *Journal of Modern Italian Studies* 15, no. 3 (2010): 354–77.

Caron, Vicki. *The Path to Vichy: Antisemitism in France in the 1930s*. Washington, DC: United States Holocaust Memorial Museum, Center for Advanced Holocaust Studies, 2005.

Casali, Antonio, and Marina Cattaruzza. *Sotto i mari del mondo: La Whitehead 1875–1990*. Rome: Laterza, 1990.

Cassels, Alan. "Fascism for Export: Italy and the United States in the Twenties." *American Historical Review* 60, no. 3 (1964): 707–12.

– "Was There a Fascist Foreign Policy? Tradition and Novelty." *The International History Review* 5, no. 2 (1983): 255–68.

Cassero, Riccardo. *Le veline del Duce. Come il Fascismo controllava la stampa*. Milan: Sperling & Kupfer, 2004.

Cassirer, Ernst. *The Myth of the State*. New Haven, CT: Yale University Press, 1946.

Castronovo, Valerio. *Giovanni Agnelli. La Fiat dal 1899 al 1945*. Turin: Einaudi, 1977.

Ceccotti, Paola. *Il fascismo a Livorno. Dalla nascita alla prima amministrazione podestarile*. Empoli: Ibiskos, 2006.

Ceci, Lucia. *The Vatican and Mussolini's Italy*. Leiden: Brill, 2016.

Cenzato, Giovanni. *Costanzo Ciano*. Milan: O. Zucchi, 1940.

Cereghino, Mario José, and Giovanni Fasanella. *Tangentopoli Nera. Malaffare, corruzione e ricatti all'ombra del fascismo nelle Carte Segrete di Mussolini*. Milan: Sperling & Kupfer, 2016.

Ceva, Luigi. *Storia delle forze armate in Italia*. Turin: Utet Università, 1999.

Chessa, Pasquale. *Dux: Benito Mussolini. Una biografia per immagini*. Milan: Mondadori, 2008.

Chiantera-Stutte, Patricia. *Von der Avantgarde zum Traditionalismus. Die radikalen Futuristen im italienischen Faschismus von 1919 bis 1931*. Frankfurt a. Main: Campus, 2002.

Chiarini, Angelo. *Costanzo Ciano*. Rome: Casa editrice Pinciana, 1940.

Childs, Timothy W. *Italo-Turkish Diplomacy and the War over Libya, 1911–1912*. Leiden: Brill, 1990.

Chiurico, Giorgio A. *Storia della rivoluzione fascista 1919–22*. Vol. 3, *Anno 1921*. Florence: Vallecchi, 1929.

Cicchino, Enzo Antonio. *Il Duce attraverso il LUCE. Una confessione cinematografica*. Milan: Mursia, 2010.

Clark, Martin. *Mussolini: Profiles in Power*. Harlow: Pearson Longman, 2014.

Collotti, Enzo. *Fascismo e politica di potenza. Politica estera 1922–1939*. Milan: La nuova italia, 2000.

Conti, Davide. *Gli uomini di Mussolini: Prefetti, questori e criminali di guerra dal fascismo alla Repubblica italiana*. Turin: Einaudi, 2017.

Cornelius, Deborah S. *Hungary in World War II: Caught in the Cauldron*. New York: Fordham University Press, 2011.

Corner, Paul. "Everyday Fascism in the 1930s: Centre and Periphery in the Decline of Mussolini's Dictatorship." *Contemporary European History* 15, no. 2 (2006): 195–222.

– *The Fascist Party and Popular Opinion in Mussolini's Italy*. Oxford: Oxford University Press, 2012.

– "Italian Fascism: Whatever Happened to Dictatorship?" *Journal of Modern History* 74, no. 2 (2002): 325–51.

– "Plebiscites in Fascist Italy: National Unity and the Importance of the Appearance of Unity." In *Voting for Hitler and Stalin*, edited by Ralph Jessen and Hedwig Richter, 173–85. Frankfurt a. Main: Campus Verlag, 2011.

– "Women in Fascist Italy. Changing Family Roles in the Transition from an Agricultural to an Industrial Society." *European History Quarterly* 23, no. 1 (1993): 51–68.

Coverdale, John F. "The Battle of Guadalajara 8–22 March 1937." *Journal of Contemporary History* 9, no. 1 (1974): 53–75.

Cristallini, Elisabetta. "De Chirico's Disregarded E42 Invitation – Published and Unpublished Documents." *Metaphysical Art* 11/13 (2014): 178–93.

Cutler, Richard W. "Three Careers, Three Names: Hildegard Beetz, Talented Spy." *International Journal of Intelligence and Counterintelligence* 22, no. 3 (2009): 515–35.

Cuzzi, Marco. *L'internazionale delle camicie nere. I CAUR, Comitati d'azione per l'universalità di Roma 1933–1939*. Milan: Mursia, 2005.

D'Alessandro, Leonardo P. *Guadalajara 1937: I Volontari fascisti e antifascisti nelle guerra di Spagna*. Rome: Carocci editore, 2017.

D'Avila, Elemo. *Vita eroica di Costanzo Ciano*. Pisa: Nistri-Lischi, 1939.

Deakin, F.W. *Die brutale Freundschaft. Hitler, Mussolini und der Untergang des italienischen Faschismus*. Cologne: Kiepenheuer & Witsch, 1964.

De Begnac, Yvon. *Palazzo Venezia. Storia di un regime*. Rome: La Rocca, 1950.

De Bono, Emilio. *Die Vorbereitungen und die ersten Operationen zur Eroberung Abessiniens*. Munich: C.H. Beck Verlag, 1936.

De Caprariis, Luca. "'Fascism for Export'? The Rise and Eclipse of the Fasci Italiani all'Estero." *Journal of Contemporary History* 35, no. 2 (2000): 151–83.

– "I fasci italiani all'estero." In *Il fascismo e gli emigranti*, edited by Emilia Franzina and Matteo Sanfilippo, 3–26. Rome: Laterza, 2003.

Dechert, Antje. *Stars all'Italiana. Kino und Körperdiskurse in Italien 1930–1965*. Cologne: Böhlau 2014.

De Felice, Renzo. *The Jews in Fascist Italy: A History*. New York: Enigma Books, 2001.

– *Mussolini il duce*. 2 vols. Turin: Einaudi, 1974/81.

– *Mussolini il fascista*. 2 vols. Turin: Einaudi, 1966/68.

De Giorgi, Laura. "In the Shadow of Marco Polo: Writing about China in Fascist Italy." *Journal of Modern Italian Studies* 15, no. 4 (2010): 573–89.

De Grand, Alexander. "Cracks in the Facade: The Failure of Fascist Totalitarianism in Italy, 1935–9." *European History Quarterly* 21, no. 4 (1991): 515–35.

– "Curzio Malaparte: The Illusion of the Fascist Revolution." *Journal of Contemporary History* 7, nos. 1/2 (1972): 73–89.

– *The Hunchback's Tailor: Giovanni Giolitti and Liberal Italy from the Challenge of Mass Politics to the Rise of Fascism, 1882–1922*. Westport: Praeger, 2001.

– "Mussolini's Follies: Fascism in Its Imperial and Racist Phase, 1935–1940." *Contemporary European History* 13, no. 2 (2004): 127–47.

De Grazia, Victoria. *The Culture of Consent: Mass Organization of Leisure in Fascist Italy*. Cambridge: Cambridge University Press, 1981.

– *How Fascism Ruled Women: Italy, 1922–1945*. Berkeley: University of California Press, 1992.

Del Boca, Angelo. "Yperit-Regen. Der Giftgaskrieg." In *Der erste faschistische Vernichtungskrieg. Die italienische Aggression gegen Äthiopien 1935–1941*, edited by Asfa-Wossen Asserate and Aram Mattioli, 45–58. Cologne: SH-Verlag, 2006.

Deletant, Dennis. "Ion Antonescu: The Paradoxes of His Regime, 1940–44." In *In the Shadow of Hitler: Personalities of the Right in Central and Eastern Europe*, edited by Rebecca Haynes and Martyn Rady, 278–94. London: I.B. Tauris, 2011.

De Ninno, Fabio. *Fascisti sul mare: La Marina e gli ammiragli di Mussolini*. Bari: Laterza, 2017.

Depkat, Volker. "The Challenges of Biography: European-American Reflections." *Bulletin of the German Historical Institute* 55 (2014): 39–48.

Di Febo, Giuliana. "Riti e propaganda: il viaggio di Ciano in Spagna (luglio 1939)." In *Fascismo e Franchismo. Relazioni, immagini, rappresentazioni*, edited by Giuliana Di Febo and Renato Moro, 245–76. Soveria Mannelli: Rubbettino, 2005.

Di Giovanni, Marco. *I periodici Livornesi tra dopoguerra e fascismo 1919–1943*. Livorno: Comune di Livorno, 1993.

Dipper, Christof. "Die italienische Zeitgeschichtsforschung heute." *Vierteljahrshefte für Zeitgeschichte* 63, no. 3 (2015): 361–77.

Di Rienzo, Eugenio. *Ciano. Vita pubblica e private del "genero di regime" nell'Italia del Ventennio Nero*. Rome: Salerno Editrice, 2018.

Djokić, Dejan. "'Leader' or 'Devil'? Milan Stojadinović, Prime Minister of Yugoslavia (1935–39), and His Ideology." In *In the Shadow of Hitler: Personalities of the Right in Central and Eastern Europe*, edited by Rebecca Haynes and Martyn Rady, 153–68. London: I.B. Tauris, 2011.

Dogliani, Patrizia. "Das faschistische Italien und das Münchner Abkommen." In *Das Münchner Abkommen von 1938 in europäischer Perspektive*, edited by Jürgen Zarusky and Martin Zückert, 53–68. Munich: Oldenbourg, 2013.

– *Il fascismo degli italiani. Una storia sociale*. Turin: UTET Liberia, 2008.

– "Propaganda and Youth." In *The Oxford Handbook of Fascism*, edited by R.J.B. Bosworth, 185–202. Oxford: Oxford University Press, 2009.

– "Sport and Fascism." *Journal of Modern Italian Studies* 5, no. 3 (2000): 326–48.

Duggan, Christopher. *Fascist Voices: An Intimate History of Mussolini's Italy*. London: Vintage Books, 2013.

– *The Force of Destiny: A History of Italy since 1796*. London: Penguin Books, 2008.

– "Political Cults in Liberal Italy, 1861–1922." In *The Cult of the Duce: Mussolini and the Italians*, edited by Stephen Gundle, Christopher Duggan, and Giuliana Pieri, 11–26. Manchester: Manchester University Press, 2013.

Durchhardt, Heinz. "Die dynastische Heirat." *Europäische Geschichte Online* (EGO), edited by Institut für Europäische Geschichte (IEG), Mainz 2010-12-03. Accessed 1 July 2017. http://www.ieg-ego.eu/duchhardth-2010-de.

Eatwell, Roger. "The Concept and Theory of Charismatic Leadership." In *Charisma and Fascism in Interwar Europe*, edited by António C. Pinto, Roger Eatwell, and Stein U. Larsen, 3–18. London: Routledge, 2007.

– "Universal Fascism? Approaches and Definitions." In *Fascism Outside Europe: The European Impulse against Domestic Conditions in the Diffusion of Global Fascism*, edited by Stein U. Larsen, 15–45. New York: Columbia University Press, 2001.

Edwards, Jill. *The British Government and the Spanish Civil War, 1936–1939*. London: Macmillan, 1979.
Edwards, Peter. "The Austen Chamberlain-Mussolini Meetings." *The Historical Journal* 14, no. 1 (1971): 153–64.
Eisenstadt, S.N., and Luis Roniger. *Patrons, Clients and Friends: Interpersonal Relations and the Structure of Trust in Society*. Cambridge: Cambridge University Press, 1984.
Erlich, Haggai. "Periphery and Youth: Fascist Italy and the Middle East." In *Fascism Outside Europe: The European Impulse against Domestic Conditions in the Diffusion of Global Fascism*, edited by Stein U. Larsen, 393–423. New York: Columbia University Press, 2001.
Esenwein, George, and Adrian Shubert. *Spain at War: The Spanish Civil War in Context, 1931–1939*. London: Longman, 1995.
Esposito, Fernando. *Mythische Moderne. Aviatik, Faschismus und die Sehnsucht nach Ordnung in Deutschland und Italien*. Munich: Oldenbourg, 2011.
Etzemüller, Thomas. "Die Form 'Biographie' als Modus der Geschichtsschreibung. Überlegungen zum Thema Biographie und Nationalsozialismus." In *Regionen im Nationalsozialismus*, edited by Michael Ruck and Karl H. Pohl, 71–90. Bielefeld: Verlag für Regionalgeschichte, 2003.
Falanga, Gianluca. *Mussolinis Vorposten in Hitlers Reich. Italiens Politik in Berlin 1933–1945*. Berlin: Links, 2008.
Falasca-Zamponi, Simonetta. *Fascist Spectacle: The Aesthetics of Power in Mussolini's Italy*. Berkeley: University of California Press, 1997.
Farinacci, Roberto. *Costanzo Ciano*. Bologna: Cappelli, 1940.
Farrell, Nicholas. *Mussolini: A New Life*. London: Weidenfeld & Nicolson, 2003.
Fatta, Corrado. "Da Verona a Norimberga." *Nuova Rivista Storica* 33 (1949): 384–421.
Favre, Franco. *La Marina nella Grande Guerra. Le operazioni navali, aeree, subacquue e terrestri in Adriatico*. Udine: Gaspari, 2008.
Ferrante, Ovidio. "Missione Aeronautica italiana in Cina." *Informazione della Difesa* 45, no. 3 (2008): 45–50.
Festorazzi, Roberto. *Tutti gli uomini di Mussolini. I gerarchi alla corte del Duce*. Milan: Cairo 2015.
Finaldi, Giuseppe. *Mussolini and Italian Fascism*. Harlow: Pearson Longman, 2008.
Finchelstein, Federico. *Transatlantic Fascism: Ideology, Violence and the Sacred in Argentina and Italy, 1919–1945*. Durham, NC: Duke University Press, 2010.
Finzi, Roberto. "The Damage to Italian Culture: The Fate of Jewish University Professors in Fascist Italy and After, 1838–1946." In *Jews in Italy under Fascist and Nazi Rule, 1922–1945*, edited by Joshua D. Zimmerman, 96–113. Cambridge: Cambridge University Press, 2005.

Fiorentino, Virgilio. *Un uomo d'azione: Costanzo Ciano*. Rome: Casa editrice Pinciana, 1928.

Firchow, Peter. "Der Faschismus und die literarische Avantgarde in England zwischen den Weltkriegen." In *Faschismus und Avantgarde*, edited by Reinhold Grimm and Jost Hermand, 35–65. Königstein: Athenäum, 1980.

Fischer, Bernd J. *Albania at War, 1939–1945.* West Lafayette: Purdue University Press, 1999.

Fischer-Galati, Stephen. "Codreanu, Romanian National Traditions and Charisma." In *Charisma and Fascism in Interwar Europe*, edited by António C. Pinto, Roger Eatwell, and Stein U. Larsen, 107–12. London: Routledge, 2007.

Fischer-Lichte, Erika. "Grenzgänge und Tauschhandel. Auf dem Weg zu einer performativen Kultur." In *Performanz. Zwischen Sprachphilosophie und Kulturwissenschaften*, edited by Uwe Wirth, 277–300. Frankfurt a. Main: Suhrkamp, 2002.

– "Performance, Inszenierung, Ritual: Zur Klärung kulturwissenschaftlicher Schlüsselbegriffe." In *Geschichtswissenschaft und "performative turn." Ritual, Inszenierung und Performanz vom Mittelalter bis zur Neuzeit*, edited by Jürgen Martschukat and Steffen Patzold, 33–54. Cologne: Böhlau, 2003.

Fisher, Margaret. "Futurism and Radio." In *Futurism and the Technological Imagination*, edited by Günter Berghaus, 229–62. Amsterdam: Rodopi, 2009.

Focardi, Filippo. *Falsche Freunde? Italiens Geschichtspolitik und die Frage der Mitschuld am Zweiten Weltkrieg*. Paderborn: Ferdinand Schöningh, 2015.

– "Italy's Amnesia over War Guilt: The 'Evil Germans' Alibi." *Mediterranean Quaterly* 25, no. 4 (2015): 5–26.

Foot, John. *Pedalare! Pedalare! A History of Italian Cycling*. London: A&C Black, 2011.

Forgacs, David. "Fascism and Italian Cinema." In *The Italian Cinema Book*, edited by Peter Bondanella, 42–9. London: Palgrave Macmillan, 2014.

Forgacs, David, and Stephen Gundle. *Mass Culture and Italian Society from Fascism to the Cold War*. Bloomington: Indiana University Press, 2007.

Foxlee, Neil. *Albert Camus's 'The New Mediterranean Culture': A Text and Its Context*. Oxford: Peter Lang, 2010.

France, Peter, and William St. Clair, eds. *Mapping Lives: The Uses of Biographies*. Oxford: Oxford University Press, 2002.

Franzinelli, Mimmo. *Fascismo anno zero: 1919: la nascita dei fasci italiani di combattimento*. Milan: Mondadori, 2019.

Galassi, Stefanie. *Pressepolitik im Faschismus. Das Verhältnis von Herrschaft und Presseordnung in Italien zwischen 1922 und 1940*. Stuttgart: Franz Steiner Verlag, 2008.

Galimi, Valeria. "The 'New Racist Man': Italian Society and the Fascist Anti-Jewish Laws." In *In the Society of Fascists: Acclamation, Acquiescence, and Agency in Mussolini's Italy*, edited by Giulia Albanese and Roberta Pergher, 149–68. New York: Palgrave Macmillan, 2012.

Garzarelli, Benedetta. *"Parleremo al mondo intero." La propaganda del fascismo all'estero*. Alessandria: Editrice dell'Orso, 2005.

Gellman, Irwin F. *Secret Affairs: Franklin Roosevelt, Cordell Hull, and Sumner Welles*. Baltimore: Johns Hopkins University Press, 1995.

Gentile, Emilio. "L'emigrazione italiana in Argentina nella politica di espansione del nazionalismo e del fascismo." *Storia Contemporanea* 17, no. 3 (1986): 355–96.

– "Der Faschismus. Eine Definition zur Orientierung." *Mittelweg 36* 16, no. 1 (2007): 81–99.

– "Fascism in Power: The Totalitarian Experiment." In *Liberal and Fascist Italy: 1900–1945*, edited by Adrian Lyttelton, 139–74. Oxford: Oxford University Press, 2002.

– "I fasci italiani all'estero. The 'Foreign Policy' of the Fascist Party." In *Fascism Outside Europe: The European Impulse against Domestic Conditions in the Diffusion of Global Fascism*, edited by Stein U. Larsen, 95–115. New York: Columbia University Press, 2001.

– "Mussolini as the Prototypical Charismatic Dictator." In *Charisma and Fascism in Interwar Europe*, edited by António C. Pinto, Roger Eatwell, and Stein U. Larsen, 113–29. London: Routledge, 2007.

– "Mussolini's Charisma." *Modern Italy* 3, no. 2 (1998): 219–35.

– "The Problem of the Party in Italian Fascism." *Journal of Contemporary History* 19, no. 2 (1984): 251–74.

– *The Sacralization of Politics in Fascist Italy*. Cambridge, MA: Harvard University Press, 1996.

Gentile, Emilio, Paul Corner, and Christopher Duggan. "Two New Books on Fascism: A Review, the Authors' Responses and the Reviewer's Comments." *Journal of Modern Italian Studies* 19, no. 5 (2014): 665–83.

Gentilli, Roberto. "La storiografia aeronautica e il problema dei gas." In *I gas di Mussolini. Il fascismo e la guerra d'Etiopia*, edited by Angelo Del Boca, 133–44. Rome: Editore riuniti, 1996.

Gerwarth, Robert. *Hitler's Hangman: The Life of Heydrich*. New Haven, CT: Yale University Press, 2012.

Gestrich, Andreas. *Geschichte der Familie im 19. und 20. Jahrhundert*. 2nd ed. Munich: Oldenbourg, 2010.

Giansanti, Luca. *Generazione littoria: il fascismo e gli universitari (1918–42)*. Vignate: Lampi di stampa, 2017.

Gilbert, Felix. "Ciano and His Ambassadors." In *The Diplomats, 1919–1939*, edited by Gordon A. Craig and Felix Gilbert, 512–36. Princeton, NJ: Princeton University Press, 1953.

Ginsborg, Paul. *Family Politics: Domestic Life, Devastation and Survival, 1900–1950*. New Haven, CT: Yale University Press, 2014.

Giovannini, Paolo, and Marco Palla, eds. *Il fascismo dalle mani sporche: dittatura, corruzione, affarismo*. Rome: Laterza, 2019.

Gobetti, Eric. "Da Marsiglia a Zagabria: Ante Pavelić e il movimento ustaša in Italia (1929–1941)." *Qualestoria* 1 (2002): 103–15.
– "The Royal Army's Betrayal? Two Different Italian Policies in Yugoslavia (1941–1943)." In *In the Society of Fascists: Acclamation, Acquiescence, and Agency in Mussolini's Italy*, edited by Giulia Albanese and Roberta Pergher, 189–210. New York: Palgrave Macmillan, 2012.
Goeschel, Christian. *Mussolini and Hitler: The Forging of the Fascist Alliance.* New Haven, CT: Yale University Press, 2018.
– "A Parallel History? Rethinking the Relationship between Italy and Germany, ca. 1860–1945." *Journal of Modern History* 88 (2016): 610–32.
– "Staging Friendship: Mussolini and Hitler in Germany in 1937." *The Historical Journal* 60, no. 1 (2017): 149–72.
Goldstein, Ivo. "Ante Pavelić, Charisma and National Mission in Wartime Croatia." In *Charisma and Fascism in Interwar Europe*, edited by António C. Pinto, Roger Eatwell, and Stein U. Larsen, 87–96. London: Routledge, 2007.
Gooch, John. *Army, State and Society in Italy, 1870–1915.* New York: St. Martin's Press, 1989.
– *Mussolini and His Generals: The Armed Forces and Fascist Foreign Policy, 1922–1940.* Cambridge: Cambridge University Press, 2007.
– "Re-Conquest and Suppression: Fascist Italy's Pacification of Libya and Ethiopia, 1922–39." *Journal of Strategic Studies* 28, no. 6 (2005): 1005–32.
Gordon, Robert S. "Race." In *The Oxford Handbook of Fascism*, edited by R.J.B. Bosworth, 296–316. Oxford: Oxford University Press, 2009.
Gori, Gigliola. "Model of Masculinity: Mussolini, the 'New Italian' of the Fascist Era." In *Superman Supreme: Fascist Body as Political Icon – Global Fascism*, edited by J.A. Mangan, 27–61. London: Frank Cass, 2000.
Griffin, Roger. "Europe for the Europeans: Fascist Myths of the European New Order, 1922–1992." In *A Fascist Century: Essays by Roger Griffin*, edited by Matthew Feldman, 132–80. Basingstoke, UK: Palgrave Macmillan, 2008.
– "The Multiplication of Man: Futurism's Technolatry Viewed through the Lens of Modernism." In *Futurism and the Technological Imagination*, edited by Günter Berghaus, 77–99. Amsterdam: Rodopi, 2009.
– *The Nature of Fascism.* London: St. Martin's Press, 1991.
– "Palingenetischer Ultranationalismus. Die Geburtswehen einer neuen Faschismusdeutung." In *Der Faschismus in Europa. Wege der Forschung*, edited by Thomas Schlemmer and Hans Woller, 17–33. Munich: De Gruyter Oldenbourg, 2014.
– "Political Modernism and the Cultural Production of 'Personalities of the Right' in Inter-War Europe." In *In the Shadow of Hitler: Personalities of the Right in Central and Eastern Europe*, edited by Rebecca Haynes and Martyn Rady, 20–37. London: I.B. Tauris, 2011.

Guerri, Giordano Bruno. *Un amore fascista. Benito, Edda e Galeazzo*. Milan: Mondadori, 2005.
– *L'arcitaliano. Vita di Curzio Malaparte*. Milan: Oscar Storia, 2000.
– *D'Annunzio. L'amante guerriero*. Milan: Mondadori, 2008.
– *Filippo Tommaso Marinetti: invenzioni, avventure e passioni di un rivoluzionario*. Milan: Mondadori, 2009.
– *Galeazzo Ciano*. 2nd ed. Milan: Bompiani, 2011.
– *Giuseppe Bottai*. Milan: Bompiani, 2010.
– *Italo Balbo. Lo squadrista, il gerarca, l'aviatore. La biografia, basata su documenti inediti, del più pericoloso rivale di Mussolini*. Milan: A Vallardi, 1984.
– *Il Malaparte illustrato*. Milan: Mondadori, 1998.
Gundle, Stephen. "Film Stars and Society in Fascist Italy." In *Re-viewing Fascism: Italian Cinema, 1922–1943*, edited by Jacqueline Reich and Piero Garofalo, 315–39. Bloomington: Indiana University Press, 2002.
– *Mussolini's Dream Factory: Film Stardom in Fascist Italy*. New York: Berghahn Books, 2016.
Gundle, Stephen, Christopher Duggan, and Giuliana Pieri, eds. *The Cult of the Duce: Mussolini and the Italians*. Manchester: Manchester University Press, 2013.
Hacke, Jens. "Selbsttäuschung aus Enttäuschung – Robert Michels' Parteiensoziologie auf dem Weg von der Demokratie in den Faschismus." In *Robert Michels' Soziologie des Parteiwesens. Oligarchien und Eliten – die Kehrseiten moderner Demokratie*, edited by Harald Bluhm and Skadi Krause, 114–31. Wiesbaden: Springer, 2012.
Hay, James. *Popular Film Culture in Fascist Italy*. Bloomington: Indiana University Press, 1987.
Hearn, Jonathan. *Theorizing Power*. Basingstoke, UK: Palgrave Macmillan, 2012.
Heiberg, Morten. "Mussolini, Franco and the Spanish Civil War." In *International Fascism, 1914–45*, edited by Gert Sørensen and Robert Mallett, 55–68. London: Frank Cass, 2002.
Heim, Susanne, Ulrich Herbert, Michael Hollmann, Horst Möller, Dieter Pohl, Sybille Steinbacher, Simone Walther-von Jena, and Andreas Wirsching, eds. *Die Verfolgung und Ermordung der europäischen Juden durch das nationalsozialistische Deutschland 1933–1945*. Vol. 14, *Besetzes Südosteuropa und Italien*, edited by Sara Berger, Erwin Lewin, Sanela Schmid, and Maria Vassilikou. Berlin: De Gruyter Oldenbourg, 2017.
Hell, Stefan. *Der Mandschurei-Konflikt. Japan, China und der Völkerbund 1931 bis 1933*. Tübingen: Universitas, 1999.
Herbert, Ulrich. *Best. Biographische Studien über Radikalismus, Weltanschauung und Vernunft 1903–1989*. 3rd ed. Bonn: J.H.W. Dietz, 1996.
Hibbert, Christopher. *Mussolini: The Rise and Fall of Il Duce*. New York: Palgrave Macmillan, 1999.

Hierro, Pablo del, and Matteo Albanese. *Transnational Fascism in the Twentieth Century: Spain, Italy and the Global Neo-Fascist Network*. London: Bloomsbury, 2016.

Hillgruber, Andreas. *Hitlers Strategie. Politik und Kriegführung 1940–1941*. Frankfurt a. Main: Bernard & Graefe, 1965.

Hof, Tobias. "Extreme Violence and Military Identity: The Italians in the Balkans (1941–1943)." *Zeitschrift für Genozidforschung. Strukturen, Folgen, Gegenwart kollektiver Gewalt* 16, no. 1 (2018): 57–84.

– "Die faschistische Internationale. Anspruch und Wirklichkeit." In *Die faschistische Herausforderung. Netzwerke, Zukunftsverheißungen und Kulturen der Gewalt in Europa 1922 bis 1945*, edited by Thomas Schlemmer and Hans Woller. Berlin: De Gruyter (forthcoming).

– *Galeazzo Ciano. Eine Studie über Außenpolitik und Faschismus in Italien*. Unpublished Habilitationsschrift, LMU Munich, 2018.

– "'Legionaries of Civilization': The Italian Military, Fascism and Violence." In *Empire, Ideology, Mass Violence: The Long 20th Century in Comparative Perspective*, edited by Tobias Hof, 97–140. Munich: Utz Verlag, 2016.

– "Narratives of 'True Peace' in Italian Fascism." Paper presented at the workshop "Europe's Orders and Discourse on Peace," 13 April 2017, Duke University, Durham, NC.

– "Of Italian Perpetrators and Victims: Forced Migration in the Italian-Yugoslavian Border Region (1922–54)." In *Authenticity and Victimhood in Twentieth-Century History and Commemoratice Culture*, edited by Randall Hansen, Achim Saupe, Andreas Wirsching, and Daqing Yang. Toronto: University of Toronto Press (forthcoming).

– "Die Tagebücher von Galeazzo Ciano." *Vierteljahrshefte für Zeitgeschichte* 60, no. 3 (2012): 321–41.

– "Widerwillige Helfer? Die Judenpolitik des italienischen Außenministeriums unter Galeazzo Ciano 1936 bis 1943." *Vierteljahrshefte für Zeitgeschichte* 68, no. 2 (2020): 181–216.

Hoffend, Andrea. *Zwischen Kultur-Achse und Kulturkampf. Die Beziehungen zwischen "Drittem Reich" und faschistischem Italien in den Bereichen Medien, Kunst, Wissenschaft und Rassenfragen*. Frankfurt a. Main: Peter Lang, 1998.

Hom, Stephanie Malia. "On the Origins of Making Italy: Massimo D'Azeglio and 'Fatta l'Italia, bisogna fare gli Italiani.'" *Italian Culture* 31, no. 1 (2013): 1–16.

Hörnqvist, Magnus. *Risk, Power and the State: After Foucault*. Abingdon: Routledge, 2010.

Howarth, David R. *Poststructuralism and After: Structure, Subjectivity and Power*. London: Palgrave Macmillan, 2013.

Hürter, Johannes. "The German Foreign Office, the Nazi Dictatorship, and the Holocaust: A Critical Commentary on Das Amt und die Vergangenheit." *Bulletin of the German Historical Institute* 49 (2011): 81–96.

Ialongo, Ernest. *Filippo Tommaso Marinetti: The Artist and His Politics*. PhD. diss., City University of New York, 2009.

Innocenti, Marco. *Ciano, il fascista che sfidò Hitler*. Milan: Mursia, 2013.

– *I gerarchi del fascismo. Storia del ventennio attraverso gli uomini del Duce*. Milan: Mursia, 1992.

Ipsen, Carl. *Dictating Demography: The Problem of Population in Fascist Italy*. Cambridge: Cambridge University Press, 1996.

Ishida, Ken D. "Racisms Compared: Fascist Italy and Ultra-Nationalist Japan." *Journal of Modern Italian Studies* 7, no. 3 (2002): 380–91.

Iuso, Pasquale. "Una politica destabilizzante e una progettualità assente: il fascismo, la Jugoslavia e gli *Ustaša* (1925–1940)." *L'Italia fascista Potenza occupant: lo scacchiere balcanico*, edited by Bruno Mantelli. *Qualestoria* 30, no. 1 (2002): 85–102.

Jareb, Mario. "The NDH's Relations with Italy and Germany." In *The Independent State of Croatia 1941–45*, edited by Sabrina P. Ramet, 61–74. London: Routledge, 2007.

Jobs, Sebastian. *Welcome Home, Boys! Military Victory Parades in New York City, 1899–1946*. Frankfurt a. Main: Campus Verlag, 2012.

Jocteau, Gian Carlo. "I nobili del fascismo." *Studi Storici* 45, no. 3 (2004): 677–726.

Jureit, Ulrike. *Generationenforschung*. Göttingen: UTB Verlag, 2006.

Juso, Raffaele. *Il processo di Verona. Una tragedia fascista*. Rome: Gangemi, 1998.

Kallis, Aristotle A. *Fascism and Genocide: The Eliminationist Drive in Fascist Europe*. London: Routledge, 2009.

– *Fascist Ideology: Territory and Expansionism in Italy and Germany, 1922–1945*. London: Routledge, 2000.

Karst, Philipp. "Deutschland 1928–1934 in italienischer Perspektive. Der Blick der italienischen Karrierediplomaten auf die deutsche Politik, Freiburg 2009." Thesis in History, Albert-Ludwigs-Universität Freiburg, 2009.

Kelly, Mark G.E. *Foucault and Politics: A Critical Introduction*. Edinburgh: University of Edinburgh Press, 2014.

Kent, Peter C. "The Vatican and the Spanish Civil War." *European History Quarterly* 16, no. 4 (1986): 441–64.

Kershaw, Ian. *Hitler.* Vol. 1, *1889–1936*. Stuttgart: Deutsche Verlagsanstalt, 1998.

– *Hitlers Macht. Das Profil der NS-Herrschaft*. 2nd ed. Munich: dtv, 2000.

Kertzer, David I. *Ritual, Politics, and Power*. New Haven, CT: Yale University Press, 1988.

Kertzer, David I., and Denis P. Hogan. *Family, Political Economy, and Demographic Change: The Transformation of Life in Casalecchio, Italy, 1861–1921*. Madison: University of Wisconsin Press, 1998.

Kirkpatrick, Ivone. *Mussolini: Study of a Demagogue*. London: Odham Books, 1964.

Klein, Thoralf. *Geschichte Chinas. Von 1800 bis zur Gegenwart*. Paderborn: UTB Verlag, 2009.

Klimke, Martin, Reinhild Kreis, and Christian F. Ostermann. "Introduction." In *Trust, but Verifiy: The Politics of Uncertainity and the Transformation of the Cold War Order, 1969–1991*, edited by Martin Klimke, Reinhild Kreis, and Christian F. Ostermann, 1–11. Stanford, CA: Stanford University Press, 2016.

Knigge, Jobst. *Das Dilemma eines Diplomaten. Otto II. von Bismarck in Rom 1940–1943*. Humboldt Universität Berlin, 2006. https://edoc.hu-berlin.de/handle/18452/14208.

– *Prinz Philipp von Hessen. Hitlers Sonderbotschafter für Italien*. Humboldt Universität Berlin, 2008. https://edoc.hu-berlin.de/handle/18452/10074.

Knox, MacGregor. "Das faschistische Italien und die 'Endlösung' 1942/43." *Vierteljahrshefte für Zeitgeschichte* 55, no. 1 (2007): 53–92.

– *Mussolini Unleashed 1939–1941: Politics and Strategy in Fascist Italy's Last War*. Cambridge: Cambridge University Press, 1982.

König, Malte. *Freundschafts- und Bündnispakt zwischen Deutschland und Italien ("Stahlpakt") vom 22. Mai 1939 und geheimer Zusatzvertrag*. Accessed 12 April 2020. http://www.1000dokumente.de.

– *Kooperation als Machtkampf. Das faschistische Achsenbündnis Berlin-Rom im Krieg 1940/41*. Cologne: SH-Verlag, 2007.

Koon, Tracy H. *Believe, Obey, Fight: Political Socialization of Youth in Fascist Italy, 1922–1943*. Chapel Hill: University of North Carolina Press, 1985.

Krusenstjern, Benigna von. *"Dass es Sinn hat zu sterben – gelebt zu haben." Adam von Trott zu Solz 1909 – 1944. Biographie*. Göttingen: Wallstein, 2009.

Kuller, Christiane. "'Kämpfende Verwaltung'. Bürokratie im NS-Staat." In *Das "Dritte Reich." Eine Einführung*, edited by Dietmar Süß and Winfried Süß, 227–45. Munich: Pantheon Verlag, 2008.

Labanca, Nicola. *Caporetto. Storia di una disfatta*. Turin: Giunti Editori, 1997.

– "Discorsi coloniali in uniforme militare." In *Storia d'Italia, Annali 18: Guerra e pace*, edited by Walter Barberis, 505–48. Turin: Einaudi, 2002.

Lagos, Katerina. "The Agony of Greek Jews, 1940–1945." *East European Jewish Affairs* 40, no. 2 (2010): 207–11.

Landy, Marcia. *Fascism in Film: The Italian Commercial Cinema, 1931–1943*. Princeton, NJ: Princeton University Press 1986.

La Rovere, Luca. "Fascist Groups in Italian Universities: An Organization at the Service of the Totalitarian State." *Journal of Contemporary History* 34, no. 3 (1999): 457–75.

– *Storia dei GUF. Organizzazione, politica e miti della gioventù universitaria fascista 1919–1943*. Turin: Bollati Boringhieri, 2003.

Lässig, Simone. "Toward a Biographical Turn? Biography in Modern Historiography – Modern Historiography in Biography." *German Historical Institute Bulletin* 35 (2004): 147–55.

La Torre, Anna, Giancarlo Celeri Bellotti, and Cecillia Sironi. "A Sample of Italian Fascist Colonialism." In *Colonial Caring: A History of Colonial and Post-Colonial Nursing*, edited by Helen Sweet and Sue Hawkins, 169–87. Manchester: Manchester University Press, 2015.

Leckie, Shirley A. "Biography Matters: Why Historians Need Well-Crafted Biographies More Than Ever." In *Writing Biography: Historians & Their Craft*, edited by Lloyd E. Ambrosius, 1–26. Lincoln: University of Nebraska Press, 2004.

Ledeen, Michael. *Universal Fascism: The Theory and Practice of the Fascist International, 1928–1936*. New York: H. Fertig, 1972.

LeGoff, Jacques. "Wie schreibt man eine Biographie." In *Der Historiker als Menschenfresser. Über den Beruf des Geschichtsschreibers*, edited by Fernand Braudel, 103–12. Berlin: Wagenbach, 1990.

Leitz, Christian. *Economic Relations between Nazi Germany and Franco's Spain, 1936–1945*. Oxford: Claredon Press, 1996.

Levi, Giovanni. "Famiglia e parentela: qualche tema di riflessione." In *Storia della famiglia italiana, 1750–1950*, edited by Marzio Barbagli and David Kertzer, 307–21. Bologna: Il Mulino, 1992.

Levis Sullam, Simon. *The Italian Executioners: The Genocide of the Jews in Italy*. Princeton, NJ: Princeton University Press 2018.

Levy, Carl. "Fascism, National Socialism and Conservatives in Europe, 1914–1945: Issues for Comparativists." *Contemporary European History* 8, no. 1 (1999): 97–126.

Lewis, Paul H. *Latin Fascist Elites: The Mussolini, Franco and Salazar Regimes*. Westport: Praeger, 2002.

Linsenmeyer, William S. "Italian Peace Feelers before the Fall of Mussolini." *Journal of Contemporary History* 16, no. 4 (1981): 649–62.

Longerich, Peter. *Goebbels: A Biography*. New York: Random House, 2015.

– *Heinrich Himmler*. Oxford: Oxford University Press, 2013.

Longo, Gisella. "I tentative per la costituzione di un'internazionale fascista: gli incontri di Amsterdam e di Montreux attraverso i verbali delle riunioni." *Storia Contemporanea* 27 (1996): 475–567.

Love, Gary. "'What's the Big Idea?' Oswald Mosley, the British Union of Fascists and Generic Fascism." *Journal of Contemporary History* 42, no. 3 (2007): 447–68.

Lu, Hanchao. *Beyond the Neon Lights: Everyday Shanghai in the Early Twentieth Century*. Berkeley: University of California Press, 1999.

Luzzatto, Sergio. *L'immagine del duce. Mussolini nelle fotografie dell'Istituto Luce*. Rome: Editore riuniti, 2001.

Lynch, Richard A. "Foucault's Theory of Power." In *Michel Foucault: Key Concepts*, edited by Dianna Taylor, 13–26. Durham, NC: Duke University Press, 2011.

MacDonald, Callum A. "Radio Bari: Italian Wireless Propaganda in the Middle East and British Countermeasures, 1934–38." *Middle Eastern Studies* 13, no. 2 (1977): 195–207.

Mack Smith, Denis. *Mussolini*. London: Weidenfeld and Nicolson, 1981.

– *Mussolini's Roman Empire*. London: Viking Press, 1976.

Malaparte, Curzio. *Kaputt*. Karlsruhe: Stahlberg Verlag, 1951.

Malatesta, Maria. "Introduction: The Italian Professions from a Comparative Perspective." In *Society and the Professions in Italy, 1860–1914*, edited by Maria Malatesta, 1–24. Cambridge: Cambridge University Press, 1995.

Mallett, Robert. "The Anglo-Italian War Trade Negotiations, Contraband Control and the Failure to Appease Mussolini, 1939–40." *Diplomacy & Statecraft* 8, no. 1 (1997): 137–67.

– "Fascist Foreign Policy and Official Italian Views of Anthony Eden in the 1930s." *The Historical Journal* 43, no. 1 (2000): 157–87.

– *The Italian Navy and Fascist Expansionism, 1935–1940*. London: Frank Cass 1998.

– *Mussolini and the Origins of the Second World War, 1933–1940*. Basingstoke, UK: Palgrave Macmillan, 2003.

Mann, Michael. *Die dunkle Seite der Demokratie. Eine Theorie der ethnischen Säuberungen*. Hamburg: Hamburger Edition, 2007.

– *Fascists*. Cambridge: Cambridge University Press, 2004.

Marchi, Vittorio, and Michele Cariello. *Cantiere F.lli Orlandi. 130 anni di storia dello stabilimento e delle sue costruzioni navali*. Livorno: Belforte Editore Libraio, 1997.

Marchicelli, Graziella. *Futurism and Fascism: The Politicization of Art and the Aestheticization of Politics, 1909–1944*. PhD. diss., University of Iowa, 1996.

Marrus, Michael R., and Robert O. Paxton. *Vichy France and the Jews*. New York: Basic Books, 1981.

Martschukat, Jürgen, and Steffen Patzold. "Geschichtswissenschaft und 'performative turn': Eine Einführung in Fragestellungen, Konzepte und Literatur." In *Geschichtswissenschaft und "performative turn." Ritual, Inszenierung und Performanz vom Mittelalter bis zur Neuzeit*, edited by Jürgen Martschukat and Steffen Patzold, 1–31. Cologne: Böhlau, 2003.

Maryks, Robert Aleksander. *"Pouring Jewish Water into Fascist Wine": Untold Stories of (Catholic) Jews from the Archive of Mussolini's Jesuit Pietro Tacchi Venturi*. Leiden: Brill, 2012.

Marzano, Arturo. "La 'guerra delle onde.' La risposta inglese e francese a Radio Bari." *Contemporanea* 15, no. 1 (2012): 3–24.

Marzari, Frank. "Projects for an Italian-Led Balkan Bloc of Neutrals, September–December 1939," *The Historical Journal* 13, no. 4 (1970): 767–88.

Matteoni, Dario. "Città e architettura: Dalla 'Livorno scomparsa' alla ricostruzione." In *Livorno, la costruzione di un'immagine. Tradizione e modernità nel Novecento*, by Francesca Cagiannelli and Dario Matteoni, 12–119. Milan: Silvana, 2003.

Mattioli, Aram. "Die vergessenen Kolonialverbrechen des faschistischen Italien in Libyen, 1923–1933." In *Völkermord und Kriegsverbrechen in der ersten Hälfte des 20. Jahrhunderts*, edited by Fritz-Bauer-Institut, 203–26. Frankfurt a. Main: Campus Verlag, 2004.

Mattioli, Aram, and Gerald Steinacher, eds. *Für den Faschismus bauen: Architektur und Städtebau im Italien Mussolinis*. Zürich: Orell Füssli, 2009.

Mazzoni, Matteo. "Costanzo Ciano, il fascismo a Livorno." *Quaderni di Farestoria* 13, nos. 2/3 (2011): 19–28.

– *Livorno all'ombra del fascio*. Florence: Leo S. Olschki, 2009.

McLean, Eden. *Mussolini's Children: Race and Elementary Education in Fascist Italy*. Lincoln: University of Nebraska Press, 2018.

Messerschmidt, Manfred. "Außenpolitik und Kriegsvorbereitung." In *Das Deutsche Reich und der Zweite Weltkrieg*. Vol. 1, *Ursachen und Voraussetzungen der deutschen Kriegspolitik*, edited by Wilhelm Deist, Manfred Messerschmidt, Hans-Erich Volkmann, and Wolfram Wette, 533–701. Stuttgart: Deutsche Verlagsanstalt, 1979.

Michaelis, Meir. "The Attitude of the Fascist Regime to the Jews in Italy." *Yad Vashem Studies* 4 (1960): 7–41.

– "Il Conte Galeazzo Ciano di Cortellazzo quale antesignano dell'Asse Roma-Berlino. La Linea 'Germanofila' di Ciano dal 1934 al 1936 alla luce di alcuni documenti inediti." *Nuovo Rivista Storica* 61 (1977): 116–49.

– "Mussolini's Unofficial Mouthpiece: Telesio Interlandi – Il Tevere and the Evolution of Mussolini's anti-Semitism." *Journal of Modern Italian Studies* 3, no. 3 (1998): 217–40.

Michels, Helmut. *Ideologie und Propaganda. Die Rolle von Joseph Goebbels in der nationalsozialistischen Außenpolitik bis 1939*. Frankfurt a. Main: Peter Lang, 1992.

Michels, Robert. *Zur Soziologie des Parteiwesens in der Modernen Demokratie*. Leipzig: Verlag von Dr. Wermer Klinkhardt, 1910.

Miller, Dawn M. "Dark Waters: Britain and Italy's Invasion of Albania, 7 April 1939." *International Journal of Intelligence and Counterintelligence* 16, no. 2 (2003): 290–323.

Mills, William C. "Sir Joseph Ball, Adrian Dingli, and Neville Chamberlain's 'Secret Channel' to Italy, 1937–40." *The International History Review* 24, no. 2 (2002): 278–317.

Momigliano, Arnaldo. "The Peace of the Ara Pacis." *Journal of the Warburg and Courtauld Institutes* 5 (1942): 228–31.

Mondini, Marco. *La politica delle armi. Il ruolo dell'esercito nell'avvento del fascismo*. Rome: Laterza 2006.

Montefusco, Gaetano. *L'ordinamento, i compiti e le attribuzioni del Ministero per la Cultura Popolare*. Rome: Unione editoriale d'Italia, 1939.

Montroni, Giovanni. "Aristocracy and Professions." In *Society and the Professions in Italy, 1860–1914*, edited by Maria Malatesta, 255–75. Cambridge: Cambridge University Press, 1995.

Moradiellos, Enrique. "The Gentle General: The Official British Perception of General Franco during the Spanish Civil War." In *The Republic Besieged: Civil War in Spain, 1936–1939*, edited by Paul Preston and Ann L. Mackenzie, 1–20. Edinburgh: Edinburgh University Press, 1996.

Morgan, Philip. *The Fall of Mussolini: Italy, the Italians, and the Second World War*. Oxford: Oxford University Press, 2007.

– *Fascism in Europe, 1919–1945*. London: Routledge, 2003.

Mori, Giorgio. "Materiali, temi e ipotesi per una storia dell'industria nella regione." In *La Toscana nel regime fascista 1922–1939*, vol. 1, edited by Andrea Binazzi and Ivo Guasti, 109–310. Florence: L.S. Olschki, 1971.

Moriconi, Emma. *Gli uomini di Mussolini. Ritratti di un ventennio*. Rome: Herald Editore, 2016.

Moro, Renato. *La Chiesa e lo sterminio degli ebrei*. Bologna: Il Mulino, 2002.

Moro, Tiberio. *Viribus Unitis: Ultimo atto*. Accessed 4 October 2020. https://www.marina.difesa.it/media-cultura/editoria/bollettino/Documents/2011/marzo/Moro.pdf.

Morsy, Laila Amin. "Britain's Wartime Policy in Egypt, 1940–42." *Middle Eastern Studies* 25, no. 1 (1989): 64–94.

Moseley, Ray. *Mussolini's Shadow: The Doublelife of Count Gaelazzo Ciano*. New Haven, CT: Yale University Press, 1999.

– *Mussolini: The Last 600 Days of Il Duce*. Lanham: Taylor Trade, 2004.

Moses, A. Dirk. "Empire, Colony, Genocide: Keywords and the Philosophy of History." In *Empire, Colony, Genocide: Conquest, Occupation, and Subaltern Resistance in World History*, edited by A. Dirk Moses, 3–54. New York: Berghahn Books, 2008.

Mosse, George L. "The Political Culture of Italian Futurism: A General Perspective." *Journal of Contemporary History* 25, nos. 2/3 (1990): 253–63.

Musella, Luigi. "Professionals in Politics. Clientelism and Networks." In *Society and the Professions in Italy, 1860–1914*, edited by Maria Malatesta, 313–36. Cambridge: Cambridge University Press, 1995.

Namier, Lewis B. *Europe in Decay: A Study in Disintegration, 1936–1940*. London: Macmillan, 1950.

Nattermann, Ruth. "Humanitäres Prinzip oder politisches Kalkül? Luca Pietromarchi und die italienische Politik gegenüber den Juden im besetzten Kroatien." In *Die "Achse" im Krieg. Politik, Ideologie und Kriegsführung 1939–1945*, edited by Lutz Klinkhammer, Amedeo Osti Guerrazzi, and Thomas Schlemmer, 319–39. Vol. 64 of *Krieg in der Geschichte*. Paderborn: Ferdinand Schöningh, 2010.

– "Politische Beobachtung im 'tono fascista.' Italienische Konsulatsberichte über das 'Dritte Reich.'" In *Fremde Blicke auf das "Dritte Reich." Berichte ausländischer Diplomaten über Herrschaft und Gesellschaft in Deutschland 1933–1945*, edited by Frank Bajohr and Christoph Strupp, 304–48. Göttingen: Wallstein Verlag 2011.

Nello, Paolo. *Dino Grandi*. Bologna: Il Mulino, 2003.

Neuwirth, Hubert. *Widerstand und Kollaboration in Albanien 1939–1944*. Wiesbaden: Harrassowitz, 2008.

Nidam-Orvieto, Iael. "The Impact of Anti-Jewish Legislation on Everyday Life and the Response of Italian Jews, 1938–1943." In *Jews in Italy under Fascist and Nazi Rule, 1922–1945*, edited by Joshua D. Zimmerman, 158–81. Cambridge: Cambridge University Press, 2005.

Oelrich, Harald. "Hitler, Mussolini und der Sport. Sportverständnis und Mythosbildung zweier Diktatoren." *Stadion. Internationale Zeitschrift für Geschichte des Sports* 24, no. 2 (1998): 289–312.

Orsini, Fabio Frassi. "La Diplomazia." In *Il regime fascista. Storia e Storiografia*, edited by Angelo Del Boca, Massimo Legnani, and Mario G. Rossi, 277–328. Rome Bari: Laterza, 1995.

Ostenc, Michel. *Ciano. Un conservateur face à Hitler et Mussolini*. Monaco: Éditions du Rocher, 2007.

Ostermann, Patrick. *Zwischen Hitler und Mussolini. Guido Manacorda und die faschistischen Katholiken*. Berlin: De Gruyter, 2018.

Osti Guerrazzi, Amedeo. "Das System Mussolini. Die Regierungspraxis des Diktators 1922 bis 1943 im Spiegel seiner Audienzen." *Vierteljahrshefte für Zeitgeschichte* 66, no. 2 (2018): 201–32.

Overy, Richard. *Der Bombenkrieg. Europa 1939–1945*. Berlin: Rowohlt, 2014.

Painter, Borden W. *Mussolini's Rome: Rebuilding the Eternal City*. New York: Palgrave Macmillan, 2005.

Panunzio, Vito. *Il "Secondo Fascismo" 1936–1943. La reazione della nuova generazione alla crisi del movimento e del regime*. Milan: Mursia, 1988.

Pardini, Giuseppe. *Curzio Malaparte: Biografia politica*. Milan: Luni, 1998.

Parlato, Giuesppe. *La sinistra fascista. Storia di un progetto mancato*. Bologna: Il Mulino, 2000.

Patriarca, Silvana. *Italian Vices: Nation and Character from the Risorgimento to the Republic*. Cambridge: Cambridge University Press 2010.

Pavolini, Alessandro. *Disperata*. Florence: Vallecchi, 1937.

Paxton, Robert O. *Anatomy of Fascism*. New York: Alfred A. Knopf, 2004.

– "Die fünf Stadien des Faschismus." *Mittelweg 36* 16, no. 1 (2007): 55–80.

– "Kultur und Zivilgesellschaft im Faschismus." In *Der Faschismus in Europa. Wege der Forschung*, edited by Thomas Schlemmer and Hans Woller, 35–44. Munich: De Gruyter Oldenbourg, 2014.

Payne, Stanley G. *A History of Fascism, 1914–1945*. Madison: University of Wisconsin Press, 1995.

– *Fascism in Spain, 1923–1977*. Madison: University of Wisconsin Press, 1999.

– "Franco, the Spanish Falange and the Institutionalisation of Mission." In *Charisma and Fascism in Interwar Europe*, edited by António C. Pinto, Roger Eatwell, and Stein U. Larsen, 53–63. London: Routledge, 2007.

Petersen, Jens. "Die Außenpolitik des faschistischen Italien als historiographisches Problem." *Vierteljahrshefte für Zeitgeschichte* 22, no. 4 (1974): 417–57.

– *Hitler-Mussolini. Die Entstehung der Achse Berlin-Rom 1933–1936*. Tübingen: Niemeyer, 1973.

– "Vorspiel zu 'Stahlpakt' und Kriegsallianz: Das Deutsch-italienische Kulturabkommen vom 23. November 1938." *Vierteljahrshefte für Zeitgeschichte* 36, no. 1 (1988): 41–77.

Piattoni, Simona. "Clientelism in Historical and Comparative Perspective." In *Clientelism, Interests, and Democratic Representation: The European Experience in Historical and Comparative Perspective*, edited by Simona Piattoni, 1–30. Cambridge: Cambridge University Press, 2001.

Pieri, Giuliana. "Portraits of the Duce." In *The Cult of the Duce: Mussolini and the Italians*, edited by Stephen Gundle, Christopher Duggan, and Giuliana Pieri, 161–77. Manchester: Manchester University Press, 2013.

Pinto, António C., Roger Eatwell, and Stein U. Larsen, eds. *Charisma and Fascism in Interwar Europe*. London: Routledge, 2007.

Podmore, Will. *Britain, Italy, Germany and the Spanish Civil War*. Lewiston: Edwin Mellen Press, 1998.

Poliakoff, Vladimir. *Europe in the Fourth Dimension*. New York: Appleton-Century, 1939.

Poliakov, Leon, and Jacques Sabille. *Jews under the Italian Occupation*. Paris: Éditions du Centre, 1955.

Ponzio, Alessio. *Shaping the New Man: Youth Training Regimes in Fascist Italy and Nazi Germany*. Madison: University of Wisconsin Press, 2015.

Preston, Paul. *Franco: A Biography*. London: HarperCollins, 1993.

– "Italy and Spain in Civil War and World War, 1936–1943." In *Spain and the Great Powers in the Twentieth Century*, edited by Paul Preston and Sebastian Balfour, 151–84. London: Routledge, 1999.

Preston, Paul, and Sebastian Balfour, eds. *Spain and the Great Powers in the Twentieth Century*. London: Routledge, 1999.

Pugliese, Stanislao G. "Death in Exile: The Assassination of Carlo Rosselli." *Journal of Contemporary History* 32, no. 3 (1997): 305–19.

Quartararo, Rosaria. "Imperial Defence in the Mediterranean on the Eve of the Ethiopian Crisis (July–October 1935)." *The Historical Journal* 20, no. 1 (1977): 185–220.

– *I rapporti italo-americani durante il fascismo (1922–1941)*. Naples: Edizioni Scientifiche Italiane, 1999.
– *Roma tra Londra e Berlino. La politica estera fascista dal 1930 al 1940*. Rome: Bonacci, 1980.
Querél, Vittorio. *Costanzo Ciano*. Rome: Tupini, 1940.
Rady, Martyn. "Ferenc Szálasi, 'Hungarism' and the Arrow Cross." In *In the Shadow of Hitler: Personalities of the Right in Central and Eastern Europe*, edited by Rebecca Haynes and Martyn Rady, 261–77. London: I.B. Tauris, 2011.
Raithel, Thomas. *Das schwierige Spiel des Parlamentarismus. Deutscher Reichstag und französische Chambre des Députés in den Inflationskrisen der 1920er Jahre*. Munich: Oldenbourg, 2005.
Rathbun, Brian C. "Trust in International Relations." In *The Oxford Handbook of Social and Political Trust*, edited by Eric M. Uslaner, 688–706. Oxford: Oxford University Press 2018.
Reich, Jacqueline. "Mussolini at the Movies: Fascism, Film and Culture." In *Re-viewing Fascism: Italian Cinema, 1922–1943*, edited by Jacqueline Reich and Piero Garofalo, 3–29. Bloomington: Indiana University Press, 2002.
Reich, Jacqueline, and Piero Garofalo, eds. *Re-viewing Fascism: Italian Cinema, 1922–1943*. Bloomington: Indiana University Press, 2002.
Reichardt, Sven. *Faschistische Kampfbünde. Gewalt und Gemeinschaft im italienischen Squadrismus und in der deutschen SA*. Cologne: Böhlau, 2002.
Reichardt, Sven, and Wolfgang Seibel. "Radikalität und Stabilität: Herrschen und Verwalten im Nationalsozialismus." In *Der prekäre Staat: Herrschen und Verwalten im Nationalsozialismus*, edited by Sven Reichardt, 7–28. Frankfurt a. Main: Campus, 2011.
Reichman, Shalom, and Amon Golan. "Irredentism and Boundary Adjustments in Post-World War I Europe." In *Irredentism and International Politics*, edited by Naomi Chazan, 51–68. London: Lynne Rienner, 1991.
Riall, Lucy. *Garibaldi: Invention of a Hero*. New Haven, CT: Yale University Press 2007.
– "The Shallow End of History? The Substance and Future of Political Biography." *Journal of Interdisciplinary History* 40, no. 3 (2010): 375–97.
Ricci, Steven. *Cinema and Fascism: Italian Film and Society, 1922–1943*. Berkeley: University of California Press, 2008.
Rintelen, Enno von. "Mussolinis Parallelkrieg im Jahre 1940." *Wehrwissenschaftliche Rundschau* 12 (1962): 16–38.
Roberts, David D. "Myth, Style, Substance and the Totalitarian Dynamic in Fascist Italy." *Contemporary European History* 16, no. 1 (2007): 1–36.
Rocco, Emanuele. *Costanzo Ciano nella grande guerra, nelle squadre dei fasci, nel Governo italiano*. Naples: Tipografia L. Di Lauro, 1940.
Rochat, Giorgio. *Le guerre italiane in Libia e in Etiopia dal 1896 al 1939*. Udine: Gaspari, 2009.

Rodogno, Davide. "Fascism and War." In *The Oxford Handbook of Fascism*, edited by R.J.B. Bosworth, 239–58. Oxford: Oxford University Press, 2009.

– *Fascism's European Empire: Italian Occupation during the Second World War*. Cambridge: Cambridge University Press, 2006.

Rodrigo, Javier. *La guerra fascista. Italia en la Guerra Civil española 1936–1939*. Madrid: Alianza Editoria, 2016.

Rofe, J. Simon. *Franklin Roosevelt's Foreign Policy and the Welles Mission*. London: Palgrave Macmillan, 2007.

Rosen, Edgar R. "Viktor Emanuel III. und die Innenpolitik des ersten Kabinetts Badoglio im Sommer 1943." *Vierteljahrshefte für Zeitgeschichte* 12, no. 1 (1964): 44–85.

Rotberg, Robert I. "Biography and Historiography: Mutual Evidentiary and Interdisciplinary Considerations." *Journal of Interdisciplinary History* 40, no. 3 (2010): 305–24.

Row, Thomas. "Mobilizing the Nation: Italian Propaganda in the Great War." *The Journal of Decorative and Propaganda Arts* 24 (2002): 141–69.

Ruck, Michael. "Führerabsolutismus und polykratisches Herrschaftsgefüge – Verfassungsstrukturen des NS-Staates." In *Deutschland 1933–1945. Neue Studien zur nationalsozialistischen Herrschaft*, edited by Karl-Dietrich Bracher, Manfred Funke, and Hans-Adolf Jacobsen, 32–56. Düsseldorf: Droste, 1993.

Sadkovich, James J. "The Italo-Greek War in Context: Italian Priorities and Axis Diplomacy." *Journal of Contemporary History* 28, no. 3 (1993): 439–64.

Salerno, Reynolds M. *Vital Crossroads: The Mediterranean Origins of the Second World War, 1935–1940*. Ithaca, NY: Cornell University Press, 2002.

Salter, Michael, and Lorie Charlesworth. "Ribbentrop and the Ciano Diaries at the Nuremberg Trial." *Journal of International Criminal Justice* 4, no. 1 (2006): 103–27.

Samarani, Guido. "An Historical Turning Point: Italy's Relations with China Before and After 8 September 1943." *Journal of Modern Italian Studies* 15, no. 4 (2010): 590–602.

Samuels, Richard J. *Machiavelli's Children: Leaders and Their Legacies in Italy and Japan*. Ithaca, NY: Cornell University Press, 2003.

Sánchez-Biosca. "The Cinematic Image of José Primo de Rivera: Somewhere between a Leader and a Saint." *Screen* 50, no. 3 (2009): 318–33.

Santini, Aldo. *Alla scoperta di Livorno e dei livornesi in 44 ritratti di scrittori, poeti, giornalisti, politici, regnanti*. Livorno: Debatte, 2009.

– *Costanzo Ciano il ganascia del fascismo*. Milan: Camunia, 1993.

Santoro, Lorenzo. *Roberto Farinacci e il Partito Nazionale Fascista 1923–1926*. Soveria Mannelli: Rubbettino, 2008.

Sarfatti, Michele. *The Jews in Mussolini's Italy: From Equality to Persecution*. Madison: University of Wisconsin Press, 2006.

Scarabello, Giovanni. *Il martirio di Venezia. Durate la Grande Guerra e l'opera della marina italiana.* 2 vols. Venice: Tip. Del Gazzettino Illustrato, 1933.

Scarantino, Anna. *"L'Impero": Un quotidiano "reazionario-futurista" degli anni venti.* Rome: Bonacci, 1981.

Schad, Martha. *Sie liebten den Führer. Wie Frauen Hitler verehrten.* Munich: Herbig, 2009.

Schieder, Wolfgang. "Faschismus im politischen Transfer. Giuseppe Renzetti als faschistischer Propagandist und Geheimagent in Berlin 1922–1941." In *Faschismus in Italien und Deutschland: Studien zu Transfer und Vergleich,* edited by Sven Reichardt and Armin Nolzen, 28–58. Göttingen: Wallstein Verlag, 2005.

– "Das italienische Experiment. Der Faschismus als Vorbild in der Krise der Weimarer Republik." *Historische Zeitschrift* 262, no. 1 (1996): 73–125.

– *Der italienische Faschismus.* Munich: C.H. Beck Verlag, 2010.

– *Mythos Mussolini: Deutsche in Audienz beim Duce.* Munich: Oldenbourg, 2013.

Schilling, Tadzio: "Mächtige Signale. Informelle Kommunikation und Herrschaft an Stalins Hof, 1927–1940." *Journal of Modern European History* 10, no. 3 (2012): 320–40.

Schlemmer, Thomas, and Hans Woller. "Der italienische Faschismus und die Juden 1922 bis 1945." *Vierteljahrshefte für Zeitgeschichte* 53, no. 2 (2005): 165–201.

Schneider, Gabriele. *Mussolini in Afrika. Die faschistische Rassenpolitik in den italienischen Kolonien 1936–1941.* Cologne: SH-Verlag, 2000.

Schönberger, Bianca: "Mütterliche Heldinnen und abenteuerlustige Mädchen. Rotkreuz-Schwestern und Etappenhelferinnen im Ersten Weltkrieg." In *Heimat – Front. Militär und Geschlechterverhältnisse im Zeitalter der Weltkriege,* edited by Karen Hagemann and Stefanie Schüler-Springorum, 108–27. Frankfurt a. Main: Campus, 2002.

Schreiber, Gerhard. "Die politische und militärische Entwicklung im Mittelmeerraum 1939/40." In *Das Deutsche Reich und der Zweite Weltkrieg.* Vol. 3, *Der Mittelmeerraum und Südosteuropa. Von der "non belligeranza" Italiens bis zum Kriegseintritt der Vereinigten Staaten,* edited by Gerhard Schreiber, Bernd Stegemann, and Detlef Bernd Vogel, 4–271. Stuttgart: Deutsche Verlagsanstalt, 1984.

Secciani, Alessandro. *I Gerarchi. Gli uomini del duce.* Novara: Ed. Nuova 2007.

Segrè, Claudio G. *Italo Balbo: A Fascist Life.* Berkeley: University of California Press, 1990.

Seibel, Wolfgang: "Staatsstruktur und Massenmord. Was kann eine historisch-vergleichende Institutionenanalyse zur Erforschung des Holocaust beitragen?" *Geschichte und Gesellschaft* 24, no. 4 (1998): 539–69.

Self, Robert C. *Neville Chamberlain: A Biography.* Aldershot: Ashgate, 2006.

Sergeant, Harriet. *Shanghai.* London: Cape, 1991.

Serra, Enrico. "Italy. The Ministry for Foreign Affairs." In *The Times Survey of Foreign Ministries of the World*, edited by Zara Steiner, 297–323. London: Times Books, 1982.

Severini, Carlo. *Costanzo Ciano*. Livorno: Confederazione fascista dei lavoratori dell'agricoltura, 1940.

Shepherd, Simon, *The Cambridge Introduction to Performance Theory*. Cambridge: Cambridge University Press, 2016.

Shorrock, William I. *From Ally to Enemy: The Enigma of Fascist Italy in French Diplomacy*. Kent: Kent State University Press, 1988.

Siebers, Tonia. *Mussolinis Medienmacht. Themen und Instrumente der Propaganda im faschistischen Italien*. Saarbrücken: VDM, 2007.

Siliato, Leonardo S. *Costanzo Ciano*. Turin: Chiantore, 1940.

Sluga, Glenda. *The Problem of Trieste and the Italo-Yugoslav Border: Difference, Identity, and Sovereignty in Twentieth-Century Europe*. Albany: State University of New York Press, 2001.

Smith, Shirley A. *Imperial Designs: Italians in China, 1900–1947*. Madison: Fairleigh Dickinson University Press, 2012.

Smyth, Howard McGaw. *Secrets of the Fascist Era: How Uncle Sam Obtained Some of the Top-Level Documents of Mussolini's Period*. Carbondale: Southern Illinois University Press, 1975.

Snowden, Frank M. *The Fascist Revolution in Tuscany, 1919–1922*. Cambridge: Cambridge University Press, 1989.

Sørensen, Gert. "The Dual State and Fascism." In *International Fascism, 1914–45*, edited by Gert Sørensen and Robert Mallett, 25–40. London: Frank Cass, 2002.

Spackman, Barbara. *Fascist Virilities: Rhetoric, Ideology, and Social Fantasy in Italy*. Minneapolis: University of Minnesota Press, 1996.

Spaulding, Stacy L. *Lisa Sergio: How Mussolini's "Golden Voice" of Propaganda Created an American Mass Communication Career*. PhD. diss., University of Maryland, 2005.

Spinosa, Antonio. *Edda una tragedia italiana*. Milan: Mondadori, 1993.

Stafford, Paul. "The Chamberlain-Halifax Visit to Rome: A Reappraisal." *The English Historical Review* 98, no. 386 (1983): 61–100.

Steinberg, Jonathan. *All or Nothing: The Axis and the Holocaust, 1941–1943*. London: Routledge, 1990.

Steiner, Zara. *The Triumph of the Dark: European International History, 1933–1939*. Oxford: Oxford University Press, 2011.

Stille, Alexander. "The Double Blind of Italian Jews: Acceptance and Assimilation." In *Jews in Italy under Fascist and Nazi Rule, 1922–1945*, edited by Joshua D. Zimmerman, 19–34. Cambridge: Cambridge University Press, 2005.

Strang, Bruce G. "War and Peace: Mussolini's Road to Munich." *Diplomacy & Statecraft* 10, nos. 2/3 (1999): 160–90.

Strauven, Wanda. "Futurist Poetics and the Cinematic Imagination: Marinetti's Cinema without Films." In *Futurism and the Technological Imagination*, edited by Günter Berghaus, 201–28. Amsterdam: Rodopi, 2009.

Sullivan, Brian R. "From Little Brother to Senior Partner: Fascist Italian Perceptions of the Nazis and of Hitler's Regime, 1930–1936." *Intelligence and National Security* 13, no. 1 (1998): 85–108.

– "'Where One Man, and Only One Man, Led.' Italy's Path from Non-Alignment to Non-Belligerency to War, 1937–1940." In *European Neutrals and Non-Belligerents during the Second World War*, edited by Neville Wylie, 119–49. Cambridge: Cambridge University Press, 2002.

Susmel, Duilio. *Vita sbagliata di Galeazzo Ciano*. Milan: Pelazzi, 1962.

Szöllösi-Janze, Margit. *Fritz Haber 1868–1934. Eine Biographie*. Munich: C.H. Beck Verlag, 1998.

– "Lebens-Geschichte – Wissenschafts-Geschichte. Vom Nutzen der Biographie für Geschichtswissenschaft und Wissenschaftsgeschichte." *Berichte zur Wissenschaftsgeschichte* 23, no. 1 (2000): 17–35.

– *Pfeilkreuzlerbewegung in Ungarn. Historischer Kontext, Entwicklung und Herrschaft*. Munich: Oldenbourg, 1989.

Tacke, Charlotte. "Die 'Nobilitierung' von Rehbock und Fasan. Jagd, 'Adel' und 'Adligkeit' in Italien und Deutschland um 1900." In *Aufsteigen und Obenbleiben in europäischen Gesellschaften des 19. Jahrhunderts. Akteure – Arenen – Aushandlungsprozesse*, edited by Karsten Holste, Dietlind Hüchtker, and Michael G. Müller, 223–48. Berlin: DeGruyter, 2009.

Talbot, George. *Censorship in Fascist Italy, 1922–43*. New York: Palgrave Macmillan, 2007.

Taylor, Dianna, ed. *Michel Foucault: Key Concepts*. Durham, NC: Duke University Press, 2011.

Terhoeven, Petra. *Liebespfand fürs Vaterland. Krieg, Geschlecht und faschistische Nation in der italienischen Gold- und Eheringsammlung 1935/36*. Tübingen: Niemeyer, 2003.

Thorne, Christopher. *The Limits of Foreign Policy: The West, the League and the Far Eastern Crisis of 1931–1933*. New York: Putnam, 1973.

Thorpe, D. Richard. *Eden: The Life and Times of Anthony Eden, First Earl of Avon, 1897–1977*. London: Chatto & Windus, 2003.

Tobia, Bruno. "Dal milite ignoto al nazionalismo monumentale fascista (1921–1940)." In *Storia d'Italia, Annali 18: Guerra e pace*, edited by Walter Barberis, 593–642. Turin: Einaudi, 2002.

Tomassini, Luigi. "La grande guerra e il biennio rosso." In *Le voci del Lavoro. 90 anni di organizzazione e di lotta della Camera del Lavoro di Livorno*, edited by Ivan Tognarini and Angelo Varni, 185–299. Naples: Edizioni scientifiche italiane, 1990.

Toscano, Mario. "Italian Jewish Identity from the Risorgimento to Fascism, 1848–1938." In *Jews in Italy under Fascist and Nazi Rule, 1922–1945*, edited by Joshua D. Zimmerman, 34–54. Cambridge: Cambridge University Press, 2005.

Tranfaglia, Nicola. *La stampa del regime 1932–1943. Le veline del Minculpop per orientare l'informazione*. Milan: Bompiani, 2005.

Trento, Angelo. "I fasci in Brasile." In *Il fascismo e gli emigranti*, edited by Emilia Franzina and Matteo Sanfilippo, 152–66. Bari: Laterza, 2003.

– "I viaggiatori d'era fascista tra curiosità ed ideologia." In *Il viaggio degli emigranti in America Latina tra Ottocento e Novecento. Gli aspetti economici, sociali, culturali*, edited by Giuseppe Moricola, 135–80. Naples: Guida, 2008.

Trifković, Srdjan. "Rivalry between Germany and Italy in Croatia, 1942–1943." *The Historical Journal* 36, no. 4 (1993): 879–904.

Troha, Nevenka. "Ethnopolitische Flurbereinigungen im italienisch-slowenisch-kroatischen Grenzgebiet." In *Zweiter Weltkrieg und ethnische Homogenisierungsversuche im Alpen-Adria-Raum: internationale Tagung, Klagenfurt*, edited by Brigitte Entner, 59–77. Klagenfurt Vienna: Drava, 2012.

Usai, Niccolò G. *Il conte di Cortellazzo Costanzo Ciano*. Rome: M. Carra, 1940.

Verna, Frank P. "Notes on Italian Rule in Dalmatia under Bastianini, 1941–1943." *The International History Review* 12, no. 3 (1990): 528–47.

Versari, Maria E. "Futurists Machine Art, Constructivism and the Modernity of Mechanization." In *Futurism and the Technological Imagination*, edited by Günter Berghaus, 149–75. Amsterdam: Rodopi 2009.

Viani, Andrea. *"Il Telegrafo" di Giovanni Ansaldo (1936–1943)*. Livorno: Belforte, 1998.

Villari, Giovanni. "A Failed Experiment: The Exportation of Fascism to Albania." *Modern Italy* 13, no. 2 (2007): 157–71.

Viñas, Ángel. "Der internationale Kontext." In *Der Spanische Bürgerkrieg. Eine Bestandsaufnahme*, by Julio Aróstegui, Josep M. Bricall, Gabriel Cardona, Manuel Tuñón de Lara, and Ángel Viñas, 187–295. Frankfurt a. Main: Suhrkamp, 1987.

Visser, Romke. "Fascist Doctrine and the Cult of the Romanità." *Journal of Contemporary History* 27, no. 1 (1992): 5–18.

Vogel-Walter, Bettina. *D'Annunzio – Abenteurer und charismatischer Führer. Propaganda und religiöser Nationalismus in Italien von 1914 bis 1921*. Frankfurt a. Main: Peter Lang, 2004.

Wakeman, Frederic, Jr. *Policing Shanghai, 1927–1937*. Berkeley: University of California Press, 1995.

Ward Price, G. *Führer und Duce wie ich sie kenne*. Berlin: Holle, 1939.

Warner, Carolyn M. "Mass Parties and Clientelism in France and Italy." In *Clientelism, Interests, and Democratic Representation: The European Experience in Historical and Comparative Perspective*, edited by Simona Piattoni, 122–51. Cambridge: Cambridge University Press, 2001.

Wasson, Ellis. *Aristocracy and the Modern World*. Basingstoke, UK: Palgrave Macmillan, 2006.

Watt, Donald C. "Hitler's Visit to Rome and the May Weekend Crisis: A Study in Hitler's Response to External Stimuli." *Journal of Contemporary History* 9, no. 1 (1974): 23–32.

– "The Rome-Berlin Axis, 1936–1940: Myth and Reality." *The Review of Politics* 22, no. 4 (1960): 519–43.

Weber, Max. *Grundriss der Sozialökonomie. III. Abteilung: Wirtschaft und Gesellschaft*. Tübingen: J.C.B. Mohr (Paul Siebeck), 1922.

Whealey, Robert H. "Mussolini's Ideological Diplomacy: An Unpublished Document." *Journal of Modern History* 39, no. 4 (1967): 432–7.

Whitaker, John T. *We Cannot Escape History*. New York: The Macmillan Company, 1943.

Wildt, Michael. *Generation des Unbedingten. Das Führungskorps des Reichssicherheitshauptamtes*. Hamburg: Hamburger Edition, 2002.

Williams, Manuela A. *Mussolini's Propaganda Abroad: Subversion in the Mediterranean and the Middle East, 1935–1940*. London: Routledge, 2006.

Willson, Perry. "Introduction: Gender and the Private Sphere in Liberal and Fascist Italy." In *Gender, Family and Sexuality: The Private Sphere in Italy, 1860–1945*, edited by Perry Willson, 1–20. Basingstoke, UK: Palgrave Macmillan, 2004.

– "Women in Mussolini's Italy, 1922–1945." In *The Oxford Handbook of Fascism*, edited by R.J.B. Bosworth, 203–20. Oxford: Oxford University Press, 2009.

Wilson, Alexandra. *The Puccini Problem: Opera, Nationalism and Modernity*. Cambridge: Cambridge University Press, 2007.

Woller, Hans. "Die Anfänge der politischen Säuberung in Italien 1943–1945. Eine Analyse des Office of Strategic Services." *Vierteljahrshefte für Zeitgeschichte* 38, no. 1 (1990): 141–90.

– *Geschichte Italiens im 20. Jahrhundert*. Munich: C.H. Beck Verlag, 2010.

– *Mussolini: Der erste Faschist – Eine Biografie*. Munich: C.H. Beck Verlag, 2016.

– "Vom Mythos der Moderation. Mussolini und die Münchner Konferenz 1938." In *Das Münchner Abkommen von 1938 in europäischer Perspektive*, edited by Jürgen Zarusky and Martin Zückert, 211–16. Munich: Oldenbourg 2013.

Wolpert, Stanley. "Rudyard Kipling." In *Encyclopedia of India*. Vol. 3. Detroit: Thomson Gale, 2006.

Wong, Aliza S. *Race and the Nation in Liberal Italy, 1861–1911: Meridionalism, Empire, and Diaspora*. New York: Palgrave Macmillan, 2006.

Wood, Benjamin. *Defying Evil: How the Italian Army Saved Croatian Jews during the Holocaust*. Palisades: History Publishing, 2012.

Woodhead, Henry G.W. *Current Comment on Events in China; In This Issue the Sino-Japanese Crisis*. Shanghai: Mercury Press, 1932.

Woodhouse, John. "Gabriele D'Annunzio: From Aestheticism to Anarchy. The Poet as Politician." In *In the Shadow of Hitler: Personalities of the Right in Central and Eastern Europe*, edited by Rebecca Haynes and Martyn Rady, 55–72. London: I.B. Tauris, 2011.

Wulf, Christoph, and Jörg Zirfas. "Bild, Wahrnehmung und Phantasie. Performative Zusammenhänge." In *Ikonologie des Performativen*, edited by Christoph Wulf and Jörg Zirfas, 7–32. Munich: Wilhelm Fink, 2005.

– eds. *Ikonologie des Performativen*. Munich: Wilhelm Fink, 2005.

Yeomans, Rory. "'For Us, Beloved Commander, You Will Never Die!' Mourning Jure Francetić, Ustasha Death Squad Leader." In *In the Shadow of Hitler: Personalities of the Right in Central and Eastern Europe*, edited by Rebecca Haynes and Martyn Rady, 188–205. London: I.B. Tauris, 2011.

Zamagni, V. "The Rich in a Late Industrialiser: The Case of Italy, 1800–1945." In *Wealth and the Wealthy in the Modern World*, edited by William D. Rubinstein, 122–66. London: St. Martin's Press, 1980.

Zanatta, Loris. "I fasci in Argentina." In *Il fascismo e gli emigranti*, edited by Emilia Franzina and Matteo Sanfilippo, 140–51. Bari: Laterza, 2003.

Zeidler, Miklós. "Gyula Gömbös: An Outsider's Attempt at Radical Reform." In *In the Shadow of Hitler: Personalities of the Right in Central and Eastern Europe*, edited by Rebecca Haynes and Martyn Rady, 121–37. London: I.B. Tauris, 2011.

Zuccotti, Susan. *The Italians and the Holocaust: Persecution, Rescue, and Survival*. New York: Basic Books, 1987.

Index